Date Due			
MAR 2 5 1980			
FEB 17 1984			
OCT - 6 1988			
APR 18 1990			
DEC 1 2 1991			

THE MOTH BOOK

THE MOTH BOOK

A POPULAR GUIDE
TO A KNOWLEDGE OF THE MOTHS OF
NORTH AMERICA

BY

W. J. HOLLAND

D.D., Ph.D., Sc.D., LL.D.

WITH FORTY-EIGHT COLOR PLATES

AND ANNOTATIONS AND A NEW FOREWORD

BY A. E. BROWER

DOVER PUBLICATIONS, INC.
NEW YORK

This Dover edition, first published in 1968, is an unabridged republication of the work originally published by Doubleday, Page and Company in 1903. This edition contains annotations and a new Foreword by A. E. Brower.

Standard Book Number: 486-21948-8
Library of Congress Catalog Card Number: 68-22887
Manufactured in the United States of America

DOVER PUBLICATIONS, INC.
180 Varick Street
New York, N. Y. 10014

TO MY HONORED FRIEND,

ANDREW CARNEGIE,

WHOSE NAME IS A SYNONYM FOR FINANCIAL

SAGACITY AND PRACTICAL BENEVOLENCE,

I DEDICATE THIS BOOK

FOREWORD TO THE DOVER EDITION

W. J. Holland's *Moth Book* has been the chief reference work for amateur lepidopterists ever since its original publication in 1903. No doubt this reprint edition will be welcomed by many moth collectors whose researches have been hampered by the book's general unavailability in recent years.

Although now more than sixty years old, *The Moth Book* remains an indispensable work, and it will continue to be a rich source of information for years and years to come. Dr. Holland's achievement seems all the more stunning when one considers the difficulties with which he had to contend. He was really a specialist on butterflies and he worked at a time when many misidentifications existed in the larger collections.

Since Dr. Holland prepared this book, a great amount of work has been done on our American moths. Types of the species have been studied so far as possible, dissected for structural details and those compared against our far greater numbers of specimens, knowledge of the total numbers of species in our fauna, and of their biology. However, we have in America north of Mexico more than 10,000 species of moths, and many genera and even whole families remain to be worked out. Research is extremely slow and difficult because many moths exhibit a wide variation in color and pattern, and frequently two or more species are so similar that they can be separated only by a close study of the genitalia or other structures, or by the biology.

Authorities on different groups began to publish corrections to *The Moth Book* soon after its initial publication. For several decades I have collected and added to these reports and for the last thirty years have been glad to supply copies of these corrections to owners of *The Moth Book*. The most recent extensive published expression on *The Moth Book* determinations is "The Lepidoptera of New York and the Neighboring States," by

W. T. M. Forbes and others, *Memoirs* 274 (1948), 329 (1954) and 371 (1960), publications of the Cornell Agricultural Experiment Station.

As a specialist on moths, I would of course like to see a thorough revision of this work, particularly since a proposed handbook of American moths seems to have fallen by the wayside, but this would require an enormous amount of work on the part of many specialists. To update the generic and specific names would necessitate rewriting large portions of the text and legends, extensive reorganization of the work, and also changes in the color plates. A revision of this scope has not been possible for this edition, in which Dr. Holland's text is reprinted unabridged and unaltered, except for the silent correction of a few typographical errors. The new footnotes (initialed A. E. B.) deal mostly with cases of misidentification, and reflect published and unpublished corrections that have come to my attention; these I have checked against the literature, with authorities on moths, and against my own moth collection and species card file. The intent has been to enable the user to associate Dr. Holland's names with the correct species of moth, and to locate the species in the latest American list, *Check List of the Lepidoptera of Canada and the United States of America* by J. McDunnough, Los Angeles, California (Part I, 1938; Part II, 1939). Check lists are needed to trace specific names and synonyms through the literature.

A. E. Brower

Augusta, Maine
February, 1968.

PREFACE TO THE ORIGINAL EDITION

WHEN a few years ago I published "The Butterfly Book," I stated in the preface to that volume that I would follow it by the preparation of a similar work upon the moths of the United States and Canada, provided the reception given that venture should seem to justify me in so doing. "The Butterfly Book" was very favorably received, and not only I, but my publishers, have been besieged with letters from all parts of the continent, urging the fulfillment of the provisional promise made by me in 1898. A prompt compliance with these requests has, however, unfortunately been impossible, owing to the fact that my official duties, which are numerous and exacting, prevent me from devoting any but the evening hours to the work of literary composition. In addition to the difficulties arising from this source, there were other and even greater difficulties which presented themselves. The species of moths known to occur in the United States and Canada vastly exceed in number the species of butterflies found within the same limits. While it was possible to bring together brief descriptions and numerous illustrations of the majority of the species of butterflies found in the region, it became evident at the outset that in dealing with the moths it would be necessary to resort to a different method. It became plain that a process of selection would have to be followed, if the volume were to be kept within proper limits as to size and cost. It would have been comparatively easy to have selected from the abundant material at my command a series of the more showy insects, and to have illustrated these, but as it is the purpose of the series of the books of which "The Moth Book" is one to provide in reasonably compact form manuals which will with tolerable completeness cover the whole field, the plan had to be materially altered. Instead, therefore, of attempting to briefly describe and figure all the thousands of species of moths which have been ascertained to occur in North America north of Mexico, the effort was made to select those species which would adequately represent the various families and the commoner and more important genera, thus providing a work which might serve as an introduction to the study. This process of selection had to be made with much patience and care. Another cause of delay arose from the fact that it is sometimes difficult to obtain perfect specimens for purposes of photographic reproduction. Even where species are well known and common, and are abundantly represented in the collections to which I have access, it has not infrequently happened that it was almost impossible to discover specimens so perfect as to allow of their being reproduced by color-photography in a satisfactory manner. Minor defects, which signify little to a working naturalist, and which can easily be eliminated from sight by a draughtsman, become very serious blemishes when resort is had to methods of photographic illustration. Much time had, therefore, to be spent in searching through various collections for the kind of material which was required, and often in remounting specimens which, while good enough for the cabinet, were not so set as to permit them to be employed in the photographic laboratory. Patience and perseverance, however, always bring in due time their reward, and I have been able to assemble enough properly prepared material to enable me in the main to accomplish my purpose.

"Brevity is the soul of wit," and this fact has not been forgotten by the writer in preparing the pages of this book. The limitations necessarily imposed by the space available precluded the preparation of lengthy descriptions. This brevity in description is, however, as the writer believes, abundantly compensated for by the illustrations in the Plates. One good recognizable figure of a species is worth reams of mere verbal description. Those who desire to go deeply into the subject, and who wish to familiarize themselves with all its technicalities, will find in the list of works named in that part of the introduction devoted to the bibliography of the subject much that they desire.

I am indebted to many scientific friends for assistance, but to no one am I more indebted than to Dr. L. O. Howard, the Entomologist of the United States Department of Agriculture and the Honorary Curator of Entomology in the United States National Museum, and to his amiable associates, Dr. William H. Ashmead and Dr. Harrison G. Dyar. With unfailing courtesy these gentlemen most generously aided me by allowing me to use the material in the National Collection, when it became necessary to do so, and in many other ways gave me invaluable help. I gratefully acknowledge the kindness of Professor J. B. Smith, of Rutgers College, who very graciously went over the Plates containing the *Noctuidæ*, thereby saving me in several instances from errors in determination. My best thanks are due to Mr. William Beutenmüller, the Curator of Entomology in the American Museum of Natural History, New York, for his most obliging courtesy and for much valued assistance. To Mrs. Beutenmüller's facile fingers I owe the frontispiece and many illustrations in the text. To Sir George F. Hampson, of the British Museum, and to the Trustees of that great institution, a debt of gratitude is due for many favors, and especially for permission to use some of the illustrations employed in their publications. From Dr. Henry Skinner, of the Academy of Natural Sciences in Philadelphia, and Mr. Jacob Doll, of the Brooklyn Institute, I received great assistance. To the Messrs. F. A. and H. S. Merrick, of New Brighton, Pa., to Dr. William Barnes, of Decatur, Ill., and to Mr. O. C. Poling, of Peoria, Ill., I return thanks for the loan of specimens used for illustration. The Honorable Walter Rothschild and Dr. Carl Jordan, of Tring, England, placed me under special obligations by permitting me to see advance proofs of the pages of their great work upon the *Sphingidæ*. To all of these gentlemen, as well as to scores of others, who have lent their aid in the preparation of the book, I extend my heartfelt thanks.

While recognizing its imperfections, I trust that the volume will accomplish much to quicken an interest, especially among the young people in our schools and colleges, in that beautiful department of scientific inquiry, which it is designed to some extent to illustrate.

DIRECTOR'S OFFICE,   W. J. H.
CARNEGIE MUSEUM, PITTSBURGH, PA.
September 8, 1903.

TABLE OF CONTENTS

PAGE

Dedication   iii
Foreword to the Dover Edition   v
Preface to the Original Edition   vii
List of Illustrations in the Text   xv
List of Color Plates   xxiii

INTRODUCTION

CHAP.   PAGE
   I. THE LIFE-HISTORY AND ANATOMY OF MOTHS . . .   3–18

How to distinguish a moth from a butterfly. *The Eggs of Moths; Caterpillars:* Structure, Form, Color, Habits, etc.; *The Pupæ of Moths:* Form, Covering, etc.; *Anatomy of Moths:* Head, Thorax, Abdomen, Legs, Wings.

  II. THE CAPTURE, PREPARATION, AND PRESERVATION OF SPECI-
        MENS   19–21

Special Instructions for Mounting and Preparing the Smaller Forms.

 III. THE CLASSIFICATION OF MOTHS   22–26

The Difficulties of Classification. Various Views Entertained by Writers. *Key to the Families of North American Heterocera.*

  IV. BOOKS ABOUT THE MOTHS OF NORTH AMERICA . . .   27–38

Early Writers. Periodicals. General Catalogues and Lists. General Works Containing Information as to the Moths of North America. Works Particularly Useful in Studying the Different Families of the Moths of North America.

THE BOOK

THE MOTHS OF NORTH AMERICA NORTH OF MEXICO.

PAGE

Family I.   The Sphingidæ 41
Family II.   The Saturniidæ 80
Family III. The Ceratocampidæ 94
Family IV.   The Syntomidæ 98
Family V.   The Lithosiidæ 103
Family VI.   The Arctiidæ 114
Family VII. The Agaristidæ 140
Family VIII. The Noctuidæ 151
Family IX.   The Nycteolidæ 288
Family X.   The Pericopidæ 289
Family XI.   The Dioptidæ 291
Family XII. The Notodontidæ 292
Family XIII. The Thyatiridæ 303
Family XIV. The Liparidæ 305
Family XV.   The Lasiocampidæ 311
Family XVI. The Bombycidæ 315
Family XVII. The Platypterygidæ 320
Family XVIII. The Geometridæ 322
Family XIX. The Epiplemidæ 356
Family XX.   The Nolidæ 357
Family XXI. The Lacosomidæ 359
Family XXII. The Psychidæ 360
Family XXIII. The Cochlidiidæ 364
Family XXIV. The Megalopygidæ 368
Family XXV. The Dalceridæ 369
Family XXVI. The Epipyropidæ 370
Family XXVII. The Zygænidæ 371
Family XXVIII. The Thyrididæ 374
Family XXIX. The Cossidæ 375
Family XXX. The Ægeriidæ 379
Family XXXI. The Pyralidæ 391
Family XXXII. The Pterophoridæ 415
Family XXXIII. The Orneodidæ 417

Family XXXIV. The Tortricidæ 417
Family XXXV. The Yponomeutidæ 423
Family XXXVI. The Gelechiidæ 424
Family XXXVII. The Xylorictidæ 428
Family XXXVIII. The Œcophoridæ 428
Family XXXIX. The Blastobasidæ 429
Family XL. The Elachistidæ 430
Family XLI. The Tineidæ 430
Family XLII. The Hepialidæ 443
Family XLIII. The Micropterygidæ 444

DIGRESSIONS AND QUOTATIONS

PAGE
The World of the Dark 77
"Splitters" and "Lumpers" 112
Sugaring for Moths 146
The Tragedy of the Night Moth (Thomas Carlyle) . . . 209
Walking as a Fine Art 270
Das Lied vom Schmetterlinge (Herder) 290
Ode to an Insect (Anacreon) 291
Nasu-no Take 301
Moth Song (Cortissoz) 310
The History of Silk Culture 316
Transformation (Henry Brooke) 321
Living and Dying (Gosse) 355
Far Out at Sea (Horne) 363
Faunal Subregions 387
Cupid's Candle (Felix Carmen) 427
Clothes-moths 434
The End of All (Tennyson) 445

LIST OF ILLUSTRATIONS IN THE TEXT

FIG.   PAGE

1. Dahlia hesperioides Pagenstecher 3
2. Egg of Peridroma saucia 5
3. Egg of Samia cecropia 5
4. Larva of Hyloicus kalmiæ 7
5. Pupa of Telea polyphemus 10
6. Pupa of cut-worm in underground cell 10
7. Front view of the head of a moth 12
8. Lateral view of the head of a moth 12
9. Antennæ of moths 13
10. Antenna of Telea polyphemus 13
11. Legs of a moth 15
12. Diagram showing the structure of the wings of a moth 16
13. Neuration of the wings of Hepialus gracilis 17
14. Figures showing the frenulum and the retinaculum . . 17
15. Figure showing the maculation of the wings of a Noctuid 18
16. Setting-needle used in mounting microlepidoptera . . 19
17. Setting-board used in mounting microlepidoptera . . 20
18. Double mount 21
19. "As it is not done" 26
20. Three joints of the antenna of Protoparce quinquemacu-
    latus 41
21. Neuration of the wings of Sesia tantalus 42
22. Pupa of Protoparce quinquemaculatus 43
23. Isoparce cupressi 48
24. Hyloicus eremitoides 50
25. Hyloicus canadensis 51
26. Protambulyx strigilis 54
27. Larva of Pholus satellitia 65
28. Larva of Pholus achemon 66
29. Larva of Darapsa myron 68
30. Parasitized larva of Darapsa myron 69

List of Illustrations in the Text

FIG.   PAGE
31. Microgaster which preys upon the larva of Darapsa myron   69
32. Pupa of Darapsa myron 69
33. Larva and moth of Sphecodina abbotti 70
34. Light form of larva of Celerio lineata 76
35. Dark form of larva of Celerio lineata 76
36. Philosamia cynthia 81
37. Cocoon of Samia cecropia 83
38. Larva of Callosamia promethea 85
39. Cocoon of Callosamia promethea 85
40. Larva of Actias luna 87
41. Larva of Telea polyphemus 88
42. Cocoon of Telea polyphemus 88
43. Larva of Automeris io 90
44. Eggs of Buck-moth 92
45. Larva of Buck-moth 92
46. Anisota rubicunda, larva and pupa 95
47. Crambidia pallida 104
48. Crambidia casta 104
49. Palpidia pallidior 105
50. Hypoprepia fucosa 106
51. Hæmatomis mexicana 107
52. Comacla simplex 107
53. Bruceia pulverina 108
54. Clemensia albata 108
55. Illice unifascia 109
56. Illice subjecta 109
57. Lerina incarnata 111
58. Dodia albertæ 117
59. Haploa lecontei 119
60. Haploa contigua 119
61. Euerythra phasma 120
62. Larva of Ecpantheria deflorata 120
63. Turuptiana permaculata 121
64. Seirarctia echo 122
65. Alexicles aspersa 122
66. Estigmene prima 122
67. Estigmene acræa 123
68. Isia isabella 125

FIG.   PAGE

69. Caterpillar and pupa of Isia isabella 125
70. Phragmatobia fuliginosa 126
71. Phragmatobia yarrowi 127
72. Apantesis anna 130
73. Kodiosoma fulva 133
74. Ectypia bivittata 133
75. Euchætias egle 135
76. Pygarctia elegans 136
77. Hypocrisias minima 136
78. Egg of Copidryas gloveri 141
79. Pupa of Copidryas gloveri 142
80. Larva and moth of Copidryas gloveri 142
81. Tuerta sabulosa 143
82. Alypia disparata 144
83. Alypia octomaculata 144
84. Alypiodes bimaculata 145
85. Apatela populi, ♀ 154
86. Apatela populi, larva 154
87. Apatela oblinita 158
88. Apharetra dentata 158
89. Apharetra pyralis 159
90. Cerma cora 161
91. Copibryophila angelica 162
92. Platyperigea præacuta 164
93. Platyperigea discistriga 164
94. Fishea yosemitæ 170
95. Momaphana comstocki 172
96. Pyrophila pyramidoides, larva 173
97. Larva of Laphygma frugiperda 174
98. Moth of Laphygma frugiperda 174
99. Podagra crassipes 178
100. Abagrotis erratica 180
101. Metalepsis cornuta 181
102. Setagrotis terrifica 181
103. Agrotis ypsilon 182
104. Pronoctua typica 185
105. Feltia subgothica 186
106. Eucoptocnemis fimbriaris 190

FIG.   PAGE

107. Mamestra picta 194
108. Trichopolia serrata 199
109. Eupolia licentiosa 199
110. Larva of Heliophila unipuncta 200
111. Pupa of Heliophila unipuncta 200
112. Moth of Heliophila unipuncta 201
113. Larvæ and eggs of Heliophila albilinea 202
114. Neleucania bicolorata 203
115. Stretchia muricina 205
116. Perigrapha prima 205
117. Xylina antennata 206
118. Asteroscopus borealis 209
119. Bellura gortynides 211
120. Gortyna immanis 212
121. Larva of Papaipema nitela 213
122. Ochria sauzælitæ 214
123. Pseudorthosia variabilis 216
124. Selicanis cinereola 216
125. Orrhodia californica 218
126. Tristyla alboplagiata 220
127. Pippona bimatris 221
128. Bessula luxa 221
129. Oxycnemis fusimacula 221
130. Boll-worm feeding on tomato 223
131. Heliothis armiger 223
132. Derrima stellata 224
133. Pseudacontia crustaria 225
134. Græperia magnifica 225
135. Trichosellus cupes 226
136. Eupanychis spinosæ 226
137. Canidia scissa 226
138. Palada scarletina 229
139. Sympistis proprius 229
140. Heliodes restrictalis 230
141. Heliosea pictipennis 230
142. Eupseudomorpha brillians 231
143. Larva of Psychomorpha epimenis 232
144. Pseudalypia crotchi 232

FIG.   PAGE

145. Larva of Euthisanotia grata 233
146. Acherdoa ferraria 234
147. Neumœgenia poetica 235
148. Autographa brassicæ 239
149. Diastema tigris 241
150. Eutelia pulcherrima 242
151. Alabama argillacea, egg, larva, and pupa 243
152. Anepischetos bipartita 245
153. Diallagma lutea 245
154. Incita aurantiaca 246
155. Trichotarache assimilis 246
156. Thalpochares ætheria 249
157. Gyros muiri 249
158. Tornacontia sutrix 250
159. Cerathosia tricolor 253
160. Hormoschista pagenstecheri 253
161. Sylectra erycata 254
162. Melanomma auricinctaria 255
163. Argillophora furcilla 255
164. Parora texana 255
165. Capnodes punctivena 277
166. Selenis monotropa 277
167. Latebraria amphipyroides 279
168. Epizeuxis americalis 280
169. Epizeuxis æmula 280
170. Zanclognatha protumnusalis 281
171. Sisyrhypena orciferalis 282
172. Hypenula cacuminalis 283
173. Hypenula opacalis 283
174. Tetanolita mynesalis 284
175. Dircetis pygmæa 284
176. Salia interpuncta 285
177. Lomanaltes eductalis 285
178. Hypena humuli 287
179. Eunystalea indiana 295
180. Euphyparpax rosea 298
181. Cargida cadmia 301
182. Hemerocampa leucostigma, moth 306

FIG.   PAGE

183. Hemerocampa leucostigma, female moth, larva, and
male and female pupæ 307
184. Hemerocampa leucostigma, full grown female larva . . 307
185. Doa ampla 309
186. Leuculodes lacteolaria 310
187. Hypopacha grisea 312
188. Malacosoma americana, eggs, larvæ, and cocoon . . . 313
189. Malacosoma disstria, mature larva 313
190. Malacosoma disstria 314
191. Larva of Bombyx mori 316
192. Cocoon of Bombyx mori 316
193. Moth of Bombyx mori 316
194. Eudeilinea herminiata 320
195. Paleacrita vernata, egg, and larva 325
196. Paleacrita vernata, male and female moths 325
197. Alsophila pometaria, egg, larva, and pupa 326
198. Moths of Alsophila pometaria 326
199. Larva of Eois ptelearia 334
200. Moth and cocoon of Eois ptelearia 335
201. Fernaldella fimetaria 337
202. Cymatophora ribearia, moth 340
203. Egg of Goose-berry span-worm 340
204. Goose-berry span-worm 341
205. Coniodes plumigeraria 346
206. Coniodes plumigeraria, larva 346
207. Nigetia formosalis 358
208. Oiketicus abboti 361
209. Thyridopteryx ephemeræformis 361
210. Harrisina americana, larva, and moth 372
211. Harrisina americana, larvæ on grape-leaf 373
212. Zeuzera pyrina 376
213. Inguromorpha basalis 378
214. Cossula magnifica 379
215. Synanthedon acerni 386
216. Desmia funeralis 392
217. Glyphodes quadristigmalis 394
218. Phlyctænodes sticticalis 395
219. Phlyctænodes sticticalis, larvæ 396

FIG.   PAGE

220. Phlyctænodes sticticalis, pupa 396
221. Hypsopygia costalis 400
222. Pyralis farinalis 401
223. Diatræa saccharalis, larvæ 403
224. Cornstalk attacked by Diatræa saccharalis 404
225. Moth and pupa of Diatræa saccharalis 405
226. The Bee-moth 406
227. Mineola juglandis 408
228. Mineola indigenella, larvæ and moth 409
229. Mineola indigenella, larval case among leaves 410
230. Zophodia grossulariæ 411
231. Canarsia hammondi 411
232. Ephestia kuehniella 412
233. Cocoons of Ephestia kuehniella 413
234. Larva of Ephestia cautella 414
235. Ephestia cautella 414
236. Plodia interpunctella 415
237. Oxyptilus periscelidactylus 416
238. Orneodes hexadactylus 417
239. Eucosma scudderiana 418
240. Ancylis comptana 419
241. Cydia pomonella 420
242. Alceris minuta 421
243. Phthorimæa operculella 424
244. Gnorimoschema gallæsolidaginis 425
245. Anarsia lineatella, larvæ 426
246. Anarsia lineatella, moths 427
247. Depressaria heracliana 428
248. Holcocera glandulella 429
249. Walshia amorphella 430
250. Bucculatrix canadensisella 431
251. Bucculatrix pomifoliella 432
252. Tineola bisselliella (The Clothes-moth) 432
253. Tinea pellionella. (The Fur-moth) 433
254. Trichophaga tapetzella. (The Carpet-moth) 434
255. Prodoxus quinquepunctella, larvæ 438
256. Prodoxus quinquepunctella, moth 439
257. Prodoxus marginatus 439

xxi

List of Illustrations in the Text

FIG.   PAGE
258. Prodoxus y-inversa 440
259. Prodoxus reticulata 440
260. Prodoxus coloradensis 440
261. Prodoxus cinereus 441
262. Pronuba yuccasella 442
263. Pronuba yuccasella, pupæ 442

LIST OF COLOR PLATES

The color plates follow page 258

I. Larvæ of Moths
II. Sphingidæ (Hawkmoths)
III. Sphingidæ (Hawkmoths), &c.
IV. Sphingidæ (Hawkmoths)
V. Sphingidæ (Hawkmoths)
VI. Sphingidæ (Hawkmoths)
VII. Sphingidæ (Hawkmoths)
VIII. Saturniidæ, Ceratocampidæ, &c.
IX. Saturniidæ, &c.
X. Saturniidæ, Ceratocampidæ, Lasiocampidæ
XI. Saturniidæ, Ceratocampidæ, Lasiocampidæ, &c.
XII. Saturniidæ, Cossidæ, Lasiocampidæ
XIII. Syntomidæ, Lithosiidæ, Arctiidæ
XIV. Arctiidæ
XV. Arctiidæ
XVI. Arctiidæ, &c.
XVII. Arctiidæ, Agaristidæ, Noctuidæ
XVIII. Noctuidæ
XIX. Noctuidæ
XX. Noctuidæ
XXI. Noctuidæ
XXII. Noctuidæ
XXIII. Noctuidæ
XXIV. Noctuidæ
XXV. Noctuidæ
XXVI. Noctuidæ

XXVII. Noctuidæ
XXVIII. Noctuidæ
XXIX. Noctuidæ
XXX. Noctuidæ
XXXI. Noctuidæ
XXXII. Noctuidæ
XXXIII. Noctuidæ
XXXIV. Noctuidæ
XXXV. Noctuidæ
XXXVI. Noctuidæ
XXXVII. Noctuidæ
XXXVIII. Pericopidæ, Dioptidæ, Liparidæ, Megalopygidæ, &c.
XXXIX. Notodontidæ
XL. Notodontidæ, Thyatiridæ, &c.
XLI. Lasiocampidæ, Hepialidæ, Psychidæ, Platypterygidæ, Lacosomidæ, &c.
XLII. Noctuidæ, Nycteolidæ, Geometridæ
XLIII. Geometridæ
XLIV. Geometridæ
XLV. Geometridæ
XLVI. Ægeriidæ
XLVII. Cochlidiidæ, Zygænidæ, Thryrididæ, Pyralidæ
XLVIII. Pyralidæ, Tortricidæ, Tineidæ, &c.

INTRODUCTION

INTRODUCTION

CHAPTER I

THE LIFE-HISTORY AND ANATOMY OF MOTHS

"I suppose you are an entomologist?"

"Not quite so ambitious as that, sir. I should like to put my eyes on the individual entitled to that name. No man can be truly called an entomologist, sir; the subject is too vast for any single human intelligence to grasp."

OLIVER WENDELL HOLMES, *The Poet at the Breakfast Table.*

THE great order of the scale-winged insects, or *lepidoptera,* by the consent of almost all naturalists has been subdivided into two suborders, the *Rhopalocera,* or Butterflies, and the *Hetero-cera,* or Moths. As Dr. David Sharp well says, "The only definition that can be given of Heterocera is the practical one that all Lepidoptera that are not butterflies are Heterocera."*

The distinction made between butterflies and moths, according to which all lepidoptera having clubbed antennæ are to be classified as Rhopalocera, or butterflies, and those without clubbed antennæ are to be classified as Heterocera, or moths, while holding good in the main, yet is found with the increase of our knowledge to have exceptions, and there are a few families of lepidoptera, apparently forming connecting links between the butterflies and the moths, in which, while most of the structural characteristics are those of the Heterocera, the antennæ are distinctly clubbed. This is true of the *Castniidæ,* found in tropical America, the *Neocastniidæ* of the Indo-Malayan region, the *Euschemonidæ* of Australia, and certain

FIG. 1.— *Dahlia hesperioides* Pagenstecher.

obscure genera of the *Agaristidæ,* among them that remarkable insect, *Dahlia hesperioides* Pagenstecher, which occurs in the

---

*Cambridge Natural History, Vol. VI. p. 366.

Bismarck Archipelago and the island of Buru. When, a few years ago, I communicated a specimen of this strange little moth to Sir George F. Hampson, he suggested that a trick had been played and that the head of a butterfly (a skipper) had been affixed to the body of a moth, but such was not the case, as a considerable series of specimens in my possession showed. The incident reveals that in classification hard and fast lines, based upon the character of a single organ, can not be always adhered to. There is scarcely any generalization in reference to organic structures which students have made which has not been found with the increase of knowledge to have its limitations. While all this is true, it is nevertheless also true that, so far as the lepidoptera of the United States and the countries of British North America are concerned, the old distinction between the two suborders, based upon the form of the antennæ, holds good, with the sole exception of the insects belonging to the genus *Megathymus*, which are by many authors classified with the *Castniidæ*, and by others with the *Hesperiidæ*. In the "Butterfly Book" I have left these insects with the *Hesperiidæ*. Leaving them out of sight, we may say that all lepidoptera found in the region with which this book deals, and which do not possess clubbed antennæ, are moths. The easiest way for the beginner who lives in the United States, or Canada, to ascertain whether the insect before him is a moth, is to first familiarize himself with the structure of the antennæ of butterflies, and then by comparison to refer the specimens before him to their proper suborder.

Moths undergo metamorphoses analogous to those through which butterflies pass. They exist first in the embryonic form as eggs. When the eggs hatch the insects appear as larvæ, or caterpillars. They are then, after undergoing a series of molts, transformed into pupæ, or chrysalids, which may be naked, or may be provided with an outer covering, known as the cocoon, which is more or less composed of silk. After remaining for some time in the pupal state, they appear as perfect four-winged, six-footed insects.

THE EGGS OF MOTHS

The eggs of moths, like those of butterflies, consist of a shell containing the embryo and the liquid food upon which it subsists until it has attained the degree of maturity which permits it to hatch, or come forth in the first larval stage. The eggs of moths have various forms. Spherical, hemispherical, cylindrical, and lenticular, or lens-shaped eggs are common. The eggs of the *Cochlidiidæ*, or Slug-moths, are broad and very flat, looking like microscopic pancakes. The surfaces of the eggs of moths are seen under a microscope to be more or less ornamented by raised lines and sculpturings. While in some

Fig. 2.—Egg of *Peridroma saucia*, greatly enlarged.

cases the eggs of moths are beautifully spotted and mottled, they are generally quite plain in color, white, pale green, bluishgreen, or brown. Like the eggs of butterflies, they are provided with a micropyle. The micropyle, in the case of such eggs as are globular, conical, or cylindrical, is situated on top. In the case of those eggs which are flattened or lenticular, the micropyle is located on the outer margin or rim.

The eggs are always laid by the female in a state of freedom upon that food-plant which is most congenial to the larva. In

Fig. 3.—Egg of *Samia cecropia*, greatly enlarged.

captivity moths will often deposit their eggs in the receptacle in which they are confined. In such cases, unless the observer knows the food-plant upon which the species feeds, he will be apt to have great difficulty in rearing the larvæ, unless by a happy chance he succeeds experimentally in ascertaining the proper plant. This may sometimes be done by introducing the leaves of a number of plants found in the neighborhood and observing those to which the young caterpillars resort.

The date of oviposition varies with different families and genera. Some moths deposit their eggs in the fall and the young insect passes the winter in the egg, emerging when the early springtime brings opening flowers and leaves. Some moths lay their eggs in the late summer and early fall; the eggs hatch shortly afterward, and the larvæ, after molting one or more times, hibernate in the caterpillar state, and in the following spring resume the process of feeding and molting until such time as they are ready to undergo further transformation. Most moths in temperate regions oviposit in the spring or early summer, and the eggs hatch shortly afterward.

THE CATERPILLARS OF MOTHS

The caterpillars of moths are of course extremely small when they first emerge from the egg. They, however, rapidly increase in relative size as they continue the process of feeding and molting, and in the case of some of the larger species become to the ignorant and uninformed even formidable in appearance. The larva of the Royal Walnut-moth, or "Hickory Horn-Devil," as it is sometimes called, is a striking object. (See Plate I, Fig. 4.) Specimens six and seven inches in length are not at all uncommon. With its curved horns and numerous spines it presents to the uninitiated a truly repellent aspect.

The larvæ of the Heterocera, like those of the Rhopalocera, are principally phytophagous, that is to say, they feed upon vegetable matter. The food of the vast majority consists of the leaves of grasses, shrubs, and trees. A few larvæ feed upon woody tissues, and bore long galleries under the bark or in the wood of trees. Others feed upon the pith of herbaceous plants. A number of species feed upon the inside of growing fruits. Only a very few species are known to be carnivorous. In Australia there occurs a Galleriid moth, the larva of which burrows into the fatty tissues of one of the great wood-boring caterpillars of the region, and preys upon it somewhat as is done by the great family of parasitic Hymenoptera, known to scientific men as the *Ichneumonidæ*. Certain Phycids and Noctuids feed upon scale-insects, in the same way in which the larva of the butterfly known as *Feniseca tarquinius* feeds upon the same class of insects. Among the *Tineidæ* there are certain species which, as is well known, feed upon hair and on horn. Every house-wife is more or less acquainted with the ravages committed by the destructive larvæ of the clothes-moth.

There is considerable variety in the form of heterocerous larvæ, and still greater variety in the manner in which their bodies are adorned by various growths and colors. The body, as is the case with the larvæ of the Rhopalocera, is composed normally of thirteen rings or somites, anterior to which is the head.

The head is usually prominent, and is provided with mandibles, or jaws, eyes, rudimentary antennæ, maxillæ, palpi, and a spinneret for the production of silk. The head may be globular, hemispherical, or conoid. It is sometimes cleft on top, or bifid. It is generally more or less retractile, or capable of being drawn back, so as to be partially concealed in the folds of the anterior somite of the body.

Of the thirteen somites forming the body of the caterpillar, the three foremost are thoracic, and each is furnished with a pair of legs which correspond to the six legs of the perfect insect, or imago. The last two somites of the body are often so closely united with each other as to be superficially indistinguishable. The somites from the third to the eleventh inclusive are provided on either side with spiracles connecting with the tracheæ, through which the creature receives the external air in order to the oxydization of the waste products of the circulation.

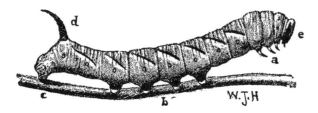

Fig. 4.—Larva of *Hyloicus kalmiæ: a,* thoracic legs; *b,* prolegs; *c,* anal proleg; *d,* anal horn; *e,* head.

The body is usually supported at the middle and at the end by prolegs, or false legs. In the majority of families there are four pairs of these prolegs, situated upon the sixth, seventh, eighth, and ninth somites, and a fifth pair situated on the thirteenth or last somite. The latter pair are called the anal prolegs. In the larvæ of the greater portion of the *Geometridæ,* and in those of numerous *Noctuidæ,* the prolegs are reduced in number, and in many of the *Psychidæ* they appear to be wholly wanting. In most of the *Geometridæ* the pair found on the ninth and thirteenth somites are the only prolegs, and therefore in order to progress the creature makes a series of movements in which the body is looped upward. These caterpillars are known as "loopers" or "measuring-worms." When, as is the case with many genera of the *Noctuidæ*, a less complete abortion of the prolegs occurs, and only a partial approximation to the movement employed by the larvæ of the *Geometridæ* is witnessed, the caterpillars are said to be "half-loopers," or "semiloopers." As examples of such caterpillars we may cite those belonging to the genus *Plusia*, in which there are only two pairs of abdominal prolegs. In the family of the *Megalopygidæ* the prolegs are supplemented by sucker-like pads on the somites ranging from the fifth to the tenth, inclusive. In the *Cochlidiidæ* the prolegs are wanting, their function being wholly assumed by such sucker-like pads, ranging on the ventral surface from the fourth to the eleventh somites, inclusive. In the *Eriocephalidæ*, which are regarded as ancestral forms, there are, as has been pointed out by Dr. T. A. Chapman, eight pairs of abdominal prolegs and an abdominal sucker situated upon the ninth and tenth somites, having the shape of a trefoil or clover leaf. These larvæ are further remarkable in having well-developed antennæ.

After the larvæ have emerged from the egg and fed for a longer or shorter period, the outer skin, or epidermis, becomes too small to admit of further growth, and the insect then molts, or sheds its skin, and resumes feeding until increased development makes another molt necessary. The number of such molts varies in the case of different species. Ordinarily, heterocerous caterpillars do not molt more than five times before transforming into pupæ, but some genera molt as often as ten times, while others only molt thrice. The skin which is cast off preserves the outline not only of the body, but also of the horn-like processes, the hairs, and various other appendages attached to the body at the time of molting. The molting period is a critical time in the life of larvæ, and those who are endeavoring to rear them should never disturb them in the least at this time.

The bodies of the larvæ of moths are covered with tubercles, the location and arrangement of which has in recent years received considerable attention from students, and is thought to furnish a clue to the lines of descent of certain families. These tubercles sometimes carry only a single hair, in other cases they carry large tufts of hairs; they may be small and inconspicuous, or they may be developed until they assume the form of great

8

spines, horns, or bulbous projections. The hairs and spines with which some larvæ are ornamented possess stinging properties. This is true of some genera among the *Saturniidæ* and the *Cochlidiidæ* in temperate America and of many genera in the same families and among the *Lasiocampidæ* in the tropics. The stinging hairs of a large caterpillar found in tropical Africa are employed by the natives in preparing the poison which they put upon their arrows. The inflammation caused by these hairs, even in the case of specimens long dead, I know from personal experience to be very severe.

The coloration of caterpillars is often very striking and beautiful, and in most cases is such as to adapt them more or less to their surroundings in life. Cases of protective mimicry are very numerous. A beautiful illustration of this is seen on Plate I, fig. 15, where the singular form of the caterpillar, combined with its green tint, suggests the serrated edge of the leaf of the elm, upon which plant it feeds. There is almost endless diversity in the modifications of form and color in the larval stages of moths, and they are as characteristic as are the forms and colors of the perfect insects.

There is much diversity in the social habits of the larvæ of moths. Some are gregarious and exist in colonies which disperse at the time of pupation; but there are a few singular instances, in which the communistic instinct perdures, and leads the entire colony to form a common cocoon, or envelope of silk, in which each individual subsequently spins a smaller cocoon for itself. In 1893 I had the pleasure of communicating some information in regard to this curious phase of insect life to the pages of the journal of the Cambridge Entomological Club (See Psyche, Vol. VI., p. 385). This habit is characteristic of certain genera of African moths, but has not thus far been observed as occurring in the case of any American species.

THE PUPÆ OF MOTHS

When the caterpillar has gone through its successive molts and attained to full development it undergoes the transformation known as pupation. From a life of freedom and motion it passes into a condition in which freedom and almost all power of motion are lost. The flexible and more or less agile body is encased in hard chitinous rings and sheathings. As a measure of protection during this stage, the insect, before transforming into a pupa, descends into the earth, and forms there a cell at a greater or lesser depth beneath the surface, or else weaves a cocoon of silk

FIG. 5.—Pupa of *Telea polyphemus*. (Riley.)

about its body. In some cases the transformation takes place at the surface of the earth under leaves or under fallen branches and the loose bark of trees. In almost all such cases there is apparently an attempt, though often slight, to throw a few strands of silk about the body of the caterpillar, if only to hold in place the loose material amidst which transformation is to occur. The forms assumed in the pupal stage are not as remarkably diversified as in the larval or imaginal stages. The pupæ of moths are generally brown or black in color, though a few are more or less variegated. The bright golden and silvery spots which ornament the pupæ of many species of butterflies, causing them to be called chrysalids, are seldom, if ever, found.

While the change into a pupa might at first sight appear to the superficial observer to be disadvantageous because of the loss of motion and the imprisonment within narrow bounds, it nevertheless distinctly marks a progression in the life of the creature. The pupal case contains within it the moth, as may easily be ascertained by a careful dissection made in the very earliest period after the change has occurred,

FIG. 6.—Pupa of Cut-worm in earthen cell. (Riley.)

and which becomes very evident at a later time when the period of the pupal life is drawing to its close.

In the cocoon or in the cell in which pupation has taken place will always be found the exuviæ, or the larval skin, etc., of the caterpillar, which have been cast off.

When the time comes for the perfect insect to emerge from the pupa, nature has provided methods by which escape from the prison cell underground, or the tightly woven cocoon, can be effected. In the case of those pupæ which lie deeply buried under the soil escape is made by means of the power possessed by the abdominal somites, or rings, of moving with a sort of spiral twist. The pupa "wriggles" itself upward through the soil until it reaches the surface, following in its course the line of least resistance, which is generally the line through which the larva burrowed downward to its hiding place. In this movement the pupæ are often aided by spinous projections at the lower edge of the somites which prevent backward motion. When emergence from a cocoon occurs, the insect is provided with the power of ejecting from its mouth a fluid, which has the property of dissolving and cutting the silken threads. When the moth first emerges from the pupa its wings are soft and flabby and its body is long and vermiform. The first act is to secure a quiet resting place. The fluids of the body are in the process of circulation rapidly absorbed from the abdominal region, and, pressing outward under the action of the heart, cause the wings to expand and assume their normal form and the other parts to acquire adjustment. There is no more interesting spectacle than to witness the rapid development of a moth from its apparently helpless condition at emergence from the pupal stage into an insect strong of wing and often gloriously beautiful in color.

THE ANATOMY OF MOTHS

The body of all lepidoptera consists of three subdivisions, the head, the thorax, and the abdomen. The head bears the principal organs of sense and of nutrition, the thorax those of locomotion, and the abdomen those of generation and in large part those of assimilation, respiration, and circulation.

The reader who desires to ascertain the names and the function of the various organs of the body of moths may consult in this connection the corresponding portion of the "Butterfly Book," in which the principal facts have been fully set forth as to the diurnal lepidoptera. The anatomy of moths does not radically differ in its main outlines from that of the Rhopalocera. The same names are applied to the parts, and the differences which occur are not so much differences in function as in outline.

In studying the head of moths we find that as a rule the head is not as prominent as is the case in butterflies. It is more retracted, as a rule, though in the case of some families, as the *Sphingidæ*, it is produced well in advance of the thorax, but even in such cases it is generally more solidly attached to the anterior part of the thorax and is less mobile than in the butterflies.

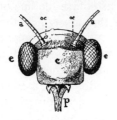

FIG. 7.—Head of a moth viewed from in front. *a*, antenna; *c*, clypeus; *e*, eye; *oc*, ocellus; *p*, proboscis.

The suctorial apparatus is formed in the moths as in the case of the butterflies by the peculiar modification of the maxillæ into semi-cylindrical and interlocking tubes forming t h e *proboscis*. This is enormously produced in some groups, enabling the insect to hover upon the wing over flowers and rob their cups of the honey which they contain. This is especially true of the *Sphingidæ* and some subfamilies of the *Noctuidæ*. In other cases, as in the family of the *Saturniidæ* and *Bombycidæ*, the proboscis is very feebly developed or aborted. In fact, we know that some of these creatures are without mouths and that they do not partake of nourishment in the winged state. They are simply animate, winged reservoirs of reproductive energy, and, when the sexual functions have been completed, they die.

The eyes of moths are often greatly developed. This is especially true of those species which are crepuscular in their habits. The eyes of the heterocera are, as in all other insects, compound. They may be naked, or may be more or less studded with hairs, or lashes, projecting from points lying at the juncture of the various facets making up the organ. This fact has been utilized to some extent in classification. Ocelli, or minute simple eyes, subsidiary to the large compound eyes, occur in some forms, just above the latter, but are generally so concealed by the covering of the head as to be only recognizable by an expert observer.

FIG. 8.—Head of a moth viewed from the side. *a*, antenna; *e*, eye; *oc*, ocellus; *m.p.*, maxillary palpus; *l.p.*, labial palpus; *p*, proboscis.

The labial palpi of moths, as of butterflies, consist of three joints, but there is far greater diversity in the development of the palpi among the moths than among the butterflies. In some cases they are but very feebly developed, in others they attain relatively enormous proportions and strangely eccentric forms. Maxillary palpi are found in some groups. The maxillary palpi have two joints.

The antennæ of moths, which, as has already been pointed out, differ greatly in form from those of butterflies, are attached to the head in the same relative location as in butterflies. Antennæ may be *filiform*, threadlike, *fusiform,* spindle-shaped, or *dilate*, more or less swollen toward the tip. They may be *simple*, i. e., without lateral projections, but this is rarely the case. The shaft may be set with cilia, or small hair-like

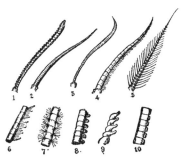

Fig. 9.—Antennæ of moths. *1*, fusiform; *2*, filiform; *3*, dilate; *4*, ciliate; *5*, bipectinate; *6*, setose-ciliate; *7*, fasciculate; *8*, dentate; *9*, serrate; *10*, lamellate.

projections on the side of the joints. Such antennæ are said to be *ciliate*. Sometimes instead of cilia we find bristle-shaped projections on the joints. These are called *setose* antennæ. In some

Fig. 10.—Antenna of *Telea polyphemus*. Plumose; doubly bipectinate. (From "Insect Life," Vol. VII. p. 40.)

forms both cilia and bristles occur on the antennæ. When the bristles are arranged in clusters on the joints of the antennæ they are said to be *fasciculate*. Many forms have tooth-like projections on the antennæ; in such cases the antennæ are described as *den-*

tate. The form and arrangement of the joints may be such as to suggest the teeth of a saw; such antennæ are said to be *serrate*. When on the lower side of the joints of the antennæ there are minute plate-like projections, the antennæ are described as *lamellate*. Many moths have *pectinate* antennæ, the projections resembling little combs, which may be arranged singly or in pairs on each joint. Occasionally, but not often, there are two pairs of such appendages on each joint. When the pectination is excessive, so as to cause the antennæ to resemble a feather, they are said to be *plumose*. Figures 9 and 10 illustrate some of these forms. In addition to the peculiarities which have just been mentioned, antennæ may be variously adorned with scales, especially upon the upper side of the shaft, and they may be notched, or provided with knot-like enlargements, in which case they are said to be *nodose*, or they may be curved, or bent in peculiar ways, when they are described as *sinuate*.

The thorax, as in butterflies, consists of three segments, the prothorax, the mesothorax, and the metathorax. The prothorax bears the tegulæ or collar-lappets, the patagia, or shoulder-lappets, and the anterior pair of legs. The mesothorax carries the second pair of legs and the fore wings. The metathorax the last pair of legs and the hind wings.

The abdomen, just as in butterflies, is normally composed of nine segments, though the modifications of the terminal segments are often such as to make it difficult to recognize so many. At the base of the thorax is situated a pair of large tracheal spiracles, and on the other segments pairs of smaller spiracles. Through these spiracles respiration is carried on. At the end of the abdomen, more or less concealed by variously arranged tufts of hair, are the organs of generation, which have in recent years been studied quite closely by a few authors and are useful in distinguishing species.

The legs of moths are composed of coxa, trochanter, femur, tibia, and tarsus, the latter composed of five joints, and armed at its end with two more or less developed hooks, or claws, known technically as the *ungues*, and also a *pulvillus*, or pad, just back of the claws on the lower side. The legs are armed with spines and spurs, and there are different sexual appendages in the males of various genera. The cut (Figure 11) shows the structure

14

of the legs. It will be well for the student to thoroughly familiarize himself with the location and names of the different parts
indicated in this and the following figure.

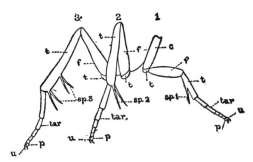

Fig. 11.—Legs of a Moth. (From "Packard's Guide," p. 231.)

1. Fore Leg. 2. Middle Leg. 3. Hind Leg.

c.	Coxa.	*u.*	Ungues.
t.	Trochanter.	*p.*	Pulvillus.
f.	Femur.	*sp.* 1.	Single anterior spur.
t.	Tibia.	*sp.* 2.	Paired medial spurs.
tar.	Tarsus.	*sp.* 3.	Two pairs of posterior spurs.

The structure of the wings of moths is essentially like that of
butterflies, and consists of a framework of hollow tubes which
support a double membrane which bears upon its surfaces the
scales, which overlap each other like the tiles upon the roof of a
house. The tubes, which are known as veins, communicate with
the respiratory system and are highly pneumatic. They are also
connected with the circulatory system, and are furnished, at least
through their basal portions, with nerves.

The fore wing has normally twelve veins. The hind wing
has also in primitive forms, as the *Hepialidæ*, twelve veins, but
in the vast majority of cases this number has been reduced, and
eight veins is the number which is found in the majority of cases
in the hind wing. The accompanying figures, with their explanations, will suffice far better than any mere verbal explanation
to explain the structure of the wings of moths. (See Figures
12 and 13.)

The relative position of vein five in relation to the median or
subcostal systems has been much utilized in recent years by
systematists in their classification of the various groups.

The fore and hind wings in some of the primitive forms are not connected with each other in the operation of flight. In the *Hepialidæ* there is a lobe near the base of the primaries which is

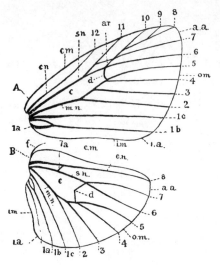

Fig. 12.—Diagram of Wings of a Moth. (After Hampson's "Moths of India," Vol. I., with modifications.)

A. Fore Wing.   B. Hind Wing.

c.m. Costal margin.	*c.n.* Costal nervure, vein 12 of fore wing,
o.m. Outer margin.	8 of hind wing.
i.m. Inner margin.	*s.n.* Subcostal nervure.
a.a. Apex.	*m.n.* Median nervure.
i.a. Inner angle.	1 *a,b,c.* Three branches of internal nervure.
c. Discoidal cell.	2, 3, 4. Three branches of median nervure.
d. Discocellulars.	5. Lower radial.
ar. Areole.	6. Upper radial.
f. Frenulum.	7, 8, 9, 10, 11. Five subcostal branches of fore wing.
	7. Subcostal nervure of hind wing.

known as the *jugum,* but it does not appear to serve the practical functions of a yoke. This is illustrated in Figure 13. In the vast majority of cases a connection between the fore and hind wings is made by means of the *frenulum* on the hind wing, which hooks into the retinaculum upon the fore wing, as illustrated in Figure 14. The form of the frenulum is of use in determining the sex of specimens, as in the case of the males it consists of a single curved, hook-like projection, whereas in the case of the females it is split up into a number of bristles. However, in some groups, as the *Phycitinæ*, the frenulum is simple in both sexes. In some of the families the frenulum is aborted, and its function is assumed by a lobe-like expansion of the basal portion of costa of the hind wing. The nomenclature of the parts of the wings of moths is not essentially different from that which is employed in describing the wings of butterflies. There are, however, certain conventional terms which have been applied by authors to the markings upon the wings, especially of the *Noctuidæ*, and Figure 15 will serve to explain and illustrate these terms.

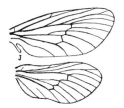

Fig. 13. — Wings of *Hepialus gracilis*. Magnified. *j*, jugum.

A great deal of useful information in regard to the anatomical structure of the Lepidoptera, and of moths in particular, may be

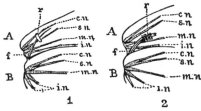

Fig. 14.—Frenulum and Retinaculum. (From "Moths of India," Vol. I.)

1. ♂ ; 2. ♀.—A. Fore Wing. B. Hind Wing.

f. Frenulum.	*s.n.* Subcostal nervure.
r. Retinaculum.	*m.n.* Median nervure.
c.n. Costal nervure.	*i.n.* Internal nervure.

derived from the study of various manuals and special papers, reference to which will be made hereafter as the various families are successively taken up and studied.

Among works to be particularly recommended in this connection are those of Professor A. S. Packard and Professor Comstock's " Manual for the Study of Insects." A very useful treatise is found in Professor David Sharp's two volumes upon the *Insecta* contained in the " Cambridge Natural History." Every student, as he advances in the study of the subject, will have frequent occasion to consult these useful books, which embody the results of the most recent researches and are invaluable for purposes of reference. An even more valuable work than these is the great "Catalogue of the Lepidoptera Phalænæ contained in the Collection of the British Museum," which is being prepared by Sir

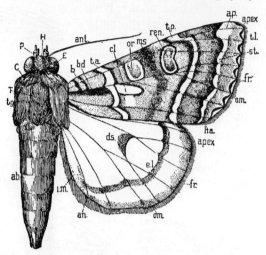

FIG. 15. — Wing of Noctuid Moth. (After Beutenmüller, "Bulletin American Museum Natural History," Vol. XIV., p. 230.) *C*, collar lappet; *tg*, patagium or shoulder lappet; *T*, thorax; *ab*, abdomen; *H*, head; *p*, palpus; *E*, eye; *ant*, antenna; *b*, basal line; *bd*, basal dash; *ta*, transverse anterior line; *cl*, claviform; *or*, orbicular; *ms*, median shade; *ren*, reniform; *tp*, transverse posterior line; *ap*, apical patch; *apex*, apex; *tl*, terminal lunules; *st*, subterminal line; *fr*, fringes; *om*, outer margin; *ha*, hind angle; *ds*, discal mark; *el*, exterior line; *an*, anal angle; *im*, inner margin.

George F. Hampson, and published by the Trustees. The endeavor in this work is to give a complete view of the entire subject in compact form, and the learned author has enlisted the coöperation of the most distinguished lepidopterists throughout the world in the prosecution of his great task. The work is of course somewhat expensive, but the working lepidopterist cannot well do without it. Much help may also be derived from the older works of Burmeister and Westwood, which, though old, are far from being obsolete and useless.

CHAPTER II

THE CAPTURE, PREPARATION, AND PRESERVATION OF SPECIMENS

"Does he who searches Nature's secrets scruple
To stick a pin into an insect?"
A. G. ŒHLENSCHLÆGER, *Aladdin's Lamp.*

EVERYTHING that has been said in "The Butterfly Book" in reference to the capture, preparation, and preservation of specimens holds good in the case of the Heterocera. Inasmuch, however, as many of the moths are exceedingly minute in form, it is worth while to state that a greater degree of care must be observed in the collection and preservation of these minute species than is necessary in the case of even the smallest butterflies. The best method of collecting the micro-lepidoptera is to put them, after they have been netted, into pill-boxes, which have glass covers, or into vials or test tubes of large size. These receptacles may be carried in a bag or pocket by the collector. When he has returned from the field, the specimens may be killed by subjecting them to the action of sulphuric ether applied to the corks of the vials, or introduced into the boxes on a camel's-hair pencil. By dipping the cork into the ether and moistening it with a drop or two and then replacing it in the vial the insect is stunned. Sometimes two or three successive applications of ether are necessary. When the insect has been killed and is still

FIG. 16.—Setting needle used in adjusting wings of micro-lepidoptera upon the glass surface of the setting board.

lax, it is fixed upon a small silver pin of a size proportionate to that of its body, and is then transferred to the setting board. Setting boards for mounting micro-lepidoptera should be made

19

differently from setting boards commonly used for butterflies and larger moths. The best form known to the writer is one, which has for many years been employed by Mr. Herbert H. Smith, the veteran collector. Small pieces of glass about one inch square, with their edges very lightly beveled, so as to remove all sharpness, are spaced upon a strip of cork fastened to a wide piece of soft pine in such a way that an interval of from one-sixteenth to one-eighth of an inch occurs between them. This serves as the groove to receive the body of the specimen. Having been fixed upon the pin the insect is placed in one of these grooves. The wings are then carefully expanded with a crooked needle fastened in a handle, as illustrated in Figure 16, and are then bound

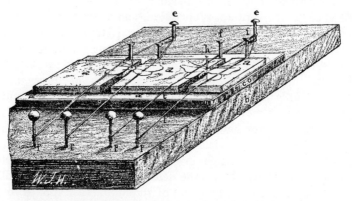

Fig. 17.—Setting board for mounting micro-lepidoptera ; *a*, pieces of glass attached to papered cork with shellac ; *b*, base of soft pine ; *co.*, cork ; *d*, white paper covering cork ; *ee*, brads, to which setting threads are tied ; *ff*, pins set firmly beyond groove to secure alignment of setting threads ; *tt*, setting threads ; *pp*, pins to which setting threads are fastened, and which are stuck into the pine base to hold down the wings in position ; *h*, small silver pin transfixing thorax of specimen.

in place by a thread which is held in place by a pin, as shown in Figure 17. Though the wings of these small insects may, when mounted, at first curl up a little under the pressure of the thread drawn across them, they generally recover their position after removal from the setting board. The advantage of mounting these insects upon glass arises from the fact that the sharp point of the needle will glide over the glass and the surface is smooth, so that they are not torn, nor are the fringes and other delicate portions injured. In doing this work it is best to use a reading-glass mounted in a frame, so that the operator can see the objects before him magnified two or three diame-ters. The mounting of micro - lepidoptera taken in the field and put into envelopes, as often has to be done, is a very trying opera-tion. After the insects have been sufficiently dried they may be set up as double mounts, the small silver pins being thrust through pieces of pith held upon a larger pin. The *Pyralidæ*, the *Tortricidæ* and all the smaller

Fig. 18.—Double mount.

micro-lepidoptera should, if possible, be collected in the way which has just been described, and it is only thus that specimens worthy of installation in a well ordered cabinet can be secured.

Larger forms may be placed in envelopes if intended to be transmitted to great distances prior to study. Larvæ may be inflated in the manner described in "The Butterfly Book." In all other particulars the directions contained in that volume may be safely followed by the student.

'As the moths around a taper,
        As the bees around a rose,
    As the gnats around a vapour,
        So the spirits group and close
Round about a holy childhood, as if drinking its repose."
E. B. Browning, *A Child Asleep.*

CHAPTER III

THE CLASSIFICATION OF MOTHS

"The filmy shapes that haunt the dusk."
TENNYSON, *In Memoriam, xciii.*

THE insects of to-day, like the animals of all other classes found upon the globe, represent lines of descent from an ancestry, which runs back into the remote geologic past. The attempt to trace the lines of descent in any order by studying the resemblance between genera and species as they exist to-day, while throwing considerable light upon the subject, can never yield wholly satisfactory results in the absence of testimony derived from the field of paleontological inquiry. The study of fossil insect life is as necessary to elucidate the story of the development of the insect world, as the study of fossil vertebrates is necessary in order to understand the manner in which existing mammals have been derived from preëxisting forms. At best descent can only be positively asserted within the lines of those groups, to which naturalists have given the name of families. Within these it is possible to declare of this or that genus that it has been possibly, or even probably, derived from the same stock as another. Reference to a common ancestral form may safely be predicated of very few families, so far as such assertion of a common parentage rests upon evidences found in the living structures of to-day.

All attempts to classify the lepidoptera in such a manner as to show the derivation of one of the existing families from another, and to maintain a lineal sequence in the order given, must necessarily prove wholly disappointing. The fact is, that the various families represent divergences from the parent stem, which may be likened to the divergence of the branches from the trunk of a tree. Any system of classification, which leaves this

22

fact out of sight, is necessarily defective, and as unnatural as it would be for a man to lop off the branches of a tree, and then, laying them down side by side, declare, as he contemplated the result of his labors, "This is a tree scientifically arranged." Inasmuch, however, as in books and cabinets serial order must be preserved, the best that the student can do is to collocate those forms, which display some traces of likeness, and give some hint of their common origin.

Exceedingly different views have been entertained by naturalists in recent years in reference to the matters which we are discussing, and various schemes of systematic arrangement have been evolved, many of which are contradictory, and not a few of which appear to the unprejudiced to be more ingenious than natural. Inasmuch as this book is intended for the use not so much of advanced students, as of those who are entering upon the study of the subject, it does not seem to the writer worth while to encumber these pages with what would necessarily be a lengthy recital of the various schemes for classification to which he has alluded. He is inclined to regard the scheme which has been adopted by Sir George F. Hampson in the preparation of his great work upon the moths of the world, which is now being issued by the Trustees of the British Museum, as upon the whole as satisfactory as any which has recently been evolved. Inasmuch, however, as Dr. Harrison G. Dyar has quite recently published a List of the Lepidoptera of the United States, which is certain for many years to come to be used very largely by American students in arranging their collections, it has seemed upon the whole to be best to conform the text of the present volume to the serial arrangement given in Dr. Dyar's List, although the writer differs very positively from the learned author of that work in his views as to the position which should be held in relation to each other of a number of genera. The last word in reference to the classification of the insects contained in this group has certainly not yet been spoken by any one, and we are very far from having attained in our studies to conclusions which may be accepted as final.

For the assistance of students the writer herewith gives a key to the families which are represented in this book, which is based upon the key given by Sir George F. Hampson in the first volume of his " Catalogue of the Lepidoptera Phalænæ," and in the preparation of which he has been assisted by Dr. Dyar.

KEY TO THE FAMILIES OF NORTH AMERICAN HETEROCERA.

Antennæ not clubbed or dilated, or frenulum present when clubbed or dilated.   Frenulum present when not otherwise indicated. . 1

1—Hind wing with cell emitting not more than six veins; wings unlike in shape. 2

Hind wing with cell emitting more than six veins; wings similar in shape 44

2—Hind wing with vein 1c absent 3

Hind wing with vein 1c present. 22

3—Fore wing with vein 5 nearer 4 than 6. 4

Fore wing with vein 5 from middle of discocellulars or nearer 6 than 4 14

4—Hind wing with vein 8 absent. . . . . .Fam. 4, *Syntomidæ.*

Hind wing with vein 8 present. 5

5—Hind wing with vein 8 remote from 7 6

Hind wing with vein 8 touching or approximate to 7 beyond cell. . . .12

6—Hind wing with vein 8 anastomosing with cell to near or beyond middle 7

Hind wing with vein 8 anastomosing with cell near base only. 9

Hind wing with vein 8 joined to cell by a bar. .Fam. 14, *Liparidæ.*

7—Ocelli present. . . . . .Fam. 6, *Arctiidæ.*

Ocelli absent 8

8—Fore wing with tufts of raised scales in the cell. .Fam. 20, *Nolidæ.*

Fore wing without such tufts. . . . . .Fam. 5, *Lithosiidæ.*

9—Antennæ with shaft more or less dilated toward tip. . . . .

. . . . .Fam. 7, *Agaristidæ.*

Antennæ with shaft not dilated 10

10—Hind wing with veins 3 and 4 stalked. . . . . . .Fam. 10, *Pericopidæ.*

Hind wing with veins 3 and 4 not stalked 11

11—Fore wing with costa and inner margin parallel, arched at base . . . .

. . . . .Fam. 9, *Nycteolidæ.*

Fore wing trigonate . . . . .Fam. 8, *Noctuidæ.*

12—Hind wing with vein 1a absent or not reaching anal angle . . . .

. . . . .Fam. 17, *Platypterygidæ.*

Hind wing with vein 1a reaching anal angle. 13

13—Frenulum present. . . . . .Fam. 28, *Thyrididæ.*

Frenulum absent. . . . . .Fam. 15, *Lasiocampidæ.*

14—Hind wing with vein 8 diverging from cell from base. 15

Hind wing with vein 8 connected or approximate to cell 16

15—Tongue absent; no tibial spurs; frenulum absent. .Fam. 2, *Saturniidæ.*

Tongue and tibial spurs present; frenulum absent. . . . .

. . . . .Fam. 3, *Ceratocampidæ.*

16—Hind wing with vein 8 remote from 7 17

Hind wing with vein 8 approximated to or united with 7 21

17—Proboscis absent; frenulum absent. . . . . .Fam. 16, *Bombycidæ.*

Proboscis present. 18

18—Hind wing with vein 8 joined to cell to near middle; vein 5 weak
. . . . .Fam. 12, *Notodontidæ.*

Hind wing with vein 8 joined to cell near base only or vein 5
strong 19

19—Fore wing with veins 3 and 4 separate 20

Fore wing with veins 3 and 4 stalked . . . . .Fam. 11, *Dioptidæ.*

20—Fore wing with vein 8 stalked with 9 . . . . .Fam. 19, *Epiplemidæ.*

Fore wing with vein 8 not stalked with 9 . . Fam. 18, *Geometridæ.*

21—Hind wing with vein 8 joined to cell by a bar . . Fam. 1, *Sphingidæ.*

Hind wing with vein 8 not joined to cell by a bar..Fam. 13, *Thyatiridæ.*

22—Wings divided into plumes. 23

Wings not divided into plumes. 24

23—Fore wing divided into four plumes . . . . .Fam. 32, *Pterophoridæ.*

Fore wing divided into six plumes. . . . . .Fam. 33, *Orneodidæ.*

24—Hind wing with vein 8 absent . . . . .Fam. 30, *Ægeriidæ.*

Hind wing with vein 8 present. 25

25—Fore wing with vein 5 from middle of discocellulars or nearer 6 than 4
. . . . Fam. 21, *Lacosomidæ.*

Fore wing with vein 5 nearer 4 than 6. 26

26—Hind wing with vein 8 anastomosing with or closely approximated
to vein 7. . . . . .Fam. 31, *Pyralidæ.*

Hind wing with vein 8 remote from 7 27

27—Vein 8 of hind wing anastomosing with cell at base 28

Vein 8 free or united to cell by a bar. 29

28—Hind wing with vein 8 joined to cell to middle; fore wing with a
branch to vein 1 below. . . . . .Fam. 24, *Megalopygidæ.*

Hind wing with vein 8 joined to cell at base; no branch to vein
1 below. . . . . .Fam. 23, *Cochlidiidæ.*

29—Mid spurs of hind tibiæ very short or absent. 30

Mid spurs of hind tibiæ, or at least one, well developed 34

30—Proboscis absent 31

Proboscis present; vein 8 joined to the cell by a bar. . . . .
. . . . Fam. 27, *Zygænidæ.*

31—Female winged. 32

Female not winged. . . . . .Fam. 22, *Psychidæ.*

32—Abdomen extending beyond hind wings. . . . . .Fam. 29, *Cossidæ.*

Abdomen not extending beyond hind wings. 33

33—Antennæ short; larvæ free. . . . . .Fam. 25, *Dalceridæ.*

Antennæ long as usual; larvæ parasitic . . . . . Fam. 26, *Epipyropidæ.*

34—Palpi obtuse. . . . . .Fam. 34, *Tortricidæ.*

Palpi more or less acute 35

35—Head at least partly roughly haired. . . . . . .Fam. 41, *Tineidæ* (part).

Head smooth, or with loosely appressed scales. 36

36—Antennæ with basal eye-cap..............Fam. 41, *Tineidæ* (part).
Antennæ without basal eye-cap............................37
37—Maxillary palpi developed...................................38
Maxillary palpi rudimentary................................39
38—Fore wing with vein 7 to outer margin........................
...........................Fam. 35, *Yponomeutidæ* (part).
Fore wing with vein 7 to costa..........Fam. 41, *Tineidæ* (part).
39—Hind wing with vein 8 more or less distinctly connected with cell;
outer margin usually sinuate............................40
Hind wing with vein 8 not connected with cell.................41
40—Fore wing with vein 7 to outer margin or apex.................
......................................Fam. 37, *Xylorictidæ*.
Fore wing with vein 7 to costa...............Fam. 36, *Gelechiidæ*.
41—Hind wing with veins 6 and 7 nearly parallel..................42
Hind wing with veins 6 and 7 approximated or stalked.......43
42—Posterior tibiæ hairy................... ⎰ Fam. 38, *Œcophoridæ*.
.... ⎱ Fam. 39, *Blastobasidæ**.
Posterior tibiæ smooth..................Fam. 35, *Yponomeutidæ*.
43—Hind wing elongated ovate, longer than fore wings ....
.... Fam. 35, *Yponomeutidæ* (part).
Hind wing lanceolate or linear, shorter than forewings ....
...................................Fam. 40, *Elachistidæ*.
44—Maxillary palpi and tibial spurs absent......Fam. 42, *Hepialidæ*.
Maxillary palpi and tibial spurs developed..Fam. 43, *Micropterygidæ*.

---

* No good character has been shown at present for the separation of the Œcophoridæ and the Blastobasidæ.

CHAPTER IV

BOOKS ABOUT NORTH AMERICAN MOTHS

THE literature of our subject is quite extensive, and the most important portions of it are contained in the publications of various learned societies and institutions.

The first references to the subject are found in the writings of Linnæus, Johanssen, Clerck, Fabricius, Cramer, Hübner, Geyer, Drury and John Abbot. The works of Clerck, Cramer, Hübner, Geyer and Drury are all illustrated, and contain figures of many of the more showy North American species. Abbot and Smith's "Rarer Lepidopterous Insects of Georgia" gives figures of a number of moths, with their larvæ and food-plants.

In 1841 the work of Dr. Thaddeus William Harris, entitled "A Report on the Insects of Massachusetts which are Injurious to Vegetation," was published. This was followed in 1852 by the work of A. Guenée on the Noctuelites, the Deltoides, and the Pyralites, constituting Volumes V.-VIII. of the "Spécies Général des Lépidoptères," forming a portion of the "Suites à Buffon." Many North American species were here described for the first time, and some of them were figured in the Atlas of Plates accompanying the work. In 1850 G. A. W. Herrich-Schæffer of Ratisbon began the publication of his "Sammlung Neuer oder Wenig Bekannter Aussereuropäischer Schmetterlinge," which, appearing in parts, was not completed until 1869. Good figures of a number of North American moths are contained in this important volume. In 1854 Francis Walker began the publication under the authority of the Trustees of the British Museum of his "List of the Specimens of Lepidopterous Insects in the Collection of the British Museum." This work, which finally grew to thirty-five volumes, the last of which appeared in 1866, contains descriptions of a multitude of moths found within the United States and Canada. Unfortunately Walker's descriptions are not always recognizable, and his classification as to families and genera was at times very careless. In 1859 Brackenridge Clemens published in the Journal of the Academy of Natural Sciences of Philadelphia, Vol. IV., pp. 97-190, a "Synopsis of the North American Sphingides." In 1860 the Smithsonian Institution issued a "Catalogue of the Described Lepidoptera of North America," compiled by the Rev. J. G. Morris. This catalogue, which was the first to appear, is now antiquated. In 1862 the same institution published a book by the same author, entitled "A Synopsis of the Described Lepidoptera of North America." It is almost wholly a compilation. The first part is devoted to the butterflies of the region. From pp. 122-314 the book is devoted to descriptions of the moths, principally extracted from the writings of Harris, Clemens, and Walker, and these are continued in the Supplement, pp. 330-350. The work is not wholly without value.

This brief review of the literature issued previous to the outbreak of the great Civil War in America, covers practically everything of importance upon the subject which had appeared up to that time. The period which has followed has been characterized by greater activity in all scientific directions, and the principal works which have appeared upon the moths of the United States during the past forty years are herewith given in a list, which, while not by any means complete, is sufficiently full to enable the student to ascertain where to find information for the prosecution of his studies, when he shall have acquainted himself with the contents of this volume.

PERIODICALS CONTAINING MUCH INFORMATION IN REGARD TO THE MOTHS OF NORTH AMERICA

Bulletins of the U. S. Department of Agriculture (Division of Entomology). (Published occasionally.)

Bulletin of the Brooklyn Entomological Society, Vols. I–VII, 1878–1885.

Bulletin of the Buffalo Society of Natural Sciences, Vols. I–IV, 1873–1884.

Canadian Entomologist, Vols. I–XXXIV, 1869–1903, London, Ontario. (Published monthly.)

Entomologica Americana, Vols. I–V, Brooklyn, 1885–1889.

Entomological News, Vols. I–XIII, 1890–1903, Philadelphia Academy of Natural Sciences. (Published monthly, except July and August.)

Insect Life, Vols. I–VII, Washington, 1888–1895.

Journal of the New York Entomological Society, Vols. I–X, 1893–1903. (Published quarterly.)

Papilio, Vols. I–III, 1881–1883, New York, Edited by Henry Edwards; Vol. IV, 1884, Philadelphia, Edited by Eugene M. Aaron.

Proceedings of the Entomological Society of Philadelphia, Vols. I–VI, 1861–1867. (Continued as the Transactions of the American Entomological Society.)

Proceedings of the Entomological Society of Washington, Vols. I–V, 1890–1903. (Published occasionally.)

Proceedings of the U. S. National Museum, Washington, Vols. I–XXVI, 1878–1903.

Psyche. Organ of the Cambridge Entomological Club, Cambridge, Mass., Vols. I–IX, 1877–1903. (Published bi-monthly.)

Transactions of the American Entomological Society, Vols. I–XXX. 1867–1903. Philadelphia Academy of Natural Sciences. (Published quarterly.)

GENERAL CATALOGUES AND LISTS

GROTE, A. R., AND ROBINSON, C. T. List of the Lepidoptera of North America, I, (Sphingidæ to Bombycidæ.) American Entomological Society, Philadelphia, 1868.

GROTE, A. R. List of the North American Platypterices, Attaci, Hemileucini, Ceratocampidæ, Lachneides, Teredines, and Hepiali with Notes (Transactions American Philosophical Society, 1874).

GROTE, A. R. A New Check List of North American Moths, New York, 1882, pp. 1–73.

BROOKLYN ENTOMOLOGICAL SOCIETY Check List of the Macro-Lepidoptera of America, North of Mexico (Brooklyn, 1882, pp. 1–25).

SMITH, JOHN B. List of the Lepidoptera of Boreal America (Philadelphia, American Entomological Society, 1891, pp. 1–124).

KIRBY, W. F. A Synonymic Catalogue of the Lepidoptera Heterocera, Vol. I, Sphinges and Bombyces, London, 1892,

DYAR, H. G. A List of North American Lepidoptera (Bulletin U. S. National Museum, No. 52), pp. i–xix, 1–723.

GENERAL WORKS CONTAINING INFORMATION AS TO THE MOTHS OF NORTH AMERICA

COMSTOCK, J. H. A Manual for the Study of Insects, Ithaca, 1895.

DRUCE, HERBERT Biologia Centrali-Americana, Insecta, Lepidoptera-Heterocera, Vols. I–II, Text; Vol. III, Plates, London, 1881–1900.

PACKARD, A. S. Guide to the Study of Insects. Numerous Editions. A Text-book of Entomology, New York, 1898.

SHARP, DAVID The Cambridge Natural History: Insects, 2 Vols.; Vol. I, 1895; Vol. II, 1899. London and New York.

STRECKER, HERMAN Lepidoptera, Rhopaloceres and Heteroceres, Indigenous and Exotic, with Descriptions and Colored Illustrations. Reading, Pa., 1872–1877. Three Supplements, 1898–1900.

WALKER, FRANCIS List of the Lepidopterous Insects in the Collection of the British Museum. Vols. I–XXXV, London, 1854–1866.

RILEY, C. V. Reports on the Noxious, Beneficial, and Other Insects of the State of Missouri. Nos. 1–9, and Index, 1869–1878.

WORKS PARTICULARLY USEFUL IN STUDYING THE DIFFERENT FAMILIES OF THE MOTHS OF NORTH AMERICA

SPHINGIDÆ

GROTE, A. R., AND ROBINSON, C. T. A Synonymical Catalogue of North America Sphingidæ. (Proceedings Ent. Soc. Philadelphia, Vol. V, 1865, pp. 149–193.)

GROTE, A. R. Catalogue of the Sphingidæ of North America. (Bulletin Buffalo Soc. Nat. Sciences, 1873, pp. 17–28.) New Check List of North American Sphingidæ, (Bulletin Buffalo Soc. Nat. Sciences, Vol. III, pp. 220–225.)

CLEMENS, B. Synopsis of the North American Sphingides. (Journal Acad. Nat. Sciences, Philadelphia, Vol. IV, 1859, pp. 97–190.)

BOISDUVAL, J. A. Sphingides, Sesiides, Castniides. Paris, 1874. Vol. I, text; and a series of Plates in the Atlas accompanying the work, which forms a portion of the "Suites à Buffon."

BUTLER, A. G. Revision of the Heterocerous Lepidoptera of the Family Sphingidæ. (Transactions Zoölogical Soc. London, Vol. IX, 1877, pp. 511–644, Plates XC–XCIV.)

SMITH, JOHN B. An Introduction to a Classification of the North American Lepidoptera. Sphingidæ. (Entomologica Americana, Vol. I, 1885, pp. 81–87.) List of the Sphingidæ of Temperate North America. (Entomologica Americana, 1888, pp. 89–94.)

A monograph of the Sphingidæ of North America North of Mexico. (Transactions American Ent. Soc., Vol. XV, 1888, pp. 49–242, Twelve Plates.)

FERNALD, C. H. The Sphingidæ of New England. Orono, Maine, 1886.

BEUTENMÜLLER, W. Descriptive Catalogue of the Sphingidæ Found within Fifty Miles of New York City. (Bull. Am. Mus. Nat. Hist., Vol. VII, pp. 275–320.)

ROTHSCHILD, HON. A Revision of the Lepidopterous Family Sphingidæ.
W., AND JORDAN, K. (Novitates Zoölogicæ, 1903.) The most complete work upon the subject as yet written.

SATURNIIDÆ

SMITH, JOHN B. A Revision of the Lepidopterous Family Saturniidæ. (Proc. U. S. National Museum, Vol. IX, pp. 414–437, Three Plates.)

PACKARD, A. S. Synopsis of the Bombycidæ of the United States. (Proc. Ent. Soc. Philadelphia, Vol. III, 1864, pp. 97–130 and 331–396.)

NEUMŒGEN, B., AND A Preliminary Revision of the Bombyces of America
DYAR, H. G. North of Mexico. (Journal New York Ent. Soc., Vol. II, pp. 121–132.)

GROTE, A. R. List of the North American Platypterices, Attaci, Hemileucini, Ceratocampidæ, Lachneides, Teredines, and Hepiali, with Notes. (Proc. Am. Philos. Soc., Vol. XIV, pp. 256–264.)

CERATOCAMPIDÆ

GROTE, A. R. List of the North American Platypterices, etc. (See Above.)

NEUMŒGEN, B., AND A Preliminary Revision of the Bombyces of America
DYAR, H. G. North of Mexico. (Journal New York Ent. Soc., Vol. II, pp. 147–152.)

SYNTOMIDÆ

HAMPSON, G. F. Catalogue of the Lepidoptera Phalænæ in the British Museum, Vol. I, 1898.

LITHOSIIDÆ

BUTLER, A. G. On the Lepidoptera of the Family Lithosiidæ, in the Collection of the British Museum. (Transactions Ent. Soc., London, 1877, pp. 325–377.)

STRETCH, R. H. Illustrations of the Zygænidæ and Bombycidæ of North America, San Francisco, 1874, pp. 242, Ten Plates. (Numerous Lithosiids are figured and described.)

HAMPSON, G. F. Catalogue of the Lepidoptera Phalænæ in the British Museum, Vol. II, 1900.

ARCTIIDÆ

HAMPSON, G. F. Catalogue of the Lepidoptera Phalænæ in the British Museum, Vol. III, 1901.

STRETCH, R. H.   Illustrations of the Zygænidæ and Bombycidæ of North America. (Numerous Arctiids are figured and described.)

BEUTENMÜLLER, W.   Descriptive Catalogue of the Bombycine Moths Found within Fifty Miles of New York City. (Bulletin Am. Mus. Nat. Hist., Vol. X., pp. 353–448.)

SMITH, JOHN B.   Preliminary Catalogue of the Arctiidæ of Temperate North America. (Canadian Entomologist, 1889, pp. 169–175, 193–200, and 213–219.)

The North American Species of Callimorpha Latreille. (Proc. U. S. Nat. Mus., 1887, pp. 342–353.)

LYMAN, H. H.   The North American Callimorphas. (Canadian Entomologist, Vol. XIX, pp. 181–191.)

GROTE, A. R.   Table of the Species of Euchætes. (Canadian Entomologist, Vol. XIV, pp. 196–197.)

AGARISTIDÆ

HAMPSON, G. F.   Catalogue of the Lepidoptera Phalænæ in the Collection of the British Museum, Vol. III, pp. 515–663, 1901.

(Consult also Stretch, Neumœgen and Dyar, and Periodicals.)

NOCTUIDÆ

HAMPSON, G. F.   Catalogue of the Lepidoptera Phalænæ in the Collection of the British Museum, Vol. IV, et seq.

GUENÉE, A.   Noctuelites. Spécies Général des Lépidoptères. Suites à Buffon, Vols. V–VIII.

GROTE, A. R.   List of the Noctuidæ of North America. (Bulletin Buffalo Soc. Nat. Sciences, Vol. II, pp. 1–77.)

Introduction to the Study of the North American Noctuidæ. (Proc. Amer. Philos. Society, Vol. XXI, pp. 134–176.)

An Illustrated Essay on the Noctuidæ of North America; with "A Colony of Butterflies," London. 1882, pp. 1–85, four colored plates.

Consult also the very numerous papers upon the Noctuidæ published by Grote in the Bulletin of the Buffalo Society of Natural Sciences; The Canadian Entomologist; the Bulletin of the U. S. Geological Survey, Vol. VI; Papilio; and recently in the publications of the Rœmer Museum at Hildesheim, Germany.

SMITH, JOHN B.	A Catalogue, Bibliographical and Synonymical, of the Species of Moths of the Lepidopterous Super-family Noctuidæ Found in Boreal America, with Critical Notes. (Bulletin U. S. Nat. Museum, No. 44, pp. 1–424.)

This is the most scholarly and complete work upon the Noctuidæ of America which has up to the present time been published, and is indispensable to the student.

Consult also the very numerous papers by Professor Smith which have been published in the Proceedings of the U. S. National Museum; the Transactions of the American Entomological Society; The Canadian Entomologist; Papilio, and other periodicals.

SMITH, JOHN B., AND DYAR, H. G.	A Revision of the Species of Acronycta and of Certain Allied Genera. (Proc. U. S. Nat. Museum, Vol. XXI, pp. 1–194.)
HULST, G. D.	The Genus Catocala. (Bulletin Brooklyn Ent. Society, Vol. VII, pp. 13–56.)

NYCTEOLIDÆ

NEUMŒGEN, B., AND DYAR, H. G.	A Preliminary Revision of the Bombyces of America North of Mexico. (Journal New York Ent. Soc., Vol. I, p. 117.)
HAMPSON, G. F.	The Fauna of British India, Moths, Vol. II, pp. 365–388.

PERICOPIDÆ

NEUMŒGEN, B., AND DYAR, H. G.	A Preliminary Revision of the Bombyces of America North of Mexico. (Journal of New York Ent. Soc., Vol. II, p. 26.)

DIOPTIDÆ

NEUMŒGEN, B., AND DYAR, H. G.	A Preliminary Revision of the Bombyces of America North of Mexico. (Journal of New York Ent. Soc., Vol. II, p. 111.)

NOTODONTIDÆ

PACKARD, A. S.	Monograph of the Bombycine Moths of America, North of Mexico. Part I, Family I, Notodontidæ. (Memoirs National Academy of Science, Vol. VII, pp. 1–390, Forty-nine Plates.)
NEUMŒGEN, B., AND DYAR, H. G.	A Preliminary Revision of the Lepidopterous Family Notodontidæ. (Transactions Am. Ent. Soc., 1894, pp. 179–208.)
SCHAUS, W.	A Revision of the American Notodontidæ. (Transactions Ent. Soc. London, 1901, pp. 257–344, Plates XI and XII.)

33

THYATIRIDÆ

GROTE, A. R.　　　　A Revision of the Species of Cymatophorina Found in the United States and British America, with Descriptions of New Species. (Proceedings Ent. Soc. Philadelphia, Vol. II, pp. 54–59.)

SMITH, JOHN B　　　Bulletin 44, U. S. National Museum, pp. 27–29.

LIPARIDÆ

NEUMŒGEN, B., AND DYAR, H. G.　　A Preliminary Revision of the Bombyces of America North of Mexico. (Journal New York Ent. Soc., Vol. II, pp. 28–30 and 57–60.)

LASIOCAMPIDÆ

NEUMŒGEN, B., AND DYAR, H. G.　　A Preliminary Revision of the Bombyces of America North of Mexico. (Journal New York Ent. Soc., Vol. II, pp. 152–160.)

BOMBYCIDÆ

HAMPSON, G. F　　　Fauna of British India, Moths, Vol. I, pp. 31–40.

PLATYPTERYGIDÆ

GROTE, A. R.　　　　On the North American Platypterygidæ. (Transactions Am. Ent. Soc., Vol. II, pp. 65–67.)
List of the North American Platypterices, etc. (Proceedings Am. Philos. Soc., Vol. XIV, pp. 256–264.)

NEUMŒGEN, B., AND DYAR, H. G.　　A Preliminary Revision of the Bombyces of America North of Mexico. (Journal New York Ent. Soc., Vol. II, pp. 61–62.)

GEOMETRIDÆ

PACKARD, A. S.　　　A Monograph of the Geometrid Moths or Phalænidæ of the United States. (U. S. Geological Survey of the Territories, Vol. X, pp. 1–607, Thirteen Plates.)

HULST, G. D.　　　　A Classification of the Geometrina of North America with Descriptions of New Genera and Species (Transactions Am. Ent. Soc., 1896, pp. 245–386.)

GUMPPENBERG, C.v.　Systema Geometrarum Zonæ Temperatioris Septentrionalis (Nova Acta der Kaiser. Leop.—Carol. Deutschen Akad. der Naturforscher, 1887–1897.)

EPIPLEMIDÆ

HULST, G. D.　　　　Transactions American Ent. Soc., Vol. XXIII, pp. 309–310.

HAMPSON, G. F.　　　Fauna of British India, Moths, Vol. III, pp. 121–137

NOLIDÆ

HAMPSON, G. F.　　　Catalogue of the Lepidoptera Phalænæ in the Collection of the British Museum, Vol. II, 1900.

34

FELT, E. P.

On Certain Grass-eating Insects. (Bulletin No. 64, Cornell Univ. Agric. Experiment Station, 1894, pp. 47–102, Fourteen Plates.)

FERNALD, C. H.

The Crambidæ of North America. (Annual Report Massachusetts Agricultural College, 1896, pp. 1–96, Nine Plates.)

RAGONOT, E. L.

Monographie des Phycitinæ et des Galleriinæ. (Romanoff's "Mémoires sur les Lépidoptères, Vols. VII–VIII, 1893–1902.) Volume VIII was completed by Sir George F. Hampson after the death of the author.

PTEROPHORIDÆ

FERNALD, C. H.

The Pterophoridæ of North America. (Special Bulletin, Mass. Agricultural College, 1898, pp. 1–64, Nine Plates.)

TORTRICIDÆ

FERNALD, C. H.

A Synonymical Catalogue of the Described Tortricidæ of North America North of Mexico. (Transactions Am. Ent. Soc., Vol. X, pp. 1–64.)

On the North American Species of Choreutis and Its Allies. (Canadian Entomologist, 1900, pp. 236–245.)

ROBINSON, C. T

Notes on American Tortricidæ. (Transactions Am. Ent. Soc., Vol. II, pp. 261–288, Plates I and IV–VIII.)

WALSINGHAM, LORD

North American Tortricidæ. Illustrations of Typical Specimens of Lepidoptera Heterocera in the Collection of the British Museum, Part IV, pp. i–xii and 1–84, Plates I–XVII.

ZELLER, P. C.

Beitræge zur Kentniss der Nordamerikanischen Nachtfalter besonders der Microlepidopteren. (Verhandlungen d. Zoöl.–Bot. Gesellsch, Wien, 1873, pp. 447–556; 1873, pp. 201–334; 1875, pp. 207–360. Treats also of Tineidæ.

TINEIDÆ, ETC.

CLEMENS, B.

The Tineina of North America, by the late Brackenridge Clemens. Being a Collected Edition of his Writings on that Group of Insects. With Notes by the Editor, H. T. Stainton, London, 1872, pp. i–xv and 1–282.

CHAMBERS, V. T.

Index to the Described Tineina of the United States and Canada. (Bulletin U. S. Geol. Survey of the Territories, Vol. IV, pp. 125–167.)

Books about North American Moths

WALSINGHAM, LORD   North American Coleophoræ.   (Transactions Ent. Soc., London, 1882, pp. 429–442, Pl. XVII.)

A Revision of the Genera Acrolophus Poey and Anaphora Clemens.   (Transactions Ent. Soc., London, 1887, pp. 137–173, Plates VII, VIII.)

Steps Toward a Revision of Chambers's Index with Notes and Descriptions of New Species.   (Insect Life, Vol. I, pp. 81–84, 113–117, 145–150, 254–258, 287–291; Vol. II, pp. 23–26, 51–54, 77–81, 116–120, 150–155, 284–286, 322–326; Vol. III, pp. 325–329, 386–389; Vol. IV, pp. 385–389.)

DYAR, H. G.   Notes on Some North American Yponomeutidæ, (Canadian Entomologist, 1900, pp. 37–41, 84–86.)

BUSCK, A.   New Species of Moths of the Superfamily Tineina from Florida.   (Proc. U. S. Nat. Mus., Vol. XXIII, pp. 225–254.)

New American Tineina.   (Journal New York Ent. Soc., Vol. VIII, pp. 234–248, Plate IX.)

A Revision of the American Moths of the Famiiy Gelechiidæ with Descriptions of New Species. (Proc. U. S. Nat. Mus., Vol. XXV, pp. 767-938.)

" When simple curiosity passes into the love of knowledge as such, and the gratification of the æsthetic sense of the beauty of completeness and accuracy seems more desirable than the easy indolence of ignorance ; when the finding out of the causes of things becomes a source of joy, and he is counted happy who is successful in the search, common knowledge of Nature passes into what our forefathers called Natural History, from whence there is but a step to that which used to be termed Natural Philosophy, and now passes by the name of Physical Science."—THOMAS HENRY HUXLEY, in *The Crayfish.*

THE MOTHS OF NORTH AMERICA,
NORTH OF MEXICO

"The laugh at entomology is nearly spent. Known professors of the science, and members of its ' Society,' may now assemble in council and communicate their observations and inquiries without fear of becoming themselves subjects for a commission *de lunatico inquirendo*, and butterfly hunters, net in hand, may now chase their game without being themselves made game of."—*Acheta Domestica.*

ORDER LEPIDOPTERA

SUBORDER HETEROCERA (MOTHS)

FAMILY I.

THE SPHINGIDÆ (HAWKMOTHS)

"The Sphinx is drowsy,
Her wings are furled."—EMERSON.

THE moths composing this family vary greatly in size. Some African species are very little more than an inch in expanse of wings. Those which occur in North America are medium-sized or large.

The body is relatively very stout, the abdomen conic, cylindric, or flattened on the ventral surface, always protruding far beyond the hind margin of the secondaries, sometimes adorned with lateral or terminal tufts capable of expansion. The thorax is stout and often advanced beyond the insertion of the wings. The head is large and generally prominent. The eyes are often large, prominent, and generally naked, never hairy. The palpi are well, but never excessively, developed. The proboscis is generally long, sometimes much longer than the body, but in a few genera among the *Ambulicinæ* greatly reduced and even obsolete. The antennæ are well developed, stouter in the male than in the female sex, thickening from the base to the middle, or in some genera to nearly the end, usually hooked at the extremity, sometimes merely curved. The joints of the antennæ in the case of the males

FIG. 20.—Greatly magnified view of the under side of three joints of the antenna of *P. quinquemaculatus*.

of some of the subfamilies are equipped at either end with peculiarly arranged fascicles of projecting hairs, or cilia, the arrangement of which, as examined under the microscope, is seen to be quite different from that which prevails in any other family of moths. The accompanying illustration (Fig. 20) shows this arrangement in the case of the common Five-spotted Hawkmoth, *(Protoparce quinquemaculatus)*.

The wings are small in comparison with the body. The front wings are very long in proportion to their width, and the costal veins are always very stoutly developed. The tip of the wing is usually pointed, and the margins are straight or evenly rounded, though in some genera, principally belonging to the subfamily *Ambulicinæ*, they have undulated or scalloped margins. The hind margin of the fore wings is always much shorter than the costal margin. The hind wings are relatively quite small. The venation of the wings is characteristic. The primaries have from eleven to twelve veins, the secondaries eight, reckoning the two internal veins, veins 1 *a* and 1 *b*, as one. Veins eight and seven are

FIG. 21.—Neuration of wings of *Sesia tantalus* Linnæus.

connected near the base of the wing by a short vein, or bar. The discal cell is relatively quite small in both wings. There is always a frenulum, though in the *Ambulicinæ* it is frequently merely vestigial. The general style of the venation is illustrated in Figure 21, which represents the structure of the wings of *Sesia tantalus* Linnæus. The hawkmoths have prodigious power of flight. A few genera are diurnal in their habits; most of them are crepuscular, flying in the dusk of evening, a few also about dawn.

The larvæ are usually large. There is great variety in their color, though the majority of the North American species are of some shade of green. They usually have oblique stripes on their sides, and most of them have a caudal horn, which in the last stages in some genera is transformed into a lenticular tubercle. In a few genera the anal horn is wanting. The anterior segments of the bodies of the larvæ are retractile. When in motion the body is long and fusiform, but when at rest the head and the anterior segments are drawn back, the rings "telescoping" into one another, and the anterior portion of the body being often raised, as illustrated in Plate I, Figure 1. It is alleged that the habit of assuming this posture, suggesting a resemblance to the Egyptian Sphinx, prompted the application of the name to these creatures. The larvæ are not gregarious, but feed solitarily upon their appropriate food-plants.

Some forms pupate in a cell deep under the soil, others spin a loose cocoon among damp fallen leaves and pupate at the surface. The pupæ are as remarkable as the larvæ. A few genera have the proboscis enclosed in a sheath which is separate along the greater portion of its course from the adjacent wall of the body. This is illustrated in Figure 22.

Fig. 22.—Pupa of *Protoparce quinquemaculatus.* (After **Riley.**)

The Hawkmoths of the United States and Canada fall into five subfamilies, the *Acherontiinæ,* the *Ambulicinæ,* the *Sesiinæ,* the *Philampelinæ,* and the *Chœrocampinæ.*

SUBFAMILY ACHERONTIINÆ
Genus HERSE Oken

(1) **Herse cingulata** Fabricius, Plate VI, Fig. 3, ♂, (The Pinkspotted Hawkmoth.)

Syn. *convolvuli,* var. Merian; *affinis* Gœze; *drurœi* Donovan; *pungens* Eschsholtz; *decolora* Henry Edwards.

This large and elegant hawkmoth, the larva of which feeds upon sweet-potato vines and various other *Convolvulaceæ,* has been confounded by writers with *H. convolvuli* Linnæus, which it resembles, but from which it is abundantly distinct. The latter species is confined to the old world. *H. cingulata,* the only species of the genus occurring in the western hemisphere, ranges from Canada to northern Patagonia, and is also found in the Galapagos and Sandwich Islands. I have a specimen taken at sea in the Atlantic, five hundred miles from the nearest land.

It settled in the cabin of a ship and was caught by the captain of the vessel.

Genus COCYTIUS Hübner

The genus *Cocytius*, which includes some of the largest hawkmoths which are known, contains five species, all of which are found in the tropics of the new world. They may easily be recognized by the fact that the third joint of the labial palpi is in both sexes prolonged into a small, sharp, conical, naked horn. The larvæ, which feed upon the *Anonaceæ*, are covered with fine hairs. Only one of the species is found within the faunal limits covered by the present work. It occurs in southern Florida, and in southern Texas as a straggler.

* (1) **Cocytius antæus** Drury, Plate VI, Fig. 1, ♀. (The Giant Sphinx.)

Syn. *caricæ* Müller (*non* Linnæus); *jatrophæ* Fabricius; *hydaspus* Cramer; *medor* Stoll; *anonæ* Shaw; *tapayusa* Moore.

The species is somewhat variable, specimens from the Antilles being often lighter in color than those from Central America, and the continental portions of its habitat. This lighter form is accepted by Rothschild & Jordan as typical, and the darker form is called by them *Cocytius antæus medor* Stoll. The difference is hardly sufficiently constant to justify the separation into two subspecies. The insect ranges from Florida into southern Brazil.

Genus PROTOPARCE Burmeister

The head is prominent. The body is stout and heavy. The tongue in both sexes is at least as long as the body. The palpi are large, ascending, and appressed to the front, having the basal joint long, the second a little shorter, but broader, and the terminal joint minute. The eyes are large, feebly lashed. The tibiæ are either without spines, or feebly armed with minute spinules. The mid tarsus is provided with a comb of long bristles. The venation of the wings is typically sphingiform. The outer margins of the primaries are evenly rounded. There is a slight projection of the secondaries at the extremity of vein 1 *b*. The prevalent colors of the wings are shades of gray, banded and mottled with darker and lighter lines and

---

*Technically, our race should be listed *C. antæus hydaspus* Cramer. Holland regularly uses only binomials, and this is the present-day practice of many authors of popular books.—A.E.B.

spots. The abdomen is generally marked on the sides by rows of yellowish spots.

The larvæ are cylindrical with the head rounded. The anal horn curves downward and is granulose. The prevalent colors are shades of green. The segments, from four to eleven inclusive, are marked on the sides with whitish diagonal stripes.

The pupa has the tongue-case free, curved, and nearly touching the pectus.

This genus, which is confined to the two Americas, includes thirty species, of which four occur within our faunal limits.

(1) **Protoparce sexta** Johanssen, Plate IV, Fig. 2, ♀. (The Tomato Sphinx.)

Syn. *carolina* Linnæus; *nicotianæ* Ménétriés; *lycopersici* Boisduval.

This is one of our commonest hawkmoths. Its larva feeds upon the potato, tomato, and other *Solanaceæ*. It ranges over the United States and is represented in Central and South America by several subspecies or local races.

(2) **Protoparce quinquemaculatus** Haworth, Plate IV, Fig. 1, ♀. See also text figures 20 and 22. (The Five-spotted Hawkmoth.)

Syn. *celeus* Hübner; *carolina* Donovan.

Like the preceding species, this hawkmoth is very common. Its larva feeds upon the *Solanaceæ* and is particularly destructive to tobacco. It is familiarly known in the South as the "tobacco fly."

(3) **Protoparce occulta** Rothschild & Jordan, Plate IV, Fig. 4, ♀. (The Occult Sphinx.)

This hawkmoth is found in a number of American collections confounded with *P. sexta = carolina* Linnæus. It may readily be distinguished by the different markings of the hind wings, the absence of the two rows of small white spots on the back of the abdomen, and by the small but conspicuous whitish dot at the end of the cell of the fore wing. It occurs in Texas and Arizona and ranges southward to Central America. Its larval habits are not known.

(4) **Protoparce rustica** Fabricius, Plate VII, Fig. 5, ♀. (The Rustic Sphinx.)

Syn. *chionanthi* Abbot & Smith.

The caterpillar of this hawkmoth feeds upon the fringe-bush

45

(Chionanthus) and the jasmine. It is a common species in the southern States and Central America, but is only occasionally found in the northern States. I have not infrequently taken specimens in southern Indiana, and it is now and then captured in Pennsylvania and even in New England.

Genus CHLÆNOGRAMMA Smith

This genus, which is very closely allied to the preceding, may be distinguished from it by the fact that the comb of long bristles of the mid tarsus, which is characteristic of *Protoparce,* is wanting or reduced to at most one or two bristles. Pulvillus and paronychium present. The eyes are smaller than in *Protoparce,* and are not lashed. There are two species in the genus, one South American, the other found in the eastern portion of the United States.

(1) **Chlænogramma jasminearum** Guérin, Plate VII, Fig. 6, ♀. (The Ash Sphinx.)

Syn. *rotundata* Rothschild.

The larva of this hawkmoth feeds upon the various species of ash *(Fraxinus)*. It is found in the middle Atlantic States and southward, and ranges as far west as the Mississippi.

Genus DOLBA Walker

Head small; eyes small and lashed. The antennæ are fusiform with a short abrupt hook at the tip. The tibiæ are not spinose. The mid tarsus has a comb.

The genus, which contains but a single species, is differentiated from all those in which the eyes are lashed by the non-spinose tibiæ.

(1) **Dolba hylæus** Drury, Plate VI, Fig. 4, ♀. (The Papaw Sphinx.)

This small, but neatly colored hawkmoth, may readily be distinguished by the figure given in our plate. Its larva, which is green, marked with lateral oblique red bands, commonly feeds upon the papaw, *(Asimina triloba),* and is generally abundant where that plant is common, as in the Valley of the Ohio. It is also said to feed upon *Prinos*. It ranges from Canada to the Gulf States and westward to Iowa and Missouri.

46

Genus ISOGRAMMA Rothschild & Jordan

This genus has been erected by Rothschild & Jordan for the reception of the single species which we figure. The learned authors say: "In the shortness of the fore tibia and first segment of the fore tarsus the only species of this genus agrees with the species of *Ceratomia,* and in the preservation of the pulvillus with *Chlænogramma,* while it differs from both genera in the fore tibia and the extreme apex of the mid tibia being armed with spines. The spinosity of the tibia is an advanced character, not acquired by *Ceratomia,* while the pulvillus is an ancestral structure already lost in *Ceratomia.*"

(1) **Isogramma hageni** Grote, Plate IV, Fig. 8, ♂. (Hagen's Sphinx.)

This obscurely colored hawkmoth, which is liable to be confounded with some of the species of *Ceratomia,* which it superficially resembles, may be distinguished at a glance by the slightly greenish shade of the primaries and by the absence of the dark-brown border of the hind wings, which is characteristic of all the species of *Ceratomia.* It occurs in Texas.

Genus CERATOMIA Harris

The tongue is reduced in size. The palpi are small. The eyes are small. The tibiæ are unarmed. There is no comb of bristles on the mid tarsus, the pulvillus is absent, the paronychium is present. The primaries are relatively large with evenly rounded outer margin. The secondaries are slightly produced at the end of vein 1 *b*.

The species have dissimilar larvæ. In the case of *amyntor* the larva has four horn-like projections on the thoracic segments ; in the case of the other two species of the genus the larvæ are distinctly and normally sphingiform.

The tongue-case of the pupa is not projecting.

(1) **Ceratomia amyntor** Hübner, Plate IV, Fig 6, ♀. (The Four-horned Sphinx.)

Syn. *quadricornis* Harris; *ulmi* Henry Edwards.

This common hawkmoth, which may be easily recognized by our figure, lives in the larval state upon the elm. It ranges from Canada to the Carolinas and westward through the Mississippi Valley, wherever its food-plant is found.

(2) **Ceratomia undulosa** Walker, Plate VI, Fig. 7, ♀. (The Waved Sphinx.)

Syn. *repentinus* Clemens; *brontes* Boisduval (*non* Drury).

This hawkmoth, which may easily be separated from its congeners by its lighter color and the distinct wavy maculation of the fore wings, lives in the larval stage upon the ash and the privet. It ranges from Maine and Canada to the Carolinas and westward into the trans-Mississippi region east of the great plains.

(3) **Ceratomia catalpæ** Boisduval, Plate IV, Fig. 7, ♀. (The Catalpa Sphinx.)

The larva feeds upon various species of catalpa, and has in recent years been charged with doing considerable damage to these trees by denuding them of their foliage. The insect ranges from New Jersey and southern Pennsylvania southward to Florida and westward through the Mississippi Valley, wherever its food-plant occurs.

Genus ISOPARCE Rothschild & Jordan

Tongue short and weak. Palpi small. Tibiæ without spines. The first protarsal segment is short. Hind tibia armed with long spurs. Comb on mid tarsus wanting; pulvillus wanting. Paronychium without lobes. Veins 6 and 7 of the hind wing on a long stalk.

(1) **Isoparce cupressi** Boisduval. (The Cypress Sphinx.)

The insect is of an almost uniform brown color on the upper surface of the wings, and may be distinguished from other species by the two conspicuous parallel dark markings on the limbal area of the fore wings. It is extremely rare in collections, only three or four specimens being as yet

Fig. 23.—*Isoparce cupressi* Boisduval.

known. It has been reported from Georgia and Florida.

Genus DICTYOSOMA Rothschild & Jordan

This genus has been erected by Messrs. Rothschild & Jordan for the reception of the single species originally described by Strecker as *Sphinx elsa.*

(1) **Dictyosoma elsa** Strecker, Plate V, Fig. 14, ♂. (The Elsa Sphinx.)

This peculiarly colored hawkmoth, which may easily be recognized by the figure in our plate, occurs in Arizona. A number of years ago Mr. Jacob Doll reared a large number of specimens from the larvæ. Since then but few specimens have been obtained, and it is as yet comparatively rare in collections.

Genus ATREIDES Holland

The generic name *Atreus* proposed by Grote and adopted on structural grounds by Rothschild & Jordan for this genus, having been preoccupied by Koch in the *Arachnida*, I have given the name *Atreides* to the genus, which contains the single species named originally *Sphinx plebeja* by Fabricius.

(1) **Atreides plebeja** Fabricius, Plate V, Fig. 6, ♂. (The Plebeian Sphinx.)

This common species feeds in its larval state upon the trumpet-vine (*Tecoma*). It ranges from Canada to the Gulf States and westward to the Mississippi, wherever its food-plant is found. It is double-brooded in the Middle States, one brood appearing in June, the second in August.

Genus HYLOICUS Hübner

This genus, which includes some thirty species, most of which are found in America, though a few occur in Europe and Asia, is represented in our faunal limits by sixteen species, of which eleven are figured in our plates. It corresponds largely with the genus *Sphinx* as defined by many recent writers.

(1) **Hyloicus eremitus** Hübner, Plate VI, Fig. 6, ♀. (The Hermit Sphinx.)
Syn., *sordida* Harris.

This hawkmoth, which is double-brooded, lives in the larval stage on spearmint (*Mentha*) and wild bergamot (*Monarda*). It ranges from New England southward to Georgia, and westward into the Mississippi Valley. It is not uncommon in western Pennsylvania, where it is double-brooded.

(2) **Hyloicus eremitoides** Strecker. (The Hermit-like Sphinx.)
Syn., *lugens* Grote (*non* Walker).

This species, which is allied to the preceding, may be easily recognized by its pale, silvery-gray color, by the almost entire absence of a dorsal stripe on the abdomen, and by the marking of the secondaries, which are grayish-white, having on the outer margin a broad band which is black inwardly, fading into darkish gray near the margin, a median irregularly curved black band, and at the insertion of the wing a black basal patch. The cut (Fig. 24) will enable the student to recognize the species, which is not common in collections. The insect is found in Kansas and the southwestern States.

FIG. 24.—*Hyloicus eremitoides.*

(3) **Hyloicus separatus** Neumœgen, Plate VI, Fig. 10, ♂. (Neumœgen's Sphinx.)

Syn. *andromedæ* Boisduval (*partim.*); *lugens* Smith (*partim.*).

This species has been confounded with others, but may easily be recognized from the figure which we give in our plate. It ranges from Colorado southward through New Mexico and Arizona into Mexico.

(4) **Hyloicus chersis** Hübner, Plate I, Fig. 1, larva ; Plate VII, Fig 8, ♀. (The Chersis Sphinx.)

This common and widely distributed species ranges from Canada to Florida, westward to the Pacific, and southward into Mexico. Several local races are recognized, that which occurs upon the Pacific coast having been named *oreodaphne* by Henry Edwards. The caterpillar feeds upon the wild-cherry, the ash, the privet, and other allied plants. The insect is double-brooded in the Middle States, appearing on the wing in the latter part of May, and again in August.

(5) **Hyloicus vancouverensis** Edwards.
Syn. *vashti* Strecker.

Form **albescens** Tepper, Plate VI, Fig. 5, ♂. (The Vancouver Sphinx.)

There are two forms of this hawkmoth, one, **Hyloicus van-**

couverensis vancouverensis in which the middle of the thorax is pale gray, and the other, **Hyloicus vancouverensis albescens,** which has a very dark thorax, and which is figured on our plate. The moth is found from northern California to British Columbia, and eastward to Montana and Alberta.

(6) **Hyloicus insolita** Lintner, Plate V, Fig. 4, ♂. (Lintner's Sphinx.)

This species, which is well represented on our plate, occurs in Texas. It is not common in collections. Rothschild & Jordan regard it as a form of *H. libocedrus* Henry Edwards, and apparently with reason.

(7) **Hyloicus perelegans** Henry Edwards. (The Elegant Sphinx.)

This hawkmoth may be distinguished by the even dark silvery-gray color of the fore wings, which are crossed by a distinct submarginal whitish band. The maculation recalls a dark *chersis* with the dark thorax and the body of *H. drupiferarum.* It is found on the Pacific coast.

(8) **Hyloicus canadensis** Boisduval.

Syn. *plota* Strecker.

This species, which is not common, is represented by the accompanying cut (Fig. 25), drawn from a specimen in the Engel Collection in the Carnegie Museum, and taken in Massachusetts. It occurs in eastern Canada, northern New York, and New England.

FIG. 25.—*Hyloicus canadensis.*

(9) **Hyloicus kalmiæ** Abbot & Smith, Plate VI, Fig. 8, ♀. (The Laurel Sphinx.)

This hawkmoth feeds in the larval stage upon *Kalmia, Chionanthus,* and *Fraxinus.* It is not uncommon in the Middle States of the Atlantic coast region, ranging from southern Canada to Georgia.

(10) **Hyloicus gordius** Cramer, Plate V, Fig. 13, ♂. (The Gordian Sphinx.)

Syn. *pœcila* Stephens.

The larva of this hawkmoth feeds upon various rosaceous plants, as the wild rose and the crab-apple. It ranges over the Atlantic region from southern Canada and New England to Georgia, and westward to Colorado.

(11) **Hyloicus luscitiosa** Clemens, Plate V, Fig. 1, ♂. (Clemens' Hawkmoth.)

The caterpillar feeds upon various species of willow. The insect occurs from Canada to the Carolinas, and westward through the eastern portion of the valley of the Mississippi.

(12) **Hyloicus drupiferarum** Abbot & Smith, Plate VII, Fig. 7, ♂. (The Wild-Cherry Sphinx.)

This common and easily recognizable species ranges over the whole of temperate North America from the Atlantic to the Pacific. The caterpillar feeds upon various trees and shrubs, but seems in the Middle Atlantic States to prefer the wild-cherry as a food-plant.

(13) **Hyloicus dolli** Neumœgen.

Form **coloradus** Smith, Plate IV, Fig. 3, ♀. (The Colorado Sphinx.)

Rothschild & Jordan recognize two forms of this species, **H. dolli dolli** Neumœgen, and **H. dolli coloradus** Smith. The latter we figure. The former is prevalently lighter in color than the form *coloradus*. The insect ranges from Colorado to Arizona.

(14) **Hyloicus sequoiæ** Boisduval, Plate V, Fig. 8, ♂. (The Sequoia Sphinx.)

Syn. *coniferarum* Walker (*partim*).

The early stages of this insect we do not remember to have seen described. It occurs on the Pacific coast. Boisduval's type was found sitting on the trunk of a red-wood tree *(Sequoia)*.

(15) **Hyloicus pinastri** Linnæus. (The Pine Sphinx.)

Syn. *saniptri* Strecker.

The late Dr. Strecker reported this species as having been found by him in the vicinity of Reading, Pennsylvania, on one or two occasions. No one else has taken it, so far as is known. It is common in Europe, and has often been figured by European writers.

Besides the species above given, there are one or two other species of the genus found in our territory.

Genus LAPARA Walker.

Head small. Palpi short and slender. Tongue very short, almost obsolete. Eyes small. Antennæ slender. Thorax stout and short. Abdomen long and cylindrical, tapering. Legs weak. Fore and mid tibiæ spinulose. The larva is without an anal horn, cylindrical, tapering slightly from the middle forward and backward, pale green, striped with white, and checkered with darker green. The caterpillars feed upon various species of pine, and are not at all sphingiform in appearance. There are reputed to be four species of the genus found in our fauna, two of which we figure. *L. halicarniæ* Strecker, of which only one specimen is known, which I have recently examined, appears to be a somewhat hypertrophied and, in consequence, aborted female of *L. coniferarum* Abbot & Smith. It is very doubtfully a valid species.

(1) **L. coniferarum** Abbot & Smith, Plate III, Fig. 16, ♀. (Abbot's Pine Sphinx.)

Syn. *cana* Martyn.

This species is somewhat variable, especially in the size of the females and in the amount of marking upon the fore wings. It is a common insect in the foot-hills of the Alleghenies about the headwaters of the Potomac River. I found the larvæ in great abundance upon pines at Berkeley Springs, West Virginia, in the summer of 1884. It ranges from Canada to Florida and westward into the basin of the Mississippi, but has never been reported from any point west of that river, south of Minnesota, so far as is known to the writer.

(2) **L. bombycoides** Walker, Plate III, Fig. 7, ♂. (The Bombyx Sphinx.)

Syn. *harrisi* Clemens.

This little hawkmoth, which may easily be recognized from the figure we give, has the same geographical distribution as the preceding species, and feeds upon the same forms of vegetation in the larval stage.

Lapara pineum Lintner (Lintner's Pine Sphinx) is a species of which thus far only two specimens have turned up. They differ from the two species we have figured in being wholly devoid of discal streaks and markings upon the fore wings. It is believed by recent authorities that these specimens represent an extreme variation of the very variable *L. coniferarum.*

SUBFAMILY AMBULICINÆ

Genus **PROTAMBULYX** Rothschild & Jordan

This genus is represented in our fauna by a single species, which occurs as a straggler into the extreme southern limits of the United States, and is represented in Florida by a local race, to which Rothschild & Jordan have given the subspecific name of *carteri* in honor of Sir Gilbert T. Carter, the Governor of the

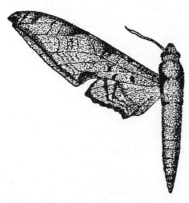

Bahamas, an ardent lepidopterist. From *A. strigilis* Linnæus, which is represented in the annexed cut, *A. carteri* may be distinguished by the fact that the fore wing is broader, less deeply excavated below the apex, and by the further fact that most of the lines and markings on the upper side of the wings and all the markings on the lower side of the wings are obsolete. While *strigilis* has not yet been reported from our territory, except as represented by the form above mentioned, it is highly probable that it will be found to occur in southern Florida.

FIG. 26.—*Protambulyx strigilis.* (Somewhat reduced.)

Genus **SPHINX** Linnæus

The type of the genus Sphinx of Linnæus is unquestionably the well-known European species named by the immortal Swede *Sphinx ocellata.* With this species the following two species, which have for many years been referred to the genus *Smerinthus* Latreille, which sinks as a synonym, are strictly congeneric.

(1) **Sphinx cerisyi** Kirby, Plate VII, Fig. *3*, ♀. (Cerisy's Sphinx.)

The larva feeds upon different species of willows. There are several forms, or subspecies, which have received names, and which run into each other to such an extent as to make it often impossible to distinguish them. These forms are *Sphinx astarte* Strecker, in which the outer margin of the fore wing is a little less dentate, and the brown markings of the same wing are a little narrower; *Sphinx ophthalmica* Boisduval, which has rather pale fore wings; *Sphinx pallidulus* Henry Edwards, in which the color of the fore wings is cinnamon-gray; and *Sphinx saliceti* Boisduval, in which the blue markings of the ocellus on the hind wing do not form a ring, but appear as two opposed crescents.

The insect is comparatively rare in the eastern part of the continent, but is not uncommon in the western States. It ranges from Canada in the north to the upper portions of the Gulf States, and westward to the Pacific, extending its habitat southward along the high lands of Mexico.

(2) **Sphinx jamaicensis** Drury.

Normal form **geminatus** Say, Plate IV, Fig. 11, ♂. (The Twin-spot Sphinx.)

This beautiful hawkmoth was originally named and described in error by Drury as coming from the Island of Jamaica. He also was so unfortunate as to have had for his type an aberrant specimen in which the ocellus of the hind wing had but one blue spot. Such specimens now and then occur, and have been obtained by breeding from the normal form, to which Say gave the name *geminatus*. Specimens also sometimes occur in which there are three blue spots in the ocellus, and Mr. Grote gave to this aberrant form the name *tripartitus*.

The caterpillar feeds upon willows, birches, and various species of wild-cherry. The insect is quite common in the Middle Atlantic States, and ranges from southern Canada to the Carolinas and northern Georgia, and westward to eastern Kansas and Iowa.

Genus CALASYMBOLUS Grote

The genus differs from *Sphinx* in the fact that the head is crested, and the hind wing is on its costal margin toward the apex produced into a somewhat broad lobe. There are three species recognized as belonging to the genus, all of which we figure.

55

(1) **Calasymbolus excæcatus** Abbot & Smith, Plate VII, Fig. 4, ♂. (The Blinded Sphinx.)

Syn. *pavonina* Geyer.

The larva feeds upon various plants of the order *Rosaceæ*, but does not strictly confine itself to these. It has been reported as found upon the willow, the hazel, iron-wood, and other allied plants. It is a common species, and in the region of Pennsylvania is double-brooded. It ranges from southern Canada to Florida and westward across the valley of the Mississippi to the borders of the great plains.

(2) **Calasymbolus myops** Abbot & Smith, Plate IV, Fig. 12, ♀. (The Small-eyed Sphinx.)

Syn. *rosacearum* Boisduval.

The food-plants and the geographical distribution of this species are very much the same as those of the preceding species, though it seems to range a little further westward, examples having been received from Colorado. It is not nearly as common as *C. excœcatus*.

(3) **Calasymbolus astylus** Drury, Plate IV, Fig. 10, ♂. (The Huckleberry Sphinx.)

Syn. *io* Gray; *integerrima* Harris.

A rather scarce species, which is found from New England to Pennsylvania. The caterpillar feeds upon various species of *Vaccinium* and allied plants. The moth is easily distinguished by the fact that the outer margins of the fore wings are almost even, whereas in *myops* they are distinctly produced at the end of vein 3, and in *excœcatus* they are scalloped. The transverse lines on the limbal area of the fore wings, which are distinct in *myops*, are almost wanting in *astylus*, and the inner margin of the primaries is heavily margined with dark brown.

Genus PACHYSPHINX Rothschild & Jordan

The genus *Pachysphinx* has been erected for the reception of the single species, two forms of which we figure on our plates. It is very different from the oriental genus *Marumba*, into which Mr. Dyar, following Kirby, has put it in his recent List. Any one who is familiar with the peculiar style of coloration of the species of *Marumba*, as well as with the structural differences, which present themselves, will recognize the propriety of the separation, which has been made.

(1) **Pachysphinx modesta** Harris, Plate VII, Fig. 1, ♂. (The Big Poplar Sphinx.)

Syn. *princeps* Walker.

Form **occidentalis** Henry Edwards, Plate VII, Fig. 2, ♀. (The Western Poplar Sphinx.)

Syn. *imperator* Strecker.

This noble hawkmoth feeds in the larval stage upon various species of the genus *Populus* and upon willows. There are a number of local races or subspecies, two of which we give ; the common eastern form and the western variety. The latter may at once be distinguished by its generally paler coloration. It ranges over the United States and as far south as northern Mexico.

Genus CRESSONIA Grote & Robinson

There is but one species in this genus. The insect is easily recognizable, in spite of the fact that it varies considerably in the color of the wings.

(1) **Cressonia juglandis** Abbot & Smith, Plate VI, Fig. 9, ♀. (The Walnut Sphinx.)

Syn. *instabilis* Martyn; *pallens* Strecker; *robinsoni* Butler.

The caterpillar feeds upon the black walnut, the butternut, and the hop-hornbeam. Some of the larvæ are green, others are reddish, but the color of the larvæ seems to have no relation to any variation in color of the perfect insects. The species is distributed from Canada to Florida and westward to the eastern boundary of the great plains.

SUBFAMILY SESIINÆ

Genus PSEUDOSPHINX Burmeister

There is but one species in this genus, which is structurally closely related to the species falling into the genus *Erinnyis*. It is a characteristic insect of the American tropics, and possesses a very wide range.

(1) **Pseudosphinx tetrio** Linnæus, Plate VI, Fig. 2, ♂. (The Giant Gray Sphinx.)

Syn. *plumeriæ* Fabricius; *rustica* Sepp; *hasdrubal* Cramer; *asdrubal* Poey; *obscura* Butler.

57

The larva of this hawkmoth has a long thread-like anal horn. It is very strikingly colored, the body being purplish black, girdled with yellow rings between the segments, and the head and anal claspers being bright red, of the color of sealing wax. It feeds upon various Euphorbiaceous plants, preferably *Plumeria*. The insect occurs not uncommonly in southern Florida.

Genus ERINNYIS Hübner

This is a moderately large genus, the species of which are all confined to the tropical or subtropical regions of the Western Hemisphere, though one species, as we shall see, occasionally occurs as a straggler far north of the metropolis of the genus.

(1) **Erinnyis alope** Drury, Plate V, Fig. 12, ♂. (The Alope Sphinx.)

Syn. *flavicans* Gœze; *fasciata* Swainson; *edwardsi* Butler.

The caterpillar is brown on the upper side, and pale green on the lower side, the colors being separated by a dark brown interrupted lateral band on either side of the body. On the third segment from the head there is a dark spot relieved by a red ring in the centre. The anal horn is quite short. The larva feeds upon *Jatropha* and *Carica*. The insect occurs in southern Florida and ranges southward as far as northern Argentina.

(2) **Erinnyis lassauxi** Boisduval.

Form **merianæ** Grote, Plate V, Fig. 2, ♀. (Madame Merian's Sphinx.)

Syn. *janiphæ* Boisduval.

This hawkmoth, which is widely distributed through the tropics of the new world, displays considerable variation, and several forms, or local races, have been recognized. The one which occurs within our territory we have figured, and the student will have no difficulty in recognizing it. The larva, which is said to closely resemble that of the next species, is reported to feed upon *Morrenia* in the West Indies. It occurs in Florida.

(3) **Erinnyis ello** Linnæus, Plate V, Fig, 10, ♂ ; Fig. 3, ♀. (The Ello Sphinx.)

This is quite the commonest of all the hawkmoths of the American tropics, and becomes a perfect drug in collections made by amateur naturalists, who venture into those regions, net in hand. It may at once be recognized by the figures we have given, which are taken from specimens bred on the Indian River by Mr. Wittfeld. The sexes are dissimilar, as the student may observe. It straggles north sparingly, even as far as Canada, and is common in the Gulf States.

(4) **Erinnyis œnotrus** Stoll, Plate V, Fig. 11, ♀. (The Œnotrus Sphinx.)

Syn. *penæus* Fabricius; *melancholica* Grote; *piperis* Grote & Robinson; *picta* Kirby.

The sexes in this species are dissimilar, the female being as represented on our plate with light fore wings, marked with dark spots and lines, while the male is prevalently quite dark on the fore wings. The species may easily be recognized by the black spots on the under side of the abdomen.

(5) **Erinnyis crameri** Schaus, Plate V, Fig 7, ♀. (Cramer's Sphinx.)

This species, which has often been confounded with the preceding, may easily be distinguished from it by the pale shoulder lappets, the absence of black spots on the under side of the abdomen, and the more evenly colored fore wings, which recall those of *E. merianæ*, from which it is at once distinguished by the absence of the white lateral markings on the abdomen. The species occurs in Florida and Texas.

(6) **Erinnyis obscura** Fabricius, Plate V, Fig. 5, ♂. (The Obscure Sphinx.)

Syn. *rustica* Schaller; *phalaris* Kirby; *stheno* Hübner; *pallida* Grote; *cinerosa* Grote & Robinson; *rhœbus* Boisduval.

This small species is well represented in our plate by a specimen which in the main conforms to the most usual style of marking. It can always be distinguished from *E. ello*, which it resembles in having a dark longitudinal shade through the fore wings, by its much smaller size, and by the absence of the white and black lateral stripes upon the abdomen, which are characteristic of the latter species. It is common in Florida.

(7) **Erinnyis domingonis** Butler, Plate V, Fig. 9, ♀. (The Domingo Sphinx.)

Syn. *obscura* Walker (*non* Fabricius); *festa* Henry Edwards.

This species, which occurs in Florida and the Antilles, may be distinguished from the preceding by the darker color of the primaries and the absence of the pale color on the outer margin of the shoulder lappets, which is characteristic of *E. obscura*. It is also considerably larger than *E. obscura*.

There remains one other closely allied species in this group, to which Cramer gave the name **caicus,** and which occurs occasionally in Florida. The body is marked like *E. ello,* the fore wings are dark with longitudinal paler stripes, the secondaries are red as in *E. crameri,* but almost wholly without the dark border found in that species, it being replaced by a series of dark stripes running inwardly from the border toward the middle of the wing. For this species, hitherto associated with the preceding in the genus *Dilophonota,* Rothschild & Jordan have erected the genus *Grammodia,* upon structural grounds.

Genus PACHYLIA Walker

This is a small genus, containing four species, of which one occurs in our territory. It is not likely to be confounded with anything else.

(1) **Pachylia ficus** Linnæus, Plate III, Fig. 12, ♀. (The Fig Sphinx.)

Syn. *crameri* Ménétriés; *lyncea* Clemens; *venezuelensis* Schaufuss; *undatifascia* Butler; *aterrima* Bönninghausen.

This great hawkmoth, which is very common in Central and South America, occurs sparingly in Florida and Texas.

Genus HEMEROPLANES Hübner

This small genus, the species of which may at once be detected by the silvery spots of the fore wings, being the only American genus of sphingids thus adorned, is characteristically neotropical. It is represented in our fauna by a single species.

(1) **Hemeroplanes parce** Fabricius, Plate III, Fig. 8, ♂. (The Silver-spotted Sphinx.)

Syn. *licastus* Stoll; *galianna* Burmeister.

The figure given on our plate is sufficiently accurate to make a verbal description unnecessary. The insect occurs in southern Florida in the vicinity of Biscayne Bay, and ranges thence southward over the Antilles into South America.

Genus EPISTOR Boisduval

Five species belong to this genus, the type of which is the species which we figure, and the only representative of the genus found in our territory.

(1) **Epistor lugubris** Linnæus, Plate II, Fig. 17, ♂. (The Mourning Sphinx.)

Syn. *fegeus* Cramer; *luctuosus* Boisduval.

There can be no difficulty in identifying this well-marked but obscurely colored hawkmoth, which occurs in Florida and Georgia, and even straggles now and then as far north as New Jersey. It is very common in the Antilles and South America. In Florida it is double-brooded, appearing on the wing in May and September. The larva feeds on the *Vitaceæ*.

Genus CAUTETHIA Grote

There are three species of this genus, only one of which occurs within the limits of the United States. The figure we give will permit of its identification without difficulty.

(1) **Cautethia grotei** Henry Edwards, Plate II, Fig. 21, ♂. (Grote's Sphinx.)

The habitat of this species is southern Florida, where it apparently is not uncommon.

Genus SESIA Fabricius

The body is depressed, fusiform, without lateral tufts, but with a broad fan-shaped anal tuft, composed of coarse flattened scales. The abdomen is produced for more than half its length beyond the hind wings. The palpi are produced and appressed, forming a short snout-like projection beyond the head. The tongue is stout, but comparatively short. The antennæ are slightly thickened at the end, and have a sharp recurved tip. The mid tibiæ have terminal spurs, and the hind tibiæ two pairs of spurs. The fore wings have eleven veins. The venation is characteristically sphingiform, and is illustrated in Figure 21. The prevalent colors are black and dark brown with white spots and bands on the wings and in some species on the abdomen. The moths fly in the hottest sunshine.

The type of the genus *Sesia* established by Fabricius is the species named *tantalus* by Linné. Rothschild & Jordan, in the latest Revision of the *Sphingidæ*, recognize five species as belonging to the genus, three of which occur within the limits of the United States, *tantalus* Linnæus, *fadus* Cramer, and the species we figure upon our plate. All three have by some recent writers been regarded as practically identical. Into the somewhat vexed question of their specific relationship it is not our purpose to enter in these pages.

(1) **S. titan** Cramer, Plate II, Fig. 16, ♂. (The White-banded Day-Sphinx.)

The white spots of the fore wings are semi-transparent. On the under side the wings are whitish at the base and on the inner margin of the secondaries. They are crossed about the middle by two parallel distinct dark bands, which are quite close to each other.

The moth sometimes strays as far north as Massachusetts. It is very common in southern Florida and throughout tropical America.

Genus HÆMORRHAGIA Grote

Moth.—Head small. Tongue as long as the body. Antennæ clavate, two-thirds the length of the costa, with a minute recurved hook at the tip. Thorax smooth, strongly projecting before the insertion of the wings. Abdomen more or less flattened beneath, and, especially in the males, adorned with a broad fan-shaped anal tuft. The primaries have eleven veins. Both primaries and secondaries are transparent about the middle; the outer margin of the former is evenly rounded, and of the latter slightly excavated between veins 1 *b* and 2.

Larva.—Characteristically sphingiform, provided with an anal horn. The epidermis in most species of the genus is more or less granulated. The caterpillars feed for the most part upon *Symphoricarpus, Lonicera, Viburnum, Cratægus,* and allied plants.

Pupa.—The pupa, which is brown in color, is enclosed in a somewhat dense cocoon, formed on the surface of the ground under fallen leaves.

(1) **Hæmorrhagia thysbe** Fabricius, Plate II, Fig. 5, ♂. (The Humming-bird Clearwing.)

Syn. *pelasgus* Cramer; *ruficaudis* Kirby; *etolus* Boisduval.

Form **cimbiciformis** Stephens, Plate II, Fig. 6, ♀.

Syn. *ruficaudis* Walker (partim); *floridensis* Grote; *uniformis* Grote & Robinson; *buffaloënsis* Grote; *pyramus* Boisduval.

This is the largest and the commonest species of the genus. It may easily be recognized by the figures given on Plate II. It is subject to considerable variation. The form *cimbiciformis* is distinguished by the absence of the dentations on the inner side of the marginal brown band of the fore wings. It has been obtained by breeding from the eggs of *H. thysbe,* and *thysbe* has been bred from it. It is a dimorphic form of the species. The caterpillar of *H. thysbe* feeds upon *Viburnum* and allied plants. The insect ranges from Canada and Nova Scotia southward to Florida and westward to the Mississippi.

(2) **Hæmorrhagia gracilis** Grote & Robinson, Plate III, Fig. 15, ♂. (The Graceful Clearwing.)

Syn. *ruficaudis* Walker (*non* Kirby) (*partim*).

The thorax and basal segments above are olive-green. The middle segments are black, the two preterminal segments are margined laterally with reddish. The anal tuft is black, divided in the middle by red hairs. On the under side the palpi, pectus, and thorax are white, and the abdomen pale red. The pale area of the thorax is traversed on either side by a stripe of reddish hair, and there are three rows of white spots on the under side of the abdomen. It occurs in the States of the Atlantic seaboard from New England to the Carolinas.

(3) **Hæmorrhagia diffinis** Boisduval. (The Snowberry Clearwing.)

Spring form **tenuis** Grote, Plate II, Fig. 2, ♀.

Syn. *fumosa* Strecker; *metathetis* Butler; *diffinis* Beutenmüller.

Summer form **diffinis** Boisduval.

Syn. *marginalis* Grote.

Summer form **axillaris** Grote & Robinson, Plate II, Fig. 3, ♂; Fig. 4, ♀.

Syn. *grotei* Butler; *æthra* Strecker.

This species is trimorphic. The life history has been in part very carefully worked out by Mr. Ellison Smythe of Blacksburg, Virginia. (See "Entomological News," Vol. XI, p. 584.) The form *diffinis* has the marginal band dentate inwardly.

The caterpillar feeds upon *Symphoricarpus, Lonicera,* and *Diervilla.* The insect has a wide range from New England to

Georgia and westward to the eastern boundaries of the great plains.

(4) **Hæmorrhagia senta** Strecker, Plate IV, Fig. 5, ♂. (The Californian Clearwing.)

Syn. *rubens* Hanham (*non* Edwards).

The head, thorax, and basal segments of the abdomen are brownish-olivaceous. The abdomen is black. The two segments immediately preceding the terminal segment are marked laterally by yellow tufts of hair. The anal tuft is wholly black. The wings are very narrowly bordered with brown. There is no rusty red spot at the apex of the primaries. The clear portions of the wing in certain lights have a bright steel-blue luster. The under side of the palpi, the pectus, and the abdomen are pale straw-yellow. In size this species is about as large as *H. diffinis.*

The perfect insect occurs in Utah and California, frequenting the blossoms of *Lupinus.*

(5) **Hæmorrhagia thetis** Boisduval, Plate II, Fig. 1, ♂. (The Thetis Clearwing.)

Syn. *palpalis* Grote; *rubens* Edwards.

Decidedly smaller than either of the two preceding species. The thorax is olive-green, passing on either side into pale yellow. This color is continued dorsally on the abdomen as far as the terminal segment, but is more or less lost in the broad yellow preanal band. The basal and middle segments of the abdomen are marked laterally with black, and the anal tuft is correspondingly marked with black on either side. The marginal band of the fore wings is narrow, as in *H. diffinis,* and is always distinctly marked above and below at the apex by a rust-red triangular spot. The wings at their insertion are more or less shaded with pale rusty red both above and below.

This species ranges from Colorado and Wyoming westward and northward to Oregon and British Columbia. It has been by Dr. Dyar made synonymous with the following species, from which it is, however, quite distinct.

(6) **Hæmorrhagia brucei** French, Plate II, Fig. 7, ♂. (Bruce's Clearwing.)

This is a small species, in size approximating *H. thetis,* from which it may be at once distinguished by the green color of the scales upon the thorax and the basal segments of the abdomen, and the fact that the anal tuft is wholly black, not divided by yellow scales in the middle as is the case in *H. thetis.*

The species is not uncommon in Colorado and Utah.

SUBFAMILY PHILAMPELINÆ
Genus PHOLUS Hübner

This is a large genus, including nineteen species, and a number of subspecies. It is confined to the Western Hemisphere. Six species occur within our territory. *P. typhon* Klug, which we have not figured, is occasionally found in Arizona. The larvæ feed upon the *Vitaceæ,* and in the case of two of the species have done at times some damage to vineyards.

(1) **Pholus satellitia** Linnæus. (The Satellite Sphinx.)

Form **pandorus** Hübner, Plate III, Fig. 6, ♂.

Syn. *ampelophaga* Walker.

This insect which is widely distributed throughout the eastern United States, and ranges northward into southern Canada, is well-known to all growers of vines. The caterpillar, when it first emerges from the egg and for several successive molts is green in color, and

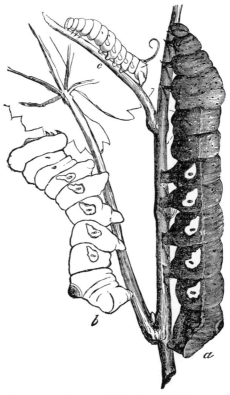

Fig. 27.—Larva of *Pholus satellitia pandorus; a,* mature larva; *b,* larva after third molt, head retracted; *c,* young larva. (After Riley.)

has at the anal extremity a very long caudal horn, which begins gradually to curl up, as represented in the accompanying cut, and after the third molt entirely disappears, being replaced by a lenticular shining eye-like prominence.   In the latter stages of development the larvæ frequently become dark brown, and Professor Riley maintains that this is invariably the case in the neighborhood of the city of St. Louis.   It is not invariably the case in other localities, as I know from experience.   I have reared a number of specimens in which the green color perdured to the time of pupation, though the brown form is very common. Like the larva of the following species, the caterpillar of *P. satellitia* has the power of withdrawing the first two segments of its body into the third, when at rest, or when suddenly alarmed. When crawling or feeding the first segments are protruded, as represented in the cut by the larger figure.

Several local races of *P. satellitia* are recognized as occurring in the Antilles and in South America, one of these, for which Mr. Grote proposed the name *posticatus,* occurs in Florida, as well as in Cuba and the Bahamas.   It may be distinguished from the form *pandorus* by its slighter build, its narrower wings, which in the case of the primaries have the outer margin straighter than in *pandorus,* and by the presence of a large roseate spot covering the anal angle of the secondaries.   There are other differences of a minor character, but those mentioned will enable the student to discriminate this form from the one we have figured.

(2) **Pholus achemon** Drury, Plate III, Fig. 5, ♂. (The Achemon Sphinx.)

Syn. *crantor* Cramer.

Like the preceding species the caterpillar of this beautiful hawkmoth feeds upon vines, and shows especial fondness for

Fig. 28.—Larva of *Pholus achemon.*   (After Riley.)

the grape.   It is also addicted to the Virginia creeper *(Ampelopsis).* The description of the habits of the larva given by

Professor C. V. Riley, "Missouri Reports," Vol. III, p. 75, is most excellent. The figure which we give is taken from that Report.

The insect ranges over the entire United States from the Atlantic to the Pacific, and from southern Canada to northern Mexico.

(3) **Pholus vitis** Linnæus, Plate III, Fig. 1, ♂. (The Vine Sphinx.)

Syn. *hornbeckiana* Harris; *linnei* Grote & Robinson; *fasciatus* Grote (*partim*).

The true *Pholus vitis*, which we figure in our plate, may easily be distinguished from its near ally, *Pholus fasciatus* Sulzer, by the absence of the pink outer marginal area on the upper two-thirds of the secondaries, by the inward prolongation of the large black spot near the inner margin of the secondaries into a well marked mesial band, and by its larger size. It occurs in Florida and in southern Texas and Arizona, whence it ranges southward over wide areas.

(4) **Pholus fasciatus** Sulzer, Plate III, Fig. 2, ♂. (The Lesser Vine Sphinx.)

Syn. *vitis* Drury (*non* Linnæus); *jussieuæ* Hübner; *strigilis* Vogel.

The caterpillar is reported as feeding upon *Jussieua* in the tropics. In our territory it feeds upon various species of *Vitaceæ*. It is quite common in the region of the Gulf States and southward, and sometimes is even taken as a straggler as far north as Massachusetts.

(5) **Pholus labruscæ** Linnæus, Plate III, Fig. 11, ♂. (The Gaudy Sphinx.)

Syn. *clotho* Fabricius.

This beautiful creature is characteristic of the tropics, where it is not uncommon. It occurs quite abundantly in southern Florida and along the borders of the Gulf, and throughout the Antilles, Central, and South America. Specimens, in spite of the subtropical habitat of the species, have been taken in Canada, illustrating the wonderful power of flight which is possessed by these insects, the frail wings of which bear them in the dusk of evening, during the few days of their existence in the winged form, from the orange-groves of the south to the banks of the St. Lawrence, a thousand leagues, across rivers, **plains, and mountains.**

Genus DARAPSA Walker

We include in this genus three species, all of which occur within our territory, and all of which we figure upon our plates.

(1) **Darapsa pholus** Cramer, Plate III, Fig. *3*, ♂. (The Azalea Sphinx.)

Syn. *choerilus* Cramer; *azaleæ* Abbot & Smith; *clorinda* Martyn.

This medium-sized hawkmoth, which is one of our commonest species in western Pennsylvania, may easily be distinguished from its very near ally, *D. myron*, by its reddish color. The caterpillar feeds upon *Viburnum* and *Azalea*.

(2) **Darapsa myron** Cramer, Plate III, Fig. 4, ♂. (The Hog Sphinx.)

Syn. *pampinatrix* Abbot & Smith; *cnotus* Hübner.

The caterpillar, of which we give a figure, feeds upon wild and domestic grape-vines, and also upon the Virginia Creeper.

It is a very common insect in the Atlantic States, and ranges as far west as Kansas and Iowa. It has been regarded as injurious to vineyards, but the damage done is inconsiderable, and the insects can easily be combated by picking off the larvæ from the vines and crushing them under foot. The reason why these insects do comparatively small damage is perhaps found in the fact that they appear to be especially subject to the attacks of a small hymenopterous parasite, belonging to the family *Ichneumonidæ*. The female ichneumon-fly deposits her eggs upon the epidermis of the young caterpillar. As soon as the eggs hatch, the grub penetrates the body of the caterpillar and feeds upon the fatty tissues lying just under the skin.

FIG. 29.—Larva of *D. myron*.
(After Riley.)

Before the caterpillar reaches maturity the grubs emerge from beneath the skin, and attaching themselves to the epidermis, proceed to weave about themselves little white cocoons, in which they are transformed into perfect insects, emerging to repeat the cycle of life. Caterpillars which have been thus parasitized do not survive the ordeal.

FIG. 30.—Parasitized larva of *D. myron*. (After Riley.)

The accompanying cut (Fig. 30), shows a larva upon which the ichneumon-flies have done their deadly work.

FIG. 31.—Microgaster which destroys larvæ of *D. myron*.

The insect, which accomplishes the task of destruction imposed upon it in the economy of nature, is very small. The figure given herewith shows it of its natural size, and also enlarged, so that its structural peculiarities may be more easily recognized. The species which we are considering shares this liability to parasitism with its congeners, as well as with the representatives of many other genera of the *Sphingidæ*. I was greatly annoyed a number of years ago by having a large series of the larvæ of the beautiful *Darapsa versicolor,* which I had collected in their early stages, destroyed by this ichneumon-fly, and the following summer, and, in fact, for several summers following, the larvæ of *D. versicolor,* which had been for awhile quite abundant in certain localities known to me, almost entirely disappeared. In one ravine, where I had obtained them by the hundreds, they were not to be found. I account for their disappearance by the unusual numbers of the parasites which had infested them that summer.

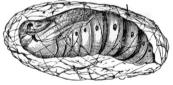

FIG. 32.—Pupa of *D. myron*

The larva of *myron* undergoes pupation in a loose cocoon of coarsely woven threads of silk, which it spins under leaves at the surface of the ground. In this respect its habits are strictly like those of the other species of the genus.

(3) **Darapsa versicolor** Harris, Plate III, Fig. 13, ♂. (The Hydrangea Sphinx.)

This lovely hawkmoth, which is accounted quite rare in localities, has been found very commonly at certain times in western Pennsylvania. Its larva feeds upon the wild hydrangea, which grows abundantly in deep wooded glens, along the margin of brooks. The insect ranges from New England to the mountains of the Carolinas and westward into the eastern border of the Mississippi Valley.

Genus SPHECODINA Blanchard

The head is broad. The proboscis is nearly as long as the body. The antennæ are fusiform, with a recurved hook at the tip. The body is broad, flattened beneath. The abdomen has a pointed anal tuft, and the segments are adorned laterally with prominent truncated tufts of coarse hairs. The wings in their outline closely resemble those of the genus Amphion. Only one species of the genus is known.

(1) **Sphecodina abbotti** Swainson, Plate II, Fig. 19, ♂. (Abbot's Sphinx.)

This beautiful hawkmoth is found throughout the Eastern States and southern Canada and ranges westward as far as Iowa

and Kansas. The larva feeds on the *Vitaceæ* and is not uncommon on *Ampelopsis*. The caterpillar is not provided with an anal horn, but has instead an eye-like tubercle, or boss, at the anal extremity. It has the habit, when disturbed, of throwing its head violently

FIG. 33.—Larva and moth of *S. abbotti.*
(After Riley.)

from side to side, a movement found in other sphingid larvæ, and also in some of the *Ceratocampidæ*.

70

Genus DEÏDAMIA Clemens

The head is small, narrow, retracted, crested. The eyes are small. The antennæ are fusiform, with the tip bent back slightly, scarcely hooked. The thorax is stout, somewhat crested. The abdomen is conic, and in the male has a small anal tuft. The fore wings, which have twelve veins, are narrow, with the inner margin sinuate. The apex of the fore wings is truncated, and the outer margin is deeply excavated opposite the end of the cell and also just above the inner angle, which is distinctly produced. The hind wings are slightly crenulate on the outer margin. There is only one species belonging to the genus.

(1) **Deïdamia inscriptum** Harris, Plate II, Fig. 15, ♂. (The Lettered Sphinx.)

The caterpillar feeds upon the wild grape-vine. The moth appears in the early spring. It is a common species in western Pennsylvania, but seems elsewhere to be regarded as quite rare. It ranges from Canada to Virginia and westward to the Mississippi.

Genus ARCTONOTUS Boisduval

This small genus, in which there are reputed to be two species, is very closely related to the genus *Proserpinus,* from which, as has been pointed out by Rothschild & Jordan, it differs in appearance "owing to the more woolly scaling." The chief structural difference is found in the fact that the antenna is not clubbed but fusiform, gradually curved, and the feet are without a pulvillus, and have only vestiges of the paronychium.

(1) **Arctonotus lucidus** Boisduval, Plate III, Fig. 14, ♂. (The Bear Sphinx.)

This insect, which hitherto has been rare in collections, appears to have a wide range along the Pacific coast, from southern California to British Columbia. It appears upon the wing very early in the spring of the year.

The name *Arctonotus terlooi* is applied to a species, reported from northern Mexico by Henry Edwards, and described by him, in which the hind wings are wholly vinous red, and the green basal band of the fore wings is wanting.

Genus AMPHION Hübner

Head small. Eyes small, hemispherical. Palpi rather short. Tongue nearly as long as the body. Antennæ fusiform with a long curved hook at the tip. Body plump, somewhat globose, the thorax projecting very little beyond the insertion of the primaries, and the abdomen terminating in a conspicuous fan-like tuft. The fore wings are comparatively short and narrow, excavated on the outer margin below the apex and above the inner angle, which is strongly produced. The inner margin is deeply sinuate. The hind wings are bluntly lobed at the anal angle. There is only one species in the genus.

(1) **Amphion nessus** Cramer, Plate II, Fig. 18, ♂. (The Nessus Sphinx.)

This species, which may easily be recognized from the figure on the plate, is not uncommon in the Middle States. It ranges from Canada to Georgia and westward to Wyoming. It flies in the daytime on cloudy days and in the late afternoon before sunset. The caterpillar feeds on *Ampelopsis* and the wild grape.

Genus POGOCOLON Boisduval

This small genus, which is closely related in many structural respects to *Proserpinus*, differs from it very decidedly in the form as well as in the habits of the insects belonging to it. In the structure of the antennæ and neuration of the wings the insects belonging to *Pogocolon* show a close relationship to the insects referred to the genus *Proserpinus*, but the form of the abdomen is wholly different, elongated, cylindrical, and not bombyliform. The moths, moreover, are crepuscular, whereas the moths referred to the genus *Proserpinus* are diurnal in their habits, in this respect resembling the species of the genus *Hæmorrhagia*. There are at least three species belonging to this genus.

(1) **Pogocolon gauræ** Abbot & Smith, Plate II, Fig. 11, ♂. (The Gaura Sphinx.)

The upper side of this small species is sufficiently delineated in the plate to require no verbal description. On the under side the wings are vinous brown, shading on the outer third into olive-green, and reproducing the maculation of the upper surface. The hind wings are deep olive at the base, passing into yellowish green outwardly.

The insect feeds in the larval stage upon various species of *Gaura*, and ranges from Georgia to Texas and as far north as southern Kansas.

(2) **Pogocolon juanita** Strecker, Plate II, Fig. 12, ♂. (Strecker's Day-sphinx.)

The moth in the general style of its maculation is very much like the preceding species, but is considerably larger, and the colors are decidedly brighter. The caterpillar is quite different in its markings from the larva of *L. gauræ*.

The habitat of this species is Texas, so far as is now known.

One other species of *Pogocolon, P. vega* Dyar, occurs in our region. It is much darker in color than the two former species, which it otherwise somewhat closely resembles.

Genus PROSERPINUS Hübner

Head small ; proboscis moderate or long ; antennæ clavate ; body stout ; abdomen with or without lateral tufts, but always with a more or less well developed anal tuft. Anterior tibiæ stout, armed with spines outwardly and at tip. Fore wings elongate, generally somewhat curved outwardly about the middle, and with the inner angle more or less distinctly produced ; more or less densely clothed with scales over their entire surface. The moths are diurnal in their habits, and mimic bumblebees in their appearance.

(1) **Proserpinus flavofasciata** Walker, Plate II, Fig. 8, ♀. (The Yellow-banded Day-sphinx.)

The head and thorax are pale yellow, the latter obscured with brownish hairs about the middle. The abdomen is black with the basal segment about the middle and the preterminal segment on either side pale yellow. The fore wings on the upper side are blackish, crossed by an oblique whitish band. The hind wings are deep black, crossed by a broad orange-yellow band. The fore wings on the under side are bright orange-yellow at the base.

This is always a rare insect in collections. It ranges, so far as is known, through British America, and southward and eastward to Maine and Massachusetts. It is found in very early summer hovering over flowers.

(2) **Proserpinus clarkiæ** Boisduval, Plate II, Fig. 10, ♀. (Clark's Day-sphinx.)

73

Syn. *victoriæ* Grote.

The head, thorax and abdomen on the upper side are prevalently pale olive-green, the fifth and the three anal segments of the abdomen being darker green. The fore wings are pale green with an oblique brownish median band, and a triangular paler brownish spot at the apex. There is a small black discal dot at the end of the cell. The hind wings are deep orange-yellow, margined with black. On the under side the wings are olive-green, darker at the base. The hind wings have a waved whitish band about their middle on the under side. The legs are greenish-white.

This species is found from Oregon to northern California, and eastward to Utah and Montana.

Genus EUPROSERPINUS Grote & Robinson

This genus is discriminated by Rothschild & Jordan from *Proserpinus* by the fact that the antenna is more abruptly hooked and slenderer at its extremity than in *Proserpinus*, and by the absence of the pulvillus and paronychium, which are found in *Proserpinus*. Two species belong to the genus, both having white hind wings margined with darker color and the under side of the pectus and the wings also white.

(1) **Euproserpinus phaëton** Grote & Robinson, Plate II, Fig. 9, ♂. (The Phaëton Sphinx.)

Syn. *errato* Boisduval.

The head and thorax above are gray, the abdomen blackish. The preterminal segment has yellow lateral tufts. The anal tuft is black. The fore wings above are of the same color as the thorax. The hind wings are yellowish-white with a broad black marginal band. Expanse 32 mm.

The habitat of this species is southern California.

(2) **Euproserpinus euterpe** Edwards. (The Euterpe Sphinx.)

This species, which is only known to the writer through an examination of the type, is discriminated from the preceding by the absence of pale tufts on the side of the abdomen and the fact that the marginal band of the hind wing is bowed inwardly and not straight as in *E. Phaëton*.

74

SUBFAMILY CHÆROCAMPINÆ

Genus XYLOPHANES Hübner

This genus, which is American, is very large, containing fifty species and many subspecies. Of these species two only are found, so far as is now known, within our territory, though it is possible that a thorough exploration of southern Florida may show that one or two of the species which are found in the Antilles also occur in that State. The student will have no difficulty in recognizing the species occurring within our borders by means of the figures which are given upon our plates.

(1) **Xylophanes pluto** Fabricius, Plate IV, Fig. 9, ♂. (The Pluto Sphinx.)

Syn. *bœrhaviæ* Fabricius; *crœsus* Dalman; *thorates* Hübner; *eson* Walker

This beautiful hawkmoth, which is very common in the Antilles, ranging southward to southern Brazil, occurs in southern Florida. The larva feeds upon *Erythroxylon*.

(2) *Xylophanes tersa* Linnæus, Plate II, Fig. 13, ♂. (The Tersa Sphinx.)

This common and easily recognized species has a wide range, occurring very rarely as far north as southern Canada, thence southward to Texas and Mexico, and as far south as northern Argentina. The larva feeds on *Bouvardia, Spermacoce,* and *Manetta.*

Genus CELERIO Oken

Head of moderate size. Eyes hemispherical, not prominent. Antennæ distinctly clavate, and armed at the tip with a minute hook. The thorax is stout, projecting for about one-third of its length beyond the insertion of the fore wings. The abdomen is conic, untufted, produced more or less at the tip, and projecting for half its length beyond the hind margins of the secondaries. The fore wings, which have eleven veins, are produced at the apex. Their outer margin is slightly and evenly bowed outwardly. Their inner margin is very slightly sinuate. The hind wings have their outer margin evenly rounded, except at the extremity of vein 1 *b*, where they are slightly produced. The genus is well represented in the Old World, and there are several South American species. Only two species occur in our territory.

(1) **Celerio lineata** Fabricius, Plate II, Fig. 14, ♂. (The Striped Morning Sphinx.)

Syn. *daucus* Cramer.

This is probably the commonest of all the North American Sphingidæ. The larva feeds upon *Portulaca*. There is considerable diversity in the maculation of the larvæ. The two figures here given represent the two most usual forms of the caterpillar. The insect ranges over the southern portions of

Fig. 34.—Light form of larva of *C. lineata*. (After Riley.)

British America to the Gulf of Mexico and southward to the Antilles and Central America. I have seen hundreds of the moths swarming about the electric lights in the streets of Denver, Cheyenne, and Colorado Springs. The moth flies con-

Fig. 35.—Dark form of larva of *C. lineata*. (After Riley.)

stantly in bright sunshine on the Laramie Plains of Wyoming in the month of August, frequenting the blossoms of thistles. I have seen it busily engaged in extracting the sweets from dew-spangled beds of Soapwort *(Saponaria)*, in the valleys of Virginia long after the sun had risen in the morning.

(2) **Celerio intermedia** Kirby, Plate II, Fig. 20, ♀. (The Galium Sphinx.)

Syn. *epilobii* Harris (*non* Boisduval); *chamænerii* Harris; *galii* Walker; *oxybaphi* Clemens; *canadensis* Guenée.

This hawkmoth, which is the North American representative of *Celerio gallii*, which is found all over the north temperate regions of the Eastern Hemisphere, ranges from Canada to

Vancouver and southward through the mountains of the Appalachian System and along the higher plateaus and mountain ranges of the West as far as Central Mexico. I have specimens taken in the Sierra Madre of Chihuahua. The identification of the species may easily be made by means of the figure on our plate.

THE WORLD OF THE DARK

> ". . . . . Sorrowing we beheld
> The night come on; but soon did night display
> More wonders than it veil'd; innumerous tribes
> From the wood-cover swarm'd, and darkness made
> Their beauties visible."
>
> SOUTHEY.

There are two worlds; the world of sunshine, and the world of the dark. Most of us are more or less familiarly acquainted with the first; very few of us are well acquainted with the latter. Our eyes are well adapted to serve us in the daylight, but they do not serve us as well in the dark, and we therefore fail to know, unless we patiently study them, what wonders this world of the dark holds within itself. There are whole armies of living things, which, when we go to sleep, begin to awaken; and when we awaken, go to sleep. The eyes of the creatures of the dark are adapted to seeing with less light than our eyes require. The broad daylight dazzles and confounds them. Sunshine has much the same effect upon them that darkness has upon us. Our twilight is their morning; our midnight is their noonday.

This is true even of many of the higher vertebrates. The lemurs, which are a low family of simians, are nocturnal in their habits. So also is the Aye-Aye of Madagascar, and that curious little member of the monkey tribe known as the Specter (*Tarsius spectrum*). No one can see the great eyes of these creatures without realizing at a glance that they love what we call darkness better than what we call light, though they are far from being evil-doers. The great family of the cats are principally nocturnal in their habits. Their eyes are capable of being used in daylight, for the beautifully contracting and expanding iris modifies the amount of light admitted to the retina

77

far more delicately and instantaneously than any device, attached to the most perfectly constructed camera, regulates the amount of light transmitted through its lens. The tiger in the jungle sees what is going on about him in the starlight as well as we see what is happening in the noontide. I have studied the eyes of lions and tigers in the dark. The yellowish-green iris in the night almost entirely disappears from view, and shrinks down into a narrow ring. The windows of the eyes have the curtains drawn back wide, so as to let in all the light which the darkness holds within itself. The great orbs then look like globes of crystal, framed in a narrow band of gold, lying on a background of the blackest velvet, while in their pellucid depths, fires, tinged with the warm glow of blood, play and coruscate.

The eyes of many birds are adapted to the dark. This is true, as everybody knows, of the owls, and of their not distant relatives, the goat-suckers. I remember having, when a boy, dissected an owl, which I found dead after a long protracted period of intensely cold weather. The thermometer had stood at twenty degrees below zero for several nights in succession. The earth was wrapped deep in snow. Upon the sleety crust I found a great horned owl, lying dead, and frozen stiff. It may have died of old age, or it may have starved to death. The instinct of the child, who takes his toys to pieces in order to see how they are made, seized me, and, with a sharp penknife as a scalpel, and a few needles set in sticks of pine, I took my owl apart, and made drawings of what I found. I did not then know the names and functions of all the parts, but the drawing of the eye, which I made, I still have in an old portfolio, and there I saw it the other day. The eye of an owl is a wonderful piece of mechanism. It is a wide-angle lens of beautiful powers of adjustment. It is adapted to taking in all the light there is, when the light is almost all gone; and it is so contrived as to shut out light, when too much of its splendor would dazzle and hurt.

Among the insects thousands and tens of thousands of species are nocturnal. This is true of the great majority of the moths. When the hour of dusk approaches stand by a bed of evening primroses, and, as their great yellow blossoms suddenly open, watch the hawkmoths coming as swiftly as meteors through the air, hovering for an instant over this blossom, probing into the sweet depths of another, and then dashing off again so quickly that the eye cannot follow them. My friend, Henry Pryer, had a great bed of evening primroses in his compound on the Bluff in Yokohama. Well I remember standing with him before the flowers, and, as the light began to fade upon the distant top of Fuji-no-yama, with net in hand capturing the hawkmoths, which came eagerly trooping to the spot. When it grew quite dark O-Chi-san held a Japanese lantern aloft to help us to see where to make our strokes. A dozen species became our spoil during those pleasant evenings. Ah! those nights in Japan! Can I ever forget them?

Did you ever reflect upon the fact that the wings of many moths, which lie concealed during the daytime, reveal their most glorious coloring only after dark, when they are upon the wing? Take as an illustration, the splendid moths of the great genus *Catocala*, the Afterwings, as we familiarly call them. The fore wings are so colored as to cause them, when they are quietly resting upon the trunks of trees in the daytime, to look like bits of moss, or discolored patches upon the bark. They furnish, in such positions, one of the most beautiful illustrations of protective mimicry which can be found in the whole realm of nature. The hind wings are completely concealed at such times. The hind wings are, however, most brilliantly colored. In some species they are banded with pink, in others with crimson; still others have markings of yellow, orange, or snowy white on a background of jet-black. One European species has bands of blue upon the wings. These colors are distinctive of the species to a greater or less extent. They are only displayed at night. The conclusion is irresistibly forced upon us that the eyes of these creatures are capable of discriminating these colors in the darkness. We cannot do it. No human eye in the blackness of the night can distinguish red from orange, or crimson from yellow. The human eye is the greatest of all anatomical marvels, and the most wonderfu piece of animal mechanism in the world, but not all of power is lodged within it. There are other allied mechanisms which have the power of responding to certain forms of radiant energy to a degree which it does not possess.

Let me commend to the study of my readers this world of the

dark of which I have been speaking. Some of the pleasantest excursions afield which can be made are those which the naturalist takes, when he has only moonlight or starlight to guide his steps. Always take a dark lantern with you. Without it you cannot see, and even with it you will not see much which it might be delightful to behold. But without a lantern you will not see a great deal, and you may in the thick wood get deeply mired in a boggy hole, or even break a limb. Your eyes are not made like those of the owl and the cat. Do not be afraid of the "night air." The air of the night has the same chemical composition as the air of the day. It is cooler, of course, and sometimes it has fog in it, but cool and even foggy air is not unhealthful. Scotchmen live half their lives in fog, but are healthy. The only things to be dreaded are the mosquitoes, carrying with them the germs of malaria, as we call it. These may be kept off if you only know how to anoint yourself with a properly prepared lotion.

FAMILY SATURNIIDÆ

"When, hypocritically clad in dressing-gown and slippers, I stopped at my guest's inner door and Fontenette opened it just enough to let me in, I saw, indeed, a wonderful sight. The entomologist had lighted up the room, and it was filled, filled! with gorgeous moths as large as my hand and all of a kind, dancing across one another's airy paths in a bewildering maze, or alighting and quivering on this thing and that. The mosquito-net, draping almost from ceiling to floor, was beflowered with them, majestically displaying in splendid alternation their upper and under colors, or, with wings lifted and vibrant, tipping to one side and another as they crept up the white mesh, like painted and gilded sails in a fairies' regatta."—G. W. CABLE.

This family is composed of moths, which are for the most part medium-sized or large. The larvæ are cocoon-makers. The perfect insects have vein 8 of the hind wings diverging from the cell from the base of the wings. The frenulum is wanting. The tongue is aborted, being at most extremely rudimentary. There are no tibial spurs on the legs. The antennæ are either singly or doubly bipectinated to the tips in the case of the males, and often in the case of the females. Bipectination of the antennæ occurs also in the family *Ceratocampidæ*, but in the latter family it never extends to the tip of the organ. The family falls into three subfamilies: the *Attacinæ;* the *Saturniinæ;* and the *Hemi-*

leucinæ.   These subfamilies may be discriminated by the help of the following Key:

Hind wings with one distinct internal vein.
    Discal cell of both wings open   -   -   -   *Attacinæ.*
    Discal cell of both wings closed   -   -   -   *Saturniinæ.*
Hind wings with two distinct internal veins   -   *Hemileucinæ.*

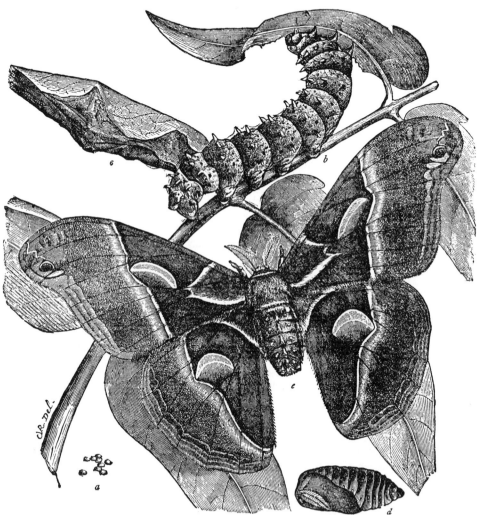

FIG. 36.—*Philosamia cynthia.*   *a.* Eggs; *b.* Larva; *c.* Cocoon; *d.* Pupa; *e.* Moth.
(After Riley.)

SUBFAMILY ATTACINÆ

Genus PHILOSAMIA Grote

This genus, which may be distinguished from all others in our fauna by the tufted abdomen of the perfect insect, is represented by a single species, which, originally imported from the eastern parts of Asia, has become thoroughly acclimatized on the Atlantic seaboard in the vicinity of the larger cities, from which, as centres, it has spread to some extent to the surrounding country.

(1) **Philosamia cynthia** Drury, Plate IX, Fig. 2, ♂. (The Ailanthus Silk-moth.)

Syn. *aurotus* Fabricius; *insularis* Vollenhoven; *vesta* Walker; *canningi* Walker; *walkeri* Felder; *pryeri* Butler.

The cut (Fig. 36) and the representation on our plate obviate all necessity for mere verbal description of the species. The insect which was originally introduced into Europe about the middle of the last century was first introduced into America in the year 1861. It was hoped that it would prove a valuable silk-bearing species, but although a good grade of coarse silk may be made from it by the process of carding, and strong and service-able fabrics are manufactured from it in China, no method of successfully and economically reeling the cocoons has yet been invented. The caterpillar feeds upon the ailanthus, and these shade trees in some places have been known to be completely defoliated by the worms.

Genus ROTHSCHILDIA Grote

This characteristically neotropical genus may always be recognized by the large more or less triangular translucent spots of the wings, and the general likeness to the species we figure upon our plate. The abdomen is without tufts. The antennæ of both sexes are doubly bipectinated. The fore wings are generally considerably produced at the apex. Two species occur within our faunal limits.

(1) **Rothschildia orizaba** Westwood, Plate X, Fig 1, ♀. (The Orizaba Silk-moth.)

From *Rothschildia jorulla* Westwood, the other species found in our territory, this is easily separated by its generally lighter color and the much larger size of the translucent spots

82

upon the wings.   Both species occur in Arizona, where they are not, however, nearly as common as they are in Mexico.

Genus SAMIA Hübner

In this genus, composed of quite large moths, characterized, as are the moths of the two preceding and the next succeeding genera, by having the discal cells open, we find that the spots on the middle of the wings are opaque, not hyaline, as in the genus *Rothschildia ;* and, furthermore, the fore wings are more rounded and less produced than in that genus.

(1) **Samia cecropia** Linnaeus, Plate VIII, Fig. 1, ♂ ; Plate I, Fig. 8, larva.   (The Cecropia Moth.)

This splendid moth, which is very common, is one of a small number of our native silk-moths, which attract more or less

FIG 37.—Cocoon of *Samia cecropia.*   (After Riley.)

popular attention, and the spring of the year in our museums is always regarded as a period in which a certain portion of the time of the entomological staff will be consumed in replying to the letters of persons who, having for once opened their eyes to the wonders of the insect world, have sent in old matchboxes through the mails specimens of this insect, generally adding the information that the species is probably "new to science" or "excessively rare," they having for the first time in their lives noticed the moth.

The larva feeds upon a great variety of deciduous trees and shrubs, though manifesting a predilection for the *Rosaceæ,* willows, maples, and the lilac.   The cocoon is a familiar object. The insect is found over the whole Atlantic seaboard, and ranges westward to the eastern margin of the great plains.

(2) **Samia gloveri** Strecker, Plate XII, Fig. 4, ♂. (Glover's Silk-moth.)

This species, which may be distinguished from the preceding by the more obscure, purplish color of the outer band, which in *S. cecropia* is bright red, ranges over the region of the Rocky Mountains from Arizona in the south to Alberta and Assiniboia in the north. A small dwarfed form has been taken upon the high mountains of Colorado, to which Neumœgen gave the sub-specific name *reducta*.

(3) **Samia columbia** Smith, Plate VIII, Fig. 8, ♂. (The Columbian Silk-moth.)

This species, which is well represented in our plate, may be discriminated from its allies by its smaller size, and by the absence of the reddish outer shading of the transverse white line which crosses the wings about their middle. It ranges from Maine to Wisconsin, never, so far as is known at present, ranging south of the forty-first parallel of north latitude. While closely allied to *S. gloveri*, it is much smaller, and the larva shows marked differences. The caterpillar feeds upon the larch.

(4) **Samia rubra** Behr, Plate VIII, Fig. 2, ♂. (The Ceanothus Silk-moth)

Syn. *ceanothi* Behr; *euryalus* Boisduval; *californica* Grote.

The species which is easily separated from its congeners by its small size and prevalently redder cast of coloration, is found on the Pacific coast, ranging eastward to Utah and Wyoming. The larva feeds upon *Ceanothus thyrsiflorus*.

Genus CALLOSAMIA Packard

The structure of the moths of this genus is much like that of the preceding genus, but the species composing it may invariably be discriminated from others by the fact that the pectinations of the antennæ of the females in the anterior pair on each joint are shorter than the posterior pair. The genus contains several species, two of which are common in portions of our territory, and the other is a straggler into our fauna from Mexico.

(1) **Callosamia promethea** Drury, Plate I, Fig. 2, larva ; Plate XI, Fig. 11, ♂ , Fig. 12, ♀. (The Spice-bush Silk-moth.)

Every country boy who lives in the Atlantic States is familiar with the cocoons, which in winter and spring he has found hanging from the twigs of the spice-bush, the sassafras, and other trees. As they dangle in the wind they are easily de-tected, though they are often wrapped in the dead leaf in which the caterpillar originally spun them. The larva of which, in addition to the figure given in Plate I, we furnish a cut herewith, is a rather striking object, the coral-red tubercles on the second and third anterior segments showing conspicuously against the bluish-green epidermis. The insect subsists in the larval stage upon a great variety of deciduous shrubs and trees, showing a

Fig. 38.—*Callosamia promethea.* *a*, Young larva; *b*, front view of head; *c*, magnified view of a segment of young larva; *d*, mature larva. (After Riley.)

Fig. 39.—Cocoon of *C. promethea.* (After Riley.)

special predilection for the *Lauraceæ, Liriodendron, Liquidambar,* and the wild-cherry. It ranges over the Atlantic States from Florida to New England into southern Canada, and thence westward through the valley of the Mississippi to the eastern boundaries of the great plains. Whether the silk produced by this common and easily reared species could be utilized in such a way as to make its production commercially profitable is a problem to be solved in the future. No one up to the present time has succeeded either in reeling or carding the silk of the cocoons.

(2) **Callosamia angulifera** Walker, Plate VIII, Fig. 3, ♂, Fig. 4, ♀. (The Tulip-tree Silk-moth.)

This species may easily be discriminated from the last named by the fact that the males are not without discal spots as in that species, but have large angular white spots, causing them to resemble in this respect the females of *C. promethea.* The larva feeds commonly on the tulip-poplar *(Liriodendron).* The cocoon is not suspended from the twigs, as in the case of *C. promethea.*

The only other species of the genus, which occurs in our fauna, is **Callosamia calleta** Westwood, which may be differentiated from the two foregoing species by the fact that it has a whitish band on the collar and at the base of the thorax.

SUBFAMILY SATURNIINÆ

The discal cells are closed. The antennæ are pectinated in both sexes to the tip. The hind wings have but one internal vein distinctly developed. But four genera representing this sub-family are found within our territory.

Genus AGAPEMA Neumœgen & Dyar

The antennæ of both sexes are doubly bipectinated, those of the female having both the anterior and posterior pectinations of equal length. Only one species is known.

(1) **Agapema galbina** Clemens, Plate IX, Fig. 3, ♂. (The Galbina Moth.)

This interesting insect occurs in southern Texas, Arizona and Mexico. The larval stages have been described by Henry Edwards (see "Entomologica Americana," Vol. IV, p. 61). The specimen figured is considerably darker than the figures given by Strecker. Specimens as light as those he depicts have never fallen into the hands of the author.

Genus ACTIAS Leach

The species of this genus may easily be discriminated by their pale green color, and the tailed hind wings. The pectinations of the antennæ in the female sex are shorter in the anterior pair on each joint than the posterior pair. The genus is quite large, but only one species occurs in temperate North America. It is better represented in the Old World.

(1) **Actias luna** Linnæus, Plate XII, Fig. **7**, ♂. (The Luna Moth.)

This common and well-known insect has an extensive range from Canada to Florida and westward to Texas and the trans-Mississippi States as far as the region of the great plains. The larva, of which we give a representation, feeds upon the various species of walnut and hickory, the sweet-gum *(Liqui-dambar)*, the persimmon *(Diospyros),* and other trees. In North Carolina it appeared to be particularly fond of the persimmon. The cocoon is thin and papery, spun among leaves, and falls to the ground in autumn. In consequence it is not nearly as often found as those of some other species, which have been described in the preceding pages.

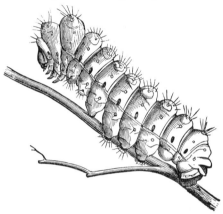

FIG. 40.—Larva of *A. luna*. (After Riley.)

Genus TELEA Hübner

This is a very small genus, including only two or three species. It is confined to the New World. The only representative in our faunal limits is the well-known species, which we figure.

(1) **Telea polyphemus** Cramer, Plate IX, Fig. 1, ♀. (The Polyphemus Moth.)

Syn. *paphia* Linnæus; *fenestra* Perry; *oculea* Neumœgen.

This very common moth feeds in the larval stage upon a great variety of trees and shrubs. I have found the caterpillar upon various species of oaks, upon the two species of *Juglans,* which grow in the Eastern States, upon hickory, basswood, elms, maples, birches, chestnuts, the sycamore *(Platanus),* wild-roses, and the beech. Other observers have reported the larva as found upon a great variety of other trees. The caterpillar,

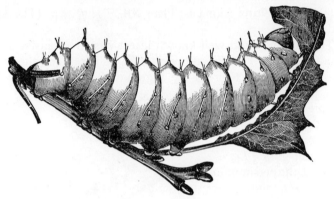

FIG. 41.—Larva of *Telea polyphemus*. (After Riley.)

which is of a beautiful shade of green, is ornamented on the sides by raised lines of silvery white, and is altogether a beautiful object, so far as coloration is concerned. The cocoon is in form like that of *Actias luna*, but is much more dense, and, after it has been spun up, is injected by the larva with a fluid, which appears to precipitate a white chalky matter through the fibers after it has dried. Efforts to reel the silk have hitherto amounted to but little. The insect is double-brooded in the southern States.

FIG. 42.—Cocoon of *Telea polyphemus*.
(After Riley.)

In Pennsylvania and northward it is single-brooded. The moth ranges across the entire continent and into Mexico in the South. We have given in Figure 5 a representation of the pupa, in Figure 10 a cut of the antenna greatly enlarged, and in Figures 41 and 42 are shown the larva and the cocoon. The latter, as is illustrated in the cut, is spun among leaves, and falls in the autumn to the ground. A number of aberrant forms and local races have been described, and there is considerable variety in the depth of the ground-color of the wings in a long series of specimens collected in the same locality. I have one or two fine melanic specimens, in which the wings are almost wholly black on the upper side. Albino specimens are also occasionally found.

Genus SATURNIA Schrank

This genus is represented in our fauna by a single species.

(1) **Saturnia mendocino** Behrens, Plate XII, Fig. 6, ♂. (The Mendocino Silk-moth.)

The insect inhabits northern California, where it is not uncommon. The larva feeds upon *Arctostaphylos tomentosa.*

Genus AUTOMERIS Hübner

Four species of this genus occur within our borders. Three of them we figure on our plates. The other, *Automeris zelleri* Grote & Robinson, may be distinguished from those we give by its much greater size, the female expanding fully five inches across the wings, and having three broad brown bands parallel to the margin of the hind wing, a large blind ocellus in the middle of that wing, and the fore wings purplish brown, marked with darker brown spots at the base, the end of the cell, and on the limbal area.

(1) **Automeris pamina** Neumœgen, Plate IX, Fig. 6, ♂. (The Pamina Moth.)

The figure we give is taken from an example of the form called *aurosea* by Neumœgen, in which the hairs along the inner margin of the hind wings are somewhat more broadly rosy red than in the specimens which he indicated as typical. The specimen was labeled by, and obtained from, the author of the species.

(2) **Automeris zephyria** Grote, Plate VIII, Fig. 5, ♀. (The Zephyr Silk-moth.)

This beautiful insect which is found in New Mexico, is well delineated in our plate, and may easily be discriminated from other species by the white transverse lines of the fore wings.

(3) **Automeris io** Fabricius, Plate IX, Fig. 4, ♂, Fig. 5, ♀. (The Io Moth.)

Syn. *corollaria* Perry; *varia*, Walker; *fabricii*, Boisduval; *argus* Neumœgen & Dyar.

This common insect, which ranges from Canada to Florida, and westward and southward to Texas and Mexico, subsists in the larval stage upon a large variety of

trees and shrubs; in fact, the caterpillar is almost omnivorous. The larva is a beautiful object, the body being green, ornamented with a lateral stripe of pink and creamy white and covered w i t h clusters of branching spines. These are possessed of stinging properties, and the caterpillar should be handled with extreme care, if painful consequences are to be avoided. In spite of this defense the larvæ are greatly liable to the a t t a c k of ichneumon wasps, which destroy multitudes of them.

FIG. 43.—Larva of *Automeris io.* (After Riley.)

Genus HYLESIA Hübner

This is a neotropical genus of small size, one species of which, common enough in Mexico, is occasionally found in Arizona. It is a true Saturnian, the secondaries having but one inner vein and the discal cells in both wings being closed.

(1) **Hylesia alinda** Druce, Plate VIII, Fig. 12, ♂. (The Alinda Moth.)

The specimens I have were taken on the Mexican border of Arizona. So far as I remember, nothing has been written upon the life-history of the species.

SUBFAMILY HEMILEUCINÆ.

The moths of this subfamily may be structurally differentiated from their near allies by the fact that the hind wings have two distinct internal veins, 1 *a* and 1 *b*. The antennæ of the male insect in the genus *Coloradia* are doubly bipectinated. In the genera *Hemileuca* and *Pseudohazis*, the antennæ of the males are singly bipectinated. In the former genus the females have bipectinated antennæ; in the latter the females have the antennæ serrate, or very feebly pectinated.

Genus COLORADIA Blake

(1) Coloradia pandora Blake, Plate X, Fig. 8, ♂. (The Pandora Moth.)

The range of this insect is from the eastern foot-hills of the Rocky Mountains to the Cascades, and from Montana to Mexico.

Genus HEMILEUCA Walker

Eight species of this genus are known from our territory, four of which we figure. *H. electra* Wright has the hind wings more or less red with a black border. *H. grotei* is a black species with a white collar, and a series of narrow white spots covering the middle of the wings, three on the fore wing, and those on the hind wing composing a narrow median band. *H. neumœgeni* is a beautiful insect with snowy white thorax and reddish brown abdomen. The wings are snowy white with orange discal marks crossed by two black bands on the primaries and one on the secondaries, the inner line of the primaries being relieved externally by an orange spot bordered with black. *H. hualapai* Neumœgen has the wings dull pink, either without markings, or crossed by two pale lines. The form with the pale transverse lines has been dubbed *sororius* by Henry Edwards.

(1) **Hemileuca maia** Drury, Plate XI, Fig. 1, ♂. (The Buck-moth.)

Syn. *proserpina* Fabricius.

In the fall of the year, when the leaves are falling and the days are still mellow and warm, the Buck-moths may be seen flitting through the air at noonday. They especially frequent the edges of groves of oaks. Upon the twigs of these trees, as well as occasionally upon willows, wild cherry-trees, and hazels, they deposit their eggs in clusters, as represented in Figure 44. The larvæ, which are gregarious and have stinging spines or bristles upon the somites, hatch in the latter part of April or in May, according to latitude, and after undergoing five molts, pupate in the ground. The moths emerge in the fall, though a few winter over in the soil until the next spring, when they emerge, or they may even remain dormant until the following fall.

The wings are semi-translucent, and in some specimens are apparently almost devoid of scales. The insects are diurnal, or semi-crepuscular in their habit, and I have never known them to be attracted to artificial light. The name "Buck-moths" is said to have been given to them because they fly at the time when deer-stalking is in order.

The insect ranges from Maine and Nova Scotia to Florida and westward to the eastern edge of the great plains. In the Carolinas it is very common, especially in groves of the Black-jack Oak, which grow on barren uplands.

FIG. 44.—Eggs of Buck-moth. (After Riley.)

(2) **Hemileuca nevadensis** Stretch, Plate XI, Fig 2, ♂. (The Nevada Buck-moth.)

Syn. *californica* Wright; *artemis* Packard.

This species, which closely resembles the preceding, may be distinguished from it by the much wider expanse of the transverse discal bands in both wings, and the much redder tuft of anal hairs.

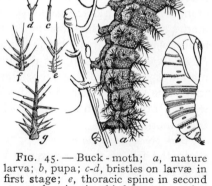

FIG. 45. — Buck - moth; *a*, mature larva; *b*, pupa; *c-d*, bristles on larvæ in first stage; *e*, thoracic spine in second stage; *f*, spine in third stage; *g*, spine in fifth stage. (After Riley.)

It may be a mere local race of *Hemileuca maia*, but most authors have recently accorded it specific rank.

(3) **Hemileuca juno** Packard, Plate XII, Fig. 8, ♂. (The Juno Moth.)

Syn. *yavapai* Neumœgen.

This beautiful moth occurs in Arizona and northern Mexico.

(4) **Hemileuca tricolor** Packard, Plate XII, Fig. 9, ♂. (The Tricolor Buck-moth.)

This species, like the preceding, is found in Arizona and in New Mexico. The larvæ feed upon the Grease-wood, according to report.

Genus PSEUDOHAZIS Grote & Robinson

This is a small genus of rather striking and exceedingly variable insects, the life histories of which have not been as thoroughly studied as is desirable. The moths appear to be diurnal in their habits, and may be found in vast numbers in the morning hours on bright days in their favorite haunts in the region of the Rocky Mountains. I have found them particularly abundant about Laramie Peak in Wyoming in the latter part of June and July. They appear to frequent flowers in company with diurnal lepidoptera, as the various species of *Argynnis*, and they may then be easily taken. Their flight is rapid. They are characteristic of the country of the sage-brush, and the ranges of the western sheep-herder.

(1) **Pseudohazis eglanterina** Boisduval.

Form **nuttalli** Strecker, Plate IX, Fig. 7, ♂ ; Plate XI, Fig. 5, ♂. (Nuttall's Sheep-moth.)

Syn. *shastaënsis* Behr; *denudata* Neumœgen.

The two figures given on our plates show two forms of this well-known insect. Whatever the amount of black or purple upon the fore wings the specimens may always be distinguished from others by the presence just beyond the discal spot of the fore wings of a longitudinal dash of Indian yellow. This is characteristic, and I have never failed to find it in a long series of specimens, no matter how the other markings varied.

(2) **Pseudohazis hera** Harris, Plate IX, Fig. 8, ♂. (The Hera Moth.)

Form **pica** Walker, Plate XI, Fig. 3, ♂ ; Fig. 4, ♀. (The Magpie Moth.)

This extremely variable moth is represented by the typical form in the figure given upon Plate IX, and in the figures given upon Plate XI by two specimens showing the form, which is most common in Colorado and Wyoming, in which the wings are greatly suffused with black. To this form Walker's name *pica* properly applies.

FAMILY CERATOCAMPIDÆ

" In Nature's infinite book of secrecy
A little I can read."—SHAKESPEARE.

This family contains moths of large or medium size, the larvæ of which do not produce cocoons, but undergo transformation in the ground. The larvæ are generally more or less ornamented with spines and bristly protuberances. The moths have the tongue developed, but nevertheless feebly. The tibial spurs are present. The frenulum is lacking. The genera belonging to this family are American, and only five of them occur within our faunal limits.

Genus ANISOTA Hübner

Of the five species, recognized as belonging to this genus and occurring within our borders, we have selected three for representation. *Anisota senatoria*, a common species found in the Atlantic States, is distinguished from its very near ally, *Anisota virginiensis*, not only by marked differences in the larval stage, but by the fact that the females are almost exactly like the female of *Anisota stigma*, profusely covered with black spots or frecklings on the wings, while the females of *virginiensis*, as shown in the plate, are almost wholly destitute of such spots. The males of these two species are almost alike, the only difference being that the male insect in the case of *virginiensis* is somewhat darker than in the case of *Anisota senatoria*, and less ochreous.

(1) **Anisota stigma** Fabricius, Plate XI, Fig. 9, ♂ ; Fig. 10, ♀. (The Stigma Moth.)

The caterpillar feeds upon various species of oak. It is ornamented with short spines upon the segments, arranged in rows, those on the second segment from the head being long and recurved. The color of the larvæ at maturity is a dull reddish brown, marked with small creamy-white and gray punctulations. The insect occurs in the Appalachian faunal region, from Canada to the Carolinas, and westward to Kansas and Missouri.

94

(2) **Anisota virginiensis** Drury, Plate VIII, Fig. 9, ♂ ; Fig. 10, ♀. (The Virginian Anisota.)

Syn. *astymone* Olivier; *pellucida* Herrich-Schæffer.

The male insect has the fore wings almost transparent about the middle, as is the case with *Anisota senatoria,* as has already been pointed out, but the female is not heavily spotted, as is the case in that species. The caterpillar feeds upon oaks. The moth has the same geographical distribution as the preceding species.

(3) **Anisota rubicunda** Fabricius, Plate VIII, Fig. 11, ♂. (The Rosy Maple-moth.)

The larva of this beautiful moth feeds commonly upon the silver-maple, which in many of our western cities has been extensively planted as a shade-tree. The depredations it commits upon the foliage have subjected it to the indignation of arbori-culturists. It was formerly very common in the city of Pittsburgh, but for many years past it has almost entirely disappeared, so that it is now regarded as a rather rare insect by local collectors. The disappearance of the moth is due no doubt to the combined influence of the electric lights, which annually destroy millions of

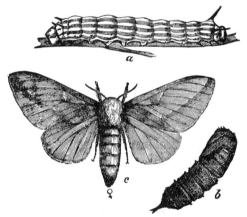

Fig. 46.—*Anisota rubicunda.* a. larva; b. pupa; c. female moth. (After Riley.)

insects, which are attracted to them, and to gas-wells, and furnaces, which lick up in their constantly burning flames other millions of insects. Perhaps the English sparrow has also had a part in the work of extermination. In Kansas the insect is very common. I recently saw in the city of Atchison numerous maples, which had almost been stripped of their leaves by these larvæ. The range of the insect is practically the same as that of the other species of the genus.

Genus ADELOCEPHALA Herrich-Schæffer

As in the preceding genus, vein 11 of the fore wing is stalked with veins 6-8, but the outer margin of the wing is not straight as in that genus, and longer than the internal margin, but it is convex and shorter than the inner margin. There are a number of species belonging to the genus, which are indigenous in Central and South America, but only one occurs within our borders.

(1) **Adelocephala bicolor** Harris, Plate X, Fig. 5, ♂ ; Fig. 6, ♀. (The Honey-locust Moth.)

Syn. *distigma* Walsh.

The larva feeds upon the Honey-locust *(Gledilschia)* and the Kentucky Coffee-tree *(Gymnocladus)*. It is a rather common insect in the valley of the Ohio, and ranges from the region of the Great Lakes southward to Georgia and Kansas.

Genus SYSSPHINX Hübner

The insects assigned to this genus by recent writers do not differ greatly in structure from those referred to the preceding genus. The principal structural differences consist in the fact that the antennæ of the females are somewhat shorter and less strongly pectinated, and the abdomen is generally longer, in some species greatly exceeding the hind· margin of the hind wings. The genus is well represented in Mexico and Central America. Only four species occur in our territory, two of which we figure.

(1) **Syssphinx albolineata** Grote & Robinson, Plate X, Fig. 7, ♂. (The White-lined Syssphinx.)

Syn. *raspa* Boisduval.

The figure we give is sufficient to enable the student to identify this species which is common in Mexico, and also occurs in southern Arizona.

(2) **Syssphinx heiligbrodti** Harvey, Plate XI, Fig. 14, ♀. (Heiligbrodt's Syssphinx.)

This very pretty moth, which may easily be determined by the help of the figure we give, is not uncommon in southern **Arizona.** The caterpillar feeds, it is said, upon Grease-wood **bushes.**

Genus CITHERONIA Hübner

This genus of large and showy moths is characteristically neotropical, having its metropolis in Central America. Three species occur in our territory, two of them having an extensive northern range.

(1) **Citheronia regalis** Fabricius, Plate I, Fig. 4, larva ; Plate X, Fig. 3, ♂ . (The Royal Walnut-moth.)
Syn. *regia* Abbot & Smith.

The caterpillar, which is known by boys as the "Hickory Horn-devil," feeds upon a great variety of trees and shrubs, showing a decided preference for the walnut and butternut, the persimmon, and several species of arborescent sumac (*Rhus*).

(2) **Citheronia sepulchralis** Grote & Robinson, Plate XLI, Fig. 5, ♀ . (The Pine-devil Moth.)
The larva, which is smaller and more obscurely colored than that of the preceding species, feeds upon various species of pine, and the insect ranges from the Carolinas northward to Massachusetts along the coast. It is not uncommon in the valley of the Potomac, and at Berkeley Springs I have found it abundant in the larval state in the months of July and August.

(3) **Citheronia mexicana** Grote & Robinson, Plate X, Fig. 4, ♂ . (The Mexican Walnut-moth.)

This species, which is in many respects very closely allied to *C. regalis,* occurs in Arizona, and southward.

Genus BASILONA Boisduval

The only representative of this genus within the limits of the United States is the species which is illustrated on our plates. There are a number of other species, which are Mexican or South American.

(1) **Basilona imperialis** Drury, Plate X, Fig. 2, ♀ ; Plate XI, Fig. 13, ♂ . (The Imperial Moth.)
Syn. *imperatoria* Abbot & Smith; *punctatissima* Neumœgen.

The larva feeds upon a vast number of trees and shrubs, and may almost be described as omnivorous. The larvæ are either brown or green, the color having nothing whatever to do with the character of the perfect insects, which emerge from the pupæ. Such cases of dichromatism among larvæ are not at all uncommon.

97

FAMILY SYNTOMIDÆ

" Whoever looks at the insect world, at flies, aphides, gnats, and innumerable parasites, and even at the infant mammals, must have remarked the extreme content they take in suction, which constitutes the main business of their life. If we go into a library or news-room, we see the same function on a higher plane, performed with like ardor, with equal impatience of interruption, indicating the sweetness of the act."—EMERSON.

This family, which quite recently has been monographed by Sir George F. Hampson, consists of moths which are small, or at most of medium size. They are diurnal in their habits, and frequent flowers. At first glance, they often are mistaken for wasps and other hymenoptera, which they mimic. The following characterization of the family is quoted from the learned author, to whom reference has just been made:

" Proboscis usually well developed, but sometimes aborted; palpi short and porrect, long and downcurved, or upturned; frons rounded; antennæ simple, ciliated, or bipectinate, usually with short branches dilated at extremity in both sexes; tibiæ with the spurs short. Fore wing usually with the terminal area broad; vein 1*a* forming a fork with 1*b*, 1*c* absent; 5 from below middle of discocellulars; 7 stalked with 8, 9. Hind wing small; vein 1*a* often absent; 1*c* absent; 8 absent, rarely rudimentary and not reaching costa; frenulum present; retinaculum bar-shaped." Hampson, *Catalogue of the Lepidoptera Phalænæ*, Vol. I, p. 20.

Eleven genera comprised within this family are recognized by recent writers as holding place in the fauna of the United States and Canada. Most of these are southern, and represent a northern movement of the great complex of genera and species referable to the family, which inhabits the hot lands of equatorial America.

Genus COSMOSOMA Hübner

This is a large genus, including at least eighty species, which are found in Central and South America. Only one species is, at present, known to occur within our faunal limits.

(1) **Cosmosoma auge** Linnæus, Plate XIII, Fig. 1, ♂. (The Scarlet-bodied Wasp-moth.)

Syn. *omphale* Hübner; *melitta* Möschler.

This beautiful little insect occurs throughout the tropics of the New World, and is not rare in southern Florida. The larval stages have been described by Dyar (see "Psyche," Vol. VII, p. 414). The caterpillar feeds upon *Mikania scandens*.

Genus SYNTOMEIDA Harris

The type of this genus is *Syntomeida ipomeæ.* Six species have thus far been assigned to it, two of these occuring in the extreme southern portions of our territory.

(1) **Syntomeida ipomeæ** Harris, Plate XIII, Fig. 3 ♀. (The Yellow-banded Wasp-moth.)

Syn. *ferox* Walker; *euterpe* Herrich-Schæffer.

This species is confined to the southern States along the borders of the Gulf of Mexico. The caterpillar, which according to report feeds upon the *Convolvulaceæ*, remains to be fully described.

(2) **Syntomeida epilais** Walker, Plate XIII, Fig. 2, ♂. (The Polka-dot Wasp-moth.)

The larva has been described by Dyar (see Journal New York Entomological Society, Vol. IV, p. 72, and "Insect Life," Vol. II, p. 360). The caterpillar feeds upon *Nerium odorum.*

Genus PSEUDOMYA Hübner

This is a small neotropical genus, including, so far as is known, but eight species, one of which occurs in the extreme southern part of Florida.

(1) **Pseudomya minima** Grote, Plate XIII, Fig. 6, ♂. (The Lesser Wasp-moth.)

The caterpillar, which has been described by Dr. H. G. Dyar in "Psyche," Vol. VIII, p. 42, feeds upon *Myginda ilicifolia.*

Genus DIDASYS Grote

Only one species has hitherto been referred to this genus. It is found in Florida.

(1) **Didasys belæ** Grote, Plate XIII, Fig. 7, ♂, Fig. 8 ♀. (The Double-tufted Wasp-moth.)

As shown in our plate, the male has the end of the abdomen ornamented by two tufts, while the female is devoid of these appendages. The insect is found on the Indian River in Florida, and southward.

Genus HORAMA Hübner

Ten species compose this genus, of which only one is found within the limits of the United States.

(1) **Horama texana** Grote, Plate XIII, Fig. 9, ♂. (The Texan Wasp-moth.)

No difficulty should be experienced in identifying this moth by the help of the figure which is given.

Genus EUCEREON Hübner

Sixty-two species, all inhabiting the hot lands of North and South America, are assigned by Hampson to this genus. The only one thus far known to occur within the limits of the United States is figured on our plate.

(1) **Eucereon confine** Herrich-Schæffer, Plate XIII, Fig. 10, ♀. (The Floridan Eucereon.)

Syn. *carolina* Henry Edwards.

This interesting little moth, which was described by Henry Edwards under the name *Nelphe carolina*, had been figured by Herrich-Schæffer under the specific name above cited thirty-two years before. It is rare in Florida, but is common in the Antilles, Mexico, and Central America.

Genus LYMIRE Walker

This is a small genus comprehending only five species. Its only representant within our borders was originally assigned by Grote to the genus *Scepsis*, which it superficially resembles.

(1) **Lymire edwardsi** Grote, Plate XIII, Fig. 11, ♀. (Edwards' Wasp-moth.)

The larval stages, thanks to the labors of Dr. H. G. Dyar, are known. The caterpillar feeds upon *Ficus pedunculata*. The insect, when pupating, spins a small cocoon of hair and silk. For fuller knowledge upon the subject the reader is referred to "Insect Life," Vol. II, p. 361.

Genus SCEPSIS Walker

Three species of this genus, which does not range far into the Mexican territory, are recognized. Two of these we figure;

the third, *Scepsis packardi* Grote, =*matthewi* Grote, is a trifle larger in size, than the other two, much paler in color, and inhabits Washington, Oregon, and British Columbia.

(1) **Scepsis fulvicollis** Hübner, Plate XIII, Fig. 12, ♀. (The Yellow-collared Scape-moth.)

Syn. *semidiaphana* Harris.

This common insect, the larva of which feeds upon grasses, has a wide range from Canada to the Gulf States, and westward to the Rocky Mountains, and southward to Chihuahua in Mexico. The moths frequent the blossoms of the golden-rod *(Solidago)* in the late summer.

(2) **Scepsis wrighti** Stretch, Plate XIII, Fig. 13, ♂. (The White-collared Scape-moth.)

The habitat of this species is southern California. The specimen figured was sent me by Mr. Wright, labeled "Type," and may be accepted as typical of the species.

Genus LYCOMORPHA Harris

A small genus of moths, diurnal in their habits, having a preference for the flowers of the *Compositæ*, upon which they may frequently be found in their habitats.

(1) **Lycomorpha grotei** Packard, Plate XIII, Fig. 14, ♀. (Grote's Lycomorpha.)

Syn. *palmeri* Packard.

This pretty little insect occurs in Colorado and thence southward to Texas. So far as recalled by the writer its larval stages have not as yet received attention from any of our American students of the lepidoptera.

(2) **Lycomorpha pholus** Drury, Plate XIII, Fig. 15, ♂.

This common insect, but not the less beautiful because it is common, is widely distributed throughout the United States. The larva is said to feed upon lichens.

Genus CTENUCHA Kirby

This genus, which includes about twenty species, is quite well represented in our fauna. Figures of all the species occurring within our territory are given in the plates.

(1) **Ctenucha venosa** Walker, Plate XIII, Fig. 20, ♂. (The Veined Ctenucha.)

From *Ctenucha cressonana,* its nearest ally, this species may be distinguished by its smaller size, the reddish tint of the stripes upon the fore wings and the edges of the shoulder lappets, and the fact that the fringe opposite the end of the cell on both wings is marked by fuscous, and not uniformly white throughout as in *C. cressonana.* The species ranges from Colorado to Mexico.

(2) **Ctenucha cressonana** Grote, Plate XIII, Fig. 21, ♂. (Cresson's Ctenucha.)

This species, which is one of the largest in the genus, may easily be recognized by the figure we give and the remarks made in connection with what has been said in regard to the preceding species.

(3) **Ctenucha brunnea** Stretch, Plate XI, Fig. 6, ♂. (The Brown-winged Ctenucha.)

Easily recognized by the pale brown color of the primaries, upon which the veins stand forth in a darker shade of brown.

(4) **Ctenucha multifaria** Walker, Plate XIII, Fig. 19, ♀. (The Californian Ctenucha.)

This species, which is closely allied to the next, may be discriminated by the fact that the fore wings are lighter in color, the collar is black, not orange spotted with black, as in *C. rubroscapus,* and the costal margin of the primaries is narrowly edged with white.

(5) **Ctenucha rubroscapus** Ménétriés, Plate XIII, Fig. 22, ♀. (Walsingham's Ctenucha.)

Syn. *walsinghami* Henry Edwards.

This species, which may be distinguished by the aid of what has been said under the preceding species, as well as by our figure, may have the edges of the shoulder lappets either red, as in our figure, or orange yellow. It is found in the Pacific States.

(6) **Ctenucha virginica** Charpentier, Plate XIII, Fig. 18, ♀. (The Virginian Ctenucha.)

Syn. *latreillana* Kirby.

This moth, which is not at all uncommon in the northern portions of the Appalachian faunal region, may be found in the latitude of New York City and Pittsburgh frequenting the blossoms of blackberries at the end of May and in June. The larva feeds, as do the larvæ of the other species, upon grasses.

Genus DAHANA Grote

Only one species, the type of the genus, is known.

(1) **Dahana atripennis** Grote, Plate XIII, Fig. 23, ♂. (The Black-winged Dahana.)

The habitat of this species is southern Florida. The insect does not appear to be common in collections.

FAMILY LITHOSIIDÆ

"You would be another Penelope: yet, they say, all the yarn she spun in Ulysses's absence did but fill Ithaca full of moths."

—SHAKESPEARE, *Coriolanus*, I, 3.

The moths belonging to this family have the larvæ of the usual form displayed by the Arctiidæ, with all of the prolegs present. They feed principally upon lichens. They pupate in cocoons spun up of silk, in which the hairs of the larva are mingled.

The perfect insects, or imagoes, are of medium size or small. As a family, they present many variations in structure, both as to the venation of the wings and secondary sexual characteristics. The following general characterization of the group is taken from Hampson, "Catalogue of the Lepidoptera Phalænæ," Vol. II, p. 80:

"Proboscis usually well developed, but often aborted; palpi usually short and porrect, sometimes reaching well beyond the frons, often upturned, rarely reaching above the vertex of the head; antennæ of male usually with bristles and cilia, often bipectinate, sometimes dilated or with tuft of scales on upper side of shaft; ocelli absent; tibiæ with the spurs usually moderate, sometimes long or absent. Fore wing typically long and narrow, but in a large section, short and broad, the narrow winged genera having vein 5, and often vein 4, absent. Hind wing with vein 8 coincident with the cell from base to one-third or to near end of cell."

About a dozen genera have thus far been recognized as represented in the fauna of the region of which this book treats.

Genus CRAMBIDIA Packard

This small genus, consisting of moths displaying delicate shades of slaty-gray, pale yellow, or pearly white upon their wings, is represented in our fauna by six species, three of

which we figure, one of them being hitherto undescribed. The genus falls into two sections, in the first being included those species in which there is no areole in the fore wing, and in the second those which have the areole developed. The first

FIG. 47.—*Crambidia pallida,* ♂ .¼.

section is represented by *Crambidia pallida,* and contains, in addition, the species named *lithosioides* and *uniformis* by Dyar ; the second section is represented by *Crambidia casta,* and contains, in addition, the species named *cephalica* by Grote & Robinson, and the species herein described and named *allegheniensis.* The structure of the insects is sufficiently well set forth in the two cuts we give, which have been kindly furnished by Sir George F. Hampson, with the permission of the Trustees of the British Museum.

(1) **Crambidia pallida** Packard. (The Pale Lichen-moth.) The moth is uniformly brownish-grey, with the hind wings a trifle paler than the fore wings. The wings on the under side are lighter than on the upper side. The species occurs in the northern Atlantic States.

(2) **Crambidia casta** Sanborn, Plate XIII, Fig. 30, ♂. (The Pearly-winged Lichen-moth.)

On the under side the fore wings and the costal area of the hind wings are fuscous, and in some specimens the upper side of the wings is also slightly touched with pale fuscous. The insect appears

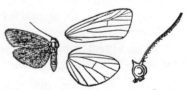

FIG. 48.—*Crambidia casta,* ♂ . ¼.

to be not uncommon in Colorado and ranges thence south and north toward the Pacific coast.

(3) **Crambidia allegheniensis,** sp. nov., Plate XIII, Fig. 31, ♂. (The Alleghenian Lichen-moth.)

The head and anterior portions of the thorax are pale yellow. The patagia are of the same color. The thorax and the abdomen on the upper side are pale slaty-gray. The legs and the tip of the abdomen on the under side are ochreous, the middle of the abdomen on the under side being dark slaty-gray. The fore wing on the upper side is slaty-gray, with the costa evenly edged with pale yellow. The hind wings are translucent white. On the under side the wings are marked as on the upper side, but paler. The insect is slightly smaller than *casta*. It occurs in western Pennsylvania. The type, which is in the collection of the author, was taken by him in East Pittsburgh.

Genus PALPIDIA Dyar

The genus is represented by only one species, so far as is now known.

(1) **Palpidia pallidior** Dyar. (Dyar's Palpidia.)

This insect, a drawing of the type of which is given in the annexed cut, has the fore wings pale ochreous, with the interspaces between the veins strongly irrorated with dark scales. The hind wings are whitish. It is as yet a rare insect in collections, and has only been recorded from Cocoanut Grove, in Dade County, Florida.

Fig. 49.—*Palpidia pallidior*, ♀ . ⅓.

Genus LEXIS Wallengren

The genus Lexis is of moderate size, all of the species referred to it, with the single exception of the one figured on our plate, being inhabitants of the Old World. The metropolis of the genus appears to be southern Asia and the adjacent islands. One species is recorded from Australia, and the species, which is the type of the genus, is found in East Africa.

(1) **Lexis bicolor** Grote, Plate XIII, Fig. 29, ♂ . (The Yellow-edged Lexis).

Syn. *argillacea* Packard.

The moth is pale slaty-grey, with the head, patagia, and anal tuft yellow. The fore wings are bordered on the costa with pale yellow, the band of this color running out to nothing before it quite reaches the apex. The specimen figured on the plate came from Colorado. It is also said to occur in Canada and the northern portions of the United States.

Genus HYPOPREPIA Hübner

A small genus of North American moths, all the species of which occur within the territory covered by this book. The insects closely resemble each other, and the student who has learned to recognize one of them cannot fail to refer the others correctly to their genus. It is not, however, so easy to discriminate the species. The following little key, which is taken from Hampson's Catalogue, Vol. II, page 515, may help the student in making correct specific references :

1. Ground-color of the fore wing wholly scarlet..............*miniata*
2. Ground-color of the fore wing yellow and crimson..........*fucosa*
3. Ground-color of the fore and hind wings yellow...........*cadaverosa*
4. Ground-color of the fore wing fuscous brown, of the hind
   wing whitish....................................*inculta*

(1) **Hypoprepia miniata** Kirby, Plate XIII, Fig. 41, ♀. (The Scarlet-winged Lichen-moth.)

Syn. *vittata* Harris; *subornata* Neumœgen & Dyar.

This rather common insect ranges from Canada to the Carolinas and westward in the region of the Great Lakes to Minnesota. It comes freely, as do all the species of the genus, to light, and I have found it very abundant at times about the lamps in the village of Saratoga, New York. I have taken it at Asheville, North Carolina, and at the White Sulphur Springs in West Virginia, but have never received specimens from low altitudes on the Virginian and Carolinian coasts.

(2) **Hypoprepia fucosa** Hübner, Plate XIII, Fig. 42, ♂. (The Painted Lichen-moth.)

Syn. *tricolor* Fitch; *plumbea* Henry Edwards.

FIG. 50.—*Hypoprepia fucosa*, ♂ . ⅓. (After Hampson.)

This species, which may be easily distinguished from the preceding by the fact that the tip of the abdomen is not marked by a dark fuscous spot, and by the narrower marginal band of the secondaries, as well as by the difference in the color of the wings, is a common species in the Atlantic States, and ranges westward into the basin of the Mississippi.

Genus HÆMATOMIS Hampson

This little genus includes, so far as is now known, but two species, both of which are Mexican, but one of which ranges into southern Arizona. The species are separated as follows by Hampson :

1. Fore wing with yellowish streaks, on costa, through cell, and
    on inner margin ....*mexicana*
2. Fore wing with pale streak on the costa only ....*uniformis*

(1) **Hæmatomis mexicana** Druce, Plate XIII, Fig. 34, ♂. (The Mexican Lichen-moth.)

With the help of the illustrations we have given the student should have no great difficulty in identifying this little moth.

Fig. 51.—*Hæmatomis mexicana,* ♂ . ⅓. (After Hampson.)

Genus COMACLA Walker

This genus is represented in our fauna by two species. One other occurs in Europe and northern Asia, and another in tropical Africa. The two American species are very much alike in appearance, and it is difficult to distinguish worn or rubbed specimens. The following key will be of some assistance:

1. Wings pale mouse gray, translucent; collar and abdomen
    ochreous; apex of fore wings rounded............*simplex* Walker

Fig. 52.—*Comacla simplex,* ♂ . ⅓. (After Hampson.)

2. Wings and body uniformly pale mouse gray, wings translucent only about the middle, sprinkled with blackish scales and marked by an obscure discal dot, apex of fore wings less rounded and more nearly square than in preceding species.*fuscipes* Grote

(1) **Comacla simplex** Walker, Plate XIII, Fig. 34, ♂. (The Mouse-colored Lichen-moth.)

Syn. *murina* Walker; *clarus* Grote & Robinson; *texana* French.

The species is common in Texas. *C. fuscipes* occurs in Arizona.

Genus BRUCEIA Neumœgen

One species is reckoned in this genus, the structural characters of which are well shown in the cut we give.

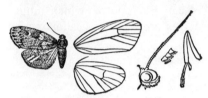

FIG. 53.—*Bruceia pulverina*, ♂ . ⅓.
(After Hampson.)

(1) **Bruceia pulverina** Neumœgen, Plate XIII, Fig. *33*, ♂ . (The Powdered Lichen-moth.)

Syn. *hubbardi* Dyar.

The insect named *hubbardi* by Dyar seems to be only a smaller form of *B. pulverina*.

Genus CLEMENSIA Packard

To this genus Sir George F. Hampson refers a dozen species. All of these are inhabitants of the hot lands of America, except the species we figure. *Cisthene lactea* Stretch is by Hampson referred to the genus *Illice*. Dr. Dyar places it in the genus *Clemensia*. The species is unknown to the writer, and does not exist in any collection which he has examined, so that we shall not attempt to discuss the vexed question of its proper location.

(1) **Clemensia albata** Packard, Plate XIII, Fig. *38*, ♂ . (The Little White Lichen-moth.)

Syn. *albida* Walker; *cana* Walker; *umbrata* Packard ; *irrorata* Henry Edwards ; *patella* Druce ; *philodina* Druce.

FIG. 54.—*Clemensia albata*, ♂ . ⅓.
(After Hampson.)

The insect ranges from New England to Mexico and westward to the Pacific coast.

Genus ILLICE Walker

This is a moderately large genus comprising nearly thirty species, the most of which are found in tropical America. It has been subdivided into three sections, or subgenera, by Hampson. In the second section, equivalent to *Ozonadia*, a genus erected by Dyar, are placed those species, in which the hind wing is slightly produced at the anal angle. Here come two of the species found in our fauna, *I. schwarziorum* and *I. unifascia*. In the third section, typical *Illice*, fall the species in which the anal angle is not produced. Here are placed five species. The student may find the following key helpful in determining his specimens:

A. Hind wing slightly produced at the anal angle.
    Lappets and markings of fore wing yellow, hind wings
      crimson, fuscous at apex.
      1. Fore wing with the band across the wing crimson on the
          inner margin......................*schwarziorum* Dyar
      2. Fore wing with the band across the wing not crimson on
          the inner margin......................*unifascia* Grote
B. Hind wing not produced at the anal angle.
    Abdomen crimson; fore wing slaty-gray in ground color.
      1. Fore wing with crimson patch on the costa.......*subjecta* Walker
      2. Fore wing without crimson patch on costa, and with a pink
          streak on the inner margin at the base....*striata* Ottolengui
      3. Fore wing with whitish patch about the middle of the inner
          margin...............................*plumbea* Stretch
    Abdomen orange or yellowish.
      1. Hind wing pale yellow, with apex blackish........*nexa* Boisduval
      2. Hind wing smoky-gray...................*faustinula* Boisduval

(1) **Illice unifascia** Grote & Robinson, Plate XIII, Fig. 36, ♀. (The Banded Lichen-moth.)

Syn. *tenuifascia* Harvey.

The insect ranges from the Ohio Valley southward to Texas, and from Virginia to Florida.

Fig. 55.—*Illice unifascia*, ♂. ¼. (After Hampson.)

The transverse band is often interrupted in the middle of the wing, and there is variation in the color of the hind wings, which, while usually red or crimson, may also be orange, or even yellow.

Fig. 56.—*Illice subjecta*, ♂. ¼. (After Hampson.)

(2) **Illice subjecta** Walker, Plate XIII, Fig. 35, ♂. (The Subject Lichen-moth.)

Syn. *packardi* Grote.

The distribution of this species is much the same as that of the preceding. Its range is slightly more northern than that of *I. unifascia.*

(3) *Illice nexa* Boisduval, Plate XIII, Fig. 37, ♂. (The Yellow-blotched Lichen-moth.)

Syn. *grisea* Packard; *deserta* Felder.

This species is found upon the Pacific coast, and is not uncommon in southern California.

Genus PTYCHOGLENE Felder

A small genus confined to the southwestern portions of our territory. The four species occurring within our fauna may be briefly characterized as follows:

1. Head, thorax, base of abdomen, basal two-thirds of primaries and basal half of secondaries bright carmine; black marginal borders of both wings strongly dentate inwardly.............................*coccinea* Henry Edwards

2. Head, thorax, and abdomen black; fore wings crimson, narrowly edged with black on inner margin, and with a black marginal band covering the wing for about one-fifth of its length, dentate inwardly opposite end of cell.   Hind wing blackish-brown, more or less broadly laved with crimson on costal margin...............*phrada* Druce

3, Head, thorax, and abdomen black; fore wing crimson, with the costal margin narrowly edged with black; terminal black band of the same width as in the preceding species, but not dentate inwardly.   Hind wing pale yellowish crimson, with the outer marginal band strongly toothed inwardly on vein 2........*sanguineola* Boisduval

4. Head, thorax, and abdomen, deep black; patagia crimson; fore wings deep crimson, very narrowly edged on external margin with black, extending on costal margin a short distance from the apex toward the base.   Hind wings deep blue-black, very narrowly edged on the costa with crimson, the crimson fascia not quite reaching the apex.............................*tenuimargo* sp. nov.

(1) **Ptychoglene phrada** Druce, Plate XIII, Fig. 28, ♂. (Druce's Lichen-moth.)

Syn. *flammans* Dyar.

(2) **Ptychoglene tenuimargo** sp. nov., Plate XIII., Fig. 17, ♀. (The Narrow-banded Lichen-moth.)

The type of this species, which I have received in recent years from Arizona and in great abundance from the State of Chihuahua in Mexico, is figured upon our plate.

Genus PYGOCTENUCHA Grote

A small genus containing three species, two of which are found within the limits of the United States. They may be discriminated as follows:

1. Uniformly black, collar-lappets and tip of abdomen ochre-yellow; size small............................*funerea* Grote
2. Head, thorax, and abdomen black shot with brilliant blue; fore coxæ, tegulæ, patagia, and anal tuft scarlet, the latter white in the female; fore wings black shot with green; hind wings black shot with blue. Fully one-third larger than preceding species............*terminalis* Walker

(1) **Pygoctenucha funerea** Grote, Plate XIII., Fig. 40, ♂. (The Funereal Lichen-moth.)

The specimen figured on our plate was kindly loaned for the purpose by the Academy of Natural Sciences of Philadelphia. The insect occurs in New Mexico.

(2) **Pygoctenucha terminalis** Walker. (The Blue-green Lichen-moth.)

Syn. *harrisi* Boisduval; *pyrrhoura* Hulst; *votiva* Henry Edwards.

This insect, referred by Hampson to his genus *Protosia*, must be placed here, *Pygoctenucha* having priority over *Protosia*, which falls as a synonym.

Genus LERINA Walker

Only one species belongs to this genus. It was originally named by Walker, and made the type of the genus. Subsequently it was redescribed by Boisduval as *Ctenucha robinsoni*, under which name it has passed current in American collections until recently.

(1) **Lerina incarnata** Walker. (The Crimson-bodied Lichen-moth.)

Syn. *robinsoni* Boisduval.

FIG. 57.—*Lerina incarnata*, ♂. ¼. (After Hampson.)

The head, tegulæ, and patagia, with the terminal half of the abdomen are deep crimson. The rest of the body and its appendages are black. The wings are bronzy-green. The insect inhabits Mexico and southern Arizona.

"SPLITTERS" AND "LUMPERS"

Every true naturalist is called upon to exercise the faculty of discrimination and the faculty of generalization. His work trains him to detect dissimilarities on the one hand and likenesses on the other. His judgments as to likeness are expressed in the genera, the famiies, the orders, which he proposes. His judgment as to dissimilarities is most frequently expressed in his views as to species. When the two faculties of discrimination and generalization are well balanced and accompanied by the habit of patient observation, ideal conditions are reached, and the work of the naturalist in classification may be expected to stand the test of time. But where, as is often the case, one of these faculties is exalted at the expense of the other, there are certain to result perversions, which will inevitably cause trouble to other students. When a man cultivates the habit of discrimination to excess, he is apt to become, so far as his labors as a systematist are concerned, "a splitter." A "splitter" magnifies the importance of trivial details; he regards minute differences with interest; he searches with more than microscopic zeal after the little things and leaves out of sight the lines of general resemblance. Huber, the celebrated naturalist, said that by patient observation he had come to be able to recognize the different ants in a hill, and, as one by one they emerged from their subterranean galleries, he knew them, as a man living upon a certain thoroughfare in a great city comes at last to know by sight the men and women who are in the habit of daily passing his windows. No doubt the critical eye can detect as great individual differences in the lower animal world as are to be detected among men. A student comes to apply himself with great zeal to searching out and describing these differences, and when he undertakes to say that because of them one form should be separated specifically from another he becomes "a splitter." I recall an entomologist whose chief weapon of research was a big microscope. He would take a minute insect and study it until he was able to number the hairs upon its head. Then he would describe it, giving it a specific name. The next specimen he would subject to the same critical process, and if the number of hairs was not just the same, or a small wart was detected here or there, or a bristle grew in a place where a bristle did not grow in the specimen previously examined, it too, was described and a specific name was given it. It was as if a man, sitting and looking out on the throng upon Broadway, should resolve to give every individual a specific name and should declare he had seen as many species of men as he had seen men passing his window. The labors of such naturalists may be highly entertaining to themselves, but they are, to say the least, provocative of unpleasant feelings in the minds of others who come after them and are compelled to deal with and review their labors.

The "lumper," on the other hand, is a man who detects no differences. "All cocoons look alike to me!" he says. Any two moths which are of approximately the same size and the same color, are, by him, declared to belong to the same species. Questions of structure do not trouble him. General re-semblances are the only things with which he deals. No matter if eggs, larvæ, legs, veins, and antennæ are different it is "all one thing" to him. His genera are "magazines," into which he stuffs species promiscuously. The "lumper" is the horror of the "splitter," the "splitter" is anathema to the "lumper"; both are the source of genuine grief and much hard-ship to conscientious men, who are the possessors of normally constituted minds and truly scientific habits. Nevertheless, we are certain to have both "splitters" and "lumpers" in the camps of science until time is no more. "This kind goeth not forth" even for "fasting and prayer."

> " Look at this beautiful world, and read the truth
> In her fair page; see every season brings
> New change to her of everlasting youth—
> Stil! the green soil, with joyous living things
> Swarms—the wide air is full of joyous wings."
> BRYANT.

FAMILY ARCTIIDÆ

"All diamonded with panes of quaint device,
Innumerable of stains, and splendid dyes,
As are the Tiger Moth's deep damask wings."

KEATS.

"There is another sort of these caterpillers, who haue no certaine place of abode, nor yet cannot tell where te find theyr foode, but, like vnto superstitious Pilgrims, doo wander and stray hither and thither (and like Mise), consume and eat vp that which is none of their owne; and these haue purchased a very apt name amongst vs Englishmen, to be called *Palmer-worms*, by reason of their wandering and rogish life (for they neuer stay in one place, but are euer wandering), although by reason of their roughnes and ruggednes some call them Beare-wormes. They can by no means endure to be dyeted, and to feede vpon some certaine herbes and flowers, but boldly and disorderly creepe ouer all, and tast of all plants and trees indifferently, and liue as they list."—TOPSELL, *History of Serpents*, p. 105 (1608).

This is a large family including many genera and reckoning, according to recent lists, over two thousand species. The family is represented in our fauna by thirty-eight genera, and at least one hundred and twenty species.

The following characterization of the family is adapted from Hampson, with special reference to the genera occurring within our territory:

Proboscis more or less aborted in the typical genera *Arctia*, *Diacrisia*, and allies, fully developed in most neotropical genera, and in *Utetheisa* and its allies; palpi slight and porrect, or well developed and upturned; ocelli present; eyes rarely hairy; antennæ pectinate or ciliate; tibial spurs typically small, but often well developed, the hind tibiæ with the medial spurs absent in a few genera and the fore tibiæ in others with curved apical claw, the mid and hind tibiæ rarely spined. Wings usually well developed. Fore wing with vein $1a$ separate from $1b$; 5 from near lower angle of cell or well below angle of discocellulars; 6 from or from near upper angle; areole present in many genera. Hind wing with vein $1a$ present; $1c$ absent;

4 often absent; 5 from near lower angle of cell or well below angle of discocellulars; 6, 7 sometimes coincident; 8 coincident with the cell from or almost from base to near middle, or extremity of the cell and even in some genera beyond the extremity of the cell. In the genus *Halisidota* vein 8 is obsolete.

The larvæ have all the prolegs and are generally profusely clothed with hairs. They pupate in cocoons woven of silk mixed with the hairs which are shed during the process of spinning. The caterpillars of some species have received the common appellation of "woolly bears," and the moths are familiarly known as "tiger-moths."

Genus HOLOMELINA Herrich-Schæffer

The names *Eubaphe* and *Crocota*, proposed by Hübner, and applied recently by some writers to this group of insects, being what are known to students as *nomina nuda*, cannot stand.

It may be said in passing that this genus from a classificational standpoint is in a very unsatisfactory condition, so far as some of the species are concerned. The "Splitters" and the "Lumpers" have been hard at work upon it, and inasmuch as the insects show very little purely structural variation, and vary greatly in color and size, there has resulted great confusion. Within the limits of the space assigned to us in the present compendium we have not the opportunity to discuss these questions, but suggest to our readers that there is here an opportunity to use both eyes and mind to advantage in solving some of the vexed points. The test of breeding should be rigorously applied, and the larval stages of the insects should be critically observed.

(1) **Holomelina ostenta** Henry Edwards, Plate XIV, Fig. 17, ♂. (The Showy Holomelina.)

This conspicuous and very beautifully colored insect ranges from Colorado through New Mexico and Arizona into Mexico.

(2) **Holomelina opella** Grote, Plate XIV, Fig. 23, ♂. (The Tawny Holomelina.)

Syn. *obscura* Strecker; *rubricosta* Ehrman.

This species is rather common in Pennsylvania and the Atlantic States as far south as Georgia.

Form **belmaria** Ehrman, Plate XIV, Fig. 24, ♀. (Ehrman's Holomelina.)

This insect, a paratype of which is figured as above cited, is regarded by Dr. Dyar as a varietal form of *H. opella*. The author is inclined to question the correctness of this determination, because all specimens of the moth so far seen, and a considerable series has come under observation, appear to be structurally different from *H. opella,* in so far forth that the fore wings are narrower, longer and more produced at the apex. The mere fact that they are always black in itself could hardly constitute a valid ground for specific discrimination.

(3) **Holomelina immaculata** Reakirt, Plate XIV, Fig. 20, ♂. (The Plain-winged Holomelina.)

The range of this species is the same as that of the preceding.

(4) **Holomelina diminutiva** Græf, Plate XIV, Fig. 22, ♀. (The Least Holomelina.)

Very common in Florida, and apparently quite constant in size and markings. It is sunk as a synonym of *aurantiaca,* form *rubicundaria,* by Dyar, but the writer is not willing to admit that this is correct.

(5) **Holomelina brevicornis** Walker, Plate XIV, Figs. 19, 21, ♀. (The Black-banded Holomelina.)

Syn. *belfragei* Stretch.

This species has also been sunk as a synonym of *aurantiaca* by recent writers, but with doubtful propriety. It is common in the Gulf States and particularly in Louisiana and Texas.

(6) **Holomelina quinaria** Grote, Plate XIV, Fig. 18, ♂. (The Five-Spotted Holomelina.)

Syn. *choriona* Reakirt; *bimaculata* Saunders.

Characterized by the creamy white spots upon the fore wings. The depth of color of the primaries varies much, from dark brown to pale ferruginous, the specimen figured being representative of the latter form. The spots also vary much in size.

> "And there's never a blade nor a leaf too mean
> To be some happy creature's place."
>
> —Lowell.

Genus DODIA Dyar

Only one species has thus far been assigned to this genus. It was named **Dodia albertæ** by Dr. Dyar in the year 1901. The description both of the genus and the species will be found in the Journal of the New York Entomological Society, Vol. IX, p. 85. The annexed cut (Fig. 58) is taken from the type of the species in the United States National Museum. The insect has thus far only been found in the Territory of Alberta.

FIG. 58.—*Dodia albertæ.*

Genus UTETHEISA Hübner

A genus of small extent, represented both in the Old World and the New by nine species, two of which occur within our territory.

(1) **Utetheisa bella** Linnæus, Plate XV, Fig. 27, ♀. (The Beautiful Utetheisa.)

Syn. *hybrida* Butler; *intermedia* Butler; *terminalis* Neumœgen & Dyar.

This common moth, which frequents the blossoms of the golden-rod (*Solidago*) in the late summer and fall, is widely distributed in the States of the Atlantic seaboard, and shows some tendency to local variation.

(2) **Utetheisa ornatrix** Linnæus, Plate XVII, Fig. 8, ♂. (The Ornamented Utetheisa.)

Syn. *stretchi* Butler; *pura* Butler.

This species may easily be distinguished from the preceding by the washed-out appearance of the primaries. In the form named *pura* by Butler the fore wings are white, immaculate, except for the red costal streak. The species is common in the Antilles, and occurs in southern Florida.

Genus HAPLOA Hübner

The genus *Haploa*, which is confined to our territory, has furnished a great deal of amusement to classificationists, who have busied themselves with the spots and markings on the wings of the species, which are very variable. In a long series of specimens of any one of the species it will be found that scarcely two are exactly alike in the amount of black or white displayed upon the fore wings. The reader will do well in this connection to consult the Proceedings of the United States National Museum, Vol. X, pp. 338-353, where Prof. John B. Smith has written upon the subject, the Canadian Entomologist, Vol. XIX, p. 181 *et seq.*, where Mr. H. H. Lyman has presented his views, and the Plate given by Mr. F. A. Merrick in the Entomological News for 1903, in which the extreme variability of *H. lecontei* in a given locality is illustrated.

(1) **Haploa clymene** Brown, Plate XVII, Fig. 7, ♂. (The Clymene Moth.)

Syn. *interruptomarginata* De Beauvois; *comma* Walker.

This is one of the most constant species of the genus, and may easily be recognized by the figure we have given upon the plate. It ranges from southern New England to Georgia, and westward to the Mississippi. The larva feeds upon *Eupatorium* it is said, and the writer believes that the statement, which has been called in question, is correct, for, although he has never reared the larvæ to maturity himself, he has observed the female moth ovipositing upon this plant in southern Indiana. It is also said to feed upon willows.

(2) **Haploa colona** Hübner, Plate XVII, Fig. 2, ♀. (The Colona Moth.)

Syn. *carolina* Harris.

Form **consita** Walker, Plate XVII, Fig. 5, ♂.

Syn. *lactata* Smith.

This species, which is the largest of the genus, is very variable in the amount of the black shown upon the fore wings. We give two extremes. Other forms are recognized. The insect has its metropolis in the southwestern States, though it occurs also very sparingly in the northern Atlantic States, and more commonly in the southern Atlantic States. It is common in Texas.

(3) **Haploa lecontei** Boisduval (Leconte's Haploa).

Form **dyari** Merrick, Plate XVII, Fig. 9, ♂.

Form **militaris** Harris, Plate XVII, Figs. 4, 10, ♂; Fig. 1, ♀.

Form **vestalis** Packard, Plate XVII, Fig. 3, ♂.

This is a protean species, of which a half dozen, or more, forms have been recognized, named, and described. We give in our cut (Fig. 59), a figure of the wings of a specimen, which agrees in its markings with the specimen figured by Boisduval, the author of the species, in his Plate given in the *Regne Animal*. Such specimens come in the form of their maculation very near the next species, which has been differentiated by Lyman under the name *confusa*. *Haploa lecontei* ranges from

Fig. 59.—*Haploa lecontei*, ♂.

New England to Georgia and westward to the Mississippi. It is a very common insect in western Pennsylvania. The caterpillar feeds upon *Triosteum perfoliatum*, and in localities where this plant is abundant the moths may be found in swarms at the end of May and the beginning of June.

(4) **Haploa confusa** Lyman, Plate XVII, Fig. 6, ♂. (Lyman's Haploa.)

This form, or species, is well represented in our plate. It appears to be constant, and is indigenous to the New England States. The specimen figured came from the neighborhood of Claremont, New Hampshire.

(5) **Haploa contigua** Walker. (The Neighbor.)

The cut we give (Fig. 60), shows the maculation of the

Fig. 60.—*Haploa contigua*, ♂

wings of this species sufficiently well to enable it to be separated at once from its congeners. It occurs in the Atlantic region from New England northward and westward. It is found in the Catskills and the Adirondacks, and probably occurs in the mountains of northern Pennsylvania, although I do not recall any reference to its having been taken in that State, nor have I seen it on the summits of the Alleghenies, where I have passed several summers.

Genus EUERYTHRA Harvey

There are two species of this genus known, **Euerythra phasma** Harvey, which is represented in the accompanying cut

(Fig. 61), and **Euerythra trimaculata**, which is figured on Plate XVI, Fig. 4. The insects occur in Texas and Arizona. They are not common in collections as yet, and so far as the

FIG. 61.—*Euerythra phasma*, ♂. ¼. (After Hampson.)

writer recalls, their larval habits have not been described. The student who desires to study the structure of the genus should consult Hampson's Catalogue, or Prof. Smith's Paper published in the Proceedings of the United States National Museum, Vol. X, p. *335 et seq.*

Genus ECPANTHERIA Hübner

This is a large genus, well represented in the tropics of America. Only two species occur within the limits of our fauna, **Ecpantheria muzina** Oberthür, which is found in Texas as a straggler from the Mexican territory, and **Ecpantheria deflorata** Fabricius, which is more commonly known by its synonymical name, *scribonia*, given to it by Stoll. The larva of this handsome moth is itself a beautiful object. It is deep black, clothed with black hairs, and at the junction of the somites, or segments of the body, it is banded with rings of crimson. The male of the perfect insect is figured on Plate XVI, Fig. 16, and in the accompanying cut we give a figure of the larva. The Eyed Tiger-moth

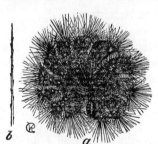

FIG. 62.—*E. deflorata; a* larva; *b* magnified hair of larva. (After Riley.)

ranges from southern New England, where it is rare, through the southern parts of the United States into Mexico. It is quite common in the Carolinas, and in my boyhood I derived much pleasure from rearing the larvæ, which fed very freely upon the plantain (*Plantago*).

Genus TURUPTIANA Walker

There are eight species in this genus, but only one of them occurs within the limits of the United States.

(1) **Turuptiana permaculata** Packard, Plate XVI, Fig. 15, ♂. (The Many-spotted Tiger-moth.)

Syn. *reducta* Grote; *cæca* Strecker.

Fig. 63.—*Turuptiana permaculata*, ♂. ¼. (After Hampson.)

This neat moth is found in Colorado and thence southward as far as Arizona and Mexico.

Genus LEPTARCTIA Stretch

There is only one species in this genus, but the single species by assuming protean colors has caused a great multiplication of names. We have figured a few of the varietal forms.

(1) **Leptarctia californiæ** Walker, Plate XIV, Fig. 25, ♀.

Form **lena** Boisduval, Plate XIV, Fig. 28, ♂.

Form **decia** Boisduval, Plate XIV, Fig. 27, ♂.

Form **dimidiata** Stretch, Plate XIV, Fig. 26, ♂.

The moth is found in southern California, where it is quite common. The student will have little trouble in recognizing the commoner varieties by the help of the figures we have given, but these are only a few of the forms which occur.

> "And with childlike credulous affection
> We behold those tender wings expand,
> Emblems of our own great resurrection,
> Emblems of the bright and better land."
> —LONGFELLOW.

Genus SEIRARCTIA Packard

(1) **Seirarctia echo** Abbot & Smith, Plate I, Fig 10, larva; Plate XVI, Fig. 23, ♀. (The Echo Moth.)

Syn. *niobe* Strecker.

This beautiful moth, the caterpillar of which feeds upon the

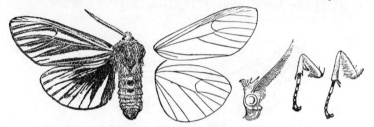

FIG. 64.—*Seirarctia echo*, ♂. ¼. (After Hampson.)

sabal palmetto, occurs in Florida, Georgia, Alabama, and Mississippi.

Genus ALEXICLES Grote

(1) **Alexicles aspersa** Grote. (The Alexicles Moth.)
This moth is referred by Hampson to *Hyphantria*. It may belong there, but I leave it in the genus erected for it by Grote. The abdomen is vermilion-colored, with black dorsal spots. The wings are dark brown, the primaries somewhat lighter than the secondaries and showing obscure darker spots, arranged in transverse bands.

FIG. 65.—*Alexicles aspersa*, ♂.

Genus ESTIGMENE Hübner

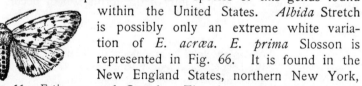

There are reputed to be four species of this genus found within the United States. *Albida* Stretch is possibly only an extreme white variation of *E. acræa*. *E. prima* Slosson is represented in Fig. 66. It is found in the New England States, northern New York, and Canada. The three species just named all agree in having the abdomen yellowish or orange above, and ornamented dorsally by a series of black

FIG. 66.—*Estigmene prima*, ♂.

spots. *E. congrua* has the abdomen white on the upper side. The genus is represented in Asia, Africa, and Tasmania, as well as in the temperate regions of North America.

(1) **Estigmene acræa** Drury, Plate, XVI, Fig. 11, ♂, Fig. 12, ♀. (The Acræa Moth.)

Syn. *caprotina* Drury; *menthastrina* Martyn; *pseuderminea* **Peck**; *californica* Packard; *packardi* Schaupp; *klagesi* Ehrman.

A western variety with the fore wings slightly shaded with brown has been dubbed *dubia* by Walker, and *rickseckeri* by Behr. In Mexico there is a local race in which the males have the hind wings white like the females, and to this race Hampson has applied the name *mexicana.* This is altogether one of

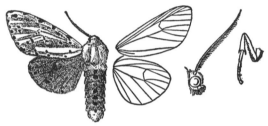

FIG. 67.—*Estigmene acræa*, ♂ . ¼. (After Hampson.)

the commonest insects in the Middle Atlantic States, and with the illustrations we have given can be easily determined.

(2) **Estigmene congrua** Walker, Plate XVI, Fig. 8, ♂. (The white-bodied Estigmene.)

Syn. *antigone* Strecker; *athena* Strecker.

A fairly common species in Pennsylvania and the Atlantic States generally, ranging westward as far as Colorado.

Genus HYPHANTRIA Harris

This small genus contains only three or four species, one of which is South African.

(1) **Hyphantria cunea** Drury. (The Fall Web-worm Moth.)

Form **punctatissima** Abbott & Smith, Plate XVI, Fig. 10, ♂ *.

---

*The specimens used on Plate XVI, Figs. 10 and 7, both unfortunately developed grease on their abdomens between the time when they were set up for the photographer, and the time when they were photographed. The abdomen in both cases is normally white, with darker markings.

Form **pallida** Packard, Plate XV, Fig. 26, ♂.

The larvæ are social in their habits, and spin great webs upon the foliage of almost all kinds of deciduous trees in the late summer and fall, and do a great deal of damage to orchards and nurseries. The insects pupate in loose cocoons, in crannies, and even under the loose surface of the soil. The species ranges over the United States from southern New England and New York to Texas and further west.

(2) **Hyphantria textor** Harris, Plate XVI, Fig. 9, ♂. (The Spotless Fall Web-worm Moth.)

This species, which is closely allied to the preceding in its habits, may be distinguished by the white antennæ, and the unspotted abdomen. There are specimens of the preceding species, which have the wings as immaculate as in *H. textor*. The range of the insect is from Canada to the Gulf, and from Nova Scotia to California.

Genus ARACHNIS Geyer

A small genus containing eight or nine species found in the southwestern States of the American Union, Mexico, and Central America.

(1) **Arachnis aulæa** Geyer, Plate XVI, Fig. 1, ♂. (The Aulæan Tiger-moth.)

Syn. *incarnata* Walker.

The insect occurs in southern Arizona and ranges thence southwardly as far as Guatemala. The larval stages have been described by Dyar in the Canadian Entomologist, Vol. XXVI, p. 307.

(2) **Arachnis picta** Packard, Plate XVI, Fig. 2, ♂. (The Painted Arachnis.)

Names have been applied to a number of color varieties of this insect. It ranges from Colorado to southern California and northern Mexico. The larva feeds upon *Lupinus*.

(3) **Arachnis zuni** Neumœgen, Plate XVI, Fig. 3, ♀. (The Zuni Tiger-moth.)

The figure we give will enable the student to recognize this pretty and rather rare species without any difficulty. It ranges from New Mexico to Arizona and southward on the tablelands.

Genus ISIA Walker

Three species belong to this genus, one found in Argentina, the other in Turkestan, and the third in the United States and Canada.

FIG. 68—*Isia isabella*, ♂ . ¼.   (After Hampson.)

(1) **Isia isabella** Abbot & Smith, Plate XVI, Fig. 13, ♀. (The Isabella Tiger-moth.)

This common insect is found everywhere in the United States. The caterpillar is the familiar "woolly bear," which may be often seen by the roadside rapidly making its way in the fall of the year to a hiding-place in which to hibernate, or, in the spring, to some spot where it may find food. It is reddish-brown in color, black at either end. When disturbed, it curls up and lies motionless, as if feigning death. To "caterpillar," in the slang phrase of the Middle West, is to silently succumb

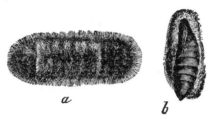

a   *b*

FIG. 69.—*Isia isabella*.   *a*. larva; *b*. pupa.

and yield to the unavoidable. The larva feeds freely upon a great variety of herbaceous plants. It is fond of the grasses, and particularly likes the leaves of the plantain (*Plantago*). There does not appear to be any marked tendency to variation in this species. Both the moth and the larva are common objects, with which every American schoolboy who has lived in the country is familiar; and unhappy is the boy who has not at some time or other in his life made the country his home. "God made the country, man made the town."

Genus PHRAGMATOBIA Stephens

A genus of modern extent, represented in Europe, Asia, and North America. The structural characteristics of the wings are displayed in Fig. 71.

(1) **Phragmatobia fuliginosa** Linnæus, Plate XIV, Fig. 31, ♀. (The Ruby Tiger-moth.)

Syn. *rubricosa* Harris.

The Ruby Tiger-moth is widely distributed, being found throughout boreal Asia, Europe, and the northern United States

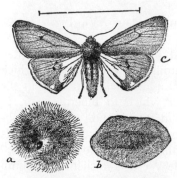

FIG. 70.—*Phragmatobia fuliginosa.*
a. larva; *b.* cocoon; *c.* imago, ♂.
From "Insect Life," Vol. I, p. 236.)

and Canada. A multitude of minor subvarietal forms have been distinguished, and to some of them names have been applied, but there is comparatively little difference between them, and the student who has once learned to recognize the species will find no difficulty in assigning to it any specimens which may come into his possession. The insect, so far as our fauna is concerned, is a northern species, quite common in New England and Canada, and ranging southward along the Appalachian Mountains into the Carolinas, where it only occurs at high elevations above sea-level. It is also found ranging southward along the Rocky Mountains. The caterpillar feeds upon a variety of herbaceous plants, and is partial to the shoots of the golden-rod (*Solidago*).

(2) **Phragmatobia brucei** Henry Edwards, Plate XIV, Fig. 30, ♂. (Bruce's Tiger.)

This species is found in Colorado upon the mountains.

(3) **Phragmatobia beani** Neumœgen, Plate XIV, Fig. 29, ♀. (Bean's Tiger-moth.)

The habitat of this species is the Rocky Mountains of Alberta and Assiniboia.

(4) **Phragmatobia yarrowi** Stretch. (Yarrow's Tiger-moth.)

Syn. *remissa* Henry Edwards.

This pretty little tiger-moth is found from the country south of Hudson Bay to British Columbia, and FIG. 71.—*P. yarrowi*, ♂ .¼. (After Hampson.) ranges thence southward along the higher mountain ranges as far as northern Arizona.

Genus MÆNAS Hübner

Only one species of this rather extensive genus, which is represented in South America by five species and by a considerable number in Africa and the Indo-Malayan region, occurs in North America.

(1) **Mænas vestalis** Packard, Plate XVI, Fig. 5, ♂. (The Vestal Tiger-Moth.)

This insect, which closely resembles *Estigmene congrua*, figured on the same plate, may be distinguished from the latter not only by structural peculiarities, but unfailingly by the ordinary observer, by the presence of the two black spots on the hind wings, as shown in our illustration.

Genus DIACRISIA Hübner

This large genus, which includes over one hundred and twenty-five species, according to the arrangement given in Hampson's Catalogue, not reckoning the species referred to the genus *Isia*, which he also places here, is represented in our fauna by four insects, of which we give illustrations.

(1) **Diacrisia virginica** Fabricius. Plate XVI, Fig. 7, ♂. (The Virginian Tiger-moth.)

The form figured on our plate is the slight variety named *fumosa* by Strecker. in which the fore wings are a little dusky at their tips as if they had been flying about in the smoke of the furnaces at Reading or Pittsburgh. Ordinarily the species is pure white. The body of the specimen on our plate is greasy, and hence too dark.

(2) **Diacrisia latipennis** Stretch, Plate XVI, Fig. 6, ♂. (The Red-legged Diacrisia.)

The coxæ and femora are pink or reddish. The insect is common in Pennsylvania, and the Atlantic States generally.

(3) **Diacrisia,rubra** Neumœgen, Plate XIV, Fig. 32, ♀. (The Ruddy Diacrisia.)

The habitat of this species is British Columbia, Oregon, and Washington.

(4) **Diacrisia vagans** Boisduval, Plate XIV, Fig. 33, ♂, Fig. 34, ♀. (The Wandering Diacrisia.)

Syn. *pteridis* Henry Edwards; *bicolor* Walker; *rufula* Boisduval; *punctata* Packard; *proba* Henry Edwards.

The insect illustrates the phenomenon of sexual dimorphism, the males and females being unlike in color. The species-makers have had some sport with it, as shown by the synonyms.

Genus HYPHORAIA Hubner

This is a sub-arctic genus, circumpolar in its distribution in the Northern Hemisphere. Three species occur in our territory, one of which we figure.

(1) **Hyphoraia parthenos** Harris, Plate XVI, Fig. 20, ♀. (The St. Lawrence Tiger-moth.)

Syn. *borealis* Mœschler.

The moth, which is one of the most beautiful in the family, is comparatively rare in collections. It occurs in northern New England, and the valley of the St. Lawrence, westward to Manitoba. It is occasionally found in the Catskills.

Genus PLATYPREPIA Dyar

One species is found in our region. It is somewhat variable in the style and number of the spots upon the wings.

(1) **Platyprepia virginalis** Boisduval, Plate XV, Fig. 18, ♂. Fig. 19. ♀. (The Ranchman's Tiger-moth.)

Syn. *ochracea* Stretch; *guttata* Boisduval.

A very beautiful insect, quite common in Colorado, Wyoming and Montana, and thence ranging westward to northern California and the region of Puget's Sound.

Genus APANTESIS Walker

The metropolis of this genus is North America, only two species attributed to it being found in the Old World. There are over twenty valid species found within our limits, and numerous so-called subspecies and varietal forms. A small treatise might be written upon these, but in a volume like this, which is designed to cover in as compact form as possible the most needed information, all that we can do is to help the student to the determination of the more important species.

(1) **Apantesis virgo** Linnæus, Plate XV, Fig. 11, ♂. (The Virgin Tiger-moth).

Found in the northern Atlantic States and Canada.

(2) **Apantesis parthenice** Kirby, Plate XV, Fig. 13, ♂. (The Parthenice Moth.)

Syn *saundersi* Grote.

The habitat of this species is the same as that of *A. virgo*, from which it may always be discriminated by its smaller size, the narrower white lines upon the fore wings and the absence of the dark spot at the origin of vein two on the hind wings, which is characteristic of the former species.

(3) **Apantesis intermedia** Stretch, Plate XI, Fig. 20, ♂. (The Intermediate Tiger-moth.)

This species which is by some authors regarded as a southern form of *A. parthenice,* is intermediate in size between *A. virgo* and *A. parthenice.* It closely resembles the latter in the maculation of the wings. but the pinkish-white stripes on the primaries are broad as in *A. virgo.*

(4) **Apantesis oithona** Strecker, Plate XVI, Fig. 30, ♂. (The Oithona Moth.)

This insect is undoubtedly genetically the same as *A. rectilinea* French. The difference is merely in the width of the pale lines on the fore wings, which, being narrower in *rectilinea,* give these wings a darker appearance.

Form **rectilinea** French, Plate XV, Fig. 1, ♀. (The Straight-lined Tiger-moth.)

This insect in its varietal forms ranges from the Atlantic States across the Mississippi Valley.

(5) **Apantesis michabo** Grote, Plate XV, Fig. 17, ♀. (The Michabo Moth.)

Syn. *minea* Slosson.

The illustration we give is sufficient to enable the student to identify this species, which is discriminated from its congeners most readily by observing the broad flesh-colored band on the costa of the fore wings. In the form *minea* the flesh-colored lines are deep-red. This is the only difference.

(6) **Apantesis arge** Drury, Plate XV, Fig. 15, ♂. (The Arge Moth.)

Syn. *dione* Fabricius; *incarnatorubra* Gœze; *cœlebs* Martyn; *nerea* Boisduval; *doris* Boisduval.

Allied to the preceding species, but ascertained by the test of breeding to be distinct. The species is very variable. The hind wings are not often as free from dark markings as the specimen, and frequently are as much spotted and blotched with black as is the figure of *A. michabo* we give. The species is found almost everywhere within the United States and Canada.

(7) **Apantesis ornata** Packard. (The Ornate Tiger-moth.)

Form **achaia** Grote & Robinson, Plate XV, Figs. 20, 24, ♂. (The Achaia Moth.)

Syn. *edwardsi* Stretch.

A variable insect to which a number of names have been given. The variety in which the hind wings are yellow is *A. ochracea* Stretch. The species is found on the Pacific coast. The larval stages have been described by Dyar, Psyche, Vol. V, p. 380, 556.

FIG. 72.—*Apantesis anna*, ♀.

(8) **Apantesis anna** Grote. (The Anna Moth.)

Form **persephone** Grote, Plate XV, Fig. 8, ♂, Fig. 10, ♀. (The Persephone Moth.)

We give in Figure 72 a cut representing a specimen of the typical *anna*, in which the hind wings are wholly black. *Persephone* is the normal form. The insect is very variable in the amount of black displayed upon the hind wings, and also to some extent in the width and extent of the light lines on the primaries. The species is found in the Atlantic States, and is not at all uncommon in western Pennsylvania. The larva has been described by Dyar.

(9) **Apantesis quenseli** Paykull, Plate XVI, Fig. 28, ♀. (The Labrador Apantesis.)

Syn. *strigosa* Fabricius: *gelida* Mœschler; *liturata* Ménétriés; *complicata* Walker; *turbans* Christoph.

This little moth is found in Labrador, Greenland, and Arctic America generally. It also occurs in Arctic Europe and Asia and upon the summits of the Swiss Alps. It doubtless will be found upon the American Alps in British Columbia.

(10) **Apantesis virguncula** Kirby, Plate XV, Fig. 9, ♂, Fig. 16, ♂. (The Little Virgin Moth.)

Syn. *dahurica* Grote (*nec* Boisduval); *speciosa* Mœschler; *otiosa* Neumœgen & Dyar.

A variable species. The form described as *otiosa* has traces of the transverse lines, characteristic of so many other species of the genus, and the fore wings have a more checkered appearance on this account. The insect occurs in the northern United States and Canada.

(11) **Apantesis proxima** Guérin-Méneville, Plate XV, Fig. 4, ♀. (The Mexican Tiger-moth.)

Syn. *docta* Walker; *mexicana* Grote & Robinson; *arizonensis* Stretch; *mormonica* Neumœgen.

Form **autholea** Boisduval, Plate XVI, Fig. 32, ♂.

From the varietal form *autholea* figured in the plate *proxima* may be discriminated by the fact that the latter has the hind wings marked with dark brown or black spots on the margins. The species occurs in southern California, Arizona, Mexico, and Central America.

(12) **Apantesis blakei** Grote, Plate XVI, Fig. 31, ♂. (Blake's Tiger-moth.)

Syn. *bolanderi* Stretch.

This species is found in the mountains of California and adjoining States.

(13) **Apantesis nevadensis** Grote & Robinson, Plate XVI, Fig. 29, ♂. (The Nevada Tiger-moth.)

Syn. *behri* Stretch.

Form **incorrupta** Henry Edwards, Plate XV, Fig. 7, ♀.

Syn. *shastaënsis* French.

As the name indicates, this species is an inhabitant of the Rocky Mountains.

(14) **Apantesis williamsi** Dodge. (Williams' Tiger-moth.) Form **determinata** Neumœgen, Plate XV., Fig. 3, ♂.

Syn. *diecki* Neumœgen.

This easily recognized species is found in Colorado and adjacent States among the mountains.

(15) **Apantesis phyllira** Drury, Plate XV, Fig. 14, ♂. (The Phyllira Moth.)

Syn. *B–atra* Gœze: *plantaginis* Martyn; *dodgei* Butler; *excelsa* Neumœgen; *favorita* Neumœgen; *lugubris* Hulst.

This species is found in the Southern States, where it is not uncommon. It is rather variable in the disposition and extent of the dark and light markings.

(16) **Apantesis figurata** Drury, Plate XV, Fig. 12, ♀, (The Figured Tiger-moth.)

Syn. *ceramica* Hübner; *f–pallida* Strecker

This is probably only a form of the preceding species, which occurs with considerable frequency. It is confined to the Southern States.

(17) **Apantesis vittata** Fabricius, Plate XV, Fig. 25, ♂, Fig. 22, ♀. (Banded Tiger-moth.)

Syn. *decorata* Saunders.

Form **radians** Walker, Plate XV, Fig. 23, ♂, Fig. 21 ♀.

Syn. *colorata* Walker; *incompleta* Butler.

Form **phalerata** Harris, Plate XV, Fig. 6, ♀.

Syn. *rhoda* Butler.

A very common and variable species, which is probably the same as *A. nais* Drury, which has the abdomen prevalently ochraceous, and not as strongly marked with black. The species seems to be, so to speak, in a liquid state. In a series of some hundreds of specimens before the writer, many of them bred from larvæ, and undoubtedly all referable to the same species, any and all of the forms, which have been named by writers, can be found, yet the bulk of them came from one narrow little ravine in western Pennsylvania. We leave the synonymy as it stands in Dyar's list, so far as the things figured on our plate are concerned, but cannot believe that these insects represent different species, as maintained by some authors.

Genus KODIOSOMA Stretch

This little Californian genus, the structure of which is abundantly illustrated by the cut we give, contains but one species, which is represented in a number of varietal forms.

(1) **Kodiosoma fulva** Stretch, Plate XIII, Fig. 45, ♂.

Form **eavesi**, Stretch, Plate XIII, Fig. 43 ♂.

Form **tricolor** Stretch, Plate XIII, Fig. 44, ♂.

There are still other forms, one of which is wholly black, and has been named *nigra* by Stretch. The moth is found in California, and is there not at all uncommon. The life-history has been thus far only imperfectly ascertained.

FIG. 73—*Kodiosoma fulva*, ♂. ¼.
(After Hampson.)

Genus ECTYPIA Clemens

Two species are referred to this genus. *E. thona* Strecker, from New Mexico is doubtfully referable to it, but the only specimen known, the type, is in too poor a condition to enable much to be told about it.

(1) **Ectypia bivittata** Clemens. (The Two-banded Ectypia.)

Syn. *nigroflava* Græf.

This very beautiful and rare moth occurs in Texas. Its characteristics are well displayed in the figure we give in the accompanying cut.

FIG. 74—*Ectypia bivittata*, ♀. ¼.
(After Hampson.)

Genus EUVERNA Neumœgen & Dyar

(1) **Euverna clio** Packard, Plate XVI, Fig. 22, ♀. (The Clio Moth.)

This chastely beautiful moth occurs in the Rocky Mountains of southern California. It is the sole representative of its genus, and is as yet rare in collections.

Genus PARASEMIA Hübner

This genus is represented in our fauna by certain varietal forms, which agree in part with those found in the Old World, and in part differ from them. There is only one species in the genus, which has a wide circumpolar distribution, and a score or more of names have been given to mere color varieties. We figure two of the commoner variations. The larva feeds on *Plantago* and *Myosotis*.

(1) **Parasemia plantaginis** Linnæus. (The Small Tiger-moth.)

Plate XVI, Fig, 25, ♂. The usual form found in Colorado and Wyoming.

Plate XVI, Fig. 26, ♂. Form named *geometrica* by Grote.

Genus ARCTIA Schrank

A circumpolar genus of the Northern Hemisphere, containing four species, which are subject to considerable variation in color and size of spots.

(1) **Arctia caia** Linnæus, Plate XV, Fig. 5, ♀. (The Great Tiger-moth.)

The specimen figured on the plate was taken in Labrador.

Form **wiskotti** Staudinger, Plate XV, Fig. 2, ♀.

Syn. *utahensis* Henry Edwards; *auripennis* Butler; *transmontana* Neumœgen & Dyar.

The specimen portrayed on the plate was taken in Colorado.

Genus PAREUCHÆTES Grote

There are three species of this genus, two of which we figure. The species may be discriminated as follows:

1. Hind wing yellowish......................................*insulata*
2. Hind wing white...*tenera*
3. Hind wing tinged with fuscous.........................*eglenensis*

(1) **Pareuchætes insulata** Walker, Plate XIV, Fig. 3, ♀. (The Yellow-winged Pareuchætes.)

Syn. *cadaverosa* Grote; *affinis* Grote; *aurata* Butler.

Found in the Gulf States and the Antilles.

(2) **Pareuchætes eglenensis** Clemens, Plate XIV, Fig. 4, ♀. (The Gray-winged Pareuchætes.)

This species occurs in the Carolinas and southward. *Pareuchætes tenera* is found in the Atlantic States and is not uncommon in Pennsylvania.

Genus EUCHÆTIAS Lyman

The following key based upon that of Hampson may enable the student to differentiate the species in his collection:

Abdomen red above.
  Fore wing with costal fascia.
    Fore wing with the costal fascia yellow . . . . *antica* Walker
    Fore wing with the costal fascia white . . . . *albicosta* Walker
  Fore wing without costal fascia.
    Hind wing with crimson patch on inner area . . . . *perlevis* Grote
  Hind wing without crimson patch on inner area.
    Fore wing uniform brownish . . . .*murina* Stretch
    Fore wing white tinged with fuscous . . . .*bolteri* Stretch
Abdomen orange above.
    Fore wing gray-brown . . . .*egle* Drury
    Fore wing brownish white with the veins white . . *oregonensis* Stretch
Abdomen whitish above . . . . *pudens* Henry Edwards

(1) **Euchætias murina** Stretch, Plate XI, Fig. 18, ♀. (The Mouse-colored Euchætias.)

The habitat of this species is Texas.

(2) **Euchætias egle** Drury, Plate I, Fig. 5, larva; Plate XVI, Fig. 21, ♀. (The Milk-weed Moth.)

Fig. 75.—*Euchætias egle,* ♂ . ¼. (After Hampson.)

The figure given above in the text and those given on the plates will suffice for the identification of this common insect, which ranges from the Atlantic to the Mississippi and beyond. The larva feeds upon Milk-weed *(Asclepias)*.

(3) **Euchætias oregonensis** Stretch, Plate XVI, Fig. 19, ♂ . (The Oregon Euchætias.)

This insect is found throughout the northern portions of the United States and Canada.

Genus PYGARCTIA Grote

A small genus containing four species all found within our territory. The following table taken from Hampson will serve for the identification of the species, taken in connection with the cut and the figures we give:

A. Fore wing with scarlet fasciæ on costa and inner margin......*spraguei*
B. Fore wing with orange fasciæ on costa and inner margin
    a. Abdomen scarlet...................................*vivida*
    b. Abdomen orange ....*abdominalis*
C. Fore wing without fasciæ...... ....*elegans*

(1) **Pygarctia elegans** Stretch, Plate XVI, Fig. 17, ♂. (The Elegant Pygarctia.)

FIG. 76.—*Pygarctia elegans*, ♂ . ¼.
(After Hampson.)

The neuration and structural characteristics of the genus are sufficiently well displayed in the accompanying cut of this species to make any verbal description unnecessary. The insect occurs in southern California, Texas, Arizona, and Mexico.

(2) **Pygarctia abdominalis** Grote, Plate XVI, Fig. 27, ♀. (The Orange-bodied Pygarctia.)

The habitat of this species is Florida.

(3) **Pygarctia spraguei** Grote, Plate XVI, Fig. 18, ♂. (Sprague's Pygarctia.)

The home of this insect is Kansas, Colorado, and adjoining States.

Genus HYPOCRISIAS Hampson

A small genus of which a single representative is found within our limits, occurring as a straggler from the Mexican fauna.

(1) **Hypocrisias minima** Neumœgen. (The Least Hypocrisias.)

Syn. *armillata* Henry Edwards.

The prevalent tints of the body and fore wings are ochreous and brown. The hind wings are yellowish white. The annexed cut will help the student to recognize the insect, when a specimen comes into his

FIG. 77—*Hypocrisias minima*, ♂.

possession. The habitat of the species is Mexico, but it is occasionally taken in southern Arizona.

Genus ÆMILIA Kirby

A small neotropical genus, represented in our fauna by two species. The insect named *occidentalis* by French is a form of *A. roseata*, in which the red of the wings has been replaced by ochreous.

(1) **Æmilia ambigua** Strecker, Plate XIV, Fig. 15, ♂. (The Red-banded Æmilia.)

Syn. *bolteri* Henry Edwards; *syracosia* Druce.

This beautiful insect is found in the Rocky Mountains of Colorado, and thence southward to northern Mexico.

(2) **Æmilia roseata** Walker, Plate XIV, Fig. 14. ♀. (The Rosy Æmilia.)

Syn. *cinnamomea* Boisduval; *sanguivenosa* Neumœgen; *significans* Henry Edwards; *occidentalis* French.

This rather rare insect occurs on the Pacific coast, and, according to report, ranges from British Columbia to Mexico. The specimen figured on the plate came from the latter country.

Genus HALISIDOTA Hübner

An extensive genus, well represented in Central and South America, and containing about a dozen species, which are found within our faunal limits. Of these we figure a number of species, enough to enable the student to recognize the genus, and the commoner species, which he is likely to encounter.

(1) **Halisidota tessellaris** Abbot & Smith, Plate XIV, Fig. 12, ♂. (The Tessellated Halisidota)

Syn. *antiphola* Walsh; *harrisi* Walsh.

The form named *Harrisi* does not differ from *tessellaris* in the imaginal stage. The sole difference is in the color of the pencils of hairs in the larvæ, which are orange in color, while in *tessellaris* they are black. This is scarcely sufficient ground upon which to establish a species.

(2) **Halisidota cinctipes** Grote, Plate XIV, Fig. 13, ♂. (The Gartered Halisidota.)

Syn. *davisi* Henry Edwards.

This species, which is southern in its habitat, and larger than its close northern ally, *tessellaris,* has the markings on the fore wings much more distinct than is the case in the latter species. The tarsi are annulated with black bands, marked with small gray points. The insect occurs in the Gulf States and in South and Central America.

(3) **Halisidota maculata** Harris, Plate XVI, Fig. 11, ♂. (The Spotted Halisidota.)

Syn. *fulvoflava* Walker; *guttifera* Herrich-Schæffer.

This species, which occurs in the northern portions of the Atlantic coast region, ranges westward to California. Several forms from the western territory have been discriminated by writers, and varietal names have been given to them. They are mere color forms.

(4) **Halisidota longa** Grote, Plate XIV, Fig. 16, ♀. (The Long-streaked Halisidota).

This species, which may easily be determined by the help of the figure we have given, occurs in Florida. The specimen delineated by the writer was taken by him at light in Jacksonville in the month of February.

(5) **Halisidota caryæ** Harris, Plate XIV, Fig. 10, ♂. (The Hickory Halisidota.)

Syn. *annulifascia* Walker; *porphyria* Herrich-Schæffer.

This well-marked and easily identified species is common in the northern Atlantic coast region, and ranges westward into the valley of the Mississippi.

(6) **Halisidota argentata** Packard, Plate XIV, Fig. 8, ♂, Fig. 9, ♀. (The Silver-spotted Halisidota.)

This pretty species is found in Colorado, and thence westward and northward to the Pacific coast. A number of subspecies have been named in this connection, but it is doubtful whether the sexes of the insects on meeting each other would recognize any specific differences themselves.

Genus HEMIHYALEA Hampson

Two species of this genus occur within the limits of the United States. *Edwardsi* is distinguished from *labecula* most easily by the fact that the inner margin of the secondaries in the former is crimson, while in the latter it is not.

(1) **Hemihyalea edwardsi** Packard, Plate XIV, Fig. 6, ♀. (Edwards' Glassy-wing.)

Syn. *translucida* Walker; *quercus* Boisduval.

This is a Californian species.

(2) **Hemihyalea labecula** Grote, Plate XIV, Fig. 7, ♂.
(The Freckled Glassy-wing.)

This insect is not uncommon in Colorado. It occurs in early summer about Manitou, and among the mountains generally.

Genus OPHARUS Walker

An extensive neotropical genus, represented within the limits of the United States by but one species.

(1) **Opharus astur** Cramer, Plate XIV, Fig. 5, ♂. (The Astur Moth.)

Syn. *albicans*, Walker; *maculicollis* Walker; *pustulata* Packard.

The insect is common in Mexico and South America, and occasionally occurs in Arizona.

Genus CALIDOTA Dyar

A neotropical genus containing a dozen species or more, two of which are found within our limits. We figure one of these; the other, *C. muricolor* Dyar, has the wings mouse-gray, semihyaline, the secondaries paler than the primaries. The head is gray in front, yellowish above; the thorax is gray, the collar edged inwardly with ochreous; the abdomen is reddish buff, with a series of black dorsal spots and broad lateral bands of the same color. The pectus and coxæ are ochreous, the legs gray. The type of the species came from Arizona.

(1) **Calidota strigosa** Walker, Plate XVI, Fig. 24, ♂.
(The Streaked Calidota.)

Syn. *cubensis* Grote; *laqueata* Henry Edwards.

This insect occurs in Florida, and is abundant in the Antilles. Its life-history has been described by Dyar in the Proceedings of the United States National Museum, for 1900. p. 268. The food-plant is *Guettarda elliptica*.

Genus EUPSEUDOSOMA Grote

Three species are attributed by Hampson to this genus, one of which, the type of the genus, we figure. It is the only species of the genus occurring within our territory.

(1) **Eupseudosoma involutum** Sepp, Plate XIV, Fig. 1, ♂.
(The Snowy Eupseudosoma.)

Syn. *nivea* Herrich-Schæffer; *floridum* Grote; *immaculata* Græf.

The life-history of this species has been given by Dyar, *i. c.*, p. 258. The food-plants are *Eugenia buxifolia, Eugenia procera,* and *Psidium pyrifera.* The insect has a wide range in tropical America, occurring from Florida to southern Brazil.

Genus BERTHOLDIA Schaus

A small neotropical genus represented in our fauna by one species.

(1) **Bertholdia trigona** Grote, Plate XIV, Fig. **2,** ♂. (Grote's Bertholdia.)

The moth flies in Colorado, New Mexico, Arizona, and northern Mexico.

FAMILY AGARISTIDÆ

"Ye lovers of marvel and fairy lore,
  Say not that the days of enchantment are o'er,
  That the well-springs of Fancy and Fable fail.

· · · · · · · · ·

There are streamlets yet where the river-sprite
  With his Harlequin changes bewilders the sight;
  There are castles yet of ivory and gold,
  Hung with floral fabrics by sunshine unroll'd,
  Within whose luxurious recesses recline
  Fays of exquisite form, quaffing exquisite wine;
  Some in gossamer veiled of ethereal dyes,
  Which have only their match in the rainbow'd skies;
  Some in richest and softest of velvets arrayed,
  Or in mail that does shame to the armourer's trade.
  These are haunting us ever for ill, or for good,
  Through earth and through air, field, forest, and flood:
  To transport our thoughts, as by magic spell,
  From the sordid objects whereon they dwell,
  To a land of the Marvellous dimly displayed,
  Where the light-winged Fancy, by wonder stayed,
  Still delighteth to hover, and joyously say:
  'Oh ! my darling elves, ye're not chased away,
  There's a region still where ye have a place—
  The mysterious world of the Insect race.' "
                    ACHETA DOMESTICA. *Episodes of Insect Life.*

The Agaristidæ compose a family of moderate size. The moths are day-flying in their habit, and in the tropics both of the Old World and the New reckon in their number some of the most resplendently colored insects found upon the globe. They are regarded as being an offshoot of the Noctuidæ.

The following description of the characteristics of the family is adapted from Hampson with reference to the forms found within our faunal limits:

'Proboscis fully developed; palpi upturned and well developed, the third joint usually naked and porrect; frons with a rounded, conical, or corneous process; antennæ cylindrical, almost simple, with slight bristles at the joints, not ciliated, and more or less distinctly dilated toward the extremity. Ocelli present; eyes sometimes hairy; tibial spurs well developed, the tibiæ rarely spined; the male claspers often very large; wings large and strongly formed. Fore wing with vein 1*a* separate from 1*b;* 1*c* absent; 5 from or from close to angle of cell; the areole present in nearly all the genera. Hind wing with vein 1*a* present; 1*c* absent; 5 obsolescent from angle of discocellulars; 6, 7 from upper angle or shortly stalked; 8 free at base, then bent downward to anastomose with the cell at a point only. All the species have silvery blue scales on the fore wings.

The larvæ are noctuiform and have all the prolegs present. The pupa is naked.'

Genus COPIDRYAS Grote

Two species belonging to this genus occur within the limits of the United States. We give illustrations of both of them.

(1) **Copidryas gloveri** Grote & Robinson, Plate XVII, Fig. 11, ♂. (Glover's Purslane-moth.)

The life-history of this rather pretty moth has been well worked out by Professor C. V. Riley and from his article published in "Insect Life," Vol. I, p. 104, we have taken the cuts which are herewith given. The drawings of the egg, pupa, and cocoon were made by Mr. C. L. Marlatt.

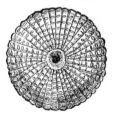

Fig. 78.—Egg of *Copidryas gloveri* greatly enlarged.

The excellent account given by Professor Riley is drawn upon for the following quotations: "The eggs are laid on the under side of the purslane leaf, either singly or in clusters of from two to five. The larva hatches in two or three days, and

is at first light green or yellowish green with darker shading across the middle of the body. In eight or nine days it attains full growth after having passed through four molts. The full grown larva is light gray or dull white with black dashes on the sides of each segment, and with the shadings of salmon pink."

FIG. 79.—Pupa and cocoon cell of *Copidryas gloveri*.

"The full-grown larvæ enter the ground for pupation, excavating a tubular burrow in the surface soil, gumming the lining and closing the opening with a thin layer of particles of soil. . . . The insect remains in this state in the neighborhood of twelve days."

In the accompanying figures we show the egg, the pupa, and the adult larva and moth. The insect is very abundant at certain times in Nebraska, Kansas, and the southwestern States generally, and ranges into northern Mexico. It appears to feed exclusively upon purslane, and as this plant is of no particular economic value, but is justly accounted as a troublesome weed, we may wish blessings upon *Copidryas gloveri*.

(2) C o p i d r y a s cosyra Druce, Plate XI, Fig. 19, ♂. (The Cosyra Moth.)

This pretty insect, which belongs to the same genus as the preceding, though assigned

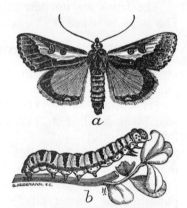

FIG. 80.—*Copidryas gloveri*. *a.* moth; *b.* larva. (After Riley.)

by the author of the species to the genus *Euthisanotia*, is found in Arizona and in Mexico. Its habits are undoubtedly very much the same as those of Glover's Purslane Moth, though up to the present time no one has described them.

Genus TUERTA Walker

Only one species of this genus, which is better represented in Africa than in America, is found within our borders.

(1) **Tuerta sabulosa** Boisduval. (The Sand-dune Moth.)

Syn. *noctuiformis* Mœschler.

The moth has the primaries grayish-brown marked with white at the insertion of the wings. The secondaries are bright orange-yellow, with a wide black marginal border, as represented in the cut. The habitat of the insect is Arizona and Mexico.

FIG. 81—*Tuerta sabulosa*, ♂ . ¼.

Genus ALYPIA Hübner

This genus is well represented within our territory. The following synopsis of the species is adapted from Hampson:

I. (*Androloma*.) Fore wing of male with a dilation of costa and
      a groove of ribbed membrane below it from base extending beyond middle. ....*mac-cullochi*
II. Fore wing of male with a postmedial dilation of costa and
      groove of ribbed membrane below it; wing elongated.
    a. Fore wing with the markings yellow . ...*disparata*
    b. Fore wing with the markings white..................*brannani*
III. (*Alypia*.) Fore wing of male without dilation of costal area
      or grove.
    A. Fore and mid tibiæ, orange; hind wings marked with
       white.
      a. Discal spot of fore wing longitudinal..........*octomaculata*
      b. Discal spot of fore wing transverse................*wittfeldi*
      Hind wings marked with yellow.
      c. Hind wing with subbasal yellow spot ....*dipsaci*
      d, Hind wing without subbasal yellow spot..........*langtoni*
    B. Mid tibiæ only orange.
      a. Wings with the spots not traversed by black veins . .*mariposa*
      b. Wings with the spots traversed by black veins ....*ridingsi*

(1) **Alypia mac-cullochi** Kirby, Plate XVII, Fig. 13, ♂ . (MacCulloch's Forester.)

Syn. *lorquini* Grote & Robinson; *similis* Stretch; *edwardsi* Boisduval.

The habitat of this species is Canada and the Rocky Mountains northward to Alaska.

(2) **Alypia disparata** Henry Edwards. (The Mexican Forester.)

Syn. *gracilenta* Græf; *desperata* Kirby.

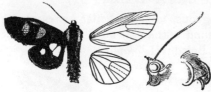

FIG. 82—*Alypia disparata*, ♂. ¼.
(After Hampson.)

The structural features of this species are shown in the accompanying cut, for the use of which we are indebted to the kindness of Sir George F. Hampson. The i n s e c t occurs in southern Texas, Arizona, and Mexico. The writer has a large series collected for him in the neighborhood of Jalapa, where it is apparently more common than farther north.

(3) **Alypia octomaculata** Fabricius, Plate XVII, Fig. 20, ♂, Fig. 21, ♀. (The Eight-spotted Forester.)

Syn. *bimaculata* Gmelin; *quadriguttalis* Hübner; *matuta* Henry Edwards.

This very common insect, which sometimes proves a veritable plague by the depredations which it commits upon the foliage of the *Ampelopsis*, which is extensively grown in our cities as a decorative vine, is found everywhere in the northern Atlantic States, and ranges westward beyond the Mississippi. One good thing which can be set down to the English sparrow is the work, which he has been observed by the writer to do in devouring the larvæ of this moth from the vines with which his home is covered.

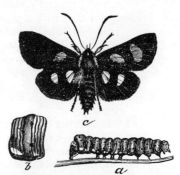

FIG. 83.—*Alypia octomaculata.*
a. larva; *b.* enlarged somite, showing markings; *c.* moth.
(After Riley.)

(4) **Alypia wittfeldi** Henry Edwards, Plate XVII, Fig. 18, ♂, Fig. 19, ♀. (Wittfeld's Forester.)

Sir George F. Hampson sinks this species as a synonym of *A. octomaculata*, but the writer cannot agree with him in this. The form of the spots on the primaries, the white at the base of the abdomen, and the white annulus near its extremity, are at all events marks quite as characteristic as those by which some other species in the genus are separated. Its habitat is southern Florida.

(5) **Alypia langtoni** Couper, Plate XVII, Fig. 16, ♂. Fig. 17, ♀. (Langton's Forester.)

Syn. *sacramenti* Grote & Robinson; *hudsonica* Henry Edwards.

This species ranges from Canada westward through British Columbia into California in the south and Alaska in the north.

(6) **Alypia mariposa** Grote & Robinson, Plate XVIII, Fig. 15. (The Californian Forester.)

This, undoubtedly the handsomest species of the genus, is confined to the Pacific coast.

(7) **Alypia ridingsi** Grote, Plate XVII, Fig. 13, ♂, Fig. 14, ♀. (Ridings' Forester.)

A common species in the Rocky Mountain region at high elevations, and ranging northward to Sitka and the valley of the Yukon.

Genus ALYPIODES Grote

Two species of this genus are Mexican, the third is found in our fauna, though also occurring south of our boundary.

(1) **Alypiodes bimaculata** Herrich-Schæffer, Plate XVII, Fig. 22. (The Two-spotted Forester.)

Syn. *trimaculata* Boisduval.

The figure in the plate represents the typical form, the figure in the cut shows the aberration named *crescens* by Walker, in

FIG. 84.—*Alypiodes bimaculata*, ♂.
(After Hampson.)

which the hind wing has a yellow spot about the middle of the wing. The insect is fairly common in southern California, New Mexico, and Arizona.

" The entomologist need not relax his endeavors day or night. Mothing is night employment."—A. S. PACKARD.

SUGARING FOR MOTHS

The day has been hot and sultry. The sun has set behind
great banks of clouds which are piling up on the northwestern
horizon. Now that the light is beginning to fade, the great
masses of cumulus, which are slowly gathering and rising higher
toward the zenith, are lit up by pale flashes of sheet-lightning.
As yet the storm is too far off to permit us to hear the boom of
the thunder, but about ten or eleven o'clock to-night we shall
probably experience all the splendor of a dashing thunder-
shower.

Along the fringe of woodland which skirts the back pastures
is a path which we long have known. Here stand long ranks
of ancient beeches; sugar maples, which in fall are glorious in
robes of yellow and scarlet; ash trees, the tall gray trunks of
which carry skyward huge masses of light pinnated foliage;
walnuts and butternuts, oaks, and tulip-poplars. On either side
of the path in luxuriant profusion are saplings, sprung from the
monarchs of the forest, young elm trees planted by the winds,
broad-leaved papaws, round-topped hawthorns, viburnums,
spreading dogwoods, and here and there in moist places clumps
of willows. Where the path runs down by the creek,
sycamores spread their gaunt white branches toward the sky,
and drink moisture from the shallow reaches of the stream, in
which duckweed, arrow-weed, and sweet pond-lilies bloom.

The woodland is the haunt of many a joyous thing, which
frequents the glades and hovers over the flowers. To-night the
lightning in the air, the suggestion of a coming storm which
lurks in the atmosphere, will send a thrill through all the swarms,
which have been hidden through the day on moss-grown trunks,
or among the leaves, and they will rise, as the dusk gathers, in
troops about the pathway. It is just the night upon which to
take a collecting trip, resorting to the well-known method of
"sugaring."

Here we have a bucket and a clean whitewash brush. We

have put into the bucket four pounds of cheap sugar. Now we will pour in a bottle of stale beer and a little rum. We have stirred the mixture well. In our pockets are our cyanide jars. Here are the dark lanterns. Before the darkness falls, while yet there is light enough to see our way along the path, we will pass from tree to tree and apply the brush charged with the sweet semi-intoxicating mixture to the trunks of the trees.

The task is accomplished! Forty trees and ten stumps have been baptized with sugar-sweetened beer. Let us wash our sticky fingers in the brook and dry them with our handkerchiefs. Let us sit down on the grass beneath this tree and puff a good Havana. It is growing darker. The bats are circling overhead. A screech-owl is uttering a plaintive lament, perhaps mourning the absence of the moon, which to-night will not appear. The frogs are croaking in the pond. The fireflies soar upward and flash in sparkling multitudes where the grass grows rank near the water.

Now let us light our lamps and put a drop or two of chloroform into our cyanide jars, just enough to slightly dampen the paper which holds the lumps of cyanide in place. We will retrace our steps along the path and visit each moistened spot upon the tree-trunks.

Here is the last tree which we sugared. There in the light of the lantern we see the shining drops of our mixture clinging to the mosses and slowly trickling downward toward the ground. Turn the light of the lantern full upon the spot, advancing cautiously, so as not to break the dry twigs under foot or rustle the leaves. Ha! Thus far nothing but the black ants which tenant the hollows of the gnarled old tree appear to have recognized the offering which we have made. But they are regaling themselves in swarms about the spot. Look at them! Scores of them, hundreds of them are congregating about the place, and seem to be drinking with as much enjoyment as a company of Germans on a picnic in the wilds of Hoboken.

Let us stealthily approach the next tree. It is a beech. What is there? Oho! my beauty! Just above the moistened patch upon the bark is a great *Catocala*. The gray upper wings are spread, revealing the lower wings gloriously banded with black and crimson. In the yellow light of the lantern the wings appear even more brilliant than they do in sunlight. How the eyes glow like spots of fire! The moth is wary. He has just alighted; he has not yet drunk deep. Move cautiously! Keep the light of the lantern steadily upon him. Uncover your poisoning jar. Approach. Hold the jar just a little under the moth, for he will drop downward on the first rush to get away. Clap the jar over him! There! you have done it! You have him securely. He flutters for a moment, but the chloroform acts quickly and the flutterings cease. Put that jar into one pocket and take out another. Now let us go to the next tree. It is an old walnut. The trunk is rough, seamed, and full of knotted excrescences. See what a company has gathered! There are a dozen moths, large and small, busily at work tippling. Begin with those which are nearest to the ground. When I was young my grandfather taught me that in shooting wild turkeys resting in a tree, it is always best to shoot the lowest fowl first, and then the next. If you shoot the gobbler which perches highest, as he comes tumbling down through the flock, he will startle them all, and they will fly away together; but if you take those which are roosting well down among the branches, those above will simply raise their heads and stare about for a moment to find out the source of their peril, and you can bag three or four before the rest make up their minds to fly. I follow the same plan with my moths, unless, perchance, the topmost moth is some unusual rarity, worth all that suck the sweets below him.

Bravo! You have learned the lesson well. You succeeded admirably in bottling those *Taraches* which were sucking the moisture at the lower edge of the sweetened patch. There above them is a fine specimen of *Strenoloma lunilinea*. Aha! You have him. Now take that *Catocala*. It is *amasia*, a charming little species. Above him is a specimen of *cara*, one of the largest and most superb of the genus. Well done! You have him, too. Now wait a moment! Have your captives ceased their struggles in your jar? Yes; they seem to be thoroughly stunned. Transfer them to the other jar for the cyanide to do its work. Look at your lantern. Is the wick trimmed? Come on then.

Let us go to the next tree. This is an ash. The moist spot

shows faintly upon the silvery-gray bark of the tree. Look sharply! Here below are a few *Geometers* daintily sipping the sweets. There is a little *Eustixis pupula*, with its silvery-white wings dotted with points of black. There is a specimen of *Harrisimemna*, the one with the coppery-brown spots on the fore wings. A good catch!

Stop! Hold still! Ha! I thought he would alight. That is *Catocala coccinata*—a fine moth—not overly common, and the specimen is perfect.

Well, let us try another tree. Here they are holding a general assembly. Look! See them fairly swarming about the spot. A dozen have found good places; two or three are fluttering about trying to alight. The ants have found the place as well as the moths. They are squabbling with each other. The moths do not like the ants. I do not blame them. I would not care to sit down at a banquet and have ants crawling all over the repast. There is a specimen of *Catocala relicta*, the hind wings white, banded with black. How beautiful simple colors are when set in sharp contrast and arranged in graceful lines! There is a specimen of *Catocala neogama*, which was originally described by Abbot from Georgia. It is not uncommon. There is a good *Mamestra*, and there *Pyrophila pyramidoides*. The latter is a common species; we shall find scores of them before we get through. Do not bother with those specimens of *Agrotis Ypsilon*; there are choicer things to be had. It is a waste of time to take them to-night. Let them drink themselves drunk, when the flying squirrels will come and catch them. Do you see that flying squirrel there peeping around the trunk of the tree? Flying squirrels eat insects. I have seen them do it at night, and they have robbed me of many a fine specimen.

Off now to the next tree!

And so we go from tree to tree. The lightning in the west grows more vivid. Hark! I hear the thunder. It is half-past nine. The storm will be here by ten. The leaves are beginning to rustle in the tree-tops. The first pulse of the tornado is beginning to be felt. Now the wind is rising. Boom! Boom! The storm is drawing nearer. We are on our second round and are coming up the path near the pasture-gate. Our collecting jars are full. We have taken more than a hundred specimens representing thirty species. Not a bad night's work. Hurry up! Here are the draw-bars. Are you through? Put out the light in your lantern. Come quickly after me. I know the path. Here is the back garden gate. It is beginning to rain. We shall have to run if we wish to avoid a wetting. Ah! here are the steps of the veranda. Come up!

My! what a flash and a crash that was! Look back and see how the big trees are bowing their heads as the wind reaches them, and the lightning silhouettes them against the gray veil of the rain. We may be glad we are out of the storm, with a good roof overhead. To-morrow morning the sun will rise bright and clear, and we shall have work enough to fill all the morning hours in setting the captures we have made. Good-night!

"It is interesting to contemplate a tangled bank, clothed with many plants of many kinds, with birds singing on the bushes, with various insects flitting about, and with worms crawling through the damp earth, and to reflect that these elaborately constructed forms, so different from each other, and dependent upon each other in so complex a manner, have all been produced by laws acting around us. These laws, taken in the largest sense, being Growth with Reproduction; Inheritance, which is almost implied by reproduction; Variability, from the indirect and direct action of the conditions of life, and from use and disuse; a Ratio of Increase so high as to lead to a Struggle for Life, and as a consequence to Natural Selection, entailing Divergence of Character and the Extinction of less improved forms. Thus, from the war of Nature, from famine and death, the most exalted object which we are capable of conceiving, namely, the production of the higher animals, directly follows. There is a grandeur in this view of life, with its several powers, having been originally breathed by the Creator into a few forms or into one, and that, whilst this planet has gone cycling on according to the fixed law of gravity, from so simple a beginning endless forms most beautiful and most wonderful have been and are being evolved."—Darwin.

FAMILY NOCTUIDÆ

"Shall mortal man be more just than God?
Shall a man be more pure than his Maker?
Behold He put no trust in His servants;
And His angels He charged with folly:
How much less in them that dwell in houses of clay,
Whose foundation is in the dust,
Which are crushed before the moth?"

JOB, *Chapter IV*, *17-19*.

The *Noctuidæ* are a huge complex of genera and species, the genera being reckoned by hundreds, and the species by thousands. Within the faunal limits intended to be covered by this book there are already known to occur in the neighborhood of three hundred and seventy-five genera, and many more than two thousand species which are referable to this family. In the arrangement of the genera and the species the author has in the main followed Dyar's Catalogue, which is based upon that of Prof. J. B. Smith, published in 1893 as "Bulletin 44 of the United States National Museum."

The moths are nocturnal in their habits. The neuration is very constant, and is described as follows by Hampson ("Moths of India," Vol. II, p. 160):

"Fore wing with vein 1*a* slight and not anastomosing with 1*b*; 1*c* absent; 2 from middle of cell; 3, 4, 5 from close to lower angle; 6 from upper angle; 8 given off from 7 and anastomosing with 9, which is given off from 10 to form an areole; 11 from cell; 12 long. Hind wing with 1*a* and *b* present; 1*c* absent; 2 from middle of cell; 3 and 4 from lower angle; 5 from near lower angle or middle of discocellulars, rarely absent, but more or less aborted in the *Acontiinæ* and *Trifinæ*. Frenulum always, proboscis almost always, present."

The larvæ are generally naked, or at most pubescent. In some of the subfamilies the larvæ are semiloopers, some of the prolegs being absent. Pupation generally takes place under

151

ground without a cocoon, the earth being fashioned in some cases into a cemented cell about the pupa.

Genus PANTHEA Hübner

(1) **Panthea furcilla** Packard, Plate XVII, Fig. 31, ♂. (The Eastern Panthea.)

Closely allied to the following species, from which it may be distinguished by the absence of the reniform spot at the end of the cell.

(2) **Panthea portlandia** Grote, Plate XVII, Fig. 30, ♂. (The Western Panthea.)

Transverse markings less diffuse than in the preceding species, and reniform spot always present.

P. furcilla occurs on the northern Atlantic, and *P. portlandia* on the northern Pacific coast.

(For the other two species consult Proceedings U. S. Nat. Museum, Vol. XXI, p. 13.)

Genus DEMAS Stephens

(1) **Demas propinquilinea** Grote, Plate XIX, Fig. 3, ♀. (The Close-banded Demas.)

The caterpillar feeds on various deciduous trees, making a case for itself by drawing two leaves together with strands of silk. It occurs in the Atlantic States.

(For the other two species of genus see Proceedings U. S. Nat. Museum, Vol. XXI, p. 22.)

Genus CHARADRA Walker

(1) **Charadra deridens** Guenée, Plate XVIII, Fig. 4, ♀. (The Laugher.)

Syn. *circulifer* Walker; *contigua* Walker.

A rather rare moth, the habitat of which is the Atlantic States, and the larva of which makes a case for itself, very much as done by the preceding species.

(2) **Charadra illudens** Walker, Plate XVIII, Fig. 5, ♂, Fig. 2, ♀. (The Sport.)

Syn. *pythion* Druce.

A Mexican species, which I admit to the fauna of our territory on the authority of George Franck of Brooklyn, who reports its occurrence in Florida.

(*3*) **Charadra decora** Morrison, Plate XVII, Fig. 29, ♂.
(The Dandy.)

Syn. *felina* Druce.

This is likewise a Mexican species, which is said to occur in Arizona, but the fact of its being found there requires verification.

One other species of the genus, *C. dispulsa* Morrison, occurs in the Southern States.

Genus RAPHIA Hübner

(1) **Raphia frater** Grote, Plate XVIII, Fig. 3, ♀. (The Brother.)

Syn. *personata* Walker; *flexuosa* Walker.

There are three species belonging to this genus in our fauna. They are closely alike in appearance. The species we figure occurs in the Eastern States. *R. abrupta* Grote is also an eastern species, while *R. coloradensis* is found in the West.

Genus APATELA Hübner

This is a large genus, well represented in the temperate regions of both the Old World and the New. The latest Catalogue of the Lepidoptera of the United States credits our fauna with seventy-five species. The genus has been monographed by Smith & Dyar. (See Proceedings U. S. Nat. Museum, Vol. XXI, pp. 1–104.) Within the compass of these pages we cannot do more than give a representation of a number of the forms, which have been described, leaving the student to further researches in the readily accessible literature of the subject.

(1) **Apatela americana** Harris, Plate XVIII, Fig. 12, ♀.
(The American Dagger-moth.)

Syn. *acericola* Guenée; *obscura* Henry Edwards; *aceris* Abbot & Smith (*non* Linnæus).

This is one of the largest species of the genus.

The caterpillar feeds upon deciduous trees of many genera, and the insect occurs from New England to Utah and south to the Gulf States.

(2) **Apatela dactylina** Grote, Plate XVIII, Fig. 17, ♂.
(The Fingered Dagger-moth).

Easily distinguished from the preceding species, which it

resembles in the markings of the fore wings, by its smaller size and the white hind wings. It ranges from Canada to Virginia and westward to the Rocky Mountains. The caterpillar lives upon alder, willow, and birch.

(*3*) **Apatela populi** Riley, Plate XVIII, Fig. 14, ♂ (The Cottonwood Dagger-moth.)

The moth, of which we reproduce the figures of the larva and imago given by Professor Riley, who first described the species,

FIG. 85.—*Apatela populi,* ♀.
(After Riley.)

ranges from Canada to the western parts of the Carolinas, thence across the continent to the Pacific coast, avoiding the warmer regions of the Gulf States and southern California. The imago is discriminated from *Apatela lepusculina* Guenée by the broader wings, especially of the female, by the paler ground-color of the primaries, and by the absence of the orbicular spot, which is very rarely as conspicuous as it appears in the figure given by Riley, and still further by the very short basal dash on the fore wings, which in *A. lepusculina* is long, reaching outwardly as a sharply defined black line one-third of the length of the cell. The larva is also quite different in important particulars from that of the species, which has been named, but with which this species is often confounded in

FIG. 86.—*Apatela populi,* larva.
(After Riley.)

collections. The caterpillar feeds upon the foliage of different species of the genus *Populus*, and is particularly common in the

States of the Mississippi Basin upon the Cottonwood (*Populus monilifera* and *Populus heterophylla*.)

(4) **Apatela innotata** Guenée, Plate XVIII, Fig. 13, ♂. (The Unmarked Dagger-moth.)

Syn. *græfi* Grote.

The figure given in the plate represents a form intermediate between those depicted by Smith & Dyar. (See Proceedings U. S. Nat. Museum, Vol. XXI, Plate II, Figs. 17, 18). The ground color is a dirty yellowish-white. The species occurs in Canada and the northern Atlantic States.

(5) **Apatela morula** Grote, Plate XVIII, Fig. 8, ♂. (The Darkish Dagger-moth.)

Syn *ulmi* Harris.

This insect occurs from Canada southward and westward to the Rocky Mountains. The caterpillar feeds upon elm, apple, and linden.

(6) **Apatela interrupta** Guenée, Plate XIX, Fig. 5, ♀. (The Interrupted Dagger-moth.)

Syn. *occidentalis* Grote & Robinson.

The larva feeds upon the *Rosaceæ*, and also upon the elm and the birch. The insect has a wide range from the Atlantic seaboard to the Rocky Mountains and from Canada to the northern portions of the Gulf States.

(7) **Apatela lobeliæ** Guenée, Plate XVIII, Fig. 9, ♂. (The Lobelia Dagger-moth.)

The caterpillar feeds upon oak, in spite of the fact that the author of the species attributed it to the *Lobelia*, which would no doubt poison it if administered. It ranges from Canada to Florida and Texas, and westward to the Rocky Mountains.

(8) **Apatela furcifera** Guenée, Plate XVIII, Fig. 10, ♂. (The Forked Dagger-moth.)

The range of this species is practically the same as that of the preceding. The larva feeds upon various species of wild-cherry.

(9) **Apatela hasta** Guenée, Plate XIX, Fig. 6, ♀. (The Dart Dagger-moth.)

Syn. *telum* Guenée.

The insect is found in the northern Atlantic States and Canada. It is smaller and darker than the preceding species, to which it is closely allied. The figure in the plate is hardly dark enough.

(10) **Apatela quadrata** Grote, Plate XVIII, Fig. 15, ♀. (The Quadrate Dagger.)

This species occurs on the Pacific coast and ranges eastward as far as Alberta in the north and Kansas in the south. The author does not recall a description of the larva.

(11) **Apatela superans** Guenée, Plate XVIII, Fig. 26, ♀. (The Chieftain Dagger.)

This is a well-marked species, which cannot easily be mistaken. It occurs in Canada, southward to the Carolinas, and westward through the valley of the Mississippi. The larva feeds on the same plants as its allies, which have been mentioned above.

(12) **Apatela lithospila** Grote, Plate XVIII, Fig. 24, ♂. (The Streaked Dagger.)

Ranges from the Atlantic to the Pacific. The larva feeds upon oak, hickory, and chestnut.

(13) **Apatela connecta** Grote, Plate XVIII, Fig. 19, ♂. (The Connected Dagger.)

The habitat of this species is found from Canada to the Carolinas and westward to the Mississippi. The larva feeds on willows.

(14) **Apatela fragilis** Guenée, Plate XIX, Fig. 1, ♂. (The Fragile Dagger-moth.)
Syn. *spectans* Walker.

This delicate little species has by some authors been referred to the genus *Microcœlia*, but is a true *Apatela*. It ranges from Canada to the Carolinas and westward to the Mississippi. The caterpillar feeds on birch and various plants belonging to the *Rosaceæ*.

(15) **Apatela vinnula** Grote, Plate XVIII, Fig. 25, ♀. (The Delightful Dagger.)

This pretty and easily recognizable species feeds in the larval stage upon the elm and ranges from the Atlantic coast to the border of the Great Plains. It comes very freely to sugar.

(16) **Apatela grisea** Walker, Plate XVIII, Fig. 11, ♀. (The Gray Dagger-moth.)
Syn. *pudorata* Morrison.

The caterpillar feeds on apple, birch, willow, elm, and arrow wood (*Euonymus*). The insect is found from Canada to Georgia and westward to Missouri and Minnesota.

(17) **Apatela albarufa** Grote, Plate XVIII, Fig. 16, ♂. (The Reddish-white Dagger.)

A somewhat variable species characterized by a very faint reddish cast upon the primaries. It ranges from the Atlantic to New Mexico and Colorado.

(18) **Apatela brumosa** Guenée, Plate XVIII, Fig. 23, ♂. (The Frosty Dagger-moth.)

Syn. *inclara* Smith.

Very closely allied to *A. impressa* Walker, but easily distinguished from that species by the lighter hind wings. The larva feeds upon willow, birch, and alder.

(19) **Apatela noctivaga** Grote, Plate XVIII, Fig. 20, ♀. (The Burglar Dagger.)

The larva feeds upon poplar and various herbaceous plants. The insect is found over almost the entire United States and southern Canada.

(20) **Apatela impressa** Walker, Plate XVIII, Fig. 21, ♂. (The Printed Dagger.)

The larva feeds upon willow, plum, hazel, currant, and blackberry. It is found from the Atlantic coast to the Rocky Mountains.

(21) **Apatela impleta** Walker, Plate XVIII, Fig. 22, ♀. (The Yellow-haired Dagger.)

Syn. *luteicoma* Grote.

The range of this species is from Canada to Florida and westward far into the valley of the Mississippi. The larva feeds on a great variety of deciduous trees and shrubs.

(22) **Apatela oblinita** Abbot & Smith, Plate XVIII, Fig. 18, ♀. (The Smeared Dagger.)

Syn. *salicis* Harris.

This is probably the commonest species of the genus. It occurs from eastern Canada to Florida and westward to the Rocky Mountains. The larva feeds on a great variety of shrubs and herbaceous plants. It never is found upon trees. It is very fond of the various species of smart-weed (*Polygonum*), and in the fall of the year it is very abundant in places where this plant grows. It does some damage to cotton-plants in the South, but by hand-

picking it can easily be kept under. The cocoon, which is composed of yellowish silk, is long and oval. There are two broods in the Middle States. The hibernating insects emerge from their cocoons in May, and lay their eggs. The caterpillars develop and the second brood of moths appears upon the wing in July. They oviposit and the caterpillars of this gene-

FIG. 87.—*Apatela oblinata*. *a*. Larva; *b*. Cocoon; *c*. Moth. (After Riley.)

ration, having made their cocoons, pass the winter in the pupal state.

Genus APHARETRA Grote

This is a small genus, the species of which have been separated from *Apatela*, in which they have been formerly placed. We give figures of both species known to occur within our territory. They have been drawn from the types, and will suffice for the identification of the perfect insects. Nothing is as yet known as to their larval stages.

(1) **Apharetra dentata** Grote. (The Toothed Apharetra.) This insect occurs in Canada and the northern portions of

FIG. 88.—*Apharetra dentata*, ♂. ⅟₁.

New York and New England. It is, however, for some reason as yet very rare in collections. The annexed cut has been drawn for me by Mr. Horace Knight from the type which is contained in the British Museum.

(2) **Apharetra pyralis** Smith. (Smith's Apharetra.)

The specimen represented in Fig. 89 is the type contained in the United States National Museum, a drawing of which I was kindly permitted to make. The species is considerably darker than the preceding.

FIG. 89.—*Apharetra pyralis*, ♂. ⅓.

It is thus far only known from the Territory of Alberta in British America.

Genus ARSILONCHE Lederer

Two species belonging to this genus are represented in our fauna. *Arsilonche colorada* was described by Smith in the Proceedings of the United States National Museum, Vol. XXII, p. 414, in 1900. The other species, which is well known, we figure.

(1) **Arsilonche albovenosa** Gœze, Plate XVIII, Fig. 6, ♂. (The White-veined Dagger.)

The abdomen in our figure is dark, the specimen being greased. It should be light, like the thorax. The insect occurs quite commonly in Canada and the northern portions of the United States, and also in Europe and northern Asia.

Genus MEROLONCHE Grote

For a full account of the three species contained in this genus the student is referred to the Proceedings of the United States National Museum, Vol. XXI, p. 179.

(1) **Merolonche lupini** Grote, Plate XVIII, Fig. 7, ♂. (The Lupine Dagger.)

Like all the species of this genus the Lupine Dagger is an inhabitant of the Pacific States. Good specimens are rare in collections.

Genus HARRISIMEMNA Grote

Only one species of this genus is thus far known.

(1) **Harrisimemna trisignata** Walker, Plate XIX, Fig. 4, ♀. (Harris's Three-spot.)

The moth ranges from Canada to Texas, and from the Atlantic to the Great Plains. The larva feeds on the winterberry and the lilac.

Genus MICROCŒLIA Guenée

This genus is like the preceding represented in our territory by but one species.

(1) **Microcœlia diphtheroides** Guenée, Plate XIX, Fig. 9, ♂ ; form **obliterata** Grote, Plate XIX, Fig. 10, ♂. (The Marbled Microcœlia.)

The form *obliterata* in which the marblings are wanting is common. The species is found in the Atlantic Subregion of the United States.

Genus JASPIDIA Hübner

This is a moderately large genus embracing five species, which occur in our fauna. We figure two of them.

(1) **Jaspidia lepidula** Grote, Plate XIX, Fig. 7, ♂. (The Marbled-green Jaspidia.)

This is a common species in the Atlantic Subregion, ranging from Canada to the Carolinas and westward to the Mississippi.

(2) **Jaspidia teratophora** Herrich-Schæffer, Plate XIX, Fig. 8, ♂. (The White-spotted Jaspidia.)

The distribution of this species is practically the same as that of the preceding.

Genus DIPHTHERA Hübner

There is but one species of this genus in our fauna.

(1) **Diphthera fallax** Herrich-Schæffer, Plate XVIII, Fig. 1, ♂. (The Green Marvel.)

This beautiful little moth is not uncommon in the Appalachian, or Atlantic, Subregion of the Continent.

Genus POLYGRAMMATE Hübner

This genus like the preceding is represented in our territory by but a single species.

(1) **Polygrammate hebraicum** Hübner, Plate XIX, Fig. 11, ♂. (The Hebrew.)

Syn. *hebræa* Guenée.

The caterpillar feeds upon the sour gum-tree (*Nyssa sylvatica*). The larval stages have been described by Dyar. (See Proceedings U. S. Nat. Museum, Vol. XXI, p. 9.) The insect is not uncommon in Pennsylvania and has much the same range as the preceding three or four species.

Genus CERMA Hübner

Three species of this genus are credited to our fauna. The one of which we give a cut has been by some authors confounded with *Polygrammate hebraicum.*

(1) **Cerma cora** Hübner. (The Cora Moth.)
Syn. *festa* Guenée.

The ground-color of this pretty little moth is white shading into vinaceous gray, upon which the darker markings stand forth conspicuously. It is quite rare, and so far as is known is confined to the Atlantic Subregion of the continent. The figure was drawn by the author from a specimen in the possession of the Brooklyn Institute, belonging to the Neumœgen Collection.

Fig. 90.—*Cerma cora*, ♂.

Genus CYATHISSA Grote

(1) **Cyathissa percara** Morrison, Plate XIX, Fig. 12, ♂. (The Darling Cyathissa.)

This pretty little species is found in the Gulf States and has been reported as ranging northward as far as Colorado. A second species of the genus has during the past year been described by Prof. J. B. Smith, from southern California, under the name *pallida.*

Genus CHYTONIX Grote

(1) **Chytonix palliatricula** Guenée, Plate XIX, Fig. 13, ♂; Fig. 14, ♂, var. (The Cloaked Marvel.)
Syn. *iaspis* Guenée.

A common species in the Northern Atlantic States. It may be found in June and July in Pennsylvania seated upon the bark of oak-trees in the forest. It comes freely to sugar and to light.

Genus COPIBRYOPHILA Smith

Of the sole species, named **angelica**, belonging to this genus, which was erected by Prof. J. B. Smith in the year 1900 (see "Proceedings U. S. Nat. Mus.," Vol. XXII, p. 416), we give a cut made from a drawing of the type, which is contained in the National Museum at Washington.

FIG. 91.—*Copibryophila angelica*, ♂ . ⅓.

Genus ALEPTINA Dyar

This genus has been erected by Dyar to accommodate the species named **inca** by him in the "Canadian Entomologist," Vol. XXXIV, p. 104. The male is figured on Plate XVII, Fig. 28. The insect is found in Arizona and Texas.

Genus BAILEYA Grote

A small genus, the species in which have been commonly referred hitherto to the genus *Leptina,* but erroneously.

(1) **Baileya ophthalmica** Guenée, Plate XVII, Fig. 25, ♀ .

Not an uncommon species in the Appalachian Subregion. It comes freely to sugar, and is rather abundant in the forests of southern Indiana.

(2) **Baileya australis** Grote, Plate XVII, Fig. 27, ♂ .

This is smaller than the preceding species, and generally lighter in color, with a very pronounced blackish apical shade on the fore wings. It occurs in the Gulf States from Florida to Texas.

(3) **Baileya doubledayi** Guenée, Plate XVII, Fig. 26, ♂ .

Of the same size as *ophthalmica,* but differently marked. From *australis* it may readily be distinguished by its larger size, and by the different marking of the apex of the fore wings.

Genus HADENELLA Grote

(1) **Hadenella pergentilis** Grote, Plate XIX, Fig. 24, ♀ .

This inconspicuous, but neatly marked little insect, belongs to the region of the Pacific coast, and ranges eastward as far as Colorado.

(2) **Hadenella subjuncta** Smith, Plate XIX, Fig. 25, ♂ .

The identification of this insect with *minuscula* Morrison, made by Dr. Dyar, is open to question. The range of this species is from the Atlantic to the mountains of Colorado, north of the Gulf States.

Genus ACOPA Harvey

(1) **Acopa carina** Harvey, Plate XIX, Fig. 16, ♂.
The habitat of this species is Texas. Three other species belonging to the region of the Southwestern States have been referred to this genus.

Genus CATABENA Walker

(1) **Catabena lineolata** Walker, Plate XIX, Fig. 15, ♂.
Syn. *miscellus* Grote.
This is a common little moth which ranges from the Atlantic States to California. It is freely attracted to light. The larva feeds on *Verbena*.

Genus CRAMBODES Guenee

(1) **Crambodes talidiformis** Guenée, Plate XIX, Fig. 17, ♂.
Syn. *conjugens* Walker.
A common species in the Appalachian Subregion, ranging westward as far as Colorado. Like the preceding species the larval form feeds on *Verbena*.

Genus PLATYSENTA Grote

(1) **Platysenta videns** Guenée, Plate XIX, Fig. 21, ♀.
Syn. *indigens* Walker; *meskei* Speyer; *atriciliata* Grote.
This species has the same range as the preceding. It is common at sugar.
(2) **Platysenta albipuncta** Smith, Plate XIX, Fig. 23, ♂.
This moth was originally described from Colorado, but it occurs all through the Southwestern States. The specimen figured came from Texas.

Genus BALSA Walker

(1) **Balsa malana** Fitch, Plate XIX, Fig. 18, ♂.
Syn. *obliquifera* Walker.

163

This is a very common species in the Atlantic States and is freely attracted to light.

Genus PLATYPERIGEA Smith

This genus has been erected by Prof. J. B. Smith for the reception of three species, two of which we figure in the annexed cuts, which have been made for me from the types through the courtesy of Dr. H. G. Dyar, of Washington. All of the species have been recorded from Colorado. They also occur in Wyoming, and I have specimens collected for me in the Freeze-out Mountains in that State. They probably have an extensive range in the Rocky Mountains.

FIG. 92.—*Platyperigea præacuta*, ♀ . ⅓.

FIG. 93.—*Platypirigea discistriga*, ♂ . ⅓.

Genus ANORTHODES Smith

* (1) **Anorthodes prima** Smith, Plate XIX, Fig. 19, ♂ .

This inconspicuous insect is quite common in central Ohio, and its range extends thence southward into the Southern States. It occurs in Kentucky, Tennessee, the Carolinas, and Georgia.

Genus CARADRINA Ochsenheimer

This is a genus of moderate extent, represented both in the Old World and the New. We have chosen a few species, familiarity with which will enable the student to recognize others.

(1) **Caradrina meralis** Morrison, Plate XIX, Fig. 22, ♂ . (The Mooned Rustic.)

Syn. *bilunata* Grote.

The moth is distributed from the Atlantic seaboard to the interior of New Mexico. It is common in Texas.

(2) **Caradrina multifera** Walker, Plate XIX, Fig. 29, ♀ . (The Speckled Rustic.)

Syn. *fidicularia* Morrison.

The habitat of this species is the Atlantic Subregion.

*Should be *A. tarda Guenée* in text and plate.—A.E.B.

(3) **Caradrina spilomela** Walker, Plate XIX, Fig. 28, ♂. (The Convivial Rustic.)

Syn. *conviva* Harvey.

This is a neotropical species found all over the hotter parts of North and South America, and ranging northward into Arizona and Texas.

(4) **Caradrina extimia** Walker, Plate XIX, Fig. 26, ♂. (The Civil Rustic.)

Syn. *civica* Grote.

The moth occurs in Colorado and thence westward to the Pacific.

(5) **Caradrina punctivena** Smith, Plate XIX, Fig. 27, ♂. (The Brown-streaked Rustic.)

The identity of this insect with *C. rufostriga* Packard has been suggested as probable. Its habitat is Colorado, among the mountains, and Labrador. It no doubt occurs at intermediate points at suitable elevations. It is evidently a strictly boreal form.

Genus PERIGEA Guenee

This is a rather extensive genus, well represented in the warmer parts of the New World, and also occurring in the Eastern Hemisphere. Twenty-four species are credited to our fauna in the latest catalogue. We figure two of the commoner species, which have a wide range.

(1) **Perigea xanthioides** Guenée, Plate XIX, Fig. 30, ♂. (The Red Groundling.)

This is not a scarce species in the Appalachian Subregion. It is particularly abundant in southern Indiana and Kentucky, where I have obtained it in large numbers.

(2) **Perigea vecors** Guenée, Plate XIX, Fig. 31, ♀. (The Dusky Groundling.)

The distribution of this species is very much the same as that of the preceding.

Genus OLIGIA Hübner

Nine species belonging to this genus are credited to our territory, of which number three are selected for illustration.

(1) **Oligia festivoides** Guenée, Plate XIX, Fig. 32, ♂. (The Festive Midget.)

Syn. *varia* Walker.

This is not an uncommon species in the Atlantic States.

(2) **Oligia fuscimacula** Grote, Plate XIX, Fig. 34, ♂. (The Brown-spotted Midget.)

A common species in the Gulf States.

(3) **Oligia grata** Hübner, Plate XIX, Fig. *33*, ♂. (The Grateful Midget.)

Syn. *rasilis* Morrison.

This species is quite widely distributed through the Atlantic States.

Genus HILLIA Grote

There are three species in this genus. They are found in the more temperate regions of our territory, being confined to the Northern States or to high elevations among the mountains of the West.

(1) **Hillia algens** Grote, Plate XIX, Fig. *35*, ♂.

This obscurely colored moth is found in Maine, northern New York, southern Canada, and among the mountains of Colorado, Wyoming, and Montana.

Genus HADENA Schrank

This is a very large genus which is represented in both the Old World and New. More than one hundred species are credited to our fauna. Of these we have selected a number for purposes of illustration, knowing that familiarity with these will enable the young collector presently to recognize other species, which he will then be able to determine with the help of accessible literature.

(1) **Hadena bridghami** Grote & Robinson, Plate XX, Fig. 2, ♂. (Bridgham's Hadena.)

A bright little species, the reddish color of the medial area of the fore wings being quite distinctive. It is found in the Appalachian Subregion.

(2) **Hadena transfrons** Neumœgen, Plate XX, Fig. 7, ♀. (Neumœgen's Hadena.)

Closely allied to the preceding species, but with darker primaries, and dark hind wings. Habitat Alberta and British Columbia.

(3) **Hadena violacea** Grote, Plate XX, Fig. 12, ♀. (The Violet Hadena.)

This species, which ranges over the region of the Rocky Mountains from Colorado to California, may be distinguished from the preceding two species by its somewhat larger size, and by the fact that the secondaries are immaculately white.

(4) **Hadena claudens** Walker, Plate XX, Fig. 6, ♂. (The Dark-winged Hadena.)

Syn. *hilli* Grote.

This species is apparently confined to the northern portion of the Atlantic Subregion.

(5) **Hadena modica** Guenée, Plate XX, Fig. 14, ♂. (The Black-banded Hadena.)

Syn. *subcedens* Walker.

Ranges from the Atlantic coast to the mountains of Colorado.

(6) **Hadena characta** Grote, Plate XX, Fig. 3, ♂. (The Double-banded Hadena.)

The habitat of this species is in the southwestern portion of the Rocky Mountains. It is not uncommon in Arizona.

(7) **Hadena mactata** Guenée, Plate XX, Fig. 8, ♀. (The Dark-spotted Hadena.)

The distribution of this species is over the Appalachian Subregion and westward to the eastern ranges of the Rocky Mountains.

(8) **Hadena turbulenta** Hübner, Plate XX, Fig. 16, ♀. (The Turbulent Hadena.)

Syn. *arcuata* Walker.

This little species is not uncommon in the Atlantic Subregion.

(9) **Hadena versuta** Smith, Plate XX, Fig. 4, ♂. (The Albertan Hadena.)

So far as is now known this species is found in the Territory of Alberta, but it probably has a wide range on the eastern slopes of the northern ranges of the Rocky Mountains.

(10) **Hadena miseloides** Guenée, Plate XX, Fig. 15, ♀. (The White-spotted Hadena.)

This is not a scarce species in the Atlantic States. It may easily be recognized by its greenish fore wings, generally marked near the middle by a large white spot.

(11) **Hadena chlorostigma** Harvey, Plate XX, Fig. 13. ♂. (The Green-spotted Hadena.)

This species is variable in color, some specimens having green spots on the disk of the fore wings, others being, as represented in the plate, almost entirely brown. It is a common species in the central portions of the Mississippi Valley, ranging thence southward. The example figured was taken at Columbus, Ohio.

(12) **Hadena fractilinea** Grote, Plate XX, Fig. 10, ♂. (The Broken-lined Hadena.)

Not a scarce species in the Appalachian Subregion.

* (13) **Hadena basilinea** Fabricius, Plate XX, Fig. 9, ♂. (The Base-streaked Hadena.)

Syn. *cerivana* Smith.

This species, which is also found in Europe, occurs in Alberta, and the northwestern portions of British North America.

(14) **Hadena passer** Guenée, Plate XIX, Fig. 36, ♂. (The Passerine Hadena.)

Syn. *incallida* Walker; *loculata* Morrison; *viralis* Grote; *conspicua* Morrison.

Not a very common species, ranging from southern Canada and the northern Atlantic States westward in the same latitudes to the Pacific, and southward into the mountains of Colorado.

(15) **Hadena burgessi** Morrison, Plate XIX, Fig. 37, ♂. (Burgess's Hadena.)

Syn. *discors* Grote.

The habitat of this well-marked species is the Atlantic Subregion and the valley of the Mississippi as far west as the Great Plains.

(16) **Hadena vultuosa** Grote, Plate XX, Fig. 11, ♂. (The Airy Hadena.)

Not a very common species, confined to the Atlantic Subregion.

(17) **Hadena lateritia** Hübner, Plate XIX, Fig. 38, ♂. (The Red-winged Hadena.)

Syn. *molochina* Hübner; *obliviosa* Walker.

Found throughout temperate North America and Europe.

(18) **Hadena dubitans** Walker, Plate XIX, Fig. 39, ♀. (The Halting Hadena.)

Syn. *insignata* Walker; *sputatrix* Grote.

---

*American races (of this Old World species) are *finitima* Guenée and *cerivana* Smith. This common species is called The Rustic Shoulder Knot in the British Isles.—A.E.B.

Much darker than the preceding species, which it somewhat resembles. It is found in the northern portions of the Atlantic Subregion.

(19) **Hadena ducta** Grote, Plate XIX, Fig. 40, ♀. (The Speckled Gray Hadena.)

The range of this species is the same as that of the last mentioned.

(20) **Hadena devastatrix** Brace, Plate XIX, Fig. 44, ♂. (The Destroying Hadena.)

Syn. *ordinaria* Walker; *contenta* Walker; *marshallana* Westwood.

Universally distributed throughout the United States and southern Canada.

(21) **Hadena arctica** Boisduval, Plate XIX, Fig. 45, ♂. The Northern Hadena.)

Syn. *amputatrix* Fitch.

A large and handsome species, easily recognizable. It ranges from Canada and New England into the Carolinas and westward to Colorado.

(22) **Hadena occidens** Grote, Plate XX, Fig. 20, ♂. (The Great Western Hadena.)

The species is distributed from Colorado to California.

(23) **Hadena verbascoides** Guenée, Plate XIX, Fig. 43, ♀. (The Mullein Hadena.)

A peculiarly marked species, which cannot easily be mistaken for anything else. It occurs in the northern Atlantic States.

(24) **Hadena nigrior** Smith, Plate XIX, Fig. 42, ♀. (The Darker Hadena.)

Allied to the preceding species, but with the light color of the costal area confined to the basal portion of the wing. Found in New England and Canada.

(25) **Hadena lignicolor** Guenée, Plate XX, Fig. 5, ♂. (The Wood-colored Hadena.)

A well-marked species, in color recalling *H. vultuosa*, but larger. It ranges from the Atlantic to Colorado and Arizona.

(26) **Hadena semilunata** Grote, Plate XXII, Fig. 41, ♂. (The Half-moon Hadena.)

Not uncommon in Colorado and ranging thence westward to the Pacific.

(27) **Hadena vinela** Smith, MS., Plate XX, Fig. 19, ♂. (The Dark Ashen Hadena.)

This species has been long distributed in collections as *Fishea enthea*, which it is not. I apply to the figure the manuscript name, which has been given me by Prof. J. B. Smith. It is found in New England and southern Canada.

Genus CALOPHASIA Stephens

The only species of this genus credited to our fauna is **C. strigata** Smith, represented in Plate XX, Fig. 17, by a female specimen, loaned to me by the United States National Museum. It occurs in Colorado and Wyoming.

Genus EPIDEMAS Smith

This genus was erected by Professor J. B. Smith for the reception of the species figured in Plate XXIII, Fig. 2, from a female specimen in the National Collection, and named by him **cinerea**. It occurs in Colorado.

Genus MACRONOCTUA Grote

(1) **Macronoctua onusta** Grote, Plate XX, Fig. 18, ♀.

There is only one species of this genus, which occurs in the southern Atlantic States.

Genus FISHEA Grote

A small genus. There are only two species known.

(1) **Fishea yosemitæ** Grote, Plate XX, Fig. 1, ♂. (The Yosemite Fishea.)

This species, which is generally referred to the genus *Aporophila* Guenée, is placed here on the authority of Prof. J. B. Smith. In addition to the figure given in the plate

FIG. 94.—*Fishea yosemitæ*, ♀ · ⅓.

we have inserted a cut drawn from the type. By the help of these the student will no doubt be able to identify the species. The insect is found in California.

Genus POLIA Hübner

A moderately large genus, which includes about twenty species in our fauna. Of these we have selected two for illustration.

(1) **Polia theodori** Grote, Plate XX, Fig. 21, ♂. (Theodore's Polia.)

The home of this species is the southwestern portion of the region of the Rocky Mountains.

(2) **Polia diversilineata** Grote, Plate XX, Fig. 22, ♂. (The Varied-banded Polia.)

Syn. *illepida* Grote.

Like the preceding species this is an inhabitant of the Rocky Mountains.

Genus DRYOBOTA Lederer

(1) **Dryobota illocata** Walker, Plate XX, Fig. 24, ♀. (The Wandering Dryobota.)

Syn. *stigmata* Grote.

A native of the Atlantic Subregion wandering as far west as Colorado.

Genus HYPPA Duponchel

The genus is found in both hemispheres. Four species are credited to North America.

(1) **Hyppa xylinoides** Guenée, Plate XX, Fig. 23, ♀. (The Common Hyppa.)

Syn. *contraria* Walker; *ancocisconensis* Morrison.

A very common species in the Atlantic Subregion. It is freely attracted to light in the spring of the year.

Genus FERALIA Grote

A small genus containing four species in our territory. The insects are generally found in groves of pine.

(1) **Feralia jocosa** Guenée, Plate XVII, Fig. 32, ♂. (The Joker.)

Found in suitable localities throughout the northern Atlantic States.

Genus MOMOPHANA Grote

The only species of this genus known is a very rare insect so far as has been ascertained. The cut we give was drawn from a unique specimen in the Neumœgen Collection at the Brooklyn Institute. The type is at Cornell University. All the specimens which have been taken have occurred in New York and Canada.

FIG. 95.—*Momophana comstocki* Grote. ¼.

Genus VALERIA Germar

This genus occurs on both sides of the Atlantic. The only species in our fauna is **Valeria opina** Grote, the male of which is figured in Plate XX, Fig. 25. It is found in California.

Genus EUPLEXIA Stephens

But one species of this genus, which is also found in Europe, occurs in North America. English entomologists call the moth "The Small Angle Shades." The scientific name is **Euplexia lucipara** Linnæus, and it is depicted on Plate XX, Fig. 26. It occurs all over the United States and Canada.

Genus TRACHEA Hübner

This genus is also found in both hemispheres. Only one species is found in America, and is confined to the Atlantic Subregion. It is known as **Trachea delicata** Grote, and the male is shown on Plate XX, Fig. 27.

Genus DIPTERYGIA Stephens

The genus *Dipterygia* is represented in the New World by the species named **scabriuscula** by Linnæus, which also occurs in Europe. There are several Asiatic species. It is shown on Plate XX, Fig. 28. It ranges from the Atlantic westward to the Rocky Mountains.

Genus ACTINOTIA Hübner

This small genus is represented in the United States and Canada by the insect to which Guenée applied the specific name

ramosula, and which is delineated on Plate XX, Fig. 29. It is very common in Pennsylvania.

Genus PYROPHILA Hübner

This genus is better represented in Europe and Asia than in America.

(1) **Pyrophila glabella** Morrison, Plate XX, Fig. 32, ♂. (The Gray Pyrophila.)

Not nearly as common as the next species, but widely distributed throughout the United States and Canada.

(2) **Pyrophila pyramidoides** Guenée, Plate XX, Fig. 30, ♂. (The American Copper Underwing.)

This insect, which is one of the commonest moths in the Atlantic Subregion, and ranges westward as far as Colorado, conceals itself under the loose bark of trees during the daytime, and comes forth at night. It sometimes fairly swarms at sugar, and becomes a veritable pest to the collector, who desires rarer things. The caterpillar does a good deal of damage to vegetation. I have recently been annoyed by the ravages inflicted by

FIG. 96.—Larva of *Pyrophila pyramidoides.* (After Riley.)

the larvæ in the spring of the year upon the foliage of imported rhododendrons, for which they seem to have a partiality in my garden. They feed freely on a great variety of shrubs and herbaceous plants.

(3) **Pyrophila tragopoginis** Linnæus, Plate XX, Fig. 31, ♂. (The Mouse-colored Pyrophila.)

Syn. *repressus* Grote.

A circumpolar species ranging throughout the temperate zone.

Genus HELIOTROPHA Lederer

The genus is represented in the Atlantic States by a species, of which a light and a dark form occur. The typical, or light form, was named **reniformis** by Grote, and is depicted on Plate XX, Fig. 33, while the dark form, named **atra** by the same author, is shown on the same plate by Figure 34.

Genus PRODENIA Guenée

A small but widely distributed genus found in all parts of the globe. Illustrations of two of the three species found in our fauna are given.

(1) **Prodenia commelinæ** Abbot & Smith, Plate XX, Fig. 36, ♀.

This species, which occurs in the Atlantic Subregion, is common in the southern portion of its range.

(2) **Prodenia ornithogalli** Guenée, Plate XX, Fig. 35, ♂.

Not as common as the preceding species, but ranging over the entire United States.

Genus LAPHYGMA Guenée

A small but widely distributed genus, represented in our fauna by but one species.

(1) **Laphygma frugiperda** Abbot & Smith, Plate XX, Fig. 37, ♂. (The Fall Army Worm.)

Syn. *macra* Guenée; *signifera* Walker; *plagiata* Walker; *autumnalis* Riley.

This destructive insect, which is found all over the Atlantic States, the Mississippi Valley, and thence southward through

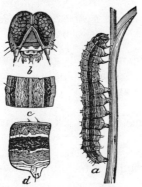 

FIG. 97.—*Laphygma frugiperda.*
a. full grown larva; *b.* head, magnified; *c* segment of body, viewed from above; *d.* viewed from side, enlarged. (After Riley.)

FIG. 98.—*Laphygma frugiperda.*
a. typical form of moth; *b. c.* varieties. (After Riley.)

—

Central and South America, feeds in its larval state upon a great variety of succulent plants, showing, however, a decided preference for the cereals. It does considerable damage to garden crops, and attacks cotton. It is said to inflict damage upon winter wheat, blue-grass, and timothy. The moth is variable in its markings. The typical form is represented on Plate XX, and by the upper figure in the annexed cut. It has frequently been mistaken by observers for the true Army Worm (*Leucania unipuncta*). Because its ravages are generally committed in the fall of the year it was named The Fall Army Worm by the late Prof. C. V. Riley. A very excellent account of the insect is given by this distinguished authority in the "Eighth Annual Report" of the State Entomologist of Missouri, p. 48, *et seq.*, which the student will do well to consult. It is from this article that the two accompanying figures have been taken.

Genus LUSSA Grote

(1) **Lussa nigroguttata** Grote, Plate XX, Fig. 38, ♂.
This little moth is found in Florida. Not much is as yet known in regard to its life-history.

Genus MAGUSA Walker

(1) **Magusa dissidens** Felder, Plate XXI, Fig. 2, ♂.
Syn. *divaricata* Grote; *angustipennis* Mœschler; *divida* Mœschler.
The sole species of the genus found within our territory, ranging from the southern Atlantic States into South America.

Genus PSEUDANARTA Henry Edwards

We figure three of the five species attributed to this genus and reported to occur within the limits of the United States.
(1) **Pseudanarta flava** Grote, Plate XX, Fig. 39, ♂. (The Yellow Pseudanarta.)
Syn. *crocea* Henry Edwards.
The range of this species is from Colorado and Arizona to the southern portions of British Columbia.
(2) **Pseudanarta singula** Grote, Plate XX, Fig. 40, ♂. (The Single Pseudanarta.)
The habitat of this species is the southwestern United States.
(3) **Pseudanarta falcata** Neumœgen, Plate XX, Fig. 41, ♂. (The Falcate Pseudanarta.)
The species occurs in Arizona and Mexico.

Genus HOMOHADENA Grote

A considerable genus, one species of which we represent.

(1) **Homohadena badistriga** Grote, Plate XXI, Fig. 1, ♂.

This is the only species of the genus, which occurs in the northern Atlantic States. Most of them are western and southern. The range of *badistriga* is from the Atlantic to Colorado.

Genus ONCOCNEMIS Lederer

An extensive genus, in which are included over forty species, most of which are found in the western and southwestern States. We have selected for representation seven of their number.

(1) **Oncocnemis dayi** Grote, Plate XXI, Fig. 4, ♂. (Day's Oncocnemis.)

Not an uncommon species in Colorado and Wyoming.

(2) **Oncocnemis tenuifascia** Smith, Plate XXI, Fig. 5, ♂. (The Narrow-banded Oncocnemis.)

The distribution of this species is the same as that of the last mentioned.

(3) **Oncocnemis occata** Grote, Plate XXI, Fig. 8, ♀. (The Harrow-moth.)

This species occurs in Texas, Colorado, and the States lying westward of these, as far as the Pacific.

(4) **Oncocnemis chandleri** Grote, Plate XXI, Fig. 7, ♀. (Chandler's Oncocnemis.)

Indigenous to the Rocky Mountains.

(5) **Oncocnemis atrifasciata** Morrison, Plate XXI, Fig. 3, ♀. (The Black-banded Oncocnemis.)

This fine species is found in the northern portions of the Atlantic Subregion. The specimen figured was taken in Maine.

(6) **Oncocnemis iricolor** Smith, Plate XXI, Fig. 6, ♀. (The Iris-colored Oncocnemis.)

So far this species has only been reported from Colorado and Wyoming.

(7) **Oncocnemis cibalis** Grote, Plate XXI, Fig. 9, ♂. (The Gray Oncocnemis.)

The only specimens so far found have been taken in Colorado.

Genus LEPIPOLYS Guenée

(1) **Lepipolys perscripta** Guenée, Plate XXI, Fig. 11, ♀.
Only one species occurs in our territory, ranging from the Atlantic to the Pacific.

Genus ADITA Grote

(1) **Adita chionanthi** Abbot & Smith, Plate XXI, Fig. 10.
A rather rare moth, which is found in the Atlantic Subregion, but is much commoner in Colorado and Wyoming. It is the only representative of its genus.

Genus COPIPANOLIS Grote

A small genus said to contain four species, which are not as distinctly separable as might be desired.
(1) **Copipanolis cubilis** Grote, Plate XXI, Fig. 12, ♀.
The habitat of this insect is the northern United States. It appears upon the wing in Pennsylvania early in April.

Genus EUTOLYPE Grote

(1) **Eutolype bombyciformis** Smith, Plate XXI, Fig. 13, ♀.
The genus represented by this species contains four others within our limits. They all occur in the Atlantic Subregion, except the species named *damalis* by Grote, which is Californian.

Genus PSAPHIDIA Walker

Of the four species of this genus occuring within our territory we give illustrations of two.
(1) **Psaphidia grotei** Morrison, Plate XXI, Fig. 14, ♀.
The home of this species is the northern Atlantic States. It occurs upon the wing very early in the spring of the year.
(2) **Psaphidia resumens** Walker, Plate XXI, Fig. 15, ♀.
Syn. *viridescens* Walker; *muralis* Grote.
The range of this insect is the same as that of the preceding species.

Genus CERAPODA Smith

Only one species of this genus is known. It was named **Cerapoda stylata** by Prof. J. B. Smith, and is shown on Plate XXIII, Fig. 1. Its habitat is Colorado.

Genus FOTA Grote

There are two species of this genus, both of which we figure. They both occur in Arizona and Mexico.

(1) **Fota armata** Grote, Plate XXI, Fig. 16, ♂.

(2) **Fota minorata** Grote, Plate XXI, Fig. 17, ♂.

We do not recall any description of the habits of these two species.

Genus PODAGRA Smith

 This genus has been quite recently erected by Smith for the reception of the species, a representation of the type of which, based upon the specimen in the United States National Museum, is given in Fig. 99.

FIG. 99.—*Podagra crassipes.*

Genus RHYNCHAGROTIS Smith

Over twenty species have been attributed to this genus. Of these we figure six.

(1) **Rhynchagrotis gilvipennis** Grote, Plate XXI, Fig. 18, ♀. (The Catocaline Dart-moth.)

This pretty species is found in the northern parts of the United States, in Canada, and British America. It is scarce in the eastern parts of its range south of Maine and the Adirondack Woods.

(2) **Rhynchagrotis rufipectus** Morrison, Plate XXI, Fig. 22, ♀. (The Red-breasted Dart-moth.)

The general distribution of this species is like the former, but it extends much farther southward.

(3) **Rhynchagrotis minimalis** Grote, Plate XXI, Fig. 21, ♀. (The Lesser Red Dart-moth.)

This species is found in Maine, southern Canada, and also in Colorado, Wyoming, and Montana.

(4) **Rhynchagrotis anchocelioides** Guenée, Plate XXI, Fig. 19, ♀.

Syn. *cupida* Grote; *velata* Walker.

A common species in the northern Atlantic Subregion, extending its habitat to the region of the Rocky Mountains.

(5) **Rhynchagrotis placida** Grote, Plate XXI, Fig. 23, ♂. (The Placid Dart-moth.)

A very common species in the northern United States, found as far westward as the Rocky Mountains.

(6) **Rhynchagrotis alternata** Grote, Plate XXI, Fig. 20, ♀. (The Greater Red Dart-moth.)

This species closely resembles in general appearance the species named *minimalis*, but may be distinguished by its larger size, and the darker color of the hind wings.

Genus ADELPHAGROTIS Smith

Of the five species belonging to the genus we select the commonest for illustration.

(1) **Adelphagrotis prasina** Fabricius, Plate XXI, Fig. 24, ♀. (The Green-winged Dart-moth.)

This insect occurs all over Canada, the northern Atlantic States, the Rocky Mountains, and British Columbia. It occurs also in Europe.

Genus PLATAGROTIS Smith

The species of this genus are confined to the more temperate regions of our territory.

(1) **Platagrotis pressa** Grote, Plate XXI, Fig. 25, ♂. (The Dappled Dart.)

Occurs in the northern portions of the Atlantic Subregion.

Genus EUERETAGROTIS Smith

Three species of the genus occur, all of them within the Atlantic Subregion.

(1) **Eueretagrotis sigmoides** Guenée, Plate XXI, Fig. 26, ♂. (The Sigmoid Dart.)

From the following species distinguished readily by its larger size, and the darker coloration of the fore wings.

(2) **Eueretagrotis perattenta** Grote, Plate XXI, Fig. 27, ♀. (The Two-spot Dart.)

A common species in the Atlantic States.

"Yon night moths that hover where honey brims over."
  JEAN INGELOW. *Songs of Seven.*

Genus ABAGROTIS Smith

Only one species is attributed to this genus. It is represented by the accompanying cut, drawn from the type in the United States National Museum. **Abagrotis erratica** is thus far only recorded from California. It is rare in collections. The color of the wings is ashen gray in some specimens; in others pale reddish.

Fig. 100.—
Abagrotis erratica.

Genus SEMIOPHORA Stephens

(1) **Semiophora elimata** Guenée, Plate XXI, Fig. 29, ♀. Form **janualis** Grote, Plate XXI, Fig. *30*, ♂. (The Variable Dart.)

Syn. *dilucidula* Morrison; *badicollis* Grote.

Not at all an uncommon species, ranging from Canada to Georgia.

(2) **Semiophora opacifrons** Grote, Plate XXI, Fig. 28, ♀. (The Black-fronted Dart.)

This species is found in the more northern portions of the Atlantic Subregion ranging into Quebec.

(3) **Semiophora tenebrifera** Walker, Plate XXI, Fig. *33*, ♂. (The Reddish Speckled Dart.)

Syn. *catharina* Grote; *manifestolabes* Morrison.

A well-marked species, the fore wings of which have a prevalently reddish cast. It ranges from New Jersey northward into Canada.

Genus PACHNOBIA Guenée

The species are mainly boreal, being found in the northern portions of our territory, principally in Canada, and on the higher mountain ranges.

(1) **Pachnobia littoralis** Packard, Plate XXI, Fig. *32*, ♂. (The Reddish Pachnobia.)

Syn. *pectinata* Grote; *ferruginoides* Smith.

The species occurs from the mountains of Colorado northward to Alberta.

(2) **Pachnobia salicarum** Walker, Plate XXI, Fig. *31*, ♂. (The Willow Pachnobia.)

Syn. *orilliana* Grote; *claviformis* Morrison.

This species, readily distinguished from all others by the well defined claviform spot, ranges from Massachusetts to Alberta and northward.

Genus METALEPSIS Grote

Two species of this genus are credited to our fauna. Of the type of one of these, preserved in the British Museum, I am able to give an excellent figure taken from Sir George F. Hampson's

FIG. 101.—*Metalepsis cornuta*, ♂ . ¼.

fine work upon the moths of the world, which is being published by the Trustees of the above named institution. The insect occurs in California.

Genus SETAGROTIS Smith

Eight species, all of them found in the northern parts of our territory or at considerable elevations among the mountains of the West, are attributed to this genus. I am able to give a figure of one of these, which Dr. Dyar kindly had drawn from the type in the United States National Museum. It occurs among the mountains of Colorado and Wyoming. The ground color of the wings is pale luteous.

FIG. 102.—*Setagrotis terrifica*, ♂ . ¼.

Genus AGROTIS Ochsenheimer

(1) **Agrotis badinodis** Grote, Plate XXI, Fig. 37, ♂ . (The Pale-banded Dart.)

Not an uncommon species in the northern Atlantic States and Canada.

(2) **Agrotis ypsilon** Rottemburg. (The Ypsilon Dart.)
Syn. *suffusa* Denis & Schiffermüller; *telifera* Harris; *idonea* Cramer.
This is an exceedingly common species, which occurs every-

where in Canada and the United States. It is also found in Europe. Its larva is one of the species, which under the name of "cut-worms," are known to inflict extensive injuries upon growing plants. They burrow into the loose soil during the day, and come forth at night and do their mischievous work. They are a

FIG. 103.—*Agrotis ypsilon.* (After Riley.)

plague to the market-gardener in particular.

(3) **Agrotis geniculata** Grote & Robinson, Plate XXI, Fig. 36, ♀. (The Knee-joint Dart.)
Not a scarce species in the northern Atlantic Subregion.

Genus PERIDROMA Hübner

This is a moderately large genus, represented in the United States and Canada by about a dozen species. Half of these we illustrate.

(1) **Peridroma occulta** Linnæus, Plate XXI, Fig. 42, ♀. (The Great Gray Dart.)
The habitat of this insect is the northern portion of our territory.

(2) **Peridroma astricta** Morrison, Plate XXI, Fig. 41, ♀. (The Great Brown Dart.)
The species is found in the northern parts of the Atlantic Subregion, and also in Colorado.

(3) **Peridroma nigra** Smith, Plate XXI, Fig. 43, ♀. (The Great Black Dart.)
Found in Colorado and Wyoming.

(4) **Peridroma saucia** Hübner, Plate XXI, Fig. 40, ♀; Egg, Text-figure No. 2. (The Common Cut-worm.)
Syn. *inermis* Harris; *ortonii* Packard.
Almost universally distributed throughout the United States and southern Canada. It also occurs in Europe.

(5) **Peridroma incivis** Guenée, Plate XXI, Fig. 39, ♂. (The Uncivil Dart.)

Syn. *alabamæ* Grote.

Ranges from the Atlantic to the Pacific.

(6) **Peridroma simplaria** Morrison, Plate XXI, Fig. 38, ♀. (The Pale-winged Dart.)

Not an uncommon species in Texas and Arizona.

Genus NOCTUA Linnæus

This is a very extensive genus, to which over forty species found in our territory are referred in recent lists.

(1) **Noctua normanniana** Grote, Plate XXI, Fig. 34, ♂. (Norman's Dart.)

Syn. *obtusa* Speyer.

Found everywhere in the Atlantic Subregion.

(2) **Noctua bicarnea** Guenée, Plate XXI, Fig. 35, ♀. (The Pink-spotted Dart.)

Syn. *plagiata* Walker.

This is likewise a common species ranging from the Atlantic as far west as Colorado.

(3) **Noctua c-nigrum** Linnæus, Plate XXII, Fig. 1, ♀. (The Black-letter Dart.)

Universally distributed through the Appalachian Subregion and also occurring in Europe.

(4) **Noctua jucunda** Walker, Plate XXII, Fig. 5, ♀. (The Smaller Pinkish Dart.)

Syn. *perconflua* Grote.

Very commonly found in the northern United States.

(5) **Noctua oblata** Morrison, Plate XXII, Fig. 3, ♂. (The Rosy Dart.)

Syn. *hilliana* Harvey.

The habitat of this species is the North. It is common in Alberta.

(6) **Noctua fennica** Tauscher, Plate XXII, Fig. 4, ♂. (The Finland Dart.)

Syn. *intractata* Walker.

A circumpolar species found throughout northern Europe, Asia, and America.

(7) **Noctua plecta** Linnæus, Plate XXII, Fig. 6, ♂. (The Flame-shouldered Dart.)

Syn. *vicaria* Walker.

The distribution of this small and well-marked species is somewhat like that of the preceding, but it extends farther to the south.

(8) **Noctua collaris** Grote & Robinson, Plate XXII, Fig. 7, ♂. (The Collared Dart.)

Occurs in the northern parts of the Atlantic Subregion.

(9) **Noctua juncta** Grote, Plate XXII, Fig, 12, ♂. (The Scribbled Dart.)

Syn. *patefacta* Smith.

The species ranges from Nova Scotia to Alberta.

(10) **Noctua haruspica** Grote, Plate XXII, Fig. 9, ♀. (The Soothsayer Dart.)

Syn. *grandis* Speyer.

Widely distributed through the northern portions of our territory.

(11) **Noctua clandestina** Harris, Plate XXII, Fig. 14, ♀. (The Clandestine Dart.)

Syn. *unicolor* Walker; *nigriceps* Walker.

A common species ranging from the Atlantic to the Rocky Mountains, and readily separated from the preceding species by the narrower and darker fore wings.

(12) **Noctua havilæ** Grote, Plate XXII, Fig. 18, ♂. (The Havilah Dart.)

A smaller species than either of the preceding. It occurs from Colorado and Wyoming westward to California.

(13) **Noctua atricincta** Smith, Plate XXII, Fig. 11, ♂. (The Black-girdled Dart.)

Thus far this species has only been reported as occurring in Alberta.

(14) **Noctua substrigata** Smith, Plate XXII, Fig. 10, ♂. (The Yellow-streaked Dart.)

This species, like the preceding, is found in Alberta. Both probably have a wider range.

(15) **Noctua calgary** Smith, Plate XXII, Fig. 13, ♂. (The Calgary Dart.)

The remarks made as to the two preceding species apply to this also.

(16) **Noctua lubricans** Guenée, Plate XXII, Fig. 8, ♂. (The Slippery Dart.)

Syn. *associans* Walker; *illapsa* Walker; *beata* Grote.

A very common species, universally distributed throughout the United States.

Genus PRONOCTUA Smith

Only one species of this genus, named **typica** by Prof. J. B. Smith, is known. It is found in Colorado and Wyoming. Through the kindness of Dr. Dyar a drawing of the type was made for me at the United States National Museum and it is reproduced in the annexed cut (Fig. 104).

FIG. 104.—*Pronoctua typica.*

Genus CHORIZAGROTIS Smith

Eight species are attributed to this genus by Dyar in his recent Catalogue of the moths of the United States. We figure three of them.

(1) **Chorizagrotis introferens** Grote, Plate XXII, Fig. 15, ♀. (The Interfering Dart.)

This insect is not scarce in Texas and Colorado, and thence ranges westward to California.

(2) **Chorizagrotis inconcinna** Harvey, Plate XXII, Fig. 22, ♀. (The Inelegant Dart.)

An obscurely colored species occuring in the southwestern States.

(3) **Chorizagrotis balanitis** Grote, Plate XXII, Fig. 17, ♂. (The Acorn Dart.)

The range of this insect is from Colorado to British Columbia.

Genus RHIZAGROTIS Smith

About a dozen species have been assigned to this genus by recent writers. We figure one of them, to which Prof. J. B. Smith has applied the name **proclivis**. It is represented by a female specimen on Plate XXII, Fig. 16. The insect occurs in Arizona and northern Mexico.

Genus FELTIA Walker

This is a considerable genus, represented by species in the northern portions of both hemispheres.

* (1) **Feltia subgothica** Haworth. (The Subgothic Dart.)

Of this common species, which is found in the northern portions of the United States and also in Canada, and which

FIG. 105.—*Feltia subgothica.*
Moth with wings expanded; moth with wings closed.

likewise occurs in Europe, we give a figure on Plate XXII. We also have reproduced a cut of the species taken from Prof. C. V. Riley's First Missouri Report. The larva is one of the commonest cut-worms, found more abundantly, however, in the West than in the East. The species has a wide range over the northern portions of the United States and through southern Canada.

(2) **Feltia herilis** Grote, Plate XXII, Fig. 20, ♂. (The Master's Dart.)

The insect ranges from the Atlantic to the Rocky Mountains.

(3) **Feltia gladiaria** Morrison, Plate XXII, Fig. 19, ♀. (The Swordsman Dart.)

Syn. *morrisoniana* Riley.

The distribution of this species is the same as that of the previous.

(4) **Feltia venerabilis** Walker, Plate XXII, Fig. 26, ♂. (The Venerable Dart.)

Widely distributed throughout the United States.

† (5) **Feltia vancouverensis** Grote, Plate XXII, Fig. 42, ♀. (The Vancouver Dart.)

Syn. *hortulana* Morrison; *semiclarata* Grote; *agilis* Grote.

I have given the above name to the specimen figured on the Plate as cited upon the authority of Prof. J. B. Smith, who has kindly examined the figure. The specimen came from Labrador.

(6) **Feltia volubilis** Harvey, Plate XXII, Fig. 23, ♀. (The Voluble Dart.)

Syn. *stigmosa* Morrison.

*The moth depicted on Plate XXII, Fig. 21, is *Feltia ducens* Walker, The Dingy Cutworm. This species, The Subgothic Dart, *F. subgothica* (*F. jaculifera* Guénee) and *F. herilis* are three of the commonest American cut-worms.—A.E.B.

†Should be *F. dissona* Möschler in text and plate.—A.E.B.

Found throughout our entire territory.

(7) **Feltia annexa** Treitschke, Plate XXII, Fig. 28, ♀. (The Added Dart.)

Syn. *decernens* Walker.

Found throughout the southern Atlantic and Gulf States and ranging into South America.

(8) **Feltia malefida** Guenée, Plate XXII, Fig. 32, ♀. (The Rascal Dart.)

This species has the same range as that of the last mentioned form.

Genus POROSAGROTIS Smith

Eleven species are assigned by Dr. Dyar in his Catalogue to this genus. As representatives of these we have chosen five for illustration.

(1) **Porosagrotis vetusta** Walker, Plate XXII, Fig. 25, ♂. (The Old Man Dart.)

Syn. *murænula* Grote & Robinson.

This pale-colored species extends in its range from the Atlantic to Colorado.

(2) **Porosagrotis fusca** Boisduval, Plate XXII, Fig. 31, ♀. (The Fuscous Dart.)

Syn. *septentrionalis* Mœschler; *patula* Walker.

The specimen figured was taken at Nain, Labrador. The insect is said also to occur in the Rocky Mountains.

(3) **Porosagrotis tripars** Walker, Plate XXII, Fig. 24, ♂; Fig. 37, ♀. (The Tripart Dart.)

Syn. *worthingtoni* Grote.

The specimens figured came from Colorado.

(4) **Porosagrotis rileyana** Morrison, Plate XXII, Fig. 33, ♀. (Riley's Dart.)

This species is spread from the Atlantic to the Rocky Mountains.

(5) **Porosagrotis dædalus** Smith, Plate XXII, Fig. 29, ♂. (The Dædalus Dart.)

The insect is peculiar to the region of the Rocky Mountains.

Genus EUXOA Hübner

This great genus, including nearly two hundred species, which are found in the region, with which this book deals, has in recent years been ranged under the name *Carneades* after the teaching of Grote, but as *Carneades*, which was erected by Bates, includes a different concept, this name was abandoned by Dr. Dyar, and the name *Paragrotis* Pratt was substituted for it. This name, however, must yield to the older name proposed by Hübner, and which we have adopted at the suggestion of Prof. J. B. Smith.

(1) **Euxoa quadridentata** Grote & Robinson, Plate XXII, Fig. 30, ♂. (The Four-toothed Dart.)

This insect is distributed from Colorado to Oregon.

(2) **Euxoa brevipennis** Smith, Plate XXII, Fig. 27, ♀. (The Short-winged Dart.)

The range of this species is the same as that of the preceding.

(3) **Euxoa olivalis** Grote, Plate XXII, Fig. 34, ♂. (The Olive Dart.)

The species occurs in Colorado and Utah.

(4) **Euxoa flavidens** Smith, Plate XXII, Fig. 38, ♂. (The Yellow-toothed Dart.)

This moth is spread through the region of the Rocky Mountains from Colorado to northern Mexico. The specimen figured came from the Sierra Madre of Chihuahua. It has been compared with the type in the National Museum at Washington.

(5) **Euxoa perpolita** Morrison, Plate XXII, Fig. 36, ♂. (The Polished Dart.)

It ranges from the States of the northern portion of the Atlantic Subregion to the mountains of Colorado.

(6) **Euxoa velleripennis** Grote, Plate XXII, Fig. 35, ♂. (The Fleece-winged Dart.)

It has the same range as the preceding species. It may at once be distinguished from it by its slighter build, and by the whiter hind wings.

(7) **Euxoa detersa** Walker, Plate XXII, Fig. 39, ♂. (The Rubbed Dart.)

Syn. *pityochrous* Grote; *personata* Morrison.

A pale and inconspicuously colored insect, which has the same distribution as the two preceding species.

(8) **Euxoa messoria** Harris, Plate XXII, Fig. 40, ♂. (The Reaper Dart.)

Syn. *spissa* Guenée; *cochrani* Riley; *repentis* Grote & Robinson; *displiciens* Walker, etc.

This wretched little creature, the larva of which is one of our most destructive cut-worms, was described seven times by Walker under different names. The more inconspicuous, or the smaller an insect, the more names it bears. The littlest bugs have the biggest names. It is thus also, sometimes, with men.

(9) **Euxoa lutulenta** Smith, Plate XXIII, Fig. 13, ♂. (The Muddy Dart.)

An inconspicuous species, which ranges from Alberta in the north to Colorado in the south, and thence westward to California.

(10) **Euxoa dissona** Mœschler, Plate XXIII, Fig. 5, ♀. (The Dissonant Dart.)

This moth is found in Labrador.

(11) **Euxoa titubatis** Smith, Plate XXIII, Fig. 6, ♂. (The Tippling Dart.)

The distribution of this species is coincident with that of the preceding.

(12) **Euxoa insulsa** Walker, Plate XXIII, Fig. 3, ♀. (The Silly Dart.)

Syn. *insignata* Walker; *expulsa* Walker; *declarata* Walker; *decolor* Morrison; *campestris* Grote; *verticalis* Grote.

This is another poor creature, which unconsciously has suffered much at the hands of the species-makers. It is found all over the United States.

(13) **Euxoa albipennis** Grote, Plate XXIII, Fig. 7, ♂. (The White-winged Dart.)

Syn. *nigripennis* Grote.

A common species in the Atlantic Subregion ranging across the valley of the Mississippi into Colorado.

(14) **Euxoa tessellata** Harris, Plate XXIII, Fig. 4, ♂. (The Tessellate Dart.)

Syn. *maizi*, Fitch; *atropurpurea* Grote.

Universally distributed throughout our region.

(15) **Euxoa basalis** Grote, Plate XXIII, Fig. 8, ♂. (The Basal Dart.)

This species is found in Colorado and Wyoming, and probably has a still wider range.

(16) **Euxoa ochrogaster** Guenée, Plate XXIII, Fig. 10, ♂.
(The Yellow-bellied Dart.)

Syn. *illata* Walker; *cinereomaculata* Morrison; *gularis* Grote; *turris* Grote.

This moth is found in the northern Atlantic States and thence westward to the foothills of the Rocky Mountains.

(17) **Euxoa furtivus** Smith, Plate XXIII, Fig. 11, ♂. (The Furtive Dart.)

The habitat of this species is the region of the Rocky Mountains.

(18) **Euxoa obeliscoides** Guenée, Plate XXIII, Fig. 12, ♀.
(The Obelisk Dart.)

Syn. *sexatilis* Grote.

Distributed over the northern Atlantic States, and across the valley of the Mississippi to Wyoming and Colorado.

(19) **Euxoa redimicula** Morrison, Plate XXIII, Fig. 9, ♂.
(The Fillet Dart.)

The insect has exactly the same range as the last mentioned species.

Genus EUCOPTOCNEMIS Grote

There is but one species of the genus recognized in our fauna. To this Guenée gave the name fimbriaris. It was afterward named *obvia* by Walker. Its habitat is New England. It is a scarce species in collections. The figure we give was taken from a specimen in the United States National Museum.

FIG. 106.—*Eucoptocnemis fimbriaris.*

Genus RICHIA Grote

A small genus of obscurely colored moths. They are found in the southwestern States.

(1) **Richia aratrix** Harvey, Plate XXIII, Fig. 14, ♂. (The Plough-girl.)

The species is found in Colorado and Texas.

(2) **Richia parentalis** Grote, Plate XXIII, Fig. 15, ♂. (The Parental Dart.)

This is a New Mexican species. It also occurs in Texas, and in the mountains of northern Mexico.

Genus ANYTUS Grote

Only a few species have been recognized as belonging to this genus. Of the five which have been named, we figure two.

(1) **Anytus privatus** Walker, Plate XXIII, Fig. 16, ♂. (The Sculptured Anytus.)

Syn. *sculptus* Grote.

A native of the Atlantic Subregion.

(2) **Anytus obscurus** Smith, Plate XXIII, Fig. 17, ♂. (The Obscure Anytus.)

Thus far this insect has only been reported from Alberta.

Genus UFEUS Grote

A small genus of rather large, plainly colored moths, having a robust habitus, which permits them to be easily distinguished from others.

(1) **Ufeus plicatus** Grote, Plate XXIII, Fig. 19, (The Pleated Ufeus.)

Syn. *barometricus* Goossens.

Distributed over the northern Atlantic States, and westward as far as California. The insect is not, however, very common.

(2) **Ufeus satyricus** Grote, Plate XXIII, Fig. 20, ♂. (The Satyr.)

This moth ranges over the northern Atlantic States, but, like the other species of the genus, does not appear to be anywhere very common.

Genus AGROTIPHILA Grote

There are seven species attributed to this genus by recent authors. We can only figure one of them.

(1) **Agrotiphila incognita** Smith, Plate XXIII, Fig. 18, ♂.

The species occurs in Alberta and westward to British Columbia.

Genus MAMESTRA Ochsenheimer

A very large genus, represented in both hemispheres by a large number of species. The caterpillars of some species are quite destructive to cultivated plants. Of the one hundred and ten or more species occurring in our territory we have selected thirty for purpose of illustration. This number of species, if correctly ascertained by the student, ought to enable him to form some idea of the general character of the complex of insects, with which we are now dealing.

(1) **Mamestra imbrifera** Guenée, Plate XXIII, Fig. 32, ♀. (The Cloudy Mamestra.)

A native of the northern Atlantic States. It is not rare in New England.

(2) **Mamestra purpurissata** Grote, Plate XXIII, Fig. 26, ♂. (The Empurpled Mamestra.)

This is a very common species in Maine and Quebec. It occurs less commonly south of these localities.

(3) **Mamestra juncimacula** Smith, Plate XIX, Fig. 41, ♂. (The Fused-spot Mamestra.)

The habitat of this species is Colorado.

(4) **Mamestra meditata** Grote, Plate XXIII, Fig. 21, ♀. (The Studied Mamestra.)

Quite a common species in the Appalachian Subregion.

* (5) **Mamestra lustralis** Grote, Plate XXIII, Fig. 22, ♀. (The Lustral Mamestra.)

Syn. *suffusa* Smith.

The range of this species is through the Atlantic States south and west to Arizona and northern Mexico.

(6) **Mamestra detracta** Walker, Plate XXIII, Fig. 24, ♂. (The Disparaged Mamestra.)

Syn. *claviplena* Grote.

The range of this insect is the same as that of the last mentioned species.

(7) **Mamestra farnhami** Grote, Plate XXIII, Fig. 23, ♀. (Farnham's Mamestra.)

A native of the eastern portions of the region of the Rocky Mountains.

(8) **Mamestra liquida** Grote, Plate XXIII, Fig. 36, ♀. (The Liquid Mamestra.)

The range of this insect is in the northwestern part of our territory as far as British Columbia.

---

*Should be *M. legitima* Grote (The Striped Garden Caterpillar) in text and plate.—A.E.B.

(9) **Mamestra radix** Walker, Plate XXIII, Fig. 25, ♂.
(Dimmock's Mamestra.)

Syn. *dimmocki* Grote; *desperata* Smith.

Distributed from Maine and Quebec across the northern parts
of the United States and the southern portions of the British
possessions to the Pacific.

(10) **Mamestra nevadæ** Grote, Plate XXIII, Fig. 33, ♀.
(The Nevadan Mamestra.)

Found in Nevada and California.

(11) **Mamestra subjuncta** Grote & Robinson, Plate XXIII,
Fig. 27, ♂. (The Harnessed Mamestra.)

Not at all an uncommon species in the Appalachian Subregion,
ranging across the Mississippi Valley to the foothills of the
Rocky Mountains.

(12) **Mamestra grandis** Boisduval, Plate XXIII, Fig. 41, ♂.
(The Grand Mamestra.)

Syn. *libera* Walker.

(13) **Mamestra trifolii** Rottemburg, Plate XXIII, Fig. 29, ♂.
(The Clover Mamestra.)

Syn. *chenopodii* Fabricius; *albifusa* Walker; *glaucovaria* Walker;
major Speyer.

Found throughout Europe, northern Asia, and the United
States and Canada. The caterpillar does at times considerable
damage to crops.

(14) **Mamestra rosea** Harvey, Plate XXIII, Fig. 30, ♀. (The
Rosy Mamestra.)

Distributed generally through the northern portions of the
United States and the southern portions of Canada and British
Columbia.

(15) **Mamestra congermana** Morrison, Plate XXIII, Fig. 31,
♀ (The Cousin German.)

This insect ranges from the Atlantic to the eastern portions
of the region of the Rocky Mountains.

(16) **Mamestra picta** Harris, Plate I, Fig. 11, larva; Plate
XXIII, Fig. 34, ♂. (The Painted Mamestra.)

Syn. *exusta* Guenée; *contraria* Walker.

This is one of the commonest species of the genus. The
caterpillar is a conspicuous object, and in the fall of the year is

generally very noticeable, feeding upon various herbaceous plants. It is a promiscuous feeder, and to enumerate all the vegetables which it attacks would almost be to provide a list of the plants of the United States. They manifest, however, a decided preference, when accessible, for the cruciferous plants, and do much damage in fields of cabbages and beets. There are two broods in the Middle States. The species does not occur on the Pacific coast, so far as is known to the writer. Its range is from the Atlantic to the eastern foothills of the Rocky Mountains.

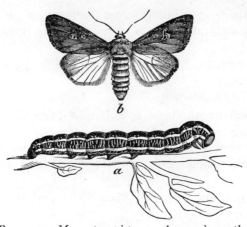

FIG. 107.—*Mamestra picta.* a. larva; b. moth.
(After Riley.)

(17) **Mamestra lubens** Grote, Plate XXIII, Fig. 28, ♂. (The Darling Mamestra.)

A denizen of the northern portions of the United States.

(18) **Mamestra latex** Guenée, Plate XXIII, Fig. 40, ♀. (The Fluid Mamestra.)

Syn. *demissa* Walker.

This insect has the same range as the preceding species.

(19) **Mamestra adjuncta** Boisduval, Plate XXIII, Fig. 38, ♀. (The Hitched Mamestra.)

This species occurs from southern Canada to the Carolinas and westward to Missouri and Minnesota.

(20) **Mamestra rugosa** Morrison, Plate XXIV, Fig. 3, ♂. (The Rugose Mamestra.)

The habitat of this species is Maine and Nova Scotia.

(21) **Mamestra lilacina** Harvey, Plate XXIII, Fig. 29, ♂. (The Lilacine Mamestra.)

Syn. *illabefacta* Morrison.

This moth ranges from the Atlantic coast to Colorado and New Mexico.

(22) **Mamestra renigera** Stephens, Plate XXIII, Fig. 35, ♀. (The Kidney-spotted Mamestra.)

Syn. *herbimacula* Guenée; *infecta* Walker.

This prettily marked little moth is found from New England and Ontario to Colorado. It occurs also in Europe.

(23) **Mamestra olivacea** Morrison, Plate XXIII, Fig. 37, ♂. (The Olivaceous Mamestra.)

For the very extensive synonymy of this insect the reader is referred to Dr. Dyar's "Catalogue of the Moths of the United States." It is too lengthy to impose upon these pages. The moth ranges over the northern portions of the United States and southern Canada.

(24) **Mamestra laudabilis** Guenée, Plate XXIV, Fig. 1, ♀. (The Laudable Mamestra.)

Syn. *indicans* Walker; *strigicollis* Wallengren.

This species extends its range from New Jersey through the southern States to Texas and southern California and northern Mexico.

(25) **Mamestra lorea** Guenée, Plate XXIV, Fig. 2, ♂. (The Bridled Mamestra.)

Syn. *ligata* Walker; *dodgei* Grote.

An obscurely colored species, which ranges from the Atlantic to the Rocky Mountains.

(26) **Mamestra erecta** Walker, Plate XXIV, Fig. 4, ♂. (The Erect Mamestra.)

Syn. *constipata* Walker; *innexa* Grote.

This little moth occurs in Texas, Arizona, and northern Mexico.

(27) **Mamestra anguina** Grote, Plate XXIV, Fig. 5, ♀. (The Snaky Mamestra.)

The insect occurs in the northern portions of our territory, and among the higher mountains of the States of Colorado and Wyoming.

(28) **Mamestra vicina** Grote, Plate XXIV, Fig. 6, ♀. (The Allied Mamestra.)

Syn. *teligera* Morrison; *acutipennis* Grote.

Ranges from the Atlantic to the Pacific.

195

(29) **Mamestra neoterica** Smith, Plate XXIV, Fig. 7, ♂.
(The Modern Mamestra.)

The range of this species is from Manitoba to Alberta, so far as is at present known.

(30) **Mamestra negussa** Smith, Plate XXIV, Fig. 8, ♀.
(The Brown-winged Mamestra.)

The species was originally described from Alberta. It occurs also in northern Montana.

Genus ADMETOVIS Grote

(1) **Admetovis oxymorus** Grote, Plate XXIV, Fig. 9, ♂.

This insect which is one of two species, which are attributed to the genus, is found from Colorado to California.

Genus BARATHRA Hübner

(1) **Barathra occidentata** Grote, Plate XXIV, Fig. 10, ♀.

This is a New Mexican species. Another species of the genus, named **curialis** by Smith, has been described by him as coming from Maine and New Hampshire.

Genus NEURONIA Hübner

(1) **Neuronia americana** Smith, Plate XXIV, Fig. 12, ♂.
(The American Neuronia.)

This is the only species of the genus represented in our territory. It occurs in Montana and Alberta.

Genus DARGIDA Walker

The only species of this genus found within the limits of the United States was named **procinctus** by Grote. It is represented by the figure of the male insect on Plate XXIV, Fig. 11. It is found from Colorado to California and Oregon.

Genus MORRISONIA Grote

Six species are attributed to this genus. We figure two of them.

(1) **Morrisonia sectilis** Guenée, Plate XXIV, Fig. 13, ♂.
Syn. *evicta* Grote.

Form **vomerina** Grote, Plate XXIV, Fig. 14, ♀.

The home of this insect is the Northern Atlantic States. It occurs in both forms in western Pennsylvania and Indiana.

(2) **Morrisonia confusa** Hübner, Plate XXIV, Fig. 15, ♂.
Syn. *infructuosa* Walker; *multifaria* Walker.
Not uncommon in **the Atlantic** Subregion.

Genus XYLOMIGES Guenée

In our fauna are found fifteen species which have been assigned to this genus. From their number we have chosen seven to put before the students of this book.

(1) **Xylomiges simplex** Walker, Plate XXIV, Fig. 17, ♂. (The Simple Woodling.)
Syn. *crucialis* Harvey.
A well marked and easily recognizable species, recalling the genus *Apatela*, so far as the pattern of the maculation is concerned. It is spread from Colorado westward to California.

(2) **Xylomiges dolosa** Grote, Plate XXIV, Fig. 20, ♂. (The Grieving Woodling.)
Distributed over the northern Atlantic States, and westward to Colorado.

(3) **Xylomiges perlubens** Grote, Plate XXIV, Fig. 19, ♂. (The Brown Woodling.)
Syn. *subapicalis* Smith.
This species belongs to the fauna of the Pacific coast, ranging eastward to Colorado.

(4) **Xylomiges pulchella** Smith, Plate XXIV, Fig. 21, ♂. (The Beautiful Woodling.)
Habitat British Columbia.

(5) **Xylomiges patalis** Grote, Plate XXIV, Fig. 18, ♀. (Fletcher's Woodling.)
Syn. *fletcheri* Grote.
Found in the Pacific States.

(6) **Xylomiges cognata** Smith, Plate XXIV, Fig. 22, ♂. (The Oregon Woodling.)
Ranges from British Columbia and Oregon eastward to Colorado.

(7) **Xylomiges indurata** Smith, Plate XXIV, Fig. 23, ♂. (The Hardened Woodling.)

Readily distinguished from *X. dolosa* by the lighter color of the primaries and the pure white secondaries, as well as by the different maculation. It is found in Colorado.

Genus SCOTOGRAMMA Smith

Of the thirteen species belonging to this genus and occurring in our fauna we depict three.

(1) **Scotogramma submarina** Grote, Plate XXIV, Fig. 24, ♂.

A native of the region of the Rocky Mountains ranging from Arizona to Montana.

(2) **Scotogramma infuscata** Smith, Plate XXIV, Fig. 25, ♂.

The figure given on the plate is taken from a specimen in the United States National Museum. The insect is found in Colorado.

(3) **Scotogramma inconcinna** Smith, Plate XXIV, Fig. 26, ♂.

This plainly colored species, like its predecessor, occurs in Colorado.

Genus ULOLONCHE Smith

A genus of moderate extent, all of the species belonging to which are western, except the one we figure, which occurs in the Atlantic Subregion.

(1) **Ulolonche modesta** Morrison, Plate XXIV, Fig. 16, ♂.
The species is not common.

Genus ANARTA Ochsenheimer

A subarctic genus, represented in both hemispheres. The insects occur either in high northern latitudes, or at great elevations upon high mountains. There are many species. We give illustrations of five of those found in our fauna.

(1) **Anarta cordigera** Thunberg, Plate XXIV, Fig. 28, ♂. (The Catocaline Anarta.)

Found in northern Canada, Labrador, Alaska, and thence southward along the summits of the higher ranges of the Rocky Mountains to Colorado. It also occurs in the north of Scotland, and from Norway to Kamschatka.

(2) **Anarta melanopa** Thunberg, Plate XXIV, Fig. 27, ♂. (The Black-mooned Anarta.)

Syn. *nigrolunata* Packard.

A circumpolar species commonly found in both hemispheres.

(3) **Anarta schœnherri** Zetterstedt, Plate XXIV, Fig. 30, ♂.
(Schœnherr's Anarta.)

Syn. *leucocycla* Staudinger.

Its habitat is Labrador, Greenland, Norway, Lapland, and arctic Asia.

(4) **Anarta richardsoni** Curtis, Plate XXIV, Fig. 29, ♀.
(Richardson's Anarta.)

Ranges from Alaska to Labrador, and has been found on the mountains of Norway.

(5) **Anarta impingens** Walker, Plate XXIV, Fig. 31, ♂.
(The Dull Brown Anarta.)

Syn. *nivaria* Grote; *curta* Morrison; *perpura* Morrison.

Found on the mountains of Colorado.

Genus **TRICHOCLEA** Grote

A small genus confined in its range to the mountain regions of the West.

(1) **Trichoclea antica** Smith, Plate XXIV, Fig. 32, ♂.

The specimen figured is one kindly loaned me from the national collection, and determined by the author of the species.

Genus **TRICHOPOLIA** Grote

Of this small genus we are able to give a figure of the type of the species named **serrata** by Professor Smith. The moth occurs in Texas.

Fig. 108.—*Trichopolia serrata.* ♂. ¼.

Genus **EUPOLIA** Smith

Fig. 109.—*Eupolia licentiosa.* ♂. ¼.

Only one species has thus far been referred to this genus. It was named **licentiosa** by Prof. J. B. Smith. The annexed cut gives a figure of the type, which is preserved in the United States National Museum. Its home is Utah.

Genus **NEPHELODES** Guenée

(1) **Nephelodes minians** Guenée, Plate XXIV, Fig. 33, ♂.

Syn. *expansa* Walker; *sobria* Walker; *violans* Guenée; *subdolens* Walker.

A common species in the Atlantic States. It is abundant in the fall of the year in western Pennsylvania.

Genus HELIOPHILA Hübner

A large genus well represented in both the eastern and the western hemispheres. Thirty-six species are credited to our fauna. Of these we give figures of eight, selecting the commoner and a few of the rarer forms.

(1) **Heliophila unipuncta** Haworth, Plate XXIV, Fig. 40, ♂. (The Army Worm.)

Syn. *extranea* Guenée.

This species, the larva of which is known as the "Northern Army Worm," or simply as the "Army Worm," is found from

the Atlantic to the Rocky Mountains, and from Canada to Texas and southward at suitable elevations upon the higher plateaus of northern Mexico. It appears occasionally in vast numbers, and is regarded by the farmer and the horticulturist as one of those pests against the ravages of which they must direct a great deal of energy. The first appearance of these insects in great numbers is recorded as having occurred in New Hampshire and Massachusetts in the year 1743. In the year 1770 they devastated the fertile fields of the valley of the Con-

FIG. 110.—Larva of *H. unipuncta.* (After Riley.)

necticut. They devoured the grasses and cereals, but neglected the pumpkins and potatoes. The chronicler of this invasion says: "Had it not been for pumpkins, which were exceedingly abundant, and potatoes, the people would have greatly suffered for food. As it was, great privation was felt on account of the loss of grass and grain." Successive attacks of the insect have been made since then upon the crops in various parts of the country. The year 1861 is memorable as having been marked by their ravages, which were

FIG. 111.—Pupa of *H. unipuncta.* (After Riley.)

particularly noticeable in the State of Missouri and in southern Illinois. An excellent account of this invasion has been published by Prof. C. V. Riley in his "Second Annual Report" as State Entomologist of Missouri. It appears from the investigations of those who are familiar with the habits of the insect that they appear in greatest numbers in years which are characterized by being wet and cool, following years in which there has been drought. Such conditions seem to be favorable to the development of the insects in great swarms. Their appearance in the fields is often at first not observed; but when, having attained considerable size, the supply of grain and grasses gives out, and they begin to migrate in vast bodies in search of provender, they at once attract attention.

Fig. 112.—Moth of *H. unipuncta.* (After Riley.)

The best remedy for these pests is to burn over grass lands in the winter, to keep the fence-rows clear of grass and weeds, and to plough under the land in the spring or the fall. Untilled grass lands on which crops are not properly rotated become centres of infection.

(2) **Heliophila pseudargyria** Guenée, Plate XXIV, Fig. 47, ♀. (The False Wainscot.)

A common species in the Atlantic States, freely attracted to sugar.

(3) **Heliophila subpunctata** Harvey, Plate XXIV, Fig. 35, ♀. (The Dark-winged Wainscot.)

Syn. *complicata* Strecker.

The range of this species is from New Mexico and Texas to Arizona.

(4) **Heliophila minorata** Smith, Plate XXIV, Fig. 41, ♂. (The Lesser Wainscot.)

This species is found in California and Oregon.

* (5) **Heliophila albilinea** Hübner, Plate XXIV, Fig. 34, ♂. (The White-lined Wainscot.)

Syn. *harveyi* Grote.

The insect is widely distributed, ranging from Nova Scotia to New Mexico and Texas, but apparently avoiding the Great Plains and the regions lying west of them.

*Technically, this should be *H. diffusa* Walker. *Albilinea* was described from Argentina, and has long been applied to this species.—A.E.B.

It is a very common species in the Atlantic States, and at times d o e s considerable injury to the crops. It has never, however, equaled in destructiveness the first species of the genus, to which we have given our attention on the preceding pages. It is said to be particularly attracted to the wheat when the grain is in the milk and the heads are just maturing. The damage done at this time is, in the Middle States, w h e r e w i n t e r wheat is commonly grown, due to the first generation of the insects. There are in fact two broods, one appearing on the wing in spring or early summer, the second in the late summer. The latter brood, which generally is more numerous than the first, produces the caterpillars, the pupæ of which yield the moths, which, coming out in the spring of the year, lay their eggs in the wheat-fields. It is said that the habit of attacking wheat in its period of maturation has lately been acquired by this insect, and is an illustration of the way in which species, long regarded as innocuous, develop with apparent suddenness destructive tendencies.

* Fig. 113—*Heliophila albilinea. a.* Larvæ; *b.* Mass of eggs laid on the stem of wheat; *c.* Egg viewed from above; *d.* Egg viewed from the side; (eggs greatly magnified). (After Riley.)

(6) **Heliophila heterodoxa**, Smith, Plate XXIV, Fig. 36, ♂. (The Heterodox Wainscot.)

The insect ranges from British **Columbia and** northern California as far east as Minnesota.

(7) **Heliophila multilinea** Walker, Plate XXIV, Fig. 39, ♂. (The Many-lined Wainscot.)

Syn. *lapidaria* Grote.

Not a scarce species in the Atlantic **States.**

*Fig. 113 could be either *H. albilinea* or *H. diffusa,* but is more probably the latter. See footnote on preceding page.—A.E.B.

(8) **Heliophila commoides** Guenée, Plate XXIV, Fig. 42, ♂. (The Comma Wainscot.)

The insect occurs from the Atlantic westward as far as Colorado. It is not very common.

Genus NELEUCANIA Smith

This is a small genus composed of species, which are, so far as is known, exclusively Western.

(1) **Neleucania bicolorata** Grote. (The Two-colored Neleucania.)

Of this species, which occurs in Colorado, New Mexico and Arizona, and probably has a still wider distribution, we are able to give a figure based upon a specimen contained in the United States National Museum.

Fig. 114.—*Neleucania bicolorata.* ♂. ¼.

Genus ZOSTEROPODA Grote

Only one species of this genus is known at present.

(1) **Zosteropoda hirtipes** Grote, Plate XXIV, Fig. 46, ♂.

The insect occurs in California.

Genus ORTHODES Guenée

Of the ten species reputed to belong to the genus and said to be found in our territory four are figured.

(1) **Orthodes crenulata** Butler, Plate XXIV, Fig. 37, ♂. (The Rustic Quaker.)

An exceedingly common species in the Atlantic States, ranging westward throughout the valley of the Mississippi.

(2) **Orthodes cynica** Guenée, Plate XXIV, Fig. 38, ♂. (The Cynical Quaker.)

Syn. *candens* Guenée; *tecta* Walker.

Quite as common as the preceding species, and having the same range.

(3) **Orthodes vecors** Guenée, Plate XIX, Fig. 20, ♂. (The Small Brown Quaker.)

Syn. *enervis* Guenée; *nimia* Guenée; *togata* Walker; *velata* Walker; *prodeuns* Walker; *griseocincta* Harvey; *nitens* Grote.

This is another small creature, which has caused the species-makers much exercise. It is found very generally throughout the Atlantic States.

(4) **Orthodes puerilis** Grote, Plate XXIV, Fig. 45, ♂. (The Boyish Quaker.)

This insect is found in northern California.

Genus HIMELLA Grote

(1) **Himella contrahens** Walker, Plate XXIV, Fig. 44, ♀.
Syn. *thecata* Morrison.

This insect is found from the northern Atlantic States southward and westward to New Mexico and Colorado.

Genus CROCIGRAPHA Grote

(1) **Crocigrapha normani** Grote, Plate XXIV, Fig. 43, ♂.
Not an uncommon insect in the northern portions of the Atlantic Subregion.

Genus GRAPHIPHORA Hübner

This is an extensive genus, represented in both hemispheres, and containing thirty-six species, which occur within our territory. We illustrate four of them.

(1) **Graphiphora culea** Guenée, Plate XXV Fig. 1, ♀.
Syn. *modifica* Morrison.

This species is quite common in the Appalachian or Atlantic Subregion.

(2) **Graphiphora oviduca** Guenée, Plate XXV, Fig. 2, ♂.
Syn. *capsella* Grote; *orobia* Harvey.

The insect has the same range as the preceding species, and is equally common.

* (3) **Graphiphora alia** Guenée, Plate XXV, Fig. 3, ♀.
Syn. *instabilis* Fitch; *insciens* Walker; *hibisci* Guenée; *confluens* Morrison.

Not a scarce species in the Atlantic Subregion.

(4) **Graphiphora garmani** Grote, Plate XXV, Fig. 5, ♂.

A rather scarce insect ranging from western Pennsylvania throughout the valley of the Mississippi as far as Illinois and Iowa.

*Should be *G. hibisci* Guenée in text and plate.—A.E.B.

Genus STRETCHIA Henry Edwards

This is an extensive genus, to which a number of Western species have been referred. It badly needs revision by a critical authority. We figure one of the best known forms.

(1) **Stretchia muricina**, Plate XXV, Fig. 5, ♂.

In addition to the figure given on the plate we annex a cut made from a drawing of a specimen contained in the collection of the late Henry Edwards, and now in the possession of the American Museum of Natural History in New York.

FIG. 115.—*Stretchia muricina.*

Genus PERIGONICA Smith

This is a small genus, which we represent by a figure of the Coloradan insect to which Prof. J. B. Smith has applied the specific name **fulminans**. The male is depicted on Plate XXV, Fig. 6.

Genus PERIGRAPHA Lederer

FIG. 116 — *Perigrapha prima.*

The only species of this genus found in our fauna has been named prima by Professor Smith. It is represented by a drawing of the type, which is contained in the American Museum of Natural History. The insect is a native of California.

Genus TRICHOLITA Grote

(1) **Tricholita signata** Walker, Plate XXV, Fig. 7, ♂.
Syn. *semiaperta* Morrison.

This is the only species of the genus found in the eastern portion of the United States. There are four other species, but they are western in their habitat.

Genus CLEOSIRIS Boisduval

This is a small genus found in Europe as well as in America. The species which has been chosen to represent the genus was named **populi** by Strecker, who first described it. It is not at all uncommon in Colorado and Wyoming. It occurs abundantly about the city of Laramie. It is represented upon Plate XXV, Fig. 8, by a female specimen.

Genus PLEROMA Smith

(1) **Pleroma obliquata** Smith, Plate XXV, Fig. 11, ♂.

The species of this genus are all found in the western half of our territory.

Genus LITHOMOIA Hübner

(1) **Lithomoia germana** Morrison, Plate XXV, Fig. 12, ♀.

This is not at all an uncommon species in the northern Atlantic States.

Genus XYLINA Ochsenheimer

An extensive genus found both in the New World and the Old. Thirty-five species are attributed to it as found in our fauna. Of this number ten are depicted in this book.

(1) **Xylina disposita** Morrison, Plate XXV, Fig. 13, ♀. (The Green-gray Pinion.)

The moth is found in the northern Atlantic States.

* (2) **Xylina petulca** Grote, Plate XXV, Fig. 9, ♀. (The Wanton Pinion.)

Not a common species, having the same range as the preceding.

(3) **Xylina antennata** Walker. (The Ashen Pinion.)

Syn. *cinerea* Riley.

The moth is a native of the Atlantic States. The larva feeds upon the apple, poplar, hickory, and other deciduous trees. It has the habit of boring into apples and peaches, and the galls which are found upon oaks. The caterpillar is green, marked with a cream-colored lateral stripe, and spots of the same color. It pupates beneath the soil in

Fig. 117.—*Xylina antennata.* *a.* Larva boring into peach. *b.* Moth.

a loose, filmy cocoon of silk, to which the particles of earth are adherent. Pupation takes place at the end of June, or the

*Should be *X. hemina* var. *lignicosta* Franclemont in text and plate.—A.E.B.

beginning of July, and the moth emerges in September and October.

(4) **Xylina laticinerea** Grote, Plate XXV, Fig. 17, ♂. (The Broad Ashen Pinion.)

The distribution of this species is the same as that of the last mentioned.

(5) **Xylina innominata** Smith, Plate XXV, Fig. 10, ♂. (The Nameless Pinion.)

The range of the Nameless Pinion is from the Atlantic to Colorado.

(6) **Xylina unimoda** Lintner, Plate XXV, Fig. 16, ♂. (The Dowdy Pinion.)

The species occurs in New England and the Middle States.

(7) **Xylina tepida** Grote, Plate XXV, Fig. 15, ♂. (The Warm Gray Pinion.)

An eastern species, not uncommon in Pennsylvania.

(8) **Xylina baileyi** Grote, Plate XXV, Fig. 19, ♀. (Bailey's Pinion.)

A rather pretty species, which has thus far only been reported from northern New York.

(9) **Xylina thaxteri** Grote, Plate XXV, Fig. 18, ♀. (Thaxter's Pinion.)

The home of this species is New England. It was originally described from Maine.

(10) **Xylina pexata** Grote, Plate XXV, Fig. 20, ♀. (The Nappy Pinion.)

Syn. *washingtoniana* Grote.

The species ranges from New England to Washington and Oregon.

Genus LITHOLOMIA Grote

There are only two species reckoned in this genus. The one, which we figure on Plate XXV, Fig. 22, by a male specimen, ranges over the entire northern portion of the United States from ocean to ocean, but is nowhere very common. The other species, *L. dunbari* Harvey, is only known from British Columbia.

Genus CALOCAMPA Stephens

The genus is found in both hemispheres. The species have a habitus which enables them to be easily recognized. Of the six occurring within the faunal limits, with which this book deals, we illustrate two.

(1) **Calocampa nupera** Lintner, Plate XXV, Fig. 24, ♂. (The American Swordgrass.)

A rather large moth, easily distinguished from the following species by the absence of the dark markings, which are found in the disk of the primaries of the latter insect. It occurs in the Atlantic Subregion.

(2) **Calocampa curvimacula** Morrison, Plate XXV, Fig. 23, ♂. (The Dot and Dash Swordgrass.)

The species is found throughout the northern portions of the United States and also in Canada.

Genus CUCULLIA Schrank

This is a considerable genus, which occurs in the temperate regions of both the Old World and the New. Four of the fourteen species attributed to our territory are chosen for representation. The larvæ feed on *Solidago* and other *Compositæ*.

(1) **Cucullia convexipennis** Grote & Robinson, Plate I, Fig. 3, larva; Plate XXV, Fig. 29, ♂. (The Brown-bordered Cucullia.)

A native of the Atlantic States.

(2) **Cucullia asteroides** Guenée, Plate XXV, Fig. 27, ♀. (The Asteroid.)

Found in the same localities as the last named species.

(3) **Cucullia speyeri** Lintner, Plate XXV, Fig. 26, ♂. (Speyer's Cucullia.)

Ranges through Colorado, Wyoming, and the adjacent regions to the west.

(4) **Cucullia intermedia** Speyer, Plate XXV, Fig. 30, ♀. (The Intermediate Cucullia.)

An Atlantic species.

Genus COPICUCULLIA Smith

(1) **Copicucullia propinqua** Smith, Plate XXV, Fig. 28. ♀. A native of Colorado and Wyoming

Genus RANCORA Smith

(1) **Rancora solidaginis** Behr, Plate XXV, Fig. 25, ♀.
Syn. *strigata* Smith.
The range of this insect is from northern California to British Columbia.

Genus LATHOSEA Grote

(1) **Lathosea pullata** Grote, Plate XXV, Fig. 32, ♂.
The species occurs in Oregon and eastward to Colorado.
(2) **Lathosea ursina** Smith, Plate XXV, Fig. 31, ♀.
A native of Colorado and the southern portions of Wyoming.

Genus ASTEROSCOPUS Boisduval

We are able to give a cut of the sole species which has been assigned from our fauna to this genus. It is based upon the type of the species which was named **borealis** by Smith, and which is preserved in the United States National Museum at Washington. The insect is a male.

Fig. 118.—*Asteroscopus borealis*. ¼.

TRAGEDY OF THE NIGHT-MOTH

Magna ausus

'Tis placid midnight, stars are keeping
    Their meek and silent course in heaven;
Save pale recluse, for knowledge seeking,
    All mortal things to sleep are given.

But see! a wandering Night-moth enters,
    Allured by taper gleaming bright;
Awhile keeps hovering round, then ventures
    On Goethe's mystic page to light.

With awe she views the candle blazing;
    A universe of fire it seems
To moth-*savante* with rapture gazing,
    Or Fount whence Life and Motion streams.

What passions in her small heart whirling,
    Hopes boundless, adoration, dread;
At length her tiny pinions twirling,
    She darts, and—puff!—the moth is dead.

Tragedy of the Night-Moth

The sullen flame, for her scarce sparkling,
  Gives but one hiss, one fitful glare;
Now bright and busy, now all darkling,
  She snaps and fades to empty air.

Her bright gray form that spread so slimly,
  Some fan she seemed of pygmy Queen;
Her silky cloak that lay so trimly,
  Her wee, wee eyes that looked so keen.

Last moment here, now gone forever,
  To nought are passed with fiery pain;
And ages circling round shall never
  Give to this creature shape again !

Poor moth ! near weeping I lament thee,
  Thy glossy form, thy instant woe;
'Twas zeal for "things too high" that sent thee
  From cheery earth to shades below.

Short speck of boundless Space was needed
  For home, for kingdom, world to thee !
Where passed unheeding as unheeded
  Thy little life from sorrow free.

But syren hopes from out thy dwelling
  Enticed thee, bade thee earth explore—
Thy frame, so late with rapture swelling,
  Is swept from earth forevermore !

Poor moth ! thy fate my own resembles.
  Me, too, a restless, asking mind
Hath sent on far and weary rambles,
  To seek the good I ne'er shall find.

Like thee, with common lot contented,
  With humble joys and vulgar fate,
I might have lived and ne'er lamented,
  Moth of a larger size, a longer date !

But Nature's majesty unveiling
  What seemed her wildest, grandest charms,
Eternal Truth and Beauty hailing,
  Like thee, I rushed into her arms.

What gained we, little moth ? Thy ashes,
  Thy one brief parting pang may show :
And thoughts like these, for soul that dashes
  From deep to deep, are—death more slow !

THOMAS CARLYLE.

Genus BELLURA Walker

We cause this genus to be represented by a figure of the species named **gortynides** by Walker. Synonyms are *densa* Walker, *vulnifica* Grote, *melanopyga* Grote. The insect is peculiar to the Atlantic States, so far as is known. The cut was drawn from a specimen in the American Museum of Natural History in New York.

FIG. 119.—*Bellura gortynides.* ♀ . ¼.

Genus SPHIDA Grote

(1) **Sphida obliqua** Walker, Plate XXV, Fig. 36, ♀ .
Syn. *obliquata* Grote & Robinson.

The range of this moth is from the Atlantic to the Mississippi. The specimen figured was taken by the writer at light in Minneapolis. It feeds in the stems of *Typha latifolia*.

Genus NONAGRIA Ochsenheimer

A rather small genus of obscurely colored moths, the larvæ of which burrow in the stems of aquatic plants, below the waterline. The genus is represented in both hemispheres. Six species belong to our fauna.

(1) **Nonagria oblonga** Grote, Plate XXV, Fig. 33, ♂ . (The Large Nonagria.)
Syn. *permagna* Grote.

This is a Southern species, thus far only recorded as found in Florida.

(2) **Nonagria subflava** Grote, Plate XXV, Fig. 34, ♀ . (The Yellowish Nonagria.)

The insect ranges from Maine to Illinois, where it is found in the vicinity of lakes and pools of water in which rushes grow.

Genus OMMATOSTOLA Grote

(1) **Ommatostola lintneri** Grote, Plate XXV, Fig. 35 ♂ .

Thus far this species has only been recorded from New York and New Jersey.

Genus ACHATODES Guenée

(1) **Achatodes zeæ** Harris, Plate I, Fig. 12, larva; Plate XXVI, Fig. 1, ♂.

This common insect, like those of the next three genera, is a stem-feeder, burrowing in the pith of its food-plants. It feeds in stems of elder (*Sambucus*), and Indian corn.

Genus GORTYNA Ochsenheimer

This genus is represented in the faunæ of both hemispheres. It is quite extensive.

(1) **Gortyna velata** Walker, Plate XXVI, Fig. 3, ♂. (The Veiled Gortyna.)

Syn. *sera* Grote & Robinson.

Not uncommon in the Atlantic States.

(2) **Gortyna nictitans** Borkhausen, Plate XXVI, **Fig. 2**, ♂.

This species, which is also found in Europe, has an extensive synonymy. It is found from the Atlantic to the Pacific, and shows in different localities slight differences in ground-color and markings, which have led to the creation of a number of subspecific distinctions by writers.

(3) **Gortyna immanis** Guenée, Plate XXVI, Fig. 4, ♀. (The Hop-vine Gortyna.)

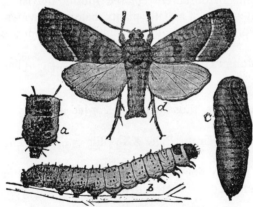

FIG. 120.—*Gortyna immanis. a.* enlarged segment of larva; *b.* larva; *c.* pupa; *d.* adult ♂ (After Howard.)

The insect is not often found south of New York and New England to any great extent, though its occurrence as far south as Maryland as a rarity has been noted. From western New York it ranges across the continent to the Pacific. As it particularly infests the hop it will not be abundant in places where that plant is not grown. In the centre of the hop-growing region of

New York and Ontario it is very abundant at times, and its depredations have been complained about by those interested in this industry. The eggs are laid on the young shoots and the little larvæ immediately bore into the stem near the tip. Here they remain until they are half an inch long, when they descend and attack the plant at the level of the ground. It has been recommended to pinch the tips which are seen to be affected and thus to kill the young worms. Various applications to be put about the roots have been advocated, for which the reader may consult "Bulletin No. 7 (New Series) of the United States Department of Agriculture." The hop-vines should at all events not be hilled up until the end of July or the beginning of August. This prevents the larvæ from having easy access to the stems at the level of the ground.

(4) **Gortyna obliqua** Harvey, Plate XXVI, Fig. 13, ♂. (The Oblique Gortyna.)

The habitat of this species is the Atlantic States and the Mississippi Valley.

Genus PAPAIPEMA Smith

* (1) **Papaipema inquæsita** Grote & Robinson, Plate XXVI, Fig. 5, ♂.

This species is, so far as we know, confined to the northern Atlantic States.

† (2) **Papaipema purpurifascia** Grote & Robinson, Plate XXVI, Fig. 7, ♂.

The range of this, as well as of all the species subsequently mentioned, is the same as that of the first species named in the genus.

‡ (3) **Papaipema nitela** Guenée, Plate XXVI, Fig. 9, ♂. Form **nebris** Guenée, Plate XXVI, Fig. 8, ♂.

The caterpillar inflicts a good deal of damage upon Indian corn by burrowing into the end of the ear when the seed is in the § milk. Those who have had to do with the preparation of roasting ears well know the unsightly larvæ, which, as they have stripped

FIG. 121—Larva of *Papaipema nitela*. (After Riley.)

the husk from the cob, have revealed their presence. Cooks know more about these things than the farmer. The farmer

---

*Should be *P. impecuniosa* Grote in text and plate.—A.E.B.

†This is now called *P. leucostigma* Harris.—A.E.B.

‡Should be *P. nebris* Guenée in text, plate and Fig. 121. Fig. 8 of Plate XXVI is *P. nebris* form *nitela* Guenée. *Nebris* is spotted, *nitela* unspotted.—A.E.B.

§The discussion of damage does not apply to any *Papaipema*, which are borers near or in the ground; it is most likely that of *Heliothis armiger* Hübner (see page 223).—A.E.B.

pulls his corn after the seed is hard and dry, but the "kitchen mechanic," who has to deal with green vegetables, often has light upon subjects which elude the observation of the grower.

(4) **Papaipema necopina** Grote, Plate XXVI, Fig. 12, ♀.

The species occurs in the Middle States, and has been more frequently found in New York than elsewhere.

(5) **Papaipema cerussata** Grote & Robinson, Plate XXVI, Fig. 10, ♀.

A pretty species, which occurs in New England and the Northern States as far west as Minnesota.

(6) **Papaipema cataphracta** Grote, Plate XXVI, Fig. 6, ♂.

The species is found in the northern Atlantic States, and is not unusual in western Pennsylvania.

(7) **Papaipema marginidens** Guenée, Plate XXVI, Fig. 11, ♂.

A rather scarce species, which has the same range as the preceding.

(8) **Papaipema furcata** Smith, Plate XXVI, Fig. 14, ♀.

The specimen shown on the plate was taken in western Pennsylvania.

Genus OCHRIA Hübner

Dr. Dyar in his recent list refers to this genus the insect which was accorded the specific name sauzælitæ by Grote. We give a figure of the moth taken from a specimen in the American Museum of Natural History, for the skilful delineation of which we are indebted to the facile fingers of Mrs. William Beutenmüller, one of the most accomplished delineators of insect life in America.

Fig. 122.—*Ochria sauzælitæ.* ⅓.

Genus PYRRHIA Hübner

(1) **Pyrrhia umbra** Hufnagel, Plate XXVI, Fig. 15, ♀.

This species, which occurs in Europe, ranges in North America from the Atlantic to the Rocky Mountains.

Genus XANTHIA Hübner

(1) **Xanthia flavago** Fabricius, Plate XXVI, Fig. 16, ♂.
Syn. *togata* Esper; *silago* Hübner.

This is likewise a European species, which has a wide range in the northern parts of the United States.

Genus JODIA Hübner

(1) **Jodia rufago** Hübner, Plate XXVI, Fig. 17, ♂. (The Red-winged Sallow.)

Syn. *honesta* Walker.

A European as well as a North American species.

Genus BROTOLOMIA Lederer

(1) **Brotolomia iris** Guenée, Plate XXVI, Fig. 19, ♀.

Not a very common moth, which occurs from New England to Colorado.

Genus TRIGONOPHORA Hübner

(1) **Trigonophora periculosa** Guenée, var. **v-brunneum** Grote, Plate XXVI, Fig. 18, ♂.

This is a very common species, having the same range as the preceding. The form we figure has the V mark on the wings heavy and dark. In the typical form this mark is light in color.

Genus CONSERVULA Grote

(1) **Conservula anodonta** Guenée, Plate XXVI, Fig. 20, ♀.

A rather scarce species, which is found in the northern part of our territory, south of Canada, and east of the Mississippi.

Genus EUCIRRŒDIA Grote

(1) **Eucirrœdia pampina** Guenée, Plate XXVI, Fig. 21, ♀.

The moth comes out late in the fall. I have often found them when a warm day has occurred in the autumn, freshly emerged, and hanging from the stems of bushes from which all the leaves had already fallen. The insect is common in the Appalachian subregion.

Genus SCOLIOPTERYX Germar

(1) **Scoliopteryx libatrix** Linnæus, Plate XXVI, Fig. 22, ♂. (The Herald.)

A common insect found in Europe and the entire temperate zone in North America. The larva feeds on willows.

Genus CHŒPHORA Grote & Robinson

(1) **Chœphora fungorum** Grote & Robinson, Plate XXVI, Fig. 23, ♀.

Not a very common moth. It is found among the Alleghanies in western Pennsylvania, and also occurs in other portions of the northern Atlantic subregion.

Genus PSEUDORTHOSIA Grote

The only species of the genus was named **variabilis** by Grote. It ranges from California to Colorado. We give a figure of the species drawn by Mrs. Beutenmüller from a specimen contained in the collection of the late Henry Edwards, and now in the American Museum of Natural History.

Fig. 123.—*Pseudorthosia variabilis*, ♂.¾.

Genus PSEUDOGLÆA Grote

(1) **Pseudoglæa blanda** Grote, Plate XXVI, Fig. 24, ♂.
Syn. *tædata* Grote; *decepta* Grote.

The habitat of the species is the Pacific States from which it ranges eastward to Texas and Colorado.

Genus ANCHOCELIS Guenee

(1) **Anchocelis digitalis** Grote, Plate XXVI, Fig. 25, ♂.

The only species in our fauna so far known is found in the northern Atlantic States.

Genus SELICANIS Smith

Under this generic name Prof. J. B. Smith in 1900 described a species from Colorado to which he gave the specific name **cinereola**. The type of this insect, which is preserved in the United States National Museum, is represented in the accompanying cut.

Fig. 124.—*Selicanis cinereola*, ♂ . ¾.

Genus TAPINOSTOLA Lederer

(1) **Tapinostola variana** Morrison, Plate XXVI, Fig. 26, ♂.

The figure we give is taken from a specimen belonging to the United States National Museum and coming from Michigan.

216

Genus FAGITANA Walker

Two species, which were formerly attributed to the genus *Pseudolimacodes* Grote, occur in the United States. We figure both of them.

(1) **Fagitana obliqua** Smith, Plate XXVI, Fig. 27, ♂.
The habitat of this species is Florida.

(2) **Fagitana littera** Guenée, Plate XXVI, Fig. 28, ♀.
Syn. *lucidata* Walker; *niveicostatus* Grote.
This is a rare insect, which occurs in the Atlantic States.

Genus COSMIA Ochsenheimer

(1) **Cosmia paleacea** Esper, Plate XXVI, Fig. 32, ♂. (The Angle-striped Sallow.)
Syn. *discolor* Walker; *infumata* Grote.
This insect is found all over northern Europe and the United States.

Genus ORTHOSIA Ochsenheimer

The genus is well represented both in the New World and the Old. Of the fifteen species reckoned as belonging to our fauna two are selected for illustration.

(1) **Orthosia bicolorago** Guenée, Plate XXVI, Fig. 29, ♂.
An eastern species, which is not uncommon.

(2) **Orthosia helva** Grote, Plate XXVI, Fig. 30, ♀.
A very common species in the Atlantic States, ranging westward as far as Colorado.

Genus PARASTICHTIS Hübner

(1) **Parastichtis discivaria** Walker, Plate XXVI, Fig. 31, ♂.
Syn. *gentilis* Grote.
Found throughout the northern Atlantic States.

Genus SCOPELOSOMA Curtis

This genus represented in Europe by a single species is represented in the United States and Canada by half a score of species. They appear upon the wing very early in the spring, when the nights are still cool and even frosty. This fact is the reason why they are for the most part not well represented in

217

collections. A good place to collect them is in maple-sugar camps, about the sap-buckets.

* (1) **Scopelosoma moffatiana** Grote, Plate XXVI, Fig. *33*, ♂. (Moffat's Sallow.)

This as well as all of the other species is found in the northern portion of the Atlantic subregion.

(2) **Scopelosoma ceromatica** Grote, Plate XXVI, Fig. *34*, ♀. (The Anointed Sallow.)

Ranges from New Jersey to Maine.

(3) **Scopelosoma walkeri** Grote, Plate XXVI, Fig. *35*, ♂. (Walker's Sallow.)

The moth is known to fly from Texas to Iowa and eastward to Maine and Canada. The larva feeds upon oaks.

(4) **Scopelosoma devia** Grote, Plate XXVI, Fig. *42*, ♂. (The Lost Sallow.)

It occurs in northern New York and Canada.

Genus ORRHODIA Hübner

FIG. 125.—*Orrhodia californica.*

The genus is found both in Europe and America. Prof. Smith has attributed to it a species to which he gave the name of **californica.** The type is in the United States National Museum and the annexed figure gives a representation of it. It is the only species of the genus in our fauna.

Genus GLÆA Hübner

(1) **Glæa viatica** Grote, Plate XXVI, Fig. *38*, ♂. (The Roadside Sallow.)

The species appears very late in the fall of the year. It ranges from Texas in the south to Massachusetts in the north.

(2) **Glæa inulta** Grote, Plate XXVI, Fig. *37*, ♂. (The Unsated Sallow.)

The moth ranges from Canada to Virginia and westward to Illinois and Iowa.

(3) **Glæa sericea** Morrison, Plate XXVI, Fig. *36*, ♂. (The Silky Sallow.)

The range of this species is much the same as that of the preceding.

*Should be *S. hesperidago* Guenée in text and plate; the synonomy is *indirecta* Walker; *græfiana* Grote; *moffatiana* Grote.—A.E.B.

Genus EPIGLÆA Grote

* (1) **Epiglæa pastillicans** Morrison, Plate XXVI, Fig. 41, ♂.
(The Round-loaf Sallow.)

The species occurs from West Virginia to Maine, and westward to Ohio.

(2) **Epiglæa decliva** Grote, Plate XXVI, Fig. 40, ♂. (The Sloping Sallow.)

Syn. *deleta* Grote.

The moth occurs from Canada to Virginia, and westward to Illinois.

Genus HOMOGLÆA Morrison

(1) **Homoglæa hircina** Morrison, Plate XXVI, Fig. 39, ♂.
(The Goat Sallow.)

The habitat of this species is the northern part of our territory. It ranges from Alberta to Nova Scotia, and southward along the Alleghany Mountains into the Western part of North Carolina.

(2) **Homoglæa carbonaria** Harvey, Plate XXV, Fig. 14, ♀.
(The Smudged Sallow.)

The species ranges from Washington and Oregon eastward to Colorado. It has been located in the genus *Euharveya*, but this name is a synonym for *Homoglæa*, according to Prof. J. B. Smith, and accordingly sinks.

Genus CALYMNIA Hübner

(1) **Calymnia orina** Guenée, Plate XXVII, Fig. 1, ♂.

Syn. *canescens* Behr.

This easily identified moth ranges over the entire temperate portion of the North American continent. The larva feeds upon oaks.

Genus ZOTHECA Grote

(1) **Zotheca tranquila** Grote, Plate XXVII, Fig. 2, ♂. (The Western Elder Moth.)

Syn. *sambuci* Behr; *viridula* Grote.

The larva feeds upon elder *(Sambucus)*. The moth ranges from northern California to British Columbia and eastward to Wyoming. The greener form was named *viridula* by Grote. The difference is hardly subspecific, as the shade of green on the wings is hardly alike in any two specimens, and the color soon fades out.

---

*Should be *E. tremula* Harvey in text and plate; the synonomy is *pastillicans* of authors.—A.E.B.

Genus IPIMORPHA Hübner

(1) **Ipimorpha pleonectusa** Grote, Plate XXVII, Fig. 3, ♂.
(The Even-lined Sallow.)

Syn. *æquilinea* Smith.

The species occurs from the Atlantic to the Rocky Mountains.

Genus ATETHMIA Hübner

(1) **Atethmia subusta** Hübner, Plate XXVII, Fig. 4, ♂.
A very common species ranging through the warmer parts of the Gulf States through Central and South America as far as Argentina.

(2) **Atethmia rectifascia** Grote, Plate XXVII, Fig. 5, ♂.
Found from New Jersey to Illinois and southward.

Genus TRICHOCOSMIA Grote

(1) **Trichocosmia inornata** Grote, Plate XXVII, Fig. 6, ♂.
The insect is found in Arizona and northern Mexico.

Genus TRISTYLA SMITH

 The genus was erected by Smith for the reception of a Californian species to which he gave the specific name **alboplagiata.** Through the kindness of the authorities of the United States National Museum I am able to give a representation of the type of this insect.

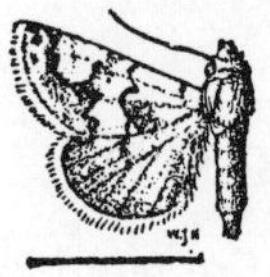

FIG. 126.—*Tristyla alboplagiata,* ♂.

Genus ANTAPLAGA Grote

A small genus composed exclusively of western species.
(1) **Antaplaga dimidiata** Grote, Plate XXVII, Fig. 7, ♂.
Hitherto only reported from Colorado.

Genus GROTELLA Harvey

(1) **Grotella dis** Grote, Plate XXVII, Fig. 8, ♂.
A small moth found in New Mexico and Arizona.

Genus PIPPONA Harvey

The only species hitherto referred to this genus is found in Texas. We give in the cut, which is herewith presented, a figure of a specimen which is contained in the American Museum of Natural History, and which was carefully drawn for this book by Mrs. Beutenmüller. It was named *bimatris* by Dr. Harvey.

FIG. 127.—*Pippona bimatris,*. ♂ ¼.

Genus BESSULA Grote

Through the kindness of the authorities of the British Museum and Sir George F. Hampson I am able to give herewith a figure

FIG. 128.—*Bessula luxa.* ♀ . ¼.

of the type of the genus and species, which is preserved in the Grote Collection. The moth occurs in New Mexico and Colorado.

Genus OXYCNEMIS Grote

FIG. 129.—*Oxycnemis fusimacula.* ♂ . ¼.

This genus is composed wholly of species which are found in the southwestern portions of our territory. Of one of these, found in California, to which Smith has applied the specific name **fusimacula**, we are permitted to give a figure taken from a specimen preserved in the American Museum of Natural History. It was drawn by Mrs. Beutenmüller.

Genus NYCTEROPHÆTA Smith

(1) **Nycterophæta luna** Morrison, Plate XXVII, Fig. 9, ♀.
Syn. *magdalena* Hulst; *notatella* Grote.

The moth ranges from Dakota and Montana southward to southern Colorado.

221

Genus COPABLEPHARON Harvey

(1) Copablepharon grandis Strecker, Plate XXVII, Fig. 10, ♂.
The species ranges from northern California and Oregon eastward to Montana.

(2) Copablepharon longipenne Grote, Plate XXVII, Fig. 11, ♀.
From the preceding species it may easily be distinguished by its much greater size. It has thus far only been found in Montana.

(3) Copablepharon album Harvey, Plate XXVII, Fig. 12, ♂.
The fore wings in this species are pure white, and not shaded with yellow, as is the case with the other two species, which have been mentioned. It occurs from Oregon to Montana and southward to Colorado.

Genus THYREION Smith

(1) Thyreion rosea Smith, Plate XXII, Fig. 13, ♀.
This insect is thus far only known to occur in Colorado.

Genus CHLORIDEA Westwood

(1) Chloridea virescens Fabricius, Plate XXVII, Fig. 14, ♂.
Syn. *rhexiæ* Abbot & Smith; *spectanda* Strecker.
Found from the Atlantic to the Pacific and from Canada southward into Mexico.

Genus HELIOCHEILUS Grote

(1) Heliocheilus paradoxus Grote, Plate XXVII, Fig. 15, ♂.
The insect ranges from the middle of the Mississippi Valley south and west. It does not appear to be common in collections.

Genus HELIOTHIS Ochsenheimer

The genus is represented in both hemispheres by a number of species. It used to be made to include a large assemblage of insects, but latterly has been restricted by authors.

(1) Heliothis armiger Hübner, Plate XXVII, Fig. 17, ♂. (The Boll-worm.)
This insect, which is known to English entomologists as the "Scarce Bordered Straw," is unfortunately not scarce in the

United States, and being of a singularly gluttonous habit in the larval stage, has become the object of execration to farmers and horticulturists. It is a very promiscuous feeder, but shows a special fondness for young Indian corn in the ear and for cotton-bolls. On account of the latter peculiarity it has received the name we have applied above. It attacks the fruit

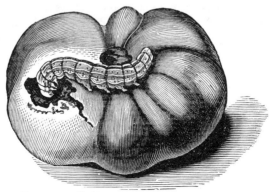

Fig. 130.—Boll-worm feeding upon a tomato. (After Riley.)

of the tomato when still green, and causes it to rot on the vines. It also feeds upon pumpkins, peas, beans, hemp, and, it is said, upon tobacco.

An excellent account of its habits has been given by Prof. C. V. Riley in his "Third Annual Report" as State Entomologist of Missouri. It is from that paper that we have extracted the figures, which are herewith given, and which serve to illustrate the life-history of the insect. The moth ranges all over the United States and southern Canada. It

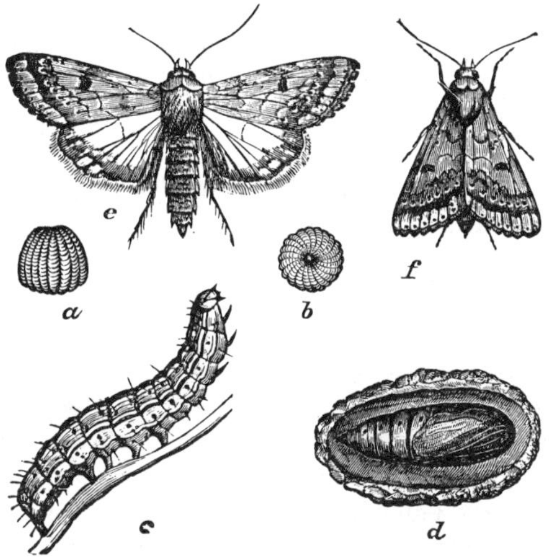

Fig. 131.—*Heliothis armiger.* a. Egg viewed from the side; b. Egg viewed from on top (both eggs magnified); c. Larva; d. Pupa; e-f. Moth. (After Riley.)

is most abundant in the southern portion of our territory, where there are from three to four broods annually. It is here in the cotton-fields and in the growing corn that the greatest damage is inflicted. There appears to be no way of applying remedies in a wholesale manner to the crops so as to prevent the depredations of this insect. The only resort is for the grower to go carefully over the fields, and where he detects the presence of the insects in their early stages, to pick them off and destroy them. In the case of corn the presence of the worm is shown by the premature drying of the silk, and in the case of cotton by the fallen flower-buds, which lie withering on the ground.

(2) **Heliothis scutosus** Fabricius, Plate XXVII, Fig. 16, ♂. (The Spotted Clover-moth.)

Syn. *nuchalis* Grote.

This species, which occurs in Europe and Asia, is also found not infrequently in the western part of our territory.

Genus DERRIMA Walker

(1) **Derrima stellata** Walker, Plate XXIX, Fig. 67, ♂. (The Pink Star-moth.)

Syn. *henrietta* Grote.

FIG. 132.—*Derrima stellata*, ♂. ¹⁄₁.

The specimen figured was taken in Maine. We also give a cut taken from a specimen in the American Museum of Natural History. It is a rare insect, but widely distributed from New England to the Mississippi through the northern tier of states.

Genus RHODOPHORA Guenée

(1) **Rhodophora gauræ** Abbott & Smith, Plate XXVII, Fig. 18, ♂.

Syn. *matutina* Hübner.

A very common species in the southern and southwestern portions of our territory. The larva feeds upon *Gaura biennis*.

(2) **Rhodophora florida** Guenée, Plate XXVII, Fig. 19, ♂.

Ranges from Canada to the Carolinas and westward as far as Utah.

(3) **Rhodophora citronellus** Grote & Robinson, Plate XXVII, Fig. 20, ♂.

This is a common species in Texas and Arizona. It occurs also in Colorado.

Genus RHODOSEA Grote

(1) **Rhodosea julia** Grote, Plate XXVII, Fig. 53, ♀.
The moth occurs in New Mexico and southward to northern Mexico. The specimen figured on the plate is contained in the United States National Museum.

Genus RHODODIPSA Grote

(1) **Rhododipsa volupia** Fitch, Plate XXVII, Fig. 22, ♂.
Habitat Colorado and Texas.

(2) **Rhododipsa miniana** Grote, Plate XXVII, Fig. 23, ♂.
The insect occurs in New Mexico.

(3) **Rhododipsa masoni** Smith, Plate XXVII, Fig. 24, ♀.
This species has thus far only been reported from Colorado.

Genus TRIOCNEMIS Grote

There is only one species of this genus, to which Grote applied the specific name **saporis**. The male is depicted on Plate XXVII, Fig. 21. It ranges from Washington and California eastward to Colorado.

Genus PSEUDACONTIA Smith

This is another genus represented thus far by one species. The insect received the specific name **crustaria** at the hands of Morrison. The figure we give was taken from a specimen contained in the United States National Museum at Washington. The insect ranges from Nebraska to Colorado and Wyoming.

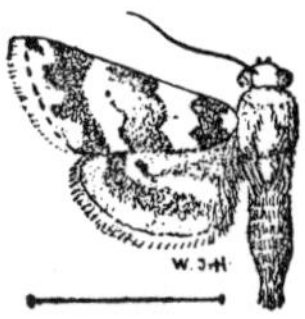

Fig. 133.—*Pseudacontia crustaria.*

Genus GRÆPERIA Grote

The only species attributed thus far to this genus is still a rare insect in collections. We give a figure of the type contained in the collection of the late Berthold Neumœgen, which is preserved at the Brooklyn Institute. The insect occurs in Texas. The fore wings are deep maroon, edged anteriorly with pale creamy white.

Fig. 134.—*Græperia magnifica,* ♂ . ⅓.

225

Genus PORRIMA Grote

(1) **Porrima regia** Strecker, Plate XXVII, Fig. 26, ♀.

This is a southern species, found in Texas, and also ranging northward as far as Kansas and Colorado.

Genus TRICHOSELLUS Grote

(1) **Trichosellus cupes** Grote.

Syn. *crotchi* Henry Edwards.

This little moth, which is the only one belonging to the genus, is represented in the annexed figure by a drawing of the type, which is preserved in the American Museum of Natural History.

FIG. 135.—*Trichosellus cupes*, ♂. ¼.

Genus EUPANYCHIS Grote

The only species belonging to the genus was originally named **spinosæ** by Guenée. Grote & Robinson subsequently called it *hirtella*. It occurs from Canada southward to the Potomac and westward to Illinois. The figure we give is from a drawing of a specimen in the United States National Museum.

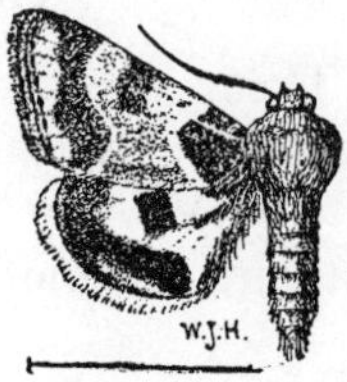

FIG. 136.—*Eupanychis spinosæ*, ♂.

Genus CANIDIA Grote

FIG. 137.—*Canidia scissa*.

This is a Floridan species, a figure of the type of which has been prepared for this book under the supervision of Sir George F. Hampson.

Genus SCHINIA Hübner

This is a very extensive genus of small and rather pretty moths, which are particularly abundant in the grassy and semiarid lands of the southwestern States. There are, however, a number of species, which occur in the Atlantic subregion.

(1) **Schinia chrysellus** Grote, Plate XXVII, Fig. 28, ♀.

The fore wings are silvery white. The insect is strikingly beautiful, and is not at all uncommon in the States of Colorado, New Mexico, and Texas.

(2) **Schinia aleucis** Harvey, Plate XXVII, Fig. 29, ♂.

This species is smaller than the preceding, which it resembles in a general way. The hind wings are darker. It occurs in Texas.

(3) **Schinia cumatilis** Grote, Plate XXVII, Fig. 30, ♂.

A beautiful species, with silvery-white wings. It may at once be distinguished from the two preceding species by the different arrangement of the bands upon the fore wings. It is found in Colorado, New Mexico, and Texas.

(4) **Schinia trifascia** Hübner, Plate XXVII, Fig. 35, ♀.
Syn. *lineata* Walker.

The moth is found from the Atlantic to the foothills of the Rocky Mountains in Colorado and Wyoming.

(5) **Schinia simplex** Smith, Plate XXVII, Fig. 32, ♀.

The home of this species is Colorado. The fore wings in some specimens are much brighter green than shown on the plate.

(6) **Schinia nundina** Drury, Plate, XXVII, Fig. 33, ♂.
Syn. *nigrirena* Haworth.

This is a strikingly marked species, which cannot easily be mistaken for anything else. It ranges from New Jersey southward and westward to Illinois and Kentucky.

(7) **Schinia acutilinea** Grote, Plate XXVII, Fig. 34, ♂.
Syn. *separata* Grote.

The moth is found in Colorado and Utah.

(8) **Schinia brucei** Smith, Plate XXVII, Fig. 37, ♂.

The home of the insect is Colorado.

(9) **Schinia lynx** Guenée, Plate XXVII, Fig. 38, ♂.

Is taken from Massachusetts to Florida and westward to the Mississippi.

(10) **Schinia roseitincta** Harvey, Plate XXVI, Fig. 36, ♂.
Syn. *exaltata* Henry Edwards.

Has been found from Colorado to Texas.

(11) **Schinia saturata** Grote, Plate XXVII, Fig. 43, ♂.

Ranges from Massachusetts to Florida, and westward to Texas and southern California.

(12) **Schinia tertia** Grote, Plate XXVII, Fig. 39, ♀.
This species is common in Texas.

(13) **Schinia albafascia** Smith, Plate XXVII, Fig. 45, ♀.
The habitat of this species is Utah and Colorado.

(14) **Schinia jaguarina** Guenée, Plate XXVII, Fig. 41, ♂.
The species ranges from western Pennsylvania to Nebraska and Colorado and southward to Texas.

(15) **Schinia arcifera** Guenée, Plate XXVII, Fig. 42, ♀.
Syn. *spraguei* Grote.
The species occurs from New England to New Mexico and southward.

(16) **Schinia packardi** Grote, Plate XXVII, Fig. 31, ♂.
Syn. *mortua* Grote; *nobilis* Grote.
Distributed from Colorado to Texas and Arizona.

(17) **Schinia thoreaui** Grote & Robinson, Plate XXVII, Fig. 46, ♂.
Ranging from the valley of the Ohio southward into Texas.

(18) **Schinia marginata** Haworth, Plate XXVII, Fig. 44, ♂.
Syn. *rivulosa* Guenée; *divergens* Walker; *contracta* Walker; *designata* Walker.
Found from New York to Iowa and thence southward.

(19) **Schinia brevis** Grote, Plate XXVII, Fig. 40, ♂.
Syn. *atrites* Grote.
This species is spread from Massachusetts to Iowa and southward to New Mexico.

Genus DASYSPOUDÆA Smith

(1) **Dasyspoudæa lucens** Morrison, Plate XXVII, Fig. 47, ♂.
A common insect in Nebraska and westward in Colorado and Wyoming.

(2) **Dasyspoudæa meadi** Grote, Plate XXVII, Fig. 48, ♂.
Ranges from Montana southward to Colorado.

Genus PSEUDANTHŒCIA Smith

(1) **Pseudanthœcia tumida** Grote, Plate XXVII, Fig. 49, ♂.
This insect occurs from Colorado to the higher plateaus of northern Mexico. It is common in Chihuahua.

Genus PALADA Smith

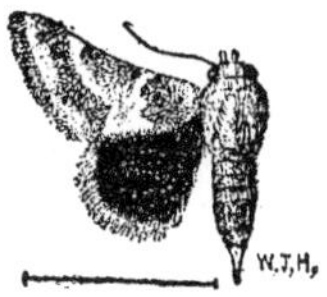

There is but one species of the genus, and we are able to give a figure of the type of this through the kindness of the authorities of the United States National Museum. It received the specific name scarletina at the hands of Prof. J. B. Smith. Its habitat is California.

Fig. 138.—*Palada scarletina*, ♀.

Genus STYLOPODA Smith

(1) **Stylopoda cephalica** Smith, Plate XXVII, Fig. 50, ♀.
This is a very common species in southern California.

Genus SYMPISTIS Hübner

This is another of the many genera among the Heliothid moths, which are represented thus far in America by but a single species. The insect was named **proprius** by Henry Edwards, and we give a figure of the type which is in his collection now in the possession of the American Museum of Natural History.

Fig. 139.—*Sympistis proprius*, ♂. ⅓.

Genus MELAPORPHYRIA Grote

This little genus contains three species. Of these we select one for illustration.

(1) **Melaporphyria oregona** Henry Edwards, Plate XXVII, Fig. 54, ♂.
The range of the species is from Colorado to Oregon.

Genus DYSOCNEMIS Grote

(1) **Dysocnemis belladonna** Henry Edwards, Plate XXVII, Fig. 55, ♂.
This beautiful little moth occurs in Utah.

Genus PSEUDOTAMILA Smith

(1) **Pseudotamila vanella** Grote, Plate XXVII, Fig. 25, ♂.
Found among the mountains of Nevada and California.

Genus MELICLEPTRIA Hübner

(1) **Melicleptria pulchripennis** Grote, Plate XXVII, Fig. 52, ♂.
Syn. *tanguida* Henry Edwards.
The range of this insect is from Colorado to California.
(2) **Melicleptria sueta** Grote, Plate XXVII, Fig. 51, ♂.
Syn. *californicus* Grote.
Is distributed from Colorado to California.

Genus HELIOLONCHE Grote

(1) **Heliolonche modicella** Grote, Plate XXVII, Fig. 58, ♂.
The moth is distributed from California to Colorado and Wyoming.

Genus OMIA Hübner

(1) **Omia nesæa** Smith, Plate XXVII, Fig. 59, ♂.
The habitat of this little moth is California.

Genus HELIOPHANA Grote

(1) **Heliophana mitis** Grote, Plate XXVII, Fig. 61, ♂.
Syn. *obliquata* Smith.

Genus HELIODES Guenée

FIG. 140.
Heliodes restric-talis, ♂.

There are but two species so far known to belong to this genus. They both occur in California, and are among the smallest of the Heliothids. We give in the annexed cut a representation of the type of the species named **restric-talis** by Prof. J. B. Smith.

Genus HELIOSEA Grote

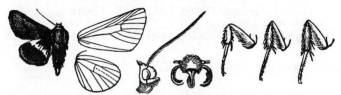

FIG. 141.—*Heliosea pictipennis*, ♂. ⅓.

The figure of the type of the genus and the species is kindly loaned me for use in this book by Sir George F. Hampson. It is taken from the "Catalogue of the Lepidoptera Phalænæ," Vol. IV. The moth occurs in California.

Genus XANTHOTHRIX Henry Edwards

(1) **Xanthothrix neumœgeni** Henry Edwards, Plate XXVII, Fig. 60, ♀.

This pretty bright colored little moth occurs in California.

Genus AXENUS Grote

(1) **Axenus arvalis** Grote, Plate XXVII, Fig. 57, ♂.

Syn. *ochraceus* Henry Edwards; *amptus* Henry Edwards.

A common insect ranging from Colorado to California and southward.

Genus HELIACA Herrich-Schæffer

Five species are attributed to this genus, of which we illustrate one.

(1) **Heliaca diminutiva** Grote, Plate XXVII, Fig. 56, ♂.

The range of this species is the same as that of the last mentioned.

Genus EUPSEUDOMORPHA Dyar

(1) **Eupseudomorpha brillians** Neumœgen.

Of this beautiful insect, which is still very rare in collections, we give a figure drawn by the writer from the type, which is contained in the Neumœgen Collection. The moth inhabits Texas.

Fig. 142.—*Eupseudomorpha brillians*, ♀ ⅓.

Genus XANTHOPASTIS Hübner

(1) **Xanthopastis timais** Cramer, Plate XI, Fig. 17, ♀.

Syn. *regnatrix* Grote.

This insect has a very wide range all over the tropics of the New World. It occurs not infrequently in the Gulf States, and occasionally ranges as far north as New York.

Genus PSYCHOMORPHA Harris

(1) **Psychomorpha epimenis** Drury, Plate III, Fig. 9, ♂.

This very beautiful little moth appears on the wing early in the spring in Pennsylvania. It is not uncommon in the Atlantic States. Hitherto it h a s been p l a c e d by many authors among the *Agaristidæ*, but we incline to the opinion that it is better located where we have put it, among the *Noctuidæ*. Larval characteristics, however, show a great likeness in this stage of development to the species included in the genus *Alypia*. The accompanying cut, which we have reproduced from the writings of Prof. C. V. Riley, may be compared in this connection with the figure of the larva of *Alypia octomaculata* given on page 144.

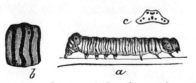

FIG. 143.—Larva of *Psychomorpha epimenis*. *a*, Full grown caterpillar; *b*, side view of segment enlarged; *c*, hump on eleventh segment. (After Riley.)

Genus PSEUDALYPIA Henry Edwards

This genus, like the preceding, has been located by some recent writers among the *Agaristidæ*. The moth is undoubtedly a Noctuid. I have placed it here in the order of arrangement, believing that upon the whole it is better located at this point in the serial arrangement than anywhere else. The figure annexed is that of the type preserved in the American Museum of Natural History. It was drawn by Mrs. Beutenmüller.

FIG. 144.—*Pseudalypia crotchi*, ♀. ⅓.

* Genus EUTHISANOTIA Hübner

(1) **Euthisanotia unio** Hübner, Plate XVII, Fig. 24, ♂. (The Pearly Wood-nymph.)

This lovely moth has a wide range throughout the eastern portions of our territory as far west as the Mississippi.

(2) **Euthisanotia grata** Fabricius, Plate XVII, Fig. 23, ♂. (The Beautiful Wood-nymph.)

Syn. *assimilis* Boisduval.

*On Plate XVII, Fig. 23 shows *E. unio* Hübner, ♂, and Fig. 24 shows *E. grata* Fabricius (The Beautiful Wood-nymph), ♂.—A.E.B.

This is a much larger species than the preceding. It has practically the s a m e range of distribution. The affinity of the genus to the g e n u s *Psychomorpha* i s clearly shown by the larva, a representation of which is given in the annexed cut taken from the writings of Prof. C. V. Riley, who devoted considerable time to the study of the life-history of these insects.

Fig. 145.—*Euthisanotia grata.* a, Full-grown larva; b, enlarged segment, side view; c, cervical shield from behind; d, anal hump from behind; e-f, top and side views of egg, enlarged. (After Riley.)

Genus CIRIS Grote

(1) **Ciris wilsoni** Grote, Plate XIX, Fig. 2, ♂.

This insect occurs in Texas and Arizona. It has also been referred to the *Agaristidæ* and to the *Zygænidæ* by various authors. There is, however, no doubt as to its being a true Noctuid.

Genus NOROPSIS Guenée

(1) **Noropsis hieroglyphica** Cramer, Plate XXVIII, Fig. 1, ♀.

This very pretty moth has a wide range in the hotter portions of America. It is found in Florida, and represents the invasion of our southern territory by the fauna of the Antilles, and South America.

Genus FENARIA Grote

(1) **Fenaria longipes** Druce, Plate XI, Fig. 16, ♂.

The species occurs in Arizona and ranges thence southwardly into Mexico.

(2) **Fenaria sevorsa** Grote, Plate XVII, Fig. 12, ♀.
Syn. *ædessa* Druce.

The species has the same range as the preceding.

> " I love the season well
> When forest glades are teeming with bright forms."
> LONGFELLOW. *An April Day.*

Genus ACHERDOA Walker

Only one species of the genus is attributed to it from our

fauna. It received the specific name **ferraria** at the hands of the late Francis Walker, and was renamed *ornata* by Neumœgen. The cut we give was drawn by Mrs. Beutenmüller from a specimen in the American Museum of Natural History. It represents the male insect.

FIG. 146.—*Acherdoa ferraria*, ♂. ¼.

Genus AON Neumœgen

(1) **Aon noctuiformis** Neumœgen, Plate XLI, Fig. 18, ♂.
. This is not an uncommon moth in southern Texas.

Genus CIRRHOPHANUS Grote

(1) **Cirrhophanus triangulifer** Grote, Plate XXVIII, Fig. 2, ♀.
The insect varies considerably in size, the specimen depicted on the plate being rather small. It is not an uncommon species in the southern States, and is also found as far north as Pennsylvania.

Genus BASILODES Guenée

(1) **Basilodes pepita** Guenée, Plate XXVIII, Fig. 7, ♀.
The genus *Basilodes* contains a number of species which are all, with the single exception of this species, natives of the southwestern portions of our territory. The present species occurs from Pennsylvania to Florida and westward to Colorado. The insect has been occasionally taken in Pittsburgh.

Genus STIRIA Grote

(1) **Stiria rugifrons** Grote, Plate XXVIII, Fig. 5, ♂.
The specimen figured on the plate was caught by the writer in southern Indiana. It is reported also from Kansas and Colorado. It probably has a wide range, but is as yet rare in collections.

Genus STIBADIUM Grote

(1) **Stibadium spumosum** Grote, Plate XXVIII, Fig. 3, ♀.
The insect ranges from New York to Colorado and southward. It is very abundant in southern Indiana, where it comes freely to sugar.

Genus PLAGIOMIMICUS Grote

There are five species reckoned as belonging to this genus. All of them are southwestern and western forms, except the one we figure.

(1) **Plagiomimicus pityochromus** Grote, Plate XXVIII, Fig. 9, ♀.

This moth is quite common in western Pennsylvania. It ranges southward and westward to the Gulf States and Colorado.

Genus FALA Grote

(1) **Fala ptycophora** Grote, Plate XXVIII, Fig. 4, ♀.

The habitat of this insect, which is the sole representative of its genus, is California.

Genus NARTHECOPHORA Smith

This is another genus in which we recognize thus far only one species.

(1) **Narthecophora pulverea** Smith, Plate XXVIII, Fig. 11, ♀.

The figure is taken from a specimen determined by the author of the species, and contained in the United States National Museum.

Genus NEUMŒGENIA Grote

The only species of this genus was named **poetica** by Grote. It is a beautiful little moth, the fore wings being bright metallic green, with a golden reflection, the light spot, which is outwardly trifid, and the costa being creamy yellow. The drawing for the annexed cut was made from the type which is preserved at the Brooklyn Institute.

Fig. 147.—*Neumœ-genia poetica*, ♂. ⅓.

Genus PLUSIODONTA Guenée

The only species of this small genus recognized as found in North America was named **compressipalpis** by Guenée. Walker renamed it *insignis*. It is represented on Plate XXVIII, Fig. 6, by a male specimen. The insect is a native of the Atlantic subregion, and is locally very common in western Pennsylvania.

Genus GONODONTA Hübner

This genus is representative of the tropical fauna of America, and but two species occur within our limits, both of them in the warmer parts of Florida.

(1) **Gonodonta unica** Neumœgen, Plate XXVIII, Fig. 10. ♂.

The larval stages have been well described by Dyar in the "Proceedings of the United States National Museum," Vol. XXIII, p. 272. The caterpillar feeds on *Anona laurifolia*, the Custard-apple.

Genus CALPE Treitschke

The genus *Calpe* is found in the temperate regions of both hemispheres. Only one species occurs in America.

(1) **Calpe canadensis** Bethune, Plate XXVIII, Fig. 8, ♀. (The Canadian Calpe.)

Syn. *purpurascens* Walker; *sobria* Walker.

The range of this species is restricted to the colder portions of our territory. It is found in Canada, rarely in northern New York, and ranges westward to Alberta.

Genus PANCHRYSIA Hübner

This genus, which is generally known under Walker's name *Deva*, is better represented in the eastern hemisphere than in the western. We figure one species of the four credited to our fauna.

(1) **Panchrysia purpurigera** Walker, Plate XXVIII, Fig. 13, ♂.

This pretty little moth, which is not very common, ranges from New England and Canada to Colorado and New Mexico.

Genus POLYCHRYSIA Hübner

Two species, both of which we figure, are attributed to this genus as occurring within our territory.

(1) **Polychrysia moneta** Fabricius, Plate XXVIII, Fig. 12, ♀.

Syn. *trabea* Smith.

This is a European insect, which is found also in Alberta and Assiniboia.

(2) **Polychrysia formosa** Grote, Plate XXVIII, Fig. 14, ♂.

So far, all the specimens which have come under the observation of the writer have been taken in New England or in New York.

Genus PLUSIA Hübner

Three of the four species attributed to the genus as found in America are represented upon our plate.

(1) **Plusia ærea** Hübner, Plate XXVIII, Fig. 16, ♂.
The moth ranges from Nova Scotia to Florida and westward to Texas and the region of the Rocky Mountains.

(2) **Plusia æroides** Grote, Plate XXVIII, Fig. 17, ♂.
The distribution of this species is almost identical with that of *Plusia ærea*. The larva feeds on various species of *Spiræa*.

(3) **Plusia balluca** Geyer, Plate XXVIII, Fig. 22, ♀.
The species is not uncommon in the northern Atlantic States.

Genus EUCHALCIA Hübner

(1) **Euchalcia contexta** Grote, Plate XXVIII, Fig. 23, ♂.
The species is found from Maine to Wisconsin, and occasionally as far south as the mountains of central Pennsylvania.

(2) **Euchalcia putnami** Grote, Plate XXVIII, Fig. 15, ♂.
Dr. Dyar with questionable correctness treats this species as a form of the European *festucæ* Linnæus. There is no doubt of the distinctness of the two.

(3) **Euchalcia venusta** Walker, Plate XXVIII, Fig. 21, ♀.
Syn. *striatella* Grote.
The range of this species is from Nova Scotia and Canada southward to the mountains of West Virginia.

Genus EOSPHOROPTERYX Dyar

(1) **Eosphoropteryx thyatiroides** Guenée, Plate XXVIII, Fig. 18, ♂.
This lovely moth is still very rare in collections. It ranges from New England and Canada to the mountains of Virginia and westward into the Valley of the Mississippi.

Genus AUTOGRAPHA Hübner

This is a large assemblage of species, about fifty being recognized as occurring in the United States. Of this number we are only able to figure about one third.

237

(1) **Autographa bimaculata** Stephens, Plate XXVIII, Fig. 19, ♂.

Syn. *u-brevis* Guenée.

This is a common species in the northern Atlantic States.

(2) **Autographa biloba** Stephens, Plate XXVIII, Fig. 24, ♂. The species is distributed widely from the Atlantic to the Pacific.

(3) **Autographa verruca** Fabricius, Plate XXVIII, Fig. 20, ♂.

Syn. *omega* Hübner; *oo* Cramer; *omicron* Hübner; *questionis* Treitschke; *rutila* Walker.

The moth is scarce in the northern Atlantic States, but has been recorded as occurring in Massachusetts. It ranges from New England to Texas and southward through Central and South America.

* (4) **Autographa rogationis** Guenée, Plate XXVIII, Fig. 25, ♂.

Syn. *hamifera* Walker; *dyaus* Grote; *includens* Walker; *culta* Lintner.

The range of this species is the same as that of the preceding.

(5) **Autographa precationis** Guenée, Plate XXVIII, Fig. 28, ♂.

The insect is found in Canada and the United States east of the Rocky Mountains.

(6) **Autographa egena** Guenée, Plate XXVIII, Fig. 29, ♂.

This is a southern species, occurring in Florida and the Gulf States, and ranging southward into South America.

(7) **Autographa flagellum** Walker, Plate XXVIII, Fig. 27, ♂.

Syn. *monodon* Grote; *insolita* Smith.

The species ranges from Quebec to Alberta.

(8) **Autographa pseudogamma** Grote, Plate XXVIII, Fig. 35, ♂.

The insect is indigenous in Quebec and Nova Scotia.

(9) **Autographa ou** Guenée, Plate XXVIII, Fig. 33, ♂.

Syn. *fratetta* Grote.

This species is almost universally distributed through the United States and southern Canada.

(10) **Autographa brassicæ** Riley, Plate XXVIII, Fig. 36, ♂.

Syn. *echinocystis* Behr.

*Should be *A. oo* Cramer (*includens* Walker).—A.E.B.

This insect, which preys upon the *Cruciferæ* in its larval state, has been well described and its habits fully set forth by Prof. C. V. Riley in the Missouri Reports. It is from his paper upon the species that we have been permitted to extract the figure which is herewith annexed of the insect in its various stages. The moth appears to be very generally distributed throughout the United States and Canada, and does a good deal to diminish the supply of the raw material from which *sauer-kraut* is made.

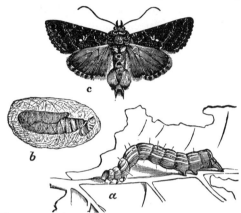

Fig. 148.—*Autographa brassicæ. a,* Full-grown larva; *b,* pupa; *c,* male moth. (After Riley.)

(11) **Autographa oxygramma** Geyer, Plate XXVIII, Fig. 30, ♂.

Syn. *indigna* Walker.

The moth is found in the southern States, and thence southward to South America.

(12) **Autographa rectangula** Kirby, Plate XXVIII, Fig. 32, ♀.
Syn. *mortuorum* Guenée.

This lovely species is northern in its range. I found it quite abundant one summer at Saratoga, New York.

(13) **Autographa vaccinii** Henry Edwards, Plate XXVIII, Fig. 34, ♂.

This species may easily be distinguished by the strongly checkered fringes of the primaries.

(14) **Autographa selecta** Walker, Plate XXVIII, Fig. 39, ♂.
Syn. *viridisignata* Grote.

This is a somewhat large species, not very attractively colored. It is northern in its range.

(15) **Autographa angulidens** Smith, Plate XXVIII, Fig. 38, ♂.

The species is found in Colorado, and probably has a wide range in the Rocky Mountains.

(16) **Autographa ampla** Walker, Plate XXVIII, Fig. 31, ♀.

This fine species is northern in its range, but extends its habitat southward along the ranges of the great mountains of the west.

(17) **Autographa basigera** Walker, Plate XXVIII, Fig. 26, ♂.
Syn. *laticlavia* Morrison.

The insect occurs in the Appalachian subregion.

(18) **Autographa simplex** Guenée, Plate XXVIII, Fig. 37, ♂.

This is one of the very commonest species of the genus, which is apparently universally distributed throughout our country.

Genus SYNGRAPHA Hübner

This genus is composed of species which are subpolar in their habitat. Of the four species which are reckoned as belonging to the fauna of North America, we illustrate two.

* (1) **Syngrapha hochenwarthi** Hochenwarth, Plate XXVIII, Fig. 41, ♂.
Syn. *divergens* Fabricius.

Found everywhere in Arctic America. The specimen figured was taken in Labrador.

† (2) **Syngrapha devergens** Hübner, Plate XXVIII, Fig. 40, ♀.
Syn. *alticola* Walker.

The species is found in Labrador, and has been reported from the high mountains of Colorado. It will probably be found to have a wide range.

Genus ABROSTOLA Ochsenheimer

We give representations of both the species which occur in our fauna.

(1) **Abrostola urentis** Guenée, Plate XXVIII, Fig. 42, ♂.

The insect, which is by no means common, is found in the Appalachian subregion.

(2) **Abrostola ovalis** Guenée, Plate XXVIII, Fig. 43, ♂.

The range of this insect is the same as that of the last mentioned.

*Should be *S. ignea* race *simulans* McDunnough in text and plate.—A.E.B.

†Should be *S. parilis* Hübner in text and plate—A.E.B.

Genus BEHRENSIA Grote

Only one species has thus far been attributed to this genus.

(1) **Behrensia conchiformis** Grote, Plate XXVIII, Fig. 44, ♂.

This little insect, which is as yet very rare in collections, is found in northern California and Oregon.

Genus DIASTEMA Guenée

(1) **Diastema tigris** Guenée.

Syn. *lineata* Walker.

The sole species belonging to the genus, which occurs within our borders, has been reported from Florida. We give in the accompanying cut an illustration of a specimen which is found in the American Museum of Natural History.

FIG. 149.—*Diastema tigris.*

Genus OGDOCONTA Butler

(1) **Ogdoconta cinereola** Guenée, Plate XXIX, Fig. 1, ♀.

Syn. *atomaria* Walker.

This is not at all an uncommon species in the Atlantic subregion. I have found it particularly abundant in southern Indiana, where it comes freely both to light and to sugar.

Genus PÆCTES Hübner

Eight species are enumerated as belonging to this genus in Dyar's recently published Catalogue. Of these we have given illustrations of three in our plates.

(1) **Pæctes abrostoloides** Guenée, Plate XXIX, Fig. 3, ♀.

The insect occurs in the Atlantic States, and ranges westward into the Mississippi Valley.

(2) **Pæctes pygmæa** Hübner, Plate XXIX, Fig. 2, ♂.

This is a southern species. The specimen from which the figure on the plate was taken was captured in Texas.

(3) **Pæctes oculatrix** Guenée, Plate XXIX, Fig. 4, ♂.

The species is by no means very common. It has a wide range from the Atlantic into the basin of the Mississippi. The specimen figured on the plate was taken in western Pennsylvania. I have specimens from Indiana and Illinois.

Genus EUTELIA Hübner

(1) **Eutelia pulcherrima** Grote.
Syn. *dentifera* Walker.

The only species of this genus known to occur within our territory is that which is figured in the accompanying cut, which

FIG. 150.—*Eutelia pulcherrima*, ♂. ⅓.

was made from the type now in the possession of the British Museum. The insect is found in New York and New Jersey, but probably has a wider southern range. It is as yet very rare in collections.

Genus MARASMALUS Grote

(1) **Marasmalus inficita** Walker, Plate XXIX, Fig. 6, ♂.
Syn. *histrio* Grote.

This species is found from the northern Atlantic States and Canada southward and westward to Texas and Colorado.

(2) **Marasmalus ventilator** Grote, Plate XXIX, Fig. 5, ♀.

This species, which is considerably larger than the preceding, has the wings more or less marked by reddish scales, which enables it to be easily discriminated from its congener. Its range is practically the same.

Genus AMYNA Guenée

(1) **Amyna octo** Guenée, Plate XXIX, Fig. 7, ♀.

This little moth has suffered more than any other known to the writer by being made the sport of the makers of synonyms. No less than nineteen synonyms have been applied to it in addition to its true name. In Dyar's Catalogue it appears under the name *orbica* Morrison, and *tecta* Grote is given as a synonym. The student who wishes to know what some of the other names are which have been given to it may consult Hampson's "Moths of India," Vol. II, p. 251. It is found throughout the hot lands of both hemispheres.

Genus PTERÆTHOLIX Grote

(1) **Pterætholix bullula** Grote, Plate XXIX, Fig. 8, ♂.
The habitat of this little moth is the Gulf States.

Genus Alabama Grote

(1) **Alabama argillacea** Hübner, Plate XXIX, Fig. 11, ♂.
(The Cotton-worm Moth).

Syn. *xylina* Say; *grandipuncta* Guenée; *bipunctina* Guenée.

The Cotton-worm Moth is one of a number of insects which annually inflict a vast amount of damage upon the crops in the southern portion of our country. In Prof. Comstock's "Report upon the insects which are injurious to cotton," published in 1879, and in the "Fourth Report of the United States Entomological Commission,"

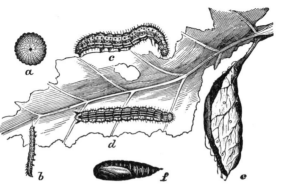

FIG. 151.—*Alabama argillacea.* *a.* Egg; *b.* immature larva; *c.* lateral view of mature larva; *d.* dorsal view of mature larva; *e.* leaf in which pupation takes place; *f.* pupa. (After Riley.)

there is given a great deal of valuable and interesting information in regard to this species. Much may also be learned about it from the study of the "Missouri Reports" published by the late Prof. C. V. Riley. The range of the insect is very broad. It sometimes, though very rarely, occurs as far north as Canada. From this northernmost location it has been found ranging southward as far as Argentina. It sometimes appears to migrate in swarms. A number of years ago, during a heavy snowstorm in November, myriads of the moths suddenly appeared in the city of Pittsburgh, and they came flying in the evening to the electric lights. From one store the proprietor said that he had swept them out by the quart. I have a few of the insects which thus appeared, and the figure on the plate is taken from one of these specimens.

Genus ANOMIS Hübner

The species belonging to this genus are mainly southern. There is considerable uncertainty as to the identification of some of the species, which were named by the older authors. Of the four reputed to be found within our limits we figure the one which is commonest.

(1) **Anomis erosa** Hübner, Plate XXIX, Fig. 12, ♀.
Occasionally found as far north as New England. Ranging thence southward into the South American continent.

Genus SCOLECOCAMPA Guenée

The only species of the genus so far known to occur in the United States was named **liburna** by Geyer. Guenée subsequently called it *ligni*. The larva feeds in decaying wood, particularly that of oaks, chestnuts, and hickories. It tunnels its way through the softer parts, and after reaching maturity makes a loose cocoon composed of a few strands of silk mixed with chips and the frass left in the burrow, from which it emerges in due season as the moth, which is represented on Plate XXIX, Fig. 16, by a male specimen.

Genus EUCALYPTERA Morrison

A small genus, the species of which are confined to the southern States and to Mexico and Central America.

(1) **Eucalyptera strigata** Smith, Plate XXIX, Fig. 9, ♂.
The habitat of this species is Texas.

Genus CILLA Grote

(1) **Cilla distema** Grote, Plate XXIX, Fig. 10, ♂.
This obscure little moth, the only representative of the genus in our territory, has hitherto only been reported from Texas.

Genus AMOLITA Grote

(1) **Amolita fessa** Grote, Plate XXIX, Fig. 13, ♂.
The moth occurs from Massachusetts to Florida and westward to Texas and Colorado.

Genus RIVULA Guenée

(1) **Rivula propinqualis** Guenée, Plate XXIX, Fig. 14, ♀.

The range of this insect is from Nova Scotia to Texas, and across the continent as far as the Rocky Mountains.

Genus PSEUDORGYIA Harvey

(1) **Pseudorgyia versuta** Harvey, Plate XXIX, Fig. 17, ♂.

This insect is thus far only known to us from Texas.

Genus DORYODES Guenée

* (1) **Doryodes bistriaris** Geyer, Plate XXIX, Fig. 15, ♂.

Syn. *acutaria* Herrich-Schæffer; *divisa* Walker; *promptella* Walker.

There are three species of the genus found in our territory, one of them, so far as is known to the writer, as yet unnamed. The insect we are considering ranges from Maine to Florida and westward to Colorado.

Genus PHIPROSOPUS Grote

(1) **Phiprosopus callitrichoides** Grote, Plate XXIX, Fig 18, ♀.

Syn. *nasutaria* Zeller; *acutalis* Walker.

The species ranges from New York to Texas.

Genus ANEPISCHETOS Smith

The only species thus far referred to this genus, which was erected by Smith in 1900 for its reception, received at the hands of that author the specific name **bipartita**. A figure of the type, which is contained in the collection of the United States National Museum, is given in the accompanying cut.

FIG. 152.
Anepischetos bipartita, ♂. ¼.

Genus DIALLAGMA Smith

FIG. 153.—*Diallagma lutea,* ♂. ¼.

This genus was erected at the same time as the preceding by the same author for the reception of the insect of which we give a representation in Fig. 153. Its habitat, as also that of the last mentioned species, is Florida.

*Should be *D. grandipennis* Barnes & McDunnough in text and plate. —A.E.B.

Genus PLEONECTYPTERA Grote

This is a genus of moderate size, which by some writers has heretofore been placed among the *Pyralidæ*, though it is undoubtedly correctly located among the *Noctuidæ*. Eight species are credited to our fauna in the latest catalogue.

(1) **Pleonectyptera pyralis** Hübner, Plate XXIX, Fig. 19, ♀. Syn. *irrecta* Walker; *floccalis* Zeller.

The insect ranges through the southern Atlantic States to Central and South America.

Genus ANNAPHILA Grote

A genus of moderate extent, embracing over a dozen species, which are found within the United States.

(1) **Annaphila diva** Grote, Plate XXIX, Fig. 20, ♂.

The habitat of this pretty little moth is California.

(2) **Annaphila lithosina** Henry Edwards, Plate XXIX, Fig. 21, ♀.

The specimen figured in the plate came from southern California.

Genus INCITA Grote

Only a single species, the type of the genus, is known. The figure we give in the annexed cut is drawn from the type in the possession of the American Museum of Natural History in New York.

FIG. 154. — *Incita aurantiaca*, ♂ . ⅓.

Genus TRICHOTARACHE Grote

The sole representative of this genus in our fauna is the insect the type of which is given in the accompanying figure, drawn for this work by Mr. Horace Knight, of London.

FIG. 155.—*Trichotarache assimilis* Grote, ♂ . ⅓.

The habitat of the moth is California.

Genus EUSTROTIA Hübner

This is quite an extensive genus, of which eighteen species are included in our fauna. Of this number we give illustrations of seven.

(1) **Eustrotia albidula** Guenée, Plate XXIX, Fig. 22, ♀.
Syn. *intractabilis* Walker.
This little moth ranges from the Atlantic to the Mississippi, and further west.

(2) **Eustrotia concinnimacula** Guenée, Plate XXIX, Fig. 23, ♀.
Not an uncommon species in the Atlantic subregion.

(3) **Eustrotia synochitis** Grote & Robinson, Plate XXIX, Fig. 24, ♂.
The distribution of this species is the same as that of the last. It occurs from Canada to Texas.

(4) **Eustrotia musta** Grote & Robinson, Plate XXIX, Fig. 25, ♂.
Found from the Atlantic to the Rocky Mountains.

(5) **Eustrotia muscosula** Guenée, Plate XXIX, Fig. 26, ♀.
The moth has the same ranges as the last mentioned species. It is very common in Indiana.

(6) **Eustrotia apicosa** Haworth, Plate XXIX, Fig. 27, ♂.
Syn. *nigritula* Guenée.
A very common species, having the same range as its predecessor.

(7) **Eustrotia carneola** Guenée, Plate XXIX, Fig. 28, ♀.
Syn. *biplaga* Walker.
What has been said of the last species applies also to this, except that it is, if anything, even more common.

Genus GALGULA Guenée

* (1) **Galgula hepara** Guenée, Plate XXIX, Fig. 31, ♂.
Syn. *externa* Walker.
Form **partita** Guenée, Plate XXIX, Fig. 32, ♂.
Syn. *vesca* Morrison; *subpartita* Guenée.
This common insect exists, as is shown in the plates, in two forms, one quite dark, the other lighter. It is an inhabitant of the Atlantic subregion, and is particularly abundant in western Pennsylvania.

*Should be *G. partita* Guenée in text and Plate XXIX (Fig. 31, ♀ ; Fig. 32, ♂). The synonomy is ♀ *hepara* Guenée; *interna* Walker, *vesca* Morrison; *subpartita* Guenée. The male of this species is quite variable; the female usually liver brown.—A.E.B.

Genus AZENIA Grote

(1) **Azenia implora** Grote, Plate XXIX, Fig. 29, ♀.
Not an uncommon insect in Arizona.

Genus LITHACODIA Hübner

(1) **Lithacodia bellicula** Hübner, Plate XXIX, Fig. 30, ♂.
This little moth may be found from the Atlantic to the Rocky
Mountains. It is the only species of its genus occurring in the
United States.

Genus PROTHYMIA Hübner

* (1) **Prothymia rhodarialis** Walker, Plate XXIX, Fig. 38, ♀.
Syn. *coccineifascia* Grote.
The species ranges from Massachusetts to Texas.
† (2) **Prothymia semipurpurea** Walker, Plate XXIX, Fig.
36, ♀.
The species has the same range as the last. The specimen
figured was taken at New Brighton, Pa., by the Messrs. Merrick,
whose ardent and successful labors as collectors of the local
fauna deserve all praise.
(3) **Prothymia orgyiæ** Grote, Plate XXIX, Fig. 37, ♂.
This is a Texan species.

Genus EXYRA Grote

(1) **Exyra semicrocea** Guenée, Plate XXIX, Fig. 35, ♀.
There are four species of the genus *Exyra* attributed to our
fauna, but only one of these is figured. The species are mainly
southern in their range. *Exyra semicrocea* is found from New
Jersey southward and westward as far as Texas.

Genus XANTHOPTERA Guenée

Two of the four species which are found within the limits
of the United States are represented upon our plates.
(1) **Xanthoptera nigrofimbria** Guenée, Plate XXIX, Fig.
33, ♂.
The insect is found in the southern portions of the Appalachian
subregion.

*Should be *P. ernestiana* Blanchard in text and plate; the synonomy
should include *rhodarialis* of authors.—A.E.B.
†Should be *P. rhodarialis* Walker in text and plate; the synonomy
is *semipurpurea* Walker; *rosalba* Grote.—A.E.B.

(2) **Xanthoptera semiflava** Guenée, Plate XXIX, Fig. 34, ♂ .

The distribution of this species is identical with that of the one last mentioned.

Genus THALPOCHARES Lederer

The only species of this genus found within our faunal limits is a native of Florida. It received the specific name **ætheria** at the hands of Mr. Grote. The illustration we give is drawn

FIG. 156.—*Thalpochares ætheria*, ♀ . 3/2.

from the type which is preserved in the British Museum, and was drawn for this book by Mr. Horace Knight under the direction of Sir George F. Hampson. The insect is not common in collections.

Genus EUMESTLETA Butler

Seven species are given by Dyar in his Catalogue as occurring within the limits of the United States. The insects have a southern and southwestern range, occurring in the Gulf States and in Arizona. We have selected one of them for illustration.

(1) **Eumestleta flammicincta** Walker, Plate XXIX, Fig. 39, ♂ .

Syn. *patula* Morrison; *patruelis* Grote.

The habitat of this insect is Florida and Texas.

Genus GYROS Henry Edwards

There is only one species of this genus known. It received the name **muiri** through Mr. Henry Edwards in honor of his friend, John Muir, the well-known writer, whose charming descriptions of the natural beauties of the western portions of our continent have established for him an enviable position in the world of letters. The moth is found in California.

FIG. 157.—*Gyros muiri*, ♂ . 1/1.

249

Genus TRIPUDIA Grote

This is a genus of considerable size, represented in the western and southwestern States by nine species, and well represented in the fauna of Mexico and Central America.

(1) **Tripudia opipara** Henry Edwards, Plate XXIX, Fig. 40, ♂.

This is a very common species in Texas.

Genus METAPONIA Duponchel

The genus is represented in both hemispheres. Three species occur in our fauna. Of these we figure two.

(1) **Metaponia obtusa** Herrich-Schæffer, Plate XXIX, Fig. 41, ♀.

Syn. *obtusula* Zeller.

The insect occurs from the valley of the Ohio southward to Texas. It is commoner in the south than in the north.

(2) **Metaponia perflava** Harvey, Plate XXIX, Fig. 42, ♀.

Not an uncommon species in Texas.

Genus CHAMYRIS Guenée

(1) **Chamyris cerintha** Treitschke, Plate XXIX, Fig. 43, ♀.

The species is found from New England and Canada southward to the Carolinas aud westward to Kansas. The larva feeds on the *Rosaceæ*. The insect is very common in Pennsylvania, Ohio, and Indiana.

Genus TORNACONTIA Smith

Two species have been attributed to this genus. One of them, which received the specific name **sutrix** at the hands of Grote, is represented in the annexed cut. It was drawn by Mrs. Beutenmüller from a specimen in the collection of the United States Museum of Natural History in New York. The insect is found in the region of the Rocky Mountains.

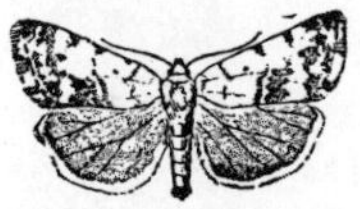

FIG. 158.—*Tornacontia sutrix*, ♂. ⅓.

Genus THERASEA Grote

This is a small genus, represented in our fauna by two species.
(1) **Therasea flavicosta** Smith, Plate XXIX, Fig. 47, ♂.
The moth occurs in the region of the Rocky Mountains.

Genus TARACHE Hübner

The genus is found in both hemispheres. It is well represented in our fauna, thirty-five species being known to occur
within the limits of the United States and Canada. Eleven of
these are figured upon our plates.
(1) **Tarache terminimacula** Grote, Plate XXIX, Fig. 46, ♀·
The species ranges from Massachusetts to Illinois.
(2) **Tarache delecta** Walker, Plate XXIX, Fig. 48, ♀.
Syn. *metallica* Grote.
The range of this species is along the Atlantic coast. It
occurs in the salt-marshes on Long Island and New Jersey, and
ranges thence southward to Texas.
(3) **Tarache flavipennis** Grote, Plate XXIX, Fig. 52, ♂.
The habitat of this species is the Pacific coast.
(4) **Tarache lactipennis** Harvey, Plate XXIX, Fig. 45, ♀.
Not at all an uncommon species in Texas.
(5) **Tarache lanceolata** Grote, Plate XXIX, Fig. 49, ♂.
This species, like the preceding, occurs in Texas.
(6) **Tarache sedata** Henry Edwards, Plate XXIX, Fig. 53 ♂.
The habitat of this insect is Arizona.
(7) **Tarache aprica** Hübner, Plate XXIX, Fig. 50, ♂.
The range of this species is from the valley of the Ohio southward to Texas and westward to Colorado.
(8) **Tarache erastrioides** Guenée, Plate XXIX, Fig. 54, ♀.
The moth is found in New England and Canada and southward so far as West Virginia and Indiana.
(9) **Tarache virginalis** Grote, Plate XXIX, Fig. 51, ♀.
The habitat of the species is from Kansas to Arizona.
(10) **Tarache binocula** Grote, Plate XXIX, Fig. 44, ♂.
The range of this species is the same as that of the preceding.
(11) **Tarache libedis** Smith, Plate XXIX, Fig. 55, ♂.
The home of this insect is New Mexico and Colorado.

Genus FRUVA Grote

The species belonging to this genus are southern and south-western in their distribution. Six are known.

(1) **Fruva apicella** Grote, Plate XXIX, Fig. 56, ♀.
Syn. *truncatula* Zeller; *accepta* Henry Edwards.
A very common species in the Gulf States.

Genus SPRAGUEIA Grote

A genus of small, but very attractively colored moths, which requent the flowers of the *Compositæ* in the later summer.

(1) **Spragueia onagrus** Guenée, Plate XXIX, Fig. 57, ♂.
The moth occurs quite abundantly in southwestern Pennsylvania and the valley of the Ohio, and ranges thence southwardly. It is common on the blossoms of the golden-rod *(Solidago.)*

(2) **Spragueia plumbifimbriata** Grote, Plate XXIX, Fig. 58, ♀.
This modestly colored species is found in Texas.

(3) **Spragueia dama** Guenée, Plate XXIX, Fig. 59, ♂.
Syn. *trifariana* Walker.
This is a common species in the southern States.

(4) **Spragueia guttata** Grote, Plate XXIX, Fig. 60, ♂.
This pretty moth ranges from Texas to Costa Rica.

Genus CALLOPISTRIA Hübner

(1) **Callopistria floridensis** Guenée, Plate XXIX, Fig. 61, ♂.
As the name indicates, the species is from Florida.

Genus METATHORASA Moore

A genus represented in both hemispheres, and particularly well in Asia.

(1) **Metathorasa monetifera** Guenée, Plate XXIX, Fig. 62, ♀.
A native of the Appalachian subregion, ranging from Canada to Florida. Thus far it does not appear to have been reported from any locality west of the Allegheny Mountains. I found it one summer quite abundantly at Saratoga, New York.

Genus EUHERRICHIA Grote

A small genus represented by three species in our fauna. *Euherrichia granitosa* occurs in Florida; *Euherrichia cervina* on the Pacific slope; and the species, which we figure, from Canada to Florida and westward to Colorado.

(1) **Euherrichia mollissima** Guenée, Plate XXIX, Fig. 63, ♂.
Syn. *rubicunda* Walker.

The specimen depicted was taken in the neighborhood of Saratoga, N. Y.

Genus CYDOSIA Westwood

A small genus represented in our fauna by three species, all of which we figure. The larva pupates in a small cocoon made of strands of silk woven into the form of a globular basket with open meshes, which is suspended from the under side of a leaf by a long cord.

(1) **Cydosia imitella** Stretch, Plate XXIX, Fig. 64, ♂.

The moth is found in the southern States.

(2) **Cydosia aurivitta** Grote & Robinson, Plate XXIX, Fig. 65, ♂.

The species occurs in Florida.

(3) **Cydosia majuscula** Henry Edwards, Plate XXIX, Fig. 66, ♀.

The habitat of the insect is the same as that of the species last mentioned.

Genus CERATHOSIA Smith

The only species of the genus was named **tricolor** by Smith. The fore wings are pure white, spotted with black, the hind wings are pale yellow. The habitat of the species is Texas.

FIG. 159.—*Cerathosia tricolor*, ♀. ⅓.

FIG. 160.—*Hormoschista pagenstecheri*, ♂. ⅓.

Genus HORMOSCHISTA Mœschler

The only species of this genus, which occurs within our territory, was originally described by Mœschler from Porto Rico. It is found in Florida and elsewhere along the borders of the Gulf of Mexico.

253

Genus PHALÆNOSTOLA Grote

There is only one species of the genus known to occur within our territory.

(1) **Phalænostola larentioides** Grote, Plate XXX, Fig. 1, ♀.

The insect ranges from New York southward to the Carolinas and westward to Missouri.

Genus PANGRAPTA Hübner

(1) **Pangrapta decoralis** Hübner, Plate XXX, Fig. 3, ♀.

Syn. *geometroides* Guenée; *epionoides* Guenée; *elegantalis* Fitch; *recusans* Walker.

The moth occurs from Nova Scotia to Florida and westward to the Mississippi.

Genus SYLECTRA Hübner

There is only one species of this genus which occurs within the faunal limits covered by this book. It was originally named

FIG. 161.—*Sylectra erycata*, ♂. ⅓.

erycata by Cramer. Subsequently Hübner applied to it the specific name *mirandalis*, which, of course, falls as a synonym. It is found in Florida, and is also quite common in the entire equatorial belt of South America. The peculiarly scalloped wings and the nodose antennæ serve to readily distinguish the insect, and it is not likely to be confounded with any other. The ground-color of the wings is luteous, variegated with reddish ochraceous.

Genus HYAMIA Walker

Three species of the genus are accredited to our fauna. Of these we figure two.

(1) **Hyamia sexpunctata** Grote, Plate XXX, Fig. 2, ♂.

The insect ranges from Massachusetts to Texas.

(2) **Hyamia perditalis** Walker, Plate XXX, Fig. 4, ♀.

Syn. *semilineata* Walker; *umbrifascia* Grote.

The range of this moth is the same as that of the preceding species. It is not uncommon in western Pennsylvania.

Genus MELANOMMA Grote

This is another genus of which we know but the one species in our territory. It received the specific name **auricinctaria**

Fig. 162.—*Melanomma auricinctaria,* ♂ . ½.

from Mr. Grote, who first described it. It occurs in the southern Atlantic States. The annexed figure is drawn from the type which is preserved in the British Museum.

Genus ARGILLOPHORA Grote

The sole representant of this species is shown in the annexed cut, which was prepared for this book by Mr. Horace Knight

Fig. 163.—*Argillophora furcilla,* ♂ . ¼.

from the type, access to which was kindly given by Sir George F. Hampson. The insect was originally reported from Alabama, but is still rare in collections. It probably has a wide range.

Genus PARORA Smith

The sole species belonging to this genus was originally described by Prof. J. B. Smith, from Texas. The accompanying cut shows a figure of the type, which is preserved in the United States National Museum. The ground-color of the wings is pale reddish ochraceous. The moth is found in Texas.

Fig. 164.—*Parora texana,* ♂ . ¼.

255

Genus HOMOPYRALIS Grote

Five species belong to this genus. We figure one of the commoner of these as representative. They come freely to sugar.

(1) **Homopyralis contracta** Walker, Plate, XXX, Fig. 5, ♀.
Syn. *zonata* Walker; *tactus* Grote.

The insect is widely distributed all over the Appalachian subregion.

Genus ISOGONA Guenée

(1) **Isogona natatrix** Guenée, Plate XXXVII, Fig. 18, ♀.
Syn. *tenuis* Grote.

The moth occurs in the southern Atlantic States.

Genus HYPSOROPHA Hübner

(1) **Hypsoropha monilis** Fabricius, Plate XXX, Fig. 6, ♂.

The species is quite abundant in northern Florida in the spring of the year. It ranges westward and northward as far as Kansas.

(2) **Hypsoropha hormos** Hübner, Plate XXX, Fig. 7, ♀.

The moth occurs from New York to Texas, and is not uncommon in the eastern half of the valley of the Mississippi.

Genus CISSUSA Walker

Ten species are attributed to this genus in the latest Catalogue of the moths of North America. They are all western and southwestern species. We have selected three of them for purposes of illustration.

(1) **Cissusa spadix** Cramer, Plate XXX, Fig. 9, ♂.
Syn. *vegeta* Morrison.

The species occurs in the southwestern portions of the United States.

(2) **Cissusa inepta** Henry Edwards, Plate XXX, Fig. 10, ♂.
Syn. *morbosa* Henry Edwards.

The moth flies in Colorado.

(3) **Cissusa sabulosa** Henry Edwards, Plate XXX, Fig. 11, ♀.

The habitat of this insect is the same as that of the preceding species.

Genus ULOSYNEDA Smith

The only species of this genus was named **valens** by Henry Edwards. It is represented on Plate XXX, Fig. 12, by a specimen of the male sex. Its home is Colorado, Wyoming, and Utah.

* Genus DRASTERIA Hübner

A widely distributed genus containing four species, which are peculiar to our fauna.

(1) **Drasteria erechtea** Cramer, Plate XXX, Fig. 14, ♀.

Syn. *sobria* Walker; *narrata* Walker; *patibilis* Walker; *agricola* Grote & Robinson; *mundula* Grote & Robinson.

This is a very common species widely distributed from Canada to Florida and westward as far as Colorado and Wyoming. It frequents grassy places and may be found from April to October.

(2) **Drasteria crassiuscula** Haworth, Plate XXX, Fig. 15, ♂.

Syn. *erichto* Guenée.

Quite as common as the preceding species, and having the same general distribution.

(3) **Drasteria cærulea** Grote, Plate XXX, Fig. 13, ♂.

Syn. *aquamarina* Felder.

The habitat of this pretty species is the Pacific coast. It is one of the very few blue moths which are known.

(4) **Drasteria conspicua** Smith, Plate XXX, Fig. 16, ♂.

This elegant moth is a native of Alberta and the adjacent territories of the British possessions.

Genus CÆNURGIA Walker

(1) **Cænurgia convalescens** Guenée, Plate XXX, Fig. 17, ♂.

Syn. *socors* Walker; *purgata* Walker.

The range of this insect is from Canada to Florida and westward to the Mississippi.

(2) **Cænurgia adversa** Grote, Plate XXX, Fig. 18, ♂.

The habitat of the species is California.

Genus EUCLIDIA Ochsenheimer

We show two of the four species which are known to occur within our faunal limits.

*Fig. 15 of Plate XXX is *D. erechtea* Cramer, ♂, not *D. crassiuscula* Haworth, which is not illustrated. *Sobria* Walker should be removed from the synonymy for (1) and inserted in that of (2).—A.E.B.

(1) **Euclidia cuspidea** Hübner, Plate XXX, Fig. 20, ♀.

The moth is found from Canada to the Carolinas and Georgia and thence westward to the Mississippi.

(2) **Euclidia intercalaris** Grote, Plate XXX, Fig. 19, ♂.

This is a rather rare species in collections. It is found in New Mexico and the southwestern States.

Genus PANULA Guenée

(1) **Panula inconstans,** Plate XXX, Fig. 21, ♂.

Not uncommon in the southern States.

Genus MELIPOTIS Hübner

This is a moderately large genus, represented in both the New World and the Old. Of the ten species known to occur within our faunal limits we show six on our plates.

(1) **Melipotis fasciolaris** Hübner, Plate XXX, Fig. 22, ♀.

This is not an uncommon insect in the Antilles, and also occurs in Florida. The specimen figured on the plate was taken in the latter locality.

(2) **Melipotis pallescens** Grote & Robinson, Plate XXX, Fig. 25, ♀.

An inhabitant of the southwestern portions of our territory, reported from Colorado, New Mexico, Texas, and Arizona.

(3) **Melipotis limbolaris** Geyer, Plate XXX, Fig. 27, ♂.

Syn. *grandirena* Haworth.

Found from New England to Florida and westward to the Mississippi.

(4) **Melipotis perlæta** Henry Edwards, Plate XXX, Fig. 26, ♀.

The species has been found in Arizona and Texas.

(5) **Melipotis jucunda** Hübner, Plate XXX, Fig. 24, ♂.

Syn. *cinis* Guenée; *agrotipennis* Harvey; *hadeniformis* Behr.

The insect ranges from New York to Florida and westward to Texas and Colorado.

(6) **Melipotis sinualis** Harvey, Plate XXX, Fig. 23, ♀

This easily recognizable species is an inhabitant of Texas and Arizona and ranges southward along the high table-lands of northern Mexico.

COLOR PLATES

1. *Hyloicus chersis* Hübner.
2. *Callosamia promethea* Drury.
3. *Cucullia convexipennis* Grote & Robinson.
4. *Citheronia regalis* Fabricius.
5. *Euchætias egle* Drury.
6. *Sibine stimulea* Clemens.
7. *Catocala innubens* Guenée.
8. *Samia cecropia* Linnæus.
9. *Prolimacodes scapha* Harris.
10. *Seirarctia echo* Abbot & Smith.
11. *Mamestra picta* Harris.
12. *Achatodes zeæ* Harris.
13. *Datana ministra* Drury.
14. *Phobetron pithecium* Abbot & Smith.
15. *Nerice bidentata* Walker.
16. *Eurycyttarus confederata* Grote & Robinson.
17. *Lycia cognataria* Guenée.
18. *Cerura multiscripta* Riley.
19. *Tortricidia testacea* Packard.

Plate I

EXPLANATION OF PLATE II

(The specimens figured are contained in the collection of W. J. Holland.)

1. *Hæmorrhagia thetis* Boisduval, ♂.
2. *Hæmorrhagia tenuis* Grote, ♀.
3. *Hæmorrhagia axillaris* Grote & Robinson, ♂.
4. *Hæmorrhagia axillaris* Grote & Robinson, ♀.
5. *Hæmorrhagia thysbe* Fabricius, ♂.
6. *Hæmorrhagia cimbiciformis* Stephens, ♀.
7. *Hæmorrhagia brucei* French, ♂.
8. *Proserpinus flavofasciata* Walker, ♀.
9. *Euproserpinus phaeton* Grote & Robinson, ♂.
10. *Proserpinus clarkiæ* Boisduval, ♀.
11. *Pogocolon gauræ* Abbot & Smith, ♂.
12. *Pogocolon juanita* Strecker, ♂.
13. *Xylophanes tersa* Linnæus, ♂.
14. *Celerio lineata* Fabricius, ♂.
15. *Deidamia inscriptum* Harris, ♂.
16. *Sesia titan* Cramer, ♂.
17. *Epistor lugubris* Linnæus, ♂.
18. *Amphion nessus* Cramer, ♂.
19. *Sphecodina abbotti* Swainson, ♂.
20. *Celerio intermedia* Kirby, ♀.
21. *Cautethia grotei* Henry Edwards, ♂.

PLATE II.

EXPLANATION OF PLATE III

(When not otherwise indicated the specimens figured are contained in the collection of W. J. Holland.)

1. *Pholus vitis* Linnæus, ♂.
2. *Pholus fasciatus* Sulzer, ♂.
3. *Darapsa pholus* Cramer, ♂.
4. *Darapsa myron* Cramer, ♂.
5. *Pholus achemon* Drury, ♂.
6. *Pholus pandorus* Hübner, ♂.
7. *Lapara bombycoides* Walker, ♂.
8. *Hemeroplanes parce* Fabricius, ♂.
9. *Psychomorpha epimenis* Drury, ♂.
10. *Dysodia oculatana* Clemens, ♂.
11. *Pholus labruscæ* Linnæus, ♂.
12. *Pachylia ficus* Linnæus, ♀.
13. *Darapsa versicolor* Harris, ♂.
14. *Arctonotus lucidus* Boisduval, ♂.
15. *Hæmorrhagia gracilis* Grote & Robinson, ♂.
16. *Lapara coniferarum*, Abbot & Smith, ♀, U.S.N.M.

PLATE III.

(The specimens figured are contained in the collection of W. J. Holland.)

1. *Protoparce quinquemaculatus* Haworth, ♀.
2. *Protoparce sexta* Johanssen, ♀.
3. *Hyloicus dolli coloradus* Smith, ♀.
4. *Protoparce occulta* Rothschild & Jordan, ♀.
5. *Hæmorrhagia senta* Strecker, ♂.
6. *Ceratomia amyntor* Geyer, ♀.
7. *Ceratomia catalpæ* Boisduval, ♀.
8. *Isogramma hageni* Grote, ♂.
9. *Xylophanes pluto* Fabricius, ♂.
10. *Calasymbolus astylus* Drury, ♂.
11. *Sphinx jamaicensis* Drury, form *geminatus* Say, ♂.
12. *Calasymbolus myops* Abbot & Smith, ♀.

PLATE IV.

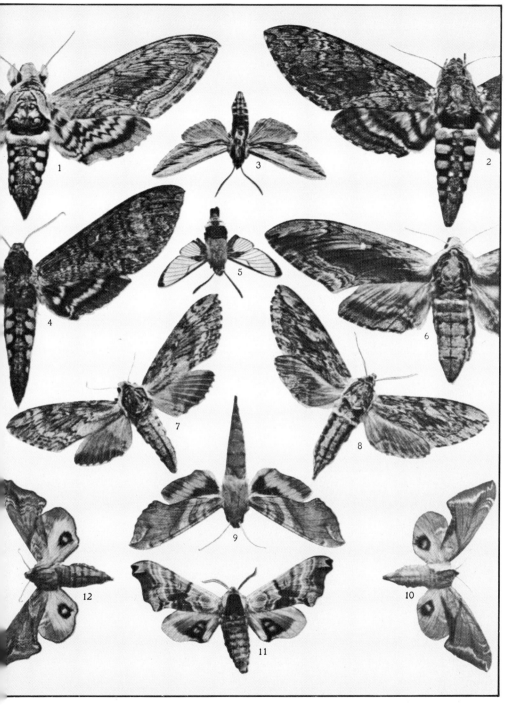

(The specimens figured are contained in the collection of W. J. Holland.)

1. *Hyloicus luscitiosa* Clemens, ♂.
2. *Errinyis lassauxi merianæ* Grote, ♀.
3. *Errinyis ello* Linnæus, ♀.
4. *Hyloicus libocedrus insolita* Lintner, ♂.
5. *Errinyis obscura* Fabricius, ♂.
6. *Atreides plebeja* Fabricius, ♂.
7. *Errinyis crameri* Schaus, ♀.
8. *Hyloicus sequoiæ* Boisduval, ♂.
9. *Errinyis domingonis* Butler, ♀.
10. *Errinyis ello* Linnæus, ♂.
11. *Errinyis œnotrus* Stoll, ♀.
12. *Errinyis alope* Drury, ♀.
13. *Hyloicus gordius* Stoll, ♂.
14. *Dictyosoma elsa* Strecker, ♂.

PLATE V.

EXPLANATION OF PLATE VI

(The specimens figured are contained in the collection of W. J. Holland.)

1. *Cocytius antæus* Drury, ♀.
2. *Pseudosphinx tetrio* Linnæus, ♂.
3. *Herse cingulata* Fabricius, ♂.
4. *Dolba hylæus* Drury, ♀.
5. *Hyloicus vancouverensis albescens* Tepper, ♂.
6. *Hyloicus eremitus* Hübner, ♀.
7. *Ceratomia undulosa* Walker, ♀.
8. *Hyloicus kalmiæ* Abbot & Smith, ♀.
9. *Cressonia juglandis* Abbot & Smith, ♀.
10. *Hyloicus separatus* Neumœgen, ♂.

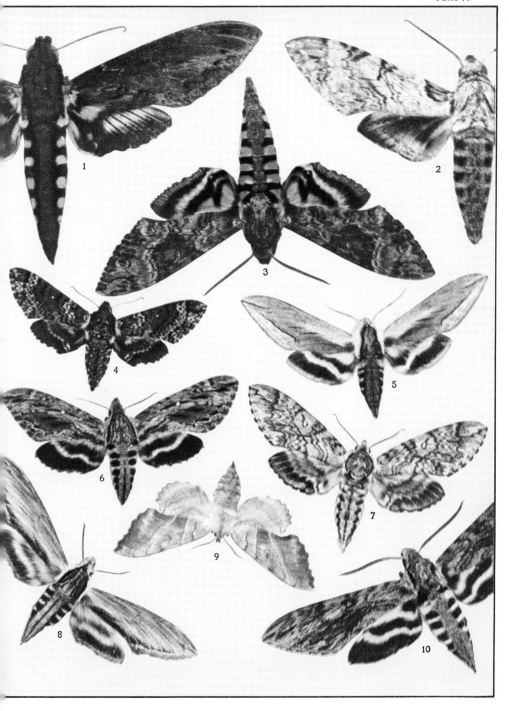

PLATE VI.

(The specimens figured are contained in the collection of W. J. Holland.)

1. *Pachysphinx modesta* Harris, ♂.
2. *Pachysphinx modesta occidentalis* Henry Edwards, ♀.
3. *Sphinx cerisyi* Kirby, ♀.
4. *Calasymbolus excæcata* Abbot & Smith, ♂.
5. *Protoparce rustica* Fabricius, ♀.
6. *Chlænogramma jasminearum* Boisduval, ♀.
7. *Hyloicus drupiferarum* Abbot & Smith, ♂.
8. *Hyloicus chersis* Hübner, ♀.

PLATE VII.

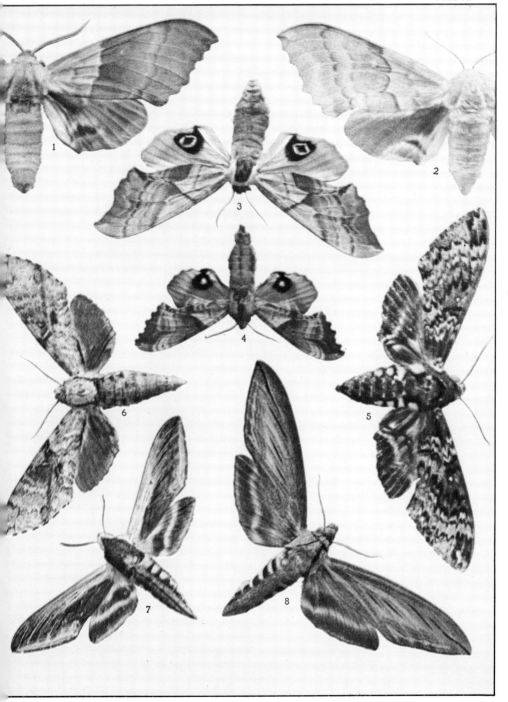

PLATE VIII.

(Except when otherwise indicated the specimens figured are contained in the collection of W. J. Holland.)

1. *Telea polyphemus* Cramer, ♀.
2. *Philosamia cynthia* Drury, ♂.
3. *Agapema galbina* Clemens, ♂, U. S. N. M.
4. *Automeris io* Fabricius, ♂.
5. *Automeris io* Fabricius, ♀.
6. *Automeris pamina aurosea* Neumœgen, ♂.
7. *Pseudohazis eglanterina nuttalli* Strecker, ♂.
8. *Pseudohazis hera* Harris, ♂.
9. *Zeuzera pyrina* Linnæus, ♂

PLATE IX.

EXPLANATION OF PLATE X

(Except when otherwise indicated the specimens figured are in the collection of W. J. Holland.)

1. *Rothschildia orizaba* Westwood, ♀.
2. *Basilona imperialis* Drury, ♀.
3. *Citheronia regalis* Fabricius, ♂
4. *Citheronia mexicana* Grote & Robinson, ♂.
5. *Adelocephala bicolor* Harris, ♂.
6. *Adelocephala bicolor* Harris, ♀.
7. *Syssphinx albolineata* Grote & Robinson, ♂.
8. *Coloradia pandora* Blake, ♂.
9. *Malacosoma disstria* Hübner, ♂, U. S. N. M.
10. *Malacosoma erosa* Stretch, ♂.
11. *Malacosoma californica* Packard, ♂.
12. *Malacosoma americana* Fabricius, ♀, U. S. N. M.

PLATE X.

EXPLANATION OF PLATE XI

(The specimens figured are contained in the collection of W. J. Holland.)

1. *Hemileuca maia* Drury, ♂.
2. *Hemileuca nevadensis* Stretch, ♂.
3. *Pseudohazis hera pica* Walker, ♂.
4. *Pseudohazis hera pica* Walker, ♀.
5. *Pseudohazis eglanterina nuttalli* Strecker, ♂.
6. *Ctenucha brunnea* Stretch, ♂.
7. *Tolype velleda* Stoll, ♂.
8. *Tolype velleda* Stoll, ♀.
9. *Anisota stigma* Fabricius, ♂.
10. *Anisota stigma* Fabricius, ♀.
11. *Callosamia promethea* Drury, ♂.
12. *Callosamia promethea* Drury, ♀.
13. *Basilona imperialis* Drury, ♂.
14. *Syssphinx heiligbrodti* Harvey, ♀.
15. *Cargida pyrrha* Druce, ♂.
16. *Fenaria longipes* Druce, ♂.
17. *Xanthopastis timais* Cramer, ♀.
18. *Euchætias murina* Stretch, ♀.
19. *Copidryas cosyra* Druce, ♂.
20. *Apantesis intermedia* Stretch, ♂.

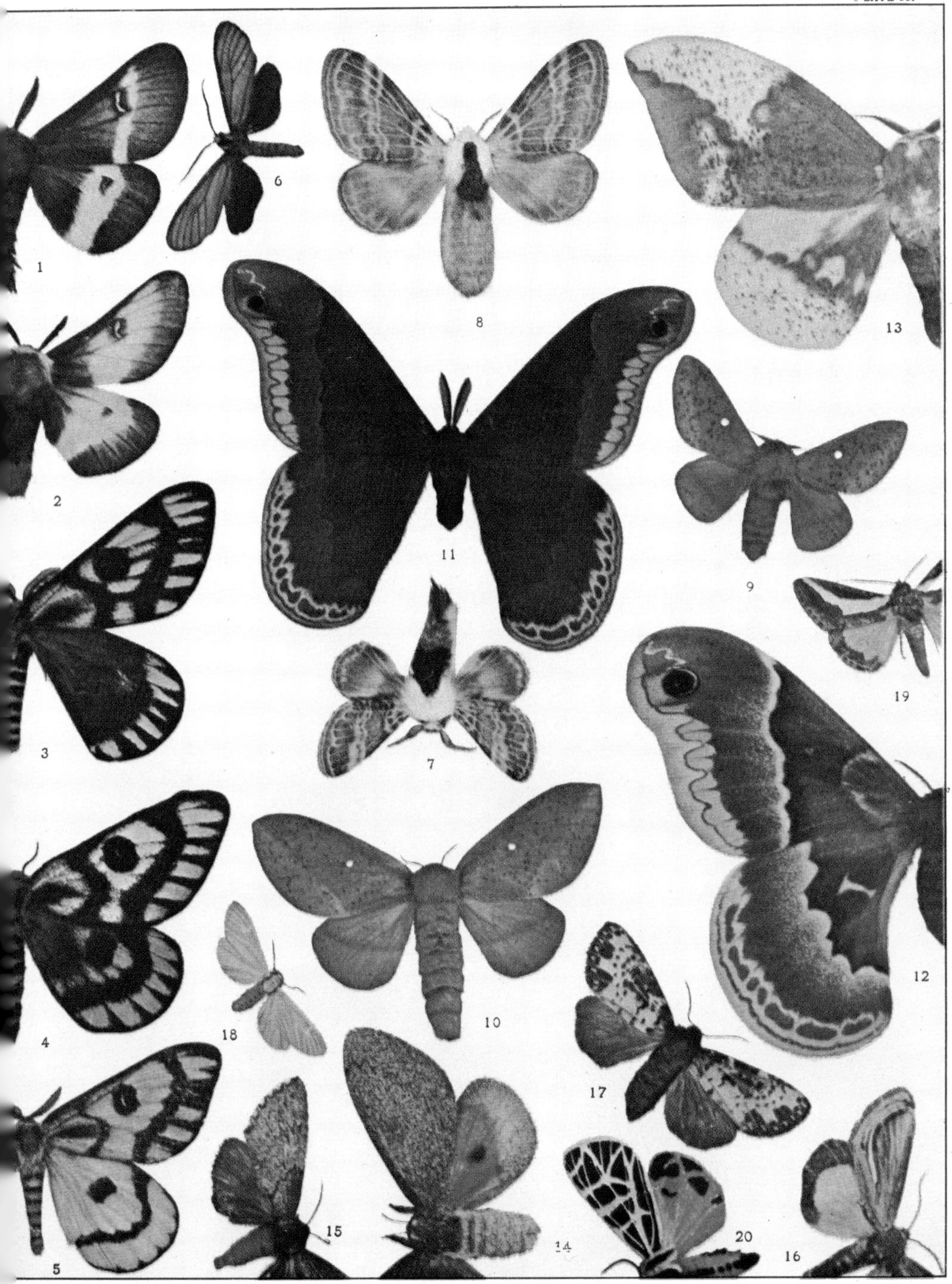
1
2
3
4
5
6
7
8
9
10
11
12
13
14
15
16
17
18
19
20

PLATE XII.

EXPLANATION OF PLATE XIII

(Unless otherwise indicated, the specimens figured are contained in the collection of W. J. Holland.)

1. *Cosmosoma auge* Linnæus, ♂.
2. *Syntomeida epilais* Walker, ♂.
3. *Syntomeida ipomeæ* Harris, ♀.
4. *Triprocris rata* Henry Edwards, ♂.
5. *Triprocris latercula* Henry Edwards, ♂, U. S. N. M.
6. *Pseudomya minima* Grote, ♂, U. S. N. M.
7. *Didasys belæ* Grote,♂,U.S.N.M.
8. *Didasys belæ* Grote, ♀.
9. *Horama texana* Grote, ♂.
10. *Eucereon confine* Herrich-Schaeffer, ♀, U. S. N. M.
11. *Lymire edwardsi* Grote, ♀.
12. *Scepsis fulvicollis* Hübner, ♀.
13. *Scepsis wrighti* Stretch, ♂, type.
14. *Lycomorpha grotei* Packard, ♀.
15. *Lycomorpha pholus* Drury, ♂.
16. *Triprocris constans* Henry Edwards, ♂.
17. *Lycomorpha fulgens* Henry Edwards, ♀.
18. *Ctenucha virginica* Charpentier, ♀.
19. *Ctenucha multifaria* Walker, ♀, U. S. N. M.
20. *Ctenucha venosa* Walker, ♂.
21. *Ctenucha cressonana* Grote, ♂.
22. *Ctenucha rubroscapus* Ménétries, ♀, U. S. N. M.
23. *Dahana atripennis*, Grote, ♂.
24. *Nola ovilla*, Grote ♂.
25. *Celama triquetrana* Fitch, ♂.
26. *Celama pustulata* Walker, ♂, U. S. N. M.
27. *Rœselia fuscula* Grote, ♀.
28. *Ptychoglene phrada* Druce, ♂.
29. *Lexis bicolor* Grote, ♂.
30. *Crambidia casta* Sanborn, ♂.
31. *Crambidia allegheniensis* Holland, ♂.
32. *Nigetia formosalis* Walker, ♂.
33. *Bruceia pulverina* Neumœgen, ♂.
34. *Comacla simplex* Walker, ♂.
35. *Illice subjecta* Walker, ♂.
36. *Illice unifascia* Grote & Robinson, ♂.
37. *Illice nexa* Boisduval, ♂.
38. *Clemensia albata* Packard, ♂, U. S. N. M.
39. *Hæmatomis mexicana* Druce,♂.
40. *Pygoctenucha funerea* Grote, ♀, Acad. Nat. Sc. Phila.
41. *Hypoprepia miniata* Kirby, ♀.
42. *Hypoprepia fucosa* Hübner, ♂.
43. *Kodiosoma eavesi* Stretch, ♂.
44. *Kodiosoma tricolor* Stretch, ♂.
45. *Kodiosoma fulva* Stretch, ♂.

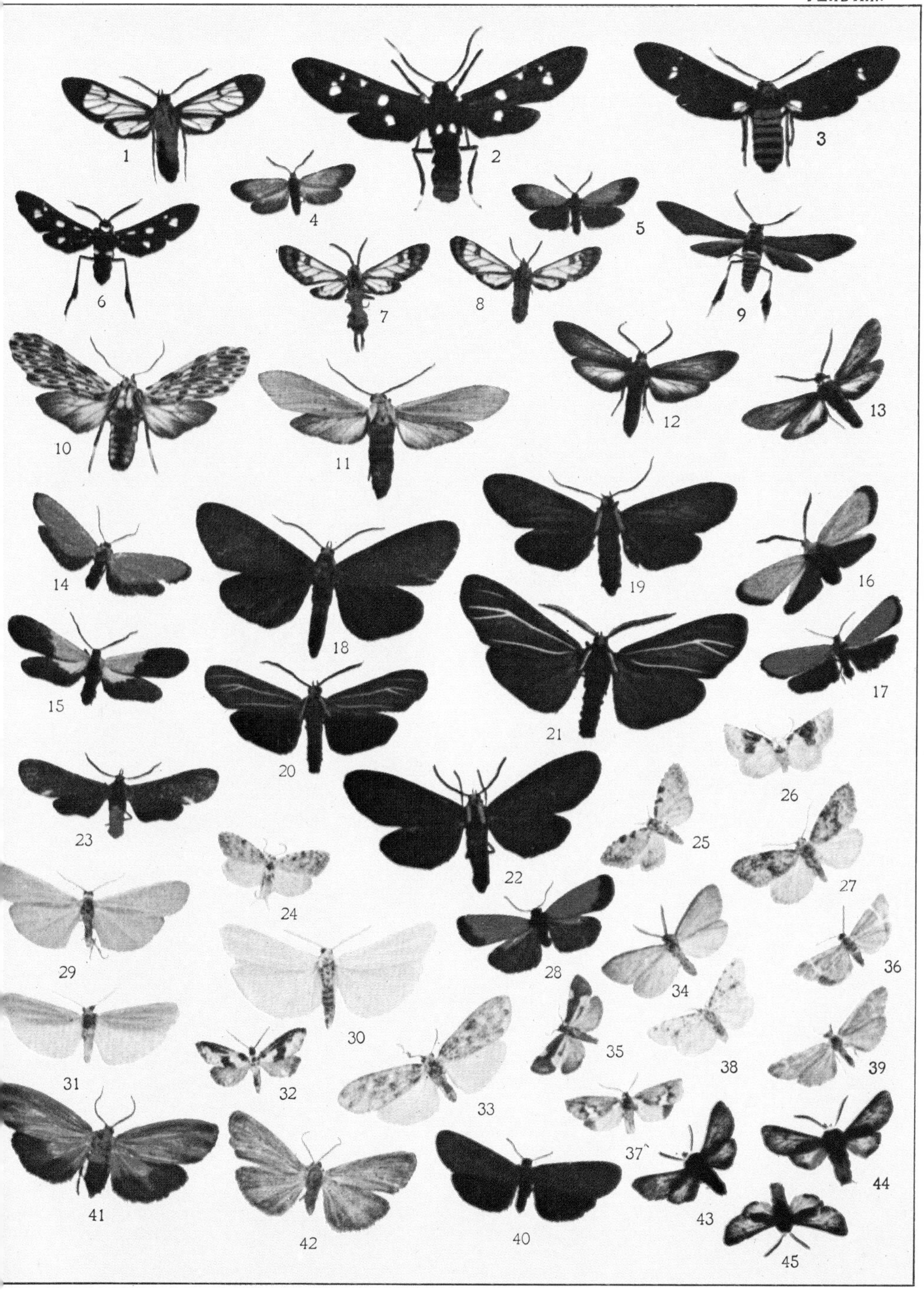
1
2
3
4
5
6
7
8
9
10
11
12
13
14
15
16
17
18
19
20
21
22
23
24
25
26
27
28
29
30
31
32
33
34
35
36
37
38
39
40
41
42
43
44
45

(Unless otherwise indicated, the specimens figured are contained in the collection of W. J. Holland.)

1. *Eupseudosoma involutum* Sepp, ♂, U. S. N. M.
2. *Bertholdia trigona* Grote, ♂.
3. *Pareuchætes insulata* Walker, ♀.
4. *Pareuchætes eglenensis*, Clemens, ♀.
5. *Opharus astur* Cramer, ♂.
6. *Hemihyalea edwardsi* Packard, ♀.
7. *Hemihyalea labecula*, Grote, ♂.
8. *Halisidota argentata* Packard, ♂.
9. *Halisidota argentata* Packard, ♀.
10. *Halisidota caryæ* Harris, ♂.
11. *Halisidota maculata* Harris, ♂.
12. *Halisidota tessellaris* Abbot & Smith, ♂.
13. *Halisidota cinctipes* Grote, ♂.
14. *Æmilia roseata* Walker, ♀.
15. *Æmilia ambigua* Strecker, ♂.
16. *Halisidota longa* Grote, ♂.
17. *Holomelina ostenta* Henry Edwards, ♂.
18. *Holomelina quinaria* Grote, ♂.
19. *Holomelina brevicornis* Walker, ♀.
20. *Holomelina immaculata* Reakirt, ♂.
21. *Holomelina brevicornis* Walker, ♀, var.
22. *Holomelina diminutiva* Græf, ♂.
23. *Holomelina opella* Grote, ♂.
24. *Holomelina belmaria* Ehrman, ♀, paratype.
25. *Leptarctia californiæ* Walker, ♀.
26. *Leptarctia dimidiata* Stretch, ♂.
27. *Leptarctia decia* Boisduval, ♂.
28. *Leptarctia lena* Boisduval, ♂.
29. *Neoarctia beani* Neumœgen, ♀, U. S. N. M.
30. *Neoarctia brucei* Henry Edwards, ♂.
31. *Phragmatobia fuliginosa* Linnæus, ♀.
32. *Diacrisia rubra* Neumœgen, ♀. U. S. N. M.
33. *Diacrisia vagans* Boisduval, ♂.
34. *Diacrisia vagans* Boisduval, ♀.

PLATE XIV.

EXPLANATION OF PLATE XV

(Unless otherwise indicated, the specimens figured are contained in the collection of W. J. Holland.)

1. *Apantesis rectilinea* French, ♀, U. S. N. M.
2. *Arctia caia*, var. *wiskotti* Staudinger, ♀.
3. *Apantesis determinata* Neumœgen, ♂.
4. *Apantesis proxima* Guérin-Méneville, ♀.
5. *Arctia caia* Linnæus, ♀.
6. *Apantesis phalerata* Harris, ♀.
7. *Apantesis nevadensis* Grote & Robinson, ♂.
8. *Apantesis persephone* Grote, ♂.
9. *Apantesis virguncula* Kirby, ♂.
10. *Apantesis persephone* Grote, ♀.
11. *Apantesis virgo* Linnæus, ♂.
12. *Apantesis figurata* Drury, ♀, U. S. N. M.
13. *Apantesis parthenice* Kirby, ♂.
14. *Apantesis phyllira* Drury, ♂.
15. *Apantesis arge* Drury, ♂.
16. *Apantesis virguncula* Kirby, ♂, var.
17. *Apantesis michabo* Grote, ♀.
18. *Platyprepia virginalis* Boisduval, ♂.
19. *Platyprepia virginalis* Boisduval, ♀.
20. *Apantesis achaia* Grote & Robinson, ♂.
21. *Apantesis radians* Walker, ♀.
22. *Apantesis vittata* Fabricius, ♀.
23. *Apantesis radians* Walker, ♂.
24. *Apantesis achaia* Grote & Robinson, ♂.
25. *Apantesis vittata* Fabricius, ♂.
26. *Hyphantria cunea* Drury, var. *pallida* Packard, ♂.
27. *Utetheisa bella* Linnæus, ♀.

PLATE XV.

EXPLANATION OF PLATE XVI

(Unless otherwise indicated, the specimens figured are contained in the collection of W. J. Holland.)

1. *Arachnis aulæa* Geyer, ♀.
2. *Arachnis picta* Packard, ♂.
3. *Arachnis zuni* Neumœgen, ♀, U. S. N. M.
4. *Euerythra trimaculata* Smith,♂, U. S. N. M.
5. *Mænas vestalis* Packard, ♂.
6. *Diacrisia latipennis* Stretch, ♂.
7. *Diacrisia virginica* Fabricius,♂.
8. *Estigmene congrua* Walker, ♂.
9. *Hyphantria cunea* Drury, ♂.
10. *Hyphantria cunea* Drury, ♂, var. *punctatissima*, Abbot & Smith.
11. *Estigmene acræa* Drury, ♂.
12. *Estigmene acræa* Drury, ♀.
13. *Isia isabella* Abbot & Smith, ♀.
14. *Acoloithus falsarius* Clemens,♂.
15. *Turuptiana permaculata* Packard, ♂.
16. *Ecpantheria deflorata* Fabricius, ♂.
17. *Pygarctia elegans* Stretch, ♂.
18. *Pygarctia spraguei* Grote, ♂.

19. *Euchætias oregonensis* Stretch, ♂.
20. *Hyphoraia parthenos* Harris, ♀, U. S. N. M.
21. *Euchætias egle* Drury, ♀.
22. *Euverna clio* Packard, ♀.
23. *Seirarctia echo* Abbot & Smith, ♀.
24. *Calidota strigosa*, Walker ♂.
25. *Parasemia plantaginis* Linnæus, ♂, U. S. N. M.
26. *Parasemia plantaginis* var. *geometrica*, Grote, ♂.
27. *Pygarctia abdominalis* Grote, ♀, U. S. N. M.
28. *Apantesis quenseli* Paykull, ♂.
29. *Apantesis nevadensis* Grote & Robinson, ♂, U. S. N. M.
30. *Apantesis oithona* Strecker, ♂, Engel Collection.
31. *Apantesis blakei* Grote, ♂, U. S. N. M.
32. *Apantesis proxima* var. *autholea*, Boisduval, ♂.

EMENDATIONS BY A. E. BROWER

9. *Hyphantria textor* Harris, ♂.

PLATE XVI.

(Except when otherwise indicated, the specimens figured are contained in the collection of W. J. Holland.)

1. *Haploa militaris* Harris, ♀.
2. *Haploa colona* Hübner, ♀.
3. *Haploa vestalis* Packard, ♂.
4. *Haploa militaris* Harris, ♂.
5. *Haploa consita* Walker, ♂.
6. *Haploa confusa* Lyman, ♂.
7. *Haploa clymene* Brown, ♂.
8. *Utetheisa ornatrix* Linnæus, ♂.
9. *Haploa dyari* Merrick, ♂, Merrick Collection.
10. *Haploa militaris* Harris, ♂, Merrick Collection.
11. *Copidryas gloveri* Grote & Robinson, ♂.
12. *Fenaria sevorsa* Grote, ♀.
13. *Androloma maccullochi* Kirby, ♂.
14. *Alypia ridingsi* Grote, ♂.
15. *Alypia mariposa* Grote & Robinson, ♀.
16. *Alypia langtoni* Couper, ♂.
17. *Alypia langtoni* Couper, ♀.
18. *Alypia wittfeldi* Henry Edwards, ♂.
19. *Alypia wittfeldi* Henry Edwards, ♀.
20. *Alypia octomaculata* Fabricius, ♂.
21. *Alypia octomaculata* Fabricius, ♀.
22. *Alypiodes bimaculata* Herrich-Schæffer, ♂.
23. *Euthisanotia grata* Fabricius, ♂.
24. *Euthisanotia unio* Hübner, ♂.
25. *Baileya ophthalmica* Guenée, ♀.
26. *Baileya doubledayi* Guenée, ♂.
27. *Baileya australis* Grote, ♂.
28. *Aleptina inca*, Dyar ♂.
29. *Charadra decora* Morrison, ♂.
30. *Panthea portlandia* Grote, ♂, U. S. N. M.
31. *Panthea furcilla* Packard, ♂, U. S. N. M.
32. *Feralia jocosa* Guenée, ♂.

EMENDATIONS BY A. E. BROWER

23. *Euthisanotia unio* Hübner, ♂.
24. *Euthisanotia grata* Fabricius, ♂.

PLATE XVII.

EXPLANATION OF PLATE XVIII

(Except when otherwise indicated, the specimens figured are contained in the collection of W. J. Holland.)

1. *Diphthera fallax* Herrich-Schæffer, ♀.
2. *Charadra illudens* Walker, ♀.
3. *Raphia frater* Grote, ♀, U. S. N. M.
4. *Charadra deridens* Guenée, ♀.
5. *Charadra illudens* Walker, ♂.
6. *Arsilonche albovenosa* Gœze, ♂.
7. *Merolonche lupini* Grote, ♂,
   Merrick Collection.
8. *Apatela morula* Grote, ♂.
9. *Apatela lobeliæ* Guenée, ♂.
10. *Apatela furcifera* Guenée, ♂.
11. *Apatela grisea* Walker, ♀.
12. *Apatela americana* Harris, ♀.
13. *Apatela innotata* Guenée, ♂.
14. *Apatela lepusculina* Guenée, ♂.
15. *Apatela quadrata* Grote, ♀.
16. *Apatela radcliffei* Harvey, ♂.
17. *Apatela dactylina* Grote, ♂.
18. *Apatela oblinita* Abbot & Smith, ♀.
19. *Apatela connecta* Grote, ♂.
20. *Apatela noctivaga* Grote, ♀.
21. *Apatela impressa* Walker, ♂.
22. *Apatela impleta* Walker, ♀.
23. *Apatela brumosa* Guenée, ♂.
24. *Apatela xyliniformis* Guenée, ♂,
   Merrick Collection.
25. *Apatela vinnula* Grote, ♀.
26. *Apatela superans* Guenée, ♀.

EMENDATIONS BY A. E. BROWER

16. *Apatela albarufa* Grote, ♂.
24. *Apatela lithospila* Grote, ♂.

PLATE XVIII.

EXPLANATION OF PLATE XIX

(Except when otherwise indicated, the specimens are contained in the collection of W. J. Holland.)

1. *Apatela fragilis* Guenée, ♂.
2. *Ciris wilsoni* Grote, ♂.
3. *Demas propinquilinea* Grote, ♀, U. S. N. M.
4. *Harrisimemna trisignata* Walker, ♀.
5. *Apatela interrupta* Guenée, ♀.
6. *Apatela hasta* Guenée, ♀.
7. *Jaspidea lepidula* Grote, ♂.
8. *Jaspidea teratophora* Herrich-Schæffer, ♂.
9. *Microcœlia diphtheroides* Guenée, ♂.
10. *Microcœlia diphtheroides* var. *obliterata*, Grote, ♂.
11. *Polygrammate hebraicum* Hübner, ♂.
12. *Cyathissa percara* Morrison, ♂, U. S. N. M.
13. *Chytonix palliatricula* Guenée, ♂.
14. *Chytonix palliatricula* Guenée, var., ♂.
15. *Catabena lineolata* Walker, ♂.
16. *Acopa carina* Harvey, ♂, U. S. N. M.
17. *Crambodes talidiformis* Guenée, ♂.
18. *Balsa malana* Fitch, ♂.

19. *Anorthodes prima* Smith, ♂.
20. *Orthodes vecors* Guenée, ♂.
21. *Platysenta videns* Guenée, ♀.
22. *Carádrina meralis* Morrison, ♂.
23. *Platysenta albipuncta* Smith, ♂.
24. *Hadenella pergentilis* Grote, ♀. U. S. N. M.
25. *Hadenella subjuncta* Smith, ♂.
26. *Caradrina extimia* Walker, ♂.
27. *Caradrina punctivena* Smith, ♂.
28. *Caradrina spilomela* Walker, ♂.
29. *Caradrina multifera* Walker, ♀.
30. *Perigea xanthioides* Guenée, ♂.
31. *Perigea vecors* Guenée, ♀.
32. *Oligia festivoides* Guenée, ♂.
33. *Oligia grata* Hübner, ♂.
34. *Oligia fuscimacula* Grote, ♂.
35. *Hillia algens* Grote, ♂.
36. *Hadena passer* Guenée, ♂.
37. *Hadena burgessi* Morrison, ♂.
38. *Hadena lateritia* Hübner, ♂.
39. *Hadena dubitans* Walker, ♀.
40. *Hadena ducta* Grote, ♀.
41. *Mamestra juncimacula* Smith, ♂.
42. *Hadena nigrior* Smith, ♀.
43. *Hadena verbascoides* Guenée, ♀.
44. *Hadena devastatrix* Brace, ♂.
45. *Hadena arctica* Boisduval, ♂.

EMENDATIONS BY A. E. BROWER

19. *Anorthodes tarda* Guenée, ♂.

Plate XIX

(Unless otherwise indicated, the specimens figured are contained in the collection of W. J. Holland.)

1. *Fishia yosemitæ* Grote, ♂.
2. *Hadena bridghami* Grote & Robinson, ♂.
3. *Hadena characta* Grote, ♂.
4. *Hadena versuta* Smith, ♂.
5. *Hadena lignicolor* Guenée, ♂.
6. *Hadena claudens* Walker, ♂.
7. *Hadena transfrons* Neumœgen, ♀.
8. *Hadena mactata* Guenée, ♀.
9. *Hadena basilinea* Fabricius, ♂.
10. *Hadena fractilinea* Grote, ♂.
11. *Hadena vultuosa* Grote, ♂.
12. *Hadena violacea* Grote, ♀.
13. *Hadena chlorostigma* Harvey, ♂.
14. *Hadena modica* Guenée, ♂.
15. *Hadena miseloides* Guenée, ♀.
16. *Hadena turbulenta* Hübner, ♀.
17. *Calophasia strigata* Smith, ♀, U. S. N. M.
18. *Macronoctua onusta* Grote, ♀, U. S. N. M.
19. *Hadena vinela* Smith, ♂.
20. *Hadena occidens* Grote, ♂, U. S. N. M.
21. *Polia theodori* Grote, ♂.
22. *Polia diversilineata* Grote, ♂.
23. *Hyppa xylinoides* Guenée, ♀.
24. *Dryobota illocata* Walker, ♀.
25. *Valeria opina* Grote, ♂, U. S. N. M.
26. *Euplexia lucipara* Linnæus, ♀.
27. *Trachea delicata* Grote, ♂.
28. *Dipterygia scabriuscula* Linnæus, ♀.
29. *Actinotia ramosula* Guenée, ♀.
30. *Pyrophila pyramidoides* Guenée, ♂.
31. *Pyrophila tragopoginis* Linnæus, ♂.
32. *Pyrophila glabella*, Morrison, ♂.
33. *Helotropha reniformis* Grote, ♀.
34. *Helotropha reniformis* var. *atra.* Grote, ♀.
35. *Prodenia ornithogalli* Guenée, ♀.
36. *Prodenia commelinæ* Abbot & Smith, ♀.
37. *Laphygma frugiperda* Abbot & Smith, ♂.
38. *Lussa nigroguttata* Grote, ♂, U. S. N. M.
39. *Pseudanarta flava* Grote, ♂.
40. *Pseudanarta singula* Grote, ♂.
41. *Pseudanarta falcata* Neumœgen, ♂.

EMENDATIONS BY A. E. BROWER

9. *Hadena cerivana* Smith, ♂.

PLATE XX

(Except when otherwise indicated the specimens are contained in the collection of W. J. Holland.)

1. *Homohadena badistriga* Grote, ♂, U. S. N. M.
2. *Magusa dissidens* Felder, ♂.
3. *Oncocnemis atrifasciata* Morrison, ♀.
4. *Oncocnemis dayi* Grote, ♂.
5. *Oncocnemis tenuifascia* Smith, ♂.
6. *Oncocnemis iricolor* Smith, ♀.
7. *Oncocnemis chandleri* Grote, ♀.
8. *Oncocnemis occata* Grote, ♀.
9. *Oncocnemis cibalis* Grote, ♂.
10. *Adita chionanthi* Abbot & Smith, ♂, U. S. N. M.
11. *Lepipolys perscripta* Guenée, ♀, U. S. N. M.
12. *Copipanolis cubilis* Grote, ♀, U. S. N. M.
13. *Eutolype bombyciformis* Smith, ♀.
14. *Psaphidia grotei* Morrison, ♀, U. S. N. M.
15. *Psaphidia resumens* Walker, ♀.
16. *Fota armata* Grote, ♂.
17. *Fota minorata* Grote, ♂.
18. *Rhynchagrotis gilvipennis* Grote, ♀.
19. *Rhynchagrotis anchocelioides* Guenée, ♀.
20. *Rhynchagrotis alternata* Grote, ♀.
21. *Rhynchagrotis placida* Grote, ♂, red variety.
22. *Rhynchagrotis rufipectus* Morrison, ♀.
23. *Rhychagrotis placida* Grote, ♂.
24. *Adelphagrotis prasina* Fabricius, ♀.
25. *Platagrotis pressa* Grote, ♂.
26. *Eueretagrotis sigmoides* Guenée, ♂.
27. *Eueretagrotis perattenta* Grote, ♀.
28. *Semiophora opacifrons* Grote, ♀.
29. *Semiophora elimata* Guenée, ♂.
30. *Semiophora elimata* var. *janualis* Grote, ♂.
31. *Pachnobia salicarum* Walker, ♂.
32. *Pachnobia littoralis* Packard, ♂.
33. *Semiophora tenebrifera* Walker, ♂.
34. *Noctua normaniana* Grote, ♂.
35. *Noctua bicarnea* Guenée, ♀.
36. *Agrotis geniculata* Grote & Robinson, ♀.
37. *Agrotis badinodis* Grote, ♂.
38. *Peridroma simplaria* Morrison, ♀.
39. *Peridroma incivis* Guenée, ♂.
40. *Peridro masaucia* Hübner, ♀.
41. *Peridroma astricta* Morrison, ♂.
42. *Peridroma occulta* Linnæus, ♀.
43. *Peridroma nigra* Smith, ♂.

PLATE XXI

EXPLANATION OF PLATE XXII

(Except when otherwise indicated the specimens figured are contained in the collection of W. J. Holland.)

1. *Noctua c-nigrum* Linnæus, ♀.
2. *Noctua phyllophora* Grote, ♀.
3. *Noctua oblata* Morrison, ♂.
4. *Noctua fennica* Tauscher, ♂.
5. *Noctua jucunda* Walker, ♀.
6. *Noctua plecta* Linnæus, ♂.
7. *Noctua collaris* Grote & Robinson, ♂.
8. *Noctua lubricans* Guenée, ♂.
9. *Noctua haruspica* Grote, ♀.
10. *Noctua substrigata* Smith, ♂.
11. *Noctua atricincta* Smith, ♂.
12. *Noctua juncta* Grote, ♂.
13. *Noctua calgary* Smith, ♂.
14. *Noctua clandestina* Harris, ♀.
15. *Chorizagrotis introferens* Grote, ♀.
16. *Rhizagrotis proclivis* Smith, ♀.
17. *Chorizagrotis balanitis* Grote, ♂.
18. *Noctua havilæ* Grote, ♂.
19. *Feltia gladiaria* Morrison, ♀.
20. *Feltia herilis* Grote, ♂.
21. *Feltia subgothica* Haworth, ♂.
22. *Chorizagrotis inconcinna* Harvey, ♀.
23. *Feltia volubilis* Harvey, ♀.
24. *Porosagrotis tripars* Grote, ♂.
25. *Porosagrotis vetusta* Walker, ♂.
26. *Feltia venerabilis* Walker, ♂.
27. *Euxoa brevipennis* Smith, ♀.
28. *Feltia annexa* Treitschke, ♀.
29. *Porosagrotis dædalus* Smith, ♂
30. *Euxoa quadridentata* Grote & Robinson, ♂.
31. *Porosagrotis fusca* Boisduval, ♂.
32. *Feltia malefida* Guenée, ♀.
33. *Porosagrotis rileyana* Morrison, ♀.
34. *Euxoa olivalis* Grote, ♂.
35. *Euxoa velleripennis* Grote, ♂.
36. *Euxoa perpolita* Morrison, ♂.
37. *Porosagrotis tripars* Walker, ♂.
38. *Euxoa flavidens* Smith, ♂.
39. *Euxoa detersa* Walker, ♂.
40. *Euxoa messoria* Harris, ♂.
41. *Hadena semilunata* Grote, ♂.

42. *Feltia vancouverensis* Morrison, ♀.

EMENDATIONS BY A. E. BROWER

21. *Feltia ducens* Walker, ♂.
42. *Feltia dissona* Möschler, ♀.

PLATE XXII

(Unless otherwise indicated, the specimens figured are contained in the collection of W. J. Holland.)

1. *Cerapoda stylata* Smith, ♂, U. S. N. M.
2. *Epidemas cinerea* Smith, ♀, U. S. N. M.
3. *Euxoa insulsa* Walker, ♀.
4. *Euxoa tessellata* Harris, ♂.
5. *Euxoa dissona* Mœschler, ♀.
6. *Euxoa titubatis* Smith, ♂.
7. *Euxoa albipennis* Grote, ♂.
8. *Euxoa basalis* Grote, ♂.
9. *Euxoa redimicula* Morrsion, ♂.
10. *Euxoa ochrogaster* Guenée, ♂.
11. *Euxoa furtivus* Smith, ♂.
12. *Euxoa obeliscoides* Guenée, ♀.
13. *Euxoa lutulenta* Smith, ♂.
14. *Richia aratrix* Harvey, ♂.
15. *Richia parentalis* Grote, ♂.
16. *Anytus privatus* Walker, ♂.
17. *Anytus obscurus* Smith, ♂.
18. *Agrotiphila incognita* Smith, ♂.
19. *Ufeus plicatus* Grote, ♂.
20. *Ufeus satyricus* Grote, ♂.
21. *Mamestra meditata* Grote, ♀.
22. *Mamestra lustralis* Grote, ♀.
23. *Mamestra farnhami* Grote, ♀.
24. *Mamestra detracta* Walker, ♂.
25. *Mamestra radix* Walker, ♂.
26. *Mamestra purpurissata* Grote, ♂.
27. *Mamestra subjuncta* Grote & Robinson, ♂.
28. *Mamestra lubens* Grote, ♂.
29. *Mamestra trifolii* Rottemburg, ♂.
30. *Mamestra rosea* Harvey, ♀.
31. *Mamestra congermana* Morrison, ♀.
32. *Mamestra imbrifera* Guenée, ♀.
33. *Mamestra nevadæ* Grote, ♀.
34. *Mamestra picta* Harris, ♂.
35. *Mamestra renigera* Stephens, ♀.
36. *Mamestra liquida* Grote, ♀.
37. *Mamestra olivacea* Morrison, ♂.
38. *Mamestra adjuncta* Boisduval, ♀.
39. *Mamestra lilacina* Harvey, ♂.
40. *Mamestra latex* Guenée, ♀.
41. *Mamestra grandis* Boisduval, ♂.

EMENDATIONS BY A. E. BROWER

22. *Mamestra legitima* Grote, ♀.

PLATE XXIII

(Except when otherwise indicated, the specimens figured are contained in the collection of W. J. Holland.)

1. *Mamestra laudabilis* Guenée, ♀.
2. *Mamestra lorea* Guenée, ♂.
3. *Mamestra rugosa* Morrison, ♂.
4. *Mamestra erecta* Walker, ♂.
5. *Mamestra anguina* Grote, ♀.
6. *Mamestra vicina* Grote, ♀.
7. *Mamestra neoterica* Smith, ♂.
8. *Mamestra negussa* Smith, ♀.
9. *Admetovis oxymorus* Grote, ♂.
10. *Barathra occidentata* Grote, ♀.
11. *Dargida procinctus* Grote, ♂.
12. *Neuronia americana* Smith, ♂.
13. *Morrisonia sectilis* Guenée, ♂.
14. *Morrisonia sectilis* var. *vomerina*, Grote, ♀.
15. *Morrisonia confusa* Hübner, ♂.
16. *Ulolonche modesta* Morrison, ♂.
17. *Xylomiges simplex* Walker, ♂.
18. *Xylomiges patalis* Grote, ♀.
19. *Xylomiges perlubens* Grote, ♂.
20. *Xylomiges dolosa* Grote, ♂.
21. *Xylomiges pulchella* Smith, ♂.
22. *Xylomiges cognata* Smith, ♂.
23. *Xylomiges indurata* Smith, ♂.
24. *Scotogramma submarina* Grote, ♂.
25. *Scotogramma infuscata* Smith, ♂, U. S. N. M.

26. *Scotogramma inconcinna* Smith, ♂, U. S. N. M.
27. *Anarta melanopa* Thunberg, ♂.
28. *Anarta cordigera* Thunberg, ♂.
29. *Anarta richardsoni* Curtis, ♀.
30. *Anarta schœnherri* Zetterstedt, ♂.
31. *Anarta impingens* Walker, ♂.
32. *Trichoclea antica* Smith, ♂, U. S. N. M.
33. *Nephelodes minians* Guenée, ♂.
34. *Heliophila albilinea* Hübner, ♂.
35. *Heliophila subpunctata* Harvey, ♀.
36. *Heliophila heterodoxa* Smith, ♂.
37. *Orthodes crenulata* Butler, ♂.
38. *Orthodes cynica* Guenée, ♂.
39. *Heliophila multilinea* Walker, ♂.
40. *Heliophila unipuncta* Haworth, ♂.
41. *Heliophila minorata* Smith, ♂.
42. *Heliophila commoides* Guenée, ♂.
43. *Crocigrapha normani* Grote, ♂.
44. *Himella contrahens* Walker, ♀.
45. *Orthodes puerilis* Grote, ♂.
46. *Zosteropoda hirtipes* Grote, ♂, U. S. N. M.

47. *Heliophila pseudargyria* Guenée, ♀.

EMENDATIONS BY A. E. BROWER

34. *Heliophila diffusa* Walker, ♂.

PLATE XXIV

(Except when otherwise indicated, the specimens figured are in the collection of W. J. Holland.)

1. *Graphiphora culea* Guenée, ♀.
2. *Graphiphora oviduca* Guenée, ♂.
3. *Graphiphora alia* Guenée, ♀.
4. *Graphiphora garmani* Grote, ♂, Merrick Collection.
5. *Stretchia muricina* Grote, ♂.
6. *Perigonica fulminans* Smith, ♂.
7. *Tricholita signata*, Walker, ♂.
8. *Cleosiris populi* Strecker, ♀, U. S. N. M
9. *Xylina petulca* Grote, ♀.
10. *Xylina innominata* Smith, ♂.
11. *Pleroma obliquata* Smith, ♂, U. S. N. M.
12. *Lithomoia germana* Morrison, ♀.
13. *Xylina disposita* Morrison, ♀.
14. *Homoglæa carbonaria* Harvey, ♀.
15. *Xylina tepida* Grote, ♂.
16. *Xylina unimoda* Lintner, ♂.
17. *Xylina laticinerea* Grote, ♂.
18. *Xylina thaxteri* Grote, ♀.
19. *Xylina baileyi* Grote, ♀.
20. *Xylina pexata* Grote, ♀.
21. *Xylina capax* Grote & Robinson.
22. *Litholomia nàpæa* Morrison, ♂.
23. *Calocampa curvimacula* Morrison, ♂.
24. *Calocampa nupera* Lintner, ♂.
25. *Rancora solidaginis* Behr, ♀.
26. *Cucullia speyeri* Lintner, ♂.
27. *Cucullia asteroides* Guenée, ♂.
28. *Copicucullia propinqua* Smith, ♀.
29. *Cucullia convexipennis* Grote & Robinson, ♂.
30. *Cucullia intermedia* Speyer, ♀.
31. *Lathosea ursina* Smith, ♀, U. S. N. M.
32. *Lathosea pullata* Grote, ♂, U. S. N. M.
33. *Nonagria oblonga* Grote, ♂, U. S. N. M.
34. *Nonagria subflava* Grote, ♀.
35. *Ommatostola lintneri* Grote, ♂, U. S. N. M.
36. *Sphida obliqua* Walker, ♀.

EMENDATIONS BY A. E. BROWER

3. *Graphiphora hibisci* Guenée, ♀.
9. *Xylina hemina* var. *lignicosta* Franclemont, ♀.

PLATE XXV

EXPLANATION OF PLATE XXVI

(Except when otherwise indicated, the specimens figured are contained in the collection of W. J. Holland.)

1. *Achatodes zeæ*, Harris ♂, U. S. N. M.
2. *Gortyna nictitans* Borkhausen, ♂.
3. *Gortyna velata*, Walker, ♂.
4. *Gortyna immanis*, Guenée, ♀.
5. *Papaipema inquæsita* Grote & Robinson, ♂.
6. *Papaipema cataphracta* Grote, ♂.
7. *Papaipema purpurifascia* Grote & Robinson, ♂.
8. *Papaipema nitela*, var. *nebris*, Guenée, ♂.
9. *Papaipema nitela* Guenée, ♂.
10. *Papaipema cerussata* Grote & Robinson, ♀.
11. *Papaipema marginidens* Guenée, ♀.
12. *Papaipema necopina* Grote, ♀.
13. *Gortyna obliqua* Harvey, ♂.
14. *Papaipema furcata* Smith, ♀.
15. *Pyrrhia umbra* Hüfnagel, ♀.
16. *Xanthia flavago* Fabricius, ♂.
17. *Jodia rufago* Hübner, ♂, U. S. N. M.
18. *Trigonophora v-brunneum* Grote, ♂.
19. *Brotolomia iris* Guenée, ♀.
20. *Conservula anodonta* Guenée, ♀, U. S. N. M.
21. *Eucirrœdia pampina* Guenée, ♀.
22. *Scoliopteryx libatrix* Linnæus, ♂.
23. *Chœphora fungorum* Grote & Robinson, ♀.
24. *Pseudoglæa blanda* Grote, ♂, U. S. N. M.
25. *Anchocelis digitalis* Grote, ♂, U. S. N. M.
26. *Tapinostola variana* Morrison, ♂, U. S. N. M.
27. *Fagitana obliqua* Smith, ♂.
28. *Fagitana littera* Guenée, ♀.
29. *Orthosia bicolorago* Guenée, ♂.
30. *Orthosia helva* Grote, ♀.
31. *Parastichtis discivaria* Walker, ♂.
32. *Cosmia paleacea* Esper, ♂.
33. *Scopelosoma moffatiana* Grote, ♂.
34. *Scopelosoma ceromatica* Grote, ♀.
35. *Scopelosoma walkeri* Grote, ♂.
36. *Glæa sericea* Morrison, ♂.
37. *Glæa inulta* Grote, ♂.
38. *Glæa viatica* Grote, ♂.
39. *Homoglæa hircina* Morrison, ♂.
40. *Epiglæa decliva* Grote, ♂.
41. *Epiglæa pastillicans* Morrison, ♂.
42. *Scopelosoma devia* Grote, ♂.

EMENDATIONS BY A. E. BROWER

5. *Papaipema impecuniosa* Grote, ♂.
7. *Papaipema leucostigma* Harris, ♂.
8. *Papaipema nebris*, var. *nitela*, Guenée, ♂.
9. *Papaipema nebris* Guenée, ♂.
33. *Scopelosoma hesperidago* Guenée, ♀.
41. *Epiglæa tremula* Harvey, ♂.

PLATE XXVI

(Except when otherwise indicated, the specimens figured are contained in the collection of W. J. Holland.)

1. *Calymnia orina* Guenée, ♂.
2. *Zotheca tranquilla* Grote, ♂.
3. *Ipimorpha pleonectusa* Grote, ♂.
4. *Atethmia subusta* Hübner, ♂, U. S. N. M.
5. *Atethmia rectifascia* Grote, ♂, U. S. N. M.
6. *Trichocosmia inornata* Grote, ♂, U. S. N. M.
7. *Antaplaga dimidiata* Grote, ♂.
8. *Grotella dis* Grote, ♂, U. S. N. M.
9. *Nycterophæta luna* Morrison, ♀.
10. *Copablepharon grandis* Strecker, ♂.
11. *Copablepharon longipenne* Grote, ♀, U. S. N. M.
12. *Copablepharon album* Harvey, ♂.
13. *Thyreion rosea* Smith, ♀, U. S. N. M.
14. *Chloridea virescens* Fabricius, ♂.
15. *Heliocheilus paradoxus* Grote, ♂.
16. *Heliothis scutosus* Fabricius, ♂.
17. *Heliothis armiger* Hübner, ♂.
18. *Rhodophora gauræ* Abbot & Smith, ♂.
19. *Rhodophora florida* Guenée, ♂.
20. *Rhodophora citronellus* Grote & Robinson, ♂.
21. *Triocnemis saporis* Grote, ♂, U. S. N. M.
22. *Rhododipsa volupia* Fitch, ♂.
23. *Rhododipsa miniana* Grote, ♂.
24. *Rhododipsa masoni* Smith, ♀.
25. *Pseudotamila vanella* Grote, ♂, U. S. N. M.
26. *Porrima regia* Strecker, ♀.
27. *Porrima gloriosa* Strecker, ♀.
28. *Schinia chrysellus* Grote, ♀.
29. *Schinia aleucis* Harvey, ♂.
30. *Schinia cumatilis* Grote, ♂.
31. *Schinia packardi*, ♂.
32. *Schinia simplex* Smith, ♀.
33. *Schinia nundina* Drury, ♂.
34. *Schinia acutilinea* Grote, ♂.
35. *Schinia trifascia* Hübner, ♀.
36. *Schinia roseitincta* Harvey, ♂.
37. *Schinia brucei* Smith, ♂.
38. *Schinia lynx* Guenée, ♂.
39. *Schinia tertia* Grote, ♀.
40. *Schinia brevis* Grote, ♂.
41. *Schinia jaguarina* Guenée, ♂.
42. *Schinia arcifera* Guenée, ♀.
43. *Schinia saturata* Grote, ♂.
44. *Schinia marginata* Haworth, ♂.
45. *Schinia albafascia* Smith, ♀.
46. *Schinia thoreaui* Grote & Robinson, ♂.
47. *Dasyspoudæa lucens* Morrison, ♂.
48. *Dasyspoudæa meadi* Grote, ♂.
49. *Pseudanthæcia tumida* Grote, ♂.
50. *Stylopoda cephalica* Smith, ♀.
51. *Melicleptria sueta* Grote, ♂.
52. *Melicleptria pulchripennis* Grote, ♂.
53. *Rhodosea julia* Grote, ♀, U. S. N. M.
54. *Melaporphyria oregona* Henry Edwards, ♂.
55. *Dysocnemis belladonna* Henry Edwards, ♂.
56. *Heliaca diminutiva* Grote, ♂.
57. *Axenus arvalis* Grote, ♂.
58. *Heliolonche modicella* Grote, ♀.
59. *Omia nesæa* Smith, ♂, U. S. N. M.
60. *Xanthothrix neumægeni* Henry Edwards, ♀.
61. *Heliophana mitis* Grote, ♂.

PLATE XXVII

(Unless otherwise indicated, the specimens figured are contained in the collection of W. J. Holland.)

1. *Noropsis hieroglyphica* Cramer, ♂.
2. *Cirrhophanus triangulifer* Grote, ♂, U. S. N. M.
3. *Stibadium spumosum* Grote, ♀.
4. *Fala ptychophora* Grote, ♂, U. S. N. M.
5. *Stiria rugifrons* Grote, ♂.
6. *Plusiodonta compressipalpis* Guenée, ♂.
7. *Basilodes pepita* Guenée, ♀.
8. *Calpe canadensis* Bethune, ♀, U. S. N. M.
9. *Plagiomimicus pityochromus* Grote, ♀.
10. *Gonodonta unica* Neumœgen, ♀, U. S. N. M.
11. *Narthecophora pulverea* Smith, ♀, U. S. N. M.
12. *Polychrysia moneta* Fabricius, var. *esmerelda*, Oberthür, ♀.
13. *Panchrysia purpurigera* Walker, ♂.
14. *Polychrysia formosa* Grote, ♂.
15. *Euchalcia putnami* Grote, ♂.
16. *Plusia ærea* Hübner, ♂.
17. *Plusia æroides* Grote, ♀.
18. *Eosphoropteryx thyatiroides* Guenée, ♂.
19. *Autographa bimaculata* Stephens, ♂.
20. *Autographa verruca* Fabricius, ♂.
21. *Euchalcia venusta* Walker, ♂.
22. *Plusia balluca* Geyer, ♂.
23. *Euchalcia contexta* Grote, ♂.
24. *Autographa biloba* Stephens, ♂.
25. *Autographa rogationis* Guenée, ♂.
26. *Autographa basigera* Walker, ♂.
27. *Autographa flagellum* Walker, ♂.
28. *Autographa precationis* Guenée, ♂.
29. *Autographa egena* Guenée, ♂.
30. *Autographa oxygramma* Geyer, ♂.
31. *Autographa ampla* Walker, ♀.
32. *Autographa rectangula* Kirby, ♀.
33. *Autographa ou* Guenée, ♂.
34. *Autographa vaccinii* Henry Edwards, ♂.
35. *Autographa pseudogamma* Grote, ♂.
36. *Autographa brassicæ* Riley, ♂.
37. *Autographa simplex* Guenée, ♂.
38. *Autographa angulidens* Smith, ♂.
39. *Autographa selecta* Walker, ♂.
40. *Syngrapha devergens* Hübner, ♀.
41. *Syngrapha hochenwarthi* Hochenwarth, ♂.
42. *Abrostola urentis* Guenée, ♂.
43. *Abrostola ovalis* Guenée, ♂.
44. *Behrensia conchiformis*, Grote, ♂, U. S. N. M.

EMENDATIONS BY A. E. BROWER

25. *Autographa oo* Cramer, ♂.
40. *Syngrapha parilis* Hübner, ♀.
41. *Syngrapha ignea* race *simulans* McDunnough, ♂.

Plate XXVIII

(Except when otherwise indicated, the specimens figured are contained in the collection of W. J. Holland.)

1. *Ogdoconta cinereola* Guenée, ♀.
2. *Pæctes pygmæa* Hübner, ♂.
3. *Pæctes abrostoloides* Guenée, ♀.
4. *Pæctes occulatrix* Guenée, ♂, Merrick Collection.
5. *Marasmalus ventilator* Grote, ♀.
6. *Marasmalus inficita* Walker, ♂.
7. *Amyna octo* Guenée, ♀, U.S.N.M.
8. *Pterœtholix bullula* Grote, ♂, U. S. N. M.
9. *Eucalyptera strigata* Smith, ♂.
10. *Cilla distema* Grote, ♂.
11. *Alabama argillacea* Hübner, ♂.
12. *Anomis erosa* Hübner, ♀.
13. *Amolita fessa* Grote, ♂, U.S.N.M.
14. *Rivula propinqualis* Guenée, ♀.
15. *Doryodes bistriaris* Geyer, ♂.
16. *Scolecocampa liburna* Geyer, ♂.
17. *Pseudorgyia versuta* Harvey, ♀, U. S. N. M.
18. *P h i p r o s o p u s callitrichoides* Grote, ♀.
19. *Pleonectyptera pyralis* Hübner, ♂.
20. *Annaphila diva* Grote, ♂.
21. *A n n a p h i l a lithosina* Henry Edwards, ♀.
22. *Eustrotia albidula* Guenée, ♀.
23. *Eustrotia c o n c i n n i m a c u l a* Guenée, ♀.
24. *Eustrotia synochitis* Grote & Robinson, ♂.
25. *E u s t r o t i a musta* Grote & Robinson, ♂.
26. *Eustrotia muscosula* Guenée, ♀.
27. *Eustrotia apicosa* Haworth, ♂.
28. *Eustrotia carneola* Guenée, ♀.
29. *Azenia implora* Grote, ♀.
30. *Lithacodia bellicula* Hübner, ♂.
31. *Galgula hepara* Guenée, ♂.
32. *Galgula hepara* var. *p a r t i t a* Guenée, ♂.
33. *Xanthoptera nigrofimbria* Guenée, ♂.
34. *Xanthoptera semiflava* Guenée, ♂.

35. *Exyra semicrocea* Guenée, ♀, U. S. N. M.
36. *Prothymia semipurpurea* Walker, ♀, Merrick Collection.
37. *Prothymia orgyiæ* Grote, ♂.
38. *Prothymia rhodarialis* Walker, ♀.
39. *Eumestleta flammicincta* Walker, ♂.
40. *Tripudia opipara* Henry Edwards, ♂.
41. *Metaponia obtusa* Herrich-Schæffer, ♀.
42. *Metaponia perflava* Harvey, ♀.
43. *Chamyris cerintha* Treitschke, ♀.
44. *Tarache binocula* Grote, ♂.
45. *Tarache lactipennis* Harvey, ♀.
46. *Tarache terminimacula* Grote, ♀.
47. *Therasea flavicosta* Smith, ♂.
48. *Tarache delecta* Walker, ♀.
49. *Tarache lanceolata* Grote, ♂.
50. *Tarache aprica* Hübner, ♂.
51. *Tarache virginalis* Grote, ♀.
52. *Tarache flavipennis* Grote, ♂.
53. *Tarache sedata* Henry Edwards, ♂.
54. *Tarache erastrioides* Guenée, ♀.
55. *Tarache libedis* Smith, ♂.
56. *Fruva apicella* Grote, ♂.
57. *Spragueia onagrus* Guenée, ♂.
58. *S p r a g u e i a plumbifimbriata* Grote, ♀.
59. *Spragueia dama* Guenée, ♂.
60. *Spragueia guttata* Grote, ♂.
61. *Callopistria floridensis* Guenée, ♂, U. S. N. M.
62. *Metathorasa monetifera* Guenée, ♀.
63. *Euherrichia mollissima* Guenée, ♂.
64. *Cydosia imitella* Stretch, ♂.
65. *Cydosia aurivitta* Grote & Robinson, ♂.
66. *Cydosia majuscula* Henry Edwards, ♀.
67. *Derrima stellata* Walker, ♂.

EMENDATIONS BY A. E. BROWER

15. *Doryodes grandipennis* Barnes & McDunnough, ♂.
31. *Galgula partita* Guenée, ♀.
32. *Galgula partita* Guenée, ♂.
36. *Prothymia rhodarialis* Walker, ♀.
38. *Prothymia ernestiana* Blanchard, ♀.

PLATE XXIX

(Except when otherwise indicated, the specimens figured are contained in the collection of W. J. Holland.)

1. *Phalænostola larentioides* Grote, ♀.
2. *Hyamia sexpunctata* Grote, ♂.
3. *Pangrapta decoralis* Hübner, ♀.
4. *Hyamia perditalis* Walker, ♀.
5. *Homopyralis contracta* Walker, ♀.
6. *Hypsoropha monilis* Fabricius, ♂.
7. *Hypsoropha hormos* Hübner, ♀.
8. *Hyblæa puera* Cramer, ♀, U. S. N. M.
9. *Cissura spadix* Cramer, ♂.
10. *Cissura inepta* Henry Edwards, ♂.
11. *Cissura sabulosa* Henry Edwards, ♀.
12. *Ulosyneda valens* Henry Edwards, ♂.
13. *Drasteria cærulea* Grote, ♂.
14. *Drasteria erechtea* Cramer, ♀.
15. *Drasteria crassiuscula* Haworth, ♂.
16. *Drasteria conspicua* Smith, ♂.
17. *Cænurgia convalescens* Guenée, ♂.
18. *Cænurgia adversa* Grote, ♂.
19. *Euclidia intercalaris* Grote, ♂.
20. *Euclidia cuspidea* Hübner, ♀.
21. *Panula inconstans* Guenée, ♂.
22. *Melipotis fasciolaris* Hübner, ♀.
23. *Melipotis sinualis* Harvey, ♀.
24. *Melipotis jucunda* Hübner, ♂.
25. *Melipotis pallescens* Grote & Robinson, ♀.
26. *Melipotis perlæta* Henry Edwards, ♀.
27. *Melipotis limbolaris* Geyer, ♂.
28. *Cirrhobolina mexicana* Behr, ♀.
29. *Syneda alhabascæ* Neumœgen, ♂.
30. *Syneda graphica* Hübner, ♂.
31. *Syneda hudsonica* Grote & Robinson, ♀.
32. *Syneda divergens* Behr, ♂.
33. *Syneda howlandi* Grote, ♂.
34. *Syneda adumbrata* Behr, ♂.
35. *Syneda alleni* Grote, ♂.
36. *Cirrhobolina deducta* Morrison, ♂.
37. *Syneda edwardsi* Behr, ♀.
38. *Syneda socia* Behr, ♂.
39. *Litocala sexsignata* Harvey, ♀.
40. *Hypocala andremona* Cramer, ♂.
41. *Agnomonia anilis* Drury, ♂.
42. *Epidromia delinquens* Walker, ♀.

EMENDATIONS BY A. E. BROWER

15. *Drasteria erechtea* Cramer, ♂.

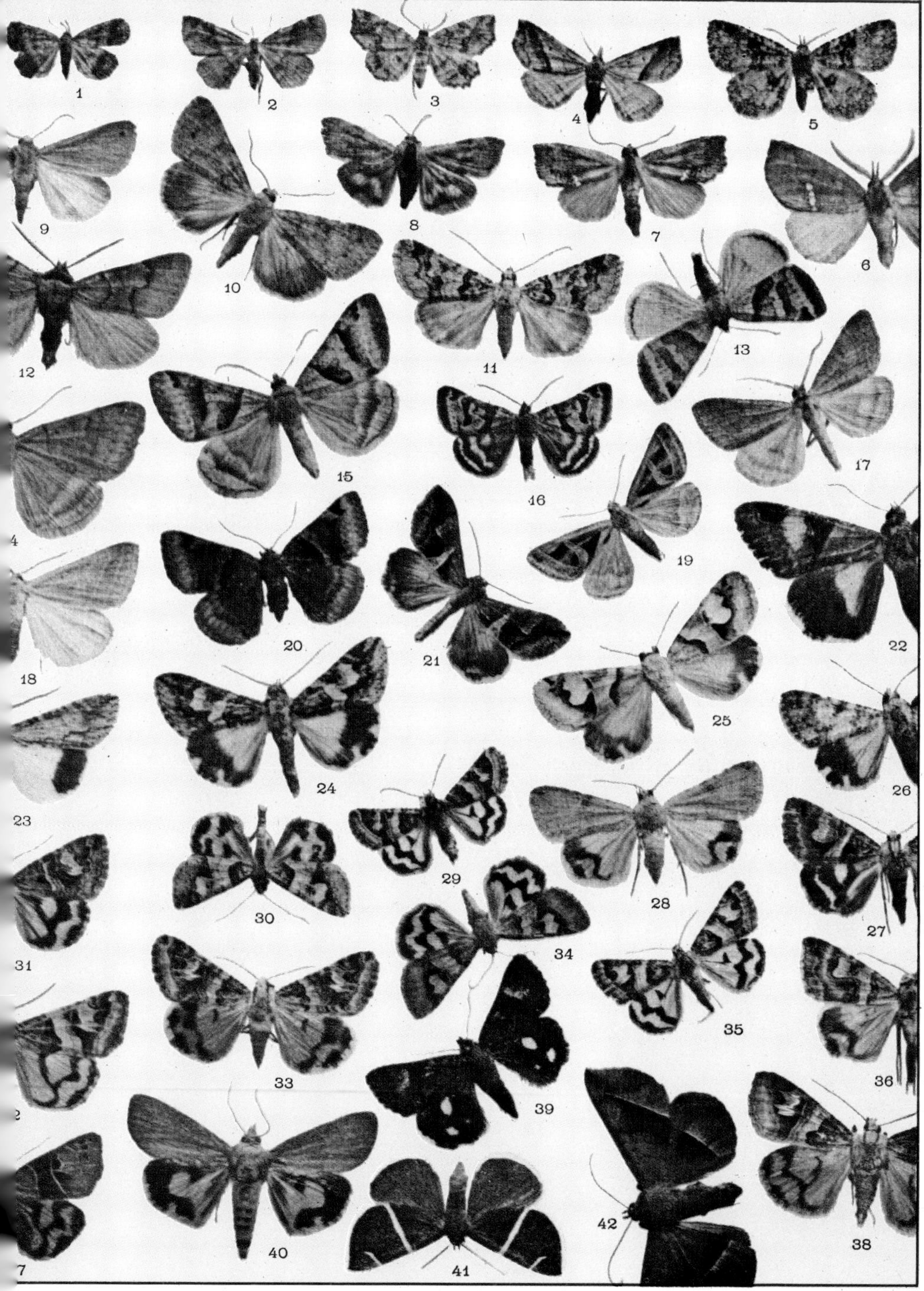
1
2
3
4
5
9
8
7
6
10
11
12
13
15
16
17
4
19
20
21
22
18
25
24
26
23
29
28
30
27
31
34
35
33
36
39
2
40
41
42
38
7

PLATE XXXI

Explanation of Plate XXXII

(The specimens figured are contained in the collection of W. J. Holland.)

1. *Catocala dejecta* Strecker, ♂.
2. *Catocala judith* Strecker ♂.
3. *Catocala tristis* Edwards, ♂.
4. *Catocala groteiana* Bailey, ♂.
5. *Catocala carolina* Holland, ♂.
6. *Catocala relicta* Walker, ♀.
7. *Catocala relicta* var. *bianca* Henry Edwards, ♂.
8. *Catocala antinympha* Hübner, ♂.
9. *Catocala cara* Guenée, ♂.
10. *Catocala badia* Grote & Robinson, ♀.
11. *Catocala muliercula* Guenée, ♂.
12. *Catocala amatrix* Hübner, ♂.
13. *Catocala amatrix* var. *nurus* Walker, ♀.
14. *Catocala olivia* Henry Edwards, ♂.
15. *Catocala alabamæ* Grote, ♀.
16. *Catocala amica* Hübner, ♂.
17. *Catocala minuta* Edwards, ♂.
18. *Catocala cælebs* Grote, ♂.
19. *Catocala lineella* Grote, ♂.
20. *Catocala nerissa* Henry Edwards, ♀.
21. *Catocala gisela* Meyer, ♀.

Emendations by A. E. Brower

4. *Catocala briseis* Edwards, ♀.
5. *Catocala flebilis* Grote, ♂.
6. *Catocala relicta* var. *clara* Beutenmüller, ♀.
7. *Catocala relicta* Walker, ♂.
12. *Catocala amatrix* var. *selecta* Walker, ♂.
13. *Catocala amatrix* Hübner, ♂.
19. *Catocala curvifascia* Brower, ♂.

PLATE XXXII

EXPLANATION OF PLATE XXXIII

(The specimens figured are contained in the collection of W. J. Holland.)

1. *Catocala californica* Henry Edwards, ♂.
2. *Catocala ultronia* Hübner, ♂.
3. *Catocala faustina* Strecker, ♂.
4. *Catocala celia* Henry Edwards, ♂.
5. *Catocala unijuga* Walker, ♀.
6. *Catocala meskei* Grote, ♂.
7. *Catocala mopsa* Henry Edwards, ♂.
8. *Catocala augusta* Henry Edwards, ♂.
9. *Catocala scintillans* Grote, ♂.
10. *Catocala hinda* French, ♂.
11. *Catocala habilis* Grote, ♂.
12. *Catocala basalis* Grote, ♂.
13. *Catocala innubens* Guenée, ♂.
14. *Catocala serena* Edwards, ♂.
15. *Catocala subnata* Grote, ♀.
16. *Catocala nebulosa* Edwards, ♀.
17. *Poaphila quadrifilaris* Hübner, ♀.
18. *Allotria elonympha* Hübner, ♂.

EMENDATIONS BY A. E. BROWER

1. *Catocala irene* Behr, ♀.
2. *Catocala celia* Henry Edwards, ♂.
4. *Catocala ultronia* Hübner, ♂.
7. *Catocala lucinda* Beutenmüller, ♀.
10. *Catocala hinda* French, ♀
12. *Catocala habilis* Grote, ♀.

PLATE XXXIII

Explanation of Plate XXXIV

(The specimens figured are contained in the collection of W. J. Holland.)

1. *Catocala illecta* Walker, ♂.
2. *Catocala andromache* Henry Edwards, ♂.
3. *Catocala consors* Abbot & Smith, ♂.
4. *Catocala delilah* Strecker, ♀.
5. *Catocala desdemona* Henry Edwards, ♂.
6. *Catocala cerogama* Guenée, ♂.
7. *Catocala osculata* Hulst, ♂.
8. *Catocala whitneyi* Dodge, ♂.
9. *Catocala abbreviatella* Grote, ♀.
10. *Catocala coccinata* Grote, ♂.
11. *Catocala parta* Guenée, ♂.
12. *Catocala cratægi* Saunders, ♂.
13. *Catocala polygama* Guenée, ♂.
14. *Catocala ilia* Cramer, ♂.
15. *Catocala aholibah* Strecker, ♀.
16. *Catocala verrilliana* Grote, ♂.
17. *Catocala uxor* Guenée, ♀.

Emendations by A. E. Brower

2. *Catocala benjamini* Brower, ♀.
13. *Catocala mira* Grote, ♂.
16. *Catocala ophelia* Henry Edwards, ♂.
17. *Catocala conspicua* Worthington, ♀.

PLATE XXXIV

(The specimens figured are contained in the collection of W. J. Holland.)

1. *Catocala amasia* Abbot & Smith, ♀.
2. *Catocala similis* Edwards, ♂.
3. *Catocala aholah* Strecker, ♂.
4. *Catocala fratercula* Grote & Robinson, ♂.
5. *Catocala jaquenetta* Henry Edwards, ♂.
6. *Catocala grynea* Cramer, ♂.
7. *Catocala præclara* Grote & Robinson, ♂.
8. *Catocala gracilis* Edwards, ♀.
9. *Catocala marmorata* Edwards, ♀.
10. *Catocala concumbens* Walker, ♂.
11. *Catocala luciana* Henry Edwards, ♂.
12. *Catocala briseis* Edwards, ♂.
13. *Catocala stretchi* Behr, ♂.
14. *Catocala cleopatra* Henry Edwards, ♀.
15. *Catocala rosalinda* Henry Edwards, ♂.
16. *Catocala somnus* Dodge, ♀.
17. *Catocala pura* Hulst, ♂.
18. *Catocala babayaga* Strecker, ♂

EMENDATIONS BY A. E. BROWER

1. *Catocala connubialis* Guenée, ♀.
2. *Catocala aholah* Strecker, ♂.
3. *Catocala similis* Edwards, ♂.
4. *Catocala micronympha* Guenée, ♂.
5. *Catocala mira* Grote, ♂.
7. *Catocala sordida* Grote, ♂.
13. *Catocala francisca* Henry Edwards, ♀.
15. *Catocala faustina* Strecker, ♂.

PLATE XXXV

Explanation of Plate XXXVI

(The specimens figured are contained in the collection of W. J. Holland.)

1. *Andrewsia messalina* Guenée, ♂.
2. *Euparthenos nubilis* Hübner, ♀
3. *Catocala palæogama* Guenée, ♂.
4. *Catocala palæogama* var. *phalanga* Grote, ♂.
5. *Catocala neogama* Abbot & Smith, ♀.
6. *Catocala piatrix* Grote, ♂.
7. *Catocala hermia* Henry Edwards, ♀.
8. *Ophideres materna* Linnæus, ♀.
9. *Strenoloma lunilinea* Grote, ♂.
10. *Toxocampa victoria* Grote, ♀.
11. *Phurys lima* Guenée, ♂.
12. *Phurys vinculum* Guenée, ♂.
13. *Celiptera frustulum* Guenée, ♀.
14. *Phoberia atomaris* Hübner, ♂.
15. *Siavana repanda* Walker, ♀.
16. *Remigia repanda* Fabricius, ♂.
17. *Palindia dominicata* Guenée, ♂.
18. *Parallelia bistriaris* Hübner, ♂.
19. *Panapoda rufimargo* Hübner. ♂.
20. *Panapoda rufimargo* var. *carneioosta* Guenée, ♂.
21. *Trama detrahens* Walker, ♂.
22. *Grammodes smithi* Guenée, ♀.
23. *Antiblemma inexacta* Walker, ♀.

Emendations by A. E. Brower

7. *Catocala pura* Hulst, ♀.
16. *Remigia texana* Morrison, ♂.

PLATE XXXVI.

(Unless otherwise indicated, the specimens figured are contained in the collection of W. J. Holland.)

1. *Thysania zenobia* Cramer, ♀.
2. *Erebus odora* Linnæus, ♀.
3. *Zale horrida* Hübner, ♂.
4. *Litoprosopus futilis* Grote & Robinson, ♂.
5. *Phæocyma lunifera* Hübner, ♀.
6. *Ypsia undularis* Drury, ♀.
7. *Pseudanthracia coracias* Guenée, ♀.
8. *Campometra amella* Guenée, ♀.
9. *Campometra mima* Harvey, ♂.
10. *Anticarsia gemmatilis* Hübner, ♂.
11. *Matigramma pulverilinea* Grote, ♀, U. S. N. M.
12. *Yrias repentis* Grote, ♂.
13. *Yrias clientis* Grote, ♂.
14. *Homoptera unilineata* Grote, ♀.
15. *Homoptera lunata* Drury, ♂.
16. *Homoptera lunata* var. *edusa* Drury, ♂.
17. *Homoptera cingulifera* Walker, ♀, Merrick Collection.
18. *Isogona natatrix* Guenée, ♂.
19. *Hormisa absorptalis* Walker, ♂.
20. *Zanclognatha lituralis* Hübner, ♀.
21. *Zanclognatha lævigata* Grote, ♂.
22. *Zanclognatha ochreipennis* Grote, ♂.
23. *Chytolita morbidalis* Guenée, ♀.
24. *Renia discoloralis* Guenée, ♂.
25. *Palthis angulalis* Hübner, ♀.
26. *Heterogramma pyramusalis* Walker, ♀.
27. *Epizeuxis denticulalis* Harvey, ♂.
28. *Epizeuxis scobialis* Grote, ♀.
29. *Epizeuxis lubricalis* Geyer, ♀.
30. *Philometra metonalis* Walker, ♂.
31. *Hormisa bivittata* Grote, ♂, U. S. N. M.
32. *Bleptina caradrinalis* Guenée, ♂.
33. *Capis curvata* Grote, ♀.

EMENDATIONS BY A. E. BROWER

14. *Homoptera obliqua* Guenée, ♀.

PLATE XXXVII

EXPLANATION OF PLATE XXXVIII

(Unless otherwise indicated, the specimens figured are contained in the collection of W. J. Holland.)

1. *Gnophæla clappiana* Holland, ♂, type.
2. *Gnophæla latipennis* Boisduval, ♂.
3. *Gnophæla vermiculata* Grote & Robinson, ♂.
4. *Composia fidelissima* Herrich-Schæffer, ♂.
5. *Daritis thetis* Klug, ♀.
6. *Phryganidia californica* Packard, ♂.
7. *Olene leucophæa* Abbot & Smith, ♂.
8. *Olene leucophæa* Abbot & Smith, ♀.
9. *Olene achatina* Abbot & Smith, ♂.
10. *Gynæphora rossi* Curtis, ♂.
11. *Gynæphora rossi* Curtis, ♀.
12. *Porthetria dispar* Linnæus, ♂.
13. *Porthetria dispar* Linnæus, ♀.
14. *Psilura monacha* Linnæus, ♂.
15. *Psilura monacha* Linnæus, ♀.
16. *Euproctis chrysorrhœa* Linnæus, ♂.
17. *Hemerocampa definita* Packard, ♂, U. S. N. M.
18. *Notolophus antiqua* Linnæus, ♂, U. S. N. M.
19. *Hemerocampa vetusta* Boisduval, ♂, U. S. N. M.
20. *Hemerocampa leucostigma* Abbot & Smith, ♂.
21. *Hemerocampa leucostigma* Abbot & Smith, ♀.
22. *Carama cretata* Grote, ♂, U. S. N. M.
23. *Lagoa crispata* Packard, ♂.
24. *Lagoa pyxidifera* Abbot & Smith, ♂.
25. *Megalopyge opercularis* Abbot & Smith, ♂.

PLATE XXXVIII.

(Unless otherwise indicated, the specimens figured are contained in the collection of W. J. Holland.)

1. *Nadata gibbosa* Abbot & Smith, ♀.
2. *Nerice bidentata* Walker, ♂.
3. *Hyparpax venus* Neumœgen, ♂, U. S. N. M.
4. *Hyparpax aurora* Abbot & Smith, ♂, U. S. N. M.
5. *Dasylophia anguina* Abbot & Smith, ♂.
6. *Dasylophia thyatiroides* Walker, ♀.
7. *Simmerista albifrons* Abbot & Smith, ♀.
8. *Harpyia cinerea* Walker, ♀, U. S. N. M.
9. *Harpyia borealis* Boisduval, ♂.
10. *Harpyia albicoma* Strecker, ♂, U. S. N. M.
11. *Harpyia scolopendrina* Boisduval, ♂.
12. *Cerura multiscripta* Riley, ♂.
13. *Schizura ipomeæ* Doubleday, var. *cinereofrons*, Packard, ♂.
14. *Schizura badia* Packard, ♀, U. S. N. M.
15. *Schizura concinna* Abbot & Smith, ♂.
16. *Schizura leptinoides* Grote, ♂.
17. *Schizura unicornis* Abbot & Smith, ♂.
18. *Hippia packardi* Morrison, ♀.
19. *Ianassa lignicolor* Walker, ♀, U. S. N. M.
20. *Litodonta hydromeli* Harvey, ♂.
21. *Misogada unicolor* Packard, ♀.
22. *Heterocampa astarte* Doubleday, ♂.
23. *Heterocampa manteo* Doubleday, ♂.
24. *Heterocampa bilineata* Packard, ♂.
25. *Heterocampa biundata* Walker, ♂.
26. *Heterocampa umbrata* Walker, ♂.
27. *Gluphisia severa* Henry Edwards, ♂, U. S. N. M.
28. *Gluphisia septentrionalis* Walker, ♂.
29. *Gluphisia wrighti* Henry Edwards, ♂.
30. *Fentonia marthesia* Cramer, ♂.
31. *Ellida caniplaga* Walker, ♀.

EMENDATIONS BY A. E. BROWER

11. *Harpyia modesta* Hudson, ♂.

PLATE XXXIX.

Explanation of Plate XL

(When not otherwise indicated, the specimens figured are contained in the collection of W. J. Holland.)

1. *Hyperæschra stragula* Grote, ♂.
2. *Heterocampa obliqua* Packard, ♂.
3. *Odontosia elegans* Strecker, ♂.
4. *Hyperæschra tortuosa* Tepper, ♀, U. S. N. M.
5. *Notodonta basitriens* Walker, ♀, U. S. N. M.
6. *Notodonta simplaria* Græf, ♀, U. S. N. M.
7. *Hyperæschra georgica* Herrich-Schæffer, ♂.
8. *Lophodonta ferruginea* Packard, ♀.
9. *Pheosia dimidiata* Herrich-Schæffer, ♂.
10. *Pheosia portlandia* Henry Edwards, ♂, U. S. N. M.
11. *Datana ministra* Drury, ♂.
12. *Datana angusi* Grote & Robinson, ♂.
13. *Datana integerrima* Grote & Robinson, ♂.
14. *Datana perspicua* Grote & Robinson, ♂.
15. *Lophodonta angulosa* Abbot & Smith, ♂.
16. *Melalopha albosigma* Fitch, ♂.
17. *Melalopha strigosa* Grote, ♂, U. S. N. M.
18. *Melalopha apicalis* Walker, var. *ornata* Grote & Robinson, ♂, U. S. N. M.
19. *Melalopha inclusa* Hübner, ♀.
20. *Apatelodes torrefacta* Abbot & Smith, ♂.
21. *Apatelodes angelica* Grote, ♂.
22. *Habrosyne scripta* Gosse, ♂.
23. *Euthyatira pudens* Guenée, ♂, Merrick Collection.
24. *Euthyatira pudens* var. *pennsylvanica* Smith, ♀, Merrick Collection.
25. *Pseudothyatira cymatophoroides* Guenée, ♂.
26. *Pseudothyatira expultrix* Grote, ♂.
27. *Bombycia tearli* Henry Edwards, ♂, U. S. N. M.
28. *Hyparpax perophoroides* Strecker, ♂, Beutenmüller Collection.

PLATE XL

PLATE XLI.

(The specimens figured are contained in the Collection of W. J. Holland.)

1. *Palthis asopialis* Guenée, ♀.
2. *Gaberasa ambigualis* Walker, ♂.
3. *Bomolocha manalis* Walker, ♀.
4. *Bomolocha baltimoralis* Guenée, ♀.
5. *Bomolocha abalinealis* Walker, ♂.
6. *Bomolocha madefactalis* Guenée, ♂.
7. *Bomolocha bijugalis* Walker, ♂.
8. *Bomolocha deceptalis* Walker, ♂.
9. *Bomolocha toreuta* Grote, ♂.
10. *Bomolocha scutellaris* Grote, ♀.
11. *Bomolocha edictalis* Walker, ♂.
12. *Hypena humuli* Harris, ♂.
13. *Hypena humuli* var., ♂.
14. *Plathypena scabra* Fabricius, ♂.
15. *Nycteola lintnerana* Speyer, ♂.
16. *Brephos infans* Mœschler, ♀.
17. *Calledapteryx dryopterata* Grote, ♂.
18. *Melanchroia geometroides* Walker, ♂.
19. *Melanchroia cephise* Cramer, ♂.
20. *Sphacelodes vulneraria* Hübner, ♂.
21. *Dyspteris abortivaria* Herrich-Schæffer, ♂.
22. *Nyctobia limitata* Walker, ♂.
23. *Cladora atroliturata* Walker, ♂.
24. *Rachela bruceata* Hulst, ♂.
25. *Paleacrita vernata* Peck, ♂.
26. *Paleacrita vernata* Peck, ♀.
27. *Eudule mendica* Walker, ♂.
28. *Eudule unicolor* Robinson, ♂.
29. *Heterophleps triguttaria* Herrich-Schæffer, ♂.
30. *Eucymatoge intestinata* Guenée, ♀.
31. *Nannia refusata* Walker, ♂.
32. *Tephroclystis absinthiata* Clerck, ♂.
33. *Venusia comptaria* Walker, ♂.
34. *Hydria undulata* Linnæus, ♀.
35. *Hydriomena latirupta* Walker, ♂.
36. *Philereme californiata* Packard, ♂.
37. *Gypsochroa sitellata* Guenée, ♂.
38. *Rheumaptera rubrosuffusata* Packard, ♂.
39. *Rheumaptera l ct:cta* Denis & Schiffermüller, ♂.
40. *Rheumaptera hastata* Linnæus, ♂.
41. *Rheumaptera hastata* Linnæus, var. ♂.
42. *Eustroma diversilineata* Hübner, ♂.
43. *Eustroma atrocolorata* Grote, ♂.
44. *Gypsochroa designata* Hufnagel, ♂.
45. *Triphosa progressata* Walker, ♂.
46. *Mesoleuca hersiliata* Guenée, ♂.
47. *Mesoleuca gratulata* Walker, ♂.
48. *Percnoptilota fluviata* Hübner, ♂.
49. *Mesoleuca intermediata* Guenée, ♂.
50. *Mesoleuca lacustrata* Guenée, ♀.
51. *Hydriomena autumnalis* Strömeyer, ♂.
52. *Hydriomena speciosata* Packard, ♂.
53. *Eustroma prunata* Linnæus, ♂.
54. *Hydriomena sordidata* Fabricius, ♂.

EMENDATIONS BY A. E. BROWER

25. *Alsophila pometaria* Harris, ♂.
26. *Alsophila pometaria* Harris, ♀.
32. *Semiothisa gnophosaria* Guenée, ♂.
33. *Hydrelia inornata* Hulst, ♂.
35. *Euphyia centrostrigaria* Wollaston, ♂.
37. *Gypsochroa stellata* Guenée, ♂.
44. *Gypsochroa emendata* Pearsall, ♂.
49. *Mesoleuca iduata* Guenée, ♀.
50. *Mesoleuca intermediata* Guenée, ♀.

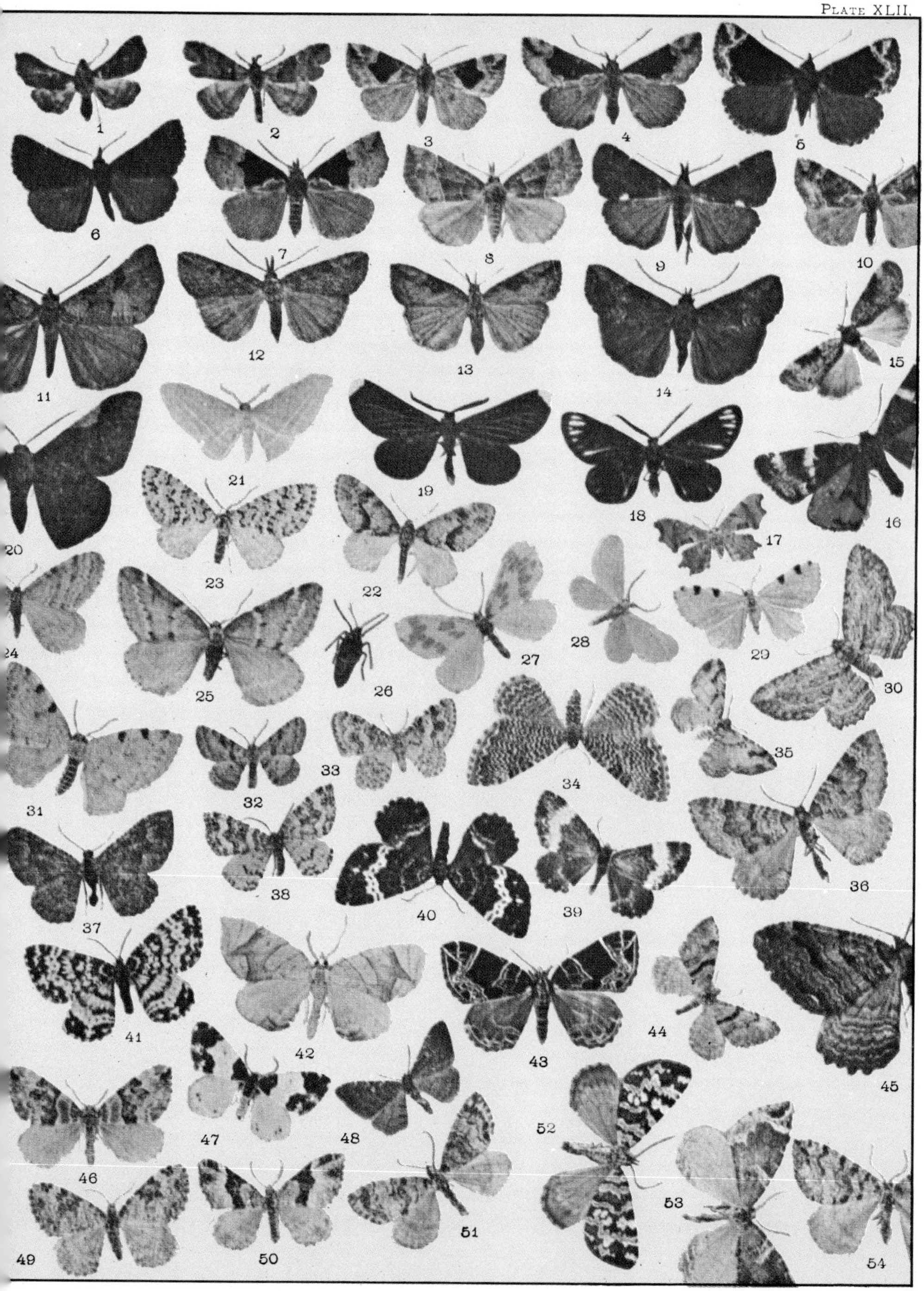
1
2
3
4
5
6
7
8
9
10
11
12
13
14
15
16
17
18
19
20
21
22
23
24
25
26
27
28
29
30
31
32
33
34
35
36
37
38
39
40
41
42
43
44
45
46
47
48
49
50
51
52
53
54

(The specimens figured are contained in the Collection of W. J. Holland.)

1. *Marmopteryx marmorata* Packard, ♂.
2. *Haematopis grataria* Fabricius, ♂.
3. *Pigea multilineata* Hulst, ♂, Type.
4. *Triphosa fervifactaria* Grote, ♂.
5. *Synelys alabastaria* Hübner, ♀.
6. *Eois inductata* Guenée, ♂.
7. *Eois ossularia* Hübner, ♂.
8. *Leptomeris magnetaria* Guenée, ♂.
9. *Leptomeris quinquelinearia* Packard, ♀.
10. *Hydriomena custodiata* Guenée, ♂.
11. *Hydriomena custodiata* Guenée, ♂, lower side.
12. *Cosymbia lumenaria* Hübner, ♀.
13. *Eois sideraria* Guenée, ♂.
14. *Leptomeris sentinaria* Hübner, ♂.
15. *Venusia duodecimlineata* Packard, ♂.
16. *Triphosa gibbicostata* Walker, ♂.
17. *Chlorochlamys chloroleucaria* Guenée, ♀.
18. *Eucrostis incertata* Walker, ♂.
19. *Racheospila hollandaria* Hulst, ♀, Type.
20. *Racheospila saltusaria* Hulst, ♂, Type.
21. *Mesoleuca rufocillata* Guenée, ♂.
22. *Erastria amaturaria* Walker, ♂.
23. *Synchlora liquoraria* Guenée, ♂.
24. *Anaplodes iridaria* Guenée, ♂.
25. *Eufidonia notataria* Walker, ♂.
26. *Epelis truncataria* Walker, ♀.
27. *Paota fultaria* Grote, ♂.
28. *Heliomata infulata* Grote, ♀.
29. *Heliomata cycladata* Grote, ♂.
30. *Orthofidonia semiclarata* Walker, ♀.
31. *Orthofidonia vestaliata* Guenée, ♂.

32. *Dasyfidonia avuncularia* Guenée, ♂.
33. *Mellilla xanthometata* Walker, ♂.
34. *Chloraspilates arizonaria* Grote, ♂.
35. *Physostegania pustularia* Guenée, ♂.
36. *Deilinea variolaria* Guenée, ♀.
37. *Sciagrapha granitata* Guenée, ♂.
38. *Deilinea behrensaria* Hulst, ♂, Type.
39. *Philobia enotata* Guenée, ♂.
40. *Macaria præatomata* Haworth, ♀.
41. *Sciagrapha heliothidata* Guenée, ♀.
42. *Sciagrapha mellistrigata* Grote, ♂.
43. *Macaria s-signata* Packard, ♂.
44. *Macaria eremiata* Guenée, ♂.
45. *Cymatophora ribearia* Fitch, ♀.
46. *Cymatophora inceptaria* Walker, ♂.
47. *Macaria hypæthrata* Grote ♂.
48. *Cymatophora successaria* Walker, ♀.
49. *Cymatophora coörtaria* Hulst, ♂.
50. *Cymatophora tenebrosata* Hulst, ♂, Type.
51. *Sympherta tripunctaria* Packard, ♀.
52. *Apæcasia defluata* Walker, ♂.
53. *Catopyrrha dissimilaria* Hübner, ♂.
54. *Catopyrrha coloraria* Fabricius, ♂
55. *Enemera juturnaria* Guenée, ♂.
56. *Platea trilinearia* Packard, ♂.
57. *Platea californiaria* Herrich-Schæffer, ♂.
58. *Caripeta divisata* Walker, ♂.
59. *Philedia punctomacularia* Hulst, ♂, Type.
60. *Nepytia semiclusaria* Walker, ♂.

EMENDATIONS BY A. E. BROWER

15. *Venusia comptaria* Walker, ♂.
25. *Eufidonia discospilata* Walker, ♂.
37. *Sciagraphia granitata* Guenée, ♂.
39. *Philobia æmulataria* Walker, ♂.
41. *Sciagraphia ocellinata* Guenée, ♂.
42. *Sciagraphia mellistrigata* Grote, ♂.

PLATE XLIII

(The specimens figured are contained in the collection of W. J. Holland.)

1. *Alcis baltearia* Hulst, ♂, *Type*.
2. *Caripeta angustiorata* Walker, ♀.
3. *Macaria glomeraria* Grote, ♀.
4. *Cleora pampinaria* Guenée, ♂.
5. *Alcis metanemaria* Hulst, ♂, *Type*.
6. *Euchœca lucata* Guenée, ♂.
7. *Melanolophia canadaria* Guenée, ♂.
8. *Cleora atrifasciata* Hulst, ♀, *Type*.
9. *Ectropis crepuscularia* Denis & Schiffermüller, ♂.
10. *Paraphia subatomaria* Wood, ♂.
11. *Paraphia unipuncta* Haworth, ♀.
12. *Apocheima rachelæ* Hulst, ♂.
13. *Lycia cognataria* Guenée, ♂.
14. *Nacophora quernaria* Abbot & Smith, ♀.
15. *Nepytia nigrovenaria* Packard, ♀.
16. *Phigalia titea* Cramer, ♂.
17. *Erannis tiliaria* Harris, ♂.
18. *Pterospoda opuscularia* Hulst, ♀, *Type*.
19. *Euchœca albovittata* Guenée, ♂.
20. *Euchœca californiata* Packard, ♂.
21. *Cingilia catenaria* Drury, ♂.
22. *Sicya macularia* Harris, ♂.
23. *Sicya macularia* Harris, var., ♀.
24. *Therina fervidaria* Hübner, ♂.
25. *Therina fiscellaria* Guenée, ♂.
26. *Therina endropiaria* Grote & Robinson, ♂.
27. *Therina athasiaria* Walker, ♂.
28. *Epimecis virginaria* Cramer, ♂.
29. *Epimecis virginaria* Cramer, ♀.
30. *Metrocampa prægrandaria* Guenée, ♂.
31. *Eugonobapta nivosaria* Guenée, ♂.
32. *Plagodis emargataria* Guenée, ♀.
33. *Plagodis serinaria* Herrich-Schæffer, ♂.
34. *Ennomos magnarius* Guenée, ♂.
35. *Ennomos subsignarius* Hübner, ♂.
36. *Plagodis keutzingi* Grote, ♂.
37. *Ania limbata* Haworth, ♀.
38. *Hyperitis amicaria* Herrich-Schæffer, ♂.
39. *Xanthotype crocataria* Fabricius, ♂.
40. *Xanthotype cælaria* Hulst, ♂.

Emendations by A. E. Brower

2. *Caripeta piniata* Packard, ♀.
32. *Plagodis alcoölaria* Guenée, ♀.
38. *Hyperitis alienaria* Herrich-Schæffer, ♂.

Plate XLIV

(The specimens figured are contained in the collection of W. J. Holland.)

1. *Gonodontis hypochraria* Herrich-Schæffer, ♂.
2. *Gonodontis duaria* Guenée, ♀.
3. *Euchlæna obtusaria* Hübner, ♂.
4. *Euchlæna serrata* Drury, ♂.
5. *Stenaspilates zalissaria* Walker, ♀.
6. *Priocycla armataria* Herrich-Schæffer, ♂.
7. *Euchlæna amœnaria* Guenée, ♂.
8. *Euchlæna astylusaria* Walker, ♂.
9. *Pherne parallelia* Packard, ♀.
10. *Syssaura infensata* Guenée, var. *biclaria* Walker, ♀.
11. *Oxydia vesulia* Cramer, ♂.
12. *Metanema determinata* Walker, ♀.
13. *Metanema inatomaria* Guenée, ♂.
14. *Gonodontis obfirmaria* Hübner, ♂.
15. *Epiplatymetra coloradaria* Grote & Robinson, ♂.
16. *Tetracis crocallata* Guenée, ♂.
17. *Sabulodes arcasaria* Walker, ♂.
18. *Sabulodes sulphurata* Packard, ♀.
19. *Sabulodes lorata* Grote, ♂.
20. *Pherne jubararia* Hulst, ♀, *Type*.
21. *Pherne placearia* Guenée, ♂.
22. *Mecoceras nitocris* Cramer, ♂.
23. *Azelina ancetaria* Hübner, ♂.
24. *Euchlæna effectaria* Walker, ♂.
25. *Euchlæna pectinaria* Denis & Schiffermüller, ♂.
26. *Sabulodes truxaliata* Guenée, ♀.
27. *Almodes terraria* Guenée, ♂.
28. *Metanema quercivoraria* Guenée, ♀.
29. *Caberodes confusaria* Hübner, ♂.
30. *Sabulodes politia* Cramer, ♂.
31. *Caberodes majoraria* Guenée, ♀.
32. *Abbotana clemitaria* Abbot & Smith, ♀.
33. *Abbotana clemitaria* Abbot & Smith, ♂, var.
34. *Sabulodes transversata* Drury, ♀.
35. *Phrygionis argenteostriata* Strecker, ♀.
36. *Palyas auriferaria* Hulst, ♂, *Type*.

EMENDATIONS BY A. E. BROWER

10. *Syssaura puber* Grote & Robinson, ♀.

PLATE XLV.

EXPLANATION OF PLATE XLVI

(The figures in this plate are taken by the kind permission of Mr. William Beutenmüller from the plates illustrating his Monograph of the Sesiidæ of North America.)

1. *Melittia satyriniformis* Hübner, ♀.
2. *Melittia snowi* Henry Edwards, ♂.
3. *Melittia grandis* Strecker, ♀.
4. *Gæa solituda* Henry Edwards, ♂.
5. *Gæa emphytiformis* Walker, ♀.
6. *Alcathoe caudata* Harris, ♂.
7. *Sannina uroceriformis* Walker, ♂.
8. *Ægeria apiformis* Linnæus, ♀.
9. *Bembecia marginata* Harris, ♀.
10. *Memythrus simulans* Grote, ♀.
11. *Memythrus polistiformis* Harris, ♂.
12. *Memythrus polistiformis* Harris, ♀.
13. *Memythrus admirandus* Henry Edwards, ♂.
14. *Memythrus tricinctus* Harris, ♀.
15. *Palmia præcedens* Henry Edwards, ♀.
16. *Parharmonia pini* Kellicott, ♂.
17. *Podosesia syringæ* Harris, ♀.
18. *Sanninoidea exitiosa* Say, ♂.
19. *Sanninoidea exitiosa* Say, ♀.
20. *Vespamima sequoiæ* Henry Edwards, ♂.
21. *Synanthedon bassiformis* Walker, ♂.
22. *Synanthedon rileyana* Henry Edwards, ♂.
23. *Synanthedon rileyana* Henry Edwards, ♀.
24. *Synanthedon pictipes* Grote & Robinson, ♀.
25. *Synanthedon pyri* Harris, ♀.
26. *Synanthedon tipuliformis* Clerck, ♀.
27. *Synanthedon albicornis* Henry Edwards, ♀.
28. *Synanthedon acerni* Clemens, ♀.
29. *Synanthedon scitula* Harris, ♀.
30. *Synanthedon neglecta* Henry Edwards, ♀.
31. *Synanthedon rutilans* Henry Edwards, ♂.
32. *Synanthedon rutilans* Henry Edwards, ♀.
33. *Synanthedon aureopurpurea* Henry Edwards, ♂.
34. *Euhagena nebraskæ* Henry Edwards, ♂.
35. *Paranthrene heucheræ* Henry Edwards, ♂.
36. *Calasesia coccinea* Beutenmüller, ♀.
37. *Albuna pyramidalis,* var. *montana* Henry Edwards, ♂.

PLATE XLVI.

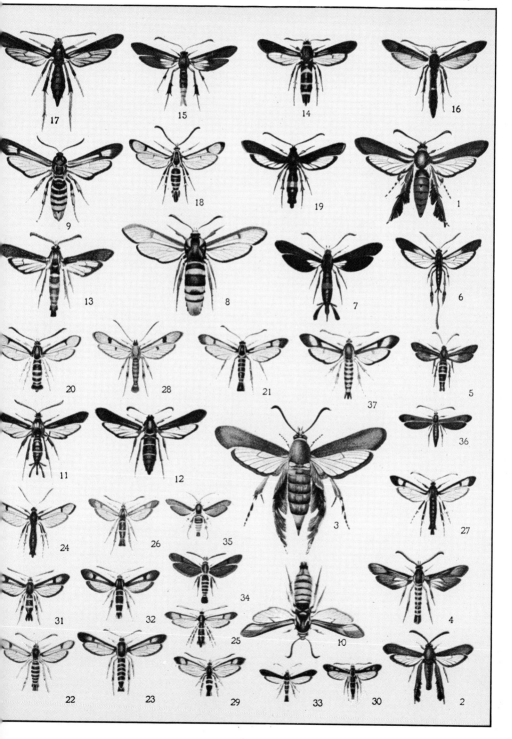

(Unless otherwise indicated, the specimens represented are contained in the collection of W. J. Holland.)

1. *Packardia geminata* Packard, ♂.
2. *Lithacodes fasciola* Herrich-Schæffer, ♂.
3. *Adoneta spinuloides* Herrich-Schæffer, ♂.
4. *Cochlidion biguttata* Packard, ♀.
5. *Euclea pænulata* Clemens, ♂.
6. *Phobetron pithecium* Abbot & Smith, ♂.
7. *Phobetron pithecium* Abbot & Smith, ♀.
8. *Prolimacodes scapha* Harris, ♀.
9. *Sibine stimulea* Clemens, ♂.
10. *Euclea indetermina* Boisduval, ♂, U. S. N. M.
11. *Tortricidia testacea* Packard, ♂.
12. *Tortricidia cæsonia* Grote, ♀, U. S. N. M.
13. *Natada nasoni* Grote, ♂, U. S. N. M.
14. *Sisyrosea textula.* Herrich-Schæffer, ♀, U. S. N. M.
15. *Euclea chloris* Herrich-Schæffer, ♀, U. S. N. M.
16. *Packardia elegans* Packard, ♀.
17. *Isochætes beutenmulleri* Henry Edwards, ♀, U. S. N. M.
18. *Alarodia slossoniæ* Packard, ♀, U. S. N. M.
19. *Adoneta pygmæa* Grote & Robinson, ♂, U. S. N. M.
20. *Heterogenea shurtleffi* Packard, ♂, U. S. N. M.
21. *Cochlidion y-inversa* Packard, ♂.
22. *Monoleuca semifascia* Walker, ♂.
23. *Euclea viridiclava* Walker, ♂.
24. *Euclea delphinii* Boisduval, ♀.
25. *Euclea nanina* Dyar, ♂.
26. *Euclea chloris* Herrich-Schæffer, ♂.
27. *Cochlidion rectilinea* Grote & Robinson, ♂

28. *Zinckenia fascialis* Cramer, ♂.
29. *Euclea chloris* Herrich-Schæffer, ♀.
30. *Thyris maculata* Harris, ♂.
31. *Thyris lugubris* Boisduval, ♂.
32. *Triprocris smithsonianus* Clemens, ♂.
33. *Pyromorpha dimidiata* Herrich-Schæffer, ♂.
34. *Harrisina americana* Guérin-Méneville, ♂.
35. *Hexeris enhydris* Grote, ♂.
36. *Meskea dyspteraria* Grote, ♂.
37. *Desmia funeralis* Hübner, ♂.
38. *Pantographa limata* Grote & Robinson, ♂.
39. *Glyphodes hyalinata* Linnæus, ♂.
40. *Cindaphia bicoloralis* Guenée, ♂.
41. *Pyrausta insequalis* Guenée, ♂.
42. *Pyrausta niveicilialis* Grote, ♀.
43. *Glyphodes nitidalis* Stoll, ♂.
44. *Pyrausta tyralis* Guenée, ♂.
45. *Evergestis straminalis* Hübner, ♂.
46. *Herculia himonialis* Zeller, ♀.
47. *Phlyctænia tertialis* Guenée, ♂.
48. *Pyrausta illibalis* Hübner, ♀.
49. *Pyrausta orphisalis* Walker, ♂.
50. *Pyrausta funebris* Ström, ♂.
51. *Pyrausta unifascialis* Packard.
52. *Pyrausta langdonalis* Grote, ♂.
53. *Pyralis farinalis* Linnæus, ♀.
54. *Pyrausta pertextalis* Lederer, ♂.
55. *Pyrausta fumalis* Guenée, ♂.
56. *Pyrausta unimacula* Grote & Robinson, ♂.
57. *Pyrausta ochosalis* Fitch, MS., ♂.
58. *Eustixia pupula* Hübner, ♂.
59. *Hypsopygia costalis* Fabricius, ♂.
60. *Conchylodes platinalis* Guenée, ♂.

EMENDATIONS BY A. E. BROWER

15. *Euclea indetermina* Boisduval, ♀.
21. *Tortricidia flexuosa* Grote, ♂.

Plate XLVII

EXPLANATION OF PLATE XLVIII

(Unless otherwise indicated, the specimens figured are contained in the collection of W. J. Holland.)

1. *Diastictis fracturalis* Zeller, ♂, U. S. N. M.
2. *Samea ecclesialis* Guenée, ♀, U. S. N. M.
3. *Agathodes monstralis* Guenée, ♂, U. S. N. M.
4. *Phlyctænodes oberthuralis* Fernald, ♂, U. S. N. M.
5. *Phlyctænodes triumphalis* Grote, ♀, U. S. N. M.
6. *Titanio proximalis* Fernald, ♂, U. S. N. M.
7. *Cornifrons simalis* Grote, ♂, U. S. N. M.
8. *Melitara fernaldialis* Hulst, ♀, U. S. N. M.
9. *Noctuelia thalialis* Walker, ♂, U. S. N. M.
10. *Nymphula obscuralis* Grote, ♀, U. S. N. M.
11. *Salobrana tecomæ* Riley, ♀.
12. *Scirpophaga perstrialis* Hübner, ♀, U. S. N. M.
13. *Herculia olinalis* Guenée, ♂, U. S. N. M.
14. *Yuma trabalis* Grote, ♀, U. S. N. M.
15. *Acrobasis betulella* Hulst, ♀, U. S. N. M.
16. *Ambesa lætella* Grote, ♂.
17. *Crambus laqueatellus* Clemens, ♂.
18. *Crambus alboclavellus* Zeller, ♂.
19. *Crambus turbatellus* Walker, ♀.
20. *Crambus trisectus* Walker, ♀.
21. *Archips cerasivorana* Fitch, ♀, U. S. N. M.
22. *Tortrix albicomana* Clemens, ♂, U. S. N. M.
23. *Amorbia humerosana* Clemens, ♀, U. S. N. M.
24. *Platynota flavedana* Clemens, ♀, var.
25. *Platynota labiosana* Zeller, ♀, U. S. N. M.
26. *Commophila macrocarpana* Walsingham, ♂, U. S. N. M.
27. *Eucosma dorsisignatana* Clemens, ♂.
28. *Cenopis groteana* Fernald, ♂.
29. *Ecdytolopha insiticiana* Zeller, ♀.
30. *Archips purpurana* Clemens, ♂.
31. *Archips parallela* Robinson, ♂.
32. *Archips rosaceana* Harris, ♀.
33. *Tosale oviplagalis* Walker, ♂.
34. *Archips argyrospila* Walker, ♀, U. S. N. M.
35. *Cenopis pettitana* Robinson, ♀, U. S. N. M.
36. *Atteva aurea* Fitch, ♂, U. S. N. M.
37. *Atteva gemmata* Grote, ♂, U. S. N. M.
38. *Semioscopis merricella* Dyar, ♀.
39. *Eulia alisellana* Robinson, ♀.
40. *Epagoge tunicana* Walsingham, ♂, U. S. N. M.
41. *Stenoma schlægeri* Zeller, ♂, U. S. N. M.
42. *Anaphora popeanella* Clemens, ♂.
43. *Acrolophus plumifrontellus* Clemens, ♂.
44. *Yponomeuta multipunctella* Clemens, ♂, U. S. N. M.
45. *Adela bella* Chambers, ♂.

EMENDATIONS BY A. E. BROWER

22. *Tortrix semipurpurana* Kearfott, ♂.
38. *Semioscopis packardella* Clemens, ♀.

PLATE XLVIII.

Genus CIRRHOBOLINA Grote

(1) **Cirrhobolina deducta** Morrison, Plate XXX, Fig. 36, ♂ .
Syn. *pavitensis* Morrison.

A common insect in Texas.

(2) **Cirrhobolina mexicana** Behr, Plate XXX, Fig. 28, ♀ .
Syn. *incandescens* Grote.

The moth occurs quite commonly in the southwestern portions of our territory from Colorado to Arizona and Texas, and thence southward on the Mexican plateaus.

Genus SYNEDA Guenée

Twenty-five species are attributed to this genus and indicated as having their habitat within the territory with which this book deals. It is possible that a final revision of the genus will lead to the discovery that some of the so-called species are merely local races or varietal forms of others. There is considerable dissimilarity between the sexes in some of the species, and it may be that there is in this fact also an element of confusion. The species which are figured on the plates are such as are for the most part well known and the identification of which is certain.

(1) **Syneda graphica** Hübner, Plate XXX, Fig. 30, ♂ .
Syn. *capticola* Walker.

The insect ranges from New York to Florida westward to the Alleghany Mountains.

(2) **Syneda divergens** Behr, Plate XXX, Fig. 32, ♂ .

The insect is western and has an ascertained range from Colorado to California.

(3) **Syneda alleni** Grote, Plate XXX, Fig. 35, ♂ .
Syn. *saxea* Henry Edwards.

The species has a northern range and is reported from Maine and Canada, Manitoba and Montana. It extends its habitat southward along the elevated table-lands of the continent to Colorado and Wyoming.

(4) **Syneda adumbrata** Behr, Plate XXX, Fig. 34, ♂ .

This is a western species ranging from Montana and Arizona in the east to the Pacific.

(5) **Syneda socia** Behr, Plate XXX, Fig. 38, ♂ .

The range of this species is practically the same as that of the last mentioned.

(6) **Syneda howlandi** Grote, Plate XXX, Fig. *33*, ♂.
Syn. *stretchi* Behr.

The insect is distributed from Colorado and Arizona westward to California.

(7) **Syneda edwardsi** Behr, Plate XXX, Fig. *37*, ♀.

The moth is thus far known only from California.

(8) **Syneda hudsonica** Grote & Robinson, Plate XXX, Fig. *31*, ♂.

This is a northern species, ranging from Ontario westward to Montana.

(9) **Syneda athabasca** Neumœgen, Plate XXX, Fig. **29**, ♂.

The moth has been taken in considerable numbers in Alberta and Assiniboia, and is also reported as occurring in British Columbia.

Genus CATOCALA Schrank

This is a very large genus represented in both hemispheres. The metropolis of the genus appears to be North America; at all events, there are more species found in our territory than occur elsewhere, though in eastern Asia and temperate Europe the genus is very well represented by many strikingly beautiful forms. There is considerable variation in the case of some of the species, and as they have always been favorites with collectors, a great deal has been written upon them, and many varietal names have been suggested. Over one hundred species are attributed to our fauna. Of these the majority are figured in our plates. We follow the order of arrangement given in Dyar's List of North American Lepidoptera.

(1) **Catocala epione** Drury, Plate XXXI, Fig. *3*, ♀. (The Epione Underwing.)

The insect is distributed from New England and Canada southward to the Carolinas and westward to Missouri and Iowa.

(2) **Catocala sappho** Strecker, Plate XXXI, Fig. **2**, ♂. (The Sappho Underwing.)

This rare species has been found from western Pennsylvania and West Virginia as far west as Illinois and as far south as Texas.

(3) **Catocala agrippina** Strecker, Plate XXXI, Fig. **1**, ♀. (The Agrippina Underwing.)

The species occurs from New York and the region of the Great Lakes southward to Texas.

* (4) **Catocala subviridis** Harvey, Plate XXXI, Fig. 4, ♂.
(The Faintly Green Underwing.)

The insect has been by some writers regarded as a variety of the preceding species. It is characterized by larger size, and brighter colored fore wings, on which the maculation is much more distinct. In certain lights there is a pronounced greenish shade visible upon the wings.

(5) **Catocala lacrymosa** Guenée, Plate XXXI, Fig. 6, ♂.
(The Tearful Underwing.)

Form **paulina** Henry Edwards, Plate XXXI, Fig. 12, ♀.
(The Paulina Underwing.)

Form **evelina** French, Plate XXXI, Fig. 9, ♀. (The Evelina Underwing.)

The range of this variable species is practically the same as that of the last mentioned.

† (6) **Catocala viduata** Guenée, Plate XXXI, Fig. 15, ♀. (The Widowed Underwing.)

Syn. *maestosa* Hulst; *guenei* Grote.

The metropolis of this species appears to be the Gulf States. It is abundant in Texas.

(7) **Catocala vidua** Abbot & Smith, Plate XXXI, Fig. 5, ♂.
(The Widow Underwing.)

Syn. *desperata* Guenée.

The insect ranges from Canada to Florida through the Appalachian subregion.

(8) **Catocala dejecta** Strecker, Plate XXXII, Fig. 1, ♂.
(The Dejected Underwing.)

The species is found in the northern portions of the Atlantic subregion.

‡ Form **carolina** *subsp. nov.*, Plate XXXII, Fig. 5, ♂. (Carrie's Underwing.)

This insect, which occurs in western Pennsylvania, appears to be a form of *dejecta*, having the same relation to that species as that which is held by *basalis* to *habilis*. It is characterized by its smaller size, and by the black stripe which runs from the base of the wing to the apex, giving it quite a different facies from *dejecta*. The type is figured upon our plate, and it may from the illustration easily be recognized.

*Should be *C: agrippina* Strecker in text and plate.—A.E.B.

†Should be *C. mæstosa* Hulst in text and plate; the synonymy is *viduata* Guenée; *guenei* Grote.—A.E.B.

‡This is *C. flebilis* Grote, a distinct species.—A.E.B.

* (9) **Catocala retecta** Grote, Plate XXXI, Fig. 8, ♀. (The Yellow-Gray Underwing.)

The moth is found from Canada to the Carolinas and westward to the Mississippi.

† (10) **Catocala flebilis** Grote, Plate XXXI, Fig. 11, ♂. (The Mourning Underwing.)

The habitat of this species is the same as that of the last mentioned.

(11) **Catocala robinsoni** Grote, Plate XXXI, Fig. 7, ♀. (Robinson's Underwing.)

The moth ranges from New England to the Mississippi and southward to Tennessee and the Carolinas. It is particularly abundant in the Ohio valley.

‡ (12) **Catocala obscura** Strecker, Plate XXXI, Fig. 14, ♂. (The Obscure Underwing.)

The moth may be found from Canada to Maryland and westward to Colorado.

(13) **Catocala insolabilis** Guenée, Plate XXXI, Fig. 10, ♀. (The Inconsolable Underwing.)

The species is found from Canada southward to the Carolinas and westward to the Mississippi.

(14) **Catocala angusi** Grote, Plate XXXI, Fig. 13, ♂. (Angus' Underwing.)

The range of this species is the same as that of the preceding.

(15) **Catocala judith** Strecker, Plate XXXII, Fig. 2, ♂. (The Judith Underwing.)

The insect occurs from New England westward in the northern portions of the Atlantic subregion.

(16) **Catocala tristis** Edwards, Plate XXXII, Fig. 3, ♂. (The Gloomy Underwing.)

The species appears to be commoner in New England than elsewhere.

§ (17) **Catocala relicta** Walker, Plate XXXII, Fig. 6, ♀. (The Relict.)

‖ Form **bianca** Henry Edwards, Plate XXXII, Fig. 7, ♂. (The Bianca Underwing.)

This fine moth is found in the northern portions of the Appalachian subregion. It is not uncommon in New England and

---

*Should be *C. luctuosa* Hulst in text and plate.—A.E.B.

†Should be *C. angusi* form *lucetta* French in text and plate.—A.E.B.

‡Should be *C. residua* Grote in text and plate. This specimen has even less contrast in pattern than The Obscure Underwing.—A.E.B.

§This is illustrated in Fig. 7, Plate XXXII, (♂).—A.E.B.

‖Should read form *clara* Beutenmüller, Plate XXXII, Fig. 6, ♀. (Clara's Underwing.).—A.E.B.

northern New York, but it is rare in western Pennsylvania. It has a westward range to Colorado and Oregon.

(18) **Catocala cara** Guenée, Plate XXXII, Fig. 9, ♂. (The Darling Underwing.)

This large and splendid species is a native of the Appalachian subregion, and in it has a wide range.

* (19) **Catocala amatrix** Hübner, Plate XXXII, Fig. 12, ♂. (The Sweetheart.)

Form **nurus** Walker, Plate XXXII, Fig. 13, ♀. (The Nurse.)

This is another fine species, which has the same geographical distribution as the last mentioned.

(20) **Catocala marmorata** Edwards, Plate XXXV, Fig. 9, ♀. (The Marbled Underwing.)

This is a rather rare species, which has a wide distribution. Its metropolis appears to be West Virginia and Kentucky, though it has been taken elsewhere.

(21) **Catocala concumbens** Walker, Plate XXXV, Fig. 10. ♀. (The Sleepy Underwing.)

This lovely moth has a wide range in the Appalachian subregion. It is very common in New England and central New York, less common in western Pennsylvania.

† (22) **Catocala californica** Edwards, Plate XXXIII, Fig. 1, ♂. (The California Underwing.)

As the name implies, the species is a native of California.

(23) **Catocala cleopatra** Henry Edwards, Plate XXXV, Fig. 14, ♀. (The Cleopatra Underwing.)

This insect is regarded by some as a varietal form of the preceding species. It has the same habitat.

(24) **Catocala luciana** Henry Edwards, Plate XXXV, Fig. 11, ♂. (The Luciana Underwing.)

Syn. *nebraskæ* Dodge.

Form **somnus** Dodge, Plate XXXV, Fig. 16, ♀.

The moth is found in Kansas, Nebraska, Colorado, and Wyoming.

(25) **Catocala babayaga** Strecker, Plate XXXV, Fig. 18, ♂. (The Babayaga Underwing.)

The habitat of the species is Arizona.

‡ (26) **Catocala stretchi** Behr, Plate XXXV, Fig. 13, ♂. (Stretch's Underwing.) The species is Californian.

*Fig. 13 of Plate XXXII shows *C. amatrix* Hübner,♂; Fig. 12 shows form *selecta* Walker, ♂.—A.E.B.

†Should be *C. irene* Behr (Irene's Underwing), a species native to the western states. Fig. 1 of Plate XXXIII shows a female specimen.—A.E.B.

‡Should be *C. francisca* Henry Edwards. Fig. 13 shows a female specimen.—A.E.B.

Noctuidæ

(27) **Catocala augusta** Henry Edwards, Plate XXXIII, Fig. 8, ♂. (The Augusta Underwing.)

Like the preceding species, this is also confined in its range to the Pacific coast.

* (28) **Catocala rosalinda** Henry Edwards, Plate XXXV, Fig. 15, ♂. (The Rosalind Underwing.)

The insect has been found in Kansas and Colorado.

(29) **Catocala pura** Hulst, Plate XXXV, Fig. 17, ♂. (The Pure Underwing.)

The moth is an inhabitant of the region of the Rocky Mountains.

(30) **Catocala unijuga** Walker, Plate XXXIII, Fig. 5, ♀. (The Once-married Underwing.)

This is a widely distributed species, the range of which is northern, extending from New England to Colorado, through Canada and the region of the Great Lakes. It is common in central New York.

(31) **Catocala meskei** Grote, Plate XXXIII, Fig. 6, ♂. (Meske's Underwing.)

By some students this species has been regarded as a variety of the preceding. Its range is the same.

† (32) **Catocala groteiana** Bailey, Plate XXXII, Fig. 4, ♂. (Grote's Underwing.)

The moth occurs from Canada to New Mexico, and has been sometimes treated as a variety of *Catocala briseis* Edwards.

‡ (33) **Catocala hermia** Henry Edwards, Plate XXXVI, Fig. 7, ♀. (The Hermia Underwing.)

The habitat of the species is Colorado and New Mexico.

(34) **Catocala briseis** Edwards, Plate XXXV, Fig. 12 ♂. (The Briseis Underwing.)

The species is an inhabitant of the northern portions of the Appalachian subregion, and is also known to occur in Colorado.

(35) **Catocala faustina** Strecker, Plate XXXIII, Fig. 3, ♂. (The Faustina Underwing.)

The specimen figured on the plate was received by the writer from the author of the species, and may be accepted as typical. The range of the moth is from Colorado to California.

(36) **Catocala parta** Guenée, Plate XXXIV, Fig. 11, ♂. (The Mother Underwing.)

*Should be *C. faustina* Strecker (The Faustina Underwing) in text and plate.—A.E.B.

†Should be *C. briseis* Edwards (The Briseis Underwing). Fig. 4 of Plate XXXII shows a female specimen.—A.E.B.

‡Should be *C. pura* Hulst (The Chaste Underwing) in text and plate. —A.E.B.

This fine species is quite common in the Appalachian sub-region and ranges northward into the region of Hudson Bay and westward as far as Colorado.

(37) **Catocala coccinata** Grote, Plate XXXIV, Fig. 10, ♂. (The Scarlet Underwing.)

The moth is recorded as occurring from Canada to Florida and Texas, and westward to the Mississippi. It is not very common.

(38) **Catocala aholibah** Strecker, Plate XXXIV, Fig. 15, ♀. (The Aholibah Underwing.)

The specimen figured on the plate was obtained from the author of the species, and may be accepted as typical. The insect is found from New Mexico and Colorado to California and Oregon.

* (39) **Catocala verrilliana** Grote, Plate XXXIV, Fig. 16, ♂. (Verrill's Underwing.)

A neat and prettily marked species which has much the same range as the preceding, though extending somewhat farther to the south.

(40) **Catocala ultronia** Hübner, Plate XXXIII, Fig. 4, ♂. (The Ultronia Underwing.)

† Form **celia** Henry Edwards, Plate XXXIII, Fig. 2, ♂. (The Celia Underwing.)

Form **mopsa** Henry Edwards, Plate XXXIII, Fig. 7, ♂. (The Mopsa Underwing.)

Besides the three forms of this variable species which we have selected for illustration, there are several others which have received subspecific names. The insect is very common, and occurs from the Atlantic to the Great Plains and from Canada to Florida.

‡ (41) **Catocala ilia** Cramer, Plate XXXIV, Fig. 14, ♂. (The Ilia Underwing.)

§ Form **uxor** Guenée, Plate XXXIV, Fig. 17, ♀. (The Wife.)

Form **osculata** Hulst, Plate XXXIV, Fig. 7, ♂. (The Beloved Underwing.)

This is a common and variable species which is found generally throughout the United States and Canada.

(42) **Catocala innubens** Guenée, Plate XXXIII, Fig. 13, ♂; Plate I, Fig. 7, larva. (The Betrothed.)

---

*Should be *C. ophelia* Henry Edwards (The Ophelia Underwing) in text and plate.—A.E.B.

†Should be form *lucinda* Beutenmüller (The Lucinda Underwing). Fig. 7 shows a female specimen.—A.E.B.

‡Fig. 14 of Plate XXXIV has abnormal hind wings; Fig. 7 is most typical of *ilia*.—A.E.B.

§Should be form *conspicua* Worthington in text and plate.—A.E.B..

Form **hinda** French, Plate XXXIII, Fig. 10, ♀. (The Hinda Underwing.)

Form **scintillans** Grote, Plate XXXIII, Fig. 9, ♂. (The Glittering Underwing.)

This is another very common and very variable species, which is found from Canada to the Carolinas and westward to the Mississippi.

(43) **Catocala nebulosa** Edwards, Plate XXXIII, Fig. 16, ♀. (The Clouded Underwing.)

This fine species is found in the Middle Atlantic and Central States east of the Mississippi. It appears to be quite common in southern Indiana.

(44) **Catocala piatrix** Grote, Plate XXXVI, Fig. 6, ♂. (The Penitent.)

The moth is found throughout the United States east of the Rocky Mountains, and as far south as Arizona. It is a common species.

(45) **Catocala neogama** Abbot & Smith, Plate XXXVI, Fig. 5, ♀. (The Bride.)

This is another common and variable species which has the same geographical distribution as that of the last-named insect.

(46) **Catocala subnata** Grote, Plate XXXIII, Fig. 15, ♀. (The Youthful Underwing.)

The species is found in the Appalachian subregion, and appears to be not uncommon in Kentucky and southern Indiana.

(47) **Catocala cerogama** Guenée, Plate XXXIV, Fig. 6, ♂. (The Yellow-banded Underwing.)

Syn. *aurella* Fisher; *eliza* Fisher.

This is a common species ranging from Canada to the Carolinas and westward to the Mississippi.

(48) **Catocala palæogama** Guenée, Plate XXXVI, Fig. 3, ♂. (The Oldwife Underwing.)

Form **phalanga** Grote, Plate XXXVI, Fig. 4, ♂. (The Phalanga Underwing.)

The moth ranges from New England to Virginia and westward to the Mississippi.

(49) **Catocala consors** Abbot & Smith, Plate XXXIV, Fig. 3, ♂. (The Consort.)

The insect is found from Pennsylvania southward and westward to Texas.

(50) **Catocala muliercula** Guenée, Plate XXXII, Fig. 11, ♂. (The Little Wife.)

The insect is an inhabitant of the central portions of the Appalachian subregion.

(51) **Catocala delilah** Strecker, Plate XXXIV, Fig. 4, ♀. (The Delilah Underwing.)

Syn. *adoptiva* Grote.

The range of this species is from southern Illinois and Kentucky southward to the Gulf and westward to Kansas and Nebraska.

(52) **Catocala desdemona** Henry Edwards, Plate XXXIV, Fig. 5, ♂. (The Desdemona Underwing.)

The species is found in the southwestern States.

* (53) **Catocala andromache** Henry Edwards, Plate XXXIV, Fig. 2, ♂. (The Andromache Underwing.)

This species is found in southern California and Arizona. I am indebted to Mr. O. C. Poling for the fine specimen of this rare moth which is figured upon the plate. It is closely allied to the preceding species.

(54) **Catocala illecta** Walker, Plate XXXIV, Fig. 1, ♂. (The Magdalen Underwing.)

Syn. *magdalena* Strecker.

The moth is found from Indiana to Nebraska and southward to Texas.

(55) **Catocala serena** Edwards, Plate XXXIII, Fig. 14, ♂. (The Serene Underwing.)

The insect ranges from Canada and New England westward into the valley of the Mississippi. It is said to also occur in eastern Siberia, but this is doubtful.

(56) **Catocala antinympha** Hübner, Plate XXXII, Fig. 8, ♂. (The Wayward Nymph.)

The moth is reported from Canada to Maryland and westward as far as the Mississippi. I have found it very abundant at Saratoga, N. Y., and even more abundant on the summits of the Allegheny Mountains about Cresson Springs in the month of August.

(57) **Catocala badia** Grote & Robinson, Plate XXXII, Fig. 10, ♀. (The Badia Underwing.)

---

*Should be *C. benjamini* Brower (Benjamin's Underwing). Fig. 2 of Plate XXXIV shows a female specimen.—A.E.B.

The species is more common in New England than elsewhere. It is rather abundant on the north shore of Massachusetts Bay, and occurs also in central New York and the Adirondacks. I have never known it to be taken in western Pennsylvania.

(58) **Catocala cœlebs** Grote, Plate XXXII, Fig. 18, ♂. (The Old-maid.)

The range of this species, which is by some students regarded as a varietal form of the preceding, is from southern Canada through New England into central New York.

(59) **Catocala habilis** Grote, Plate XXXIII, Fig. 11, ♂.
* Form **basalis** Grote, Plate XXXIII, Fig. 12, ♂.

The moth occurs from Canada to Virginia and westward to the Mississippi. The form *basalis* has a black longitudinal streak from the base of the fore wing along the lower side of the cell.

(60) **Catocala abbreviatella** Grote, Plate XXXIV, Fig. 9, ♀.

The insect occurs from Minnesota and Illinois southward to Texas and westward to Utah.

(61) **Catocala whitneyi** Dodge, Plate XXXIV, Fig. 8, ♂. (Whitney's Underwing.)

The moth, which is probably only a varietal form of the preceding species, has the same range. The specimen figured on the plate was received from the author of the species.

† (62) **Catocala polygama** Guenée, Plate XXXIV, Fig. 13, ♂. (The Polygamist.)

Form **cratægi** Saunders, Plate XXXIV, Fig. 12, ♂. (The Hawthorn Underwing.)

A common and variable species ranging all over the Appalachian subregion.

‡ (63) **Catocala amasia** Abbot & Smith, Plate XXXV, Fig. 1, ♂. (The Amasia Underwing.)

Syn. *sancta* Hulst.

The geographical range of the species is from New York and Illinois southward to the Gulf of Mexico.

(64) **Catocala similis** Edwards, Plate XXXV, Fig. 3, ♂.

Syn. *formula* Grote.

Form **aholah** Strecker, Plate XXXV, Fig. 2, ♂.

The moth occurs from Rhode Island to Texas. It is a widely distributed but not very common species.

*Form *basalis* Grote is the usual female of *habilis* Grote.—A.E.B.

†Should be *C. mira* Grote (The Wonderful Underwing). A male specimen is shown in Fig. 5, Plate XXXV.—A.E.B.

‡Should be *C. connubialis* Guenée (The Connubial Underwing). Fig. 1 of Plate XXXV is a female specimen. The synonymy should read: *sancta* Hulst; *amasia* Abbot & Smith.—A.E.B.

* (65) **Catocala fratercula** Grote & Robinson, Plate XXXV, Fig. 4, ♂. (The Little Sister.)

† Form **jaquenetta** Henry Edwards, Plate XXXV, Fig. 5, ♂.

Form **gisela** Meyer, Plate XXXII, Fig. 21, ♀.

The species is very variable within certain limits, and is widely distributed over the United States and Canada from the Atlantic to the Pacific.

(66) **Catocala olivia** Henry Edwards, Plate XXXII, Fig. 14, ♂. (The Olivia Underwing.)

The species is a native of Texas.

‡ (67) **Catocala præclara** Grote & Robinson, Plate XXXV, Fig. 7, ♂.

The insect belongs within the more northern portions of the Appalachian subregion. The specimen figured was taken in Massachusetts.

(68) **Catocala grynea** Cramer, Plate XXXV, Fig. 6, ♂.

The moth is found from Canada to the Carolinas and westward to the Mississippi.

(69) **Catocala alabamæ** Grote, Plate XXXII, Fig. 15, ♀.

The habitat of the species is, as indicated by the name, the state of Alabama.

(70) **Catocala gracilis** Edwards, Plate XXXV, Fig. 8, ♀. (The Graceful Underwing.)

The species occurs from Canada to the southern States on the Atlantic seaboard and westward to the valley of the Ohio.

(71) **Catocala minuta** Edwards, Plate XXXII, Fig. 17, ♂. (The Little Underwing.)

The moth is indigenous in the Eastern and Middle States.

(72) **Catocala amica** Hübner, Plate XXXII, Fig. 16, ♂.

§ Form **lineella** Grote, Plate XXXII, Fig. 19, ♂.

Form **nerissa** Henry Edwards, Plate XXXII, Fig. 20, ♀.

This small species is subject to considerable variation. It has a wide range from Ontario to Texas, and from the Atlantic to the Great Plains.

" Place and time requiring, let this insect fly.
It hovers round the wick—with the wind of its wings the flame is extinguished." *Súdraka, The Mrichchakati, or, The Toy-cart.*

*Should be .*C. micronympha* Guenée (The Little Bride) in text and plate.—A.E.B.

†This is *C. mira* Grote,♂. See footnote † on page 268.—A.E.B.

‡Should be *C. sordida* Grote in text and plate.—A.E.B.

§This is form *curvifascia* Brower.—A.E.B.

WALKING AS A FINE ART

THE first act of all animals is that of absorption. Feeding is a primal necessity. The senses of smell, of touch, and of taste are involved in it. Sight has little to do with it at first, but is soon awakened. Coincident with this act among the lower animals is that of locomotion. Man, whose desire to annihilate space has become a supreme passion, approaches the act of locomotion later than all other animals. Young ducks and geese fly from the Arctic Circle to Florida a few months after they have been hatched. Babies do not often begin to crawl until they are twice as old, and rarely walk until more than a year of life has been passed. There is nothing more interesting than the sight of a child just beginning to walk. The look of glad surprise and immense satisfaction which is displayed when a few successful steps have been taken is delightful to the observer. The triumphs of the most successful men do not in later years afford them so much momentary pleasure as is experienced by the little fellow who realizes that at last after many failures he has "got his legs."

In much of our going to and fro on this small globe we are aided by adventitious helps. Stephenson, Fulton, and the fathers of the science of magnetism and electricity have done much to pave the way for our rapid transportation from one spot to another. But there are some places to which we cannot be hauled, and we have not yet reached the point where we can dispense with the use of our pedal extremities.

Happy is the man who has acquired the love of walking for its own sake! There is no form of exercise more health-giving, none which tends more thoroughly to invigorate, if it be wisely undertaken. The effect of the act is to quicken the venous circulation; to send the blood to the lungs, there to be purified by contact with the oxygen of the atmosphere; to harden and strengthen the muscles of the legs and to bring those of the arms and the chest into play. People who walk do not have over-loaded veins. The shop-girl who stands behind the counter all day suffers from varicosis, but the man or woman who walks avoids it. Standing is harder than walking; it is more fatiguing, and brings no return of health to the system.

270

In walking, the best results are secured when there is no burden upon the mind. The man who carries the load of daily care with him when he walks derives less benefit from the act than the man who dismisses all concern and simply gives himself over to the act. It is a mistake to suppose that it is an advantage in walking to have some definite object of pursuit. The woman who is advised by her physician to walk should not select as her path some busy street upon which she is certain to be diverted by the opportunity to unite with her exercise a number of shopping excursions. The man who goes out to walk should not choose a much frequented part of the town where he is sure to meet business friends and acquaintances. The person who desires to derive the best results from his strolls should select a retired spot in park or country where the "madding throng" does not resort. It is hard to make Americans realize the importance of these suggestions. The demand is forever that exercise, if taken at all, shall have an aim ulterior to itself, in the pursuit of which the upbuilding of the system shall take place as a collateral incident. The popularity of golf is due to the fact that it answers the demand of a great class of persons to be amused while they are being invigorated. It is one of the least objectionable forms, in which the pill of exercise is sugar-coated for consumption by a race which is slowly but surely working itself to death in office, mill and factory.

Walking for its own sake is pursued to a far greater extent in England and in Germany than in America. We may well learn to imitate our cousins on the eastern side of the Atlantic in this regard.

If walking is to be pursued with an object, there is nothing which may be chosen as an aim better than the pursuit of that knowledge which is the end of the naturalist. To become acquainted with the fields and the flowers which bloom in them, with the forests and the myriad forms of animate life which frequent them, is an aim which leads far away from the cares and pursuits of the weary, workday world. I met the other day a friend, who, with quick step and alertness depicted in every feature, was hurrying along one of the avenues in the capital. I marveled at his gait, for I knew that the winters of fourscore and five years rested upon his head. "How is it that you have found the fountain of eternal youth?" I said. "My dear boy," he replied, "I have found it by living near to nature's heart, and by having my beloved science of entomology to refresh and quicken me in my daily walks."

Would you cultivate walking as a fine art, learn to see and to hear what the world, which man has not made nor has entirely marred, is telling you of the wonders of that life which she kindly nourishes upon her bosom.

"Cleon sees no charm in nature—in a daisy, I;
Cleon hears no anthem ringing in the sea and the sky,
Nature sings to me forever—earnest listener, I;
State for state, with all attendants, who would change! Not I."

Genus ALLOTRIA Hübner

(1) **Allotria elonympha** Hübner, Plate XXXIII, Fig. 18, ♂.
This handsome little species is found in the Appalachian subregion. It is the sole species of the genus.

Genus ANDREWSIA Grote

(1) **Andrewsia messalina** Guenée, Plate XXXVI, Fig. 1, ♂.
Syn. *belfragiana* Harvey; *jocasta* Strecker.
The insect has been found to range from Kansas to Texas. It appears on the wing in the latter state in May.

Genus EUPARTHENOS Grote

(1) **Euparthenos nubilis** Hübner, Plate XXXVI, Fig. 2, ♀.
The moth occurs from the northern Atlantic States to Arizona.

Genus HYPOCALA Guenée

(1) **Hypocala andremona** Cramer, Plate XXX, Fig. 40, ♂.
Syn. *hilli* Lintner.
The insect is characteristic of the neotropical fauna. It occurs as a straggler into Texas, and is found very commonly throughout Mexico, Central America, and South America.

Genus LITOCALA Harvey

(1) **Litocala sexsignata** Harvey, Plate XXX, Fig. 39, ♀.
The species occurs through the region of the Rocky Mountains to California.

Genus TOXOCAMPA Guenée

(1) **Toxocampa victoria** Grote, Plate XXXVI, Fig. 10, ♀.
This is a northern species found from New England to British Columbia and ranging southward along the higher mountain ranges of the west.

Genus PHOBERIA Hübner

(1) **Phoberia atomaris** Hübner, Plate XXXVI, Fig. 14, ♂.
Syn. *orthosioides* Guenée; *forrigens* Walker; *ingenua* Walker.
The moth has been taken from Maine to Texas and westward as far as the Great Plains.

Genus SIAVANA Walker

(1) **Siavana repanda** Walker, Plate XXXVI, Fig.15, ♀.
Syn. *auripennis* Grote.
The moth ranges from the Valley of the Ohio southward to the Gulf of Mexico. It is not uncommon in Florida.

Genus PALINDIA Guenée

This is an extensive neotropical genus, represented by but two species, which have thus far been taken within our territory.
(1) **Palindia dominicata** Guenée, Plate XXXVI, Fig. 17, ♂.
The moth occasionally occurs in Texas. It is very common in Central and South America.

Genus PANAPODA Guenée

(1) **Panapoda rufimargo** Hübner, Plate XXXVI, Fig. 19, ♂.
Syn. *rubricosta* Guenée; *cressoni* Grote.
Form **carneicosta** Guenée, Plate XXXVI, Fig. 20, ♂.
Syn. *scissa* Walker; *combinata* Walker.
The insect is found through the Appalachian subregion. It is quite common in parts of New England, and at certain times has been taken abundantly in western Pennsylvania.

Genus PARALLELIA Hübner

(1) **Parallelia bistriaris** Hübner, Plate XXXVI, Fig. 18, ♂.
Syn. *amplissima* Walker.
The insect occurs from Nova Scotia to Florida and westward to the Rocky Mountains.

Genus AGNOMONIA Hübner

(1) Agnomonia anilis Drury, Plate XXX, Fig. 41, ♂.
Syn. *sesquistriaris* Hübner.
The moth is found from Pennsylvania to Missouri and Texas.
It is common in Florida.

Genus REMIGIA Guenée

＊ **(1) Remigia repanda** Fabricius, Plate XXXVI, Fig. 16, ♂.
Syn. *latipes* Guenée; *perlata* Walker; *indentata* Harvey; *texana* Morrison.
The species, which is somewhat variable, is said to occur in Labrador, but the writer, though he has at various times received large collections from that country, is not in possession of any direct evidence of the correctness of the statement. The insect does, however, occur in northern Canada and ranges thence southwardly to Argentina, keeping, so far as is known, to the eastern side of the Rocky Mountains and the Andes.

Genus GRAMMODES Guenée

A moderately large genus, which is represented in both hemispheres. Three species occur in our fauna, of which we figure one.

(1) Grammodes smithi Guenée, Plate XXXVI, Fig. 22, ♀.
The moth occurs in the Gulf States and in Mexico. The specimen figured was taken in southern Texas.

Genus EPIDROMA Guenée

(1) Epidroma delinquens Walker, Plate XXX, Fig. 42, ♀.
The moth, which is common enough in Central and South America, has recently been found to occur in southern Florida.

Genus POAPHILA Guenée

This is a genus of large size, the insects belonging to which occur in the warmer regions of America. We figure but one of the twelve species, which are attributed to our fauna.

(1) Poaphila quadrifilaris Hübner, Plate XXXIII, Fig. 17, ♀.
The insect is known to occur from Massachusetts to Florida along the coast.

*Should be *R. texana* Morrison in text and plate.—A.E.B.

Genus PHURYS Guenée

Six species occurring within our territory are given as belonging to this genus in the latest list of the lepidoptera of North America. Of these we illustrate two.

(1) **Phurys vinculum** Guenée, Plate XXXVI, Fig. 12, ♂.
The species occurs in the Gulf States and southward.

(2) **Phurys lima** Guenée, Plate XXXVI, Fig 11, ♂.
The range of this insect is the same as that of the preceding species. It may be easily distinguished by the presence of the small round dark dot near the base of the fore wings on the inner margin.

Genus CELIPTERA Guenée

(1) **Celiptera frustulum** Guenée, Plate XXXVI, Fig. 13, ♀.
Syn. *discissa* Walker; *elongatus* Grote.
The moth is found from Canada to the Gulf of Mexico east of the Rocky Mountains.

Genus ANTICARSIA Hübner

Of the two species of the genus found within our limits we give a figure of the one which most commonly occurs.

(1) **Anticarsia gemmatilis** Hübner, Plate XXXVII, Fig. 10, ♂.
The moth is found through the valley of the Mississippi from Wisconsin to Texas.

Genus ANTIBLEMMA Hübner

(1) **Antiblemma inexacta** Walker, Plate XXXVI, Fig. 23, ♂.
Syn. *canalis* Grote.
This is a variable insect, to which a number of subspecific names have been given, based upon slight differences in the markings of the wings. It is found in the Southern States, and ranges thence to the southern portions of the South American continent.

Genus LITOPROSOPSUS Grote

(1) **Litoprosopsus futilis** Grote & Robinson, Plate XXXVII, Fig. 4, ♂.
The insect occurs in Florida and Georgia and also in the hotter portions of America.

Genus OPHIDERES Boisduval

This is a large genus of remarkably showy insects, which are more numerously found in the tropics of the Old World than in the New. There are several very beautiful species which are found in South America. Only one occurs sparingly as a straggler into our fauna. It is now and then taken in Florida. It is commoner in South America and is also found in Africa.

(1) **Ophideres materna** Linnæus, Plate XXXVI, Fig. 8, ♀.
Syn. *hybrida* Fabricius; *calaminea* Cramer.
The insect is rare in Florida.

Genus STRENOLOMA Grote

(1) **Strenoloma lunilinea** Grote, Plate XXXVI, Fig. 9, ♂.
This fine moth is quite common in the valley of the Ohio, and ranges from Pennsylvania southward and westward as far as Missouri and the Gulf of Mexico.

Genus CAMPOMETRA Guenée

The species of this genus are principally found in the southern and southwestern portions of our territory.

(1) **Campometra amella** Guenée, Plate XXXVII, Fig. 8, ♀.
Syn. *integerrima* Walker; *stylobata* Harvey.
The species ranges from Florida to Texas.
(2) **Campometra mima** Harvey, Plate XXXVII, Fig. 9, ♂.
The moth occurs from Colorado to Texas and Arizona.

Genus TRAMA Harvey

Three species are assigned to this genus in recent lists.
(1) **Trama detrahens** Walker, Plate XXXVI, Fig. 21, ♂.
Syn. *arrosa* Harvey.
The habitat of this species is the Southern States.

Genus MATIGRAMMA Grote

A small genus, the species of which are southern, or southwestern, in their distribution.

(1) **Matigramma pulverilinea** Grote, Plate XXXVII, Fig. 11, ♀.
The moth is found from Florida to Texas.

Genus CAPNODES Guenée

The genus is well represented in the tropics of both hemispheres. There is but one species in our fauna, **Capnodes punctivena** Smith, a representation of which is given in the accompanying cut, drawn from the type in the National Museum.

Fig. 165.—*Capnodes punctivena*, ♂ . ¼.

Genus YRIAS Guenée

Not a large genus, the species of which are confined to the southwestern portions of our territory.

(1) **Yrias clientis** Grote, Plate XXXVII, Fig. 13, ♂ .
The insect is found in Arizona.
(2) **Yrias repentis** Grote, Plate XXXVII, Fig. 12, ♂ .
The moth, like its predecessor, is found in Arizona.

Genus ZALE Hübner

(1) **Zale horrida** Hübner, Plate XXXVII, Fig. 3, ♂ .
The moth is found throughout the United States east of the region of the Great Plains.

Genus SELENIS Guenée

The only species of the genus which occurs within our borders is **monotropa** Grote. It is found in Texas. The annexed

Fig. 166.—*Selenis monotropa*, ♂ . ¼.

cut was drawn from the type of the species which is preserved in the British Museum. It was made by Mr. Horace Knight, under the supervision of Sir George F. Hampson.

277

Genus PHEOCYMA Hübner

(1) **Pheocyma lunifera** Hübner, Plate XXXVII, Fig. 5, ♀.
Syn. *lineola* Walker.
Found in the Appalachian subregion.

Genus YPSIA Guenée

(1) **Ypsia undularis** Drury, Plate XXXVII, Fig. 6, ♀.
The moth occurs from Canada to Florida and westward to Colorado.

Genus PSEUDANTHRACIA Grote

(1) **Pseudanthracia coracias** Guenée, Plate XXXVII, Fig, 7, ♀.
The insect, which is far from common in collections, has practically the same range as the preceding species, of which it appears at first glance to be a miniature reproduction.

Genus HOMOPTERA Boisduval

This is quite an extensive genus, species of which occur both in the Old World and the New. Some twenty or more so-called species are attributed to our fauna, but several of these will no doubt prove to be mere varieties or local races of others. We give figures of three of the commoner forms in our plates.

(1) **Homoptera lunata** Drury, Plate XXXVII, Fig. 15, ♂.
Form **edusa** Drury, Plate XXXVII, Fig. 16, ♂.
Syn. *putrescens* Guenée; *saundersi* Bethune; *viridans* Walker; *involuta* Walker.
Almost universally distributed throughout the United States and Canada.

(2) **Homoptera cingulifera** Walker, Plate XXXVII, Fig. 17, ♀.
Syn. *intenta* Walker; *woodi* Grote.
The moth occurs from Massachusetts to Florida and westward to the region of the Great Plains.

* (3) **Homoptera unilineata** Grote, Plate XXXVII, Fig. 14, ♀.
The insect ranges from eastern Canada to the Carolinas and westward to the Mississippi. It appears to be quite common in eastern Massachusetts. The specimen figured on the plate was taken at Magnolia, Massachusetts.

*Should be *H. obliqua* Guenée in text and plate.—A.E.B.

Genus LATEBRARIA Guenée

(1) **Latebraria amphipyroides** Guenée.

There is only one species of the genus known to occur within the faunal limits covered by this book. It is a straggler from the South American and Mexican territories, in which it is quite common. The accompanying cut based upon a drawing made from a specimen contained in the collection of the United States National Museum at Washington, will, no doubt, enable the student to r e a d i l y recognize the

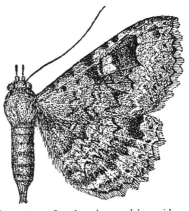

FIG. 167.—*Latebraria amphipyroides*, ♂. ⅓.

species, which is not likely to be confounded with anything else.

Genus EREBUS Latreille

This is a genus of large moths most in evidence in the tropics of the New World. Only one species occurs in the United States.

(1) **Erebus odora** Linnæus, Plate XXXVII, Fig. 2, ♀.
Syn. *agarista* Cramer.

This great moth is very common in the tropical regions of America. It occurs quite abundantly in southern Florida and the warmer portions of the Gulf States, and is universally distributed over the countries of Central America and throughout tropical South America. It is found as a straggler into the northern portions of the United States, and has even been taken in Canada. I have in my collection a specimen which was taken at Leadville, Colorado, in a snowstorm which occurred there one Fourth of July. The insect, blown to that lofty and desolate spot, was caught fluttering about in the drifts.

Genus THYSANIA Dalman

(1) **Thysania zenobia** Cramer, Plate XXXVII, Fig. 1, ♀.

This is another great South American moth, which occasionally occurs within our territory. It has been taken in Florida and southern Texas. It is a very abundant species in Mexico and South America.

Genus EPIZEUXIS Hübner

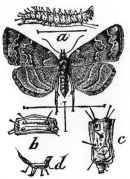

FIG. 168.—*Epizeuxis americalis.* a, Larva enlarged; b, Dorsal view of larval segment; c, Lateral view of do.; d, Cremaster of pupa. (After Riley, "Insect Life," Vol. IV, p. 111.)

This is a genus of considerable size. The larvæ feed upon dried leaves for the most part. Eleven species are attributed to our fauna, five of which we figure.

(1) **Epizeuxis americalis** Guenée.
Syn. *scriptipennis* Walker.

The range of this insect is from Canada to Texas east of the Rocky Mountains. It is exceedingly common in the woods of the Appalachian subregion, and is one of the moths which are most commonly attracted to sugar. The life history has been well ascertained, and has been entertainly described by Professor C. V. Riley in the Fourth Volume of "Insect Life." The reader is referred to the account there given for fuller details.

(2) **Epizeuxis æmula** Hübner.
Syn. *mollifera* Walker; *herminioides* Walker; *effusalis* Walker; *concisa* Walker.

The range and the habits of this species are very much the same as those of the last mentioned species. Like it, the insect is also very frequent at sugar, and on a warm summer night, in the forests of southern Indiana, I have seen as many as twenty of these moths at one time, congregated about a spot on the trunk of a tree, which had been moistened with beer in which sugar had been dissolved.

(3) **Epizeuxis lubricalis** Geyer, Plate XXXVII, Fig. 29, ♀.
Syn. *phœalis* Guenée; *surrectalis* Walker.

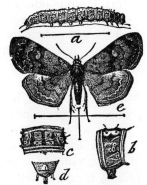

FIG. 169.—*Epizeuxis æmula.* a, Larva enlarged; b, Segment of larva viewed laterally; c, do. viewed dorsally; d, Tip of pupa; e, Moth. (After Riley, "Insect Life," Vol. IV, p. 110.)

The species occurs generally throughout the United States and Canada.

(4) **Epizeuxis denticulalis** Harvey, Plate XXXVII, Fig. 27, ♂.

The insect is found from the Atlantic to the Mississippi and from Canada to the Carolinas.

(5) **Epizeuxis scobialis** Grote, Plate XXXVII, Fig. 28, ♀.

The moth occurs from New England to the Trans-Mississippi States, east of the Great Plains.

Genus ZANCLOGNATHA Lederer

The genus is of moderate size. All of the species known are found in the Appalachian subregion, and have within it a wide range.

(1) **Zanclognatha lævigata** Grote, Plate XXXVII, Fig. 21, ♂.

The species is somewhat variable in the amount of dark shading upon the fore wings. It is distributed from Canada to the southern states.

(2) **Zanclognatha protumnusalis** Walker.

Syn. *minimalis* Grote.

The moth has much the same range as the last-mentioned species. Its life history has been accurately ascertained, and Professor C. V. Riley has given us an account of the habits of the insect in the paper to which reference has already been made.

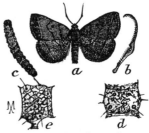

FIG. 170.—*Zanclognatha protumnusalis.* a, Moth; b, Male antenna; c, Larva; d, Dorsal view of larval segment; e, lateral view of do.; b, d, e, Enlarged. (After Riley, "Insect Life," Vol. IV, p. 111.)

The types of both Walker's and Grote's insects are preserved in the British Museum, and there is no doubt of their identity.

(3) **Zanclognatha ochreipennis** Grote, Plate XXXVII, Fig. 22, ♂.

The habitat and the habits of this species are much the same as those of the preceding.

(4) **Zanclognatha lituralis** Hübner, Plate XXXVII, Fig. 20, ♀.

The moth is widely distributed throughout the Appalachian subregion.

Genus HORMISA Walker

This is a small genus of which there are known to be four species inhabiting our territory. We figure the two commonest of these.

(1) **Hormisa absorptalis** Walker, Plate XXXVII, Fig. 19, ♂.
Syn. *nubilifascia* Grote.

The moth ranges from Canada to Virginia and westward to Illinois.

(2) **Hormisa bivittata** Grote, Plate XXXVII, Fig. 31, ♂.

The moth, which is not common in collections, is found from Quebec and Maine to Wisconsin and Iowa, and southward as far as Pennsylvania and Ohio.

Genus SISYRHYPENA Grote

FIG. 171.—*Sisyrhypena orciferalis,* ♂. ¼.

(1) **Sisyrhypena orciferalis** Walker.
Syn. *pupillaris* Grote; *harti* French.

The figure which we give was drawn for this book from the type of the species which is in the collection of Mr. Grote in the British Museum. The insect occurs in the southern States.

Genus PHILOMETRA Grote

Three species are reckoned as belonging to this genus. We give a figure of one of them.

(1) **Philometra metonalis** Walker, Plate XXVII, Fig. 30, ♂.
Syn. *goasalis* Walker; *longilabris* Grote.

The moth is found from Nova Scotia and the region of Hudson Bay to Virginia and westward to Illinois.

Genus CHYTOLITA Grote

(1) **Chytolita morbidalis** Guenée, Plate XXXVII, Fig. 23, ♀.
The moth is not at all uncommon in the Atlantic subregion.

Genus HYPENULA Grote

One species is reckoned as belonging to this genus.

Fig. 172.—*Hypenula cacuminalis,* ♂ . ¼.

(1) Hypenula cacuminalis Walker.

Syn. *biferalis* Walker; *opacalis* Grote.

The moth is a native of the southern portions of our territory.
The figure we give is taken from Walker's type, which is preserved in the British Museum. We also give a figure of a specimen preserved in the American Museum of Natural History, and which was determined by Mr. Grote as his species, to which he gave the name opacalis. The comparison of the two figures will serve to illustrate the variability of the species.

Fig. 173.—*Hypenula opacalis* Grote, ♂ . ¼.

Genus RENIA Guenée

There are eight species belonging to the genus which are found within the region covered by this book. One of the commonest of these is selected for illustration.

(1) **Renia discoloralis** Guenée, Plate XXXVII, Fig. 24, ♂ .

Syn. *fallacialis* Walker; *generalis* Walker; *thraxalis* Walker.

The insect is very common in the Appalachian subregion.

Genus BLEPTINA Guenée

(1) **Bleptina caradrinalis** Guenée, Plate XXXVII, Fig. 32, ♂ .

Syn. *cloniasalis* Walker.

The moth occurs from Canada to the Gulf of Mexico, and westward to the Rocky Mountains.

Genus TETANOLITA Grote

Three species are assigned to this genus in the latest lists. Of these, we have selected the one which is the type of the genus for purposes of illustration. The specific name **mynesalis** was originally applied to the insect by Walker. Subsequently Grote gave it the name *lixalis*. The cut hereto annexed was drawn

FIG. 174.— *Tetanolita mynesalis,* ♂ . ¼.

from Walker's type, which is contained in the collections of the British Museum. The moth ranges from Pennsylvania to Illinois and southward to the Gulf of Mexico.

Genus HETEROGRAMMA Guenée

(1) **Heterogramma pyramusalis** Walker, Plate XXXVII, Fig. 26, ♀.

Syn. *gyasalis* Walker; *rurigena* Grote.

The species is found from Canada to the Gulf of Mexico and westward to the region of the Great Plains. It is the only species in the genus.

Genus GABERASA Walker

(1) **Gaberasa ambigualis** Walker, Plate XLII, Fig. 2, ♂.

Syn. *bifidalis* Grote; *indivisalis* Grote.

The male moth has the fore wings bifid. Grote described the female, which has not bifid wings, under the name *indivisalis*. The moth occurs from Canada to Texas.

Genus DIRCETIS Grote

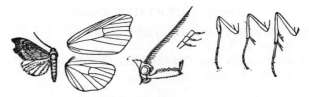

FIG. 175.— *Dircetis pygmæa* Grote, ♀ . ¼.

There are two species of the genus which are found within our borders. We give in the cut a figure of the type of Grote's species to which he applied the name **pygmæa**. It is found from Florida to Texas along the shores of the Gulf of Mexico.

Genus PALTHIS Hübner

Two species of the genus are found within the United States. We figure both of them.

(1) **Palthis angulalis** Hübner, Plate XXXVII, Fig. 25, ♀.
Syn. *aracinthusalis* Walker.

The insect is very common everywhere from Canada to the Gulf of Mexico east of the Great Plains.

(2) **Palthis asopialis** Guenée, Plate XLII, Fig. 1, ♀.

The distribution of the species is the same as that of the preceding.

Genus CAPIS Grote

(1) **Capis curvata** Grote, Plate XXXVII, Fig. 33, ♀.

The insect is found in Maine, northern New York, and Canada. It is the only species belonging to the genus.

Genus SALIA Hübner

Two species belonging to the genus are found within our territory. We figure in the accompanying cut the type of one of these, which received the specific name **interpuncta** at the hands of Mr. Grote.

FIG. 176.—*Salia interpuncta,* ♀. ¼.

The moth is found from Massachusetts to Arizona.

Genus LOMANALTES Grote

(1) **Lomanaltes eductalis** Walker.
Syn. *lætulus* Grote.

The figure of the moth which we give was drawn for this book by Mrs. Beutenmüller of New York from a specimen contained in the collections of the American Museum of Natural History. The insect ranges from Nova Scotia to

FIG. 177.—*Lomanaltes eductalis,* ♂. ¼.

Minnesota and southward to New York and Pennsylvania.

285

Genus BOMOLOCHA Hübner

Sixteen species occurring within our limits are attributed to this genus in the latest List of the Lepidoptera of North America. Nine of these we illustrate.

(1) **Bomolocha manalis** Walker, Plate XLII, Fig. 3, ♂.

The moth ranges from Canada and Minnesota southward to the valleys of the Potomac and the Ohio.

(2) **Bomolocha baltimoralis** Guenée, Plate XLII, Fig. 4, ♀.
Syn. *benignalis* Walker; *laciniosa* Zeller.

The geographical distribution of the species practically coincides with that of the last.

(3) **Bomolocha bijugalis** Walker, Plate XLII, Fig. 7, ♀.
Syn. *fecialis* Grote; *pallialis* Zeller.

The insect occurs from Canada to Florida and westward to the Rocky Mountains.

(4) **Bomolocha scutellaris** Grote, Plate XLII, Fig. 10, ♂.

The moth is found from New England to British Columbia, but does not range far to the south.

(5) **Bomolocha abalinealis** Walker, Plate XLII, Fig. 5, ♂.

The habitat of the insect extends from New England and Canada westward to Illinois and southward to Pennsylvania and the Virginias.

(6) **Bomolocha madefactalis** Guenée, Plate XLII, Fig. 6, ♂.
Syn. *achatinalis* Zeller; *damnosalis* Walker; *caducalis* Walker; *profecta* Grote.

The insect is found from the Middle States southward to Texas.

(7) **Bomolocha toreuta** Grote, Plate XLII, Fig. 9, ♂.
Syn. *albisignalis* Zeller.

The moth ranges over the same region as the last-mentioned species.

(8) **Bomolocha deceptalis** Walker, Plate XLII, Fig. 8, ♂.
Syn. *perangulalis* Harvey.

The moth is found from Canada to Virginia.

(9) **Bomolocha edictalis** Walker, Plate XLII, Fig. 11, ♂.
Syn. *lentiginosa* Grote; *vellifera* Grote.

The range of the species is the same as that of the last mentioned.

Genus PLATHYPENA Grote

Only one species of the genus is known to occur within our territory.

(1) **Plathypena scabra** Fabricius, Plate XLII, Fig. 14, ♂.

Syn. *erectalis* Guenée; *palpalis* Haworth; *crassatus* Haworth; *obesalis* Stephens.

Universally distributed through the United States and Canada east of the Rocky Mountains.

Genus HYPENA Schrank

The genus is found in all parts of the globe. Three species are known to be found in our territory. Of these we figure the one which is commonest.

(1) **Hypena humuli** Harris, Plate XLII, Fig. 12, ♂ ; Fig. 13, ♀, *var.*

Syn. *evanidalis* Robinson; *germanalis* Walker.

This insect, the larva of which does considerable damage to the hop, is widely distributed over the whole of the United States and Canada. It is somewhat variable in the shade of the wings and the amount of maculation upon them. For an account of the habits of the insect and the best manner to guard against the ravages which the larva commits the reader is referred to the excellent article by Dr. L. O. Howard of the Department of Agriculture in Washington upon insects injurious to the hop-vine, which was published as the Seventh Bulletin of the New Series of Bulletins issued by the Division of Entomology of the Department.

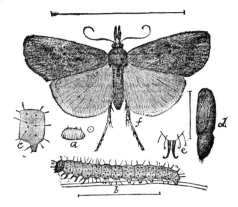

FIG. 178.—*Hypena humuli.* a, egg; b, larva; c, segment of do.; d, pupa; e, tip of do.; f, adult. a, c, e, greatly enlarged. (After Howard, Bull. U. S. Dept. Agric., New Series, No. 7, p. 44.)

> *Arm.* Who was Samson's love, my dear Moth?
> *Moth.* A woman, master.
> —SHAKESPEARE, *Love's Labor's Lost, I, 2.*

FAMILY NYCTEOLIDÆ

"An vnredy reue thi residue shal spene,
That menye moththe was maister ynne, in a mynte-while."
PIERS PLOWMAN (C) xiii, 216.

THE *Nycteolidæ* are related to the *Noctuidæ*, many of the genera, especially in the Old World, containing moths which are green in color and frequent trees. The apex of the fore wing is more or less produced to a point. The larvæ have eight pairs of legs, and are fleshy, with the anal somite tapering to a point. They are either naked or slightly pubescent. But two genera are found in the United States.

Genus NYCTEOLA Hübner

The genus is represented in both the Old World and the New. Two species are found in the United States. *

(1) **Nycteola revayana** Scopoli, form **lintnerana** Speyer, Plate XLII, Fig. 15, ♂.

A large number of synonyms and subspecific forms have been erected by authors who have dealt with this species. The form which we figure is the one which is most commonly encountered in our territory.

Genus HYBLÆA Fabricius

This genus is extensively developed in the warmer portions of the Eastern Hemisphere, but is represented by only one species in our region.

(1) **Hyblæa puera** Cramer, Plate XXX, Fig. 8, ♀.

Syn. *saga* Fabricius; *mirificum* Strecker.

The insect, which is common in the tropics of the two hemispheres, occurs occasionally in Florida. The specimen figured on our plate is contained in the collection of the United States National Museum.

*N. *cinereana* Neumœgen & Doll is also found in the Eastern U. S., and *N. columbiana* Henry Edwards on the West Coast.—A.E.B.

FAMILY PERICOPIDÆ

(HYPSIDÆ Auctorum)

" Loose to the wind their airy garments flew,
Thin glittering textures of the filmy dew,
Dipt in the richest tincture of the skies,
Where light disports in ever-mingling dyes,
While every beam new transient colours flings,
Colours that change whene'er they wave their wings."

POPE.—*Rape of the Lock.*

The following characterization of the family is taken from Hampson's "*Moths of India,*" Vol. I, p. 495: "Proboscis present. Palpi smoothly scaled; the third joint long and naked. Legs smooth; mid tibiae with one pair of spurs, hind tibiae with two pairs. Frenulum present. Fore wing with vein 1a separate from 1b; 1c absent; 5 from near lower angle of cell. Hind wing with veins 1a and 1b present, 1c absent; 5 from near lower angle of cell; 8 free from the base and connected by a bar with 7 at middle of cell.

"*Larva* with all the legs present, sparsely covered with long hairs.

"*Cocoon* slight."

Genus DARITIS Walker

A small genus of rather showy moths, which is represented in our fauna by two species.

(1) **Daritis thetis** Klug, Plate XXXVIII, Fig. 5, ♀.
The insect occurs in southern Arizona.

Genus COMPOSIA Hübner

(1) **Composia fidelissima** Herrich-Schæffer, Plate XXXVIII, Fig. 4, ♂.

Syn. *olympia* Butler.

This very beautiful moth is found throughout the Antilles and in southern Florida. It is the only representative of its genus which occurs within our territory.

Genus GNOPHÆLA Walker

Three species of this genus are found within the limits of the United States. Others occur in Mexico and Central America.

(1) **Gnophæla latipennis** Boisduval, Plate XXXVIII, Fig. 2, ♂.

Syn. *hopfferi* Grote & Robinson; *discreta* Stretch; *arizonæ* French; *morrisoni* Druce.

The habitat of this species is the southwestern portion of our territory and northern Mexico.

(2) **Gnophæla vermiculata** Grote & Robinson, Plate XXXVIII, Fig. 3, ♂.

Syn. *continua* Henry Edwards.

The moth is found from southern Colorado westward and south-westward.

(3) **Gnophæla clappiana** Holland, Plate XXXVIII, Fig. 1, ♂.

The figure on our plate represents the type of the species, which was taken at Colorado Springs. It occurs from central Colorado to Arizona.

DAS LIED VOM SCHMETTERLINGE

"Liebes, leichtes, luft'ges Ding,
Schmetterling,
Das da über Blumen schwebet,
Nur von Thau und Blüten lebet,
Blüte selbst, ein fliegend Blatt,
Das, mit welchem Rosenfinger!
Wer bepurpurt hat?

War's ein Sylphe, der dein Kleid
So bestreut,
Dich aus Morgenduft gewebet,
Nur auf Tage dich belebet?
Seelchen, und dein kleines Herz
Pocht da unter meinem Finger,
Fühlet Todesschmerz.

Fleuch dahin, O Seelchen, sei
Froh und frei,
Mir ein Bild, was ich sein werde,
Wenn die Raupe dieser Erde
Auch wie du ein Zephyr ist
Und in Duft und Thau und Honig
Jede Blüte küsst."

HERDER.

FAMILY DIOPTIDÆ

"Genius detects through the fly, through the caterpillar, through the grub, through the egg, the constant individual; through countless individuals the fixed species, through many species the genus, through all genera the steadfast type; through all the kingdoms of organized life the eternal unity."—RALPH WALDO EMERSON.

The moths belonging to this family are, so far as is known, closely related in many respects to the *Geometridæ*. They differ, however, in having veins 3 and 4 of the hind wing arising from a common stalk at the lower angle of the cell. The family is well represented in the tropics of the New World, but is only known in our territory by the genus *Phryganidia* Packard, which occurs in southern California.

Genus PHRYGANIDIA Packard

(1) **Phryganidia californica** Packard, Plate XXXVIII, Fig. 6, ♂.

The moth, which is obscurely colored, is one of the least attractive insects belonging to the family which it represents. Many of the species are very bright and gay in color, as any student of the fauna of South America knows. The home of the species, as the name implies, is California, to the southern portion of which it is confined.

"Happy insect, what can be
In happiness compared to thee?
Fed with nourishment divine,
The dewey morning's gentle wine!
Nature waits upon thee still,
And thy verdant cup does fill;
'Tis filled wherever thou dost tread
Nature's self thy Ganymede.

"Thou dost drink and dance and sing,
Happier than the happiest king!
All the fields which thou dost see,
All the plants belong to thee,
All the summer hours produce,
Fertile made with early juice,
Man for thee does sow and plough,
Farmer he, and landlord thou."

From the Greek of Anacreon.

FAMILY NOTODONTIDÆ

"The Beauty which old Greece or Rome
Sung, painted, wrought, lies here at home;
We need but eye and ear
In all our daily walks to trace
The outlines of incarnate grace,
The hymns of gods to hear."

WHITTIER.

The Notodontidæ have been characterized by Sir George F. Hampson as follows: "A family of moths superficially resembling the Noctuidæ. Mid tibia with one pair of spurs; hind tibia with two pairs; tarsi short and hairy. Fore wing with vein 1a forming a fork with 1b at the base; 1c absent; vein 5 from the middle of the discocellulars, or rarely from just below the upper angle of the cell. Hind wings with two internal veins; vein 5 from the centre of the discocellulars or rarely absent; 8 free from the base, curved, and running close along the subcostal nervure or joined to it by a bar.

"*Larva* without the anal prolegs, and carrying the anal somites more or less erect; these often bear paired processes and are sometimes swollen; the other somites are often prominently humped.

"*Pupa* naked."

An elaborate and very useful monograph dealing with the insects composing this family has been written by Professor A. S. Packard, and is published in the Memoirs of the National Academy of Science, Vol. VII, pp. 87–284. The student will do well to refer to this.

Genus APATELODES Packard

(1) **Apatelodes torrefacta** Abbot & Smith, Plate XL, Fig. 20, ♂.

The insect is not uncommon in the Appalachian subregion. It ranges from Canada to the southern States and as far west as the Mississippi.

(2) **Apatelodes angelica** Grote, Plate XL, Fig. 21, ♂ .

Syn. *hyalinopuncta* Packard.

The distribution of this species is the same as that of the preceding. It is rather common in western Pennsylvania.

Genus MELALOPHA Hübner

Six species and a number of subspecies have been recognized as belonging to this genus and are found in the region with which this book deals. Of four of these we give figures.

(1) **Melalopha apicalis** Walker, Plate XL, Fig. 18, ♂ .

Syn. *vau* Fitch; *indentata* Packard.

The figure upon our plate, cited above, represents the form of the species to which Grote & Robinson applied the name *ornata* and of which the name *incarcerata* Boisduval is a synonym. The insect is widely distributed all over the United States.

(2) **Melalopha inclusa** Hübner, Plate XL, Fig. 19, ♀ .

Syn. *americana* Harris.

The insect is very widely distributed over the Appalachian subregion. The larva feeds upon the leaves of various species of the genus *Populus*.

(3) **Melalopha strigosa** Grote, Plate XL, Fig. 17, ♂ .

The habitat of this species is the northern portion of the Appalachian subregion.

(4) **Melalopha albosigma** Fitch, Plate XL, Fig. 16, ♂ .

Widely distributed over the United States. Easily discriminated from the other species by the broad brown shade on the apical half of the outer margin of the primaries, succeeded near the costa by a distinct s-shaped white line.

Genus DATANA Walker

Thirteen species which are properly referred to this genus are found within our limits. Of these we give figures of the four which are most commonly found.

(1) **Datana ministra** Drury, Plate I, Fig. 13, larva; Plate XL, Fig. 11, ♂ .

This is a very common species, found throughout the Appalachian subregion. The larvæ are gregarious and may be found in great masses upon the leaves of the walnut and allied trees in the latter part of August and early September.

(2) **Datana angusi** Grote & Robinson, Plate XL, Fig. 12, ♂ .

The habits and the distribution of this species are very much the same as those of the preceding.

(3) **Datana perspicua** Grote & Robinson, Plate XL, Fig. 14, ♂.

More nearly allied to *D. ministra* than to any other species of the genus, but readily distinguished from that insect by the paler color of the secondaries and the lighter, more yellowish color of the primaries.

(4) **Datana integerrima** Grote & Robinson, Plate XL, Fig. 13, ♂.

The darker color of the primaries and the more numerous transverse bands enable this species to be at once separated from the other species which we have figured.

Genus HYPERÆSCHRA Butler

(1) **Hyperæschra stragula** Grote, Plate XL, Fig. 1, ♂.
Syn. *scitipennis* Walker.

The moth is found throughout the United States. With the help of the illustration we have given there should be no difficulty whatever in determining it.

(2) **Hyperæschra georgica** Herrich-Schæffer, Plate XL, Fig. 7, ♂.

The moth is found in the Appalachian subregion, and is commoner in the southern portions of its range than in the more northern portions thereof. It is, however, not very rare in Pennsylvania.

(3) **Hyperæschra tortuosa** Tepper, Plate XL, Fig. 4, ♀.

The insect is as yet quite rare in collections. Its habitat is Colorado and Arizona.

Genus ODONTOSIA Hübner

(1) **Odontosia elegans** Strecker, Plate XL, Fig. 3, ♂.

This elegant insect is found from Canada to Colorado and appears to be commoner in the region of the Rocky Mountains than elsewhere.

Genus NOTODONTA Ochsenheimer

The genus is represented in both hemispheres. There are two species which belong to our fauna. We give illustrations of both of them.

(1) **Notodonta basitriens** Walker, Plate XL, Fig. 5, ♀.

The moth is found in the Atlantic States.

(2) **Notodonta simplaria** Græf, Plate XL, Fig. 6, ♀.

The moth, which is by no means common, occurs in the northern portions of the Appalachian subregion.

Genus PHEOSIA Hübner

(1) **Pheosia dimidiata** Herrich-Schæffer, Plate XL, Fig. 9, ♂.

Syn. *rimosa* Packard; *californica* Stretch.

The moth, which is far from common, ranges from Canada and New England westward to the region of the Rocky Mountains.

(2) **Pheosia portlandia** Henry Edwards, Plate XL, Fig. 10, ♂.

Syn. *descherei* Neumœgen.

The species replaces in the northwestern States the form, which has been described as *dimidiata*. Whether this is a valid species or a local race of the preceding is a question which is still open to discussion.

Genus LOPHODONTA Packard

(1) **Lophodonta ferruginea** Packard, Plate XL, Fig. 8, ♀.

The moth is not rare in the Appalachian subregion. The caterpillar feeds upon the linden (*Tilia*).

(2) **Lophodonta angulosa** Abbot & Smith, Plate XL, Fig. 15, ♂.

The insect is found in the same region as the last mentioned, and its habits are very much the same.

Genus EUNYSTALEA Grote

(1) **Eunystalea indiana** Grote.

This is one of the rarest insects of the family to which it belongs. Besides the type, which the writer believes to be contained in the collection of the British Museum, there is only one other specimen known, which is found in the collection of Dr. Barnes, to whom the author is indebted for the privilege of being allowed to make the cut which is given herewith. The insect occurs in Florida.

FIG. 179.—*Eunystalea indiana,* ♂. ¼.

Genus NADATA Walker

(1) **Nadata gibbosa** Abbot & Smith, Plate XXXIX, Fig. 1, ♀.

This insect, the distribution of which is almost universal throughout our territory, has been described under a number of varietal or subspecific names, founded for the most part upon trifling variations in the ground-color of the wings.

Genus NERICE Walker

(1) **Nerice bidentata** Walker, Plate I, Fig. 15, larva; Plate XXXIX, Fig. 2, ♂.

The larva feeds upon the elm. The insect has a wide range through the Appalachian subregion.

Genus SYMMERISTA Hübner

(1) **Symmerista albifrons** Abbot & Smith, Plate XXXIX, Fig. 7, ♀.

A very common insect in the Appalachian subregion, ranging from the Atlantic westward as far as the region of the Rocky Mountains.

Genus HIPPIA Mœschler

(1) **Hippia packardi** Morrison, Plate XXXIX, Fig. 18, ♀.

A rather scarce insect in collections. Its habitat is Texas.

Genus DASYLOPHIA Packard

(1) **Dasylophia anguina** Abbot & Smith, Plate XXXIX, Fig. 5, ♂.

Syn. *cuculifera* Herrich-Schæffer; *punctata* Walker; *cana* Walker; *signata* Walker.

The moth ranges from the Atlantic to the Rocky Mountains.

(2) **Dasylophia thyatiroides** Walker, Plate XXXIX, Fig. 6, ♀.

Syn. *interna* Packard; *tripartita* Walker.

The habitat of the moth is the Appalachian subregion. The specimen figured was taken in Indiana.

Genus LITODONTA Harvey

(1) **Litodonta hydromeli** Harvey, Plate XXXIX, Fig. 20, ♂.

The moth, which is the sole representative of the genus in

our fauna, is not at all uncommon in Texas and Arizona, and ranges southward into northern Mexico.

Genus HETEROCAMPA Doubleday

Eleven species belonging to this somewhat extensive genus are recognized as occurring within the limits with which this book deals. Six of these have been selected for illustration.

(1) **Heterocampa astarte** Doubleday, Plate XXXIX, Fig. 22, ♂.

Syn. *varia* Walker; *menas* Harris.

The moth is not uncommon in the southern States and ranges northward as far as Pennsylvania and Ohio.

(2) **Heterocampa obliqua** Packard, Plate XL, Fig. 2, ♂.

The insect occurs in the northern portions of the Appalachian subregion.

(3) **Heterocampa umbrata** Walker, Plate XXXIX, Fig. 26, ♂.

Syn. *semiplaga* Walker; *pulverea* Grote & Robinson; *athereo* Harris.

The moth is rather common in the Appalachian subregion, ranging from the Atlantic as far west as the Mississippi.

(4) **Heterocampa manteo** Doubleday, Plate XXXIX, Fig. 23, ♂.

Syn. *cinerascens* Walker; *subalbicans* Grote.

The distribution of this species is the same as that of the last mentioned.

(5) **Heterocampa biundata** Walker, Plate XXXIX, Fig. 25, ♂.

Syn. *olivatus* Packard; *mollis* Walker.

Like the preceding species, this is a native of the eastern portion of our territory, and occurs from Canada southward to Georgia.

(6) **Heterocampa bilineata** Packard, Plate XXXIX, Fig. 24, ♂.

Syn. *turbida* Walker; *associata* Walker; *ulmi* Harris.

Not uncommon in the eastern States.

Genus MISOGADA Walker

(1) **Misogada unicolor** Packard, Plate XXXIX, Fig. 21, ♀.

Syn. *marina* Packard; *cinerea* Schaus (*non* Packard); *sobria* Walker.

This is the sole species of the genus. It inhabits the Appalachian subregion.

Genus EUHYPARPAX Beutenmüller

The only species of the genus as yet known is that to which

Beutenmüller applied the name **rosea**. It is a native of Colorado, and is as yet very rare in collections, only one specimen, the type, being known. This is found in the collection of the American Museum of Natural History in New York. The moth is pale rosy red in color, and marked as shown in the cut, which was drawn from the type by Mrs. Beutenmüller.

FIG. 180.—*Euhyparpax rosea*, ♂ · ¼·

Genus IANASSA Walker

(1) **Ianassa lignicolor** Walker, Plate XXXIX, Fig. 19, ♀.
Syn. *virgata* Packard; *lignigera* Walker.

The habitat of the species is the Appalachian subregion. Two other species, both of them inhabiting the southwestern portions of our territory, are known to belong to the genus.

Genus SCHIZURA Doubleday

(1) **Schizura ipomœæ** Doubleday, form **cinereofrons** Packard, Plate XXXIX, Fig. 13, ♂.

The species is widely distributed throughout the United States. Several subspecific or varietal forms have been described, and a number of synonyms have been created for the species. For a knowledge of these the reader may refer to the Monograph by Professor Packard, to which allusion has already been made.

(2) **Schizura concinna** Abbot & Smith, Plate XXXIX, Fig. 15, ♂.
Syn. *nitida* Packard.

This is also a widely distributed species. The larva feeds upon the *Rosaceæ*.

(3) **Schizura unicornis** Abbot & Smith, Plate XXXIX, Fig. 17, ♂.
Syn. *edmandsi* Packard; *humilis* Walker; *conspecta* Henry Edwards.

This is a very common species of wide distribution. Its habits are much the same as those of the last mentioned.

(4) **Schizura badia** Packard, Plate XXXIX, Fig. 14, ♀.
Syn. *significata* Walker.
The habitat of the species is the Appalachian subregion.
(5) **Schizura leptinoides** Grote, Plate XXXIX, Fig. 16, ♂.
Syn. *mustelina* Packard.
The insect ranges through the Atlantic States westward to the Mississippi.

Genus HYPARPAX Hübner

(1) **Hyparpax aurora** Abbot & Smith, Plate XXXIX, Fig. 4, ♂.
Syn. *rosea* Walker; *venusta* Walker.
The moth occurs in the Appalachian subregion, but is more common in Virginia than elsewhere, so far as the observations of the writer extend.
(2) **Hyparpax venus** Neumœgen, Plate XXXIX, Fig. 3, ♂.
The habitat of the insect is Colorado.
(3) **Hyparpax perophoroides** Strecker, Plate XL, Fig. 28, ♂.
The insect has thus far been reported only from Florida. I am indebted to Mr. Beutenmüller for the loan of the specimen, which is figured upon the plate.

Genus CERURA Schrank

The genus is found in both hemispheres. Two species are attributed to it as being found in the United States.
(1) **Cerura scitiscripta** Walker, form **multiscripta** Riley, Plate I, Fig. 18, larva; Plate XXXIX, Fig. 12, ♂.
The moth is known to occur from New England to Mexico.

Genus HARPYIA Ochsenheimer

(1) **Harpyia borealis** Boisduval, Plate XXXIX, Fig. 9, ♂.
The range of the species is through the Appalachian subregion.
(2) **Harpyia cinerea** Walker, Plate XXXIX, Fig. 8, ♀.
The moth occurs almost everywhere throughout the United States and southern Canada.
(3) **Harpyia scolopendrina** Boisduval, Plate XXXIX, Fig. 11, ♂.
Syn. *aquilonaris* Lintner.
* Form **albicoma** Strecker, Plate XXXIX, Fig, 10, ♂.

*This line should read: (4) *Harpyia modesta* Hudson, Plate XXXIX, Fig. 11, ♂.—A.E.B.

The insect is a denizen of Canada and the northern portions of the United States from the Atlantic to the Pacific.

Genus FENTONIA Butler

(1) **Fentonia marthesia** Cramer, Plate XXXIX, Fig. 30, ♂.
Syn. *tessella* Packard; *turbida* Walker.

The moth, which is by no means common, has a wide range through the Appalachian subregion.

Genus GLUPHISIA Boisduval

(1) **Gluphisia septentrionalis** Walker, Plate XXXIX, Fig. 28, ♂.
Syn. *clandestina* Walker; *trilineata* Packard.

Widely distributed throughout the entire territory.

(2) **Gluphisia wrighti** Henry Edwards, Plate XXIX, Fig. 29, ♂.
Syn. *albofascia* Henry Edwards; *rupta* Henry Edwards; *formosa* Henry Edwards.

The moth is found in southern California and Arizona, as well as in northern Mexico.

(3) **Gluphisia severa** Henry Edwards, Plate XXXIX, Fig. 27, ♂.
Syn. *danbyi* Neumœgen; *avimacula* Hudson; *slossoni* Packard.

The species, which is somewhat variable in the maculation of the wings, is found in the northern portions of our territory.

Genus ELLIDA Grote

(1) **Ellida caniplaga** Walker, Plate XXXIX, Fig. 31, ♀.
Syn. *transversata* Walker; *gelida* Grote.

The moth in Pennsylvania is double-brooded. The first brood appears upon the wing in the early spring. The caterpillar feeds upon the linden (*Tilia*). The second brood is matured about the end of July. The insect is not common in collections, because its habits have not been hitherto understood.

Genus CARGIDA Schaus

(1) **Cargida cadmia** Guenée.
Syn. *obliquilinea* Walker.

The moth is a native of the southern States, and ranges from Texas southward to Costa Rica. The cut which we give is drawn from the type of Walker's species, which is contained in the British Museum. The insect is rare as yet in collections, though specimens coming from Central America are far more

Fig. 181.—*Cargida cadmia*, ♂ . ¼.

numerous in cabinets than specimens obtained from points within the limits of the United States.

(2) **Cargida pyrrha** Druce, Plate XI, Fig. 15, ♂ .
The insect occurs in southern Arizona and in Mexico.

Genus CRINODES Herrich-Schæffer

(1) **Crinodes beskei** Hübner, Plate XLI, Fig. 4, ♂ .
This very peculiar moth is the only representative of its genus which occurs within our territory. There are numerous species found in the tropics of the New World. The habitat of the present species is Arizona and Mexico.

NASU-NO TAKE

Nasu-no Take is a volcano in the interior of Japan. Tora-san came into my room on the upper floor of the tea-house where we had made our stay while exploring the summit of the moun-tain, which was in eruption at the time. Tora-san was my *fidus Achates.* He could make an insect-box or repair a jinrickisha, for he was "an honorable carpenter." He did not disdain, when necessity demanded, to prove himself a capable cook, though this was not his calling. He could provide a meal of "America-no Chow" or "Nippon-no Chow," the *cuisine* of Anglo-Saxon and of Japanese being alike familiar to him. He was best of all an enthusiastic entomologist, and much preferred sugaring for moths to making curries. "Danna-san," he said, "Nasu-no Take have got many moth Tokio no have got." "Yea, verily! good Tora-san." "Danna-san, me catchee moth

301

ko komban sugar way. Danna-san go long?" "With all my heart! Sayo!" And so it was arranged.

In the oak-forest below the tea-house we sugared the trees. When the night came on we went with our lanterns to the spot. The black shadows clung to the woodland path. As the lanterns went bobbing along the narrow way, each turn produced a weird and beautiful effect. The gnarled old pines, the oaks and the bamboos, the wild yams festooning the shrubbery, thrust forth for a moment into relief against the universal darkness, were fascinating to look upon. Here and there white lilies held up their stately blossoms, and starry flowers, from which the moths fled as we came along, bloomed everywhere. The effect of moving lights in shrubbery and forest-growths is always charming.

But the captures of that night were more memorable than all the witchery of the strange and beautiful scenery in the midst of which we walked. The gems of our catch were a dozen perfect specimens of the great Snowy Underwing, the most beautiful as well as one of the rarest species of the splendid genus to which it belongs. I never pull out the drawer in the cabinet, where these things have rested full many a day since then, without seeing visions and dreaming dreams of the happy past. How much "globe-trotters" miss when they are not students of nature! The memory of one such night spent in the wild woods is worth the memory of weeks spent in palaces.

> " The insect legions, prank'd with gaudiest hues,
> Pearl, gold and purple, swarm'd into existence.
> Minute and marvellous creations these.
> .   .   .   .   some proudly shone
> Like living jewels; some grotesque, uncouth,
> And hideous   .   .   .   .
> Those lived deliciously on honey-dews,
> And dwelt in palaces of blossomed bells.
> Millions on millions, wing'd and plumed in front,
> Fill'd the dim atmosphere with hum and hurry.
>   MONTGOMERY. — *Pelican Island.*

FAMILY THYATIRIDÆ

"Feeble though the insect be,
Allah speaks through that to thee!
As within the moonbeam I,
God in glory sits on high,
Sits where countless planets roll,
And from thence controls the whole:
There with threads of thousand dyes
Life's bewildered web he plies,
And the hand which holds them all
Lets not e'en the feeblest fall."
ŒHLENSCHLÆGER.—*Aladdin's Lamp.*

The family has been characterized as follows by Sir George F. Hampson, in his work upon the moths of India:

"A family of moths resembling the *Noctuidæ* in appearance.

Proboscis present. Antennæ usually rather thickened and flattened. Mid tibia with one pair of spurs, hind tibia with two pairs. Fore wing with vein 1*a* short and slight, not forming a fork with 1*b;* 1*c* absent; 5 from the center of the discocellulars; veins 7 and 8 stalked; and 9 and 10 stalked, and almost or quite anastomosing with veins 7 and 8 to form an areole. Hind wing with two internal veins; vein 5 from the center of the discocellulars, or generally from below the center; veins 6 and 7 given off not far from the base; 8 bent down and quite or almost touching 7 after the bifurcation.

Larva noctuiform, with five pairs of prolegs."

Genus HABROSYNE Hübner

(1) **Habrosyne scripta** Gosse, Plate XL, Fig. 22, ♂ .

The moth is quite common locally in the northern States of the Atlantic seaboard, and ranges westward to the central portions of the Valley of the Mississippi.

303

Genus PSEUDOTHYATIRA Grote

(1) **Pseudothyatira cymatophoroides** Guenée, Plate XL, Fig. 25, ♂.

Form **expultrix** Grote, Plate XL, Fig. 26, ♂.

The moth, which occurs in the two forms which we have delineated on the plate, is a native of the northern portions of the Appalachian subregion. It is common in Pennsylvania.

Genus EUTHYATIRA Smith

(1) **Euthyatira pudens** Guenée, Plate XL, Fig. 23, ♂.

Form **pennsylvanica** Smith, Plate XL, Fig. 24, ♀.

The moth emerges in the very early spring, and may be found where it is common, seated about three inches from the end of twigs in the woodlands, with its wings folded about the twig in such a way as to elude the observation of those who are not familiar with its habits. The form *pennsylvanica* is found in both sexes in every brood. It represents a curious case of dimorphism.

Genus BOMBYCIA Hübner

(1) **Bombycia improvisa** Henry Edwards, Plate XL, Fig. 27, ♂.

Syn. *tearli* Henry Edwards.

The habitat of the insect is on the Pacific slope, in the northern portions of the coast ranges.

> "Then rapidly with foot as light
> As the young musk-roe's, out she flew
> To cull each shining leaf that grew
> Beneath the moonlight's hallowing beams
> For this enchanted wreath of dreams,
> Anemones and Seas of Gold,
>   And new-blown lilies of the river,
> And those sweet flowrets that unfold
>   Their buds on Camadeva's quiver."
>   THOMAS MOORE.—*Lalla Rookh.*

FAMILY LIPARIDÆ

"The study of entomology is one of the most fascinating of pursuits. It takes its votaries into the treasure-houses of Nature, and explains some of the wonderful series of links which form the great chain of creation. It lays open before us another world, of which we have been hitherto unconscious, and shows us that the tiniest insect, so small perhaps that the unaided eye can scarcely see it, has its work to do in the world, and does it."—REV. J. G. WOOD.

The following characterization of the family is adapted from the pages of Sir George F. Hampson's "Moths of India," Vol. I, p. 432:

'A family of moths generally of nocturnal flight, though some genera, as *Aroa* of the Eastern Hemisphere and *Hemerocampa*, are more or less diurnal in their habits. The perfect insects are mostly clothed with long hair-like scales upon the body. The males have the antennæ highly pectinated, the branches often having long terminal spines, and spines to retain them in position. The females often have a largely developed anal tuft of hair for covering the eggs. The proboscis is absent. The legs are hairy. The frenulum is present, except in the genus *Ratarda*, which does not occur in America. The fore wing with vein 1*a* not anastomosing with 1*b*; 1*c* absent except in *Ratarda*; 5 from close to lower angle of cell. Hind wing with two internal veins; 5 from close to lower angle of cell, except in the eastern genera *Gazalina* and *Porthesia*, 8 nearly touching 7 at middle of cell and connected with it by a bar.

Larva hairy; generally clothed with very thick hair or with thick tufts of hair, and forming a cocoon into which these hairs are woven, they being often of a very poisonous nature.'

Genus GYNÆPHORA Hübner

(1) **Gynæphora rossi** Curtis, Plate XXXVIII, Fig. 10, ♂, Fig. 11, ♀.

The genus is arctic, and the species is found in the arctic

regions of America, the specimens figured having been received by the writer from Point Barrow in Alaska.

Genus NOTOLOPHUS Germar

(1) **Notolophus antiqua** Linnæus, Plate XXXVIII, Fig. 18, ♂.
Syn. *nova* Fitch.

The moth is found in Europe and in the northern portions of the United States and in Canada.

Genus HEMEROCAMPA Dyar

The females in this genus are wingless, or have the wings at most rudimentary. The eggs are deposited in masses, generally upon the surface of the cocoon from which the female has emerged. The larvæ are voracious feeders; and as the species are generally very prolific, the insects inflict a great deal of damage upon vegetation.

(1) **Hemerocampa vetusta** Boisduval, Plate XXXVIII, Fig. 19, ♂.
Syn. *cana* Henry Edwards; *gulosa* Henry Edwards.

The insect replaces on the Pacific coast the following species, which in its habits it closely resembles.

(2) **Hemerocampa leucostigma** Abbot & Smith, Plate XXXVIII, Fig. 20, ♂, Fig. 21, ♀. (The White-marked Tussock Moth.)
Syn. *leucographa* Geyer; *intermedia* Fitch; *borealis* Fitch; *obliviosa* Henry Edwards.

The moth is widely distributed in the Appalachian subregion, and its ravages upon shade-trees and shrubbery are matter of familiar observation. The insect is double-brooded in the more

FIG. 182.—*H. leucostigma*, ♂. ¼. (After Riley.)

northern portions of its range, and triple-brooded farther south. The first generation is matured from eggs which, having been deposited in the fall of the year, remain *in situ* upon the cocoons upon which they were deposited until they are hatched by the heat of the sunshine of spring. The caterpillars rapidly develop, and the second generation, which is always much more numerous than the first, begins to appear about the middle of July in the latitude of New York and Philadelphia.

A third generation follows in the month of September. This generation lays the eggs from which the larvæ which appear in the following spring are hatched.

The female, as has already been stated, is wingless, and lives solely for the purpose of oviposition. Having laid her eggs, which she covers with the hairy scales which she plucks from the abdomen, and mingles with a viscid secretion, which she deposits with the eggs, and which on drying becomes hard and brittle, she dies. The young larva on being hatched has the power of spinning a thin thread of silk, with which it lowers itself from its resting-place when disturbed,

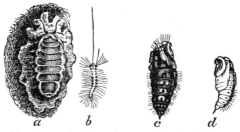

FIG. 183.—*H. leucostigma.* *a*, female; *b*, young larva, magnified; *c*, female pupa; *d*, male pupa. (After Riley.)

and by means of which it regains the place from which it has dropped. This power is lost as the insect develops after successive molts. The mature caterpillar is a rather striking and not unbeautiful creature. The head is brilliant vermilion in color; the body is white banded with black, and adorned with black-tipped tufts and bundles of cream-colored hairs. There is considerable disparity in the size of the larvæ and the pupæ of the two sexes, as is partially shown in Fig. 183. The larva and the pupa of the female moth are generally twice as large as those of the male.

The best means of combating the ravages of this insect is to see to it that in the fall and winter the cocoons, which may be found adhering to the twigs of trees and shrubs and secreted in the nooks and crannies of fences, are gathered together and destroyed. It is also useful to spray the young foliage of trees which are liable to attack with any one

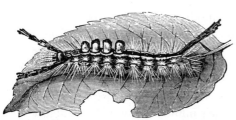

FIG. 184.—*H. leucostigma.* Larva of female moth. (After Riley.)

307

of the preparations which are made by reputable firms for the purpose of destroying the larvæ of this and other destructive insects which attack our shade-trees. The spraying should take place at intervals when the young larvæ are observed to be moving upward upon the trunks of the trees.

(3) **Hemerocampa definita** Packard, Plate XXXVIII, Fig. 17, ♂.

This species, which is closely allied to the last, is found in the northern Atlantic States. What has been said as to the habits of *H. leucostigma* applies also to this insect.

Genus OLENE Hübner

(1) **Olene achatina** Abbot & Smith, Plate XXXVIII, Fig. 9, ♂.
Syn. *parallela* Grote & Robinson; *tephra* Hübner; *cinnamomea* Grote & Robinson.

The moth, which is somewhat variable in the style and intensity of the dark markings upon the wings, is found in the Appalachian subregion, but is somewhat more frequent in the south than in the north.

(2) **Olene leucophæa** Abbot & Smith, Plate XXXVIII, Fig. 7, ♂, Fig. 8, ♀.
Syn. *basiflava* Packard; *atrivenosa* Palm; *manto* Strecker.

This is likewise a variable insect, the range of which is practically coincident with that of the last-mentioned species.

Genus PORTHETRIA Hübner

(1) **Porthetria dispar** Linnæus, Plate XXXVIII, Fig. 12, ♂, Fig. 13, ♀. (The Gypsy Moth.)

This well-known insect is a native of the Old World. A number of years ago, a gentleman interested in entomology, and residing at the time in Cambridge, Massachusetts, received from a friend in Europe a number of cocoons of the moth, from which the insects in due season emerged. A few of the number were prepared and mounted in his cabinet, and the remainder were allowed to escape through the window of the room in which they were. Unchecked by the presence of parasites, which in their native habitat keep their numbers down, they rapidly multiplied and became a scourge. Fully a million of dollars has thus far been expended in the effort to exterminate them. In spite of all the exertion which has been put forth, the insect appears to have obtained a permanent foothold in the New England States, though in recent years the destruction wrought has not been very great, owing to the incessant vigilance which is maintained by the civic authorities in repressing the nuisance.

Genus PSILURA

(1) **Psilura monacha** Linnæus, Plate XXXVIII, Fig. 14, ♂, Fig. 15, ♀.

This is another insect which is said to have been imported from Europe, and is reputed to have found a foothold on the soil of the New World. The specimens figured on our plate are from a brood which the writer is informed by Mr. George Franck, of Brooklyn, to have been found in the eastern suburbs of that place. Mr. Franck has assured me that it is certainly already well domiciled in the region.

Genus EUPROCTIS Hübner

(1) **Euproctis chrysorrhœa** Linnæus, Plate XXXVIII, Fig. 16, ♂. (The Brown-tail Moth.)

This insect, like the two preceding species, is an importation from Europe. It has become domiciled in the vicinity of Boston, Massachusetts, and is very common in the vicinity of Magnolia, Beverly Farms, and Manchester-on-the-Sea.

Genus DOA Neumœgen & Dyar

The only species of the genus, named **ampla** by Grote, is a native of Colorado, and ranges thence southward through Arizona to the higher mountain plateaus of Mexico. It also occurs not infrequently in northwestern Texas. It may easily be recognized with the help of the accompanying cut, which is drawn from a specimen in the collection of the writer.

FIG. 185.—*Doa ampla*, ♂ . ¼.

" Maidens, like moths, are ever caught by glare,
And Mammon wins his way where seraphs might despair."
BYRON.—*Childe Harold*, Canto I.

Genus LEUCULODES Dyar

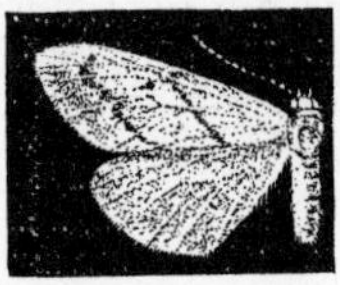

The genus is thus far represented in our fauna by but a single species, to which Hulst applied the specific name **lacteolaria.** It is a native of Arizona. The figure which is herewith given was drawn by the writer from the type which is preserved in the United States National Museum.

FIG. 186.—*Leuculodes lacteolaria,* ♂ . ¼.

MOTH-SONG

"What dost thou here,
Thou dusky courtier,
Within the pinky palace of the rose?
Here is no bed for thee,
No honeyed spicery,—
But for the golden bee,
And the gay wind, and me,
Its sweetness grows.
Rover, thou dost forget ;—
Seek thou the passion-flower
Bloom of one twilight hour.
Haste, thou art late!
Its hidden savors wait.
For thee is spread
Its soft, purple coverlet;
Moth, art thou sped ?
—Dim as a ghost he flies
Thorough the night mysteries."

ELLEN MACKAY HUTCHINSON CORTISSOZ.

FAMILY LASIOCAMPIDÆ

"Now busily convened upon the bud
  That crowns the genial branch, they feast sublime,
  And spread their muslin canopy around,
  Pavilioned richer than the proudest kings."

The *Lasiocampidæ* have been characterized as follows by Sir George F. Hampson, in "The Moths of India," Vol. I, p. 402:

"Moths mostly of large size. Palpi porrect and generally large. Proboscis absent; eyes small; antennæ bipectinate in both sexes; legs generally with minute terminal pairs of spurs to mid and hind tibiæ and rather hairy. Fore wing with vein 1*a* not forked with *b;* 1*c* rarely present; the cell medial in position; veins 6 and 7 from the angle; veins 9 and 10 always stalked and from before the angle. Hind wing with two internal veins; 6 and 7 arising very near the base; 8 curved and almost touching 7, or connected with it by a bar, thus forming a precostal cell; accessory costal veinlets generally present. Frenulum absent.

Larva with lateral downwardly-directed tufts of hair, and often subdorsal tufts or dorsal humps on anterior somites thickly clothed with hair.

Cocoon closely woven of silk and hair."

Seven genera belonging to the family are recognized as occurring within our faunal limits.

Genus GLOVERIA Packard

(1) **Gloveria arizonensis** Packard, Plate XLI, Fig. 3, ♀.
Syn. *dentata* Henry Edwards.
The moth is found in Arizona and northern Mexico.
(2) **Gloveria psidii** Sallé, Plate XLI, Fig. 2, ♂.
The habitat of the species is the same as that of the foregoing.
(3) **Gloveria howardi** Dyar, Plate XLI, Fig. 1, ♀.
The specimen figured on the plate is one of several which are contained in the collection of the United States National Museum,

and which constituted the material upon which the original description of the species was based by Dr. Dyar.

Genus ARTACE Walker

(1) **Artace punctistriga** Walker, Plate XII, Fig. 5, ♂.
Syn. *rubripalpis* Felder.
This rather rare little moth has its habitat in the southern Atlantic States.

Genus TOLYPE Hübner

Five species are accounted as belonging to this genus. We give illustrations of the one which is commonest.
(1) **Tolype velleda** Stoll, Plate XI, Fig. 7, ♂, Fig. 8, ♀.
The species is found throughout the Appalachian subregion.

Genus HYPOPACHA Neumœgen & Dyar

The only species known to belong to this genus was named **grisea** by Neumœgen. The only specimen of which the writer has knowledge is the type which is contained in the collection of the Brooklyn Institute. Of this I have, through the kindness of the authorities of that institution, been permitted to make a drawing, which is reproduced in the annexed cut. The habitat of the species is Arizona.

FIG. 187.—*H. grisea*, ♂. ¾.

Genus MALACOSOMA Hübner

(1) **Malacosoma americana** Fabricius, Plate X, Fig. 12, ♀.
Syn. *decipiens* Walker; *frutetorum* Boisduval.
The species, which is commonly known as "The American Tent-caterpillar," is widely distributed throughout the Appalachian subregion, and at times inflicts considerable injury upon the foliage of trees. It especially affects trees belonging to the *Rosaceæ*, as the wild cherry and wild plum, and attacks apple-orchards with avidity. The great white webs woven by the caterpillars are familiar objects in the rural landscape, detested by the fruit-grower, and equally despised by the man who loves to see trees in perfect leaf. An orchard cobwebbed by the tent-caterpil-

lar is not pleasant to contemplate. The best way to combat these destructive insects is to diligently search for their webs when they first are being formed, and to cut off the branches to which they are attached and burn them. By following this method carefully, their ravages may be held in check.

(2) **Malacosoma californica** Packard, Plate X, Fig. 11, ♂.

Syn. *pseudoneustria* Boisduval.

The species, which is in its habits very closely allied to the preceding, has its home upon the Pacific coast.

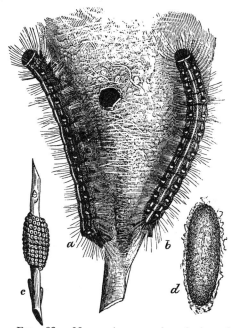

FIG. 188.—*M. americana.* *a,* lateral view of larva; *b,* dorsal view of larva; *c,* mass of eggs; *d,* cocoon. (After Riley.)

FIG. 189.— *M. disstria,* larva. (After Riley.)

(3) **Malacosoma disstria** Hübner, Plate X, Fig. 9, ♂ ; form **erosa** Stretch, Plate X, Fig. 10 , ♂ .

Syn. *sylvatica* Harris; *drupacearum* Boisduval; *thoracicoides* Neumœgen & Dyar; *sylvaticoides* Neumœgen & Dyar; *thoracica* Stretch; *perversa* Neumœgen & Dyar.

The moth is universally distributed through the United States and Canada. It appears to be rather variable, and a number of subspecies or varietal forms have been recognized. Many of the races, if such they can be called, differ so little from the typical stock that it hardly appears worth while to regard the names which have been applied to them as other than synonyms.

The habits of the larvæ are almost identical with those of the species to which reference has already been made. Like them, they prefer to attack the

313

Rosaceæ, although they also at times feed upon other trees. The hickories of various species and the walnuts are not exempt from their ravages. The writer has never observed them feeding upon oaks, birch, or beeches. An excellent account of the habits of these creatures may be found in Riley's Missouri Reports, Number III, from which the illustrations here given have been taken. The means of holding the insects in check are the same which have been recommended in the case of *M. americana*.

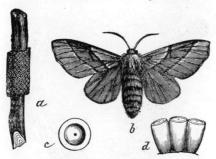

Fig. 190.—*M. disstria. a*, egg mass; *b*, moth; *c*, egg viewed from top; *d*, eggs viewed from side; *c, d*, magnified. (After Riley.)

Genus HETEROPACHA Harvey

(1) **Heteropacha rileyana** Harvey, Plate VIII, Fig. **7** ♀.

The moth is not uncommon in the Valley of the Mississippi, ranging from western Pennsylvania to Kansas and Missouri, and southward into Texas.

Genus EPICNAPTERA Rambur

(1) **Epicnaptera americana** Harris, Plate XLI, Fig. 19, ♂, Fig. 20, ♀.

Syn. *occidentis* Walker; *carpinifolia* Boisduval.

There are a number of color forms of this insect which have received names, and which appear to be local races of some measure of stability in the regions where they occur. We have given in our plate the form which is common in the Mississippi Valley. The specimens figured were bred from larvæ reared by Mr. Tallant at Columbus, Ohio.

" The Baron was an entomologist. Both the Fontenettes thought we should be fascinated with the beauty of some of his cases of moths and butterflies."

G. W. CABLE

FAMILY BOMBYCIDÆ

"And thou, the insect of an hour,
  O'er Time to triumph wouldst pretend;
  With nerves of grass wouldst brave the power
  Beneath which pyramids must bend!"
                              CARL GUSTAF AF LEOPOLD.

The *Bombycidæ* were originally confined to the Asiatic continent, and more particularly to the southeastern portions of that great land mass. The family is quite small and includes only a few genera. Of these the genus *Bombyx* is the only one which is well known. The family has been characterized as follows by Sir George F. Hampson, in "The Moths of India," Vol. I, p. 31:

"Proboscis absent, palpi rather small or absent; antennæ bipectinated in both sexes; legs hairy, without spurs. Frenulum absent; vein 5 of both wings from or from above the middle of the discocellulars; veins 7, 8, and 9 of the fore wing generally more or less bent downward; vein 1*a* forming or not forming a fork with 1*b*; 1*c* absent or present. Hind wing with two or three internal veins; vein 8 arising from the base of 7, or free from the base with a bar between them; the inner margin irregular and in part turned over.

Larva elongate and not hairy; dorsal humps on some of the somites, or a horn on the terminal somite, or paired dorsal spines.

Cocoon formed of fine silk of great commercial value."

Genus BOMBYX Linnæus

(1) **Bombyx mori** Linnæus.

The silk-worm of commerce is not known to exist in a feral or wild state in the regions where it is now most commonly

315

reared. In this respect it is like many other domesticated animals. The caterpillar, of which a figure is herewith given, feeds upon

FIG. 191.—Larva of *Bombyx mori*. (After Riley.)

the leaves of the white mulberry, and will also feed freely upon the leaves of the Osage orange, an American hedge-plant. The

FIG. 192.—Cocoon of *B. mori*. (After Riley.)

insect was introduced at an early date into the American colonies, but its culture has not as yet risen in the New World to great proportions, though the manufacture of silk from imported material is at the present day an important American industry. The culture of silk is an industry which might be best undertaken and maintained in the Southern States of the American Union, where climatic conditions are wholly favorable to it. The Caro-linas and Georgia appear to fur-nish the best climate for the development of this industry, and it is believed by those who are most conversant with the matter that in time the rearing of the silk-worm may become in these States an exceedingly important and profitable branch of industry. Southern California and Arizona

FIG. 193.—Moth of *B. mori*. (After Riley.)

are also likely to become centers in which the growing of raw silk may be successfully pursued.

THE HISTORY OF SILK-CULTURE

The greater portion of the silk of commerce is produced by the larvæ of the moth known as *Bombyx mori*. The insect, through ages of human culture, has become thoroughly domesticated. It has been wrongly maintained that the moth known as *Theophila huttoni*, and which is found in China and western India, is the ancestral or feral form from which the domesticated *Bombyx mori* has been derived. The common silkworm does not exist in a wild state anywhere so far as is known, and is as much a domestic animal as the Jersey cow or the greyhound. Chinese literature clearly shows that the silk-industry originated in that country. The Emperor Hwang-Ti, whose reign was in the eighteenth century B.C., fostered the culture of silk, and his empress, Si-Ling-Chi, who gave her personal attention to the breeding of silk-worms and the manufacture of silk, was deified in consequence, and is reputed to be "the goddess of silk-worms." The methods of securing the silk and weaving fabrics from it were held secret by the Chinese for nearly two thousand years, and only after ages was a knowledge of the art transmitted to Corea, and thence to Japan. Silk in very small quantities was imported into Greece and Rome from China by way of Persia. Aristotle was the first writer in Europe to give a correct account of the manner in which silk is produced. He is supposed to have derived his information from those who had accompanied Alexander the Great on his victorious march into India. The price of silken fabrics in the West at the beginning of the Christian era, owing to the cost of transportation, was so great that only the very rich could possess garments of this material. Their use was restricted to wealthy women. For a man to use silken clothing was esteemed a sign of luxurious effeminacy. Under the reigns of Tiberius, Vespasian, and Diocletian the use of silken apparel by men was positively interdicted; but gradually, with the increase of importation of raw silk from Persia and its manufacture into stuffs in Asia Minor and elsewhere, the habit of using it grew, and its cost was slowly lowered. Under the reign of the Emperor Justinian, in the sixth century, positive steps to foster sericulture as an imperial monopoly were taken. Silk-looms operated by women were established in the palace at Constantinople, and Justinian endeavored, in view of the loss of the supply of raw silk brought about by a war with Persia, to induce the Prince of Abyssinia to secure to him supplies of the article by a circuitous route. Relief was finally brought to the embarrassed imperial manufacturer when two Nestorian monks, who had lived long in China and had learned all the processes of silk-culture, were induced to go back to that far-away land and bring to Constantinople a stock of the eggs of the silk-worm. As it was among the Chinese a capital offense to reveal the secrets of the trade or to export the eggs from which the worms are hatched, the two priests had to proceed with the utmost caution. They concealed the eggs in the hollows of the bamboo staffs which they carried as pilgrims. From these eggs, thus transported to Constantinople in A.D. 555, all of the silk-worms in Europe, Africa, Asia Minor, and America until as recently as 1865 were descended. It was not until the last-mentioned year that any importation of fresh eggs of the silk-worm from China took place. Those two bamboo sticks held within themselves the germ of a vast industry, countless costly wardrobes, the raiment of kings, queens, and emperors, and untold wealth.

From the time of Justinian onward the growth of silk-culture in Greece and Asia Minor was rapid. It was introduced into Spain by the Saracens at the beginning of the eighth century. It found lodgment in Sicily and Naples in the twelfth century, and in the next century was taken up in Genoa and Venice. It was not begun in France until the latter part of the sixteenth century, but in the seventeenth century it made great progress in France, as well as in Belgium and Switzerland. The weaving of silk had begun at an earlier date than this in France, Germany, and England. Attempts made to introduce the culture of the mulberry-tree and of the silk-worm in Great Britain have always signally failed. The climate appears to be against the industry. James I, who had failed in his attempts to foster sericulture in England, undertook to plant the industry in Virginia in 1609. But the eggs and mulberry-trees he sent out were lost by shipwreck. In 1619 and the years immediately following the attempt was renewed, and the raising of silk-worms was enjoined by statute and encouraged by bounties. In spite of every effort, little came of the attempt, the colonists finding the growth of tobacco to be far more profitable. In Georgia and the Carolinas similar attempts were made, and from 1735 to 1766 there were exported to England considerable quantities of raw silk from these colonies. From

1760 onward the industry declined. Sericulture was at this time taken up in Connecticut and flourished there more than anywhere else for many years, though the raw silk was not exported, but woven on the spot into various fabrics. The production of raw silk in Connecticut for many years amounted to a sum of not less than $200,000 annually. In 1830 an effort was made to introduce into the United States the so-called Chinese mulberry (*Morus multicaulis*). A popular craze in regard to this plant and the profits of silk-culture was begotten. Fabulous prices were paid for cuttings of the *Morus multicaulis,* as much even as five dollars for twigs less than two feet in length. Hundreds of people came to believe that the possession of a grove of these trees would be the avenue to fortune. But in 1839 the bubble burst, and many persons who had invested the whole of their small earnings were ruined. It was discovered that the trees would not withstand frost and were practically worthless, as compared with the white mulberry (*Morus alba*). "Colonel Mulberry Sellers" remains in American literature a reminder of those days, and of the visionary tendencies of certain of our people.

The manufacture of silk thread and of silken fabrics was begun in the United States at an early date. Machinery for reeling, throwing, and weaving silk was invented, and the importation of raw silk was begun. The industry has steadily grown until at the present time silk-manufacture has come to be an important industry, in which nearly a hundred millions of dollars are invested. The annual production of silken goods amounts to a sum even greater than the capital employed and gives employment to seventy-five thousand persons. So much for the industrial importance of one small species of those insects to which this volume is devoted.

> " It was brown with a golden gloss, Janette,
> It was finer than silk of the floss, my pet ;
> 'T was a beautiful mist falling down to your wrist,
> 'T was a thing to be braided, and jewelled, and kissed—
> 'T was the loveliest hair in the world, pet."
>
> CHARLES G. HALPINE. —*Janette's Hair.*

FAMILY PLATYPTERYGIDÆ

"Above the wet and tangled swamp
White vapors gathered thick and damp,
And through their cloudy curtaining
Flapped many a brown and dusky wing—
Pinions that fan the moonless dun,
ut fold them at the rising sun."
WHITTIER.

The family has been described as follows by Sir George F. Hampson, "Moths of India," Vol. I, p. 326:

"Small or moderate-sized moths of somewhat slender build, generally with the apex of the fore wing falcate.

Palpi slender and slightly scaled, often very minute. Fore wing with vein 1*b* forked at the base; 1*c* absent; 5 from close to the lower angle of cell. Hind wing with one or two internal veins; 1*a* short when present; 5 from near lower angle of cell; the discocellulars angled; the origin of veins 6 and 7 before the angle of cell; 8 bent down and nearly or quite touching 7.

Larva smooth, with the anal prolegs absent, except in the genus *Euchera;** the anal somite usually with a long process, the others often humped.

Cocoon spun among leaves."

Genus EUDEILINEA Packard

FIG. 194.—*E. herminiata*, ♂ . ¼.

The only species of the genus known in our fauna is the one named **herminiata** by Guenée. It is a rather rare little moth in collections, being probably overlooked by collectors on account of its insignificant size and its general resemblance to commoner species. It is found in the Appalachian subregion.

* Not American.

320

Genus ORETA Walker

(1) **Oreta rosea** Walker, Plate XLI, Fig. 24, ♀.
Syn. *americana* Herrich-Schæffer; *formula* Grote.
The moth is a native of the eastern portions of our territory.
(2) **Oreta irrorata** Packard, Plate XLI, Fig. 6, ♀.
The range of this species is coincident with that of the last.

Genus DREPANA Schrank

(1) **Drepana arcuata** Walker, Plate XLI, Fig. 23, ♂.
Syn. *fabula* Grote.
Form **genicula** Grote, Plate XLI, Fig. 22, ♂.
The species, which is dimorphic, inhabits the Appalachian subregion. The form *genicula* occurs in the spring, the form *arcuata* in the summer.

Genus FALCARIA Haworth

The genus is common to both hemispheres.
(1) **Falcaria bilineata** Packard, Plate XLI, Fig. 7, ♀.
The insect, which is by no means common, is a native of the eastern portion of our territory.

TRANSFORMATION

" Who that beholds the summer's glistering swarms,
Ten thousand thousand gaily gilded forms,
In volant dance of mix'd rotation play,
Bask in the beam, and beautify the day;
Who 'd think these airy wantons, so adorn,
Were late his vile antipathy and scorn,
Prone to the dust, or reptile thro' the mire,
And ever thence unlikely to aspire ?
Or who with transient view, beholding, loaths
Those crawling sects, whom vilest semblance cloaths;
Who, with corruption, hold their kindred state,
As by contempt, or negligence of fate;
Could think, that such, revers'd by wondrous doom,
Sublimer powers and brighter forms assume;
From death their future happier life derive,
And tho' apparently entomb'd, revive;
Chang'd, thro' amazing transmigration rise,
And wing the regions of unwonted skies;
So late depress'd, contemptible on earth,
Now elevate to heaven by second birth."

HENRY BROOKE. —*Universal Beauty.*

FAMILY GEOMETRIDÆ

". . . The sylvan powers
Obey our summons; from their deepest dells
The Dryads come, and throw their garlands wild
And odorous branches at our feet; the Nymphs
That press with nimble step the mountain-thyme
And purple heath-flower come not empty-handed,
But scatter round ten thousand forms minute
Of velvet moss or lichen, torn from rock
Or rifted oak or cavern deep: the Naiads too
Quit their loved native stream, from whose smooth face
They crop the lily, and each sedge and rush
That drinks the rippling tide: the frozen poles,
Where peril waits the bold adventurer's tread,
The burning sands of Borneo and Cayenne,
All, all to us unlock their secret stores
And pay their cheerful tribute."

J. TAYLOR.—*Norwich*, 1818.

The *Geometridæ* are a very large and universally distributed family of moths. There is no country where there is any vegetation where they do not occur. Even in the inhospitable regions of the far North, upon the verge of the eternal ice, they may be found. They are more or less frail in their habit, with considerable expanse of wing in proportion to the size of the body. They are semidiurnal or crepuscular. They have been characterized as follows by Sir George F. Hampson:

". . . Proboscis present or rarely absent. Legs and tarsi slender, elongate, and naked, or slightly clothed with hair. Fore wing with vein 1*a* forming a fork with 1*b*. 1*c* absent; vein 5 from or from above middle of the discocellulars, 7 rising from 8, 9. Hind wing with the frenulum usually present, but absent in a few genera. Vein 1*a* very short, apparently absent in some forms; vein 1*b* running to anal angle; 1*c* absent. 8 with a well-developed precostal spur.

Larvæ with the three anterior pairs of abdominal claspers totally aborted, and progressing by bringing the posterior somites close to the thoracic, looping the medial somites. In a few ancestral forms there is tendency to develop additional prolegs and to a more ordinary mode of progression."

The larvæ, which are commonly known as "measuring-worms," "span-worms," or "loopers," have the power in many cases of attaching themselves by the posterior claspers to the stems and branches of plants, and extending the remainder of the body outwardly at an angle to the growth upon which they are resting, in which attitude they wonderfully resemble short twigs. Dichromatism is often revealed among them, part of a brood of caterpillars being green and the remainder brown or yellowish. Various explanations of this phenomenon have been suggested. In not a few cases the females are wingless.

Over eight hundred species of *Geometridæ* are known to occur within the limits of the United States and Canada, and when the region shall have been exhaustively explored, there is little doubt that this number will be greatly increased. It is impossible within the limits of this book to mention and depict all of these species. We have therefore confined ourselves to the description through our plates of one hundred and seventy species, which are either more commonly encountered, or are possessed of some striking character. Incidentally occasion has been taken to figure a few of the types of species in the collection of the author which have never before been delineated.

The student who desires to familiarize himself with the family with which we are now dealing will derive much assistance from the writings of Packard and Hulst, the titles of which he will find in the portion of the Introduction of this book devoted to the literature of the subject.

SUBFAMILY DYSPTERIDINÆ
Genus DYSPTERIS Hübner

(1) **Dyspteris abortivaria** Herrich-Schæffer, Plate XLII, Fig. 21, ♂. (The Bad-wing.)

This pretty little moth may be easily recognized by the fact that the hind wings are so much smaller than the fore wings.

It is the only species of the genus found within our territory. It is not uncommon in the Appalachian subregion.

Genus NYCTOBIA Hulst

Three species belong to this genus. One of them is selected for illustration.

(1) **Nyctobia limitata** Walker, Plate XLII, Fig. 22, ♂.

Syn. *lobophorata* Walker; *vernata* Packard.

The habitat of this moth is identical with that of the last-mentioned species. It is not at all uncommon in Pennsylvania.

Genus CLADORA Hulst

(1) **Cladora atroliturata** Walker, Plate XLII, Fig. 23, ♂. (The Scribbler.)

Syn. *geminata* Grote & Robinson.

A neatly marked species, which is the sole representative of the genus in our fauna. The moths may be found in the early spring seated upon the trunks of trees in the forest. It is a native of the Appalachian subregion.

Genus RACHELA Hulst

Four species of this genus have been characterized by the late Dr. Hulst. The only one which occurs in the eastern portions of the continent we figure.

(1) **Rachela bruceata** Hulst, Plate XLII, Fig. 24, ♂.

The moth is found in the northern Atlantic States. It is not uncommon in western Pennsylvania.

SUBFAMILY HYDRIOMENINÆ

Genus PALEACRITA Riley

There are reputed to be three species of the genus found in the United States. Only one of them, because of its economic importance, has received much attention thus far.

* (1) **Paleacrita vernata** Peck, Plate XLII, Fig. 25, ♂, Fig. 26, ♀. (The Spring Canker-worm.)

Syn. *sericeiferata* Walker; *autumnata* Packard; *merricata* Dyar.

There are two insects known as canker-worms. One of these, the smaller of the two, is properly named the Spring

*P. vernata Peck is not illustrated. See footnote on page 326.—A.E.B.

Canker-worm, because the great majority of the moths issue from the ground in the spring. It has been a great pest in orchards, and formerly in our Eastern cities was a nuisance, not only because of the injury which it inflicted upon the foliage of shade-trees, but because of the annoying manner in which the larvæ, pendent from the branches by long threads of silk, were blown about over things and persons beneath them. It was to effect their destruction that the English sparrow was originally imported into this country. The ravages of the insects upon the foliage of trees in parks and gardens have measurably decreased since this step was taken, but in the open country, especially in

FIG. 195.—*Paleacrita vernata. a,* mature larva; *b,* egg, magnified, natural size shown in mass at side; *c,* enlarged segment of larva, side view; *d,* do., viewed dorsally. (After Riley.)

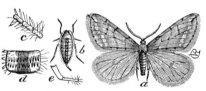

FIG. 196.—*Paleacrita vernata. a,* male; *b,* female; *c,* joint of antenna; *d,* joint of abdomen; *e,* ovipositor. (After Riley.)

the Valley of the Mississippi, the insects are still numerous enough to do much harm to orchards. The females being apterous, the best method of preventing the multiplication of the insects upon trees is to prevent them from climbing up upon the foliage and ovipositing. A simple device, which has proved very effective, is to tie a piece of rope about the trunk of the tree which it is intended to protect, and to insert between the rope and the bark strips of tin, which, having been put into place, should be bent downwardly and outwardly, so as to form a collar with a downward flare. The insects have been found not to be inclined to pass such a barrier, and they will congregate just below it, and may there be captured and destroyed. Birds are the chief enemies of the canker-worm, and every wise orchardist will see to it that all species of insectivorous birds are not molested in his neighborhood, but are encouraged to find in his trees a hospitable welcome. The small amount of fruit which the birds take as toll is amply compensated for by the work which they perform in keeping down insect pests, such as the one under consideration. It is the part of wisdom in every way to protect the birds.

The canker-worm is widely distributed from the Atlantic to the Pacific.

Genus ALSOPHILA Hübner

Only one species of the genus occurs within our limits.

* (1) **Alsophila pometaria** Harris. (The Fall Canker-worm.) Syn. *restituens* Walker.

The Fall Canker-worm in many respects closely resembles the preceding species, but a critical eye can at once detect great differences both in the form and markings of the caterpillar and of the mature insect. The moths generally emerge from the

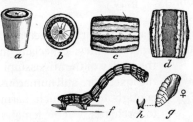

pupal state in the late fall, or during mild spells of weather in the winter, and may even continue to come forth until the spring is well advanced. The eggs are not laid as those of the preceding species, singly under the scales of bark,

FIG. 197.—*Alsophila pometaria.* a, egg, side view; b, do., top view; c, side view of segment of larva; d, top view of segment of larva; f, mature larva; g, pupa; h, cremaster. (After Riley.)

but are deposited in a compact mass fastened to the twigs by a strong gluey secretion, and are loosely covered with gray hairs, which the female rubs from her abdomen. The caterpillars are not ornamented on the back by a multitude of fine lines, but have a broad brown stripe along the dorsal line. The moths are larger than those of the Spring Canker-worm, and have a distinct whitish spot on the costa of the primaries near the apex. The caterpillar undergoes but two molts, and matures very rapidly. It has rudimentary prolegs on the eighth somite. The precautionary

FIG. 198.—*A. pometaria.* a, male; b, female; c, female antenna; d, segment of body of female, enlarged. (After Riley.)

measures which have proved effective in combating the Spring Canker-worm are not efficacious in dealing with this species. To effectively destroy them the best means is to spray the foli-

A. pometaria Harris is pictured on Plate XLII. Fig. 25, ♂; Fig. 26, ♀. —A.E.B.

age, just as the buds are opening, with some one of the poisonous mixtures which are prepared as insecticides. One of the very best means of keeping down the ravages of the insects is to encourage the cherry-birds (*Ampelis*) to stay about the place. They wage relentless war upon the pests.

Genus EUDULE Hübner

(1) **Eudule mendica** Walker, Plate XLII, Fig. 27, ♂. (The Beggar.)

Syn. *biseriata* Herrich-Schæffer.

This delicate little moth is widely distributed throughout the Appalachian subregion. It has been commonly placed in the genus *Euphanessa*.

(2) **Eudule unicolor** Robinson, Plate XLII, Fig. 28, ♂. (The Plain-colored Eudule.)

The insect, which has been in most lists attributed to the genus *Ameria*, ranges from Colorado to Texas and Arizona.

Genus NANNIA Hulst

(1) **Nannia refusata** Walker, Plate XLII, Fig. 31, ♀. (Harvey's Geometer.)

Syn. *harveiata* Packard.

This is a common species in the spring of the year in the northern Atlantic States.

Genus HETEROPHLEPS Herrich-Schæffer

(1) **Heterophleps triguttaria** Herrich-Schæffer, Plate XLII, Fig. 29, ♂. (The Three-spotted Fillip.)

Syn. *quadrinotata* Walker; *hexaspilata* Walker.

This pretty little moth is widely distributed throughout the entire United States, and is very generally associated with the preceding species in locality and time of appearance.

Genus TEPHROCLYSTIS Hübner

This is a very extensive genus, composed for the most part of small and inconspicuous species. It is found in both hemispheres. We select, for purposes of illustration, one of the commoner species, which is found in both Europe and America.

327

* (1) **Tephroclystis absinthiata** Clerck, Plate XLII, Fig. 32, ♂. (The Absinth.)

Syn. *minutata* Treitschke; *notata* Stephens; *elongata* Haworth; *absynthiata* Guenée; *coagulata* Guenée; *geminata* Packard.

This inconspicuous little creature illustrates the truth of the remark, already made, that the smaller the insect the more and the lengthier the names which it bears or which have been imposed upon it.

Genus EUCYMATOGE Hübner

(1) **Eucymatoge intestinata** Guenée, Plate XLII, Fig. 30, ♀.

Syn. *impleta* Walker; *indoctrinata* Walker.

The moth is almost universally distributed throughout the United States. It is found in the spring of the year seated upon the trunks of trees, the gray bark of which it assimilates in color.

Genus VENUSIA Curtis

The genus is common to both hemispheres. *Venusia cambrica* Curtis is found in Europe and the United States. Two other species of the genus occur in our territory, and of both of these we give figures.

† (1) **Venusia duodecimlineata** Packard, Plate XLIII, Fig. 15, ♂.

The moth is very widely, if not universally, distributed throughout temperate North America.

‡ (2) **Venusia comptaria** Walker, Plate XLII, Fig. 33, ♂.

Syn. *condensata* Walker; *inclinataria* Walker; *inclinata* Hulst; *perlineata* Packard.

The species is common in the eastern portions of the United States.

Genus EUCHŒCA Hübner

(1) **Euchœca albovittata** Guenée, Plate XLIV, Fig. 19, ♂. (The White-striped Black.)

Syn. *propriaria* Walker; *reciprocata* Walker.

The moth is found from the Atlantic to the Pacific and ranges well up into Alaska, whence I have obtained specimens taken at Sitka and on Lake Labarge, in the Valley of the Yukon.

(2) **Euchœca californiata** Packard, Plate XLIV, Fig. 20, ♂. (The Californian Black.)

The moth inhabits the Pacific States.

**T. absinthiata Clerck* is European. The species described and pictured (Fig. 32, Plate XLII) is *Semiothisa gnophosaria* Guenée; syn. *infectata* Walker; *reductaria* Walker; *cæsiria* Hulst.—A.E.B.

†Should be *V. comptaria* Walker in text and plate.—A.E.B.

‡The species illustrated in Fig. 33, Plate XLII is *Hydrelia inornata* Hulst.—A.E.B.

(3) **Euchœca lucata** Guenée, Plate XLIV, Fig. 6, ♂. (The Woodland Black.)

The insect is distributed from western Pennsylvania and West Virginia to Illinois, and northward to Manitoba. It is not rare about Pittsburgh.

Genus HYDRIA Hübner

(1) **Hydria undulata** Linnæus, Plate XLII, Fig. 34, ♀. (The Scallop-shell Moth.)

This neatly marked species is found in both Europe and America. It is the only species of the genus in the United States.

Genus PHILEREME Hübner

The species of this genus are all Western in their habitat.

(1) **Philereme californiata** Packard, Plate XLII, Fig. 36, ♂. The specimen figured was taken on the slopes of Mt. Shasta.

Genus EUSTROMA Hübner

This is quite an extensive genus found in both the New World and the Old. Of the nine species recognized thus far as occurring within the United States, we figure three.

(1) **Eustroma diversilineata** Hübner, Plate XLII, Fig. 42, ♂. (The Diverse-line Moth.)

The moth is not at all uncommon in the Appalachian subregion.

(2) **Eustroma prunata** Linnæus, Plate XLII, Fig. 53, ♂. (The Plum Moth.)

Syn. *ribesiaria* Boisduval; *triangulatum* Packard; *montanatum* Packard.

The insect is found in both Europe and North America.

(3) **Eustroma atrocolorata** Grote, Plate XLII, Fig. 43, ♂. (The Dark-banded Geometer.)

A denizen of the Appalachian subregion. It is one of the most beautiful of the geometrid moths found in the Atlantic States.

Genus RHEUMAPTERA Hübner

A genus of moderate size, the species of which are found in the temperate and boreal regions of both hemispheres.

(1) **Rheumaptera hastata** Linnæus, Plate XLII, Fig. 40, ♂, Fig. 41, ♀, var. (The Spear-mark.)

The species is very variable, and half a dozen forms have been named. The only differences existing between these forms are in the relative amount of black and white upon the upper side of the wings. The moth is found all through northern Europe and Asia, and is widely distributed through the northern United States and Canada as far west as Alaska, where it is very common.

(2) **Rheumaptera luctuata** Denis & Schiffermüller, Plate XLII, Fig. 39, ♂.

The remarks made as to the preceding species apply equally well to the present. I have received it in recent years in great numbers from Alaska.

(3) **Rheumaptera rubrosuffusata** Packard, Plate XLII, Fig. 38, ♂.

The moth is a native of the Pacific States.

Genus PERCNOPTILOTA Hulst

This genus is represented in North America by a single species, **Percnoptilota fluviata** Hübner, which is shown on Plate XLII, Fig. 48, by a male specimen. The moth also occurs in Europe and northern Asia, and has been described under at least fifteen different names. The synonymy is too extensive to burden the pages of this book with it.

Genus MESOLEUCA Hübner

This is an extensive genus found in the temperate regions of the northern hemisphere on both sides of the Atlantic.

(1) **Mesoleuca ruficillata** Guenée, Plate XLIII, Fig. 21, ♂.

The habitat of the species is the northern United States and southern Canada.

(2) **Mesoleuca gratulata** Walker, Plate XLII, Fig. 47, ♂.
Syn. *brunneiciliata* Packard.

The insect is found in the Pacific subregion.

* (3) **Mesoleuca lacustrata** Guenée, Plate XLII, Fig. 50, ♀.

This is not an uncommon species in Europe and the northern portions of the United States and in Canada.

† (4) **Mesoleuca intermediata** Guenée, Plate XLII, Fig. 49, ♀.

The moth occurs in the Atlantic States.

(5) **Mesoleuca hersiliata** Guenée, Plate XLII, Fig. 46, ♂.
Syn. *flammifera* Walker.

The home of the species is in the region of the Rocky Mountains. It is not uncommon in Colorado.

*Should be *M. intermediata* Guenée in text and plate.—A.E.B.
†Should be *M. iduata* Guenée in text and plate.—A.E.B.

Genus HYDRIOMENA·Hübner

This is a very extensive genus, which is well represented in the temperate portions of both the Eastern and the Western Hemisphere. There are nearly thirty species which have been reported to occur in our fauna.

(1) **Hydriomena sordidata** Fabricius, Plate XLII, Fig. 54, ♀.
Syn. *rectangulata* Fabricius; *bicolorata* Borkhausen; *birivata* Borkhausen.

The insect is found all over the northern United States and Canada, and is common in Europe. Various varietal forms have been described, based upon differences, more or less constant, in the markings of the wings.

(2) **Hydriomena autumnalis** Strömeyer, Plate XLII, Fig. 51, ♂.

This is another species which is found in Europe, and also occurs in the Pacific subregion of North America. It has an extensive synonymy, for a knowledge of which the student may refer to Staudinger & Rebel's Catalogue of the Moths of the Palæarctic Region, or to Dyar's List.

(3) **Hydriomena speciosata** Packard, Plate XLII, Fig. 52, ♂.

The home of this pretty species is in the southwestern portions of the United States. It occurs in Texas, Arizona, and southern California.

* (4) **Hydriomena latirupta** Walker, Plate XLII, Fig. 35, ♂.
Syn. *lascinata* Zeller.

The insect is found almost everywhere in the United States and Canada.

(5) **Hydriomena custodiata** Guenée, Plate XLIII, Fig. 10, ♂, *upper side;* Fig. 11, ♂, *under side.*
Syn. *gueneata* Packard.

The moth is an inhabitant of the Pacific subregion.

Genus TRIPHOSA Stephens

(1) **Triphosa progressata** Walker, Plate XLII, Fig. 45, ♂.
Syn. *indubitata* Grote; *dubitata* Packard.

The species occurs in the northern portions of the Pacific subregion.

" Soft-buzzing Slander; silly moths that eat
An honest name." THOMSON. —*Liberty*, Pt. IV, 609.

*Should be *Euphyia centrostrigaria* Wollaston in text and plate—A.E.B.

Genus CŒNOCALPE Hübner

This is a moderately large genus, almost all the species of which are found in the Pacific subregion or in the southwestern portions of the United States.

(1) **Cœnocalpe gibbocostata** Walker, Plate XLIII, Fig. 16, ♂.
Syn. *costinotata* Walker; *strigularia* Minot; *œneiformis* Harvey.
The moth is one of the few species of the genus found in the Atlantic States.

(2) **Cœnocalpe fervifactaria** Grote, Plate XLIII, Fig. 4, ♂.
This rather pretty insect is found in the region of the Rocky Mountains.

Genus MARMOPTERYX Packard

(1) **Marmopteryx marmorata** Packard, Plate XLIII, Fig. 1, ♂. (The Marble-wing.)
The insect ranges from Colorado in the east to California in the west.

Genus GYPSOCHROA Hübner

* (1) **Gypsochroa designata** Hufnagel, Plate XLII, Fig. 44, ♂.
Syn. *propugnata* Denis & Schiffermüller; *propugnaria* Treitschke.
The moth occurs in both Europe and North America.

† (2) **Gypsochroa sitellata** Guenée, Plate XLII, Fig. 37, ♂.
Syn. *hæsitata* Guenée; *impauperata* Walker; *albosignata* Packard.
The species is quite widely distributed throughout the United States.

SUBFAMILY MONOCTENIINÆ

Genus PAOTA Hulst

(1) **Paota fultaria** Grote, Plate XLIII, Fig. 27, ♂.
The habitat of the species is Arizona.

Genus HÆMATOPSIS Hübner

(1) **Hæmatopsis grataria** Fabricius, Plate XLIII, Fig. 2, ♂. (The Chickweed Moth.)
Syn. *saniara* Hübner; *successaria* Walker.
This common but none the less beautiful little moth is often seen by the roadsides, where it has the habit of clinging to the stems of grasses, and of flying up when the footsteps of the passer-by approach. It is a native of the Appalachian subregion,

---

*Should be *G. emendata* Pearsall in text and plate. Syn. *gynandrata* Pearsall.—A.E.B.

†For *G. sitellata* Guenée read *G. stelatta* Guenée in text and plate. —A.E.B.

and ranges from the Atlantic to the Mississippi and beyond. The larva feeds on chickweed.

SUBFAMILY STERRHINÆ
Genus ERASTRIA Hübner

(1) **Erastria amaturaria** Walker, Plate XLIII, Fig. 22, ♂.
This insect, which is not likely to be mistaken for anything else, is a native of the Appalachian subregion. It is common in Pennsylvania.

Genus PIGEA Guenée

(1) **Pigea mutilineata** Hulst, Plate XLIII, Fig. 3, ♂.
The insect is found in Arizona. The specimen figured is one of the types of the species which was loaned to Dr. Hulst, and upon which he based his description.

Genus COSYMBIA Hübner

(1) **Cosymbia lumenaria** Hübner, Plate XLIII, Fig. 12, ♀.
Syn. *pendulinaria* Guenée; *quadriannulata* Walker.
This is a common species in the Atlantic subregion.

Genus SYNELYS Hulst

This is a small genus containing eight or nine species, all of which are found in the Southern States, except two.
(1) **Synelys alabastaria** Hübner, Plate XLIII, Fig. 5, ♀.
Syn. *reconditaria* Walker; *ennucleata* Packard (*non* Guenée).
The moth is very common in the Appalachian subregion.

Genus LEPTOMERIS Hübner

(1) **Leptomeris quinquelinearia** Packard, Plate XLIII, Fig. 9, ♀. (The Five-lined Geometer.)
A common species everywhere in the United States.
(2) **Leptomeris sentinaria** Hübner, Plate XLIII, Fig. 14, ♂.
Syn. *spuraria* Christoph; *gracilior* Butler.
The habitat of this insect is the northern portion of the Appalachian subregion.
(3) **Leptomeris magnetaria** Guenée, Plate XLIII, Fig. 8, ♂. (The Magnet Moth.)
Syn. *rubrolinearia* Packard; *rubrolineata* Packard.
The insect is found in the Pacific subregion.

Genus EOIS Hübner

(1) **Eois ptelearia** Riley. (The Herbarium Moth.)

The moth which is the subject of consideration is interesting because of the fact that in recent years it has become known as a destructive herbarium pest. The larvæ attack the flowers, to

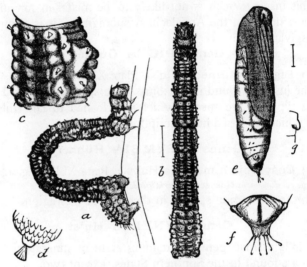

FIG. 199.—*Eois ptelearia.* *a*, larva, from side; *b*, do., from above; *c*, side view of abdominal segment; *d*, tubercle of same; *e*, pupa; *f*, cremaster; *g*, abdominal projection. All figures greatly enlarged. (After C. V. Riley, " Insect Life," Vol. IV, p. 109.)

some extent the leaves, and also to a less extent the hard fruits and seeds of specimens collected in the Southwestern States and in Mexico. Their ravages were first detected at the United States National Museum in the year 1890. Strangely enough, they show no appetite for species belonging to the flora of the Eastern and Northern States. It is believed that the insect is native to the region the plants of which it devours, but thus far no entomologist has reported its occurrence in the section of country from which it is supposed to come. The damage it is able to inflict upon specimens is very great, because of the very rapid multiplication of individuals which takes place.

An exceedingly interesting account of the insect and its

destructive work was given by the late Professor C. V. Riley in "Insect Life," Vol. IV, p. 108 *et seq.* From this article the cuts which are herewith given have been extracted. Botanists cannot too carefully guard against this and other insect plagues which multiply in their collections. A solution of corrosive sublimate and arsenic, such as is commonly employed for poisoning herbarium specimens, will do much to prevent the ravages of the larvæ; but, as is pointed out by Professor Riley in the article to which reference has been made, additional safety from attack will be secured if all specimens, as they are received in the herbarium, are subjected to at least twenty-four hours' exposure to the fumes of bisulphide of carbon in an air-tight box or receptacle. This substance, as experience

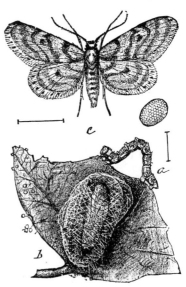

Fig. 200.—*Eois ptelearia. a,* larva; *b,* cocoon; *c,* moth; *d,* egg. All figures greatly enlarged. (After C. V. Riley, "Insect Life," Vol. IV, p. 110.)

has shown, is destructive to all forms of insect life. Care should, however, be exercised in its use, as the fumes mixed with atmospheric gases make a highly explosive compound. The operation should never be undertaken in the presence of flame. It is not even safe to allow the fumes of carbon bisulphide to mingle in large quantity with the atmosphere of an apartment which is lighted by electricity. Accidental sparking, owing to some defect of the wires, may cause an explosion. Several bad accidents have occurred from the use in careless hands of this otherwise most valuable insecticide.

(2) **Eois ossularia** Hübner, Plate XLIII, Fig. 7, ♂.

The moth, which has an extensive synonymy, which we will omit, is widely distributed throughout the United States.

(3) **Eois inductata** Guenée, Plate XLIII, Fig. 6, ♂.

Syn. *consecutaria* Walker; *sobria* Walker; *suppressaria* Walker.

335

The species is indigenous in the Appalachian subregion.

(4) **Eois sideraria** Guenée, Plate XLIII, Fig. 13, ♂.

Syn. *californiaria* Packard; *californiata* Packard; *pacificaria* Packard.

The species ranges over the northern portions of the United States.

SUBFAMILY GEOMETRINÆ

Genus CHLOROCHLAMYS Hulst

(1) **Chlorochlamys chloroleucaria** Guenée, Plate XLIII, Fig. 17, ♀.

Syn. *indiscriminaria* Walker; *densaria* Walker; *deprivata* Walker.

The insect ranges from the Atlantic to the Pacific. It is freely attracted to light in the evening.

Genus EUCROSTIS Hübner

(1) **Eucrostis incertata** Walker, Plate XLIII, Fig. 18, ♂.

Syn. *oporaria* Zeller; *gratata* Packard.

Not at all uncommon in the Appalachian subregion.

Genus RACHEOSPILA Guenée

A small genus, characteristic of the hot lands of the American continents. One species, *R. lixaria*, is found in the Appalachian subregion as far north as the Middle States; the four remaining species found within our territory have thus far been reported only from Florida.

(1) **Racheospila hollandaria** Hulst, Plate XLIII, Fig. 19, ♀.

The specimen depicted on the plate is the type of the species, which was taken by the writer on the upper waters of the St. Johns River.

(2) **Racheospila saltusaria** Hulst, Plate XLIII, Fig. 20, ♂.

The specimen depicted on the plate is likewise the type of the species and came from the same locality as the preceding species.

Genus SYNCHLORA Guenée

(1) **Synchlora liquoraria** Guenée, Plate XLIII, Fig. 23, ♂.

Syn. *tricoloraria* Packard.

A species which is very widely distributed throughout the United States.

Genus ANAPLODES Packard

(1) **Anaplodes iridaria** Guenée, Plate XLIII, Fig. 24, ♂.
Syn. *rectaria* Grote.
The moth ranges from Colorado to California.

SUBFAMILY FERNALDELLINÆ

Genus FERNALDELLA Hulst

The genus is the only representative of the subfamily. There are two species in the genus, both of them natives of the region of the Rocky Mountains. One of these, originally named **fimetaria** by Grote & Robinson, and subsequently named *halesaria* by Zeller, is represented in the accompanying cut. It is a very common insect in central Texas as well as in Colorado and Arizona.

FIG. 201.—*Fernaldella fimetaria*, ♂. ⅓.

SUBFAMILY ENNOMINÆ

Genus EPELIS Hulst

(1) **Epelis truncataria** Walker, Plate XLIII, Fig. 26, ♀.
This species, the only representative of the genus, ranges through the northern and cooler portions of the Appalachian subregion, westward to the Rocky Mountains.

Genus EUFIDONIA Packard

(1) **Eufidonia notataria** Walker, Plate XLIII, Fig. 25, ♂.
This neatly marked moth is found in the Appalachian subregion.

Genus ORTHOFIDONIA Packard

(1) **Orthofidonia semiclarata** Walker, Plate XLIII, Fig. 30, ♀.
Syn. *viatica* Harvey.
The moth is a native of the Atlantic States.
(2) **Orthofidonia vestaliata** Guenée, Plate XLIII, Fig. 31, ♂.
Syn. *junctaria* Walker.

*Should be *E. discospilata* Walker in text and plate. Synonyms are *quadripunctaria* Morrison and *fidoniata* Walker. *E. notataria* is similar but blacker in color, with similar range. Its synonyms are *convergaria* Walker and *bicolorata* Minot.—A.E.B.

The habitat of this insect is the same as that of the preceding species, but it ranges a little farther to the West, and has been reported from Colorado.

Genus DASYFIDONIA Packard

(1) **Dasyfidonia avuncularia** Guenée, Plate XLIII, Fig. 32, ♂.

This very pretty moth occurs from Colorado to California. It is the sole species in the genus.

Genus HELIOMATA Grote

There are reputed to be three species in this genus. Two of them we figure.

(1) **Heliomata infulata** Grote, Plate XLIII, Fig. 28, ♀.

The habitat of the species is the Atlantic region of the continent.

(2) **Heliomata cycladata** Grote, Plate XLIII, Fig. 29, ♂.

The moth ranges from the Atlantic States westward as far as Montana. It is nowhere very common.

Genus MELLILLA Grote

(1) **Mellilla inextricata** Walker, Plate XLIII, Fig. 33, ♂.

Syn. *xanthometata* Walker; *snoviaria* Packard.

The insect is a native of the Atlantic States.

Genus CHLORASPILATES Packard

(1) **Chloraspilates bicoloraria** Packard, form **arizonaria**, Plate XLIII, Fig. 34, ♂.

The moth is found in the region of the Rocky Mountains.

Genus PHYSOSTEGANIA Warren

(1) **Physostegania pustularia** Guenée, Plate XLIII, Fig. 35, ♂.

A native of the Atlantic States, ranging westward into the Valley of the Mississippi.

Genus DEILINEA Hübner

(1) **Deilinea variolaria** Guenée, Plate XLIII, Fig. 36, ♀.

Syn. *intentata* Packard.

338

The moth occurs quite commonly in the Atlantic subregion.

(2) **Deilinea behrensaria** Hulst, Plate XLIII, Fig. 38, ♂.

A native of the Pacific subregion. The specimen figured is one of the types.

Genus SCIAGRAPHIA Hulst

(1) **Sciagraphia granitata** Guenée, Plate XLIII, Fig. 37, ♂. (The Granite Moth.)

This small moth, which is a common species in the Appalachian subregion, has been described under no less than nineteen names by various authors. The student who is curious as to the synonymy may consult Dyar's List.

* (2) **Sciagraphia heliothidata** Guenée, Plate XLIII, Fig. 41, ♀. (The Sun-flower Moth.)

Syn. *ocellinata* Guenée; *restorata* Walker; *subcolumbata* Walker; *duplicata*, Packard.

The moth occurs throughout the region of the Great Plains and the Rocky Mountains.

(3) **Sciagraphia mellistrigata** Grote, Plate XLIII, Fig. 42, ♂. (The Honey-streak.)

The insect is found in the northern portions of the United States, and ranges westward and southward, being not at all uncommon in northern Texas and in Colorado.

Genus PHILOBIA Duponchel

† (1) **Philobia enotata** Guenée, Plate XLIII, Fig. 39, ♂.

Syn. *æmulataria* Walker; *sectomaculata* Morrison; *notata* Cramer (*non* Linnæus).

The insect appears to be common everywhere throughout the United States and Canada.

Genus MACARIA Curtis

A considerable genus, represented in both hemispheres.

(1) **Macaria s-signata** Packard, Plate XLIII, Fig. 43, ♂.

The species occurs from Colorado westward to California.

(2) **Macaria eremiata** Guenée, Plate XLIII, Fig. 44, ♂.

Syn. *retectata* Walker; *gradata* Walker; *retentata* Walker; *subcinctaria* Walker.

The habitat of the species is the Appalachian subregion.

(3) **Macaria hypæthrata** Grote, Plate XLIII, Fig. 47, ♂.

---

*Should be *S. ocellinata* Guenée in text. Fig. 41, Plate XLIII, is a male specimen. The common name is no longer valid, and the synonymy is simply *duplicata* Packard.—A.E.B.

†Should be *P. æmulataria* Walker in text and plate; the synonymy simply *sectomaculata* Morrison.—A.E.B.

The insect flies in Colorado and adjoining States.

(4) **Macaria præatomata** Haworth, Plate XLIII, Fig. 40, ♀.
Syn. *consepta* Walker.

Not a rare species in the Atlantic States.

(5) **Macaria glomeraria** Grote, Plate XLIV, Fig. 3, ♀.

The range of this species is the same as that of the preceding.

Genus CYMATOPHORA Hübner

(1) **Cymatophora ribearia** Fitch, Plate XLIII, Fig. 45, ♀.
(The Gooseberry Span-worm.)

Syn. *sigmaria* Guenée; *annisaria* Walker; *aniusaria* Walker; *grossulariata* Saunders.

The gooseberry and the currant are subject in the United States and Canada to the attack of various insects, which do a great deal of damage to them. One of the most frequent causes

Fig. 202.—*Cymatophora ribearia*, ♀ . ¼. (After Riley.)

of injury to these plants are the larvæ of the Gooseberry Span-worm, which is represented in Fig. 204. It is, when mature, about an inch in length, bright yellow in color, marked with dark-brown spots upon the segments. The eggs, which are laid by the mature female at the end of June or the beginning of July, are very minute, but upon examination under the microscope are seen to be beautifully ornamented with deep pits or sculpturings. They are pale bluish-green. The eggs are attached by the female to the stems and branches of the plants, not far from the ground. Being almost microscopic in size, they readily elude observation, and this, it is known, accounts for the fact that the insects are often, by the transplantation of the shrubs, transferred from one locality to another in which they have been previously unknown. The eggs, having been laid, remain through the summer and fall and all of the succeeding winter in a dormant state, and do not hatch until early in the following spring, when the leaves are beginning to put out upon the bushes. As soon as the

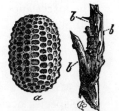

Fig. 203. — Egg of Gooseberry Span-worm. *a*, enlarged; *b*, natural size. (After Riley.)

eggs are hatched, the larvæ begin to feed upon the young leaves, and they mature very quickly, the rate of their development being marked by a corresponding devastation of the plants upon which they have established themselves. Pupation takes place at the end of May or in the beginning of June. The caterpillar burrows into the loose soil about the roots of the bushes, or simply crawls under loose leaves, and, without spinning a cocoon, undergoes transformation into a chrysalis, which is smooth and of a shining mahogany color. In this state the insects remain for about two weeks, when they emerge as moths, and the cycle of life is repeated.

FIG. 204.—Gooseberry Span-worm, *a*, *b*, larvæ; *c*, pupa. (After Riley.)

The most effectual method of combating the larvæ is to sprinkle the bushes with powdered white hellebore. This is a good remedy, not only for the species we are considering, but for several other insects which are likely to occur upon the plants at the same time.

(2) **Cymatophora inceptaria** Walker, Plate XLIII, Fig. 46, ♂ .

Syn. *argillacearia* Packard; *modestaria* Hulst.

A native of the Appalachian subregion.

(3) **Cymatophora successaria** Walker, Plate XLIII, Fig. 48, ♀ .

Syn. *perarcuata* Walker.

Form **coortaria** Hulst, Plate XLIII, Fig. 49, ♂ .

A widely distributed species, which is not at all uncommon in the Middle Atlantic States.

(4) **Cymatophora tenebrosata** Hulst, Plate XLIII, Fig. 50, ♂ .

341

The specimen represented upon the plate is one of Dr. Hulst's types. The moth is found in Arizona.

Genus SYMPHERTA Hulst

(1) **Sympherta tripunctaria** Packard, Plate XLIII, Fig. 51, ♀.
The moth is found in northern California, and ranges north-ward into British Columbia.

Genus APÆCASIA Hulst

(1) **Apæcasia defluata** Walker, Plate XLIII, Fig. 52, ♂.
Syn. *subæquaria* Walker.
The habitat of the species is the northern portion of the Appalachian subregion.

Genus CATOPYRRHA Hübner

(1) **Catopyrrha coloraria** Fabricius, Plate XLIII, Fig. 54, ♂.
Syn. *accessaria* Hübner; *cruentaria* Hübner; *atropunctaria* Walker.
Form **dissimilaria** Hübner, Plate XLIII, Fig. 53, ♂.
The insect, which in the mature form presents many varietal differences, due to variation in the form and shade of the markings, is found in the Appalachian subregion.

Genus ENEMERA Hulst

(1) **Enemera juturnaria** Guenée, Plate XLIII, Fig. 55, ♂.
The moth is found in the region of the Rocky Mountains, westward to California and northward to Alaska.

Genus CARIPETA Walker

(1) **Caripeta divisata** Walker, Plate XLIII, Fig. 58, ♂.
Syn. *albopunctata* Morrison.
The insect is found in the Atlantic States.
* (2) **Caripeta angustiorata** Walker, Plate XLIV, Fig. 2, ♀.
Syn. *piniaria* Packard.
The moth, which is as yet quite rare in collections, is, like the preceding species, a native of the Appalachian subregion.

Genus PLATEA Herrich-Schæffer

(1) **Platea californiaria** Herrich-Schæffer, Plate XLIII, Fig. 57, ♂.
Syn. *uncanaria* Guenée.

*Should be *C. piniata* Packard in text and plate; the synonymy *seductaria* Strecker.—A.E.B.

The moth flies from Colorado to California.

(2) **Platea trilinearia** Packard, Plate XLIII, Fig. 56, ♂.

Syn. *dulcearia* Grote.

The insect ranges from northern Wyoming to Arizona.

Genus PHILEDIA Hulst

(1) **Philedia punctomacularia** Hulst, Plate XLIII, Fig. 59, ♂.
The insect, which is found in the Pacific States, is represented on the plate by a figure of the type.

Genus NEPYTIA Hulst

(1) **Nepytia nigrovenaria** Packard, Plate XLIV, Fig. 15, ♀.
The insect is a native of the Pacific subregion.

(2) **Nepytia semiclusaria** Walker, Plate XLIII, Fig. 60, ♂.

Syn. *pulchraria* Minot; *pellucidaria* Packard; *pinaria* Packard.

The moth occurs in the northern portions of the United States.

Genus ALCIS Curtis

(1) **Alcis sulphuraria** Packard, form **baltearia** Hulst, Plate XLIV, Fig. 1, ♂.

This insect, which is somewhat variable, is represented in the plate by the type of the form to which the Rev. Dr. Hulst applied the name *baltearia*. The species is widely distributed throughout the United States.

(2) **Alcis metanemaria** Hulst, Plate XLIV, Fig. 5, ♂.

The moth occurs in Arizona and southern California. The figure on the plate is that of the type of the species.

Genus PARAPHIA Guenée

(1) **Paraphia subatomaria** Wood, Plate XLIV, Fig. 10, ♂.

Syn. *nubecularia* Guenée; *mammurraria* Guenée; *impropriata* Walker; *exsuperata* Walker.

Form **unipuncta** Haworth, Plate XLIV, Fig. 11, ♀.

Syn. *unipunctata* Guenée; *triplipunctaria* Fitch.

The moth, which is variable in the shade of the wings and the markings, is found in the Appalachian subregion.

Genus PTEROSPODA Dyar

(1) **Pterospoda opuscularia** Hulst, Plate XLIV, Fig. 18, ♀.
The insect is a native of California. The specimen figured on

the plate is the type upon which Dr. Hulst based the description of the species.

Genus CLEORA Curtis

(1) **Cleora pampinaria** Guenée, Plate XLIV, Fig. 4, ♂.

Syn. *sublunaria* Guenée; *frugallaria* Guenée; *collecta* Walker; *tinctaria* Walker; *fraudulentaria* Zeller.

The moth is a native of the Appalachian subregion, ranging from the Atlantic to the Mississippi and beyond.

(2) **Cleora atrifasciata** Hulst, Plate XLIV, Fig. 8, ♀.

The specimen figured on the plate is the unique type which was described by Hulst in "Entomologica Americana," Vol. III, p. 214. The species has been overlooked in Dyar's List.

Genus MELANOLOPHIA Hulst

(1) **Melanolophia canadaria** Guenée, Plate XLIV, Fig. 7, ♂.
Syn. *signataria* Walker; *imperfectaria* Walker; *contribuaria* Walker.

A common species in the early spring throughout the United States.

Genus ECTROPIS Hübner

(1) **Ectropis crepuscularia** Denis & Schiffermüller, Plate XLIV, Fig. 9, ♂.

This species, which is found alike in Europe and America, has an extensive synonymy, for a knowledge of which the student may refer to Dyar's List or to Staudinger & Rebel's Catalogue. The species is widely distributed throughout the continent of North America.

Genus EPIMECIS Hübner

(1) **Epimecis virginaria** Cramer, Plate XLIV, Fig. 28, ♂, Fig. 29, ♀.

Syn. *hortaria* Fabricius; *liriodendraria* Abbot & Smith; *disserptaria* Walker; *amplaria* Walker.

The insect is found in the Appalachian subregion, but is far more common in the South than in the North. I have taken it in Pennsylvania on rare occasions, but it has been found in great abundance by me in Florida.

Genus LYCIA Hübner

(1) **Lycia cognataria** Guenée, Plate I, Fig. 17, larva; Plate XLIV, Fig. 13, ♂.

Syn. *sperataria* Walker.

This is a common species in the Atlantic States. The larva depicted on the plate is brown. In every brood there are many specimens of the larvæ which are green, and some are even yellowish. The moth has in the vicinity of Pittsburgh latterly shown a fondness for ovipositing upon imported rhododendrons, and the caterpillars have proved troublesome.

Genus NACOPHORA Hulst

(1) **Nacophora quernaria** Abbot & Smith, Plate XLIV, Fig. 14, ♀.

The species is not as common as the last, but is not rare. It has the same habitat, being a native of the Appalachian subregion.

Genus APOCHEIMA Hübner

The genus is found in the boreal regions of both hemispheres. Only one species occurs in our fauna.

(1) **Apocheima rachelæ** Hulst, Plate XLIV, Fig. 12, ♂. (Rachel's Moth.)

The moth is found in Montana, Assiniboia, and northward to Alaska.

Genus CONIODES Hulst

(1) **Coniodes plumigeraria** Hulst. (The Walnut Span-worm.)

In recent years the groves of English walnuts in southern California have been found to be liable to the attack of a span-worm, which previously had been unknown or unobserved. The trees had up to that time been regarded as singularly immune from the depredations of insect pests, and considerable alarm and apprehension were felt when it was found that a small caterpillar had begun to ravage them. The insect feeds also upon the leaves of various rosaceous plants, and upon the oak. The taste for the foliage of the English walnut has evidently been recently acquired.

An excellent article upon these insects was published in 1897 by D. W. Coquillet in the "Bulletins of the United States Department of Agriculture," New Series, No. 7, p. 64. From this

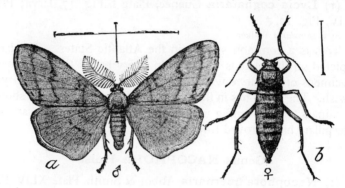

FIG. 205.—*C. plumigeraria.* *a*, male; *b*, female, magnified. (After Coquillet, " Bull. U. S. Dept. Agric.," New Series, No. 7, p. 66.)

article we have taken the accompanying cuts, and from it we draw some of the facts herein set forth. In describing the insect Mr. Coquillet says: " The color of the caterpillar is a light pinkish gray, varied with a darker gray or purplish, or sometimes with

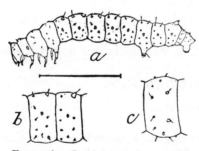

FIG. 206.—*C. plumigeraria.* *a*, larva, magnified; *b*, segment viewed laterally; *c*, do. viewed dorsally. (After Coquillet, "Bull. U. S. Dept. Agric.," New Series, No. 7, p. 65.)

black and yellow, but never marked with distinct lines; the piliferous spots are black or dark brown, and the spiracles are orange yellow, ringed with black, and usually situated on a yellow spot. The worms become full grown in the latter part of April or during the month of May; they then enter the earth to a depth of from two to four inches and form small cells, but do not spin cocoons. The change to the chrysalis takes place shortly after the cells are completed, and the chrysalis remains unchanged throughout the entire summer and until early in the following year, when they are changed into moths, which emerge from the ground from the first week in January to the last week in March. The male moth

346

is winged, but the female is wingless and is so very different in appearance from the male that no one not familiar with the facts in the case would ever suspect both belong to the same species."

The best means of combating these pests has been found to be to spray the trees, when the caterpillars are just hatching, with a solution of Paris green and water, one pound of the poison to two hundred gallons of water.

Genus PHIGALIA Duponchel

(1) **Phigalia titea** Cramer, Plate XLIV, Fig. 16, ♂.
Syn. *titearia* Guenée; *revocata* Walker; *strigataria* Minot.
The species is found in the Appalachian subregion, and is very common in Pennsylvania.

Genus ERANNIS Hübner

(1) **Erannis tiliaria** Harris, Plate XLIV, Fig. 17, ♂. (The Linden Moth.)
The species ranges from the Atlantic coast to the Rocky Mountains.

Genus CINGILIA Walker

(1) **Cingilia catenaria** Drury, Plate XLIV, Fig. 21, ♂. (The Chain-streak Moth.)
Syn. *humeralis* Walker.
The range of this species is much the same as that of the one which has just been mentioned above.

Genus SICYA Guenée

(1) **Sicya macularia** Harris, Plate XLIV, Fig. 22, ♂, Fig. 23, ♀, var.
This species has an extensive synonymy, the insects being variable in the amount of red which they show on the yellow ground-color of the wings. The student who wishes to go into these matters may consult Dyar's List. The insect is very generally distributed throughout our territory.

Genus THERINA Hübner

(1) **Therina endropiaria** Grote & Robinson, Plate XLIV, Fig. 26, ♂.

A native of the Appalachian subregion.

(2) **Therina athasiaria** Walker, Plate XLIV, Fig. 27, ♂.

Syn. *siccaria* Walker; *seminudata* Walker; *seminudaria* Packard; *bibularia* Grote & Robinson.

The habitat of this species is the same as that of the preceding.

(3) **Therina fiscellaria** Guenée, Plate XLIV, Fig. 25, ♂.

Syn. *flagitaria* Guenée; *panisaria* Walker; *æqualiaria* Walker.

The insect ranges from the Atlantic to Colorado.

(4) **Therina fervidaria** Hübner, Plate XLIV, Fig. 24, ♂.

Syn. *pultaria* Guenée; *sciata* Walker; *invexata* Walker.

The moth is quite common in the Atlantic States.

Genus METROCAMPA Latreille

(1) **Metrocampa prægrandaria** Guenée, Plate XLIV, Fig. 30, ♂.

Syn. *perlata* Guenée; *perlaria* Packard; *viridoperlata* Packard.

The home of the species is the northern part of the United States and southern Canada.

Genus EUGONOBAPTA Warren

(1) **Eugonobapta nivosaria** Guenée, Plate XLIV, Fig. 31, ♂. (The Snowy Geometer.)

Syn. *nivosata* Packard.

This is a very common species in the Appalachian subregion. It is particularly abundant in western Pennsylvania.

Genus ENNOMOS Treitschke

The genus is found in both Europe and America. Three species are attributed to our fauna, two of which we figure.

(1) **Ennomos subsignarius** Hübner, Plate XLIV, Fig. 35, ♂.

Syn. *niveosericeata* Jones.

The moth ranges from the Atlantic westward as far as Colorado.

(2) **Ennomos magnarius** Guenée, Plate XLIV, Fig. 34, ♂. (The Notch-wing.)

Syn. *alniaria* Packard (*non* Linnæus); *autumnaria* Mœschler (*non* Werneburg); *lutaria* Walker.

This is one of the larger and more conspicuous species of the family. It is rather a common insect in the northern United States, and appears on the wing most abundantly in the late summer and early fall.

Genus XANTHOTYPE Warren

(1) **Xanthotype crocataria** Fabricius, Plate XLIV, Fig. 39, ♂. (The Crocus Geometer.)

Syn. *citrina* Hübner.

Form **cælaria** Hulst, Plate XLIV, Fig. 40, ♂.

Quite a common species in the Appalachian subregion. The insect shows great variability in the a mount of the dark spots and cloudings upon the upper side of the wings.

Genus PLAGODIS Hübner

(1) **Plagodis serinaria** Herrich-Schæffer, Plate XLIV, Fig. 33, ♂.

Syn. *subprivata* Walker; *floscularia* Grote.

A common species of the Appalachian subregion, particularly abundant among the Alleghany Mountains.

(2) **Plagodis keutzingi** Grote, Plate XLIV, Fig. 36, ♂.

Syn. *keutzingaria* Packard.

The habitat of this species is identical with that of the preceding.

* (3) **Plagodis emargataria** Guenée, Plate XLIV, Fig. 32, ♀.

Syn. *arrogaria* Hulst.

The range of the moth is throughout the northern portions of the Atlantic subregion.

Genus HYPERITIS Guenée

† (1) **Hyperitis amicaria** Herrich-Schæffer, Plate XLIV, Fig. 38, ♂.

Syn. *nyssaria* Guenée; *exsimaria* Guenée; *insinuaria* Guenée; *laticincta* Walker; *subsinuaria* Guenée; *neoninaria* Walker; *neonaria* Packard; *æsionaria* Walker.

A very variable species, which has a wide distribution throughout the eastern portions of our territory.

Genus ANIA Stephens

(1) **Ania limbata** Haworth, Plate XLIV, Fig. 37, ♀.

Syn. *vestitaria* Herrich-Schæffer; *resistaria* Herrich-Schæffer; *filimentaria* Guenée.

By no means rare in the eastern portions of our territory.

---

*Should be *P. alcoölaria* Guenée in text and plate.—A.E.B.

†Should be *H. alienaria* Herrich-Schæffer in text and plate; the synonomy *persinuaria* Guenée; *subsinuaria* Guenée; *nyssaria* Guenée; *æsionaria* Walker.—A.E.B.

Genus GONODONTIS Hübner

(1) **Gonodontis hypochraria** Herrich-Schæffer, Plate XLV, Fig. 1, ♂.

Syn. *refractaria* Guenée; *mestusata* Walker.

The insect ranges from the Atlantic coast to the central portions of the Rocky Mountains. It is very variable in color and in the distribution of the spots and markings.

(2) **Gonodontis duaria** Guenée, Plate XLV, Fig. 2, ♀.

Syn. *hamaria* Guenée; *agreasaria* Walker; *adustaria* Walker.

The distribution of this species is coincident with that of the preceding.

(3) **Gonodontis obfirmaria** Hübner, Plate XLV, Fig. 14, ♂.

The moth is found in the Atlantic States. It is common in western Pennsylvania.

Genus EUCHLÆNA Hübner

(1) **Euchlæna serrata** Drury, Plate XLV, Fig. 4, ♂. (The Saw-wing.)

Syn. *serrataria* Packard; *concisaria* Walker.

This rather large and showy species is not at all uncommon in the eastern portions of the region with which this book deals.

(2) **Euchlæna obtusaria** Hübner, Plate XLV, Fig. 3, ♂.

Syn. *propriaria* Walker; *decisaria* Walker.

Like the preceding species, a native of the eastern half of the continent.

(3) **Euchlæna effectaria** Walker, Plate XLV, Fig. 24, ♂.

Syn. *muzaria* Walker.

A denizen of the Appalachian subregion.

(4) **Euchlæna amœnaria** Guenée, Plate XLV, Fig. 7, ♂.

Syn. *deplanaria* Walker; *arefactaria* Grote & Robinson.

The habitat of the insect is the same as that of the preceding species.

(5) **Euchlæna astylusaria** Walker, Plate XLV, Fig. 8, ♂.

Syn. *madusaria* Walker; *oponearia* Walker; *vinosaria* Grote & Robinson.

A native of the Atlantic States.

(6) **Euchlæna pectinaria** Denis & Schiffermüller, Plate XLV, Fig. 25, ♂.

Syn. *deductaria* Walker.

Found from the Atlantic to the Mississippi.

Genus EPIPLATYMETRA Grote

(1) **Epiplatymetra coloradaria** Grote & Robinson, Plate XLV, Fig. 15, ♂.

The insect is common in Wyoming and Colorado.

Genus PHERNE Hulst

(1) **Pherne parallelia** Packard, Plate XLV, Fig. 9, ♀.
Syn. *paralleliaria* Packard.

The moth is a native of the Pacific subregion.

(2) **Pherne jubararia** Hulst, Plate XLV, Fig. 20, ♀.

The insect occurs in the State of Washington. The specimen depicted in the plate is the type of the species originally described by Hulst.

(3) **Pherne placearia** Guenée, Plate XLV, Fig. 21, ♂.
Syn. *mellitularia* Hulst.

The habitat of the species is California.

Genus METANEMA Guenée

(1) **Metanema inatomaria** Guenée, Plate XLV, Fig. 13, ♂.

A widely distributed species, found throughout the entire territory.

(2) **Metanema determinata** Walker, Plate XLV, Fig. 12, ♀.
Syn. *carnaria* Packard.

The moth occurs in the northern portions of the Appalachian subregion.

(3) **Metanema quercivoraria** Guenée, Plate XLV, Fig. 28, ♀.
Syn. *æliaria* Walker; *trilinearia* Packard.

The insect has a wide range in the Appalachian subregion.

Genus PRIOCYCLA Guenée

(1) **Priocycla armataria** Herrich-Schæffer, Plate XLV, Fig. 6, ♂.

Very commonly found in the eastern portions of our territory.

Genus STENASPILATES Packard

(1) **Stenaspilates zalissaria** Walker, Plate XLV, Fig. 5, ♀.

The moth occurs in the region of the Gulf of Mexico, and is common in Florida.

Genus AZELINA Guenée

(1) **Azelina ancetaria** Hübner, Plate XLV, Fig. 23, ♂.

Syn. *hubneraria* Guenée; *hubnerata* Packard; *honestaria* Walker; *peplaria* Hübner; *stygiaria* Walker; *atrocolorata* Hulst; *morrisonata* Henry Edwards.

A very common and a very variable species, which is widely distributed throughout the entire continent, except in the colder portions.

Genus SYSSAURA Hübner

* (1) **Syssaura infensata** Guenée, Plate XLV, Fig. 10, ♀, var. **biclaria** Walker.

Syn. *ephyrata* Guenée; *olyzonaria* Walker; *æquosus* Grote & Robinson; *sesquilinea* Grote; *æmearia* Walker; *puber* Grote & Robinson; *varus* Grote & Robinson; *juniperaria* Packard.

This species, which has a very extensive range in the southern Atlantic and Gulf States, has been frequently redescribed, as a reference to the above synonymy will show.

Genus CABERODES Guenée

(1) **Caberodes confusaria** Hübner, Plate XLV, Fig. 29, ♂.

Syn. *remissaria* Guenée; *imbraria* Guenée; *superaria* Guenée; *ineffusaria* Guenée; *floridaria* Guenée; *phasianaria* Guenée; *interlinearia* Guenée; *varadaria* Walker; *arburaria* Walker; *amyrisaria* Walker; *myandaria* Walker, etc.

This is a very common moth, universally found throughout the temperate portions of the territory with which this book deals. It is somewhat variable, but there is hardly any excuse for the application to it of the multitude of names which have been given. The student is likely to recognize it in any of its slightly varying forms from the figure we have supplied in our plate.

(2) **Caberodes majoraria** Guenée, Plate XLV, Fig. 31, ♀.

Syn. *pandaria* Walker.

This is a larger species than the preceding, with more delicate wings. It ranges from the Atlantic to the Rocky Mountains.

Genus OXYDIA Guenée

(1) **Oxydia vesulia** Cramer, Plate XLV, Fig. 11, ♂.

This moth has a very lengthy synonymy, which we will not attempt to give. It is one of the larger species found within our territory, and ranges from Florida and Texas southward to the Valley of the Rio de la Plata in South America.

*Should be *S. puber* Grote & Robinson in text and plate; the synonomy *varus* Grote & Robinson; *aquosus* Grote & Robinson; *biclaria* Hulst; *juniperata* Packard; *perizomaria* Hulst; *sesquilinea* Grote.—A.E.B.

Genus TETRACIS Guenée

(1) **Tetracis crocallata** Guenée, Plate XLV, Fig. 16, ♂.
Syn. *allediusaria* Walker; *aspilata* Guenée.
This is a common species in the Atlantic subregion.

Genus SABULODES Guenée

(1) **Sabulodes sulphurata** Packard, Plate XLV, Fig. 18, ♀.
Syn. *imitata* Henry Edwards.
A native of the Appalachian subregion.

(2) **Sabulodes arcasaria** Walker, Plate XLV, Fig. 17, ♂.
Syn. *depontanata* Grote.
The moth has the same habitat as the preceding species.

(3) **Sabulodes lorata** Grote, Plate XLV, Fig. 19, ♂.
Common in the eastern portions of our territory.

(4) **Sabulodes truxaliata** Guenée, Plate XLV, Fig. 26, ♀.
The insect ranges from Colorado to California.

(5) **Sabulodes transversata** Drury, Plate XLV, Fig. 34, ♀.
Syn. *transmutans* Walker; *contingens* Walker; *transfindens* Walker; *goniata*
Guenée; *transvertens* Walker; *transposita* Walker; *incurvata* Guenée.
This is one of the commonest species which are found in the
Atlantic subregion. It is very abundant in Pennsylvania in the
late summer and early autumn. There is also a brood which
appears in the early summer.

(6) **Sabulodes politia** Cramer, Plate XLV, Fig. 30, ♂.
The moth, which is found in Florida, and southward through
the warmer portions of America, has a very extensive synonymy,
which will be found in Dyar's List.

Genus ABBOTANA Hulst

(1) **Abbotana clemataria** Abbot & Smith, Plate XLV, Fig.
32, ♀, Fig. 33, ♂, var.
Syn. *transferens* Walker; *transducens* Walker.
A somewhat variable species, which is widely distributed
through the Appalachian subregion. It is not uncommon in
Pennsylvania.

"Moths, which the night-air of reality blows to pieces."
CLIVE HOLLAND.—*My Japanese Wife.*

SUBFAMILY MECOCERATINÆ

Genus MECOCERAS Guenée

(1) **Mecoceras nitocris** Cramer, Plate XLV, Fig. 22, ♂.

Syn. *nitocraria* Hübner; *peninsularia* Grote.

The habitat of the species is Florida.

Genus ALMODES Guenée

(1) **Almodes terraria** Guenée, Plate XLV, Fig. 27, ♂.

Syn. *stellidaria* Guenée; *squamigera* Felder; *balteolata* Herrich-Schæffer; *assecoma* Druce; *calvina* Druce; *rivularia* Grote.

This is a tropical species, the sole representative of its genus found within our borders. It ranges from Florida southward into Central and South America.

SUBFAMILY PALYADINÆ

Genus PALYAS Guenée

(1) **Palyas auriferaria** Hulst, Plate XLV, Fig. 36, ♂.

The specimen figured in the plate is the type which was loaned by the writer to the author of the species.

Genus PHRYGIONIS Hübner

(1) **Phryigonis argenteostriata** Strecker, Plate XLV, Fig. 35, ♀.

Syn. *cerussata* Grote; *obrussata* Grote.

This moth, like the preceding species, is a native of Florida.

SUBFAMILY SPHACELODINÆ

Genus SPHACELODES Guenée

(1) **Sphacelodes vulneraria** Hübner, Plate XLII, Fig. 20, ♂.

Syn. *floridensis* Holland.

The moth is found from the southern portions of North Carolina along the Atlantic coast to Florida, and ranges southward into South America.

SUBFAMILY MELANCHROIINÆ

Genus MELANCHROIA Hübner

(1) **Melanchroia cephise** Cramer, Plate XLII, Fig. 19, ♂.

Found throughout the region of the Gulf southward to South America.

(2) **Melanchroia geometroides** Walker, Plate XLII, Fig. 18, ♂.

Syn. *mors* Lucas.

The moth occurs in Florida and southern Texas, and ranges thence southward into Brazil.

SUBFAMILY BREPHINÆ

Genus BREPHOS Ochsenheimer

(1) **Brephos infans** Mœschler, Plate XLII, Fig. 16, ♀. (The Infant.)

This is a boreal insect which occurs upon the White Mountains in New Hampshire, in northern Maine, and ranges thence northwardly to Labrador.

LIVING AND DYING

" Then let me joy to be
Alive with bird and tree,
And have no haughtier aim than this,
To be a partner in their bliss.

So shall my soul at peace
From anxious carping cease,
Fed slowly like a wholesome bud
With sap of healthy thoughts and good

That when at last I die
No praise may earth deny,
But with her living forms combine
To chant a threnody divine."

EDMUND GOSSE.—*The Farm.*

FAMILY EPIPLEMIDÆ

" And I will purge thy mortal grossness so,
That thou shalt like an airy spirit go.
Peaseblossom! Cobweb! Moth! and Mustardseed!"
SHAKESPEARE.—*Midsummer Night's Dream*, III, I.

This is a family of small moths in many respects closely allied to the *Geometridæ*, so far as the structure and general appearance of the mature insects are concerned. The larvæ are, however, quite different. The family has been described as follows by Hampson, "The Moths of India," Vol. III, p. 121:

"Proboscis and frenulum present. Fore wing with vein 1*a* separate from 1*b*; 1*c* absent; 5 from or from above the middle of the discocellulars; 7 widely separated from 8, and usually stalked with 6. Hind wing with two internal veins; vein 5 from or from above the middle of the discocellulars; 8 free from the base.

Larvæ with five pairs of prolegs and sparsely clothed with hair."

The family is much better represented in the tropics of the New World than in our territory, and even better represented in the tropics of the Old World than of the New. Only four genera are known to occur within the United States, *Philagraula*, *Callizia*, *Calledapteryx*, and *Schidax*. Of these we have selected one for purposes of illustration.

Genus CALLEDAPTERYX Grote

(1) **Calledapteryx dryopterata** Grote, Plate XLII, Fig. 17, ♂.
Syn. *erosiata* Packard.

This little moth, which may easily be distinguished by its deeply eroded or scalloped wings, is not uncommon in the Appalachian subregion. It has the habit of alighting upon old rails and the trunks of trees, and, before composing itself on its new station, of waving its wings three or four times upward and downward. This peculiar habit enables the collector to quickly recognize it.

356

FAMILY NOLIDÆ

"I would bee unwilling to write anything untrue, or uncertaine out of mine owne invention; and truth on every part is so deare unto mee, that I will not lie to bring any man in love and admiration with God and his works, for God needeth not the lies of men."—TOPSELL, writing upon the Unicorn in *The Historie of Four-footed Beasts*.

This is a small family of quite small moths, which have by many authors been associated with the *Lithosiidæ*. They are characterized by the presence of ridges and tufts of raised scales upon the fore wings. They frequent the trunks of trees, and the larvæ feed upon lichens growing upon the bark. The caterpillars have eight pairs of legs and are thinly clad with minute hairs. Four genera occur within the limits with which this book deals.

Genus CELAMA Walker

Seven species occurring within our territory are attributed to this genus.

(1) **Celama triquetrana** Fitch, Plate XIII, Fig. 25, ♂.
Syn. *trinotata* Walker; *sexmaculata* Grote.

The moths may be found in the early spring of the year, sitting upon the trunks of trees in the forest. They are easily recognized by the three black tufts of raised scales upon the costa of the fore wing.

(2) **Celama pustulata** Walker, Plate XIII, Fig. 26, ♂.
Syn. *nigrofasciata* Zeller; *obaurata* Morrison.

This species, like the preceding, is common in the Appalachian subregion. It may be at once distinguished from the former by the wide black band running across the middle of the primaries.

Genus NOLA Leach

There are three species of the genus found within our fauna. We select the commonest for purposes of illustration.

(1) **Nola ovilla** Grote, Plate XIII, Fig. 24, ♂.

357

The habits of this insect are much like those of the species described under the preceding genus. It is found associated with them at the same time and in the same localities. The moth has a considerable range in the Atlantic States, and is always very abundant in the forests of Pennsylvania in the early spring. It seems to prefer the trunks of beeches and oaks.

Genus RŒSELIA Hübner

(1) **Rœselia fuscula** Grote, Plate XIII, Fig. 27, ♀.
Syn. *conspicua* Dyar.

This moth is a native of Colorado, where it is not uncommon. An allied species, *Rœselia minuscula* Zeller, is found in the Atlantic States.

Genus NIGETIA Walker

(1) **Nigetia formosalis** Walker, Plate XIII, Fig. 32, ♂.
Syn. *melanopa* Zeller.

This rather pretty little creature is common in the woodlands

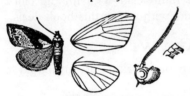

of the Appalachian subregion. It is freely attracted to sugar, and when sugaring for moths in southern Indiana I have taken it very frequently. In fact, it appears to be commoner in southern Indiana than in any other locality where I

FIG. 207.—*N. formosalis*, ♂ . ♀.
(After Hampson.)

have found it, though it is by no means rare in Pennsylvania.

" . . . all you restless things,
That dance and tourney in the fields of air:

. . . . . .

Your secret 's out! I know you for the souls
Of all light loves that ever caused heartache,
Still dancing suit as some new beauty toles!
Nor can you e'er your flitting ways forsake,
Till the just winds strip off your painted stoles,
And sere leaves follow in your downward wake."

EDITH M. THOMAS.

FAMILY LACOSOMIDÆ

" Everything lives by a law; a central balance sustains all."

C. L. von Kuebel.

This is a small family of moths peculiar to the Western Hemisphere. While the perfect insects show structural resemblances to the *Platypterygidæ*, the caterpillars, which have the habit of constructing for themselves portable cases out of leaves, which they drag about with them, resemble in some respects the *Psychidæ*. The young larva of *Cicinnus melsheimeri*, immediately after hatching, draws together two small leaves with strands of silk, and makes between them its hiding-place. Afterward, when more mature, it detaches two pieces of leaves and makes out of them a case which it carries about with it, and which it can desert at will. When at rest it ties the case to a station selected with a few strands of silk, which it bites off when it desires again to start on a journey among the branches. The larva of *Lacosoma* makes a case by doubling a leaf at the midrib, cutting it off at the petiole, and taking it with it as a portable house. There are only two genera of this family in our fauna. It is more abundantly represented in the tropics of South America.

Genus CICINNUS Blanchard

(1) **Cicinnus melsheimeri** Harris, Plate XLI, Fig. 17, ♀. (Melsheimer's Sack-bearer.)

Syn. *egenaria* Walker.

The species occurs in the eastern portions of our territory. It is not uncommon in Pennsylvania.

Genus LACOSOMA Grote

(1) **Lacosoma chiridota** Grote, Plate XLI, Fig. 21, ♂. (The Scalloped Sack-bearer.)

The distribution of this species is the same as that of the foregoing. It occurs quite frequently in western Pennsylvania. Specimens from Florida in the possession of the author are smaller and much darker in color.

359

FAMILY PSYCHIDÆ

" The habits of insects are very mines of interesting knowledge, and it is impossible carefully to watch the proceedings of any insect, however insignificant, without feeling that no writer of fiction ever invented a drama of such absorbing interest as is acted daily before our eyes, though to indifferent spectators."

J. G. WOOD.

A family of small or medium-sized moths, the larvæ of which feed in a case composed of silk covered with bits of leaves, grass, twigs, or other vegetable matter, which are often arranged in a very curious manner. From this fact has arisen the custom of calling the caterpillars "basket-worms." In certain species found in Asia and Africa, these "baskets," or "cases," are spiral in form, and so closely resemble the shells of snails that they were, in fact, originally sent to the British Museum as shells by the first person who collected them. The pupa is formed within the larva-case. The males are winged, but the females are without wings. The female in almost all of the genera is possessed of a very lowly organization, being maggot-like, and in truth being little more than an ovary. She is known to deposit her eggs in the larval skin which lines the sack in which she was developed. Copulation takes place through the insertion of the abdomen of the winged male into the sack where the female is concealed. Parthenogenesis is ascertained to occur in one at least of the genera. The moths are obscurely colored. The wings of the males have numerous scales upon them, but they are in many species so loosely attached that they are lost in the first few moments of flight. In consequence the male insects appear to have diaphanous wings.

Eight genera, including the genus *Solenobia*, which has by most authors heretofore been reckoned among the *Tineidæ*, are attributed by Dyar to this family as occurring within our territory. Much remains to be learned both as to the structure and the life-history of these interesting, but obscure, moths.

360

Genus OIKETICUS Guilding

The genus is found in the hotter parts of America, the typical species having originally been found in Central America. It is also represented in southern Asia and in Australia. Three species occur in the United States—one in southern California, another in New Mexico, and a third in Florida. The latter species was named **abboti** by Grote, and the male is delineated in Fig. 208. The wings are pale smoky brown, with darker

FIG. 208.— *Oiketicus abboti,* ♂ . ¼.

maculation at the end of the cell and just beyond in the primaries.

Genus THYRIDOPTERYX Stephens

(1) **Thyridopteryx ephemeræformis** Haworth, Plate XLI, Fig. 12, ♂ .

Syn. *coniferarum* Packard.

The common "Bag-worm," as it is usually called, occurs throughout the Appalachian subregion, from the Atlantic to the

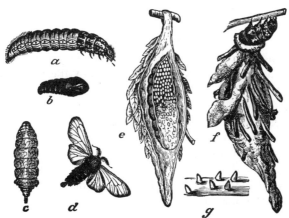

FIG. 209.— *Thyridopteryx ephemeræformis.* (Bag-worm.) *a*, larva; *b*, male pupa; *c*, female pupa; *d*, male moth; *e*, female chrysalis in cocoon, showing eggs *in situ ; f*, full-grown larva; *g*, young larvæ with small cones of silk over them. (After Riley.)

borders of the Great Plains. It is a very promiscuous feeder, attacking trees and shrubs of many genera, but, so far as is known, abstaining from the *Gramineæ*. It evinces special fondness for the conifers, and above all for the red cedar and arborvitæ. It has proved very injurious to shade-trees in some of our cities, and its ravages in St. Louis and Washington have been made the subject of repeated comment in the literature of economic entomology. A very full and interesting account of the habits of this peculiar insect was published by the late Professor C. V. Riley in the "First Annual Report of the State Entomologist of Missouri," to which the reader will do well to refer. The "bag," or "basket," of the male insect is smaller than that of the female. The males escape from the lower end of the case in the winged form, and having copulated with the females, which remain in their cases and are apterous and sluggish, die. The female deposits her eggs, which are soft and yellow, in the sack where she has her home, and ends her existence by leaving what little of her body remains after the ova have been extruded, as a sort of loose plug of desiccated tissue at the lower end of the sack. The eggs remain in the case till the following spring, when they hatch. The young larvæ emerge, and placing themselves upon the leaves, where they walk about on their fore feet, with their anal extremities held up perpendicularly, proceed to construct about themselves little cones of vegetable matter mixed with fine silk. After a while they cease to hold these cones erect, and seizing the leaves and branches with their feet, allow the bag to assume a pendant position. They moult within their cases four times before reaching maturity and pupating.

The remedy for these insects is to simply collect the cases which may be found in the fall and winter hanging from the branches, and burn them. In one of the parks in St. Louis several years ago, the superintendent caused the cases to be collected, and they were destroyed by the bushel, with great benefit to the trees the next summer.

Genus EURYCYTTARUS Hampson

This is a small genus of very small case-bearing moths, two species of which are known to occur in the United States. *E. carbonaria* is found in Texas. The other species, which we figure, is a native of the Appalachian subregion.

(1) **Eurycyttarus confederata** Grote & Robinson, Plate I, Fig. 16, larval case; Plate XLI, Fig. 8, ♂.

The insects feed upon grasses and herbaceous plants in the larval state. When ready to pupate they attach their cases to the under side of rails, the stringers of fences, and fallen branches of trees. The insect is very common in western Pennsylvania and in the city of Pittsburgh.

FAR OUT AT SEA

" Far out at sea—the sun was high,
　　While veered the wind and flapped the sail;
　We saw a snow-white butterfly
　　Dancing before the fitful gale
　　　Far out at sea.

The little wanderer, who had lost
　　His way, of danger nothing knew;
Settled a while upon the mast;
　　Then fluttered o'er the waters blue
　　　Far out at sea.

Above, there gleamed the boundless sky;
　　Beneath, the boundless ocean sheen;
Between them danced the butterfly,
　　The spirit-life of this vast scene,
　　　Far out at sea.

The tiny soul that soared away,
　　Seeking the clouds on fragile wings,
Lured by the brighter, purer ray
　　Which hope's ecstatic morning brings'—
　　　Far out at sea.

Away he sped, with shimmering glee,
　　Scarce seen, now lost, yet onward borne!
Night comes with wind and rain, and he
　　No more will dance before the morn,
　　　Far out at sea.

He dies, unlike his mates, I ween
　　Perhaps not sooner or worse crossed;
And he hath felt and known and seen
　　A larger life and hope, though lost
　　　Far out at sea."

　　　　　　　R. H. HORNE.—*Genius.*

363

FAMILY COCHLIDIIDÆ

"The rearing of larvæ . . . when joined with the entomological collection, adds immense interest to Saturday afternoon rambles, and forms an admirable introduction to the study of physiology."

HERBERT SPENCER, in *Education*.

This family, which has generally been known as the *Limacodidæ*, is described as follows by Hampson, "The Moths of India," Vol. I, p. 371:

"Fore wing with two internal veins; vein 1*b* forked at the base. Hind wing with vein 8 arising free, then bent down and usually anastomosing shortly with 7 near the base of the cells; three internal veins.

Larva limaciform, and either bearing series of spinous stinging tubercles, or smooth and segmented, or unsegmented with very thick transparent cuticle; the head, legs, and claspers small and often retractile.

Cocoon hard and compact; round or oval in shape, with a lid for the escape of the imago prepared by the larva."

These curious insects, the larvæ of which are commonly known as "slug-caterpillars," are better represented in the tropics of both hemispheres than in the more temperate regions. Nevertheless our fauna contains quite a large number of genera and species. Of the majority of these we give illustrations.

Genus SIBINE Herrich-Schæffer

(1) **Sibine stimulea** Clemens, Plate I, Fig. 6, larva; Plate XLVII, Fig. 9, ♂. (The Saddle-back.)

Syn. *ephippiatus* Harris.

The green caterpillars with their little brown saddle on the back are familiar to every Southern boy who has wandered in the corn-fields, and many a lad can recall the first time he came in contact with the stinging bristles as he happened to brush against the beastie. Nettles are not to be compared in stinging power to the armament of this beautifully colored larva.

Genus EUCLEA Hübner

(1) **Euclea nanina** Dyar, Plate XLVII, Fig. 25, ♂.
Syn. *nana* Dyar (*non* Herrich-Schæffer).

The moth is a native of Florida. The writer took it in some numbers, in the spring of the year 1884, on the upper waters of the St. Johns.

(2) **Euclea delphinii** Boisduval, Plate XLVII, Fig. 24, ♀. (The Spiny Oak-slug.)
Syn. *strigata* Boisduval; *quercicola* Herrich-Schæffer; *tardigrada* Clemens; *ferruginea* Packard; *argentatus* Wetherby.

Form **viridiclava** Walker, Plate XLVII, Fig. 23, ♂.
Syn. *monitor* Packard.

Form **pænulata** Clemens, Plate XLVII, Fig. 5, ♂.

This is a very variable species. It occurs in the eastern portion of our territory, and is not at all uncommon.

(3) **Euclea indetermina** Boisduval, Plate XLVII, Fig. 10, ♂.
Syn. *vernata* Packard.

The species is found in the States of the Atlantic seaboard.

* (4) **Euclea chloris** Herrich-Schæffer, Plate XLVII, Figs. 15 and 29, ♀, Fig. 26, ♂.
Syn. *viridis* Reakirt; *fraterna* Grote.

The insect has the same range as the species last mentioned.

Genus MONOLEUCA Grote & Robinson

The insects belonging to this genus are subtropical so far as they are known to occur in the United States. The genus is well represented in Central and South America.

(1) **Monoleuca semifascia** Walker, Plate XLVII, Fig. 22, ♂.
The moth is found in the Gulf States.

Genus ADONETA Clemens

(1) **Adoneta spinuloides** Herrich-Schæffer, Plate XLVII, Fig. 3, ♂.
Syn. *voluta* Clemens; *ferrigera* Walker; *nebulosus* Wetherby.

This is a common species in western Pennsylvania, and is widely distributed through the Appalachian subregion.

(2) **Adoneta pygmæa** Grote & Robinson, Plate XLVII, Fig. 19, ♂. (The Pygmy Slug.)
The moth has thus far been found only in Texas.

*Fig. 15 of Plate XLVII is *E. indetermina* Boisduval, ♀.—A.E.B.

Genus SISYROSEA Grote

(1) **Sisyrosea textula** Herrich-Schæffer, Plate XLVII, Fig. 14, ♀.

Syn. *inornata* Grote & Robinson.

The insect occurs in the eastern portion of our territory. It is not rare about Pittsburgh.

Genus NATADA Walker

(1) **Natada nasoni** Grote, Plate XLVII, Fig. 13, ♂. (Nason's Slug.)

Syn. *daona* Druce; *rude* Henry Edwards.

The moth ranges from the southern portions of the Atlantic coast westward and southward to Texas and Mexico.

Genus PHOBETRON Hübner

(1) **Phobetron pithecium** Abbot & Smith, Plate I, Fig. 14, larva; Plate XLVII, Fig. 6, ♂, Fig. 7, ♀. (The Monkey Slug.)

Syn. *abbotana* Hübner; *nigricans* Packard; *hyalinus* Walsh; *tetradactylus* Walsh; *nondescriptus* Wetherby.

The perfect insects are quite dissimilar in the two sexes. The larva, which is a very curious object, feeds upon the *Rosaceæ*, the *Cupuliferæ*, and various low-growing shrubs, as the sassafras, alder, and *Spiræa*. The species is found in the Appalachian sub-region, and was quite common in western North Carolina in former years, and may be so still. The larvæ are generally to be found close to the ground.

Genus ISOCHÆTES Dyar

(1) **Isochætes beutenmülleri** Henry Edwards, Plate XLVII, Fig. 17, ♀.

This is a rare little insect, which has practically the same distribution as the preceding species.

Genus ALARODIA Mœschler

(1) **Alarodia slossoniæ** Packard, Plate XLVII, Fig. 18, ♀. (Slosson's Slug.)

This remarkable little species inhabits in the larval stage the mangroves which grow in the swampy lands on the southern coast of Florida. A good account of its habits has been published by Dr. Dyar in the "Journal of the New York Entomological Society," Vol. V, and indeed the student who desires to know about the habits of this and all other species of the *Cochlidiidæ* found in North America must consult the writings of this author, who has made these insects the subject of special and exhaustive inquiry.

Genus PROLIMACODES

(1) **Prolimacodes scapha** Harris, Plate I, Fig. 9, larva; Plate XLVII, Fig. 8, ♀. (The Skiff Moth.)

Syn. *undifera* Walker.

The moth has a wide distribution throughout the Appalachian subregion. The larva feeds upon a great variety of shrubs and trees. It appeared to me in my boyhood, when I reared it often, to have a particular fondness for the leaves of the sycamore (*Platanus*).

Genus COCHLIDION Hübner

(1) **Cochlidion biguttata** Packard, Plate XLVII, Fig. 4, ♀.

Syn. *tetraspilaris* Walker.

A native of the eastern portions of the region.

(2) **Cochlidion rectilinea** Grote & Robinson, Plate XLVII, Fig. 27, ♂.

The insect is quite common locally, and has the same distribution as the preceding species.

* (3) **Cochlidion y-inversa** Packard, Plate XLVII, Fig. 21, ♂.

The distribution of the species is the same as that of the two preceding. The larva frequents hickory.

Genus LITHACODES Packard

(1) **Lithacodes fasciola** Herrich-Schæffer, Plate XLVII, Fig. 2, ♂.

Syn. *divergens* Walker.

The caterpillar feeds on a great variety of low shrubs and trees; it is especially fond of the leaves of the various species of wild cherry. It is common in western Pennsylvania, and is well distributed throughout the Appalachian subregion.

Genus PACKARDIA Grote & Robinson

(1) **Packardia elegans** Packard, Plate XLVII, Fig. 16, ♀.

Syn. *nigripunctata* Goodell.

*Should be *Tortricidia flexuosa* Grote. See *Tortricidia* on page 368. —A.E.B.

The larvæ feed upon a great variety of trees and shrubs, and are commonly found in the deep glens and ravines of the Appalachian subregion, where there is much shade and moisture. The insect is not uncommon in the vicinity of Pittsburgh.

(2) **Packardia geminata** Packard, Plate XLVII, Fig. 1, ♂.

The larvæ frequent places exactly opposite in character to those resorted to by the previous species, being fond of dry open woods, and living upon low shrubs and bushes. The insect is a native of the Appalachian subregion.

Genus HETEROGENEA Knoch

(1) **Heterogenea shurtleffi** Packard, Plate XLVII, Fig. 20, ♂.

This, which is one of the very smallest of all the *Cochlidiidæ*, feeds in its larval stage upon black oak, chestnut, beech, and ironwood. The genus is found both in the Old World and the New.

Genus TORTRICIDIA Packard

(1) **Tortricidia flexuosa** Grote, form **cæsonia** Grote, Plate XLVII, Fig. 12, ♀.

A native of the Appalachian subregion, the larva feeding on chestnut, oak, hickory, and wild cherry. It is not uncommon in western Pennsylvania.

(2) **Tortricidia testacea** Packard, Plate I, Fig. 19, larva; Plate XLVII, Fig. 11, ♂.

The insect, which has the same habitat as the preceding species, feeds upon the same species of plants. It is not uncommon at light in western Pennsylvania.

FAMILY MEGALOPYGIDÆ

" Simple and sweet is their food : they eat no flesh of the living."

C. L. von Kuebel.

This is a small family characteristic of the neotropical regions, and represented by three or four genera, which have a foothold in the southern portions of our territory.

Genus CARAMA Walker

(1) **Carama cretata** Grote, Plate XXXVIII, Fig. 22, ♂.
Syn. *pura* Butler.

The insect feeds in its larval stage upon the red-bud (*Cercis*). The caterpillars are gregarious at first, but during the later part of their life separate. The cocoon is made in the ground. The insect occurs from New Jersey and southern Pennsylvania southward in the Appalachian region at comparatively low elevations.

Genus MEGALOPYGE Hübner

(1) **Megalopyge opercularis** Abbot & Smith, Plate XXXVIII, Fig. 25, ♂.

Syn. *lanuginosa* Clemens; *subcitrina* Walker.

The moth is found in Georgia and the region of the Gulf States.

Genus LAGOA Harris

(1) **Lagoa crispata** Packard, Plate XXXVIII, Fig. 23, ♂. (The White Flannel-moth.)

The caterpillar feeds upon the flowering blackberry (*Rubus villosus*), and ranges from Massachusetts southward along the coast.

(2) **Lagoa pyxidifera** Abbot & Smith, Plate XXXVIII, Fig. 24, ♂. (The Yellow Flannel-moth.)

This is a rare moth in collections. It is no doubt common enough in its proper locality, but thus far few collectors have succeeded in finding it. Its home is on the seaboard of the Southern States.

FAMILY DALCERIDÆ

> " So man, the moth, is not afraid, it seems,
> To span Omnipotence, and measure night
> That knows no measure, by the scanty rule
> And standard of his own, that is to-day,
> And is not ere to-morrow's sun go down."
>
> COWPER.—*The Task*, VI, 211.

This is another family which is represented in our fauna only by a small number of species. Besides the insect known as *Dalcerides ingenita* Henry Edwards, there is only one other species referable to the family known to occur within the United States. This insect is **Pinconia coa** Schaus, a moth which is not uncommon in Mexico, and occurs in Arizona as a straggler into our territory. *Dalcerides ingenita* is likewise an inhabitant of Arizona. In Central and South America the *Dalceridæ* are more numerously found. Of *Pinconia coa* we give a representation on Plate VIII, Fig. 6.

FAMILY EPIPYROPIDÆ

" So, naturalists observe, a flea
Has smaller fleas that on him prey;
And these have smaller still to bite 'em,
And so proceed *ad infinitum*."

SWIFT.—*A Rhapsody.*

The *Epipyropidæ* are a very remarkable little family of parasitic moths, of which, as yet, comparatively little is known. Professor J. O. Westwood of Oxford, in the year 1876, published an account of a lepidopterous insect, the larva of which lived upon *Fulgora candelaria*, the great tree-hopper, which is abundant at Hong-Kong and elsewhere in southeastern Asia. The caterpillar, according to Westwood, feeds upon the white, cottony secretion, which is found at the base of the wings of *Fulgora*. In 1902 Dr. Dyar described another species, the moth of which was bred from a larva which was found attached to the body of a tree-hopper belonging to the genus *Issus*. The specimen came from New Mexico, and was taken at Las Vegas Hot Springs. The moth, cocoon, and an alcoholic specimen of the larva are preserved in the United States National Museum. Mr. Champion, the veteran explorer of Central America, who has done so much to instruct us as to the biology of those lands, has recorded in a note in the Proceedings of the Entomological Society of London for 1883, p. xx, that a similar phenomenon was observed by him while collecting in Central America. There is here a field of interesting study for some patient observer whose home is in New Mexico. Dr. Dyar named the New Mexican insect **Epipyrops barberiana.**

" The little fleas that do so tease,
Have smaller fleas that bite 'em,
And these again have lesser fleas,
And so *ad infinitum*."

SWIFT. As popularly but incorrectly quoted.

370

FAMILY ZYGÆNIDÆ

" Every traveller is a self-taught entomologist."
OLIVER WENDELL HOLMES. — *The Autocrat of the Breakfast-table.*

The *Zygænidæ* are not very well represented in the fauna of North America. They are more numerous in the Old World than in the New, and the genera found in the New World are mainly aberrant. The family has been characterized as follows by Hampson, "Moths of India," Vol. I, p. 228: "Closely allied to the *Syntomidæ*, but distinguished by vein 1a of the fore wing being present, except in *Anomœotes*[1]; vein 8 of the hind wing present and connected with 7 by a bar; veinlets in the cell of both, with wings generally present. Frenulum present except in *Himantopterus.*[1]

Larva short and cylindrical.
Pupa in a silken cocoon."

Genus ACOLOITHUS Clemens

(1) **Acoloithus falsarius** Clemens, Plate XVI, Fig. 14, ♂.
Syn. *sanborni* Packard.
The larva feeds upon the grape and the Virginia creeper (*Ampelopsis*). The insect is not scarce in the Atlantic States.

Genus PYROMORPHA Herrich-Schæffer

(1) **Pyromorpha dimidiata** Herrich-Schæffer, Plate XLVII, Fig. 33, ♂.
Syn. *perlucidula* Clemens.
The insect is not very common. It is a native of the eastern portions of the territory with which this book deals.

Genus TRIPROCRIS Grote

There are eight species assigned to this genus in recent lists. They are all found in the southwestern portions of our territory.
(1) **Triprocris rata** Henry Edwards, Plate XIII, Fig. 4, ♂.
A native of Arizona.

[1] Genera found in Asia and Africa.

371

(2) **Triprocris latercula** Henry Edwards, Plate XIII, Fig. 5, ♂.

Has the same habitat as the preceding species.

(3) **Triprocris constans** Henry Edwards, Plate XIII, Fig. 16, ♂.

The moth occurs in New Mexico.

(4) **Triprocris smithsonianus** Clemens, Plate XLVII, Fig. 32, ♂.

The insect is not uncommon in the southern portions of Colorado, and is found in New Mexico and northern Texas.

Genus HARRISINA Packard

Three species belonging to the genus occur within the United States. Two of these are indigenous to Texas and Arizona. The other has a wide range through the Appalachian subregion. We have selected it for illustration.

(1) **Harrisina americana** Guérin-Méneville, Plate XLVII, Fig. 34, ♂.

Syn. *texana* Stretch.

The habits of this insect have been so well described by Professor C. V. Riley that we cannot do better than quote some passages from his account, which is to be found in the "Second Annual Report of the State Entomologist of Missouri," at page 85. He says: "During the months of July and August, the leaves of the grape-vine may often be found denuded of their softer parts, with nothing but the veins, and sometimes only a few of the larger ribs left skeleton-like, to tell the mischief that has been done. Very frequently only portions of the leaf will be thus denuded, and in that event, if we examine such a leaf closely, we shall find the authors of the mischief drawn up in line upon the yet leafy tissue with their heads all toward the margin, cutting away with their little jaws and retreating as they feed.

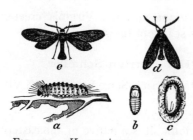

FIG. 210.—*H. americana.* *a,* larva; *b,* pupa; *c,* cocoon; *d, e,* moths. (After Riley.)

These soldier-like files are formed by worms in black and yellow uniforms which produce a moth popularly known as the American Procris. The eggs from which they hatch are laid in small clusters on the under side of the leaves, and while the worms are small, they leave untouched the most delicate veins of the leaf, which then presents the appearance of fine network, as shown in the right of the figure (211); but when they become older and stronger they devour all but the larger ribs, as shown at the left of the figure. . . . When full grown

FIG. 211.—*Harrisina americana.* Larvæ.
(After Riley.)

these worms disperse over the vines or forsake them entirely, and each spins for itself a small, tough, whitish, flattened cocoon, within which, in about three days, it changes to a chrysalis, three tenths of an inch long, broad, flattened, and of a light shining yellowish-brown color. In about ten days afterwards the moths begin to issue."

The insect is double-brooded. It is common in the Appalachian subregion, ranging from the Atlantic to the borders of the Great Plains in the West.

FAMILY CHALCOSIIDÆ

"Daughters of the air."—DE LA FONTAINE.

This family is represented in our fauna by but a single insect, belonging to the genus *Gingla*, established by Walker. It is an obscure little moth known as **Gingla laterculæ** Dyar. Its habitat is Arizona.

FAMILY THYRIDIDÆ

"And yet I will exercise your promised patience by saying a little of the Caterpillar, or the Palmer-fly or worm, that by them you may guess what a work it were in a discourse but to run over those very many flies, worms, and little living creatures with which the sun and summer adorn and beautify the river-banks and meadows, both for the recreation and contemplation of us Anglers: pleasures which, I think, myself enjoy more than any other man that is not of my profession."

IZAAK WALTON. — *The Compleat Angler,* Chap. V, Pt. 1

The *Thyrididæ* are a small family of moths revealing decided affinity to the *Pyralidæ*. They have been characterized as follows by Hampson, "Moths of India," Vol. I, p. 352: "Moths generally with hyaline patches and striæ on the wings. Palpi obliquely upturned and slender. Antennæ almost simple. Fore wing with vein 1*a* forming a fork with 1*b* at base; 1*c* absent; 5 from near lower angle of cell. Hind wing with two internal veins; vein 8 nearly touching vein 7 just before or after the end of the cell. Mid tibia with one pair of spurs; hind tibia with two pairs.

Larva pyraliform, with five pairs of legs."

Six genera are attributed to this family in the last list of the species found within the United States which has been published. Of four of these we give illustrations.

Genus THYRIS Laspeyres

(1) **Thyris maculata** Harris, Plate XLVII, Fig. *30, ♂*. (The Spotted Thyris.)

Syn. *perspicua* Walker.

The moth is a native of the Eastern States. It is not common.

(2) **Thyris lugubris** Boisduval, Plate XLVII, Fig. *31, ♂*. (The Mournful Thyris.)

Syn. *sepulchralis* Boisduval; *nevadæ* Oberthür.

The range of the species is coincident with that of its only other congener in the United States.

Genus DYSODIA Clemens

(1) **Dysodia oculatana** Clemens, Plate III, Fig. 10, *♂*. (The Eyed Dysodia.)

Syn. *plena* Walker; *fasciata* Grote & Robinson; *montana* Henry Edwards; *aurea* Pagenstecher.

The species is widely distributed throughout the entire United States. It is very common in western Pennsylvania.

Genus HEXERIS Grote

(1) **Hexeris enhydris** Grote, Plate XLVII, Fig. 35, ♂.
Syn. *reticulina* Beutenmüller.

The moth occurs in the subregion of the Gulf.

Genus MESKEA Grote

(1) **Meskea dyspteraria** Grote, Plate XLVII, Fig. 36, ♂.

The moth is found in Florida and the region of the Antilles.

FAMILY COSSIDÆ

> " Bright insect, ere thy filmy wing,
> Expanding on the breath of spring,
> Quivered with brief enjoyment,
> 'T was thine for years immured to dwell
> Within a lone and gloomy cell,
> To eat,—thy sole employment."—*Acheta Domestica.*

The *Cossidæ*, " Goat-moths," or " Carpenter-worms," as they are familiarly called, have sorely puzzled systematists. Some writers have been inclined to regard them as allied to the *Tortricidæ*. We assign them the position in the linear series which is accorded them by Hampson and also by Dyar. They form a very distinctly defined group, whatever their relationships may be. They are succinctly described by Hampson in " The Moths of India," Vol. I, p. 304, as follows: " Proboscis absent; palpi usually minute or absent; antennæ bipectinated to tip or with distal half simple in both sexes, or wholly simple in female. Tibiæ with spurs absent or minute. Fore wing with vein 1*b* forked at base; 1*c* present; an areole formed by veins 7 and 10; veins 7 and 8 forking after the areole; the inner margins usually more or less lobed. Hind wing with three internal veins; vein 8 free from the base or connected with 7 by an erect bar at end of cell. Both wings with forked veinlets in cell. The female may have as many as nine bristles to the frenulum.

Larva. Smooth, with a few hairs; internal feeders, boring galleries in wood or the pith of reeds, etc., and often doing considerable damage.

Pupa in a cocoon formed of silk and chips of wood."

Six genera are recognized as occurring within our fauna.

Genus ZEUZERA Latreille

(1) **Zeuzera pyrina** Linnæus, Plate IX, Fig. 9, ♂. (The Leopard-moth.)

Syn. *hypocastrina* Poda; *æsculi* Linnæus; *hilaris* Fourcroy; *decipiens* Kirby.

This insect is a native of the Old World, but has within recent years become introduced and acclimated on Long Island, and has

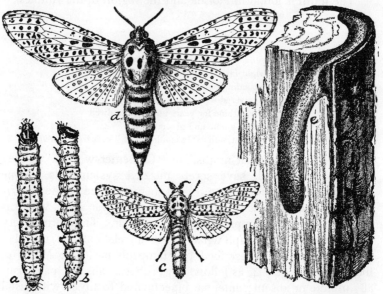

FIG. 212.—The Leopard-moth. *a*, dorsal view of larva; *b*, lateral view of do.; *c*, male; *d*, female; *e*, burrow in wood made by larva. (After Pike, "Insect Life," Vol. IV, p. 317.)

multiplied to a great extent in the environs of the city of Brooklyn. It has already inflicted much damage upon trees, and, apparently being firmly established, is destined to work still greater injury. It is a promiscuous feeder, but evinces a particular fondness for elms and maples.

The eggs are generally laid near the crotch of the tree, and watch should be kept in the spring of the year to detect their presence and destroy them before they are hatched.

Genus COSSUS Fabricius

The genus is found on both sides of the Atlantic. *Cossus cossus* Linnæus is a large species which does great damage to trees in Europe. As I am writing, my friend, Dr. Ortmann, relates that when he was a boy of eleven, living in his native village in Thuringia, his attention was called to a notice posted by the Bürgermeister offering a reward for information which would lead to the detection and punishment of the individuals who by boring into the trunks of a certain fine avenue of birch-trees, upon which the place prided itself, had caused great injury to them. Already the instincts of the naturalist had asserted themselves, and the prying eyes of the lad had found out the cause of the trouble. He went accordingly to the office of the Bürgermeister and informed him that he could tell him all about the injury to the trees. The official sat wide-mouthed and eager to hear. "But you must assure me, before I tell you, that the reward you offer will surely be paid to me." "Yes, yes, my little man; do not be in doubt on that score. You shall certainly be paid." "Well, then, Herr Bürgermeister, the holes from which the sap is flowing were not made by boys who were after the birch-sap to make beer, but by the *Weidenbohrer*."[1] A small explosion of official dignity followed. The act of the presumptuous boy was reported to a stern parent, and the result was, in Yankee phrase, a "licking," which was certainly undeserved.

(1) **Cossus centerensis** Lintner, Plate XII, Fig. 1, ♂.

The insect is quite rare. It is found in the Atlantic States.

(2) **Cossus undosus** Lintner, Plate XLI, Fig. 9, ♀.

Syn. *brucei* French.

The moth occurs in the region of the Rocky Mountains. The specimen figured was taken on the Arkansas River in Colorado, near Canyon City.

It is undoubtedly the most attractively marked and most elegant species found in our territory.

[1] The common German name for the *Cossus*.

Genus PRIONOXYSTUS Grote

There are two species of this genus found in the United States. One of them, *Prionoxystus macmurtrei* Guérin-Méneville = *querciperda* Fitch, is a rather rare species. It bores its larval passages in oak. The female, which resembles the female of the other species, is quite large, sometimes four inches in expanse of wing. The male, on the other hand, is quite diminutive. I have never seen a male much more than an inch and a half in expanse of wing. The species has been taken most frequently in recent years in western Pennsylvania by local collectors. The other species, **Prionoxystus robiniæ** Peck, is very common. It frequents various trees, but shows a preference for the wood of the common locust (*Robinia pseudacacia*) and various species of the genus *Populus*. The male is depicted on Plate XLI, Fig. 11, and the female by Fig. 10 on the same plate. The insect is widely distributed throughout the United States. I have found the males exceedingly abundant about the electric lights in some of our Western cities, as St. Paul and Omaha.

Genus INGUROMORPHA Henry Edwards

Two species of this genus occur within our limits. Both are found in the extreme southern portions of the United States. *I. arbeloides* Dyar is a native of Arizona. **I. basalis** Walker, which is shown in the annexed figure, is found in Florida and Mexico.

The general color of the fore wings is pale ashen-gray, with the outer border dull ochreous, marked with dark-brown striæ, and broader spots and blotches toward the outer margin. The hind wings are darker gray.

*
FIG. 213.—*Inguromorpha basalis*, ♂ . ⅟₁.
Type of *slossoni*.

> " I recognize
> The moths, with that great overpoise of wings
> Which makes a mystery of them how at all
> They can stop flying."
> E. B. BROWNING.—*Aurora Leigh.*

*The illustrations on pages 378 and 379 are transposed. The moth pictured on page 378 is *Cossula magnifica*, and that on page 379 is *Inguromorpha basalis.*—A.E.B.

Genus COSSULA Bailey

Only one species of this genus is known from our fauna. It occurs in Florida and Mexico. It was named **magnifica** by Strecker, and subsequently also by Bailey. Druce in the year 1891 applied to it the specific name *norax*. It is represented in the annexed cut one third larger than the size of life. It is as yet a rare insect in collections, only a few specimens having been found. No doubt it is

FIG. 214.—*Cossula magnifica*, ♂. ⅔.

*

locally common, and when some shrewd observer discovers its haunts and mode of life, we shall all have a good supply of specimens in our cabinets.

Genus HYPOPTA Hübner

Nine species are said to belong to this genus and are reputed to occur within our territory. They are all Southern or Southwestern forms.

(1) **Hypopta bertholdi** Grote, Plate XII, Fig. 2, ♀.

The specimen figured on the plate came from California. The author has also received it from Colorado.

(2) **Hypopta henrici** Grote, Plate XII, Fig. 3, ♂.

The moth is found in Arizona and New Mexico.

FAMILY ÆGERIIDÆ

" I 'll follow you, I 'll lead you about a round
Through bog, through bush, through brake, through brier."
SHAKESPEARE.—*Midsummer Night's Dream*, III, 1.

The name *Sesia* being, according to the laws of priority, strictly applicable to a genus of the *Sphingidæ*, as has been pointed out on page 61, the name of the family which we are now considering must be that which is given above. The name " *Sesiidæ* " must yield to the name " *Ægeriidæ*." This is on some accounts regrettable, as the former name has for many years been consistently applied to the family by many authors.

*See note on opposite page.—A.E.B.

The name which we use has also been applied by a multitude of writers, and is already well established in use in certain quarters.

The *Ægeriidæ* are diurnal in their habits, flying in the hottest sunshine. They are very rapid on the wing. Their larvæ are borers, feeding on the inner bark or the pith of trees and lesser plants. The pupæ are generally armed with hook-like projections, which enable them to progress in a forward direction in the galleries in which they are formed. Some of the genera have at the cephalic end a sharp cutting projection, which is used to enable the insect to cut its way out of the chamber before the change into a moth takes place. The moths have been described as follows by Hampson in "The Moths of India," Vol. I, p. 189: "Antennæ often dilated or knobbed. Legs often with thick tufts of hair; mid tibiæ with one pair of spurs; hind tibiæ with two pairs. Frenulum present. Wings generally more or less hyaline; fore wing with veins 1a and 1b forming a fork at base; 1c absent; veins 4 to 11 given off at almost even distances from the cell. Hind wing with three internal veins; vein 8 coincident with 7."

The American species have been very thoroughly monographed by Mr. Beutenmüller, the amiable and accomplished Curator of the Section of Entomology in the American Museum of Natural History in New York. It is through his kindness that the author is able to give on Plate XLVI of the present volume so many illustrations of the species which are found in our fauna. The student who desires to know more about these things must consult Mr. Beutenmüller's great work.

Genus MELITTIA Hübner

(1) **Melittia satyriniformis** Hübner, Plate XLVI, Fig. 1, ♀.
Syn. *cucurbitæ* Harris; *ceto* Westwood; *amœna* Henry Edwards.

The larva of the insect is commonly known as the "Squash-borer," or the "Pumpkin-borer." The insect has an extensive range from New England to the Argentine States. It attacks the *Cucurbitaceæ* generally, laying the eggs upon all parts of the plant, but preferably upon the stems, into which the caterpillar bores, and in which it develops until the time of pupation, when it descends into the ground, makes a cell beneath the surface in which it hibernates, and is transformed into a chrysalis the following spring. The moths emerge, according to locality, from June to August. It is said to be double-brooded in the southern parts of our region, but is single-brooded in the Northern States.

(2) **Melittia snowi** Henry Edwards, Plate XLVI, Fig. 2, ♂.

This species is very closely allied to the preceding, but the fore wings are devoid of the metallic tints which appear in that species, and there are other minor differences which present themselves upon comparison of the two forms. The life-history remains to be worked out. It is thus far known only from Kansas.

(3) **Melittia grandis** Strecker, Plate XLVI, Fig. 3, ♀.

The insect is reported to occur in Texas and Arizona.

Genus GÆA Beutenmüller

(1) **Gæa emphytiformis** Walker, Plate XLVI, Fig. 5, ♀.

The types of this species are found in the British Museum. Nothing is known definitely as to its true locality, except that the specimens came from the United States. Of course the life-history is also unknown. It is to be hoped that some reader of this book will rediscover the species and let us all know its true history.

(2) **Gæa solituda** Henry Edwards, Plate XLVI, Fig. 4, ♂.

The species occurs in Kansas and in Texas, but the history of its mode of development from egg to imago remains to be written.

Genus EUHAGENA Henry Edwards

There is only one species of this genus known at the present time. It was named **nebraskæ** by Henry Edwards in the year 1881. A male specimen is depicted on Plate XLVI, Fig. 34. The species may easily be recognized by its red wings. Its early history is unknown. I received several specimens of the insect some time ago from a friend who sent them to me, but so wretchedly packed that nothing came to hand but fragments. The well-meaning sender had done them up in cotton as if they were birds' eggs, and of course they were all smashed. Never wrap cotton about moths or butterflies, and then ram cotton down into the box to make the specimens ride well. Particularly avoid the "ramming" process.

Genus ALCOTHOE Henry Edwards

(1) **Alcothoe caudata** Harris, Plate XLVI, Fig. 6, ♂.

The larvæ bore in the roots of various species of clematis. The insect is widely distributed, occurring from Canada to Florida, and westward to the Mississippi. The moths come out in April and May in the South, and from June to August in the North. The larvæ hibernate in their galleries in various stages of growth.

Genus SANNINA Walker

(1) **Sannina uroceriformis** Walker, Plate XLVI, Fig. 7, ♂.
Syn. *quinquecaudatus* Ridings.

The larva feeds on the tap-root of the persimmon (*Diospyros*) at a depth of from eighteen to twenty-two inches under the ground. The species occurs from Virginia to Florida, and westward as far as the food-plant ranges.

Genus PODOSESIA Mœschler

(1) **Podosesia syringæ** Harris, Plate XLVI, Fig. 17, ♀.
Syn. *longipes* Mœschler.

The larvæ feed on the ash and the lilac. They tunnel their passages straight into the wood for many inches. They cut their way out almost to the surface just before pupating, leaving only a thin layer of fiber to close the end of the gallery; this is broken through by the emergent pupa as it comes forth from its cocoon, and then the pupal envelope is split and the perfect winged insect appears. The moths are on the wing in western Pennsylvania in June, and are to be found on the blossoms of *Syringa*.

Genus MEMYTHRUS Newman

(1) **Memythrus tricinctus** Harris, Plate XLVI, Fig. 14, ♀.

The larvæ infest the small trunks of willows and poplars. The moths appear in the latter part of June and the beginning of July; the caterpillars hibernate in their galleries. Transformation occurs in a tough cocoon located at the outer end of the gallery. The species is found in New England and the Middle States, ranging westward as far as Ohio and Michigan.

(2) **Memythrus polistiformis** Harris, Plate XLVI, Fig. 11, ♂, Fig. 12, ♀.

The insect, which is popularly known as the "Grape-root Borer," ranges from Vermont to the Carolinas, and westward as far as Missouri. It inflicts considerable damage upon both wild and cultivated grape-vines. The moth resembles the wasps of the genus *Polistes*, whence the name.

(3) **Memythrus simulans** Grote, Plate XLVI, Fig. 10, ♀.

The insect, which is known to occur from New England to Minnesota, not ranging below the Potomac and the Ohio, feeds in its larval stage upon the wood of the red oak.

(4) **Memythrus admirandus** Henry Edwards, Plate XLVI, Fig. 13, ♂.

The habitat of the species is Texas.

Genus PALMIA Beutenmüller

(1) **Palmia præcedens** Henry Edwards, Plate XLVI, Fig. 15, ♀.

The moth is known to occur in North Carolina. It is very rare in collections as yet, and nothing is known of its life-history.

Genus ÆGERIA Fabricius

(1) **Ægeria apiformis** Clerck, Plate XLVI, Fig. 8, ♀.

Syn. *vespiformis* Hufnagel; *crabroniformis* Denis & Schiffermüller.

This insect, which in England is known as the "Hornet-moth," because of its resemblance to a hornet, is found abundantly in Europe, but less commonly in North America. Its larva lives in the roots and lower portions of the trunks of poplars and willows, and requires two years in which to undergo transformation.

Genus BEMBECIA Hübner

(1) **Bembecia marginata** Harris, Plate XLVI, Fig. 9, ♀.

Syn. *pleciæformis* Walker; *odyneripennis* Walker; *rubi* Riley; *flavipes* Hulst.

The insect, which is popularly known as the "Blackberry-borer," is not at all uncommon. The grub-like larvæ infest the roots of blackberries and raspberries, and when mature eat their way up about three inches through the pith of the dead cane, and cutting their way outwardly, leave only a thin layer of the epidermis between themselves and the outer air. The pupa is armed at its head with a triangular chisel-shaped process, with which it cuts through the epidermis of the plant, and then wriggling forward, until half of the body is extruded, the pupal case bursts, and the moth emerges. The males come out in the early afternoon, the females about four o'clock, copulation occurs almost immediately, and the female begins to oviposit before the sun sets. The moths appear at the end of July and throughout August in Pennsylvania. The larvæ overwinter in the canes.

Genus VESPAMIMA Beutenmüller

(1) **Vespamima sequoiæ** Henry Edwards, Plate XLVI, Fig. 20, ♂.

Syn. *pinorum* Behrens.

This species is said to be very destructive to coniferous trees upon the Pacific slope. The larvæ do their mischievous work at the forking of the branches.

Genus PARHARMONIA Beutenmüller

(1) **Parharmonia pini** Kellicott, Plate XLVI, Fig. 16, ♂.

The species is found from Canada to New Jersey. The larvæ live under the bark of pine-trees. The moths appear in July and August.

Genus SANNINOIDEA Beutenmüller

(1) **Sanninoidea exitiosa** Say, Plate XLVI, Fig. 18, ♂, Fig. 19, ♀.

Syn. *persica* Thomas; *pepsidiformis* Hübner; *xiphiæformis* Boisduval.

This is the well-known "Peach-borer." The larvæ infest the trunks of peach-trees and wild cherries near the ground, and also attack the upper roots. The species ranges from Canada to Florida, and westward to the Rocky Mountains. It does a large amount of damage in peach-orchards.

Genus ALBUNA Henry Edwards

(1) **Albuna pyramidalis** Walker, form **montana** Henry Edwards, Plate XLVI, Fig. 37, ♂.

This is a variable species, of which several varieties have been described. It ranges from Nova Scotia into New England, and westward to the Pacific in the same latitudes. Nothing is known of its early history or food-plants.

384

Genus SYNANTHEDON Hübner

(*Sesia* auctorum.)

The name *Sesia* being properly restricted to a genus of the *Sphingidæ*, we apply to the genus the name proposed by Hübner in the "Verzeichniss Bekannter Schmetterlinge," p. 129. This appears to be the proper and logical method of procedure under the circumstances.

The genus is very extensive. Fifty-eight species are found in our fauna, of which we delineate eleven.

(1) **Synanthedon rileyana** Henry Edwards, Plate XLVI, Fig. 22, ♂, Fig. 23, ♀.

Syn. *brunneipennis* Henry Edwards; *hyperici* Henry Edwards.

The species ranges from the Virginias and Carolinas westward through Ohio and Illinois as far as California and Oregon.

(2) **Synanthedon rutilans** Henry Edwards, Plate XLVI, Fig. 31, ♂, Fig. 32, ♀.

Syn. *aureola* Henry Edwards; *hemizonæ* Henry Edwards; *lupini* Henry Edwards; *perplexa* Henry Edwards; *impropria* Henry Edwards; *washingtonia* Henry Edwards; *madariæ* Henry Edwards.

This insect is known as the "Strawberry-borer." It not only infests the crown of these plants, which it generally destroys, but also frequently attacks raspberries and blackberries at the crown of the roots. It ranges from Nova Scotia westward across the continent, and in the Mississippi Valley southward into northern Texas.

(3) **Synanthedon neglecta** Henry Edwards, Plate XLVI, Fig. 30, ♀.

The insect is found in California and Washington. Its early stages are unknown.

(4) **Synanthedon bassiformis** Walker, Plate XLVI, Fig. 21, ♂.

Syn. *lustrans* Grote; *consimilis* Henry Edwards; *bolli* Henry Edwards; *eupatorii* Henry Edwards; *sexfasciata* Henry Edwards; *infirma* Henry Edwards; *imitata* Henry Edwards.

The larva feeds in the stems of *Eupatorium purpureum*. The insect ranges from New England to Texas.

(5) **Synanthedon tipuliformis** Clerck, Plate XLVI, Fig. 26, ♀.

The insect, which is found in Europe and Asia, and has also

been transported to Australia, is an importation into this country from Europe. It feeds in the stems of gooseberry- and currant-bushes.

(6) **Synanthedon pictipes** Grote & Robinson, Plate XLVI, Fig. 24, ♀.

Syn. *inusitata* Henry Edwards.

The larvæ feed under the bark of plums, wild and cultivated cherry-trees, peach-trees, the June-berry (*Amelanchier*), and the chestnut. The eggs are laid on the trunks and the branches of the trees. The moths are on the wing in June and July.

(7) **Synanthedon acerni** Clemens, Plate XLVI, Fig. 28, ♀.

Syn. *acericolum* Gennadius.

This is the common "Maple-borer." The larvæ tunnel in the sap-wood and do a great deal of damage to trees, especially in our larger cities. At times trees are completely girdled by the galleries made by the insects, and are thus killed; at other times they are so weakened that on the occasion of high winds or storms they are broken off and greatly disfigured. The insects emerge from the pupæ early in the morning, and may be seen at times in small swarms about the trunks of the trees, ovipositing upon the bark. The time of emergence is the latter part of May and the beginning of June. The pupæ are formed in small cocoons composed of silk and pellets of excrement interwoven upon the surface. Just before the moths emerge, the chrysalids work their way partially out of the tunnels in which they are, and then the outer sheathing of the pupa splits open and the perfect insect crawls forth, in a few moments to be upon the wing; for the development of the power of flight is with this species, as with almost all the *Ægeriidæ*, exceedingly rapid.

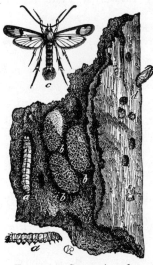

FIG. 215.—*S. acerni. a*, larvæ; *b*, cocoons; *c*, male; *d*, pupa projecting from burrow. (After Riley.)

The moth is found from New England as far west as Nebraska.

(8) **Synanthedon aureopurpurea** Henry Edwards, Plate XLVI, Fig. *33, ♂*.

The moth occurs in Texas. No history of its habits has as yet been written.

(9) **Synanthedon pyri** Harris, Plate XLVI, Fig. 25, ♀.

Syn. *kœbelei* Henry Edwards.

This is a common species everywhere, infesting the bark of pear- and apple-trees. In the vicinity of Pittsburgh many trees have been killed by these mischievous little creatures.

(10) **Synanthedon scitula** Harris, Plate XLVI, Fig. 29, ♀.

Syn. *gallivorum* Westwood; *hospes* Walsh; *æmula* Henry Edwards.

The larvæ inhabit the bark of chestnut, dogwood, oak, willow, hickory, and the galls of oaks. The moth ranges from Canada to Virginia, and westward through the Valley of the Ohio.

* (11) **Synanthedon albicornis** Henry Edwards, Plate XLVI, Fig. 27, ♀.

Syn. *proxima* Henry Edwards; *modesta* Kellicott.

The moth is not known to occur south of the Potomac and the Ohio. It ranges from New England to Oregon. The larvæ feed upon the trunks and shoots of willows.

Genus CALESESIA Beutenmüller

(1) **Calesesia coccinea** Beutenmüller, Plate XLVI, Fig. *36,* ♀.

The habitat of this rare insect is New Mexico. The male and the early stages are as yet unknown.

Genus PARANTHRENE Hübner

(1) **Paranthrene heucheræ** Henry Edwards, Plate XLVI, Fig. *35, ♂*.

There are several species in the genus found in the United States, which are all, as yet, rare in collections, and little is known as to their life-history. The present species has been found in New Mexico.

FAUNAL SUBREGIONS

This volume is an attempt to bring together into compact form an account of the commoner and more striking species of

---

*This moth is found from the Rocky Mountains to the Pacific, whereas the closely similar species *S. proxima* Henry Edwards occurs eastward to the Atlantic.—A.E.B.

moths which are found in the United States and Canada. The area is vast, and zoölogists as well as botanists have for the purposes of science subdivided the region into what are known as "faunal subregions," or "botanical subregions." These subdivisions of the territory are entirely natural and are based upon a knowledge of the flora and fauna of each area. Both flora and fauna are more or less dependent upon conditions of soil, rainfall, and temperature.

Beginning with the Atlantic coast, we find a large area extending from Nova Scotia, Quebec, and Ontario, southward through New England, the Middle States, and the Eastern Central States as far south as the Carolinas and northern Georgia, Alabama, and Mississippi, westward into Arkansas, Missouri, and eastern Kansas, then northward through eastern Iowa and Minnesota, in which, with some slight variations, the predominant features of the vegetation and of the fauna are alike. In a broad way this territory is known as the Appalachian subregion. It has been subdivided into two parts, to the more northern of which has been applied the name Canadian, and to the southern the name Carolinian. These minor subdivisions of the broader subregion are quite natural, and are based upon the fact that certain groups of plants and animals are characteristic of the one which are not characteristic of the other; yet upon the whole the character of the vegetation and of the animal life of the two lesser areas is in most respects quite similar. The genera are practically the same throughout these territories. It was, when the country was first discovered by white men, a region of trees, except in northern Indiana and parts of Illinois, Iowa, and Minnesota, where there were prairies; but on these prairies, where trees grew, they were for the most part representatives of the same genera which were found through the eastern parts of the domain, and in many cases were the same species. Accompanying the plants are the insects which feed upon them.

Beginning on the extreme southern portions of the coast of North Carolina and running along the coast of South Carolina through eastern and southern Georgia, northern Florida, and westward along the Gulf of Mexico, we have a strip of territory preserving many of the floral and faunal peculiarities of the Appalachian subregion, but possessing distinctive features of its own.

We detect here the influence of warmer skies and the life of the not-far-off tropics. It is the region of the long-leaved pine, the cypress, the live-oak, the evergreen magnolia, and the palmetto. It is the subregion of the Gulf. It has a fauna of its own.

In the extreme southern portion of Florida and on the outlying islands we find established a northern offshoot of the plant-life and of the fauna of the West Indies. The conditions are distinctly tropical here.

A sharp division takes place west of the Mississippi River, at those points where the heavily wooded lands terminate and are succeeded by the grassy, woodless plains, which lie between the western borders of the Valley of the Mississippi and the eastern ranges of the Rocky Mountains. While the Great Plains are traversed by numerous river valleys, in which there is abundant arboreal vegetation, nevertheless the whole region in part only preserves the faunal and floral characteristics of the Appalachian subregion. The southern part of this territory, lying in New Mexico, western Texas, and Arizona, with which, in part, southern California is identified, has a large number of genera and species which range southward along the plateaus and treeless highlands of Mexico and Central America. This may be called the Arizonian or Sonoran subregion.

The northern half of the belt of the Great Plains is invaded by forms of both plant and animal life which are related to types predominant in the colder regions of the continent. This is especially true where the plains reach a great altitude above the level of the sea. This subregion may be called the Dakotan. It stretches from northern Colorado northward to the British provinces of Assiniboia and Alberta.

West of the Great Plains is a territory traversed from north to south by the ranges of the Rocky Mountains, in which there occurs a commingling of genera and species, some coming in from the far north on the higher ranges, others coming in from the south on the lower levels, and a multitude of forms mingling with these which show the influence of migration both from the Great Plains and from the Pacific slope. The region of the Rocky Mountains is a region in which there are singular complexities, owing to the great differences in elevation. Species of the arctic zone may be found having their habitat within a few miles of species which are in many cases distinctly subtropical. On the high peaks holarctic genera occur, and in the valleys genera which have their metropolis in Mexico. In a general sense the territory may be called the Coloradan subregion.

The Pacific subregion includes central and northern California and the valleys lying between the coast and the western outliers of the central cordillera. The subregion extends northward into British Columbia. There is shown here a distinct resemblance to the fauna of Europe and temperate Asia.

Beginning in Labrador on the east and extending across the entire northern portion of the continent into Alaska is a region which we may call the *Holarctic* subregion, in which the genera and species alike of plants and animals are for the most part the same which are found in similar latitudes in the Eastern Hemisphere. In Alaska there is evidence of a distinct connection between the flora and fauna of Asia. Greenland and Labrador, together with some of the adjacent islands, show remarkable affinities to the flora and fauna of boreal Europe and the Alps.

Various subdivisions of these broader areas have been suggested, but in the main the subregions which the writer has indicated suffice to show the differences in these tracts.

> ". . . From every chink
> And secret corner, where they slept away
> The wintry storms—or rising from their tombs
> To higher life—by myriads, forth at once,
> Swarming they pour, of all the varied hues
> Their beauty-beaming parent can disclose.
> Ten thousand forms ! ten thousand different tribes !
> People the blaze."
>
> THOMSON.—*Summer.*

FAMILY PYRALIDÆ

"All multiplicity rushes to be resolved into unity. Anatomy, osteology, exhibit arrested or progressive ascent in each kind; the lower pointing to the higher forms, the higher to the highest, from the fluid in an elastic sack, from radiate, mollusk, articulate, vertebrate, up to man; as if the whole animal world were only a Hunterian Museum to exhibit the genesis of mankind."— EMERSON.

The *Pyralidæ* constitute an enormous complex of subfamilies, genera, and species. They are found in all the temperate and tropical parts of the world, but are more numerous in hot lands than in the colder portions of the globe. Nearly eight hundred species belonging to this family are already known to occur within the United States and Canada, and the region will undoubtedly yet yield many new species to science. We cannot in these pages undertake to give even an outline of the genera and the species, but we have selected a few for illustration in order that the student, encountering these interesting insects, may be able to at least recognize their relative position in the great suborder with which this book deals.

The moths of this family are described as follows by Sir George F. Hampson in the Proceedings of the Zoölogical Society of London for 1898, page 590: "Proboscis and maxillary palpi usually well developed; frenulum present. Fore wing with vein $1a$ usually free, sometimes forming a fork with $1b$; $1c$ absent; 5 from near lower angle of cell; 8, 9 almost always stalked. Hind wing with veins $1a$, b, c present; 5 almost always from near lower angle of cell; 8 approximated to 7 or anastomosing with it beyond the cell.

Larva elongate, with five pairs of prolegs. Pupa with segments 9–11 and sometimes also 8 and 12 movable, not protruding from cocoon on emergence."

The *Pyralidæ* have been divided into a number of subfamilies. Of the subfamilies represented in our fauna, we shall in the following pages give illustrations of a few species which are commonly encountered or possess interesting traits. While it is to be wished that we might be able to give a monographic view of the entire family, such a procedure is wholly out of the question, in view of the limits imposed upon us in the matter of space by such a volume as that which has been undertaken.

SUBFAMILY PYRAUSTINÆ

The genera of this family may be distinguished by the fact that the median nervure is not pectinated upon the upper side, or is at most very slightly pectinated, by the absence of tufts of scales in the cell of the fore wing, and by the further fact that vein 10 of the fore wing rises from the cell. In the hind wing, vein 7 and vein 8 almost invariably anastomose.

Fifty-seven genera are found in our territory, represented by two hundred and twenty-four species.

Genus ZINCKENIA Hübner

(1) **Zinckenia fascialis** Cramer, Plate XLVII, Fig. 28, ♂.

Syn. *angustalis* Fabricius; *recurvalis* Fabricius; *diffascialis* Hübner; *albifascialis* Boisduval.

The moth is found all over the temperate and subtropical regions of both hemispheres. It is common in the southern portions of the United States.

Genus DESMIA Westwood

(1) **Desmia funeralis** Hübner, Plate XLVII, Fig. 37, ♂. (The Grape-leaf Folder.)

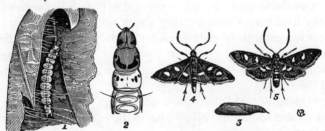

FIG. 216.—*Desmia funeralis.* 1, larva secreted between folds of leaf; 2, head of larva, magnified; 3, pupa; 4, male moth; 5, female moth. (After Riley.)

The caterpillar of this pretty little moth feeds upon the leaves of various wild and cultivated grapes, showing a preference for those species the leaves of which are thin and tender. The caterpillar is of a transparent green color, and is very lively when disturbed. The insects, which do considerable damage in vineyards, may be kept down by crushing the larvæ and the pupæ when found in the folded leaves, which are easily detected. The moth is found from Canada to the Gulf east of the Great Plains.

Genus SAMEA Guenée

(1) **Samea ecclesialis** Guenée, Plate XLVIII, Fig. 2, ♀.
Syn. *castellalis* Guenée; *luccusalis* Walker; *disertalis* Walker.
The insect is widely distributed throughout the hotter parts of the Western Hemisphere. It is common in Florida and ranges south as far as Argentina.

Genus DIASTICTIS Hübner

(1) **Diastictis fracturalis** Zeller, Plate XLVIII, Fig. 1, ♂.
This is a neatly marked species, which is found in Texas and Arizona, and ranges southward into Mexico and Central America.

Genus CONCHYLODES Guenée

(1) **Conchylodes platinalis** Guenée, Plate XLVII, Fig. 60, ♂.
Syn. *ovulalis* Guenée; *erinalis* Walker; *magicalis* Felder; *concinnalis* Hampson.
The moth is found in western Pennsylvania and southward through the southern portions of the United States into South America.

Genus PANTOGRAPHA Lederer

(1) **Pantographa limata** Grote & Robinson, Plate XLVII, Fig. 38, ♂.
Syn. *suffusalis* Druce.
The insect occurs from Maine to Patagonia.

Genus AGATHODES Guenée

(1) **Agathodes monstralis** Guenée, Plate XLVIII, Fig. 3, ♂.
Syn. *designalis* Guenée; *floridalis* Hulst.
The moth ranges from Florida to the Rio de la Plata in South America.

Genus GLYPHODES Guenée

This is a large genus, represented in both hemispheres by numerous species. We give figures of three.

(1) **Glyphodes nitidalis** Stoll, Plate XLVII, Fig. 43, ♂. (The Pickle-worm.)

The insect feeds in its larval stage upon cucumbers and melons, into which the caterpillar bores. A good account of its habits is given by Riley in the "Second Annual Report of the State Entomologist of Missouri," page 67. It has, like most of the *Pyralidæ*, a wide range, and extends from the southern portions of the United States to the southern portions of South America.

(2) **Glyphodes hyalinata** Linnæus, Plate XLVII, Fig. 39, ♂.
Syn. *marginalis* Stoll; *lucernalis* Hübner; *hyalinatalis* Guenée.

The range of this species is very much the same as that of the last mentioned.

(3) **Glyphodes quadristigmalis** Guenée. (The Privet-moth.)

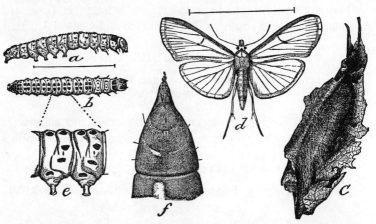

FIG. 217.—*Glyphodes quadristigmalis.* *a*, lateral view of larva; *b*, dorsal view; *c*, cocoon; *d*, moth; *e*, lateral view of two segments of larva, enlarged; *f*, anal segment of pupa from below, greatly enlarged. (After Riley, "Insect Life," Vol. I, p. 24.)

This moth has in recent years proved at times troublesome as an enemy of privet-hedges in the southern portions of the country. As many as four broods of the moths have been detected in one summer in Washington, D. C. The insect has a wide range, being known to occur in the West Indies and Central America.

Genus PHLYCTÆNODES Guenée

This is a genus well represented in both hemispheres. There are over thirty species found in the United States.

(1) **Phlyctænodes triumphalis** Grote, Plate XLVIII, Fig. 5, ♂ .

This species, which is found in the vicinity of San Luis Obispo, California, was described by Grote in the "Canadian Entomologist," Vol. XXXIV, p. 295. It does not appear in Dyar's List.

(2) **Phlyctænodes sticticalis** Linnæus. (The Sugar-beet Moth.)

Syn. *fuscalis* Hübner; *tetragonalis* Haworth; *sordida* Butler.

The moth, of which we give an enlarged representation in Fig. 218, has becmee in recent years the object of attention in those portions of the West in which the cultivation of the sugar-beet has become an industry of magnitude. It has done considerable damage to the crop in Nebraska. There are two and perhaps three broods produced in a year. The insect multiplies with great rapidity, and large areas planted with the beet have been defoliated by the

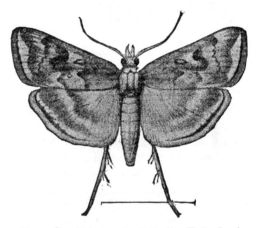

FIG. 218.—*Phlyctænodes sticticalis.* Twice the size of life. (After Riley, "Insect Life," Vol. V, p. 320.)

caterpillars in comparatively a short time. The larvæ hibernate in cases woven of silk to which particles of earth are adherent, and which are formed at a small depth under the surface of the soil. By harrowing the ground it has been ascertained that many of the cases are thrown up, and are emptied of the larvæ by the meadow-larks and other insectivorous birds, or are killed by the frosts of winter. Many of them, however, escape such treatment, being possessed of vitality enough to withstand a great degree of cold. It has been suggested that a better way in which to rid the fields of the pests is to apply Paris green to the beets, in a solution composed of one pound of the poison to two hundred gallons of water. The spraying of the plants by the mixture is said to have proved efficacious in cases where the

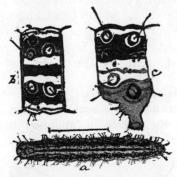

FIG. 219.—*P. sticticalis.* *a*, larva, magnified; *b*, dorsal view of segment of do.; *c*, lateral view of segment. (After Riley, "Insect Life," Vol. V, p. 321.)

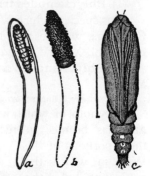

FIG. 220.—*P. sticticalis.* *a*, outline of larval case; *b*, cocoon of parasite in larval case; *c*, pupa, enlarged. (After Riley, "Insect Life," Vol. V, p. 321.)

application was made as soon as it was ascertained that the insects were at work upon the leaves. Nature in this case, as in multitudes of others, comes to the assistance of the agriculturist, and there is a parasite which destroys many of the larvæ. The cocoon of one of these is shown in Fig. 220.

The moth occurs in Europe as well as in America, and it is possible that the insect has been imported from the Old World.

(3) **Phlyctænodes oberthuralis** Fernald, Plate XLVIII, Fig. 4, ♂.

The species occurs in California and Arizona.

Genus TITANIO Hübner

(1) **Titanio proximalis** Fernald, Plate XLVIII, Fig. 6, ♂.

The moth is a native of California. The genus to which it belongs is represented in our fauna by a number of species.

"And your spoil shall be gathered like the gathering of the caterpillar."
ISAIAH.—XXXIII, 4.

Genus PHLYCTÆNIA Hübner

(1) **Phlyctænia tertialis** Guenée, Plate XLVII, Fig. 47, ♂.
Syn. *plectilis* Grote & Robinson; *syringicola* Packard.

This is a common species in the eastern portion of the region. It is very abundant about Pittsburgh. The genus is represented in our fauna by a dozen species.

Genus CINDAPHIA Lederer

(1) **Cindaphia bicoloralis** Guenée, Plate XLVII, Fig. 40, ♂.
Syn. *julialis* Walker; *incensalis* Lederer; *amiculatalis* Berg; *pulchripictalis* Hampson.

The moth occurs from New York and New England southward to the temperate regions of South America. It is the only representative of the genus in our fauna.

Genus PYRAUSTA Schrank

This is a very large genus, which is well represented in both hemispheres. There are about sixty species known to occur within our territory.

(1) **Pyrausta pertextalis** Lederer, Plate XLVII, Fig. 54, ♂.
Syn. *gentilis* Grote; *thesealis* Zeller.

The species ranges from New England to the extreme southern portions of our region.

(2) **Pyrausta langdonalis** Grote, Plate XLVII, Fig. 52, ♂.

The moth occurs in western Pennsylvania and Ohio and Indiana.

(3) **Pyrausta orphisalis** Walker, Plate XLVII, Fig. 49, ♂.
Syn. *adipaloides* Grote & Robinson.

The insect is not uncommon in the Middle Atlantic States.

(4) **Pyrausta fumalis** Guenée, Plate XLVII, Fig. 55, ♂.
Syn. *orasusalis* Walker; *badipennis* Grote.

The species is found in the eastern portions of our territory. It is not uncommon in Pennsylvania.

(5) **Pyrausta illibalis** Hübner, Plate XLVII, Fig. 48, ♀.
Syn. *arsaltealis* Walker; *euphœsalis* Walker; *guttulosa* Walker; *fascialis* Walker; *subjectalis* Lederer; *magniferalis* Walker.

The moth, which is somewhat variable in its markings, is found in the Appalachian subregion.

(6) **Pyrausta unifascialis** Packard, Plate XLVII, Fig. ¯1, ♂.

Syn. *subolivalis* Packard; *hircinalis* Grote; *obnigralis* Hulst.

The moth is known to occur in the northern portions of the United States and to range westward to California.

(7) **Pyrausta insequalis** Guenée, Plate XLVII, Fig. 41, ♂.

Syn. *subsequalis* Guenée; *madetesalis* Walker; *repletalis* Walker; *efficitalis* Walker.

The species inhabits the Appalachian subregion.

(8) **Pyrausta ochosalis** Fitch, MS., Plate XLVII, Fig. 57, ♂.

This species, which is not at all uncommon in Pennsylvania, is in many collections confounded with *P. generosa* Grote & Robinson, which it resembles in a general way. The insect is prevalently smaller than the latter species, and the markings are different. The species has been correctly discriminated in the collection of the United States National Museum from *P. generosa*, and the name applied to it in manuscript by Fitch is there given it. I have used this name in designation of the species.

(9) **Pyrausta tyralis** Guenée, Plate XLVII, Fig. 44, ♂.

Syn. *erosnealis* Walker; *diffissa* Grote & Robinson; *bellulalis* Hulst.

The species ranges from the Valley of the Ohio southward to Texas.

(10) **Pyrausta unimacula** Grote & Robinson, Plate XLVII, Fig. 56, ♂.

The insect is common in Pennsylvania and the Valley of the Ohio.

(11) **Pyrausta funebris** Ström, Plate XLVII, Fig. 50, ♂.

Syn. *octomaculata* Linnæus; *glomeralis* Walker.

This pretty and distinctly marked species, which in the pattern of its wings recalls the markings of the genus *Alypia*, is found in the northern parts of temperate North America and in Europe.

(12) **Pyrausta niveicilialis** Grote, Plate XLVII, Fig. 42, ♀.

The moth is found from New England to western Pennsylvania and the Valley of the Ohio as far west as southern Indiana.

Genus EUSTIXIA Hübner

(1) **Eustixia pupula** Hübner, Plate XLVII, Fig. 58, ♂.

The insect is found throughout the Appalachian subregion. It is freely attracted to light and also to sugar. It is common in Indiana.

Genus CORNIFRONS Lederer

(1) **Cornifrons simalis** Grote, Plate XLVIII, Fig. 7, ♂.
The range of the moth is from Montana to Oregon.

nus NOCTUELIA Guenée

(1) **Noctuelia thalialis** Walker, Plate XLVIII, Fig. 9, ♂.
Syn. *peruviana* Walker; *gelidalis* Walker; *novalis* Grote; *costæmaculalis* Snellen.
The insect is found in the Gulf States and southward through South America.

SUBFAMILY NYMPHULINÆ

The insects composing this family are generally found in the vicinity of water, the larvæ feeding for the most part upon aquatic plants. Four genera belonging to the subfamily are recognized as occurring within our limits. We give an illustration of one of the commoner species.

Genus NYMPHULA Schrank

(1) **Nymphula obscuralis** Grote, Plate XLVIII, Fig. 10, ♀.
The insect occurs from Maine to Minnesota, and southward into Pennsylvania and West Virginia.

SUBFAMILY SCOPARIINÆ

The *Scopariinæ* are represented in our fauna by the genus *Scoparia* alone. Seven species belonging to this genus are attributed to it in the last published list of the Lepidoptera of the United States.

SUBFAMILY PYRALINÆ

Five genera belonging to this subfamily occur within our territory. Of these we have selected for illustration specimens representing three of the genera.

Genus HYPSOPYGIA Hübner

(1) **Hypsopygia costalis** Fabricius, Plate XLVII, Fig. 59, ♂.
(The Clover-hay Worm.)
Syn. *fimbrialis* Denis & Schiffermüller.

This troublesome little species is no doubt an importation from Europe, where it is very common. It has spread from the Atlantic to the Rocky Mountains. It has the habit of infesting stacks of clover-hay, and often does a great deal of damage by weaving its webs of fine whitish silk mixed with excrement in the hay and devouring the leaves. Many cases have been reported in which hay had been rendered entirely unfit for use by the presence of these pests. As the larvæ feed upon dried clover, it has been recommended to make it a point not to stack new hay in places where the old hay is known to have been infected. Furthermore, as the larvæ are known to prefer hay which is somewhat moist, it is recommended to make it a point to stack the hay in such a manner that it cannot be subjected to an excess of moisture. This may be done by building the stacks upon a framework of rails elevated a little distance above the ground, so as to permit of the circulation of air beneath.

FIG. 221.—*Hypsopygia costalis.* 1–2, larvæ; 3, cocoon; 4, pupa; 5–6, moth; 7, larva covered with silken web. (After Riley.)

Genus PYRALIS Linnæus

(1) **Pyralis farinalis** Linnæus, Plate XLVII, Fig. 53, ♀. (The Meal Snout-moth.)

This is a cosmopolitan species, being quite abundant everywhere. It manifests a decided preference for cereals in almost any form, and feeds upon meal, bran, and even the straw and husks. It undergoes

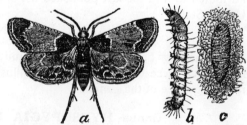

FIG. 222.—*Pyralis farinalis.* *a*, moth; *b*, larva; *c*, cocoon. (After Chittenden, "Bull. U. S. Dept. Agric.," New Series, Vol. IV, p. 119.) All figures twice the size of life.

transformation quite rapidly and is known to produce as many as four generations in a year. The caterpillars prefer the dark corners of meal-bins and the nooks of granaries and elevators which are least disturbed, and here will, unless they are detected and their ravages checked, establish centers of infection, from which they will go forth to do a vast amount of mischief. The caterpillars form long cases or tunnels of silk mixed with the debris of their food, in which they are quite effectually concealed from view. The best remedy is cleanliness, and frequent moving of stored products.

Genus HERCULIA Walker

(1) **Herculia olinalis** Guenée, Plate XLVIII, Fig. 13, ♂.
Syn. *trentonalis* Lederer.
The species is widely distributed throughout the United States and Canada. The larvæ feed upon the leaves of the oak.

(2) **Herculia himonialis** Zeller, Plate XLVII, Fig. 46, ♀.
The moth is found from New England to Pennsylvania. It is not uncommon among the Alleghany Mountains about Cresson.

SUBFAMILY CHRYSAUGINÆ

This is a small subfamily, represented in our fauna by nine genera. Two of these we have selected for representation.

Genus SALOBRANA Walker

(1) **Salobrana tecomæ** Riley, Plate XLVIII, Fig. 11, ♀.
This curious little moth feeds in its larval state upon the interior of the seed-pods of the common trumpet-vine (*Tecoma*). The eggs are deposited when the pods are forming, and the larvæ develop within them until in the fall, when they become dormant, hibernating in their burrows until the following spring, when they prepare for their escape by making an orifice in the outer shell of the pod and transforming into pupæ. An excellent account of their habits has been given by the late Professor C. V. Riley in the "American Entomologist," Vol. III, p. 288. The moth is found in the southwestern portions of the United States, in the West Indies, and in Mexico and Central America.

Genus TOSALE Walker

(1) **Tosale oviplagalis** Walker, Plate XLVIII, Fig. 33, ♂.
Syn. *nobilis* Grote; *anthæcioides* Grote & Robinson.
This is a common insect in western Pennsylvania, coming freely to sugar. It ranges from the eastern portions of our territory southward into South America.

SUBFAMILY SCHŒNOBIINÆ

This is a small subfamily of peculiar moths in which the proboscis is wanting, and which are represented in our territory by four genera and a dozen or more species. Of these we have selected one for illustration.

Genus SCIRPOPHAGA Treitschke

(1) **Scirpophaga perstrialis** Hübner, Plate XLVIII, Fig. 12, ♀.
Syn. *serriradiellus* Walker; *macrinellus* Zellner.
The habitat of this moth is the southern part of Florida.

SUBFAMILY CRAMBINÆ

The *Crambinæ*, or "Grass-moths," as they are commonly called, constitute a large subfamily. The North American species have been well described and delineated by Fernald in his little book entitled "The Crambidæ of North America," which was published in 1896. To this the student will do well to refer. There are fourteen genera in our territory, and over eighty species. Only a few of these can be represented in our plates.

Genus CRAMBUS Fabricius

(1) **Crambus laqueatellus** Clemens, Plate XLVIII, Fig. 17, ♂.
Syn. *semifusellus* Walker.
The moth ranges from New England to Texas. Like all the other species of the genus, it feeds in its larval state upon the grasses.

(2) **Crambus alboclavellus** Zeller, Plate XLVIII, Fig. 18, ♂.
The insect is very common in the Appalachian subregion.

(3) **Crambus turbatellus** Walker, Plate XLVIII, Fig. 19, ♀.
Syn. *bipunctellus* Zeller.

The insect occurs from Canada and New England in the North to the Potomac and the Ohio in the South.

(4) **Crambus trisectus** Walker, Plate XLVIII, Fig. 20, ♀.

Syn. *interminellus* Walker; *exsiccatus* Zeller; *biliturellus* Zeller.

This is a very common and widely distributed species, ranging from the Atlantic to the Pacific through more temperate latitudes.

Genus DIATRÆA Guilding

(1) **Diatræa saccharalis** Fabricius. (The Larger Corn-stalk Borer.)

Syn. *leucaniellus* Walker; *lineosellus* Walker; *obliteratellus* Zeller; *crambidoides* Grote.

As early as the year 1828 the attention of the world was called to the damage inflicted upon the sugar-cane in the West Indies by the larva of a lepidopterous insect. The author of the paper in which it was described was the Rev. Lansdown Guilding, who was awarded a gold medal by the Society of Arts for his account of the insect. About thirty years later, attention was called to the ravages of a similar insect in the island of Mauritius, into which it had been introduced. From the West Indies the insect was transported to Louisiana, and a study of its pernicious habits was accurately made in the year 1881 by Dr. L. O. Howard of the

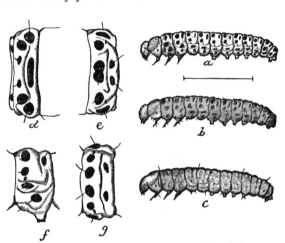

Fig. 223.—*D. saccharalis. a, b, c,* varieties of larva, enlarged; *d,* third thoracic segment; *e,* eighth abdominal segment; *f,* abdominal segment from side; *g,* same from above, enlarged. (After Howard, "Insect Life," Vol. IV, p. 101.)

United States Department of Agriculture. It had been known in Louisiana as a pest since 1855.

The ravages of the insect are not confined to the sugar-cane. It attacks with equal avidity sorghum and the stalks of the common Indian corn, or maize. The insect has gradually worked its way northward from the region of the Gulf, having found lodgment here and there throughout the Southern States, and is now known to occur quite abundantly at times as far north as Maryland. It is double-brooded in Virginia.

The most serious damage is inflicted upon the crop where the larvæ attack young stalks. Plants which are older and well established, though they may suffer to some extent from the insects, are generally not damaged sufficiently to prevent the maturing and hardening of the grain; but where the stalks are young and quite tender, they fail to mature, are stunted, sicken, and ultimately die. The accompanying figure shows the dwarfed and sickly appearance of such a stalk, which has been invaded by the borer. The life-history of the insect has been briefly given by Howard as follows: "In early spring the parent moth lays her eggs upon the young cane near the axils, and the young borer penetrates the stalk at or near the joint, and commences to tunnel, usually upward, through the soft pith. The larval growth is rapid, and the borer is active,

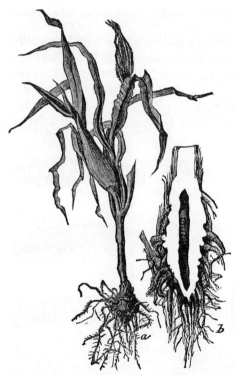

FIG. 224.—*D. saccharalis.* *a*, appearance of corn-stalk infested by larva; *b*, stalk cut open to show larval tunnel and pupa. (After Howard, "Insect Life," Vol. IV, p. 99.)

and frequently leaves the stalk at one place and enters at another, making several holes in the course of its growth. When ready to transform, it burrows to the surface, making a hole for the exit of the future moth, and transforms to the pupa state. There are several generations in the course of a season, and the insect hibernates in the larval state within the stalks."

The fact that the insect makes its home in the winter months in the dry stalks furnishes the means for most effectually combating its attacks. The remedy is found in destroying the stalks, either by burning them or by gathering them up and feeding them to live stock. It is well known that where crops are rotated, and the stalks are not left standing in the fields all winter, the insect does not succeed in inflicting much damage. Careful and intelligent tillage of the soil, cleanliness in the fields, will do much to prevent the increase of these insects, as well as of many other injurious species which might be named. In addition to feeding

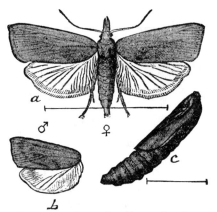

Fig. 225.—*D. saccharalis.* *a*, female, enlarged; *b*, wings of male; *c*, pupa, enlarged. (After Howard, "Insect Life," Vol. IV, p. 95.)

upon sugar-cane, sorghum, and corn, it has been ascertained that the insect will attack "Gama-grass" (*Tripsacum dactyloides*), and it is recommended to burn over fields in which this grass grows in proximity to corn-fields. The student who is desirous to know more about this insect may consult the pages of "Insect Life," Vol. IV, p. 95, where Dr. Howard has written at length upon its habits. It is from this article that much of the information contained in the preceding paragraphs has been drawn.

SUBFAMILY GALLERIINÆ

This is a subfamily the larvæ of at least one species of which have the remarkable habit of making their abode in the hives of

405

bees, where they feed upon the wax and destroy the young of the insects upon whose industry they prey.

Genus GALLERIA Fabricius

(1) **Galleria mellonella** Linnæus. (The Bee-moth.)

Syn. *cereana* Linnæus; *cerella* Fabricius; *obliquella* Walker.

The Bee-moth was undoubtedly introduced into this country from Europe. It is a well-known enemy of the apiarist, and has been active in doing mischief on this side of the Atlantic for more

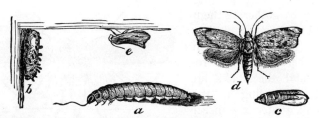

FIG. 226.—The Bee-moth. *a*, larva; *b*, cocoon; *c*, pupa; *d*, female moth with wings expanded; *e*, male moth with wings closed. (After Riley.)

than a century, while it has been known from time immemorial in Europe as one of the most dreaded pests of the hive. The moth is double-brooded, the first generation appearing on the wing in the latter part of May and the beginning of June, and the second in August. We cannot do better than to quote in this connection the following account of the insect which is given by Professor C. V. Riley in the " First Annual Report of the State Entomologist of Missouri," p. 166:

" During the daytime these moths remain quietly ensconced in some angle of the hive, but, as night approaches, they become active, and the female uses her best endeavors to get into the hive, her object being to deposit her eggs in as favorable a place as possible. Wire-gauze contrivances are of no avail to keep her out, as she frequently commences flying before all the bees have ceased their work. But even if she were entirely prevented from entering the hive, she could yet deposit her eggs on the outside, or, by means of her extensile ovipositor, thrust them in between the slightest joint or crack, and the young worms hatching from them would readily make their way into the hive. The moment the worm is hatched, it commences spinning a silken tube for its protection, and this tube is enlarged as it increases in size. The worm cuts its channels right through the comb, feeding on the wax, and destroying the young bees on its way. When full-grown, it creeps into a corner of the hive or under some ledge at the bottom, and forms a tough white cocoon of silk mingled with its own black excrement, as shown in Figure 226, *b*. In due time the moth emerges from this cocoon.

A worm-infested hive may generally be known by the discouraged aspect which the bees present, and by the bottom-board being covered with pieces of bee-bread mixed with the black gunpowder-like excrement of the worm. . . . If a hive is very badly infested with the worm, it is better to drive out the bees and secure what honey and wax there may be left than to preserve it as a moth-breeder to infest the apiary. If put into a new hive, the bees may do something; and if they do not, there is no loss, as they would have perished, finally, from the ravages of the worm."

SUBFAMILY EPIPASCHIINÆ

This subfamily is represented in our fauna by fourteen genera and about thirty species. The insects may generally be recognized and separated from allied forms by the fact that the cell of the fore wing is adorned by tufts of raised scales. We have only space to give an illustration of a single genus and species.

Genus YUMA Hulst

(1) **Yuma trabalis** Grote, Plate XLVIII, Fig. 14, ♀.
Syn. *adulatalis* Hulst.

The insect is found in Colorado and Wyoming, and ranges southward into Texas. Almost all of the *Epipaschiinæ* found within our territory are native to the West and the Southwest, only a few species being found in the eastern portions of the United States.

SUBFAMILY PHYCITINÆ

This is a very extensive group of moths, which have been admirably monographed by the late Mons. E. L. Ragonot of Paris, in the "Mémoires sur les Lépidoptères," Vols. VII and

VIII. There are represented in our fauna over sixty genera and more than two hundred species. We can give our readers merely a glimpse into this corner of the field, but trust that what they shall see may impel them to undertake for themselves the pleasant task of diligent exploration, assuring them that they will find here a world of wonders with which to deal.

Genus ACROBASIS Zeller

(1) **Acrobasis betulella** Hulst, Plate XLVIII, Fig. 15, ♀.

This is a common species, ranging from New England to Colorado. There are nearly a dozen other species of the genus known to occur in our fauna, and no doubt many more which have not yet been discovered and described.

Genus MINEOLA Hulst

(1) **Mineola juglandis** Le Baron. (The Walnut Case-bearer.)

This little moth lives in its larval stage upon the leaves of the hickory and walnut. It has the habit of drawing together

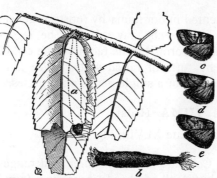

FIG. 227.—*M. juglandis.* *a*, case woven between leaves; *b*, case; *c, e*, wing of *M. indigenella* and variety; *d*, wing of *M. juglandis.* (After Riley.)

two of the opposite leaves attached to the long petiole, and between them it builds a case, which is quite straight and is composed of silk, attached to which is excrementitious matter, which is neatly and closely applied to the whole. In this case the larva lives until the cooler airs of autumn warn it to leave the petiole of the compound leaf, which will fall presently, and it then anchors its little case to the twig near by, and in a half-grown state prepares for the cold winds and icy temperature of winter. When again spring sends the sap up the branches, and the leaves begin to unfold, it cuts the bands of silk which held the case in place, and completing its development upon freshly grown and sapid food, it is transformed into a pupa, from which the moth presently emerges. The moth closely resembles the next species, but the student, by the study of its habits and of the case, which is always straight, and not crooked, as is that of the following species, may at once discriminate it.

(2) **Mineola indigenella** Zeller. (The Rascal Leaf-crumpler.)
Syn. *nebulo* Walsh; *zelatella* Hulst.

This moth is common in the Valley of the Mississippi and in Ontario, but does not appear to be very common in the Eastern States, and is unknown in the extreme southern portions of our region. It is very common in western Pennsylvania.

Professor C. V. Riley describes its habits as follows: "It is one of those insects which is hardly noticed while it is carrying on its most destructive work; for it is most voracious during the leafy months of May and June, and is then more or less hidden by the foliage of the tree,

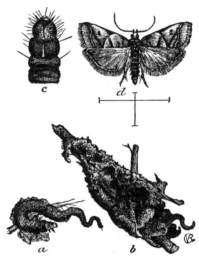

FIG. 228.—*M. indigenella.* *a*, case; *b*, case wrapped in debris of leaves; *c*, head of larva; *d*, moth, enlarged. (After Riley.)

which it so effectually helps to denude. But the nakedness of winter, though it does not reveal the surreptitious worm, lays bare and renders conspicuous its little house, and these houses— these larval cases—whether closely attached in clusters to the twigs as in Figure 228, *b*, or hidden in a few seared and silk-sewn leaves as at Figure 229, are unerring tokens of past injury to the tree, and symbols of increased injury in the future, unless removed. The bunches of leaves anchored to the tree by strong silken cables and breasting defiantly every winter's wind are, indeed, significant insignia upon which is written in characters, if not in words—'result of careless culture and unpardonable neglect.'

There is but one brood a year, and the larva, about one-third

409

grown, invariably passes the winter protected in its case. At this season of the year it is always of a deep reddish-brown

color. As the leaves expand in spring it rouses from its winter lethargy, and after 'heaving anchor'—to use a nautical expression—by severing the silken connections of its case, travels in search of food, and having found it, secures its case again, and breaks its long fast. Toward the end of May it acquires its growth, when the earlier brown color frequently takes on a more or less decided deep green hue. It is a smooth worm with the head and thoracic joints as represented

FIG. 229.—Cluster of leaves hiding larval case of *M. indigenella*. (After Riley.)

at *c*. The case at this time usually presents the appearance of Figure 228, *a*, being crooked and twisted like a little horn, gradually enlarging, cornucopia-fashion, from tip to mouth, and reminding one strongly of a piece of bird-dung. It is formed of the worm's excrement and other debris, interwoven with silk, and is completely lined on the inside with a carpet of the last-named material. The worm leaves it for feeding purposes mostly during the night. The chrysalis is formed inside this case, and the moths commence to make their appearance during the fore part of June, and later as we go farther north."

The insect feeds principally upon the *Rosaceæ*, and is very injurious to orchards, attacking apple-trees, plums, quinces, cherries, and certain varieties of pears, especially the Seckel pear.

Genus AMBESA Grote

(1) **Ambesa lætella** Grote, Plate XLVIII, Fig. 16, ♂.
The moth is not uncommon in Colorado, Wyoming, and Utah. It is found in the sage-brush in August.

Genus MELITARA Walker

(1) **Melitara fernaldialis** Hulst, Plate XLVIII, Fig. 8, ♀.
The insect is not at all uncommon in Arizona, and is also said to occur in Mexico.

Genus ZOPHODIA Hübner

(1) **Zophodia grossulariæ** Riley. (The Gooseberry Fruit-worm.)

Syn. *turbitella* Grote.

The larva of this little moth, which is glass-green, feeds upon currants and gooseberries as they are forming upon the branches, hollowing out their interiors, and often fastening a cluster of them together with a web of silk. The berries attacked by the larvæ do not generally fall to the ground, but shrivel up where they are, attached to the stalk. The caterpillars transform into pupæ on the ground, under leaves and among rubbish. There is but one brood during the year.

FIG. 230.—*Z. grossulariæ.* Moth and cocoon. (After Riley.)

The insect is widely distributed from New England and southern Canada westward and southward into the Valley of the Ohio and the upper portions of the Mississippi Valley.

Genus CANARSIA Hulst

(1)**Canarsia hammondi** Riley. (The Apple-leaf Skeletonizer.)

The larva of this little moth feeds upon the parenchyma, or soft green pulpy covering of the leaves, of the apple and allied trees, leaving the framework of veins and veinlets untouched. Sometimes it devours all of the upper surface of the leaf and completely skeletonizes it; more frequently it only eats portions here and there. In the fall of the year orchards are often made to appear quite sear and blighted by the inroads of the minute larvæ, which are gregarious and are at times found literally in millions upon the trees.

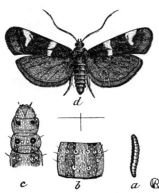

FIG. 231.—*C. hammondi. a,* larva; *b,* enlarged dorsal view of segment; *c,* enlarged view of head and anterior segments; *d,* moth. (After Riley.)

The insect has an extensive range, and is found from New

411

England and Ontario southward through the valleys of the Ohio and the Mississippi as far as northern Texas.

By weakening the trees the larvæ cause the fruit to fall prematurely, and not a little damage is thus caused to the crop. It has been recommended to treat trees which are infested by the insect to a dust-bath made of air-slaked lime. It is said that this has the effect of destroying the larvæ. A better method of procedure is to give the trees a spraying with a very weak solution of one or the other of the coal-oil emulsions which are in use as disinfectants in orchards.

Genus EPHESTIA Guenée

(1) **Ephestia kuehniella** Zeller. (The Flour-moth.)
Syn. *gitonella* Druce.

This wretched pest, the original habitat of which is not known, has within recent years caused a great deal of trouble and expense to millers and dealers in grain on both sides of the Atlantic. It is believed by many European entomologists to be of American origin, but this cannot be proved. Others hold that

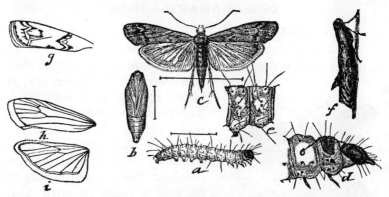

FIG. 232.—*E. kuehniella.* (All figures greatly enlarged.) *a*, larva; *b*, pupa; *c*, moth; *d*, enlarged head of larva; *e*, enlarged segment; *f*, moth at rest; *g*, front wing, showing characteristic markings; *h*, *i*, neuration of wings. (After Riley, "Insect Life," Vol. II, p. 166.)

it is an importation from the Orient, and it goes under the name of the Mediterranean Flour-moth in some localities. Wherever the creature came from, it is a decided plague. Rapidly multiplying, it takes possession of mills and grain-warehouses, and seems to defy attempts to eradicate it. Each female lays from six to seven hundred eggs, and the process of generation seems, where buildings are warm, to go on continuously. Moving and airing the wheat does no good, as the insect seems to multiply in the pipes in which flour is transported in a mill from one place to another by air-pressure. Much damage is done by the habit which the larvæ possess of gnawing the fine gauze of the screens in a flour-mill.

When the insect has once established itself in an elevator or mill, the only remedy appears to be to shut down, and thorough-ly clean the place from top to bottom, and keep shut down and go on cleaning until not a nook or cranny is known to harbor the larvæ, cocoons, or moths. The accompanying illustrations, which are taken from the pages of "Insect Life," Vol. II, will enable the student to recognize this creature in its various stages of development.

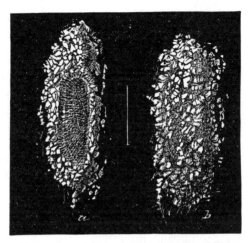

FIG. 233.—*a*, Enlarged view of cocoon of Flour-moth from below, showing pupa through thin silk which was attached to a beam. *b*, Cocoon viewed from above, with meal clinging to it. (After Riley, "Insect Life," Vol. II, p. 167.)

Thus far it has not become universally distributed throughout the country, but it has appeared in alarming numbers in some parts of Canada and New England. In England, Germany, and Belgium its attacks have been the subject of frequent comment. It shares an unenviable reputation with another species of the same genus, which we shall presently speak of, and with a species of *Plodia*, of which we shall also have something to say.

> "Bee to the blossom, moth to the flame;
> Each to his passion; what's in a name?"
> HELEN HUNT JACKSON.—*Vanity of Vanities.*

413

(2) **Ephestia cautella** Walker. (The Dried-currant Moth.)

Syn. *cahiritella* Zeller; *pasulella* Barrett; *desuetella* Walker.

FIG. 234.— *E. cautella.* Larva, twice size of life. (After Chittenden, "Bull. U. S. Dept. Agric.," New Ser., No. 8, p. 8.)

This insect, which in many respects closely resembles the preceding species, like it is destructive to stored food-products. It is known to feed upon Zante currants, raisins, cacao-beans, or chocolate-nuts, on flax-seed, flax-meal, and figs. It is regarded as probable that upon occasion it may develop a tendency to feed upon almost any substance which, containing nutriment, accords in its general character with the commodities which have been named. It is especially likely to attack dried fruits of any kind in which there is sugar or oil. That the insect has been introduced from abroad into our fauna is beyond reasonable doubt. Its ravages on the other side of the Atlantic have been described by writers long ago, while its appearance in this country seems to date from about the time of the Atlanta Cotton Exposition.

Just as most of the common weeds in our fields are of European origin, having been brought over in the seeds which were originally imported, or at a later time in the hay and straw which are used to stuff crates and packing-boxes, so many of the destructive insects, which have greatly multiplied in America, are foreign in their origin. It is not without reason that the government maintains a set of officers, whose function it is to inspect vegetable importations for the purpose of quarantin-

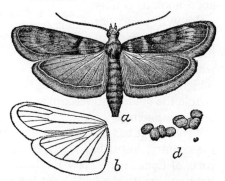

FIG. 235.—*E. cautella. a*, moth; *b*, venation of wings; *d*, eggs. All figures enlarged. (After Chittenden, "Bull. U. S. Dept. Agric.," New Ser., No. 8, p. 8.)

ing those which appear to be likely to introduce insect pests. Had the custom of quarantining plants been instituted earlier, our farmers would to-day be happier.

Genus PLODIA Guenée

(1) **Plodia interpunctella** Hübner. (The Indian-meal Moth.)
Syn. *zeæ* Fitch.

The larva of this moth has a propensity to feed upon almost anything edible which comes in its way. It feeds upon Indian meal with particular avidity, but does not disdain grain of any kind, whole or ground. It breeds in all sorts of dried fruits and vegetables. It eats English walnuts, is said to invade beehives, and is known at times to damage herbariums and to attack collections of dried insects. There is nothing which seems to come amiss to its appetite, and

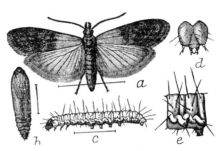

FIG. 236.—*P. interpunctella. a*, moth; *b*, pupa; *c*, larva; *d*, front view of head of larva; *e*, lateral view of segment of larva. All figures enlarged. (After Chittenden, "Bull. U. S. Dept. Agric.," New Ser., No. 4, p. 119.)

it is, when established in a house or store-room, a veritable nuisance. There are, according to the temperature of the building which it inhabits, from four to seven generations a year, and the reader of these lines will do well to remember that if the thing has establis   itself under his roof it will require industry, patience, and great regard to cleanliness and order to get rid of it.

FAMILY PTEROPHORIDÆ

"Nature never did betray
The breast that loved her; 't is her privilege,
Through all the years of this our life, to lead
From joy to joy."
WORDSWORTH.

The Plume-moths, as they are called, constitute a comparatively small family of elegant insects, in which the wings are divided in such a manner as to suggest feathers. The hind wings are generally trifid, sometimes quadrifid; the fore wings are generally bifid, sometimes trifid. The larvæ are slow in movement, clumsy in appearance, and live on the surface of leaves. They are generally hairy. The pupæ are very remarkable, being soft and hairy like the caterpillars, and attached in pendant position by the cremaster, very much as the chrysalids of some butterflies, though a few have rudimentary cocoons in the form of strands of silk thrown about them. There are six genera and about sixty species of Plume-moths known to occur in the United States. We can take space to represent only one of these species.

Genus OXYPTILUS Zeller

(1) **Oxyptilus periscelidactylus** Fitch. (The Grape-vine Plume.)

An exceedingly readable and very interesting account of the habits of this insect, which is universally distributed over the

whole Appalachian subregion, is given by the late Professor Riley in the "Fourth Missouri Report." The moths may generally be found in vineyards and about grape-vines, when they are beginning to put out their leaves. The eggs are laid on the branches before they begin to blossom, and about the time the third bunch of grapes on a given shoot is beginning to mature, it will be found that the terminal leaves have been drawn together with a few strands of silk, and in the tangle thus prepared, under cover from heat and rain, will be found the curious little caterpillars of the Plume-moth. The accompanying cut, taken from the paper of Professor Riley to which allusion has been made, will serve to tell the story better than can be done in brief compass by words.

FIG. 237.—The Grape-vine Plume. *a*, larvæ; *b*, pupa; *c*, enlarged view of process on back of pupa; *d*, moth; *e*, lateral view of segment of larva. (After Riley.)

The damage done by the insects is not usually very great, and it is an easy matter for the vine-grower, when he discovers the leaves drawn together in the way pointed out, to pluck off the end of the shoot and destroy the insects.

FAMILY ORNEODIDÆ

"Very close and diligent looking at living creatures, even through the best microscope, will leave room for new and contradictory discoveries."

GEORGE ELIOT.

This is a very small family of moths, represented in our fauna by but a single genus and species. The moth has both the fore and the hind wings divided into six plumes, as is the case in all the insects of the family.

Genus ORNEODES Latreille

(1) **Orneodes hexadactyla** Linnæus. (The Six-plume Moth.)

The moth, which measures half an inch in expanse of wings, is found in Europe and in the cooler portions of North America, exclusive of the arctic regions. It has been reported to occur as far south as Missouri, but is more commonly found in New England, New York, Canada, Manitoba, and the Northwestern States on the Pacific coast. It is nowhere apparently a common insect, or else is overlooked by collectors on account of its small size.

FIG. 238.—*O. hexadactyla.* ⚥.

FAMILY TORTRICIDÆ

"Die Kritik nimmt oft dem Baume
Raupen und Blüthen mit einander."
JEAN PAUL RICHTER.

The *Tortricidæ* constitute a very large assemblage of genera and species. Because of the habit of the larvæ of many species of rolling up the leaves of the plants on which they feed, these insects have been often called "Leaf-rollers." Many of the larvæ live in the inside of the stems of plants, or burrow in fruits, and the famous "jumping-beans" of New Mexico and Arizona are simply the seeds of a species of *Croton* or *Sebastiania* in which is lodged the larva of a species of Tortricid, which has the power, by changing its position on the inside of the seed, of making the seed move. In the case of Croton seeds the insect is *Cydia saltitans* Westwood; in the case of Sebastiania seeds the insect imparting the motion to the thing is the larva of *Enarmonia sebastianiæ*.

It is quite impossible for us in a work of the present scope to give even an epitome of the nearly five hundred species of Tortricids which are at present known to occur within the limits of the United States and Canada. We shall content ourselves with an account of a few species, which will serve to show the reader what a mine of interesting inquiry presents itself to view in this single family of beautiful little moths.

Genus EUCOSMA Hübner

(1) **Eucosma scudderiana** Clemens. (The Misnamed Gall-moth.)

Syn. *saligneana* Clemens; *affusana* Zeller.

The moth was called "the Misnamed Gall-moth" by Professor

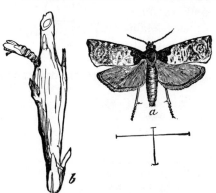

Riley because Clemens had given it a specific name which implied that it was a denizen of willow-trees or willow-galls, when in fact it has been ascertained to live in the galls of the Golden-rod (*Solidago*). The insect is not uncommon in western Pennsylvania, and is possibly an inquiline or intruder in the galls, which are produced by another species, *Gnorimoschema gallæsolidaginis* Riley.

FIG. 239.—*E. scudderiana. a*, moth; *b*, larval skin protruding from a gall of the Golden-rod. (After Riley.)

(2) **Eucosma dorsisignatana** Clemens, Plate XLVIII, Fig. 27, ♂.

Syn. *similana* Clemens; *distigmana* Walker; *clavana* Zeller; *graduatana* Walsingham.

418

This is a common species in the Appalachian subregion. It is found abundantly in western Pennsylvania.

Genus ANCYLIS Hübner

(1) **Ancylis comptana** Frölich. (The Strawberry Leaf-roller.)

Syn. *conflexana* Walker; *fragariæ* Walsh & Riley.

This little insect has proved a very destructive foe of the strawberry in parts of the Mississippi Valley. There are two broods annually. The insects roll up the leaves, and feeding upon the tender paren- chyma, cause the plants to wither and dry. So bad have the ravages of the larvæ proved in some places that horticultur- ists have been led to abandon growing straw- berries in those localities. The insect is found in

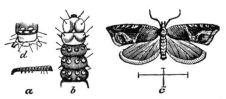

FIG. 240.—*A. comptana. a*, larva, natural size; *b*, enlarged view of anterior portion of larva; *c*, moth; *d*, anal segment of larva. (After Riley.)

Canada and in the portions of the United States immediately south of the Great Lakes. Although the moth occurs in western Pennsylvania, no great loss from its attacks has as yet been re- ported from this part of the country.

Genus ECDYTOLOPHA Zeller

(1) **Ecdytolopha insiticiana** Zeller, Plate XLVIII, Fig. 29, ♀.

The larva of this species has the habit of boring under the bark and causing gall-like excrescences to appear upon the twigs of the common locust (*Robinia*).

Genus CYDIA Hübner

(1) **Cydia pomonella** Linnæus. (The Coddling-moth.)

This well-known and most destructive little insect is estimated to inflict an annual loss upon the fruit-growers of America which amounts in the aggregate to tens of millions of dollars. Every one is familiar with the pinkish worm which is encountered at the heart of apples and pears. But for every apple and pear

which survives the attacks of these insects and develops sufficiently to come to market and to the mouth of the consumer,

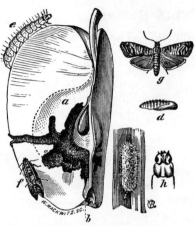

there are scores of apples
and pears the development
of which is entirely ruined,
and they fall to the ground
undersized and worthless.
There are two broods of the
insects annually. The second brood hibernates in the
cocoon. We quote again
from Riley: "The same
temperature which causes
our apple-trees to burst their
beauteous blossoms releases
the coddling-moth from its
pupal tomb, and though its
wings are still damp with
the imprint of the great
Stereotyping Establishment
of the Almighty, they soon

FIG. 241.—*C. pomonella.* *a*, burrow in
apple; *b*, point where egg is laid; *e*, full-
grown larva; *d*, pupa; *f*, moth at rest;
g, moth with wings expanded; *h*, enlarged
head of larva; *i*, cocoon. (After Riley.)

dry and expand under the genial spring-day sun, and enable each
to seek its companion. . . . The moths soon pair, and the female
flits from blossom to blossom, deftly depositing in the calyx of
each a tiny yellow egg. As the fruit matures, the worm develops.
In thirty-three days, under favorable circumstances, it has become
full-fed; when, leaving the apple, it spins up in some crevice,
changes to a chrysalis in three days, and issues two weeks afterwards as moth, ready to deposit again, though not always in the
favorite calyx this time, as I have frequently found the young
worm entering from the side."

The best remedy for the coddling-moth is to destroy all wind-
falls and immature fruit lying upon the ground. Make it a duty
to keep the wind-fallen fruit garnered up once a week and fed to
the pigs. Let the pigs into the orchard, if possible. Bind bands
of hay about the trees. The caterpillars will form their cocoons
among the hay in preference to any other place. Once a week
crush the hay with the cocoons in it, and move the band up and
down. Burn the wisp of hay if it gets full of cocoons, and bind

420

on another. The coddling-moth is an importation from Europe. Not all the live stock brought into America from Europe, biped or hexapod, has turned out well.

Genus ALCERIS Hübner

(1) **Alceris minuta** Robinson. (The Green Apple Leaf-tier.)
Syn. *malivorana* Le Baron; *vacciniivorana* Packard; *variolana* Zeller.

The larvæ of this insect feed in the early spring upon the young leaves of apple- and pear-trees, which they crumple up and tie together with threads of silk. Under the folded leaves they live and at last undergo their transformation into the pupal state. The caterpillars are green in color, and very nimble when disturbed, dropping to the ground or lowering themselves quickly upon a strand of silk. The chrysalis, as shown in the annexed cut, has a peculiar horn-like boss or projection at the upper end. The insect does much damage in the spring by preventing the proper expansion of the leaves in the terminal buds and by devouring the blossoms. The writer has for several years been greatly interested in observing the manner in which these pernicious little creatures

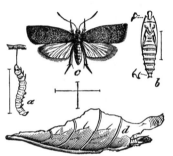

FIG. 242.—*Alceris minuta.* *a,* larva; *b,* pupa; *c,* moth; *d,* folded apple-leaf concealing pupa. (After Riley.)

have steadily robbed him of all fruit upon a couple of dwarf pear-trees which are growing at the rear of his city home. It has been found that a thorough spraying with a strong infusion of tobacco stems and slaked lime brings their work to a speedy end, and it is recommended to fruit-growers to resort to the application of this old-fashioned remedy when needed.

Genus EPAGOGE Hübner

(1) **Epagoge tunicana** Walsingham, Plate XLVIII, Fig. 40, ♂.

This rather neatly marked moth, which may be accepted as a good representative of its genus, inhabits the Pacific subregion.

Genus CENOPIS Zeller

(1) **Cenopis pettitana** Robinson, Plate XLVIII, Fig. 35, ♀.
The habitat of this species is the Appalachian subregion.
(2) **Cenopis groteana** Fernald, Plate XLVIII, Fig. 28, ♂.
The insect is not uncommon in the Valley of the Ohio.

Genus ARCHIPS Hübner

(1) **Archips rosaceana** Harris, Plate XLVIII, Fig. 32, ♀.
Syn. *vicariana* Walker; *gossypiana* Packard; *arcticana* Mœschler.
This is a common species found all over the northern portions of the United States and southern Canada. The larvæ inflict considerable damage at times upon roses and the foliage of allied plants.
(2) **Archips purpurana** Clemens, Plate XLVIII, Fig. 30, ♂.
Syn. *gurgitana* Robinson; *lintneriana* Grote.
In many respects this species is very closely allied to the last mentioned, from which it may be distinguished by the darker, more smoky color of the primaries. It has the same distribution as *rosaceana*.
(3) **Archips cerasivorana** Fitch, Plate XLVIII, Fig. 21, ♀.
The larva of this insect, as its name implies, is addicted to feeding upon the leaves of various species of wild cherry. It is found in the northern portions of the United States and southern Canada.
(4) **Archips parallela** Robinson, Plate XLVIII, Fig. 31, ♂.
The species ranges from New England westward into the Valley of the Mississippi.
(5) **Archips argyrospila** Walker, Plate XLVIII, Fig. 34, ♀.
Syn. *furvana* Robinson; *v-signatana* Packard.
The species, which is not at all uncommon, ranges through the northern portions of the United States from the Atlantic to the Pacific.

Genus PLATYNOTA Clemens

(1) **Platynota flavedana** Clemens, Plate XLVIII, Fig. 24, ♀.
Syn. *concursana* Walker; *laterana* Robinson.
The moth is a native of the Appalachian subregion.
(2) **Platynota labiosana** Zeller, Plate XLVIII, Fig. 25, ♀.

The insect is found in the southwestern portion of our territory, having been reported from Colorado and Texas.

Genus TORTRIX Linnæus

* (1) **Tortrix albicomana** Clemens, Plate XLVIII, Fig. 22, ♂.
The moth flies in the eastern portions of our region, being commoner in the Atlantic States than elsewhere.

Genus EULIA Hübner

(1) **Eulia alisellana** Robinson, Plate XLVIII, Fig. 39, ♀.
The insect is common in the Valley of the Ohio. It occurs in western Pennsylvania, Ohio, and Indiana.

Genus AMORBIA Clemens

(1) **Amorbia humerosana** Clemens, Plate XLVIII, Fig. 23, ♀.
The species is indigenous in the northern portions of the Appalachian subregion.

Genus COMMOPHILA Hübner

(1) **Commophila macrocarpana** Walsingham, Plate XLVIII, Fig. 26, ♀.
The insect is a native of the Pacific subregion.

FAMILY YPONOMEUTIDÆ

" Thus hath the candle sing'd the moth."
SHAKESPEARE.— *Merchant of Venice*, I, 9.

This is a family of moderate size, represented in our fauna by twenty-two genera and over sixty species. The species have a characteristic facies, which when once recognized will enable the student to readily separate them from their allies. We are able to figure only three species, owing to the necessary limitations of space.

Genus YPONOMEUTA Latreille

(1) **Yponomeuta multipunctella** Clemens, Plate XLVIII, Fig. 44, ♂.
Syn. *ordinatellus* Walker; *euonymella* Chambers; *orbimaculella* Chambers; *wakarusa* Gaumer.

*The specimen pictured in Fig. 22, Plate XLVIII, appears to be *Tortrix semipurpurana* Kearfott. It does not resemble *T. albicomana* Clemens or any variation of the latter.—A.E.B.

The insect is found in the Appalachian subregion, but more particularly in the southeastern portions thereof.

Genus ATTEVA Walker

(1) **Atteva aurea** Fitch, Plate XLVIII, Fig. *36*, ♂ .
Syn. *compta* Clemens.

The insect is common in the southern portions of our region, being distributed from the Gulf States southward and westward in o Mexico and lands still farther South.

(2) **Atteva gemmata** Grote, Plate XLVIII, Fig. *37*, ♂ .
Syn. *fastuosa* Zeller; *floridana* Neumœgen.

The moth is found in the warmer parts of Florida.

FAMILY GELECHIIDÆ

" He buildeth his house as a moth." Job.—xxvii, 18.

This is a very extensive family of small moths which possess habits of considerable interest to students. Many of them are

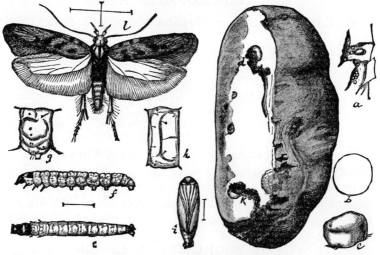

Fig. 243.—*P. operculella.* *a*, section of tuber showing eye and eggs deposited about it, natural size; *b*, egg, dorsal view; *c*, egg, lateral view, greatly enlarged; *d*, *k*, mines of larva in potato; *j*, pupa at end of mine, seen through skin of potato, somewhat reduced; *e*, larva, dorsal view; *f*, larva, lateral view; *g*, larva, third abdominal segment, lateral view; *h*, do., dorsal view, still more enlarged; *i*, pupa; *l*, moth, enlarged. (After Riley, "Insect Life," Vol. IV, p. 239.)

known to be more or less injurious to vegetables, in which they either burrow in their larval state, or upon the foliage of which they prey. We can speak of only a few of them.

Genus PHTHORIMÆA Meyrick

(1) Phthorimæa operculella Zeller. (The Potato-moth.)
Syn. *terrella* Walker; *solanella* Boisduval; *tabacella* Ragonot.

This insect, represented in Fig. 243, the ravages of which upon potatoes in Algiers and other Mediterranean countries have been well known for many years, and which has more recently caused much mischief in New Zealand and Australia, has quite recently found lodgment in California, having been apparently accidentally imported from Australia. In Algiers it is known in certain years to have destroyed fully two thirds of the potato-crop. It is a dangerous and annoying pest. The best remedy for it is said to be the total destruction of infected potatoes, and the protection of the stored tubers from access by the ovipositing females.

Genus GNORIMOSCHEMA Busck

(1) Gnorimoschema gallæsoli-daginis Riley. (The Solidago Gall-moth.)

The man who has loitered by the waysides in the country must often have noticed the manner in which the stems of the common golden-rod are frequently swollen and enlarged about two thirds of their length from the root. This swelling may be caused by the larvæ of several insects, but one of the most frequent causes of the abnormal growth is the larva of a little moth to which the above sesquipedalian name has been given. The life-

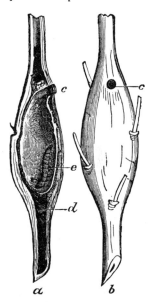

FIG. 244.—Galls of the Solidago Gall-moth. (After Riley.) *a*, section of gall showing burrow at *d*, larva at *e; b*, gall, opening at *c*.

history of the insect was carefully worked out by Professor Riley, and from his interesting paper upon the subject, contained

425

in the "First Missouri Report," the accompanying cut has been taken. It shows a gall as it appears from the outside, and also a section of a gall, revealing the home which the larva constructed for itself in the enlargement of the stem.

The moth is very common in many parts of the country, but particularly in western Pennsylvania.

Genus ANARSIA Zeller

(1) **Anarsia lineatella** Zeller. (The Peach-twig Borer.)
Syn. *pruniella* Clemens.

The insect which we are considering was in all probability introduced into California, where it is now most firmly established, from Asia, probably from Japan. The eggs are deposited at the point where the leaves are attached to the stems, or where the stem of the fruit is located. The larvæ make minute burrows under the bark of the twigs and into the stem of the fruit, and thus cause damage both to the trees and to the peaches. The insect is double-brooded. The larvæ are secretive, and hide so effectually that it is said to be very difficult to detect them. The insect remains in the pupal state about ten days, when the moth emerges. The imago is about half an inch in expanse of wing. The fore wings are of a beautiful gray color, clouded on the costa with darker markings. The insects of the second generation hibernate as larvæ in their burrows in the bark of the twigs.

FIG. 245.—*A. lineatella. a*, new shoot of peach withering from attack of larva; *b*, larva, enlarged; *c*, pupa, enlarged. (After Marlatt, "Bull. U. S. Dept. Agric.," New Ser., No. 10, p. 11.)

A very full and excellent account of the habits of this insect has been published in the "Bulletin of the United States Department of Agriculture" by Mr. C. L. Marlatt. It is from this paper that we have been with great kindness permitted to draw the illustrations which are herewith given.

As a means of combating this pest, it has been recommended to spray the peach-trees, just as the leaves are beginning to open in the spring, with a solution of one pound of lime and one pound of Paris green mixed in two hundred gallons of water. It is also recommended to spray the trees in February, or even in January, with kerosene emulsion, which is said to penetrate the little burrows in which the larvæ hibernate and kill them. The latter method is undoubtedly preferable.

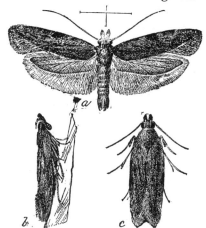

FIG. 246.—*A. lineatella.* *a*, moth with wings expanded; *b*, *c*, moths with wings folded. All figures enlarged. (After Marlatt, "Bull. U. S. Dept. Agric.," New Ser., No. 10, p. 12.)

CUPID'S CANDLE

" Round her flaming heart they hover,
Lured by loveliness they go
Moth-like, every man a lover,
Captive to its gleam and glow.

Old and young, the blind and blinking,—
Fascinated, frenzied things,—
How they flutter, never thinking
What a doom awaits their wings!

It is all the same old story,—
Pleasure hung upon a breath:
Just a chance to taste of glory
Draws a legion down to death.

Fire is dangerous to handle;
Love is an uncertain flame;
But the game is worth the candle
When the candle 's worth the game! "

FELIX CARMEN, in *Life*, Vol. XLI, p. 494.

FAMILY XYLORICTIDÆ

A small family which contains in our fauna two genera and nine species. The group may be represented by **Stenoma schlægeri** Zeller, which is portrayed on Plate XLVIII, Fig. 41, by a male specimen. The insect is very common in the Appalachian subregion, and is particularly abundant in western Pennsylvania.

FAMILY ŒCOPHORIDÆ

"Entomology is a science, not a pastime."—WESTWOOD.

This is another comparatively small family of interesting insects, numbering in our fauna about ninety species, which are distributed into thirteen genera. We can represent only a couple of them, for the purpose of showing the readers of " The Moth Book" what they are like.

Genus DEPRESSARIA Haworth

(1) **Depressaria heracliana** De Geer. (The Parsnip Webworm.)

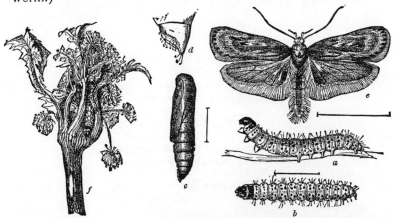

FIG. 247.—*D. heracliana.* *a*, larva, side view; *b*, dorsal view; *c*, pupa; *d*, anal extremity of pupa; *e*, moth, enlarged; *f*, umbel of parsnip webbed together by the larvæ, natural size. (After Riley.)

Syn. *heraclei* Retzius; *umbellana* Fabricius; *umbellella* Zetterstedt; *pastinacella* Duponchel; *ontariella* Bethune.

The Parsnip Web-worm is an importation from Europe,

where it has been known from time immemorial as an enemy of umbelliferous plants. A full account of the insect is given by Riley in "Insect Life," Vol. I, p. 94. To this the reader may refer. The remedy for the insect is to gather the portions of the plants which have become infested, and to burn them. The insects, many of which conceal themselves in the stems or are hidden in the foliage, are thus most conveniently destroyed.

Genus SEMIOSCOPIS Hübner

* (1) **Semioscopis merricella** Dyar, Plate XLVIII, Fig. 38, ♀.

This is not at all an uncommon insect in western Pennsylvania. There are numerous specimens in the collection of the writer which have been taken during the past twenty years.

FAMILY BLASTOBASIDÆ

This is a considerable family of minute moths, as representative of which we have selected for illustration a species of the genus **Holcocera,** to which Professor Riley applied the specific name **glandulella,** because it infests acorns. The Acorn-moth is an inquiline; that is to say, it takes possession of the remnants of the repast left in the acorn by the grub of a weevil, which has developed within the fruit and forsaken its burrow in order to undergo transformation elsewhere.

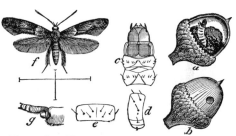

FIG. 248.—*H. glandulella.* a, acorn showing larva; *b,* acorn showing opening left for moth; *c,* enlarged view of head of larva; *d,* lateral view of segment; *e,* dorsal view of segment; *f,* moth; *g,* nodule to which antenna articulates. (After Riley.)

Between the weevil and the larva of the moth very little is left of the contents of the acorn, and farmers who expect to derive sustenance for their hogs from the oak-mast are often disappointed. The accompanying cut shows the different stages in the development of the larva, and also the moth. The insect is quite common in Pennsylvania, Ohio, and Indiana.

*Should be *S. packardella* Clemens in text and plate.—A.E.B.

FAMILY ELACHISTIDÆ

This is a large family of moths, many of which are almost microscopic in size, but all are very beautiful. One of the larger species we have selected for illustration. It lives in the galls which its presence produces in the stems of the False Indigo (*Amorpha fruticosa*). It belongs to the genus **Walshia**, and was described under the specific name **amorphella** by Clemens.

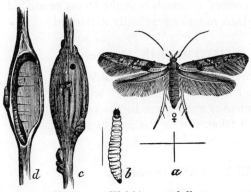

FIG. 249.—*Walshia amorphella.*

In its habits it reminds us somewhat of the moth with the frightful name which lives in the galls of the Golden-rod, about which something has already been said. The accompanying cut, which has been taken from Professor Riley's "Second Missouri Report," shows at *a* a figure of the female moth enlarged. The larva, which is a soft white little affair, is delineated at *b*, and the figures *c* and *d* show the galls as they appear. The insect is found in the Appalachian subregion.

FAMILY TINEIDÆ

"Lay not up for yourselves treasures upon earth, where moth and rust doth corrupt, and where thieves break through and steal: but lay up for yourselves treasures in heaven, where neither moth nor rust doth corrupt, and where thieves do not break through nor steal." MATTHEW.—VI, 19, 20.

The *Tineidæ* are a very great family of moths, some of which are of moderate size, but most of which are very minute. Among them there are many insects which are exceedingly beautiful, although they are so small, while many of them have great economic importance, being destructive or beneficial. Of a few of these we shall take opportunity to speak briefly.

Genus BUCCULATRIX Zeller

(1) **Bucculatrix canadensisella** Chambers. (The Birch-leaf Bucculatrix.)

This little insect in its larval stage is known to infest the leaves of the birch and the wild cherry. The caterpillars feed upon the parenchyma of the leaves, attacking both the upper and the lower sides, and completely skeletonizing them. Forests of birches in New England are known to have been completely stripped of living tissue in the fall of the year, in such a manner as to suggest that a fire had passed over the trees. The larvæ are sluggish in their movements, when disturbed dropping down by a silken cord. The cocoons are white and ribbed, as represented in the annexed figure. They turn dark after they have been spun up for some time. The insect is not uncommon in Rhode Island, and is

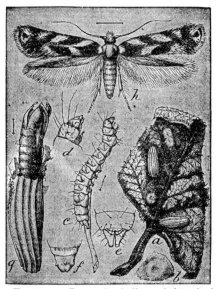

FIG. 250.—*B. canadensisella. a*, skeletonized birch-leaf; *b*, pseudo-cocoon; *c*, larva; *d*, head of same; *e*, anal segments of do.; *f*, anal segment of pupa; *g*, cocoon with extended pupal skin; *h*, moth. All figures magnified. (After Packard, "Insect Life," Vol. V, p. 14.)

known to occur throughout New England, northern New York, and Canada. It probably has even a wider range, and may be found in the mountains of Pennsylvania, where its food-plant is abundant. The best account of its habits has been given by Professor A. S. Packard in "Insect Life," Vol. V, p. 14.

(2) **Bucculatrix pomifoliella** Clemens. (The Apple-leaf Bucculatrix.)

Syn. *pomonella* Packard; *curvilineatella* Packard.

The minute moth, a greatly enlarged figure of which is given in the annexed cut, has the habit of denuding the leaves of apple-trees of their parenchyma. While it does not appear to have wrought great destruction generally, nevertheless there are instances on record where it has done much damage in orchards. The larvæ have the habit of forming their cocoons in company, attaching them to the twigs in great clusters, as represented in Fig. 251. This fact has led to the recommendation that the trees, when infested, should be lightly pruned all over in the fall, and the twigs carefully collected and

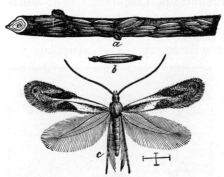

FIG. 251.—*B. pomifoliella. a*, cocoons clustered upon end of twig; *b*, cocoon, greatly enlarged; *c*, moth, very greatly magnified. (After Riley.)

burned. As the cocoons are located at the ends of the twigs, this may be a partially effective remedy. Another remedy is to thoroughly spray the trees with coal-oil emulsion or with linseed-oil. The greasy application is said to destroy the pupæ in the thin papery cocoons.

Genus TINEOLA Herrich-Schæffer

(1) Tineola bisselliella Hummel. (The Clothes-moth.)

Syn. *crinella* Treitschke; *destructor* Stephens; *biselliella* Zeller; *lanariella* Clemens.

There are several species of Tineid insects which attack garments made of woolen fiber and furs. One of the commonest and most widely distributed of these is the insect which we are now considering. In Pennsylvania and in Maryland and southward, so far as observation shows, this is the commonest of the "Clothes-moths." The damage, it is needless to say, is not done by the

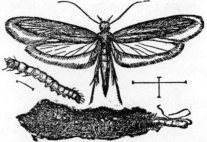

FIG. 252.—*T. bisselliella.* (After Riley.)

432

imago, or perfect insect, but by the larva, or caterpillar. This is represented in all its destructive ugliness in the annexed cut. Its food is animal fibers, and it constructs for itself a cocoon of bits of wool or hair, in which transformation into a pupa finally takes place. It is partial to all animal hair. It feeds upon furs, woolens, carpets, horsehair mattresses, and even to some extent upon silken fabrics, though it has no positive preference for the latter. The insect, like all the others of its class, has been introduced into this country from the Old World. In a separate article the writer will speak of the best method of preventing its ravages.

Genus TINEA Linnæus

(1) **Tinea pellionella** Linnæus. (The Fur-moth.)

Syn. *flavescentella* Haworth; *merdella* Zeller; *dubiella* Stainton; *griseella* Chambers.

This insect makes for itself a movable case in which it travels about in the larval stage. Its food is very much the same as that of the preceding species, and it is equally destructive. The moth differs from the pale-colored Clothes-moth in having the fore wings darker. They are, in fact, quite gray, mottled with darker

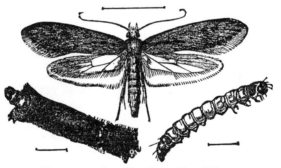

FIG. 253.—*T. pellionella.* (After Riley.)

gray, as shown in the cut which we have herewith caused to be reproduced. A comparison between the figures of this and the succeeding species will enable the student to readily discriminate them. The lower left-hand figure gives a good representation of the case made out of bits of hair in which the caterpillar performs its migrations. The insect is many-brooded, according to the temperature of its domicile. In the warmer parts of the country the processes of generation no doubt go on continuously.

In the colder parts of the country winter arrests development temporarily.

The insect is widely distributed all over the continent, and in fact all over the world.

Genus TRICHOPHAGA Ragonot

(1) **Trichophaga tapetzella** Linnæus. (The Carpet-moth.)

The nature and habits of this species are very closely allied to those of the last two species of which we have spoken. Like

them, it was originally introduced into America from the Old World. It differs from them in the larval state in that, instead of simply making a cocoon for itself out of bits of hair as the Clothesmoth, or forming a movable case for itself as the Fur-

FIG. 254.—*T. tapetzella.* (After Riley.)

moth, it weaves together, out of the debris of the material in which it is carrying on its ravages, long galleries lined inside with strands of silk. These long, tortuous galleries, cut through the pile of carpets, are familiar objects to the careful housewife, whose horror and anxiety have often been expressed to the writer. It is one of the sad prerogatives of the entomologist to be made from time to time the recipient of the household woes of his neighbors, who discover that the moth and the buffalo-bug "corrupt," and that the white ant and the cockroach "steal."

The perfect insect, as shown in the annexed cut, is in appearance a very different moth from either of the foregoing species.

CLOTHES-MOTHS

"The moth shall eat them up like a garment, and the worm shall eat them like wool."   ISAIAH.—LI, 8.

From the accounts which have been given in the preceding pages of the three species of Clothes-moths, the ravages of which are commonly encountered in the household, it has been learned that they may each be discriminated from the other by the habits of the larvæ. The Carpet-moth makes a gallery of the substance on which it feeds; the Fur-moth makes a small portable case, which it carries with it; while the insect which we have called the Clothes-moth lives for the most part free until the time of pupation, when it constructs for itself a cocoon out of bits of fiber.

All of these three species are equally destructive, and there is no question which is more frequently asked of the writer than how best to destroy the insects when once they have found lodgment in a house, and how to prevent their attacks.

All of these creatures "love darkness better than light, their deeds being evil." When it is suspected that furs or garments are infected by their presence, the first step which should be taken is to expose them to full sunlight, the hotter the better. Garments in which moths are known to exist should be hung up in the open air. And this airing and exposure to sunlight should not be for an hour or two, but, if possible, it should extend over a number of days, and should take place in the latter part of May or the early part of the month of June, at which time the female moth is engaged in ovipositing. Where it is impossible to air and expose to sunlight the fabrics which have been attacked, as is sometimes the case with carpets in dark corners, they should be thoroughly saturated with benzine. It is needless to say that this operation should never be undertaken in the presence of a candle or other exposed light. Furniture in carpeted rooms should in the spring of the year be removed from the place where it has long stood, and the spot should be thoroughly sponged with benzine. A solution of corrosive sublimate in alcohol, so weak that it will not leave any white mark upon a black feather which has been dipped into it and afterward dried, may be applied effectively to carpets and to fabrics which are exhibited in museum cases. At the Carnegie Museum we make it a rule to spray all substances which might be exposed to the attack of moths, when hung in cases, with a solution of corrosive sublimate and strychnine in alcohol.

In carpet warehouses and in establishments where woolen goods are stored in quantity it is well to have on the roof of the building an apartment fitted up with large air-tight chests. Into these chests, or compartments, fabrics supposed to have been attacked by moths may be put and exposed for twenty-four or

435

more hours to the fumes of carbon bisulphide. This fluid should be placed in large quantity in shallow pans at the bottom of the disinfecting-chambers, in such a way that it will not come directly in contact with the fabrics. Being volatile, the fumes will gradually fill the entire chamber, and will destroy all animal life. Inasmuch as carbon bisulphide, as has already been stated elsewhere in this book, is, when mixed with atmospheric air, highly explosive, no lights should be allowed to come near the chests, or the apartment in which the disinfection is taking place. The writer has in his own household made it a rule in the spring of the year to take all rugs and have them placed in a large chest about four feet long, three feet wide, and three feet deep, at the bottom of which there is a slatted support beneath which is a long, shallow pan. Into this pan the bisulphide is poured. The rugs are loosely placed in the chest, and then it is closed tightly and they are left there for forty-eight hours.

The storage of furs and woolen garments during the summer months is an important matter. The one thing to be perfectly ascertained before placing garments in storage is that they are thoroughly disinfected and that not a single female moth capable of depositing fertile eggs is present. This fact being known with certainty, all that it is necessary to do is to place the garments in clean air-tight receptacles and close them up so that nothing can get into them. Garments may be put into perfectly tight paper bags with all openings pasted shut with a piece of tough paper. The boxes in which tailors send home garments are good storage receptacles, provided the garments are free from pests when put into them and provided every opening in the box is pasted shut with a piece of paper. It is not an altogether unwise precaution to put in "moth-balls" or crystals of naphthaline or bits of camphor, but it must be borne in mind that neither naphthaline nor camphor will kill the larvæ of moths that have once found access to the garments upon which they are in the habit of feeding. A great deal of money has been uselessly expended upon such substances, when all that is necessary is simply to insure the exclusion of the pests.

The annual loss occasioned by these minute yet most annoying insects is vast, and it is not unreasonable to say that their mischievous depredations cost the citizens of the United States annually a sum of money which is enough in amount at the present time to pay the interest upon the national debt.

Genus ADELA Latreille

The moths of this genus are remarkable for the enormous length of their antennæ in proportion to their size. We have represented one of the commoner species on Plate XLVIII, Fig. 45. It received the specific name **bella** at the hands of the late Mr. V. T. Chambers. The base of the antennæ is black, and the extremity is white. This fact has prevented the photographer from getting a full representation of the length of the organ in our cut. This is much to be regretted, and the student must add in his imagination to the antennæ, as they are shown, a thread-like extension, extending fully three eighths of an inch beyond the apparent ending of the organs as depicted. The moths may be found in shaded woods in June feeding upon the flowers of *Asclepias*.

Genus PRODOXUS Riley

The relation of the insect world to the life of plants has been the subject of a great deal of interesting inquiry in recent years. It has been discovered that many genera and species depend for their fructification and consequently for their continued preservation upon the agency of insects. Without the kind attention which they receive from the tiny creatures of the air, they would not produce seed, and the race would speedily become extinct. One of the most beautiful illustrations of the interdependence of the world of plants and the world of insects has been discovered in the case of the Tineid genus *Pronuba*. This insect has become specialized to a remarkable degree, as we shall have occasion to show in speaking of it. In fact, without its agency the pollenation of the plants belonging to the genus *Yucca* is never accomplished. But, curiously enough, associated with it and closely resembling it superficially is a genus of moths which does not possess the power of pollenizing the Yucca, but which is represented by many species the larvæ of which feed in the stems of the various species of Yucca. The Yucca plants depend for the perpetuation of the species upon the moth *Pronuba*. The moth *Prodoxus* depends upon the Yucca plants for life, and thus

437

indirectly upon the labor of *Pronuba*. The whole story is one of the most interesting in the annals of insect life, and the student who is curious to know all about its interesting details should consult the fourth volume of "Insect Life," where Professor Riley has with minute patience worked out the wonderful story, with all the skill of a Sherlock Holmes.

(1) **Prodoxus quinquepunctella** Chambers. (The Bogus Yucca Moth.)

Syn. *decipiens* Riley; *paradoxica* Chambers.

This little moth, which superficially resembles *Pronuba yuccasella*, has no maxillary tentacle such as is found in the latter insect. Its absence is characteristic, in fact, of all the species of the genus. The ovipositor is homologous to that of *Pronuba*, but is a stronger instrument intended for making incisions in the tender bark of the stem, while the ovipositor of *Pronuba* is a long, slender organ which is used to thrust the egg into the ovarian cavity of the growing seed-vessel.

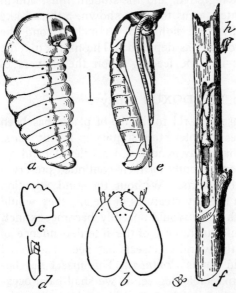

FIG. 255.—*P. quinquepunctella*. *a*, larva; *b*, head from above; *c, d*, left jaw and antenna; *e*, pupa; *f*, infested stem, showing burrows, castings, cocoons, and pupa-shell, *h*. All enlarged. (After Riley.)

The larvæ of the various species of *Prodoxus* are without feet, quite maggot-like, and remain in their burrows in the stems of the Yucca plants, not descending to the ground to pupate, as do those of *Pronuba*. The pupæ, when the time for emergence arrives, protrude themselves from the stems, and the moth escapes from the pupal skin, very much in the way in which the same act is performed by various species 'of

438

wood-burrowing Ægerians. The cut, Fig. 255, taken from the writings of Professor C. V. Riley, has more value as an explanation of the facts in the case than a whole page of verbal description would have. The species of the genus *Prodoxus* all appear upon the wing before those of the genus *Pronuba*, the former having no function to perform in connection with the fertilization of the flowers, and being on the spot to oviposit while the flower-stems are still soft and easily capable of being cut into by the ovipositor of the female, while *Pronuba* must wait until the flowers are opening and the tissues of these portions of the plant are ready for the peculiar operations which the perpetuation of the life both of the plant and the insect call for.

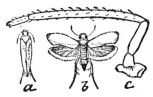

FIG. 256.— *P. quinquepunctella*. *a*, moth with wings folded; *b*, moth with wings expanded; *c*, enlarged maxillary palpus. (After Riley.)

(2) **Prodoxus marginatus** Riley.

The accompanying cut serves to show the characteristic features of this species of the genus. The figure at *a* gives a view of the last abdominal segment of the female magnified twenty-six diameters. The basal joint of the ovipositor is represented at *bjo*, the terminal joint at *tjo*, and the oviduct at *ov*. Figure *c* represents the claspers of the male viewed from above. A view of the fore wing magnified five times is given at *pr.*, and by it the species may be known.

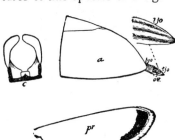

FIG. 257.—*P. marginatus*. (After Riley, " Insect Life," Vol. IV, p. 373.)

(3) **Prodoxus y-inversa** Riley.

The main characteristics of a third species of the genus are given in Fig. 258. The left front wing is represented at *a*, the hair-line beneath serving to show the natural size of the wing. By looking at the figure upside down the reader will understand why the specific name which was given to the moth originally suggested itself. The genitalia of the male moth are represented at *b* enlarged fourteen diameters. This view is taken from above and gives the dorsal aspect of these organs. At *c* we have a lateral view of the same parts magnified eighteen diameters. The ovi-

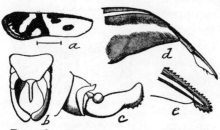

positor of the female is shown at *d* exserted from the anal joint of the abdomen. At *e* there is given another lateral view of the tip of the ovipositor much more enlarged. This view shows the peculiar saw-like structure of the organ, by help of which incisions are made

FIG. 258.—*P. y-inversa.* (After Riley, "Insect Life," Vol. IV, p. 373.)

in the soft outer bark of the growing stems of the Yucca. Both this and the preceding species are found in California.

(4) **Prodoxus reticulata** Riley.

This pretty little moth, the habits of which are much the same as those of the preceding three species, is a native of the State of Colorado. The figure represents a female with her wings expanded, and the drawing is magnified more than three times the size of life. The insect is undoubtedly, so far as the mark-

FIG. 259.—*P. reticulata.* (After Riley, "Insect Life," Vol. IV, p. 374.)

ings of the wings are concerned, the most attractive species in the entire genus.

(5) **Prodoxus coloradensis** Riley.

Fig. 260 is devoted to the illustration of the salient specific features of a fifth insect belonging to the genus *Prodoxus.* As

FIG. 260.—*P. coloradensis.* (After Riley, "Insect Life," Vol. IV, p. 374.)

the name implies, this species, like the preceding, is found in Colorado. The front wing is shown four times the size of life, the hair-line below the figure indicating the natural size. The genitalia of the male are shown at *b* viewed from above, and at *c* viewed laterally.

(6) **Prodoxus cinereus** Riley.

This species is known to breed in the flower-stems of *Yucca whipplei*. The best way in which to set the species before the

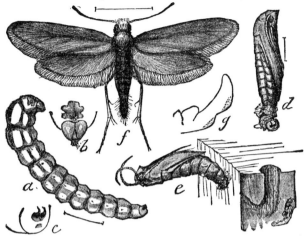

FIG. 261.—*P. cinereus.* *a*, larva; *b*, head and first thoracic joint; *c*, anal hooks; *d*, pupa; *e*, pupal shell protruding from stalk; *f*, adult female; *g*, side view of clasper of adult male. All figures greatly enlarged. (After Riley, "Insect Life," Vol. V, p. 306.)

reader seems to be to reproduce, as we have done, the figure given by the author of the species, in which its characteristic features are carefully depicted. It is found in California.

Genus PRONUBA Riley

(1) **Pronuba yuccasella** Riley. (The Yucca Moth.)

No discovery in recent years has been more interesting to students of insect and plant life than that which was made in 1872 by Professor Riley, of the intimate relationship which subsists between the beautiful plants, known as Yuccas, and the genus of moths to which the present species belongs. It has been ascertained that the fructification of the various species of Yucca is almost absolutely dependent upon the agency of the female moth ; and, strangely enough, it has also been ascertained that the pollenation of the flowers is not the result of mere accidental attrition of the wings and other organs of the insect when engaged in seeking for nectar in the flower and when engaged in laying her eggs, but that she deliberately collects the pollen with her mouth, which is peculiarly modified to enable her to do this, and then applies the pollen to the stigma with in-

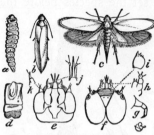

finitely better care than it could be done by the most skilful horticulturist using the most delicate human appliances.

There are several species of the genus *Pronuba*, and they hold a positive and well-ascertained relationship to the various species of the plants in the economy of which they perform so important a function. *Pronuba yuccasella* pollenizes in the Eastern States the blossoms of the common *Yucca filamentosa*, and on the Western plains it performs the act for the blossoms of *Yucca angustifolia*.

Fig. 262.—*P. yuccasella.* a, larva; b, female moth with closed wings; c, do. with wings expanded; d, side view of larval segment; e, head of larva from below; f, do. from above; g, thoracic leg of do.; h, maxilla; i, mandible; j, spinneret and labial palpi; k, antenna, enlarged. (After Riley, "Insect Life," Vol. IV, p. 360.)

Yucca brevifolia is pollenized by *Pronuba synthetica*. *Yucca whipplei* is pollenized by *Pronuba maculata*. No doubt there are other species of Yucca which will be ultimately discovered to have species of *Pronuba* which are adapted in their organs to the work of pollenation according to their peculiar requirements.

The larva of *Pronuba*, after it has attained to full size, drops to the ground, having three pairs of thoracic legs, which enable it to move about and burrow into the earth. It then undergoes transformation into the pupal state. The chrysalis, which is depicted in Fig. 263, has the back armed with peculiar spinous processes, which enable it to make its way through the loose soil.

The student who desires to become fully acquainted with this interesting chapter in insect life must consult the altogether admirable papers written upon the subject by Professor Riley, to whom we are indebted for almost all that we know in regard to the subject. These papers may be found in the Publications of the St. Louis Academy of Science, the "Fifth

Fig. 263.—*P. yuccasella.* l, male chrysalis; m, female chrysalis. (After Riley, "Insect Life," Vol. IV, p. 368.)

Annual Report of the State Entomologist of Missouri," and in the fourth and fifth volumes of "Insect Life."

Genus ACROLOPHUS Poey

(1) **Acrolophus plumifrontellus** Clemens, Plate XLVIII, Fig. 43, ♂.

Syn. *bombycina* Zeller.

As a representative of this well-marked genus, quite a number of species of which are found in our fauna, we have selected the species which is most common in the Appalachian subregion. The other species are mainly Southern and Western.

Genus ANAPHORA Clemens

(1) **Anaphora popeanella** Clemens, Plate XLVIII, Fig. 42, ♂.

Syn. *agrotipennella* Grote; *scardina* Zeller.

The insect ranges from the Atlantic States to the Rocky Mountains. There are other species in the genus, which are found in the South and the West.

FAMILY HEPIALIDÆ

This family is composed of large or moderately large insects. They are very peculiar in their structure, and are now by systematists generally accorded a position of inferiority at the bottom of the series of lepidopterous families, being regarded as representing an ancestral stock. Some go even so far as to deny that they are lepidoptera at all. This is, however, an untenable position.

Genus STHENOPIS Packard

(1) **Sthenopis argenteomaculatus** Harris, Plate XLI, Fig. 14, ♂. (The Silver-spotted Ghost-moth.)

Syn. *argentata* Packard; *alni* Kellicott.

The larvæ feed at first upon the roots of the alder, and then enter the stems. The insect is found in the northern portions of the United States and Canada. The moths have the habit of dancing in the air at sunset, and perform very peculiar gyrations over the spot where oviposition is to take place.

(2) **Sthenopis quadriguttatus** Grote, Plate XLI, Fig. 13, ♂.

Syn. *semiauratus* Neumœgen & Dyar.

The range of this species is the same as that of the preceding. It occurs rather abundantly in Assiniboia and Alberta.

Genus HEPIALUS Fabricius

(1) **Hepialus hyperboreus** Mœschler, Plate XLI, Fig. 15, ♂.
Syn. *pulcher* Grote; *macglashani* Henry Edwards.
The moth is found in New England and southern Canada.
(2) **Hepialus gracilis** Grote. (The Graceful Ghost-moth.)
This species, the neuration of the wings of which is represented in the text at Fig. 12, is not an uncommon species in the northern portions of our territory.
(3) **Hepialus lemberti** Dyar, Plate XLI, Fig. 16, ♂. (Lembert's Ghost-moth.)
The moth is found in California. It is not as yet common in collections.

FAMILY MICROPTERYGIDÆ

This family is represented in our fauna by two genera of minute insects and six species. They are remarkable because revealing certain anatomical features which are believed to point to an ancestral connection between them and other orders of insects. One of the remarkable features which they reveal is the persistence in them of mandibles in the pupæ, which are lost in the imaginal form in the genus *Micropteryx*, which is not represented in our fauna, but are persistent in the genus *Eriocephala*, which does occur in North America.

We have arrived at last at the end of our necessarily compacted but rather extensive survey of the families of moths represented in the fauna of the United States and Canada. We have thrown the doors of our subject open to the curious. We have thrown them wide open. Much has been omitted which might have been said; possibly some things have been said which will have little interest for the general reader; but, upon the whole, we feel, in bringing this book to its end, that we have given a fuller and more complete review of the whole subject to American students than has ever been essayed in any book by any other writer. Throughout the task has been to a large degree a labor of love, with the purpose of popularizing knowledge and helping those who have eyes to see and ears to hear, to understand something of the wonders of a world which becomes the more wonderful the more we know of it.

THE FINAL GOAL

"O, yet we trust that somehow good
　　Will be the final goal of ill,
　　To pangs of nature, sins of will,
Defects of doubt and taints of blood;

That nothing walks with aimless feet;
　　That not one life shall be destroyed,
　　Or cast as rubbish to the void,
When God hath made the pile complete;

That not a worm is cloven in vain,
　　That not a moth with vain desire
　　Is shrivelled in a fruitless fire,
Or but subserves another's gain."

TENNYSON.—*In Memoriam*, I, III.

THE END

When the moon shall have faded out from the sky, and the sun shall shine at noonday a dull cherry-red, and the seas shall be frozen over, and the ice-cap shall have crept downward to the equator from either pole, and no keels shall cut the waters, nor wheels turn in mills, when all cities shall have long been dead and crumbled into dust, and all life shall be on the very last verge of extinction on this globe; then, on a bit of lichen, growing on the bald rocks beside the eternal snows of Panama, shall be seated a tiny insect, preening its antennæ in the glow of the worn-out sun, representing the sole survival of animal life on this our earth, — a melancholy "bug."

INDEX

A

Abagrotis, genus; erratica, 180
abalinealis, Bomolocha, 286
Abbot, John, 27
Abbotana, genus; clemataria, transducens, transferens, 353
abbotana, Phobetron, 366
abboti, Oiketicus, 361
abbotti, Sphecodina, 70
abbreviatella, Catocala, 268
Abdomen, 14, 18
abdominalis, Pygarctia, 136
abortivaria, Dyspteris, 323
Abrostola, genus; ovalis urentis, 240
abrostoloides, Pæctes, 241
abrupta, Raphia, 153
Absinth, The, 328
absinthiata, Tephroclystis, 328
absorptalis, Hormisa, 282
absynthiata, Tephroclystis, 328
accepta, Fruva, 252
accessaria, Catopyrrha, 342
acericola, Apatela, 153
acericolum, Synanthedon, 386
aceris, Apatela, 153
acerni, Synanthedon, 386
achaia, Apantesis, 130
achatina, Olene, 308
achatinalis, Bomolocha, 286
Achatodes, genus; zeæ, 212
achemon, Pholus, 66
Acherdoa, genus; ferraria, ornata, 234
Acherontiinæ, 43
"Acheta Domestica," quoted, 140
Acoloithus, genus; falsarius, sanborni, 371
Acopa, genus; carina, 163
Acorn-moth, The, 429
acræa, Estigmene, 122, 123
Acrobasis, genus; betulella, 408
Acrolophus, genus; bombycina, plumifrontellus, 443
Actias, genus, 86; luna, 87, 88
Actinotia, genus, 172; ramosula, 173
acutalis, Phiprosopus, 245
acutaria, Doryodes, 245
acutilinea, Schinia, 227
acutipennis, Mamestra, 195
Adela, genus; bella, 437
Adelocephala, genus, 96; bicolor, distigma, 96
Adelphagrotis, genus; prasina, 179
adipaloides, Pyrausta, 397
Adita, genus; chionanthi, 177
adjuncta, Mamestra, 194
Admetovis, genus; oxymorus, 196
admirandus, Memythrus, 383
Adoneta, genus; ferrigera, nebulosus, pygmæa, spinuloides, voluta, 365
adoptiva, Catocala, 267
adulatalis, Yuma, 407
adumbrata, Syneda, 259
adustaria, Gonodontis, 350
adversa, Cænurgia, 257
ædessa, Fenaria, 233

Ægeria, genus; paiformis, crabroniformis, vespiformis, 383
Ægeriidæ, Family, 25, 36, 379
æliaria, Metanema, 351
Æmilia, genus; ambigua, bolteri, cinnamomea, occidentalis, Red-banded, Rosy, sanguivenosa, significans, syracosia, 137
æmula, Epizeuxis, 280; Synanthedon, 387
æmulataria, Philobia, 339
æqualiaria, Therina, 348
æquilinea, Ipimorpha, 220
æquosus, Syssaura, 352
ærea, Plusia, 237
æroides, Plusia, 237
æsculi, Zeuzera, 376
æsionaria, Hyperitis, 349
ætheria, Thalpochares, 249
æthra, Hæmorrhagia, 63
affinis, Herse, 43
affusana, Eucosma, 418
Agapema, genus, 86; galbina, 86
agarista, Erebus, 279
Agaristidæ, 3, 24, 32, 140, 232, 233
Agathodes, genus; designalis, floridalis, monstralis, 393
agilis, Feltia, 186
Agnomonia, genus; anilis, sesquistriaris, 274
agreasaria, Gonodontis, 350
agricola, Drasteria, 257
agrippina, Catocala, 260
agrotipennella, Anaphora, 443
agrotipennis, Melioptis, 258
Agrotiphila, genus; incognita, 191
Agrotis, genus; badinodis, 181; geniculata, idonea, suffusa, telifera, ypsilon, 182
aholah, Catocala, 268
aholibah, Catocala, 265
Ailanthus, 82
Alabama, genus; argillacea, bipunctina, grandipuncta, xylina, 243
alabamæ, Catocala, 269; Peridroma, 183
alabastaria, Synelys, 333
Alarodia, genus; slossoniæ, 366
albafascia, Schinia, 228
albarufa, Apatela, 157
albata, Clemensia, 108
albertæ, Dodia, 117
albescens, Hyloicus, 50
albicans, Opharus, 139
albicoma, Harpyia, 299
albicomana, Tortrix, 423
albicornis, Synanthedon, 387
albicosta, Euchætias, 135
albida, Clemensia, 108; Estigmene, 122
albidula, Eustrotia, 247
albifascialis, Zinckenia, 392
albifrons, Symmerista, 296
albifusa, Mamestra, 193
albilinea, Heliophila, 201
albipennis, Euxoa, 189
albipuncta, Platysenta, 163
albisignalis, Bomolocha, 286
alboclavellus, Crambus, 402
albofascia, Gluphisia, 300
albolineata, Syssphinx, 96

Index

alboplagiata, Tristyla, 220
albopunctata, Caripeta, 342
albosigma, Melalopha, 293
albosignata, Gypsochroa, 332
albovenosa, Arsilonche, 159
albovittata, Euchœca, 328
album, Copablepharon, 222
Albuna, genus; montana, pyramidalis, 384
Alceris, genus; malivorana, minuta, vacciniivorana, variolana, 421
Alcis, genus; baltearia, metanemaria, sulphuraria, 343
Alcothoe, genus; caudata, 382
Aleptina, genus; inca, 162
aleucis, Schinia, 227
Alexicles, genus; aspersa, 122
algens, Hillia, 166
alia, Graphiphora, 204
alinda, Hylesia, 90
alisellana, Eulia, 423
allediusaria, Tetracis, 353
allegheniensis, Crambidia, 104
alleni, Syneda, 259
Allotria, genus; elonympha, 272
Almodes, genus; assecoma, balteolata, calvina, rivularia, squamigera, stellidaria terraria, 354
alni, Sthenopis, 443
alniaria, Ennomos, 348
alope, Erinnyis, 58
Alsophila, genus; pometaria, restituens, 326
alternata, Rhynchagrotis, 179
alticola, Syngrapha, 240
Alypia, genus, 143, 232; bimaculata, 144; brannani, 143; desperata, 144; dipsaci, 143; disparata, 143, 144; edwardsi, 143; gracilenta, 144; hudsonica, 145; langtoni, 143, 145; lorquini, mac-cullochi, 143; mariposa, 143, 145; matuta, 144; octomaculata, 143, 144; quadriguttalis, 144; ridingsi, 143, 145; sacraments, 145; similis, 143, wittfeldi, 143, 144
Alypiodes, genus; bimaculata, trimaculata 145
amasia, Catocala, 148, 268
amatrix, Catocala, 263
amaturaria, Erastria, 333
Ambesa, genus; lætella, 410
ambigua, Æmilia, 137
ambigualis Gaberasa, 284
Ambulycinæ, 41, 42, 54
Amelanchier, 386
amella, Campometra, 276
Ameria, genus, 327
americalis, Epizeuxis, 280
americana, Apatela, 153; Epicnaptera, 314; Harrisina, 372; Malacosoma, 312; Melalopha, 293; Neuronia, 196; Oreta, 321
amica, Catocala, 269
amicaria, Hyperitis, 349
amiculatalis, Cindaphia, 397
amœna, Melittia, 380
amœnaria, Euchlæna, 350
Amolita, genus; fessa, 244
Amorbia, genus; humerosana, 423
Amorpha fruticosa, 430
amorphella, Walshia, 430
ampelophaga, Pholus, 65
Ampelopsis, 66, 70, 72, 144, 371
Amphion, genus, 72; nessus, 72
amphipyroides, Latebraria, 279
ampla, Autographa, 240; Doa, 309
amplaria, Epimecis, 344
amplissima, Parallelia, 273
amplus, Axenus, 231
amputatrix, Hadena, 169
Amyna, genus; octo, orbica, tecta, 242

amyntor, Ceratomia, 47
amyrisaria, Caberodes, 352
Anacreon, Ode to an Insect, quoted, 291
Anal angle, 18
Anaphora, genus; agrotipennella, popeanella scardina, 443
Anaplodes, genus; iridaria, rectaria, 337
Anarsia, genus; lineatella, pruniella, 426
Anarta, genus; Black-mooned, Catocaline, cordigera, 198; curta, Dull Brown, impingens, leucocycla, 199; nigrolunata, 198; nivaria, perpura, richardsoni, Richardson's, schœnherri, Schœnherr's, 199
Anatomy of moths, 10
ancetaria, Azelina, 352
anchocelioides, Rhynchagrotis, 178
Anchocelis, genus; digitalis, 216
ancocisconensis, Hyppa, 171
Ancylis, genus; fragariæ, comptana, conflexana, 419
andremona, Hypocala, 272
Andrewsia, genus; belfragiana, jocasta, messalina, 272
andromache, Catocala, 267
andromedæ, Hyloicus, 50
Anepischetos, genus; bipartita, 245
angelica, Apatelodes, 293; Copibryophila, 162
anguina, Dasylophia, 296; Mamestra, 195
angulalis, Palthis, 285
angulidens, Autographa, 239
angulifera, Callosamia, 86
angulosa, Lophodonta, 295
angusi, Catocala, 262; Datana, 293
angustalis, Zinckenia, 392
angustiorata, Caripeta, 342
angustipennis, Magusa, 175
Ania, genus; filimentaria, limbata, resistaria, vestitaria, 349
anilis, Agnomonia, 274
Anisota, genus, 94; astymone, pellucida, rubicunda, 95; senatoria, stigma, 94; Virginian, 95; virginiensis, 94, 95
aniusaria, Cymatophora, 340
anna, Apantesis, 130
Annaphila, genus; diva, lithosina, 246
annexa, Feltia, 187
annisaria, Cymatophora, 340
annulifascia, Halisidota, 138
anodonta, Conservula, 215
Anomis, genus; erosa, 244
Anona laurifolia, 236
anonæ, Cocytius, 44
Anomœotes, genus, 371
Anorthodes, genus; prima, 164
antæus, Cocytius, 44
Antaplaga, genus; dimidiata, 220
Antennæ, 3, 4, 13, 18; of Eriocephalid larvæ, 8; of Telea polyphemus, 13
antennata, Xylina, 206
anthœcioides, Tosale, 402
Antiblemma, genus; canalis, inexacta, 275
antica, Euchætias, 135; Trichoclea, 199
Anticarsia, genus; gemmatilis, 275
antigone, Estigmene, 123
antinympha, Catocala, 267
antiphola, Halisidota, 137
antiqua, Notolophus, 306
Ants, 147
Anytus, genus; Obscure, obscurus, privatus, Sculptured, sculptus, 191
Aon, genus; noctuiformis, 234
Apæcasia, genus; defluata, subæquaria, 342
Apantesis, genus, 129; achaia, anna, arge, 130; arizonensis, autholea, 131; b-atra, 132; behri, blakei, bolanderi, 131; ceramica, 132; cœlebs, 130; colorata, 132;

Apantesis—*Continued*
complicata, dahurica, 131; decolorata, determinata, diecki, 132; dione, 130; docta, 131; dodgei, 132; doris, edwardsi, 130; excelsa, favorita, figurata, f-pallida, 132; gelida, 131; incarnatorubra, 130; incompleta, 132; incorrupta, 131; intermedia, 129; liturata, 131; lugubris, 132; mexicana, 131; michabo, minea, 130; mormonica, 131; nais, 132; nerea, 130; nevadensis, 131; ochracea, 130; oithona, 129; ornata, 130; otiosa, 131; parthenice, 129; persephone, 130; phalerata, 132; proxima, quenseli, 131; radians, 132; rectilinea, 129; rhoda, 132; saundersi, 129; shastaensis, speciosa, strigosa, turbans, 131; virgo, 129; virguncula, 131; vittata, williamsi, 132
Apatela, genus, 153, 157, 197; acericola, aceris, 153; albarufa, 157; americana, 153; brumosa, 157; connecta, 156; dactylina, 153; fragilis, 156; furcifera, græfi, 155; grisea, 156; hasta, 155; impleta, impressa, inclara, 157; innotata, interrupta, 155; lepusculina, 154; lithospila, 156; lobeliæ, 155; luteicoma, 157; morula, 155; noctivaga, oblinita, 157; obscura, 153; occidentalis, 155; populi, 154; pudorata, quadrata, 156; salicis, 157; spectans, superans, 156; telum, ulmi, 155; vinnula, 156
Apatelodes, genus; angelica, hyalinopuncta 293; torrefacta, 292
Apex of wing, 18
Apical patch, 18
apicalis, Melalopha, 293
apicella, Fruva, 252
apicosa, Eustrotia, 247
apiformis, Ægeria, 383
Apharetra, genus; dentata, 158; pyralis, Smith's, 159; Toothed, 158
Apocheima, genus; rachelæ, 345
Aporophila, genus, 170
Apple-leaf Skeletonizer, The, 411
Apple-leaf Tier, The Green, 421
aprica, Tarache, 251
aquamarina, Drasteria, 257
aquilonaris, Harpyia, 299
Arachnis, genus; aulæa, incarnata, Painted, picta, zuni, 124
aracinthusalis, Palthis, 285
aratrix, Richia, 190
arbeloides, Inguromorpha, 378
arburaria, Caberodes, 352
arcasaria, Sabulodes, 353
Archips, genus; arcticana, argyrospila, cerasivorana, furvana, gossypiana, gurgitans, lintnerana, parallela, purpurana, rosaceana vicariana, v-signatana, 422
arcifera, Schinia, 228
Arctia, genus, 114, 134; auripennis, caia transmontana, utahensis, wiskotti, 134
arctica, Hadena, 169
arcticana, Archips, 422
Arctiidæ, 24, 31, 114
Arctonotus, genus, 71; lucidus, terlooi, 71
Arctostaphylos tomentosa, 89
arcuata, Drepana, 321; Hadena, 167
arefactaria, Euchlæna, 350
arge, Apantesis, 130
argentata, Halisidota, 138; Sthenopis, 443
argentatus, Euclea, 365
argenteomaculatus, Sthenopis, 443
argenteostriata, Phrygionis, 354
argillacea, Alabama, 243; Lexis, 105
argillacearia, Cymatophora, 341
Argillophora, genus; furcilla, 255
argus, Automeris, 89

argyrospila, Archips, 422
arizonæ, Gnophæla, 290
arizonaria, Chloraspilates, 338
arizonensis, Apantesis, 131; Gloveria, 311
armata, Fota, 178
armataria, Priocycla, 351
armiger, Heliothis, 222
armillata, Hypocrisias, 136
Army Worm, The, 200
Army Worm, The Fall, 174
Aroa, genus, 305
arrogaria, Plagodis, 349
arrosa, Trama, 276
arsaltealis, Pyrausta, 307
Arsilonche, genus; albovenosa, colorada, 159
Artace, genus; punctistriga, rubripalpis, 312
artemis, Hemileuca, 92
arvalis, Axenus, 231
Asclepias, 135, 437
asdrubal, Pseudosphinx, 57
Ashmead, William H., viii.
Asimina triloba 46
asopialis, Palthis, 285
aspersa, Alexicles, 122
aspilata, Tetracis, 353
assecoma, Almodes, 354
assimilis, Euthisanotia, 232; Trichotarache, 246
associans, Noctua, 185
associata, Heterocampa, 297
astarte, Heterocampa, 297; Sphinx, 55
asteroides, Cucullia, 208
Asteroscopus, genus; borealis, 209.
astricta, Peridroma, 182
astur, Opharus, 139
astylus, Calasymbolus, 56
astylusaria, Euchlæna, 350
astymone, Anisota, 95
aterrima, Pachylia, 60
Atethmia, genus; rectifascia, subusta, 220
athabasca, Syneda, 260
athasiaria, Therina, 348
athena, Estigmene, 123
athereo, Heterocampa, 297
atomaria, Phoberia, 273; Ogdoconta, 241
atra, Heliotropha, 173
Atreides, genus, 49; plebeja, 49
Atreus, genus, 49
atriciliata, Platysenta, 163
atricincta, Noctua, 184
atrifasciata, Cleora, 344; Oncocnemis, 176
atripennis, Dahana, 103
atrites, Schinia, 228
atrivenosa, Olene, 308
atrocolorata, Azelina, 352; Eustroma, 329
atroliturata, Cladora, 324
atropunctata, Catopyrrha, 342
atropurpurea, Euxoa, 189
Attacinæ, 80, 81
Atteva, genus; aurea, compta, fastuosa, floridana, gemmata, 424
auge, Cosmosoma, 98
augusta, Catocala, 264
aulæa, Arachnis, 124
aurantiaca, Incita, 246
aurea, Atteva, 424; Dysodia, 375
aurella, Catocala, 266
aureola, Synanthedon, 385
aureopurpurea, Synanthedon, 387
auricinctaria, Melanomma, 255
auriferaria, Palyas, 354
auripennis, Arctia, 134; Siavana, 273
aurivitta, Cydosia, 253
aurora, Hyparpax, 299
aurosea, Automeris, 89
aurotus, Philosamia, 82
australis, Baileya, 162

Index

autholea, Apantesis, 131
Autographa, genus 237; ampla, 240; angulidens, 239; basigera, 240; biloba, bimaculata, brassicæ, culta, dyaus, echinocystis,
egena, flagellum, fratella, hamifera, includens, 238; indigna, 239; insolita, 238;
laticlavia, 240; monodon, 238; mortuorum,
239; omega, omicron, oo, ou, 238; oxygramma, 239; precationis, pseudogamma, questionis, 238; rectangula, 239; rogationis,
rutila, 238; selecta, 239; simplex, 240;
u-brevis, 238; vaccinii, 239; verruca, 238;
viridisignata, 239
Automeris, genus, 89; argus, aurosea, corollaria, fabricii, io, pamina, varia, zelleri,
zephyria, 89
autumnata, Paleacrita, 324
autumnalis, Hydriomena, 331; Laphygma,
174
autumnaria, Ennomos, 348
avimacula, Gluphisia, 300
avuncularia, Dasyfidonia, 338
Axenus, genus; amplus, arvalis, ochraceus,
231
axillaris, Hæmorrhagia, 63
Aye-Aye, 77
azaleæ, Darapsa, 68
Azelina, genus; ancetaria, atrocolorata,
honestaria, hubneraria, hubnerata, morrisonata, peplaria, stygiaria, 352
Azenia genus; implora, 248

B

babayaga, Catocala, 263
badia, Catocala, 267; Schizura, 299
badicollis, Semiophora, 180
badinodis, Agrotis, 181
badipennis, Pyrausta, 397
badistriga, Homohadena, 176
Bad-wing, The, 323
Bag-worm, The, 361
Bailey, J. S., 36
Baileya, genus; australis, doubledayi, ophthalmica, 162
baileyi, Xylina, 207
balanitis, Chorizagrotis, 185
balluca, Plusia, 237
baltearia, Alcis, 343
balteolata, Almodes, 354
baltimoralis, Bomolocha, 286
Balsa, genus; malana, obliquifera, 163
Barathra, genus; curialis, occidentata, 196
barberiana, Epipyrops, 370
Barnes, Dr. William, ix
barometricus, Ufeus, 191
Basal dash, 18; line, 18
basalis, Catocala, 261 268; Euxoa, 189;
Inguromorpha, 378
basiflava, Olene, 308
basigera, Autographa, 240
basilinea, Hadena, 168
Basilodes, genus; pepita, 234
Basilona, genus; imperatoria, imperialis
punctatissima, 97
basitriens, Notodonta, 295
bassiformis, Synanthedon, 385
b-atra, Apantesis, 132
Bats, 147
beani, Phragmatobia, 126
beata, Noctua, 185
Bee-moth, The, 406
Beggar, The, 327
behrensaria, Deilinea, 339
Behrensia, genus; conchiformis, 241
behri, Apantesis, 131
belæ, Didasys, 99

belfragiana, Andrewsia, 272
belfragei, Holomelina, 116
bella, Adela, 437; Utetheisa, 117
belladonna, Dysocnemis, 229
bellicula, Lithacodia, 248
bellulalis, Pyrausta, 398
Bellura, genus; densa, gostynides, melanopyga, vulnifica, 211
belmaria, Holomelina, 116
Beloved, The, 265
Bembecia, genus; flavipes, marginata, odyneripennis, pleciæformis, rubi, 383
benignalis, Bomolocha, 286
beskei, Crinodes, 301
Bessula, genus; luxa, 221
bertholdi, Hypopta, 379
Bertholdia, genus; Grote's, trigona, 140
Betrothed, The, 265
betulella, Acrobasis, 408
Beutenmuller, W. 31, 32, 36, 380
beutenmulleri, Isochætes, 366
bianca, Catocala, 262
bibularia, Therina, 348
bicarnea, Noctua, 183
biclaria, Syssaura, 352
bicolor, Adelocephala, 96; Diacrisia, 128,
Lexis, 105
bicolorago, Orthosia, 217
bicoloralis, Cindaphia, 397
bicoloraria, Chloraspilates, 338
bicolorata, Eufidonia, 337; Hydriomena,
331; Neleucania, 203
bidentata, Nerice, 296
biferalis, Hypenula, 283
bifidalis, Gaberasa, 284
biguttata, Cochlidion, 367
bijugalis, Bomolocha, 286
bilineata, Falcaria, 321; Heterocampa, 297
biliturellus, Crambus, 403
biloba, Autographa, 238
bilunata, Caradrina, 164
bimaculata, Alypia, 144; Alypiodes, 145;
Autographa, 238; Holomelina, 116
bimatris, Pippona, 221
binocula, Tarache, 251
bipartita, Anepischetos, 245
biplaga, Eustrotia, 247
bipunctellus, Crambus, 402
bipunctina, Alabama, 243
birivata, Hydriomena, 331
biselliella, Tineola, 432
biseriata, Eudule, 327
bisselliella, Tineola, 432
bistriaris, Doryodes, 245; Parallelia, 273
biundata Heterocampa, 297
bivittata, Ectypia, 133; Hormisa, 282
Black, The Californian, The White-striped,
328; Woodland, 329
blakei, Apantesis, 131
blanda, Pseudoglæa, 216
Blastobasidæ, 26, 429
Bleptina, genus; caradrinalis, cloniasalis, 283
bœrhaviæ, Xylophanes, 75
Boisduval, J. A., 30
bolanderi, Apantesis, 131
bolli, Synanthedon, 385
Boll-worm, The, 222
bolteri, Æmilia, 137; Euchætias, 135
Bombycia, genus; improvisa, tearli, 304
Bombycidæ, Family, 12, 25, 34, 315
bombyciformis, Eutolype, 177
bombycina, Acrolophus, 443
bombycoides, Lapara, 53
Bombyx, genus; mori, 315
Bomolocha, genus; abalinealis, achatinalis,
albisignalis, baltimoralis, benignalis, bijugalis, caducalis, damnosalis, deceptalis,

Bomolocha—*Continued*
edictalis, fecialis, laciniosa, lentiginosa, madefactalis, manalis, pallialis, perangulalis, profecta, scutellaris, toreuta, vellifera, 286
Books about North American Moths, 27
borealis, Asteroscopus, 209; Harpyia, 290; Hemerocampa, 306; Hyphoraia, 128
Borer, The Peach-twig, 426
Bouvardia, 75
brannani, Alypia, 143
brassicæ, Autographa, 238
Breeding larvæ, 5
Brephinæ, Subfamily, 355
Brephos, genus; infans, 355
brevis, Schinia, 228
brevicornis, Holomelina, 116
brevipennis, Euxoa, 188
Bride, The, 266
bridghami, Hadena, 166
brillians, Eupseudomorpha, 231
briseis, Catocala, 264
British Museum, Trustees, ix
brontes, Ceratomia, 48
Brooke, Henry, quoted, 321
Brother, The, 153
Brotolomia, genus; iris, 215
Browning, E. B., quoted, 21, 378
Brown-tail Moth, The, 309
bruceata, Rachela, 324
brucei, Cossus, 377; Hæmorrhagia, 64; Phragmatobia, 126; Schinia, 227
Bruceia, genus; hubbardi, pulverina, 108
brumosa, Apatela, 157
brunnea, Ctenucha, 102
brunneiciliata, Mesoleuca, 330
brunneipennis, Synanthedon, 385
Bryant, W. C., quoted, 113
Bucculatrix, genus; Apple-leaf, Birch-leaf, canadensiselia, curvilineatella, pomifoliella, pomonella, 431
Buck-moth, 91; Nevada, 92; Tricolor, 93
Budgeon, Miss, Acheta Domestica, quoted, 375
buffaloensis, Hæmorrhagia, 63
bullula, P7erætholix, 243
burgessi, Hadena, 168
Busck, A., 38
Butler, A. G., 30
"Butterfly Book, The," 4
Byron, quoted, 309

C

Caberodes, genus; amyrisaria, arburaria, confusaria, floridaria, imbraria, ineffusaria, interlinearia, majoraria, myandaria, pandaria, phasianaria, remissaria, superaria, varadaria, 352
Cable, G. W., quoted, 80; 314
cacuminalis, Hypenula, 283
cadaverosa, Hypoprepia, 106
cadmia, Cargida, 300
caducalis, Bomolocha, 286
cæca, Turuptiana, 121
cælaria, Xanthotype, 349
Cænurgia, genus; adversa, convalescens, purgata, socors, 257
cærulea, Drasteria, 257
cæsonia, Tortricidia, 368
cahiritella, Ephestia, 414
caia, Arctia, 134
caicus, Erinnyis, 60
calaminea, Ophideres, 276
calasymbolus, genus, 55; astylus, excæcatus, integerrima, io, myops, pavonina, rosacearum, 56

Calesesia, genus; coccinea, 387
calgary, Noctua, 184
Calidota, genus; cubensis, laqueata, muricolor, Streaked, strigosa, 139
californiæ, Leptarctia, 121
californiaria, Eois, 336; Platea, 342
californiata, Eois, 336; Euchœca, 328; Philereme, 329
californica, Catocala, 263; Estigmene, 123; Hemileuca, 92; Malacosoma, 313; Orrhodia, 218; Pheosia, 295; Phryganidia, 291; Samia, 84
californicus, Melicleptria, 230
Calledapteryx, genus; dryopterata, erosiata 356
calleta, Callosamia, 86
callitrichoides, Phiprosopus 245
Callizia, genus, 356
Callopistria, genus; floridensis, 252
Callosamia, genus, 84; angulifera, calleta, 86; promethea, 84
Calocampa, genus, 207; curvimacula, nupera, 208
Calophasia, genus; strigata, 170
Calpe, genus; canadensis, Canadian, purpurascens, sobria, 236
calvina, Almodes, 354
Calymnia, genus; canescens, orina, 219
cambrica, Venusia, 328
"Cambridge Natural History," 17
campestris, Euxoa, 189
Campometra, genus; amella, integerrima, mima, stylobata, 276
cana, Clemensia, 108; Dasylophia, 296; Hemerocampa, 306; Lapara, 53
canadaria, Melanolophia, 344
canadensis, Calpe, 236; Celerio, 76; Hyloicus 51
canadensisella, Bucculatrix, 431
canalis, Antiblemma, 275
Canarsia, genus; hammondi, 411
candens, Orthodes, 203
canescens, Calymnia, 219
Canidia, genus; scissa, 226
caniplaga, Ellida, 300
Canker-worm, The Fall, 326; The Spring, 324
canningi, Philosamia, 82
Capis, genus; curvata, 285
Capnodes, genus; punctivena, 277
caprotina, Estigmene, 123
capsella, Graphiphora, 204
capticola, Syneda, 259
Capture of specimens, 19
cara, Catocala, 148, 263
Caradrina, genus; bilunata, 164; civica conviva, extimia, 165; fidicularia, meralis, multifera, 164; punctivena, rufostriga, spilomela, 165
caradrinalis, Bleptina, 283
Carama, genus; cretata, pura, 368
carbonaria, Eurycyttarus, 362; Homoglæa, 219
Cargida, genus; cadmia, obliquilinea, 300 pyrrha, 301
Carica, 58
caricæ, Cocytius, 44
carina, Acopa, 163
Caripeta, genus; albopunctata, angustiorata divisata, piniaria, 342
Carlyle, Thomas, quoted, 210
Carmen, Felix, quoted, 427
carnaria, Metanema, 351
Carnegie, Andrew, Dedication to, v
Carneades, genus, 188
carneola, Eustrotia, 247
carolina, Catocala, 261; Eucereon, 100; Haploa, 118; Protoparce, 45

Carpenter-worms, 375
Carpet-moth, The, 434
carpinifolia, Epicnaptera, 314
Carter, Sir Gilbert T., 54
caryæ, Halisidota, 138
Case-bearer, The Walnut, 408
casta, Crambidia, 104
castellalis, Samea, 393
Castniidæ, 3, 4
Catabena, genus; lineolata, miscellus, 163
Catalogues and Lists, 29
catalpæ, Ceratomia, 48
cataphracta, Papaipema, 214
catenaria, Cingilia, 347
Caterpillars, 6; Coloration of, 9; gregarious, 9
catharina, Semiophora, 180
Catocala, genus, 79, 147, 148, 260; abbreviatella, 268; adoptiva, 267; agrippina, 260;
   aholah, 268; aholibah, 265; alabamæ, 269;
   amasia, 268; amatrix, 263; amica, 269
   andromache, 267; angusi, 262; antinympha,
   267; augusta, 264; aurella, 266; babayaga,
   263; badia, 267; basalis, 261, 268; bianca,
   262; briseis, 264; californica, cara, 263;
   carolina, 261; celia, 265; cerogama, 266;
   cleopatra, 263; coccinata, 263; cœlebs,
   268; concumbens, 263; consors, 266;
   cratægi, 268; dejecta, 261; delilah, 267;
   desdemona, 267; desperata, 261; eliza,
   266; epione, 260; evelina, 261; faustina,
   264; flebilis, 262; formula, 268; fratercula,
   gisela, gracilis, 269; groteiana, 264; grynea,
   269; guenei, 261; habilis, 268; hermia,
   264; hinda, 266; ilia, 265; illecta, 267;
   innubens, 265; insolabilis, 262; jaquenetta,
   269; judith, 262; lacrymosa, 261; lineella,
   269; luciana, 263; mæstosa, 261; magdalena,
   267; marmorata, 263; meskei, 264; minuta,
   269; mopsa, 265; muliercula, 267; nebraskæ,
   263; nebulosa, neogama, 266; nerissa,
   269; nurus, 263; obscura, 262; olivia, 269;
   osculata, 265; palæogama, 266; parta,
   264; paulina, 261; phalanga, piatrix, 266;
   polygama, 268; præclara, 269; pura, 264;
   relicta, retecta, robinsoni, 262; rosalinda,
   268; sappho, 260; scintillans, 266; serena,
   267; similis, 268; somnus, stretchi, 263;
   subnata, 266; subviridis, 261; tristis, 262;
   ultronia, 265; unijuga, 264; uxor, verrilliana, 265; vidua, viduata, 261; whitneyi,
   268
Catopyrrha, genus; accessaria, atropunctaria,
   coloraria, cruentaria, dissimilaria, 342
caudata, Alcothoe, 382
cautella, Ephestia, 414
Cautethia, genus, 61; grotei, 61
ceanothi, Samia, 84
Ceanothus thyrsiflorus, 84
cecropia, Samia, 83, 84
Celama, genus; nigrofasciata, obaurata,
   pustulata, sexmaculata, trinotata, triquetrana, 357
Celerio, genus, 75; canadensis, chamænerii,
   daucus, epilobii, galii, intermedia, lineata
   oxybaphi, 76
celeus, Protoparce, 45
celia, Catocala, 265
Celiptera, genus; discissa, elongatus, frustulum, 275
Cenopis, genus; groteana, pettitana, 422
centerensis, Cossus, 377
cephalica, Crambidia, 104; Stylopoda, 229
cephise, Melanchroia, 354
ceramica, Apantesis, 132
Cerapoda, genus; stylata, 177
cerasivorana, Archips, 422
Cerathosia, genus; tricolor, 253

Ceratocampidæ, Family, 24, 31, 70, 80, 94
Ceratomia, genus, 47; amyntor, 47; brontes
   48; catalpæ, 48; quadricornis, 47; repentinus, 48; ulmi, 47; undulosa, 48
Cercis, 369
cereana, Galleria, 406
cerella, Galleria, 406
cerintha, Chamyris, 250
Cerisyi, Sphinx, 54
cerivana, Hadena, 168
Cerma, genus; cora, festa, 161
cerogama, Catocala, 266
ceromatica, Scopelosoma, 218
cerussata, Papaipema, 214; Phrygionis, 354
Cerura, genus; multiscripta, scitiscripta, 209
cervina, Euherrichia, 253
ceto, Melittia, 380
Chalcosiidæ, Family, 373
chamænerii, Celerio, 76
Chambers, V. T., 37
Chamyris, genus; cerintha, 250
chandleri, Oncocnemis, 176
Chapman, T. A., 8
characta, Hadena, 167
Charadra, genus; circulifer, contigua, 152,
   decora, 153; deridens, 152; dispulsa,
   felina, 153; illudens, python, 152
chenopodii, Mamestra, 193
chersis, Hyloicus, 50
chionanthi, Adita, 177; Protoparce, 45
Chionanthus, 46, 51
chiridota, Lacosoma, 359
Chlænogramma, Genus, 46; jasminearum
   rotundata, 46
Chloraspilates, genus; arizonaria, bicoloraria, 338
Chloridea, genus; rhexiæ, spectanda, virescens, 222
chloris, Euclea, 365
Chlorochlamys, genus; chloroleucaria, densaria, deprivata, indiscriminaria, 336
chloroleucaria, Chlorochlamys, 336
chlorostigma, Hadena, 168
Chœphora, genus; fungorum, 216
chœrilus, Darapsa, 68
Chœrocampinæ, Subfamily, 75
choriona, Holomelina, 116
Chorizagrotis, genus; balanitis, inconcinna
   introferens, 185
Chrysauginæ, Subfamily, 401
chrysellus, Schinia, 227
chrysorrhœa, Euproctis, 309
Chytolita, genus; morbidalis, 282
Chytonix, genus; iaspis, palliatricula, 161
cibalis, Oncocnemis, 176
Cicinnus, genus; egenaria, melsheimeri, 359
Cilla, genus; distema, 244
cimbiciformis, Hæmorrhagia, 63
Cindaphia, genus; amiculatalis, bicoloralis,
   incensalis, julialis, pulchripictalis, 397
cinerascens, Heterocampa, 297
cinerea, Epidemas, 170; Harpyia, 299;
   Misogada, 297; Xylina, 206
cinereofrons, Schizura, 298
cinereola, Ogdoconta, 241; Selicanis, 216
cinereomaculata, Euxoa, 190
cinereus, Prodoxus, 441
cinerosa, Erinnyis, 59
Cingilia, genus; catenaria, humeralis, 347
cingulata, Herse, 43
cingulifera, Homoptera, 278
cinis, Melipotis, 258
cinnamomea, Æmilia, 137; Olene, 308
circulifer, Charadra, 152
Ciris, genus; wilsoni, 233
Cirrhobolina, genus; deducta, incandescens,
   pavitensis, mexicana, 259

Cirrhophanus, genus; triangulifer, 234
Cissusa, genus; inepta, morbosa, sabulosa, spadix, vegeta, 256
Cisthene lactea, 108
Citheronia, genus; mexicana, regalis, regia, sepulchralis, 97
citrina, Xanthotype, 349
citronellus, Rhodophora, 224
civica, Caradrina, 165
Cladora, genus; atroliturata, geminata, 324
clandestina, Gluphisia, 300; Noctua, 184
clappiana, Gnophæla, 290
clarkiæ, Proserpinus, 73
clarus, Comacla, 107
Classification of moths, 22
claudens, Hadena, 167
clavana, Eucosma, 418
claviform spot, 18
claviformis, Pachnobia, 180
claviplena, Mamestra, 192
Clearwing, Bruce's, 64; Californian, 64; Graceful, 63; Humming-bird, 62; Snowberry, 63; Thetis, 64
clemataria, Abbotana, 353
Clematis, 382
Clemens, Brackenridge, 28, 30, 37
Clemensia, genus; albata, albida, cana, irrorata, patella, philodina, umbrata, 108
cleopatra, Catocala, 263
Cleora, genus; atrifasciata, collecta, fraudulentaria, frugallaria, pampinaria, sublunaria, tinctaria, 344
Cleosiris, genus; populi, 205
clientis, Yrias, 277
clio, Euverna, 133
cloniasalis, Bleptina, 283
clorinda, Darapsa, 68
Clothes-moth, The, 432, 434
clotho, Pholus, 67
Clover-hay Worm, The, 399
clymene, Haploa, 118
c-nigrum, Noctua, 183
cnotus, Darapsa, 68
coa, Pinconia, 369
coagulata, Tephroclystis, 328
coccinata, Catocala, 149, 265
coccinea, Calesesia, 387; Ptychoglene, 110
coccineifascia, Prothymia, 248
Cochlidiidæ, Family, 8, 9, 25, 35, 364
Cochlidion, genus; biguttata, rectilinea tetraspilaris, y-inversa, 367
cochrani, Euxoa, 189
Cocytius, genus, 44; anonæ; antæus; caricæ; hydaspus; jatrophæ; medor; tapayusa, 44
Coddling-moth, The, 419
cœlebs, Apantesis, 130; Catocala, 268
Cœnocalpe, genus; costinotata, fervifactaria, gibbocostata, œneiformis, strigularia, 332
cognata, Xylomiges, 197
cognataria, Lycia, 345
Collar lappet, 18
collaris, Noctua, 184
collecta, Cleora, 344
colona, Haploa, 118
colorada, Arsilonche, 159
coloradaria, Epiplatymetra, 351
coloradensis, Prodoxus, 440; Raphia 153
Coloradia, genus, 90, 91; pandora, 91
coloradus, Hyloicus, 52
coloraria, Catopyrrha, 342
colorata, Apantesis, 132
columbia, Samia, 84
Comacla, genus; clarus, fuscipes, murina, simplex, texana, 107
comma, Haploa, 118
commelinæ, Prodenia, 174
commoides, Heliophila, 203

Commophila, genus; macrocarpana, 423
complicata, Apantesis, 131; Heliophila, 201
Composia, genus; fidelissima, olympia, 289
Compositæ, 101, 252
compressipalpis, Plusiodonta, 235
compta, Atteva, 424
comptana, Ancylis, 419
comptaria, Venusia, 328
Comstock, J. H., 29
comstocki, Momophana, 172
conchiformis, Behrensia, 241
Conchylodes, genus; concinnalis, erinalis magicalis, ovulalis, platinalis, 393
concinna, Schizura, 298
concinnalis, Conchylodes, 393
concinnimacula, Eustrotia, 247
concisa, Epizeuxis, 280
concisaria, Euchlæna, 350
concumbens, Catocala, 263
concursana, Platynota, 422
condensata, Venusia, 328
confederata, Eurycyttarus, 363
confine, Eucereon, 100
conflexana, Ancylis, 419
confluens Graphiphora, 204
confusa, Haploa, 119; Morrisonia, 197
confusaria, Caberodes, 352
congermana, Mamestra, 193
congrua, Estigmene, 123
coniferarum, Hyloicus, 52; Lapara 53; Thyridopteryx, 361
Coniodes, genus; plumigeraria, 345
conjungens, Crambodes, 163
connecta, Apatela, 156
consecutaria, Eois, 335
consepta, Macaria, 340
Conservula, genus; anodonta, 215
consimilis, Synanthedon, 385
consita, Haploa, 118
consors, Catocala, 266
Consort, The, 266
conspicua, Drasteria, 257; Hadena. 168· Rœselia, 358
conspecta, Schizura, 298
constipata, Mamestra, 195
contenta, Hadena, 169
contexta, Euchalcia, 237
contigua, Charadra, 152; Haploa, 119
contingens, Sabulodes, 353
continua, Gnophæla, 290
contracta, Homopyralis, 256; Schinia 228
contrahens, Himella, 204
contraria, Hyppa, 171; Mamestra, 193
contribuaria, Melanolophia, 344
convalescens, Cænurgia, 257
convexipennis, Cucullia, 208
conviva, Caradrina, 165
Convolvulaceæ, 99
convolvuli, Herse, 43
coörtaria, Cymatophora, 341
copablepharon, genus; album, grandis longipenne, 222
Copibryophila, genus; angelica, 162
Copicucullia, genus; propinqua, 208
Copidryas, genus, 141; cosyra, 142; gloveri 141
Copipanolis, genus; cubilis, 177
Coquillet, D. W., 346
cora, Cerma, 161
coracias, Pseudanthracia, 278
cordigera, Anarta, 198
Cornifrons, genus; simalis, 399
Corn-stalk Borer, The Larger, 403
cornuta, Metalepsis, 181
corollaria, Automeris, 89
Cortissoz, Ellen Mackay Hutchinson, quoted, 310

Index

Cosmia, genus; discolor, infumata, paleacea, 217
Cosmosoma, genus; auge, melitta, omphale, 98
Cossidæ, Family, 25, 35, 375
Cossula, genus; magnifica, norax, 379
Cossus, genus; brucei, centerensis, undosus, 377
costæmaculalis, Noctuelia, 399
costalis, Hypsopygia, 399
costinotata, Cœnocalpe, 332
Cosymbia, genus; lumenaria, pendulinaria quadriannulata, 333
cosyra, Copidryas, 142
Cotton-worm, 243
Cowper, quoted, 369
Coxa, 14, 15
crabroniformis, Ægeria, 383
Crambidia, genus; allegheniensis, casta cephalica, lithosioides, pallida, uniformis, 104
Crambinæ, Subfamily, 402
Crambodes, genus; conjungens, talidiformis 163
Crambus, genus; alboclavellus, 402; biliturellus, 403; bipunctellus, 402; exsiccatus, interminellus, 403; laqueatellus, semifusellus, 402; trisectus, 403; turbatellus 402
crameri, Erinnyis, 59; Pachylia, 60
crantor, Pholus, 66
crassatus, Plathypena, 287
crassipes, Podagra, 178
crassiuscula, Drasteria, 257
cratægi, Catocala, 268
Cratægus, 62
crenulata, Orthodes, 203
crepuscularia, Ectropis, 344
cressonana, Ctenucha, 102
Cressonia, genus; 57; instabilis, juglandis pallens, robinsoni, 57
cretata, Carama, 368
crinella, Tineola, 432
Crinodes, genus; beskei, 301
crispata, Lagoa, 369
crocallata, Tetracis, 353
crocataria, Xanthotype, 349
crocea, Pseudanarta, 175
Crocigrapha, genus; normani, 204
Crocota, genus, 115
crœsus, Xylophanes, 75
crotchi, Pseudalypia, 232; Trichosellus, 226
Croton, 417
crucialis, Xylomiges, 197
Cruciferæ, 239
cruentaria, Catopyrrha, 342
crustaria, Pseudacontia, 225
Ctenucha, genus, 101; brunnea, cressonana, latreillana, multifaria, rubroscapus, 102; venosa, 101; virginica, walsinghami, 102
cubensis, Calidota, 139
cubilis, Copipanolis, 177
cuculifera, Dasylophia, 296
Cucullia, genus; Asteroid, asteroides, Brown-bordered, convexipennis, intermedia, Intermediate, speyeri, Speyer's, 208
cucurbitæ, Melittia, 380
culea, Graphiphora, 204
culta, Autographa, 238
cumatilis, Schinia, 227
cunea, Hyphantria, 123
cupes, Trichosellus, 226
cupida, Rhynchagrotis, 178
Cupid's Candle, 427
cupressi, Isoparce, 48
Cupuliferæ, 366
curialis, Barathra, 196

curta, Anarta, 199
curvata, Capis, 285
curvilineatella, Bucculatrix, 431
curvimacula, Calocampa, 208
Custard-apple, 236
custodiata, Hydriomena, 331
Cyathissa, genus; Darling, pallida, percara 161
cycladata, Heliomata, 338
Cydia, genus; pomonella, 419; saltitans, 418
Cydosia, genus; aurivitta, imitella, majuscula, 253
Cymatophora, genus; aniusaria, annisaria, 340; argillacearia, coortaria, 341; grossulariata, 340; inceptaria, modestaria, perarcuata, 341; ribearia, sigmaria, 340; successaria, tenebrosata, 341
cymatophoroides, Pseudothyatira, 304
cynica, Orthodes, 203
cynthia Philosamia, 81, 82

D

dactylina, Apatela, 153
dædalus, Porosagrotis, 187
Dagger (Dagger-moth), American, 153; Burglar, 157; Chieftain, Connected, 156; Cottonwood, 154; Darkish, Dart, 155; Delightful, 156; Fingered, 153; Forked, 155; Fragile, 156; Frosty, 157; Gray, 156; Interrupted, Lobelia, 155; Lupine, 159; Printed, 157; Quadrate, 156; Reddish-white, Smeared, 157; Streaked, 156; Unmarked, 155; White-veined, 159; Yellow-haired, 157
Dahana, genus; atripennis, 103
Dahlia hesperioides, 3
dahurica, Apantesis, 131
Dalceridæ, Family, 25, 35, 369
Dalcerides, genus; ingenita, 369
dama, Spraguea, 252
damalis, Eutolype, 177
damnosalis, Bomolocha, 286
danbyi, Gluphisia, 300
Dandy, The, 153
Darapsa, genus, 68; azaleæ, chœrilus, clorinda, cnotus, myron, pampinatrix, pholus 68; versicolor, 69
Dargida, genus; procinctus, 196
Daritis, genus; thetis, 289
Dark, World of the, 77
Dart (Dart-moth), Acorn, 185; Added, 187; Basal, 189; Black-fronted, 180; Black-girdled, 184; Black-letter, 183; Calgary, 184; Catocaline, 178; Clandestine, Collared, 184; Dædalus, 187; Dappled, 179; Dissonant, 189; Fillet, 190; Finland, 183; Flame-shouldered, 184; Fleece-winged, Four-toothed, 188; Furtive, 190; Fuscous, 187; Great Black, Great Brown, Great Gray, 182; Greater Red, Green-winged, 179; Havilah, 184; Inelegant, Interfering, 185; Lesser Red, 178; Masters, 186; Muddy, 189; Norman's, 183; Obelisk, 190; Old Man, 187; Olive, 188; Pale-banded, 181; Pale-winged, 183; Parental, 190; Pink-speckled, 185; Placid, 178; Polished, 188; Rascal, 187; Reaper, 188; Red-breasted, 178; Reddish-speckled, 180; Riley's, 187; Rosy, 183; Rubbed, 188; Scribbled, 184; Short-winged, 188; Sigmoid, 179; Silly, 189; Slippery, 185; Smaller Pinkish, 183; Soothsayer, 184; Subgothic, Swordsman, 186; Tessellate, Tippling, 189; Tripart, 187; Two-spot, 179; Uncivil, 183; Vancouver, 186; Variable, 180; Venerable, Voluble, 186; White-winged, 189; Yellow-bellied, 190; Yellow-streaked, 184; Yellow-toothed, 188; Ypsilon, 182

Darwin, quoted, 150
Dasyfidonia, genus; avuncularia, 338
Dasylophia, genus; anguina, cana, cuculifera, interna, punctata, signata, thyatiroides, tripartita, 296
Dasyspoudæa, genus; lucens, meadi, 228
Datana, genus; angusi, 293; integerrima, 294; ministra, 293; perspicua, 294
daucus, Celerio, 76
davisi, Halisidota, 137
dayi, Oncocnemis, 176
Day-sphinx, White-banded, 62
decepta, Pseudoglæa, 216
deceptalis, Bomolocha, 286
decernens, Feltia, 187
decia, Leptarctia, 121
decipiens, Malacosoma, 312; Prodoxus, 438; Zeuzera, 376
decisaria, Euchlæna, 350
declarata, Euxoa, 189
decliva, Epiglæa, 219
decolor, Euxoa, 189
decolora, Herse, 43
decolorata, Apantesis, 132
decora, Charadra, 153
decoralis, Pangrapta, 254
deducta, Cirrhobolina, 259
deductaria, Euchlæna, 350
definita, Hemerocampa, 308
deflorata, Ecpantheria, 120
defluata, Apæcasia, 342
Deidamia, genus, 71; inscriptum, 71
Deilinea, genus, 338; behrensaria, 339; intentata, variolaria, 338
dejecta, Catocala, 261
delecta, Tarache, 251
deleta, Epiglæa, 219
delicata, Trachea, 172
delilah, Catocala, 267
delinquens, Epidroma, 274
delphinii, Euclea, 365
Demas, genus; Close-banded, propinquilinea, 152
demissa, Mamestra, 194
densa, Bellura, 211
densaria, Chlorochlamys, 336
dentata, Apharetra, 158; Gloveria, 311
denticulalis, Epizeuxis, 281
dentifera, Eutelia, 242
denudata, Pseudohazis, 93
deplanaria, Euchlæna, 350
depontanata, Sabulodes, 353
Depressaria, genus; heracliana, heraclei, ontariella, pastinacella, umbellana, umbellella, 428
deprivata, Chlorochlamys, 336
deridens, Charadra, 152
Derrima, genus; henrietta, stellata, 224
descherei, Pheosia, 295
desdemona, Catocala, 267
deserta, Illice, 110
designalis, Agathodes, 393
designata, Gypsochroa, 332; Schinia, 228
Desmia, genus, funeralis, 392
desperata, Alypia, 144; Catocala, 261; Mamestra, 193
Destruction of insects by electric lights, 95
destructor, Tineola, 432
desuetella, Ephestia, 414
determinata, Apantesis, 132; Metanema, 351
detersa, Euxoa, 188
detracta, Mamestra, 192
detrahens, Trama, 276
Deva, genus, 236
devastatrix, Hadena, 169
devergens, Syngrapha, 240
devia, Scopelosoma, 218

Diacrisia, genus, 114, 127; bicolor, 128; fumosa, 127; latipennis, proba, punctata, pteridis, Red-legged, rubra, Ruddy, rufula, vagans, 128; virginica, 127; Wandering, 128
Diallagma, genus, lutea, 245
Diastema, genus; lineata, tigris, 241
Diastictis, genus; fracturalis, 393
Diatræa, genus; crambidoides, leucaniellus, lineosellus, obliteratellus, saccharalis, 403
Dictyosoma, genus, 48; elsa, 49
Didasys, genus; belæ, 99
diecki, Apantesis, 132
Diervilla, 63
diffascialis, Zinckenia, 392
diffinis, Hæmorrhagia, 63
diffissa, Pyrausta, 398
digitalis, Anchocelis, 216
Dilophonota, genus, 60
dilucidula, Semiophora, 180
dimidiata, Antaplaga, 220; Leptarctia, 121; Pheosia, 295; Pyromorpha, 371
diminutiva, Heliaca, 231; Holomelina, 116
dimmocki, Mamestra, 193
dione, Apantesis, 130
Dioptidæ, Family, 25, 33, 291
Diospyros, 87, 382
Diphthera, genus; fallax, 160
diphtheroides, Microcœlia, 160
dipsaci, Alypia, 143
Dipterygia, genus, scabriuscula, 172
Dircetis, genus; pygmæa, 284
dis, Grotella, 220
Discal mark, 18
discissa, Celiptera, 275
discistriga, Platyperigea, 164
discivaria, Parastichtis, 217
discolor, Cosmia, 217
discoloralis, Renia, 283
discopilata, Eufidonia, 337
discors, Hadena, 168
discreta, Gnophæla, 290
disertalis, Samea, 393
dispar, Porthetria, 308
disparata, Alypia, 143, 144
displiciens, Euxoa, 189
disposita, Xylina, 206
dispulsa, Charadra, 153
disserptaria, Epimecis, 344
dissidens, Magusa, 175
dissimilaria, Catopyrrha, 342
dissona, Euxoa, 189
disstria Malacosoma, 313
distema, Cilla, 244
distigma, Adelocephala, 96
distigmana, Eucosma, 418
diva, Annaphila, 246
divaricata, Magusa, 175
divergens, Lithacodes, 367; Schinia, 228; Syneda, 259; Syngrapha, 240
diversilineata, Eustroma, 329; Polia, 171
divida, Magusa, 175
divisa, Doryodes, 245
divisata, Caripeta, 342
Doa, genus; ampla, 309
docta, Apantesis, 131
dodgei, Apantesis, 132; Mamestra, 195
Dodia, genus; albertæ, 117
Dolba, genus, 46; hylæus, 46
Doll, Jacob, ix, 49
dolli, Hyloicus, 52
dolosa, Xylomiges, 197
domingonis, Erinnyis, 59
dominicata, Palindia, 273
doris, Apantesis, 130
dorsisignatana, Eucosma, 418
Doryodes, genus; acutaria, bistriaris, divisa, promptella, 245

Index

doubledayi, Baileya, 162
Double mount, 21
Drasteria, genus; agricola, aquamarina, cærulea, conspicua, crassiuscula, erechtea, erichto, mundula, narrata, patibilis, sobria, 257
Drepana, genus; arcuata, fabula, genicula, 321
Dried-currant Moth, The, 414
Druce, Herbert, 29
drupacearum, Malacosoma, 313
drupiferarum, Hyloicus, 52
druræi, Herse, 43
Dryobota, genus; illocata, stigmata, Wandering, 171
dryopterata, Calledapteryx, 356
duaria, Gonodontis, 350
dubia, Estigmene, 123
dubiella, Tinea, 433
dubitans, Hadena, 168
dubitata, Triphosa, 331
ducta, Hadena, 169
dulcearia, Platea, 343
dunbari, Litholomia, 207
duodecimlineata, Venusia, 328
duplicata, Sciagraphia, 339
Dyar, Harrison G., ix, 23, 29, 31, 33, 34, 35, 38
dyari, Haploa, 118
dyaus, Autographa, 238
Dysocnemis, genus; belladonna, 229
Dysodia, genus, 374; aurea, 375; Eyed, 374; fasciata, montana, oculatana, 374; plena, 375
dyspteraria, Meskea, 375
Dyspteridinæ, Subfamily, 323
Dyspteris, genus: abortivaria, 323

E

eavesi, Kodiosoma, 133
ecclesialis, Samea, 393
Ecdytolopha, genus; insiticiana, 419
echinocystis, Autographa, 238
echo, Seirarctia, 122
Ecpantheria, genus; deflorata, muzina, scribonia, 120
Ectropis, genus; crepuscularia, 344
Ectypia, genus; bivittata, nigroflava, Two-banded, 133
edictalis, Bomolocha, 286
edmandsi, Schizura, 298
eductalis, Lomanaltes, 285
edusa, Homoptera, 278
edwardsi, Alypia, 143; Apantesis, 130; Erinnyis, 58; Hemihyalea, 138; Lymire, 100; Syneda, 260
effectaria, Euchlæna, 350
efficitalis, Pyrausta, 398
effusalis, Epizeuxis, 280
egena, Autographa, 238
egenaria, Cicinnus, 359
Eggs, of moths, 4, 5
eglanterina, Pseudohazis, 93
egle, Euchætias, 135
eglenensis, Pareuchætes, 134
Elachistidæ, Family, 26, 430
electra, Hemileuca, 91
elegans, Odontosia, 294; Pygarctia, 136
elegantalis, Pangrapta, 254
elimata, Semiophora, 180
Eliot, George, quoted, 417
eliza, Catocala, 266
Ellida, genus; caniplaga, gelida, transversata, 300
ello, Erinnyis, 58
elongata, Tephroclystis, 328

elongatus, Celiptera, 275
elsa, Dictyosoma, 49
emargataria, Plagodis, 349
Emerson, R. W., quoted, 41, 98, 288, 291, 391
emphytiformis, Gæa, 381
Enarmonia sebastianæ, 418
End of All, 445
endropiaria, Therina, 347
Enemera, genus; juturnaria, 342
enervis, Orthodes, 203
enotata, Philobia, 339
English sparrow, 95
enhydris, Hexeris, 375
Ennominæ, Subfamily, 337
Ennomos, genus; alniaria, autumnaria, lutaria, magnarius, niveosericeata, subsignarius, 348
ennucleata, Synelys, 333
enthea, Fishea, 170
Eois, genus, 334; californiaria, californiata, 336; consecutaria, inductata, ossularia, 335; pacificaria, 336; ptelearia, 334; sideraria, 336; sobria, suppressaria, 335
Eosphoropteryx, genus; thyatiroides, 237
Epagoge, genus; tunicana, 421
Epelis, genus; faxoni, truncataria, 337
ephemeræformis, Thyridopteryx, 361
Ephestia, genus, 412; cahiritella, cautella, desuetella, 414; gitonella, kuehniella, 412; pasulella, 414
ephippiatus, Sibine, 364
ephyrata, Syssaura, 352
Epicnaptera, genus; americana, carpinifolia, occidentis, 314
Epidemas, genus; cinerea, 170
Epidroma, genus; delinquens, 274
Epiglæa, genus; decliva, deleta, pastillicans, 219
epilais, Syntomeida, 99
epilobii, Celerio, 76
Epimecis, genus; amplaria, disserptaria, hortaria, liriodendraria, virginaria, 344
epimenis, Psychomorpha, 232
epione, Catocala, 260
epionoides, Pangrapta, 254
Epipaschiinæ, Subfamily, 407
Epiplatymetra, genus; coloradaria, 351
Epiplemidæ, Family, 25, 34, 356
Epipyropidæ, Family, 25, 35, 370
Epipyrops, genus, barberiana, 370
Epistor, genus, 61; fegeus, luctuosus, lugubris, 61
Epizeuxis, genus; æmula, americalis, concisa, 280; denticulalis, 281; effusalis, herminioides, lubricalis, mollifera, phæalis, 280; scobialis, 281; scriptipennis, surrectalis, 280
Erannis, genus; tiliaria, 347
Erastria, genus; amaturaria, 333
erastrioides, Tarache, 251
Erebus, genus; agarista, odora, 279
erechtea, Drasteria, 257
erecta, Mamestra, 195
erectalis, Plathypena, 287
cremiata, Macaria, 339
eremitoides, Hyloicus, 49
eremitus, Hyloicus, 49
erichto, Drasteria, 257
Erinnyis, genus, 57, 58; alope, 58; caicus, 60; cinerosa, crameri, domingonis, 59; edwardsi, ello, fasciata, 58; festa, 59; flavicans, janiphæ, lassauxi, 58; melancholica, 59; merianæ, 58, 59; obscura, œnotrus, pallida, penæus, picta, phalaris, piperis, rhœbus, rustica, 59
Eriocephala, genus, 444

erinalis, Conchylodes, 393
Eriocephalidæ, 8
erosa, Anomis, 244; Malacosoma, 313
erosiata, Calledapteryx, 356
erosnealis, Pyrausta, 398
erratica, Abagrotis, 180
errato, Euproserpinus, 74
erycata, Sylectra, 254
eson, Xylophanes, 75
Estigmene, genus, 122; acræa, 122, 123;
   albida, 122; antigone, athena, californica,
   caprotina, congrua, dubia, klagesi, menthastrina, mexicana, packardi, 123; prima,
   122; pseuderminea, rickseckeri, White-
   bodied, 123
etolus, Hæmorrhagia, 62
Eubaphe, genus, 115
Eucalyptera, genus; strigata, 244
Eucereon, genus, carolina, confine, Floridan,
   100
Euchætias, genus; albicosta, antica, bolteri,
   egle, Mouse-colored, murina, Oregon,
   oregonensis, perlevis, pudens, 135
Euchalcia, genus; contexta, festucæ, putnami, striatella, venusta, 237
Euchlæna, genus; amœnaria, arefactaria,
   astylusaria, concisaria, decisaria, deductaria, deplanaria, effectaria, madusaria,
   muzaria, obtusaria, oponearia, pectinaria,
   propriaria, serrata, serrataria, vinosaria,
   350
Euchœca, genus; albovittata, californiata,
   328; lucata, 329; propriaria, reciprocata
   328
Eucirrœdia, genus; pampina, 215
Euclea, genus; argentaria, chloris, delphinii,
   ferruginea, fraterna, indetermina, monitor,
   nana, nanina, pænulata, quercicola, strigata, tardigrada, vernata, viridiclava,
   viridis, 365
Euclidia, genus, 257; cuspidea, intercalaris,
   258
Eucoptocnemis, genus; fimbriaris, obvia, 190
Eucosma, genus; affusana, clavana, distigmana, dorsisignatana, graduatana, saligneana, scudderiana, similana, 418
Eucrostis, genus; gratata, incertata, oporaria,
   336
Eucymatoge, genus; impleta, indoctrinata,
   intestinata, 328
Eudeilinea, genus; herminiata, 320
Eudule, genus; biseriata, mendica, Plain-
   colored, unicolor, 327
Eueretagrotis, genus; perattenta, sigmoides,
   179
Euerythra, genus; phasma, trimaculata, 120
Eufidonia, genus; bicolorata, discopilata,
   fidoniata, notataria, quadripunctaria, 337
Eugenia, buxifolia, procera, 140
Eugonobapta, genus; nivosaria, nivosata, 348
Euhagena, genus; nebraskæ, 381
Euharveya, genus, 219
Euherrichia, genus; cervina, granitosa, gran-
   itosa, mollissima, rubicunda, 253
Euhyparpax, genus; rosea, 298
Eulia, genus; alisellana, 423
Eumestleta, genus; flammicincta, patruelis,
   patula, 249
Eunystalea, genus; indiana, 295
euonymella, Yponomeuta, 423
Euonymus, 157
Eupanychis, genus; hirtella, spinosæ, 226
Euparthenos, genus; nubilis, 272
eupatorii, Synanthedon, 385
Euphanessa, genus, 327
euphœsalis, Pyrausta, 397
Euplexia, genus; lucipara, 172

Eupolia, genus; licentiosa, 199
Euproctis, genus; chrysorrhœa, 309
Euproserpinus, genus, 74; errato, euterpe,
   phaeton, 74
Eupseudomorpha, genus; brillians, 231
Eupseudosoma, genus; floridum, immaculata,
   involutum, nivea, Snowy, 139
euryalus, Samia, 84
Eurycyttarus, genus; carbonaria, 362; con-
   federata, 363
Euschemonidæ, 3
Eustixia, genus; pupula, 398
Eustroma, genus; atrocolorata, diversilineata,
   montanatum, prunata, ribesiaria, triangu-
   latum, 329
Eustrotia, genus; albidula, apicosa, biplaga,
   carneola, concinnimacula, intractabilis,
   muscosula, musta, nigritula, synochitis,
   247
Eutelia, genus; dentifera, pulcherrima, 242
euterpe, Euproserpinus, 74; Syntomeida, 99
Euthisanotia, genus, 142, 232; assimilis,
   grata, unio, 232
Euthyatira, genus; pennsylvanica, pudens,
   304
Eutolype, genus; bombyciformis, damalis,
   177
Euverna, genus; clio, 133
Euxoa, genus, 187; albipennis, atropurpurea,
   basalis, 189; brevipennis, 188; campestris,
   189; cinereomaculata, 190; cochrani, declarata, decolor, 189; detersa, 188; displiciens, dissona, expulsa, 189; flavidens,
   188; furtivus, gularis, illata, 190; insignata,
   insulsa, lutulenta, maizi, 189; messoria,
   188; nigripennis, 189; obeliscoides, ochrogaster, 190; olivalis, perpolita, personata,
   pityochrous, quadridentata, 188; redimicula, 190; repentis, 189; sexatilis, 190;
   spissa, tessellata, titubatis, 189; turris,
   190; velleripennis, 188; verticalis, 189
evanidalis, Hypena, 287
evelina, Catocala, 261
evicta, Morrisonia, 196
exaltata, Schinia, 227
excæcatus, Calasymbolus, 56
excelsa, Apantesis, 132
exitiosa, Sanninoidea, 384
expansa, Nephelodes, 199
expulsa, Euxoa, 189
expultrix, Pseudothyatira, 304
exsiccatus, Crambus, 403
eximaria, Hyperitis, 349
exsuperata, Paraphia, 343
Exterior line, 18
externa, Galgula, 247
extimia, Caradrina, 165
extranea, Heliophila, 200
exusta, Mamestra, 193
Exuviæ, larval, 9
Exyra, genus; semicrocea, 248
Eyes; of cats, 78; of moths, 12, 18; of nocturnal animals, 77; of owls, 78

F

fabricii, Automeris, 89
fabula. Drepana, 321
fadus, Sesia, 62
Fagitana, genus; littera, lucidata, niveicostatus, obliqua, 217
Fala, genus, ptycophora, 235
Falcaria, genus; bilineata, 321
falcata, Pseudanarta, 175
fallacialis, Renia, 283
fallax, Diphthera, 160
Fall Web-worm, 123

Index

falsarius, Acoloithus, 371
False Indigo, 430
Families of North American moths, Key to, 24
Far out at Sea, 362
farinalis, Pyralis, 400
farnhami, Mamestra, 192
"Far Out at Sea," 363
fascialis, Pyrausta, 397; Zinckenia, 392
fasciata, Dysodia, 375; Erinnyis, 58
fasciatus, Pholus, 67
fasciola, Lithacodes, 367
fasciolaris, Melipotis, 258
fastuosa, Atteva, 424
Faunal Subregions, 387
faustina, Catocala, 264
faustinula, Illice, 109
favorita, Apantesis, 132
faxoni, Epelis, 337
fecialis, Bomolocha, 286
fegeus, Epistor, 61
felina, Charadra, 153
Felt, E. P., 37
Feltia, genus, 186; agilis, 186; annexa,
  decernens, 187; gladiaria, herilis, hortulana,
  186; malefida, 187; morrisoniana, semiclarata, stigmosa, subgothica, vancouverensis, venerabilis, volubilis, 186
Femur, 14, 15
Fenaria, genus; ædessa, longipes, sevorsa
  233
fenestra, Telea, 87
Feniseca tarquinius, 6
fennica, Noctua, 183
Fentonia, genus; marthesia, tessella, turbida,
  300
Feralia, genus; jocosa, 171
Fernald, C. H., 31, 37
Fernaldella, genus; fimetaria, halesaria, 337
Fernaldellinæ, Subfamily, 337
fernaldialis, Melitara, 410
ferox, Syntomeida, 99
ferraria, Acherdoa, 234
ferrigera, Adoneta, 365
ferruginea, Euclea, 365; Lophodonta, 295
ferruginoides, Pachnobia, 180
fervidaria, Therina, 348
fervifactaria, Cœnocalpe, 332
fessa, Amolita, 244
festa, Cerma, 161; Erinnyis, 59
festivoides, Oligia, 165
festucæ, Euchalcia, 237
ficus, Pachylia, 60
Ficus pedunculata, 100
fidelissima, Composia, 289
fidicularia, Caradrina, 164
fidoniata, Eufidonia, 337
figurata, Apantesis, 132
filimentaria, Ania, 349
Fillip, The Three-spotted, 327
fimbrialis, Hypsopygia, 399
fimbriaris, Eucoptocnemis, 190
fimetaria, Fernaldella, 337
Final Goal, The, 445
fiscellaria, Therina, 348
Fishea, genus; enthea, Yosemite, yosemitæ,
  170
flagellum, Autographa, 238
flagitaria, Therina, 348
flammans, Ptychoglene, 110
flammicincta, Eumestleta, 249
flammifera, Mesoleuca, 330
Flannel-moth, White, Yellow 369
flava, Pseudanarta, 175
flavago, Xanthia, 214
flavedana, Platynota, 422
flavescentella, Tinea, 433
flavicans, Erinnyis, 58

flavicosta, Therasea, 251
flavidens, Euxoa, 188
flavipennis, Tarache, 251
flavipes, Bembecia, 383
flavofasciata, Proserpinus, 73
flebilis, Catocala, 622
fletcheri, Xylomiges, 197
flexuosa, Raphia, 153; Tortricidia, 368
Flight, Great powers of, 67
floccalis, Pleonectyptera, 246
florida, Rhodophora, 224
floridalis, Agathodes, 393
floridana, Atteva, 424
floridaria, Caberodes, 352
floridensis, Callopistria, 252; Hæmorrhagia,
  63; Sphacelodes, 354
floridum, Eupseudosoma, 139
floscularia, Plagodis, 349
Flour-moth, The, 412
fluviata, Percnoptilota, 330
Flying Squirrels, 149
Fontaine, De La, quoted, 373
Forester, Californian, 145; Eight-spotted,
  144; Langton's, 145; MacCulloch's, 143;
  Mexican, 144; Ridings', Two-spotted, 145;
  Wittfeld's, 144
formosa, Gluphisia, 300
formosa, Polychrysia, 236
formosalis, Nigetia, 358
formula, Catocala, 268
formula, Oreta, 321
forrigens, Phoberia, 273
Fota, genus; armata, minorata, 178
f-pallida, Apantesis, 132
fractilinea, Hadena, 168
fracturalis, Diastictis, 393
fragariæ, Ancylis, 419
fragilis, Apatela, 156
fratella, Autographa, 238
frater, Raphia, 153
fratercula, Catocala, 269
fraterna, Euclea, 365
fraudulentaria, Cleora, 344
Fraxinus, 46, 51
Frenulum, 16, 17
Fringes, 18
frugallaria, Cleora, 344
frugiperda, Laphygma, 174
Fruit-worm, The Gooseberry, 411
frustulum, Celiptera, 275
frutetorum, Malacosoma, 312
Fruva, genus; accepta, apicella, truncatula,
  252
fucosa, Hypoprepia, 106
Fulgora candelaria, 370
fuliginosa, Phragmatobia, 126
fulminans, Perigonica, 205
fultaria, Paota, 332
fulva, Kodiosoma, 133
fulvicollis, Scepsis, 101
fulvoflava, Halisidota, 138
fumalis, Pyrausta, 397
fumosa, Diacrisia, 127; Hæmorrhagia, 63
funebris, Pyrausta, 398
funeralis, Desmia, 392
funerea, Pygoctenucha, 111
fungorum, Chœphora, 216
furcata, Papaipema, 214
furcifera, Apatela, 155
furcilla, Argillophora, 255; Panthea, 152
Fur-moth, The, 433
furtivus, Euxoa, 190
furvana, Archips, 422
fusca, Porosagrotis, 187
fuscalis, Phlyctænodes, 395
fuscimacula, Oligia, 166
fuscipes, Comacla, 107

fuscula, Rœselia, 358
fusimacula, Oxycnemis, 221
futilis, Litoprosopus, 275

G

Gaberasa, genus; a m b i g u a l i s, bifidalis, divisalis, 284
Gæa, genus; emphytiformis, solituda, 381
galbina, Agapema, 86
Galgula, genus; externa, hepara, partita, subpartita, vesca, 247
galianna, Hemeroplanes, 60
galii, Celerio, 76
gallæsolidaginis, Gnorimoschema, 418, 425
Galleria, genus; cereana, cerella, mellonella, obliquella, 406
Galleriinæ, Subfamily, 405
gallivorum, Synanthedon, 387
Gall- moth, The Misnamed, 418; The Solidago, 425
Gama-grass, 405
garmani, Graphiphora, 204
Gaura biennis, 224
gauræ, Pogocolon, 72; Rhodophora, 224
Gazalina, genus, 305
Gelechiidæ, Family, 26, 38, 424
gelida, Apantesis, 131; Ellida, 300
gelidalis, Noctuelia, 399
geminata, Cladora, 324; Tephroclystis, 328
geminatus, Sphinx, 55
gemmata, Atteva, 424
gemmatilis, Anticarsia 275
generalis, Renia, 283
generosa, Pyrausta, 398
genicula, Drepana, 321
geniculata, Agrotis, 182
gentilis, Parastichtis, 217; Pyrausta, 397
Geometer, Crocus, 349; Dark-banded, 329; Five-lined, 333; Harvey's, 327; Snowy, 348
Geometers, 149
geometrica, Parasemia, 134
Geometridæ, Family, 7, 25, 34, 322
Geometrinæ, Subfamily, 336
geometroides, Melanchroia, 355; Pangrapta, 254
georgica, Hyperæschra, 294
germana, Lithomoia, 206
germanalis, Hypena, 287
gibbocostata, Cœnocalpe, 332
gibbosa, Nadata, 296
gilvipennis, Rhynchagrotis, 178
Gingla, genus; laterculæ, 373
gisela, Catocala, 269
gitonella, Ephestia, 412
Ghost-moth; Graceful, Lembert's, 444; Silver-spotted, 443
glabella, Pyrophila, 173
gladiaria, Feltia, 186
Glæa, genus; inulta, sericea, viatica, 218
glandulella, Holcocera, 429
Glassy-wing, Edwards', 138; Freckled, 139
glaucovaria, Mamestra, 193
Gleditschia, 96
glomeralis, Pyrausta, 398
glomeraria, Macaria 340
gloveri, Copidryas, 141; Samia, 84
Gloveria, genus; arizonensis, dentata, howardi, psidii, 311
Glover's Purslane-moth, 141
Gluphisia, genus; albofascia, avimacula, clandestina, danbyi, formosa, rupta, septentrionalis, severa, slossoni, trilineata, wrighti, 300
Glyphodes, genus; hyalinata, hyalinatalis, lucernalis, marginalis, nitidalis, quadristigmalis, 394

Gnophæla, genus; arizonæ, clappiana, continua, discreta, hopfferi, latipennis, morrisoni, vermiculata, 290
Gnorimoschema, genus, 425; gallæsolidaginis, 418, 425
goasalis, Philometra, 282
Goat-moths, 375
goniata, Sabulodes, 353
Gonodonta, genus; unica, 236
Gonodontis, genus; adustaria, agreasaria duaria, hamaria, hypochraria, mestusata obfirmaria, refractaria, 350
Gooseberry Fruit-worm, The, 411
Gooseberry Span-worm, The, 340
gordius, Hyloicus, 51
Gortyna, genus; immanis, Hop-vine, nictitans, 212; obliqua, Oblique, 213; sera, Veiled, velata, 212
gortynides, Bellura, 211
Gosse, Edmund, quoted, 355
gossypiana, Archips, 422
gracilenta, Alypia, 144
gracilior, Leptomeris, 333
gracilis, Catocala, 269; Hæmorrhagia, 63; Hepialus, 444
gradata, Macaria, 340
graduatana, Eucosma, 418
græfi, Apatela, 155
Græperia, genus; magnifica, 225
Grammodes, genus; smithi, 274
Grammodia, genus, 60
grandipuncta, Alabama, 243
grandirena, Melipotis, 258
grandis, Copablepharon, 222; Mamestra, 193; Melittia, 381; Noctua, 184
granitata, Sciagraphia, 339
granitosa, Euherrichia, 253
Grape-leaf Folder, The, 392
Grape-vine Plume, The, 416
graphica, Syneda, 259
Graphiphora, genus; alia, capsella, confluens, culea, garmani, hibisci, insciens, instabilis, modifica, orobia, oviduca, 204
Grass-moths, 402
grata, Euthisanotia, 232; Oligia, 166
grataria, Hæmatopsis, 332
gratata, Eucrostis, 336
gratulata, Mesoleuca, 330
Grease-wood, 96
Green Apple-leaf Tier, The, 421
grisea, Apatela, 156; Hypopacha, 312; Illice, 110
griseella, Tinea, 433
griseocincta, Orthodes, 203
grossulariæ, Zophodia, 411
grossulariata, Cymatophora, 340
Grote, A. R., 29, 30, 31, 32, 34, 35, 36
groteana, Cenopis, 422
grotei, Hæmorrhagia, 63; Hemileuca, 91; Lycomorpha, 101; Psaphidia, 177
groteiana, Catocala, 264
Grotella, genus; dis, 220
Groundling; Dusky, Red, 165
grynea, Catocala, 269
gueneana, Hydriomena, 331
Guenée, A., 27, 32, 36
guenei, Catocala, 261
Guettarda elliptica, 139
Guilding, Lansdown, 403
gularis, Euxoa, 190
gulosa, Hemerocampa, 308
Gumppenberg, C. v., 34
gurgitans, Archips, 422
guttata, Platyprepia, 128; Spragueia, 252
guttifera, Halisidota, 138
guttulosa, Pyrausta, 397
gyasalis, Heterogramma, 284

Index

Gymnocladus, 96
Gynæphora, genus; rossi. 305
Gypsochroa, genus; albosignata. designata
  hæsitata, impauperata, propugnata, pro-
  pugnaria, sitellata, 332
Gypsy Moth, The, 308
Gyros, genus; muiri, 249

H

habilis, Catocala, 268
Habrosyne, genus; scripta, 303
Hadena, genus, 166; Airy, 168; Albertan, 167;
  amputatrix, arctica, 169; arcuata, 167;
  Base-streaked, basilinea, 168; Black-
  banded, 167; bridghami, Bridgham's, 166;
  Broken-lined, Burgess', burgessi, cerivana,
  168; characta, 167; chlorostigma, 168;
  claudens, 167; conspicua, 168; contenta,
  169; Dark Ashen, 170; Darker, 169;
  Dark-spotted, Dark-winged. 167; Destroying, devastatrix, 169; discors, 168; Double-
  banded, 167; dubitans, 168; ducta, 169;
  fractilinea, 168; Great Western, 169;
  Green-spotted, 168; Half-Moon, 169; Halting, 168; hilli, 167; incallida, insignata,
  lateritia, 168; lignicolor, 169; loculata, 168;
  mactata, 167; marshallana, 169; miseloides, modica, 167; molochina, 168;
  Mullein, 169; Neumœgen's, 166; nigrior,
  Northern, 169; obliviosa, 168; occidens,
  ordinaria, 169; passer, Passerine, Red-
  winged, 168; semilunata, Speckled Gray,
  169; sputatrix, 168; subcedens, 167;
  transfrons, 166; Turbulent, turbulenta,
  167; verbascoides, 169; versuta, 167;
  vinela, 170; violacea, Violet, 167; viralis,
  vultuosa, 168; White-spotted, 167; Wood-
  colored, 169
Hadenella, genus, 162; minuscula, 163;
  pergentilis, subjuncta, 162
hadeniformis, Melipotis, 258
Hæmatomis, genus; mexicana, uniformis, 107
Hæmatopsis, genus; grataria, saniaria, successaria, 332
Hæmorrhagia, genus, 62, 72; æthra, axillaris,
  63; brucei, 64; buffaloensis, cimbiciformis,
  diffinis, 63; etolus, 62; floridensis, fumosa,
  gracilis, grotei, marginalis, metathetis
  63; palpalis, 64; pelasgus, 62; pyramus,
  63; rubens, 64; ruficaudis, 62, 63; senta,
  64; tenuis, 63; thetis, 64; thysbe, 62;
  uniformis, 63
hæsitata, Gypsochrea, 332
hageni, Isogramma, 47
halesaria, Fernaldella, 337
halicarniæ, Lapara, 53
Halisidota, genus, 115, 137; annulifascia,
  138; antiphola, 137; argentata, caryæ,
  138; davisi, 137; fulvoflava, 138; Gartered
  137; guttifera, 138; harrisi, 137; Hickory,
  longa, Long-streaked, maculata, porphyria, Silver-spotted, Spotted, 138; Tessellated, tessellaris, 137
Halpine, Charles G., quoted, 319
hamaria, Gonodontis, 350
hamifera, Autographa, 238
hammondi, Canarsia, 411
Hampson, Sir George F., ix, 18, 23, 31, 32,
  33, 34, 35, 36, 37, 98, 103, 114, 140, 151,
  288, 289, 292, 303, 306, 311, 315, 320,
  322, 356, 364, 371, 374, 375, 380, 391
Haploa, genus, 117; Leconte's, 118; Lyman's,
  119; carolina, clymene, colona, comma,
  118; confusa, 119; consita, 118; contigua,
  119; dyari, interruptomarginata, lactata,
  lecontei, militaris, vestalis, 118

Harpyia, genus; albicoma, aquilonaris, borealis, cinerea, scolopendrina, 299
Harris, Thaddeus William, 27
Harris' Three-spot, 159
harrisi, Halisidota 137; Lapara, 53; Pygoctenucha, 111
Harrisimemna, 149, 159; trisignata, 159
Harrisina, genus; americana, texana, 372
harti, Sysyrhypena, 282
haruspica, Noctua, 184
harveiata, Nannia 327
harveyi, Heliophila, 201
hasdrubal, Pseudosphinx, 57
hasta, Apatela, 155
hastata, Rheumaptera, 329
havilæ, Noctua, 184
Hawkmoth, 78; Clemens', 52; Five-Spotted,
  45
Head; anatomy of, 12, 18; larval, 7
hebræa, Polygrammate, 160
hebraicum, Polygrammate, 160, 161
Hebrew, The, 160
heiligbrodti, Syssphinx, 96
Heliaca, genus; diminutiva, 231
Heliochilus, genus; paradoxus, 222
Heliodes, genus; restrictalis, 230
Heliolonche, genus; modicella, 230
Heliomata, genus; cycladata, infulata, 338
Heliophana, genus; mitis, obliquata, 230
Heliophila, genus, 200; albilinea, 201; commoides, 203; complicata, 201; extranea,
  200; harveyi, 201; heterodoxa, lapidaria,
  202; minorata, 201; multilinea, 202;
  pseudargyria, subpunctata, 201; unipuncta, 200
Heliosea, genus; pictipennis, 230
heliothidata, Sciagraphia, 339
Heliothis, genus; armiger, 222; nuchalis
  scutosus, 224
Heliotropha, genus; atra, reniformis, 173
helva, Orthosia, 217
Hemerocampa, genus, 305; borealis, cana,
  305; definita, 307; gulosa, intermedia,
  leucographa, leucostigma, obliviosa, vetusta, 306
Hemeroplanes, genus, 60; galianna, licastus,
  parce, 60
Hemihyalea, genus; Edwards', edwardsi,
  138; Freckled, labecula, 139; quereus,
  translucida, 138
Hemileuca, genus, 91; artemis, californica,
  92; electra, grotei, hualapai, 91; juno, 92;
  maia, neumœgeni, 91; nevadensis, 92;
  proserpina, sororius, 91; tricolor, 93;
  yavapai, 92
Hemileucinæ, Subfamily, 80, 81, 90
hemizonæ, Synanthedon, 385
henrici, Hypopta, 379
henrietta, Derrima, 224
hepara, Galgula, 247
Hepialidæ, Family, 15, 16, 26, 443
Hepialus, genus; gracilis, hyperboreus, lemberti, macglashani, pulcher, 444
hera, Pseudohazis, 93
heraclei, Depressaria, 428
heracliana, Depressaria, 428
herbimacula, Mamestra, 195
Herculia, genus; himonialis, olinalis, trentonalis, 401
Herder, Das Lied vom Schmetterlinge, 290
herilis, Feltia, 186
hermia, Catocala, 264
herminiata, Eudeilinea, 320
herminioides, Epizeuxis, 280
Herrich-Schæffer, G. A. W., 27
Herse, genus, 43; affinis, cingulata, convolvuli, decolora, druræi, pungens, 43

hersiliata, Mesoleuca, 330
hertaria, Epimecis, 344
Heterocampa, genus; associata, astarte, athereo, bilineata, biundata, cinerascens, manteo, menas, mollis, obliqua, olivatus, pulverea, semiplaga, subalbicans, turbida, ulmi, umbrata, varia, 297
Heterocera, defined, 3
heterodoxa, Heliophila, 202
Heterogenea, genus; shurtleffi, 368
Heterogramma, genus; gyasalis, pyramusalis, rurigena, 284
Heteropacha, genus; rileyana, 314
Heterophleps, genus; hexaspilata, quadrinotata, triguttaria, 327
heucheræ, Paranthrene, 387
hexadactyla, Orneodes, 417
hexaspilata, Heterophleps. 327
Hexeris, genus; enhydris, reticulina, 375
hibisci, Graphiphora, 204
"Hickory Horn-devil," 6, 97
hieroglyphica, Noropsis, 233
hilaris, Zeuzera, 376
hilli, Hadena, 167; Hypocala, 272
Hillia, genus; algens, 166
hilliana, Noctua, 183
Himantopterus. genus, 371
Himella, genus; contrahens, thecata, 204
himonialis, Herculia, 401
hinda, Catocala, 266
Hippia, genus; packardi, 296
hircina, Homoglæa, 219
hircinalis, Pyrausta, 398
hirtella, Eupanychis, 226
hirtipes, Zosteropoda, 203
histrio, marasmalus, 242
Hoboken, 147
hochenwarthi, Syngrapha, 240
Holcocera, genus; glandulella, 429
Holland, Clive, quoted, 353
hollandaria, Racheospila, 336
Holmes, O. W., quoted, 3, 371
Holomelina, genus, 115; choriona, belfragei, belmaria, bimaculata, Black-banded, brevicornis, diminutiva, Ehrman's, Five-spotted, immaculata, Least, Plain-winged, 116; obscura, opella, ostenta, rubricosta, Showy, Tawny, 115
Homoglæa, genus; carbonaria, hircina, 219
Homohadena, genus; badistriga, 176
Homoptera, genus; cingulifera, edusa, intenta, involuta, lunata, putrescens, saundersi, unilineata, viridans, woodi, 278
Homopyralis, genus; contracta, tactus, zonata, 256
honesta, Jodia, 215
honestaria, Azelina, 352
Honey-locust, 96
Honey-streak, The, 339
hopfferi, Gnophæla, 290
Hops, 287
Horama, genus; texana, 100
Hormisa, genus; absorptalis bivittata, nubilifascia, 282
hormos, Hypsoropha, 256
Hormoschista, genus; pagenstecheri, 253
hornbeckiana, Pholus, 67
Horne, R. H., quoted, 363
horrida, Zale, 277
hortaria, Epimecis. 346
hortulana, Feltia, 186
hospes, Synanthedon, 387
Howard, L. O., viii, 403, 405
howardi, Gloveria, 311
howlandi, Syneda, 260
hualapai, Hemileuca, 91
Huber, 112

hubbardi, Bruceia, 108
hubneraria, Azelina, 352
hubnerata, Azelina, 352
hudsonica, Alypia, 145; Syneda, 260
Hulst, Rev. G. D., 33, 34, 36
humeralis, Cingilia, 347
humerosana, Amorbia, 423
humilis, Schizura, 298
humuli, Hypena, 287
Huxley, Thomas Henry, quoted, 38
hyalinata, Glyphodes, 394
hyalinatalis, Glyphodes, 394
hyalinopuncta, Apatelodes 293
hyalinus, Phobetron, 366
Hyamia, genus; perditalis, semilineata, sexpunctata, umbrifascia, 254
Hyblæa, genus; mirificum, puera, saga, 288
hybrida, Ophideres, 276; Utetheisa, 117
Hydria, genus; undulata, 329
Hydriomena, genus; autumnalis, bicolorata, birivata, custodiata, gueneata, lascinata, latirupta, rectangulata, sordidata, speciosata, 331
hydromeli, Litodonta, 296
hylæus, Dolba, 46
Hylesia, genus; 90; alinda, 90
Hyloicus, genus, 49; albescens, 50; andromedæ, 50; canadensis, 51; chersis, 50; coloradus, 52; coniferarum, 52; dolli, 52; drupiferarum, 52; eremitus, 49; eremitoides, 49; gordius, 51; insolita, 51; kalmiæ, 51; libocedrus, 51; lugens, 49, 50; luscitiosa, 52; oreodaphne, 50; perelegans, 51; pinastri, 52; plota, 51; pœcila, 51; saniptri, 52; separatus, 50; sequoiæ, 52; sordida, 49; vancouverensis, 50; vashti, 50
Hyloicus kalmiæ, larva of, 7
hypæthrata, Macaria, 339
Hyparpax, genus; aurora, perophoroides, rosea. venus, venusta, 299
Hypena, genus; evanidalis, germanalis, humuli, 287
Hypenula, genus; biferalis, cacuminalis, opacalis, 283
Hyperæschra, genus; georgica, scitipennis, stragula, tortuosa, 294
hyperboreus, Hepialus, 444
hyperici, Synanthedon, 385
Hyperitis, genus; æsionaria, amicaria, exsimaria, insinuaria, laticincta, neonaria, neoninaria, nyssaria, subsinuaria, 349
Hyphantria, genus, 122, 123; cunea, 123; pallida, 124; punctatissima, 123; textor, 124
Hyphoraia, genus; borealis, parthenos, 128
Hypocala, genus; andremona, hilli, 272
hypocastrina, Zeuzera, 376
hypochraria, Gonodontis, 350
Hypocrisias, genus; armillata, Least, minima, 136
Hypopacha, genus; grisea, 312
Hypoprepia, genus; cadaverosa, fucosa, inculta, miniata, plumbea, subornata tricolor, vittata, 106
Hypopta, genus; bertholdi, henrici, 379
Hyppa, genus; ancocisconensis, Common, contraria, xylinoides, 171
Hypsopygia, genus; costalis, fimbrialis, 399
Hypsoropha, genus; hormos, monilis, 256

I

Ianassa, genus; lignicolor, lignigera, virgata, 298
iaspis, Chytonix, 161
Ichneumon-flies, 69
Ichneumonidæ, 6, 68
idonea, Agrotis, 182

Index

ilia, Catocala, 265
illabefacta, Mamestra, 194
illapsa, Noctua, 185
illata, Euxoa, 190
illecta, Catocala, 267
illepida, Polia, 171
illibalis, Pyrausta, 397
Illice, genus, 108; deserta, 110; faustinula, 109; grisea, 110; nexa, 109, 110; packardi, plumbea, schwarziorum, striata, subjecta, tenuifascia, unifascia, 109
illocata, Dryobota, 171
illudens, Charadra, 152
imbraria, Caberodes, 352
imbrifera, Mamestra, 192
imitata, Sabulodes, 353; Synanthedon, 385
imitella, Cydosia, 253
immaculata, Eupseudosoma, 139; Holomelina, 116
impauperata, Gypsochroa, 332
imperator, Pachysphinx, 57
imperatoria, Basilona, 97
imperfectaria, Melanolophia, 344
imperialis, Basilona, 971
impingens, Anarta, 199
impleta, Apatela, 157; Eucymatoge, 328
implora, Azenia, 248
impressa, Apatela, 157
impropria, Synanthedon, 385
impropriata, Paraphia, 343
improvisa, Bombycia, 304
inatomaria, Metanema, 351
inca, Aleptina, 162
incallida, Hadena, 168
incandescens, Cirrhobolina, 259
incarcerata, Melalopha, 293
incarnata, Arachnis, 124; Lerina, 111
incarnatorubra, Apantesis, 130
incensalis, Cindaphia, 397
inceptaria, Cymatophora, 341
incertata, Eucrostis, 336
Incita, genus; aurantiaca, 246
incivis, Peridroma, 183
inclara, Apatela, 157
inclinata, Venusia, 328
inclinataria, Venusia, 328
includens, Autographa, 238
inclusa, Melalopha, 293
incognita, Agrotiphila, 191
incompleta, Apantesis, 132
inconcinna, Chorizagrotis, 185; Scotogramma, 198
inconstans, Panula, 258
incorrupta, Apantesis, 131
inculta, Hypoprepia, 106
incurvata, Sabulodes, 353
indentata, Melalopha, 293; Remigia, 274
indetermina, Euclea, 365
indiana, Eunystalea, 295
Indian-meal Moth, The, 415
indicans, Mamestra, 195
indigenella, Mineola, 409
indigens, Platysenta, 163
indigna, Autographa, 239
indiscriminaria, Chlorochlamys 336
indivisalis, Gaberasa, 284
indoctrinata, Eucymatoge, 328
indubitata, Triphosa, 331
inductata, Eois, 335
indurata, Xylomiges, 197
ineffusaria, Caberodes, 352
inepta, Cissusa, 256
inermis, Peridroma, 182
inexacta, Antiblemma, 275
inextricata, Mellilla, 338
infans, Brephos, 355
infecta, Mamestra, 195

infensata, Syssaura, 352
inficita, Marasmalus, 242
infirma, Synanthedon, 385
infructuosa, Morrisonia, 197
infulata, Heliomata, 338
infumata, Cosmia, 217
infuscata, Scotogramma, 198
ingenita, Dalcerides, 369
ingenua, Phoberia, 273
Inguromorpha, genus; arbeloides basalis, 378
innexa, Mamestra, 195
innominata, Xylina, 207
inornata, Sisyrosea, 366; Trichocosmia, 220
innotata, Apatela, 155
innubens, Catocala, 265
inquæsita, Papaipema, 213
insciens, Graphiphora, 204
inscriptum, Deidamia, 71
insequalis, Pyrausta, 398
insignata, Euxoa, 189; Hadena, 168
insignis, Plusiodonta, 235
insinuaria, Hyperitis, 349
insiticiana, Ecdytolopha, 419
insolabilis, Catocala, 262
insolita, Autographa, 238; Hyloicus, 51
insularis, Philosamia, 82
insulata, Pareuchætes, 134
instabilis, Cressonia, 57; Graphiphora, 204
insulsa, Euxoa, 189
integerrima, Calasymbolus, 56; Campometra, 276; Datana, 294
intenta, Homoptera, 278
intentata, Deilinea, 338
interlinearia, Caberodes, 352
intermedia, Apantesis, 129; Celerio, 76; Cucullia, 208; Hemerocampa, 308; Utetheisa, 117
intermediata, Mesoleuca, 330
interminellus, Crambus, 403
interna, Dasylophia, 296
interpuncta, Salia, 285
interpunctella, Plodia, 415
interrupta, Apatela, 155
interruptomarginata, Haploa, 118
intestinata, Eucymatoge, 328
intractabilis, Eustrotia, 247
intracta, Noctua, 183
introferens, Chorizagrotis, 185
inulta, Glæa, 218
inusitata, Synanthedon, 386
invexata, Therina, 348
involuta, Homoptera, 278
involutum, Eupseudosoma, 139
io, Automeris, 89; Calasymbolus, 56
Ipimorpha, genus; æquilinea, pleonectusa, 220
ipomœæ, Schizura, 298; Syntomeida, 99
iricolor, Oncocnemis, 176
iridaria, Anaplodes, 337
iris, Brotolomia, 215
irrecta, Pleonectyptera, 246
irrorata, Clemensia, 108; Oreta, 321
isabella, Isia, 124
Isaiah, quoted, 396, 434
Isia, genus, 125, 127; isabella, 125
Isogona, genus; natatrix, tenuis, 256
Isochætes, genus; beutenmulleri, 366
Isogramma, genus, 47; hageni, 47
Isoparce, genus, 48; cupressi, 48
Issus, genus, 370

J

Jackson, Helen Hunt, quoted, 413
jaguarina, Schinia, 228
jamaicensis, Sphinx, 55

Janette's Hair, 319
janiphæ, Erinnyis, 58
janualis, Semiophora, 180
Japan, 79, 307
jaquenetta, Catocala, 269
jasminearum, Chlænogramma, 46
Jaspidia, genus; lepidula, Marbled-green, teratophora, White-spotted, 160
Jatropha, 58
jatrophæ, Cocytius, 44
Jean Ingelow, quoted, 179
Job, quoted, 151, 424
jocasta, Andrewsia, 272
jocosa, Feralia, 171
Jodia, genus; honesta, rufago, 215
Joker, The, 171
Jordan, Dr. Karl, ix, 31
jorulla, Rothschildia, 82
juanita, Pogocolon, 73
jubararia, Pherne, 351
jucunda, Melipotis, 258; Noctua, 183
judith, Catocala 262
juglandis, Cressonia, 57; Mineola, 408
Juglans, 87
Jugum, 16
julia, Rhodosea, 225
julialis, Cindaphia, 397
Jumping beans, 417
juncimacula, Mamestra, 192
juncta, Noctua, 184
junctaria, Orthofidonia, 337
June-berry, 386
juniperaria, Syssaura, 352
juno, Hemileuca, 92
Jussieua, 67
jussieuæ, Pholus, 67
juturnaria, Enemera, 342

K

Kalmia, 51
kalmiæ, Hyloicus, 51
Keats, quoted, 114
Kentucky Coffee-tree, 06
keutzingaria, Plagodis, 349
keutzingi, Plagodis, 349
Key to families of North American moths, 24
Killing specimens, 19
Kirby, W. F., 29
klagesi, Estigmene, 123
Kodiosoma, genus; eavesi, fulva, nigra, tricolor, 133
kœbelei, Synanthedon, 387
Kuebel, C. L. von, quoted, 359, 368
kuehniella, Ephestia, 412

L

labecula, Hemihyalea, 139
labiosana, Platynota, 422
labruscæ, Pholus, 67
laciniosa, Bomolocha, 286
Lacosoma, genus; chiridota, 359
Lacosomidæ, Family, 25, 35, 359
lacrymosa, Catocala, 261
lactata, Haploa, 118
lacteolaria, Leuculodes, 310
lactipennis, Tarache, 251
lacustrata, Mesoleuca, 330
lætella, Ambesa, 410
lætulus, Lomanaltes, 285
lævigata, Zanclognatha, 281
Lagoa, genus; crispata, pyxidifera, 369
lanariella, Tineola, 432
lanceolata, Tarache, 251
langdonalis, Pyrausta, 397
langtoni, Alypia, 143, 145

languida, Melicleptria, 230
lanuginosa, Megalopyge, 369
Lapara, genus, 53; bombycoides, cana, coniferarum, halicarniæ, harrisi, pineum, 53
Laphygma, genus; autumnalis, frugiperda, macra, plagiata, signifera, 174
lapidaria, Heliophila, 202
Lappet, collar and shoulder, 18
laqueata, Calidota, 139
laqueatellus, Crambus, 402
larentioides, Phalænostola, 254
Larvæ; food of, 6
lascinata, Hydriomena, 331
Lasiocampidæ, Family, 9, 24, 34, 311
lassauxi, Erinnyis, 58
Latebraria, genus; amphipyroides, 279
laterana, Platynota, 422
laterculæ, Gingla, 373
lateritia, Hadena, 168
latex, Mamestra, 194
laticincta, Hyperitis, 349
laticinerea, Xylina, 207
laticlavia, Autographa, 240
latipennis, Diacrisia, 128; Gnophæla, 290
latipes, Remigia, 274
latirupta, Hydriomena, 331
Lathosea, genus; pullata, ursina, 209
latreillana, Ctenucha, 102
laudabilis, Mamestra, 195
Laugher, The, 152
Lauraceæ, 85
Leaf-rollers, 417
lecontei, Haploa, 118
Legs of moths, 14, 15
lemberti, Hepialus, 444
lena, Leptarctia, 121
lentiginosa, Bomolocha, 286
Leopard-moth, The, 376
lepidula, Jaspidia, 160
Lepipolys, genus; perscripta, 177
Leptarctia, genus; californiæ, decia dimidiata, lena, 121
Leptina, genus, 162
leptinoides, Schizura, 299
Leptomeris, genus, gracilior, magnetaria, quinquelinearia, rubrolinearia, rubrolineata, sentinaria, spuraria, 333
lepusculina, Apatela, 154
Lerina, genus; incarnata, robinsoni, 111
leucocycla, Anarta, 199
leucographa, Hemerocampa, 308
leucophæa, Olene, 308
leucostigma, Hemerocampa, 308
Leuculodes, genus; lacteolaria, 310
Lexis, genus; argillacea, bicolor, 105
libatrix, Scoliopteryx, 215
libedis, Tarache, 251
libera, Mamestra, 193
libocedrus, Hyloicus, 51
Libraries, Readers in, 98
liburna, Scolecocampa, 244
licastus, Homeroplanes, 60
licentiosa, Eupolia, 199
Lichen-moth; Allgehenian, 104; Banded, 109; Blue-green, Crimson-bodied, 111; Druce's, 110; Funereal, 111; Little White, 108: Mouse-colored, 107; Narrow-banded, 110; Powdered, 108; Subject, 109; Mexican, 107; Painted, 106; Pale, Pearly-winged, 104; Scarlet-winged, 106; Yellow-blotched, 110
ligata, Mamestra, 195
ligni, Scolecocampa, 244
lignicolor, Ianassa, 298; Hadena, 169
lignigera, Ianassa, 298
lilacina, Mamestra, 194
lima, Phurys, 275

Index

limata, Pantographa, 393
limbata, Ania, 349
limbolaris, Melipotis, 258
limitata, Nyctobia, 324
lineata, Celerio, 76; Diastema, 241; Schinia, 227
lineatella, Anarsia, 426
lineella, Catocala, 269
lineola, Pheocyma, 278
lineolata, Catabena, 163
Lines, on wings of Noctuid moth, 18
linnei, Pholus, 67
lintnerana, Archips, 422; Nycteola, 288
lintneri, Ommatostola, 211
Liparidæ, Family, 24, 34, 305
liquida, Mamestra, 192
Liquidambar, 85, 87
liquoraria, Synchlora, 336
liriodendraria, Epimecis, 344
Liriodendron, 85
Lithacodes, genus; divergens, fasciola, 367
Lithacodia, genus; bellicula, 248
Litholomia, genus; dunbari, napæa, 207
Lithomoia, genus; germana, 206
Lithosiidæ, Family, 24, 31, 103
lithosina, Annaphila, 246
lithosioides, Crambidia, 104
lithospila, Apatela, 156
Litocala, genus; sexsignata, 272
Litodonta, genus, hydromeli, 296
Litoprosopus, genus; futilis, 275
littera, Fagitana, 217
Little Wife, The, 267
littoralis, Pachnobia, 180
lituralis, Zanclognatha, 281
liturata, Apantesis, 131
Living and Dying, 354
lixaria, Racheospila, 336
Lobelia 155
lobeliæ, Apatela, 155
lobophorata, Nyctobia, 324
loculata, Hadena, 168
Lomanaltes, genus; eductalis, lætulus, 285
longa, Halisidota, 138
Longfellow, H. W., quoted, 121, 233
longilabris, Philometra, 282
longipenne, Copablepharon, 222
longipes, Fenaria, 233; Podosesia, 382
Lonicera, 62, 63
"Loopers," 8
Lophodonta, genus; angulosa, ferruginea, 295
lorata, Sabulodes, 353
lorea, Mamestra, 195
lorquini, Alypia, 143
Lowell, James Russell, quoted, 116
lubens, Mamestra, 194
lubricalis, Epizeuxis, 280
lubricans, Noctua, 185
lucata, Euchœca, 329
luccusalis, Samea, 393
lucens, Dasyspoudæa, 228
lucernalis, Glyphodes, 394
luciana, Catocala, 263
lucidata, Fagitana, 217
lucidus, Arctonotus, 71
lucifera, Pheocyma, 278
lucipara, Euplexia, 172
luctuata, Rheumaptera, 330
luctuosus, Epistor, 61
lugens, Hyloicus, 49, 50
lugubris, Apantesis, 132; Epistor, 61; Thyris, 374
lumenaria, Cosymbia, 333
luna, Actias, 87; Nycterophæta, 221
lunata, Homoptera, 278
lunilinea, Strenoloma, 276

lupini, Merolonche, 159; Synanthedon, 385
Lupinus, 64, 124
luscitiosa, Hyloicus, 52
Lussa, genus; nigroguttata, 175
lustralis, Mamestra, 192
lustrans, Synanthedon, 385
lutaria, Ennomos, 348
lutea, Diallagma, 245
luteicoma, Apatela, 157
lutulenta, Euxoa, 189
luxa, Bessula, 221
Lycia, genus; cognataria, sperataria, 345
Lycomorpha, genus; grotei, palmeri, pholus, 101
lycopersici, Protoparce, 45
Lyman, H. H., 32, 118
Lymire, genus; edwardsi, 100
lyncea, Pachylia, 60
lynx, Schinia, 227

M

Macaria, genus, 339; consepta, 340; eremiata, 339; glomeraria, 340; gradata, hypæthrata, 339; præatomata, 340; retectata, retentata, s-signata, subcinctaria, 339
mac-cullochi, Alypia, 143
macglashani, Hepialus, 444
Mackay, C. W., quoted, 272
macmurtrei, Prionoxystus, 378
macra, Laphygma, 174
macrinellus, Scirpophaga, 402
macrocarpana, Commophila, 423
Macronoctua, genus; onusta, 170
mactata, Hadena, 167
macularia, Sicya, 347
maculata, Halisidota, 137; Thyris, 374
maculicollis, Opharus, 139
madariæ, Synanthedon, 385
madefactalis, Bomolocha, 286
madetesalis, Pyrausta, 398
madusaria, Euchlæna, 350
Mænas, genus; vestalis, 127
mæstosa, Catocala, 261
magdalena, Catocala, 267; Nycterophæta, 221
magicalis, Conchylodes, 393
magnarius, Ennomos, 348
magnetaria, Leptomeris, 333
magniferalis, Pyrausta, 397
magnifica, Cossula, 379; Græperia, 225
Magusa, genus; angustipennis, dissidens, divaricata, divida, 175
maia, Hemileuca, 91
maizi, Euxoa, 189
majoraria, Caberodes, 352
majuscula, Cydosia, 253
Malacosoma, genus; americana, 312; californica, 313; decipiens, 312; disstria, drupacearum, erosa, 313; frutetorum, 312; perversa, pseudo-neustria, sylvaticoides, thoracica, thoracicoides, 313
malana, Balsa, 163
Malaporphyria, genus; oregona, 229
malefida, Feltia, 187
malivorana, Alceris, 421
Mamestra, genus, 191; acutipennis, 195; adjuncta, 194; albifusa, 193; Allied, anguina, 195; Brown-winged, 196; chenopodii, 193; claviplena, Cloudy, 192; Clover, congermana, 193; constipata, 195; contraria, Cousin-German, 193; Darling, demissa, 194; desperata, 193; detracta, 192; dimmocki, Dimmock's, 193; Disparaged, 192; dodgei, 195; Empurpled, 192; Erect, erecta, 195; exusta, 193; farnhami, Farnham's, 192; Fluid, 194; Fused-spot,

Mamestra—*Continued*
192; glaucovaria, Grand, grandis, Harnessed, 193; herbimacula, 195; Hitched, illabefacta, 194; imbrifera, 192; indicans, infecta, innexa, 195; juncimacula, 192, latex, 194; Laudable, laudabilis, 195; libera, 193; ligata, 195; lilacina, Lilacine; 194; Liquid, liquida, 192; lorea, 195; lubens, 194; Lustral, lustralis, meditata, 192; Modern, negussa, neoterica, 196; nevadæ, Nevadan, 193; olivacea, Olivaceous, 195; Painted, picta, 193; purpurissata, 192; radix, 193; renigera, 195; rosea, Rosy, 193; rugosa, Rugose, 194; Snaky, strigicollis, 195; Studied, 192; subjuncta, 193; suffusa, 192; teligera, 195; trifolii, 193; vicina, 195
mammurraria, Paraphia, 343
manalis, Bomolocha, 286
Mandibles of larvæ, 7
Manetta, 75
manifestolabes, Semiophora, 180
manteo, Heterocampa, 297
manto, Olene, 308
"Manual for the Study of Insects," by Comstock, 17
Maple-borer, The, 386
Maple-trees, 95
Marasmalus, genus; histrio, inficita, ventilator, 242
Marble-wing, The, 332
Margin of wings, 18
marginalis, Glyphodes, 394
marginalis, Hæmorrhagia, 63
marginata, Bembecia, 383; Schinia, 228
marginatus, Prodoxus, 439
marginidens, Papaipema, 214
marina, Misogada, 297
mariposa, Alypia, 143, 145
Marlatt, C. L., 426
Marmopteryx, genus; marmorata, 332
marmorata, Catocala, 263; Marmopteryx, 332
marshallana, Hadena, 169
Marumba, genus, 56
Marvel, The Cloaked, 161; The Green, 160
masoni, Rhododipsa, 225
materna, Ophideres, 276
Matigramma genus; pulverilinea, 276
Matthew, quoted, 430
matthewi, Scepsis, 101
matuta, Alypia, 144
matutina, Rhodophora, 224
meadi, Dasyspoudæa, 228
Meal Snout-moth, The, 400
"Measuring-worms," 8
Mecoceras, genus; nitocraria, nitocris, peninsularia, 354
Mecoceratinæ, Subfamily, 354
Median. shade, 18
medita, Mamestra, 192
medor, Cocytius, 44
Megalopyge, genus; lanuginosa, opercularis, subcitrina, 369
Megalopygidæ, 8, 25, 35, 368
Melalopha, genus; albosigma, americana, apicalis, incarcerata, inclusa, indentata, ornata, strigosa, vau, 293
melancholica, Erinnyis, 50
Melanchroia, genus; cephise, 354; geometroides, mors, 355
Melanchroiinæ, Subfamily, 354
Melanolophia, genus; canadaria, contribuaria, imperfectaria, signataria, 344
Melanomma, genus; auricinctaria, 255
melanopa, Nigetia, 358
melanopyga, Bellura, 211

Melicleptria, genus; californicus, languida, pulchripennis, sueta, 230
Melipotis, genus; agrotipennis, cinis, fasciolaris, grandirena, hadeniformis, jucunda, limbolaris, pallescens, perlæta, sinualis 258
Melitara, genus; fernaldialis, 410
melitta, Cosmosoma, 98
Melittia, genus; amœna, ceto, cucurbitæ, 380; grandis, 381; satyriniformis, 380; snowi, 381
Mellilla, genus; inextricata, snoviaria, xanthometata, 338
mellistrigata, Sciagraphia, 339
mellitularia, Pherne, 351
mellonella, Galleria, 406
melsheimeri, Cicinnus, 359
Memythrus, genus, 382; admirandus, 383; polistiformis, 382; simulans, 383; tricinctus, 382
menas, Heterocampa, 297
mendica, Eudule, 327
mendocino, Saturnia, 89
Mentha, 49
menthastrina, Estigmene, 123
meralis, Caradrina, 164
merdella, Tinea, 433
merianæ, Erinnyis, 58, 59
Merolonche, genus; lupini, 159
merricata, Paleacrita, 324
merricella, Semioscopis, 429
Merrick, F. A., ix, 118
Merrick, H. S., ix
Meskea, genus; dyspteraria, 375
meskei, Catocala, 264; Platysenta, 163
Mesoleuca, genus; brunneiciliata, flammifera, gratulata, hersiliata, intermediata, lacustrata, ruficillata, 330
messalina, Andrewsia, 272
messoria, Euxoa, 188
mestusata, Gonodontis, 350
Metalepsis, genus; cornuta, 181
metallica, Tarache, 251
Metamorphoses, 4
Metanema, genus; æliaria, carnaria, determinata, inatomaria, quercivoraria trilinearia, 351
metanemaria, Alcis, 343
Metaponia, genus; obtusa, obtusula, perflava, 250
metathetis, Hæmorrhagia, 63
Metathorasa, genus; monetifera, 252
metonalis, Philometra, 282
Metrocampa, genus; perlaria, perlata, prægrandaria, viridoperlata, 348
mexicana, Apantesis, 131; Cirrhobolina, 259; Citheronia, 97; Estigmene, 123; Hæmatomis, 107
michabo, Apantesis, 130
Micrococlia, genus, 156, 160; diphtheroides, Marbled, obliterata, 160
Microgaster, 69
Micropterygidæ, Family, 26, 444
Micropteryx, genus, 444
Micropyle, 5
Midget, Brown-spotted, 166; Festive, 165; Grateful, 166
Mikania scandens, 99
militaris, Haploa, 118
mima, Campometra, 274
minea, Apantesis, 130
Mineola, genus, 408; indigenella, 409; juglandis, 408; nebulo, zelatella, 409
miniana, Rhododipsa, 225
minians, Nephelodes, 199
miniata, Hypoprepia, 106
minima, Hypocrisias, 136; Pseudomya, 99

minimalis, Rhychagrotis, 178, 179; Zanclognatha, 281
ministra, Datana, 293
minorata, Fota, 178; Heliophila, 201
minuscula, Hadenella, 163; Rœselia, 358
minuta, Alceris, 421; Catocala, 269
minutata, Tephroclystis, 328
mirificum, Hyblæa, 288
miscellus, Catabena, 163
miseloides, Hadena, 167
Misnamed Gall-moth, The, 418
Misogada, genus; cinerea, marina, sobria,
  unicolor, 297
mitis, Heliophana, 230
modesta, Pachysphinx, 57; Synanthedon,
  387; Ulolonche, 198
modestaria, Cymatophora, 341
modica, Hadena, 167
modicella, Heliolonche, 230
modifica, Graphiphora, 204
moffatiana, Scopelosoma, 218
mollifera, Epizeuxis, 280
mollis, Heterocampa, 297
mollissima, Euherrichia, 253
molochina, Hadena, 168
Molts, larval, 8
Momophana, genus; comstocki, 172
monacha, Psilura, 309
Monarda, 49
moneta, Polychrysia, 236
monetifera, Metathorasa, 252
monilis, Hypsoropha, 256
monitor, Euclea, 365
monodon, Autographa, 238
Monoleuca, genus; semifascia, 365
monotropa, Selenis, 277
mopsa, Catocala, 265
monstralis, Agathodes, 393
montana, Albuna, 384; Dysodia, 375
montanatum, Eustroma, 329
Montgomery, James, quoted, 302
Moore, Thomas, quoted, 304
morbidalis, Chytolita, 282
morbosa, Cissusa, 256
mori, Bombyx, 315
mormonica, Apantesis, 131
Morrenia, 58
Morris, Rev. J. G., 28
Morrisonia, genus, 196; confusa, 197; evicta,
  196; infructuosa, multifaria, 197; sectilis,
  vomerina, 196
morrisonata, Azelina, 352
morrisoni, Gnophæla, 290
morrisoniana, Feltia, 186
mors, Melanchroia, 355
mortua, Schinia, 228
mortuorum, Autographa, 239
morula, Apatela, 155
Moths; Achaia, 130; Acorn, 429; Acraea, 123;
  Alinda, 90; Anna, 130; Arge, 130; Astur,
  139; Carpet, 434; Chain-streak, 347;
  Clio, 133; Clymena, 118; Colona, 118;
  Cora, 161; Cosyra, 142; Cotton-worm, 243;
  Diverse-line, 329; Dried-currant, 414;
  Echo, 122; Fall Web-worm, 123; Flour,
  412; Fur, 433; Galbina, 86; Glover's
  Purslane-, 141; Granite, 339; Gypsy, 308;
  Harrow, 176; Hera, 93; Herbarium, 334;
  Honey-locust, 96; Imperial, 97; Indian-
  meal, 415; Io, 89; Juno, 92; Leopard, 376;
  Linden, 347; Luna, 87; Magnet, 333;
  Magpie, 93; Michabo, 130; Milk-weed,
  135; Oithona, 129; Pandora, 91; Parthenice,
  129; Persephone, 130; Plum, 329; Poly-
  phemus, 87; Potato, 425; Privet, 394;
  Mexican Walnut-, 97; Pine-devil, 97;
  Rosy Maple-, 95; Royal Walnut-, 97;

Moths—Continued
  Sand-dune, 143; Scallop-shell, 329; Six-
  plume, 417; Skiff, 367; Solidago Gall-, 425;
  Spotless Fall Web-worm, 124; Stigma, 94;
  Sugar-beet, 395; Sun-flower, 339; Yucca,
  441
Moth-Song, 310
Muir, John, 249
muiri, Gyros, 249
muliercula, Catocala, 267
multifaria, Ctenucha, 102; Morrisonia, 197
multifera, Caradrina, 164
multilinea, Heliophila, 202
multilineata, Pigea, 333
multipunctella, Yponomeuta, 423
multiscripta, Cerura, 299
mundula, Drasteria, 257
muraenula, Porosagrotis, 187
muralis, Psaphidia, 177
muricina, Stretchia, 205
muricolor, Calidota, 139
murina, Comacla, 107; Euchætias, 135
muscosula, Eustrotia, 247
musta, Eustrotia, 247
mustelina, Schizura, 299
muzaria, Euchlæna, 350
muzina, Ecpantheria, 120
myandaria, Caberodes, 352
Myginda ilicifolia, 99
mynesalis, Tetanolita, 284
myops, Calasymbolus, 56
Myosotis, 134
myron, Darapsa, 68

N

Nacophora, genus; quernaria, 345
Nadata, genus; gibbosa, 296
nais, Apantesis, 132
nana, Euclea, 365
nanina, Euclea, 365
Nannia, genus; harveiata, refusata, 327
napæa, Litholomia, 207
narrata, Drasteria, 257
Narthecophora, genus; pulverea, 235
nasoni, Natada, 366
Nasu-no Take, 301
nasutaria, Phiprosopus, 245
Natada, genus; daona, nasoni, rude, 366
natatrix, Isogona, 256
nebraskæ, Catocala, 263; Euhagena, 381
nebulo, Mineola, 409
nebulosa, Catocala, 266
nebulosus, Adoneta, 365
necopina, Papaipema, 214
neglecta, Synanthedon, 385
negussa, Mamestra, 196
Neighbor, The, 119
Neleucania, genus; bicolorata 203
Nelphe carolina, 100
Neocastniidæ, 3
neogama, Catocala, 149, 266
neonaria, Hyperitis, 349
neoninaria, Hyperitis, 349
Nephelodes, genus; expansa, minians, sobria,
  subdolens, violans, 199
Nepytia, genus; nigrovenaria, pellucidaria,
  pinaria, pulchraria, semiclusaria, 343
nerea, Apantesis, 130
Nerice, genus; bidentata, 296
Nerium odorum, 99
nesæa, Omia, 230
nessus, Amphion, 72
Neumœgen, B., 31, 33, 34, 35
neumœgeni, Hemileuca, 91; Xanthothrix 231
Neumœgenia, genus; poetica, 235
Neuronia, genus; americana, 196

nevadæ, Mamestra, 193; Thyris, 374
nevadensis, Apantesis, 131; Hemileuca, 92
nerissa, Catocala, 269
nexa, Illice, 109, 110
nicotianæ, Protoparce, 45
Nigetia, genus; formosalis, melanopa, 358
Night air, 80
nigra, Kodiosoma, 133; Peridroma, 182
nigricans, Phobetron, 366
nigriceps, Noctua, 184
nigrior, Hadena, 169
nigripennis, Euxoa, 189
nigrirena, Schinia, 227
nigritula, Eustrotia, 247
nigrofasciata, Celama, 357
nigrofimbria, Xanthoptera, 248
nigroflava, Ectypia, 133
nigroguttata, Lussa, 175
nigrolunata, Anarta, 198
nigrovenaria, Nepytia, 343
nimia, Orthodes, 203
niobe, Seirarctia, 122
nitela, Papaipema, 213
nitens, Orthodes, 203
nitida, Schizura, 298
nitidalis, Glyphodes, 394
nitocraria, Mecoceras, 354
nitocris, . ecoceras, 354
nivaria, Anarta, 199
nivea, Eupseudosoma, 139
niveicilialis, Pyrausta, 398
niveicostatus, Fagitana, 217
niveosericeata, Ennomos, 348
nivosaria, Eugonobapta, 348
nivosata, Eugonobapta, 348
nobilis, Schinia, 288; Tosale, 402
noctivaga, Apatela, 157
Noctua, genus, 183; associans, 185; atricincta,
  184; beata, 185; bicarnea, 183; calgary,
  clandestina, collaris, 184; c-nigrum, fennica, 183; grandis, haruspica, havilæ, 184;
  hilliana, 183; illapsa, 185; intractata,
  jucunda, 183; juncta, 184; lubricans, 185;
  nigriceps, 184; normanniana, oblata, obtusa, 183; patefacta, 184; perconflua,
  plagiata, 183; plecta, substrigata, unicolor, vicaria, 184
Noctuelia, genus; costæmaculalis, gelidalis,
  novalis, peruviana, thalialis, 399
Noctuidæ, Family, 7, 24, 32, 151
noctuiformis, Aon, 234; Tuerta, 143
Nola, genus; ovilla, 357
Nolidæ, Family, 24, 34, 357
Nonagria, genus; Large, oblonga, permagna,
  subflava, Yellowish, 211
nondescriptus, Phobetron, 366
notata, Philobia, 339; Tephroclystis, 328
notataria, Eufidonia, 337
notatella, Nycterophæta, 221
Notch-wing, The, 348
Notodonta, genus, 294; basitriens, simplaria,
  295
Notodontidæ, Family, 25, 33, 292
Notolophus, genus; antiqua, nova, 306
norax, Cossula, 379
normani, Crocigrapha, 204
normanniana, Noctua, 183
Noropsis, genus; hieroglyphica, 233
nova, Notolophus, 306
novalis, Noctuelia, 399
nubecularia, Paraphia, 343
nubilifascia, Hormisa, 282
nubilis, Euparthenos, 272
nuchalis, Heliothis, 224
nundina, Schinia, 227
nupera, Calocampa, 208
Nurse, The, 263

nurus, Catocala, 263
nuttalli, Pseudohazis, 93
Nycteola. genus; lintnerana revayana, 288
Nycteolidæ, Family, 24, 33, 288
Nycterophæta, genus; luna magdalena,
  notatella, 221
Nyctobia, genus; limitata, lobophorata,
  vernata, 324
Nymphula, genus; obscuralis, 399
Nymphulinæ, Subfamily, 399
Nyssa sylvatica, 161
nyssaria, Hyperitis, 349

O

obaurata, Celama, 357
obeliscoides, Euxoa, 190 .
oberthuralis, Phlyctænodes, 396
obesalis, Plathypena, 287
obfirmaria, Gonodontis, 350
oblata, Noctua, 183
oblinita, Apatela, 157
obliqua, Fagitana, 217; Heterocampa, 297;
  Sphida, 211
obliquata, Heliophana, 230; Pleroma, 206;
  Sphida, 211
obliquella, Galleria, 406
obliquifera, Balsa, 163
obliquilinea, Cargida, 300
obliterata, Microcœlia, 160
obliviosa, Hadena, 168; Hemerocampa, 305
oblonga, Nonagria, 211
obnigralis, Pyrausta, 398
obrussata, Phrygionis, 354
obscura, Apatela, 153; Catocala, 262; Erinnyis, 59; Holomelina, 115; Pseudosphinx,
  57
obscuralis, Nymphula, 399
obscurus, Anytus, 191
obtusa, Noctua, 183; Metaponia, 250
obtusaria, Euchlæna, 350
obtusula, Metaponia, 250
obvia, Eucoptocnemis, 190
occata, Oncocnemis, 176
occidens, Hadena, 169
occidentalis, Æmilia, 137; Apatela, 155;
  Pachysphinx, 57
occidentata, Barathra, 196
occidentis, Epicnaptera, 314
occulta, Peridroma, 182; Protoparce, 45
ocellata, Sphinx, 54
Ocelli, 12
ocellinata, Sciagraphia, 339
ochosalis, Pyrausta, 398
ochracea, Apantesis, 130; Platyprepia, 128
ochraceus, Axenus, 231
Ochria, genus; sauzælitæ, 214
ochreipennis, Zanclognatha, 281
ochrogaster, Euxoa, 190
octo, Amyna, 242
octomaculata, Alypia, 143, 144; Pyrausta,
  398
oculatana, Dysodia, 374
oculatrix, Pæctes, 241
oculea, Telea, 87
Ode to an Insect, 291
Odontosia, genus; elegans, 294
odora, Erebus, 279
odyneripennis, Bembecia, 383
Œcophoridæ, Family, 26, 428
Œhlenschlæger, quoted, 303
œmearia, Syssaura, 352
œneiformis, Cœnocalpe, 332
œnotrus, Erinnyis, 59
Ogdoconta, genus; atomaria, cinereola, 241
Oiketicus, genus; abboti, 361
oithona, Apantesis, 129

Index

Olene, genus; achatina, atrivenosa, basiflava, cinnamomea, leucophæa, manto,
  parallela, tephra, 308
Oligia, genus; festivoides, 165; fuscimacula
  grata, rasilis, 166; varia, 165
olinalis, Herculia, 401
olivacea, Mamestra, 195
olivalis, Euxoa, 188
olivatus, Heterocampa, 297
olivia, Catocala, 269
olympia, Composia, 289
olyzonaria, Syssaura, 352
omega, Autographa, 238
Omia, genus; nesæa, 230
omicron, Autographa, 238
Ommatostola, genus; lintneri, 211
omphale, Cosmosoma, 98
onagrus, Spragueia, 252
Oncocnemis, genus; atrifasciata, Black-
  banded, chandleri, Chandler's, cibalis,
  dayi, Day's, Gray, iricolor, Iris-colored,
  Narrow-banded, occata, tenuifascia, 176
ontariella, Depressaria, 428
onusta, Macronoctua, 170
oo, Autographa, 238
opacalis, Hypenula, 283
opacifrons, Semiophora, 180
opella, Holomelina, 115
opercularis, Megalopyge, 369
operculella, Phthorimæa, 424, 425
Opharus, genus; albicans, astur, maculicollis,
  pustulata, 139
Ophideres, genus; calaminea, hybrida, materna, 276
ophthalmica, Baileya, 162; Sphinx, 55
opipara, Tripudia, 250
opina, Valeria, 172
oponearia, Euchlæna, 350
oporaria, Eucrostis, 336
opuscularia, Pterospoda, 343
orbica, Amyna, 242
Orbicular spot, 18
orbimaculella, Yponomeuta, 423
orciferalis, Sysyrhypena, 282
ordinaria, Hadena, 169
ordinatellus, Yponomeuta, 423
oregona, Melaporphyria, 229
oregonensis, Euchætias, 135
oreodaphne, Hyloicus, 50
Oreta, genus; americana, formula, irrorata,
  rosea, 321
orgyiæ, Prothymia, 248
orilliana, Pachnobia, 180
orina, Calymnia, 219
orizaba, Rothschildia, 82
ornata, Acherdoa, 234; Apantesis, 130;
  Melalopha, 293
ornatrix, Utetheisa, 117
Orneodes, genus; hexadactyla, 417
Orneodidæ, Family, 25, 417
ornithogalli, Prodenia, 174
orobia, Graphiphora, 204
orosusalis, Pyrausta, 397
orphisalis, Pyrausta, 397
Orrhodia, genus; californica, 218
Orthodes, genus; candens, crenulata, cynica,
  enervis, griseocincta, nimia, nitens, prodeuns, 203; pueriiis, 204; tecta, togata,
  vecors, velata, 203
Orthofidonia, genus; junctaria, semiclarata,
  vestaliata, viatica, 337
Orthosia, genus; bicolorago, helva, 217
orthosioides, Phoberia, 273
Ortmann, A. E., 377
ortonii, Peridroma, 182
osculata, Catocala, 265
ossularia, Eois, 335

ostenta, Holomelina, 115
otiosa, Apantesis, 131
ou, Autographa, 238
ovalis, Abrostola, 240
oviduca, Graphiphora, 204
ovilla, Nola, 357
oviplagalis, Tosale, 402
Oviposition, Time of, 5
ovulalis, Conchylodes, 393
Owls, 78
oxybaphi, Celerio, 76
Oxycnemis, genus; fusimacula, 221
Oxydia, genus; vesulia, 352
oxygramma, Autographa, 239
oxymorus, Admetovis, 196
Oxyptilus, genus; periscelidactylus, 416
Ozonadia, genus, 108

P

Pachnobia, genus; claviformis, ferruginoides,
  littoralis, orilliana, pectinata, Reddish,
  salicarum, Willow, 180
Pachylia, genus, 60; aterrima, crameri, ficus,
  lyncea, undatifascia, venezuelensis, 60
Pachysphinx, genus, 56; imperator, modesta,
  occidentalis, princeps, 57
pacificaria, Eois, 336
Packard, A. S., p. 30, 31, 33, 34, 35, 145
packardi, Estigmene, 123; Hippia 296;
  Mice, 109; Scepsis, 101; Schinia, 228
Packardia, genus; elegans, 367; geminata,
  368; nigripunctata, 367
Pæctes, genus; abrostoloides oculatrix,
  pygmæa, 241
pænulata, Euclea, 365
pagenstecheri, Hormoschista, 253
Palada, genus; scarletina, 229
palæogama, Catocala, 266
paleacea, Cosmia, 217
Paleacrita, genus; autumnata, merricata,
  sericeiferata, vernata, 324
Paleontology, 22
Palindia, genus; dominicata, 273
pallens, Cressonia, 57
pallescens, Melipotis, 258
pallialis, Bomolocha, 286
palliatricula, Chytonix, 161
pallida, Crambidia, 104; Cyathissa, 161;
  Erinnyis, 59; Hyphantria, 124
pallidior, Palpidia, 105
pallidulus, Sphinx, 55
palmeri, Lycomorpha, 101
Palmer-worms, 114
Palmia, genus; præcedens, 383
palpalis, Hæmorrhagia, 64; Plathypena, 287
Palpi, 7, 12
Palpidia, genus; pallidior, 105
Palthis, genus; angulalis, asopialis, aracinthusalis, 285
Palyadinæ, subfamily, 354
Palyas, genus; auriferaria, 354
pamina, Automeris, 89
pampina, Eucirrœdia, 215
pampinaria, Cleora, 344
pampinatrix, Darapsa, 68
Panapoda, genus; carneicosta, combinata,
  cressoni, rubricosta, rufimargo, scissa 273
Panchrysia, genus; purpurigera, 236
pandaria, Caberodes, 352
pandora, Coloradia, 91
pandorus, Pholus, 65
Pangrapta, genus; decoralis, elegantalis,
  epionoides, geometroides, recusans, 254
panisaria, Therina, 348
Panthea, genus; Eastern, furcilla, portlandia,
  Western, 152

Pantographa, genus; limata, suffusalis, 393
Panula, genus; inconstans, 258
Paota, genus; fultaria, 332
Papaipema, genus, 213; cataphracta, cerussata, furcata, 214; inquæsita, 213; marginidens necopina, nitela, 213, 214; purpurifascia, 213
Pawpaw, The, 46
paphia, Telea, 87
paradoxica, Prodoxus, 438
paradoxus, Heliochilus, 222
Paragrotis, genus, 188
parallela, Archips, 422; Olene, 308
Parallelia, genus; amplissima, bistriaris, 273
parallelia, Pherne, 351
paralleliaria, Pherne, 351
Paranthrene, genus; heucheræ, 387
Paraphia, genus; exsuperata, impropriata, mammurraria, nubecularia, subatomaria, triplipunctaria, unipuncta, unipunctata, 343
Parasemia, genus; geometrica, plantaginis, 134
Parasitized larva, 69
Parastichtis, genus; discivaria, gentilis, 217
parce, Hemeroplanes, 60
parentalis, Richia, 190
Pareuchætes, genus; églenensis, Gray-winged, insulata, 134; tenera, 134, 135; Yellow-winged, 134
Parharmonia, genus; pini, 384
Parora, genus; texana, 255
parta, Catocala, 264
parthenice, Apantesis, 129
parthenos, Hyphoraia, 128
partita, Galgula, 247
passer, Hadena, 168
pastillicans, Epiglæa, 219
pastinacella. Depressaria, 428
pasulella, Ephestia, 414
Patagium, p. 18
patalis, Xylomiges, 197
patefacta, Noctua, 184
patella, Clemensia, 108
patibilis, Drasteria, 257
patruelis, Eumestleta, 249
patula, Eumestleta, 249; Porosagrotis, 187
paulina, Catocala, 261
pavitensis, Cirrhobolina, 259
pavonina, Calasymbolus, 56
Parsnip Web-worm, The, 428
Peach-borer, The, 384
Peach-twig Borer, The, 426
pectinaria, Euchlæna, 350
pectinata, Pachnobia, 180
pelasgus, Hæmorrhagia, 62
pellionella, Tinea, 433
pellucida, Anisota, 95
pellucidaria, Nepytia, 343
penæus, Erinnyis, 59
pendulinaria, Cosymbia, 333
peninsularia. Mecoceras, 354
Penitent, The, 266
pennsylvanica, Euthyatira, 304
pepita, Basilodes, 234
peplaria, Azelina, 352
pepsidiformis, Sanninoidea, 384
perangulalis, Bomolocha, 286
perarcuata, Cymatophora, 341
perattenta, Eueretagrotis, 179
percara, Cyathissa, 161
Percnoptilota, genus; fluviata, 330
perconflua, Noctua, 183
perditalis, Hyamia, 254
perelegans, Hyloicus, 51
perflava, Metaponia, 250
pergentilis, Hadenella, 162

Pericopidæ, Family, 24, 33, 289
periculosa, Trigonophora, 215
Peridroma, genus, 182; alabamæ, 183; astricta, 182; incivis, 183; inermis, nigra, occulta, ortonii, saucia, 182; simplaria, 183
Perigea, genus; vecors, xanthioides, 165
Perigonica, genus; fulminans, 205
Perigrapha, genus; prima, 205
Periodicals containing information as to moths, 28
periscelidactylus, Oxyptilus, 416
perlaria, Metrocampa, 348
perlata, Metrocampa, 348; Remigia, 274
perlæta, Melipotis, 258
perlevis, Euchætias, 135
perlineata, Venusia, 328
perlubens, Xylomiges, 197
perlucidula, Pyromorpha, 371
permaculata, Turuptiana, 121
permagna, Nonagria, 211
perophoroides, Hyparpax, 299
perplexa, Synanthedon, 385
perpolita, Euxoa, 188
perpura, Anarta, 199
perscripta, Lepipolys, 177
persephone, Apantesis, 130
persica, Sanninoidea, 384
Persimmon, 87, 382
personata, Euxoa, 188; Raphia, 153
perspicua, Datana, 294; Thyris, 374
perstrialis, Scirpophaga, 402
pertextalis. Pyrausta, 397
peruviana, Noctuelia, 399
perversa, Malacosoma, 313
pettitana, Cenopis, 422
petulca, Xylina, 206
pexata, Xylina, 207
phæalis, Epizeuxis. 280
phaeton, Euproserpinus, 74
Phalænostola, genus: larentioides, 254
phalanga, Catocala, 266
phalaris. Erinnyis, 59
phalerata, Apantesis, 132
phasianaria, Caberodes. 352
phasma, Euerythra, 120
Pheocyma, genus; lineola, lucifera, 278
Pheosia, genus; californica, descherei, dimidiata, portlandia, rimosa, 295
Pherne, genus; jubararia, mellitularia, parallelia, paralleliaria, placearia, 351
Phigalia, genus; revocata, strigataria, titea, titearia, 347
Philagraula, genus, 356
Philedia, genus; punctomacularia, 343
Philereme, genus; californiata, 329
Philobia, genus; æmulataria, enotata, notata, sectomaculata, 339
philodina, Clemensia, 108
Philometra, genus; goasalis, longilabris, metonalis, 282
Philosamia, genus, 82; aurótus, canningi, 82; cynthia, 81, 82; insularis, pryeri, vesta, walkeri, 82
Phiprosopus, genus; acutalis, callitrichoides, nasutaria, 245
Phlyctænia, genus; plectilis, syringicola, tertialis, 397
Phlyctænodes genus; fuscalis, 395; oberthuralis, 396; sordida, sticticalis, tetragonalis, triumphalis, 395
Phoberia, genus; atomaria, forrigens, ingenua, orthosioides, 273
Phobetron, genus; abbotana, hyalinus, nigricans, nondescriptus, pithecium, tetradactylus, 366

Index

Pholus, genus, 65; achemon, 66; ampelophaga, 65; clotho, 67; crantor, 66; fasciatus, hornbeckiana, jussieuæ, labruscæ, linnei, 67; pandorus, 65; posticatus, 66; satellitia, 65; strigilis, 67; typhon, 65; vitis, 67
pholus, Darapsa, 68; Lycomorpha, 101
phrada, Ptychoglene, 110
Phragmatobia, genus; beani, brucei, fuliginosa, 126; remissa, 127; rubricosa, 126; yarrowi, 127
Phryganidia, genus; californica, 291
Phrygionis, genus; argenteostriata, cerussata, obrussata, 354
Phthorimæa, genus, 425; operculella, 424, 425; solanella, tabacella, terrella, 425
Phurys, genus; lima, vinculum, 275
Phycitinæ, Subfamily, 407
Physostegania, genus; pustularia, 338
piatrix, Catocala, 266
pica, Pseudohazis, 93
Pickle-worm, The, 394
picta, Arachnis, 124; Erinnyis, 59; Mamestra, 193
pictipennis, Heliosea, 230
pictipes, Synanthedon, 386
Piers Plowman, quoted, 288
Pigea, genus; multilineata, 333
pinaria, Nepytia, 343
pinastri, Hyloicus, 52
Pinconia, genus; coa, 369
pineum, Lapara, 53
pini, Parharmonia, 384
piniaria, Caripeta, 342
Pinion; Ashen, 206; Bailey's, Broad Ashen, Dowdy, 207; Green Gray, 206; Nameless, Nappy, Thaxter's, 207; Wanton, 206; Warm Gray, 207
pinorum, Vespamima, 384
piperis, Erinnyis, 59
Pippona, genus; bimatris, 221
pithecium, Phobetron, 366
pityochromus, Plagiomimicus, 235
pityochrous, Euxoa, 188
placearia, Pherne, 351
placida, Rhynchagrotis, 178
plagiata, Laphygma, 174; Noctua, 183
Plagiomimicus, genus; pityochromus, 235
Plagodis, genus; arrogaria, emargataria, floscularia, keutzingaria, keutzingi, serinaria, subprivata, 349
plantaginis, Parasemia, 134
Plantago, 120, 125, 134
Platagrotis, genus; pressa, 179
Platanus, 87, 367
Platea, genus; californiaria, 342; dulcearia, trilinearia, 343; uncanaria 342
Plathypena, genus; crassatus, erectalis, obesalis, palpalis, scabra, 287
platinalis, Conchylodes, 393
Platynota, genus; concursana, flavedana, labiosana, laterana, 422
Platyperigea, genus; discistriga, præacuta, 164
Platyprepia, genus; guttata, ochracea, virginalis, 128
Platypterygidæ, Family, 24, 34, 320
Platysenta, genus; albipuncta, atriciliata, indigens, meskei, videns, 163
plebeja, Atreides, 49
pleciæformis, Bembecia, 383
plecta, Noctua, 184
plectilis Phlyctænia, 397
plena, Dysodia, 375
pleonectusa, Ipimorpha, 220
Pleonectyptera, genus; floccalis, irrecta, pyralis, 246

Pleroma, genus; obliquata, 206
plicatus, Ufeus. 191
Plodia, genus; interpunctella, zeæ, 415
plota, Hyloicus, 51
plumbea, Hypoprepia, 106; Illice, 109
plumbifimbriata, Spragueia, 252
Plume, The Grape-vine, 416
Plumeria, 58
plumeriæ, Pseudosphinx, 57
plumifrontellus, Acrolophus, 443
plumigeraria, Coniodes, 345
Plusia, genus, 8, 237; ærea, æroides, balluca, 237
Plusiodonta, genus; compressipalpis, insignis, 235
pluto, Xylophanes, 75
Poaphila, genus; quadrifilaris, 274
Podagra, genus; crassipes, 178
Podosesia, genus; longipes, syringæ, 382
pœcila, Hyloicus, 51
poetica, Neumœgenia, 235
Pogocolon, genus, 72; gauræ, 72; juanita, vega, 73
Polia, genus; diversilineata, illepida, Theodore's, theodori, Varied-banded, 171
Poling, O. C., ix
polistiformis, Memythrus, 382
politia, Sabulodes, 353
Polychrysia, genus; formosa, moneta, trabea, 236
polygama, Catocala, 268
Polygamist, The, 268
Polygonum, 157
Polygrammate, genus; hebræa, hebraicum, 160
polyphemus, Telea, 87
pometaria, Alsophila, 326
pomifoliella, Bucculatrix, 431
pomonella, Bucculatrix, 431
Pope, Alexander, quoted, 289
popeanella, Anaphora, 443
populi, Apatela, 154; Cleosiris, 205
Populus, 57, 155, 378
Porosagrotis, genus; dædalus, fusca, murænula, patula, rileyana, septentrionalis, tripars, vetusta, worthingtoni, 187
porphyria, Halisidota, 138
Porrima, genus; regia, 226
Porthesia, genus, 305
Porthetria, genus; dispar, 308
portlandia, Panthea, 152; Pheosia, 295
posticatus, Pholus, 66
Potato-moth, The, 425
præacuta, Platyperigea, 164
præcedens, Palmia, 383
præclara, Catocala, 269
prægrandaria, Metrocampa, 348
præatomata, Macaria, 340
prasina, Adelphagrotis, 179
precationis, Autographa, 238
pressa, Platagrotis, 179
prima, Anorthodes, 164; Estigmene, 122, Perigrapha, 205
princeps, Pachysphinx, 57
Prinos, 46
Priocycla, genus; armataria, 351
Prionoxystus, genus; macmurtrei, querciperda, robiniæ, 378
privatus, Anytus, 191
Privet-moth, The, 394
proba, Diacrisia, 128
Proboscis, 12
procinctus, Dargida, 196
proclivis, Rhizagrotis, 185
Prodenia, genus; commelinæ, ornithogalli, 174
prodeuns, Orthodes, 203

Prodoxus, genus; cinereus, 441; coloradensis, 440; decipiens, 438; marginatus, 439; paradoxica, quinquepunctella, 438; reticulata, 440; y-inversa, 439
profecta. Bomolocha, 286
progressata, Triphosa, 331
Prolegs, abdominal, anal, 7
Prolimacodes, genus; undifera, scapha, 367
promethea, Callosamia, 84
promptella, Doryodes, 245
Pronoctua, genus; typica, 185
Pronuba, genus, 441; maculata, synthetica, 442; yuccasella, 441
propinqua, Copicucullia, 208
propinqualis, Rivula, 245
propinquilinea, Demas, 152
propriaria, Euchœca, 328; Euchlæna, 350
proprius, Sympistis, 229
propugnata, Gypsochroa, 332
propugnaria, Gypsochroa 332
proserpina, Hemileuca, 91
Proserpinus, genus, 72, 73, 74; clarkiæ, flavofasciata, 73
Protambulyx, genus, 54; strigilis, carteri, 54
Prothymia, genus; coccineifascia, orgyiæ, rhodarialis, semipurpurea, 248
Protoparce, genus, 44; carolina Linnæus; carolina Donavan; celeus; chionanthi; lycopersici; nicotianæ occulta, 45; quinquemaculatus, 41, 43, 45; rustica sexta, 45
Protosia, genus, 111
protumnusalis, Zanclognatha, 281
proxima, Apantesis, 131; Synanthedon, 387
proximalis, Titanio, 396
prunata, Eustroma, 329
pruniella, Anarsia, 426
Pryer, Henry, 79
pryeri, Philosamia 82
Psaphidia, genus; grotei, muralis, resumens, viridescens, 177
Pseudacontia, genus; crustaria, 225
Pseudalypia, genus; crotchi, 232
Pseudanarta, genus; crocea, falcata, Falcate, flava, Single, singula, Yellow, 175
Pseudanthœcia, genus; tumida, 228
Pseudanthracia, genus; coracias, 278
pseudargyria, Heliophila, 201
pseuderminea, Estigmene, 123
pseudogamma, Autographa, 238
Pseudoglæa, genus; blanda, decepta, tædata, 216
Pseudohazis, genus, 93; denudata, eglanterina, hera, nuttalli, pica, shastaensis, 93
Pseudolimacodes, genus, 217
Pseudomya, genus; minima, 99
pseudoneustria, Malacosoma, 313
Pseudorgyia, genus; versuta, 245
Pseudorthosia, genus; variabilis, 216
Pseudosphinx, genus, 57; asdrubal, hasdrubal, obscura, plumeriæ, rustica, tetrio, 57
Pseudotamila, genus; vanella, 229
Pseudothyatira, genus; cymatophoroides, expultrix, 304
psidii, Gloveria, 311
Psidium pyrifera, 140
Psilura, genus; monacha, 309
Psychidæ, Family, 7, 25, 35, 360
Psychomorpha, genus; epimenis, 232
ptelearia, Eois, 334
Pterætholix, genus; bullula, 243
pteridis, Diacrisia, 128
Pterophoridæ, Family, 25, 37, 415
Pterospoda, genus; opuscularia, 343
Ptychoglene, genus; coccinea, flammans, phrada, sanguineola, tenuimargo, 110
ptycophora, Fala, 235
puber, Syssaura, 352

pudens, Euchætias, 135; Euthyatira, 304
pudorata, Apatela, 156
puera, Hyblæa, 288
puerilis, Orthodes, 204
pulchella, Xylomiges, 197
pulcher, Hepialus, 444
pulcherrima, Eutelia, 242
pulchraria, Nepytia, 343
pulchripennis, Melicleptria, 230
pulchripictalis, Cindaphia, 397
pullata, Lathosea, 209
pultaria, Therina, 348
pulverea, Heterocampa, 297; Narthecophora, 235
pulverilinea, Matigramma, 276
pulverina, Bruceia, 108
Pulvillus, 14, 15
punctata, Dasylophia, 296; Diacrisia, 128
punctatissima, Basilona, 97; Hyphantria, 123
punctistriga, Artace, 312
punctivena, Capnodes, 277; Caradrina, 165
punctomacularia, Philedia, 343
pungens, Herse, 43
Pupæ, 9
pupillaris, Sysyrhypena, 282
pupula, Eustixia, 149, 398
pura, Carama, 368; Catocala, 264; Utetheisa, 117
purgata, Cænurgia, 257
purpurana, Archips, 422
purpurascens, Calpe, 236
purpurifascia, Papaipema. 213
purpurigera, Panchrysia, 236
purpurissata, Mamestra, 192
pustularia, Physostegania, 338
pustulata, Celama, 357; Opharus, 139
putnami, Euchalcia, 237
putrescens, Homoptera, 278
Pygarctia, genus; abdominalis, elegans, Elegant, Orange-bodied, spraguei, Sprague's, vivida, 136
pygmæa, Adoneta, 365; Dircetis, 284; Pæctes, 241
Pygoctenucha, genus; funerea, harrisi, pyrrhoura, terminalis, votiva, 111
Pyralidæ, Family, 21, 25, 36, 246, 391
Pyralinæ, Subfamily, 399
Pyralis, genus; farinalis, 400
pyralis, Apharetra, 159; Pleonectyptera, 246
pyramidalis, Albuna, 384
pyramidoides, Pyrophila, 149, 173
pyramus, Hæmorrhagia, 63
pyramusalis, Heterogramma, 284
Pyrausta, genus; adipaloides, arsaltealis, badipennis, 397; bellulalis, diffissa, efficitalis, erosnealis, 398; euphœsalis, fascialis, fumalis, 397; funebris, generosa, 398; gentilis, 397; glomeralis, 398; guttulosa, 397; hircinalis, 398; illibalis, 397; insequalis, 398; langdonalis, 397; madetesalis, 398; magniferalis, 397; niveicilialis, obnigralis, ochosalis, octomaculata, 398; orasusalis, orphisalis, pertextalis, 397; repletalis, 398; subjectalis, 397; subolivalis, subsequalis, 398; thesealis, 397; tyralis, 398; unifascialis, 397; unimacula, 398
Pyraustinæ, Subfamily, 392
pyri, Synanthedon, 387
pyrina, Zeuzera, 376
Pyromorpha, genus; dimidiata, perlucidula, 371
Pyrophila, genus; glabella, Gray, Mouse-colored, pyramidoides, repressus, tragopoginis, 173
pyrrha, Cargida, 301
Pyrrhia, genus; umbra, 214
pyrrhoura, Pygoctenucha, 111

Index

pythion, Charadra, 152
pyxidifera, Lagoa, 369

Q

quadrata, Apatela, 156
quadriannulata, Cosymbia, 333
quadricornis, Ceratomia, 47
quadridentata, Euxoa, 188
quadrifilaris, Poaphila, 274
quadriguttalis, Alypia, 144
quadriguttatus, Sthenopis, 443
quadrinotata, Heterophleps, 327
quadripunctaria, Eufidonia, 337
quadristigmalis, Glyphodes, 394
Quaker, Boyish, 204; Cynical, Rustic, Small
    Brown, 203
quinquecaudatus, Sannina, 382
quinquelinearia, Leptomeris, 333
quinquemaculatus, Protoparce, 45
quinquepunctella, Prodoxus, 438
quenseli, Apantesis, 131
quercicola, Euclea, 365
querciperda, Prionoxystus, 378
quercivoraria, Metanema, 351
quercus, Hemihyalea, 138
quernaria, Nacophora, 345
questionis, Autographa, 238

R

Rachela, genus; bruceata, 324
rachelæ, Apocheima, 345
Racheospila, genus; hollandaria, lixaria,
    saltusaria, 336
radians, Apantesis, 132
radix, Mamestra, 193
Ragonot, E. L., 37, 408
ramosula, Actinotia, 173
Rancora, genus; solidaginis, strigata, 209
Raphia, genus; abrupta, coloradensis, flex-
    uosa, frater, personata, 153
Rascal Leaf-crumpler, The, 409
rasilis, Oligia, 166
raspa, Syssphinx, 96
Ratarda, genus, 305
reciprocata, Euchœca, 328
reconditaria, Synelys, 333
rectangula, Autographa, 239
rectangulata, Hydriomena, 331
rectaria, Anaplodes, 337
rectifascia, Atethmia, 220
rectilinea, Apantesis, 129; Cochlidion, 367
recurvalis, Zinckenia, 392
recusans, Pangrapta, 254
redimicula, Euxoa, 190
reducta, Turuptiana, 121
refractaria, Gonodontis, 350
refusata, Nannia, 327
regalis, Citheronia, 97
regia, Citheronia, 97; Porrima, 226
regnatrix, Xanthopastis, 231
Relict, The, 262
relicta, Catocala, 149, 262
Remigia, genus; indentata, latipes, perlata,
    repanda, texana, 274
remissa, Phragmatobia, 127
remissaria, Caberodes, 352
Renia, genus; discoloralis, fallacialis, gener-
    alis, thraxalis, 283
Reniform spot, 18
reniformis, Heliotropha, 173
renigera, Mamestra, 195
repanda, Remigia, 274; Siavana, 273
repentinus, Ceratomia, 48
repentis, Euxoa, 189; Yrias, 277
repletalis, Pyrausta, 398

repressus, Pyrophila, 173
resistaria, Ania, 349
restituens, Alsophila, 326
restrictalis, Heliodes, 230
restorata, Sciagraphia, 339
resumens, Psaphidia, 177
retecta, Catocala, 262
retectata, Macaria, 339
retentata, Macaria, 339
reticulata, Prodoxus, 440
reticulina, Hexeris, 375
Retinaculum, 17
revayana, Nycteola, 288
revocata, Phigalia, 347
Rheumaptera, genus; hastata, 329; luctuata,
    rubrosuffusata, 330
rhexiæ, Chloridea, 222
Rhizagrotis, genus; proclivis, 185
rhoda, Apantesis, 132
rhodarialis, Prothymia, 248
Rhododendrons, 173
Rhododipsa, genus; masoni, miniana, volupia,
    225
Rhodophora, genus; citronellus, florida,
    gauræ, matutina, 224
Rhodosea, genus; julia, 225
rhœbus, Erinnyis, 59
Rhopalocera, 3
Rhynchagrotis, genus; alternata, 179; ancho-
    celioides, cupida, gilvipennis, 178; mini-
    malis, 178, 179; placida, rufipectus, velata,
    178
ribearia, Cymatophora, 340
ribesiaria, Eustroma, 329
richardsoni, Anarta, 199
Richia, genus; aratrix, parentalis, 190
Richter, Jean Paul, quoted, 417
rickseckeri, Estigmene, 123
ridingsi, Alypia, 143, 145
Riley, C. V., 30, 141, 154, 175, 201, 223,
    232, 233, 239, 243, 280, 281, 335, 362,
    401, 406, 409, 420, 425
rileyana, Heteropacha, 314; Porosagrotis,
    187; Synanthedon, 385
rimosa, Pheosia 295
Rivula, genus; propinqualis, 245
rivularia, Almodes, 354
rivulosa, Schinia, 228
Robinia, pseudacacia, 378, 419
robiniæ, Prionoxystus, 378
Robinson, C. T., 29, 30, 37
robinsoni, Catocala, 262; Cressonia, 57;
    Lerina, 111
Rœselia, genus; conspicua, fuscula, minuscula,
    358
rogationis, Autographa, 238
Rosaceæ, 83, 155, 366, 410
rosaceana, Archips, 422
rosacearum, Calasymbolus, 56
rosalinda, Catocala, 268
rosea, Euhyparpax, 298; Hyparpax, 299;
    Mamestra, 193; Oreta 321; Thyreion, 222
roseitincta, Schinia, 227
rossi, Gynæphora, 305
Rothschild, Hon. Walter, ix, 31
Rothschildia, genus, 82, 83; jorulla, orizaba,
    82
rotundata, Chlænogramma, 46
Royal Walnut-moth, 6
rubens, Hæmorrhagia, 64
rubi, Bembecia, 383
rubicunda, Anisota, 95; Euherrichia, 253
rubra, Diacrisia, 128; Samia, 84
rubricosa, Phragmatobia, 126
rubricosta, Holomelina, 115
rubripalpis, Artace, 312
rubrolinearia, Leptomeris, 333

rubrolineata, Leptomeris, 333
rubroscapus, Ctenucha, 102
rubrosuffusata, Rheumaptera, 330
rude, Natada, 366
rufago, Jodia, 215
ruficaudis, Hæmorrhagia, 62, 63
ruficillata, Mesoleuca, 330
rufipectus, Rhynchagrotis, 178
rufostriga, Caradrina, 165
rufula, Diacrisia, 128
rugifrons, Stiria, 234
rugosa, Mamestra, 194
rupta, Gluphisia, 300
rurigena, Heterogramma, 284
Rustic; Brown-streaked, Civil, Convivial, 165; Mooned, Speckled, 164
rustica, Erinnyis, 59; Protoparce, 45; Pseudosphinx, 57
rutila, Autographa, 238
rutilans, Synanthedon, 385

S

Sabal palmetto, 122
Sabulodes, genus; arcasaria, contingens, depontanata, goniata, imitata, incurvata, lorata, politia, sulphurata, transfindens, transmutans, transposita, transvertens, truxaliata, 353
sabulosa, Cissusa, 256; Tuerta, 143
Sack-bearer, Melsheimer's, Scalloped, 359
sacramenti, Alypia, 145
Saddle-back, The, 364
saga, Hyblæa, 288
Salia, genus; interpuncta, 285
salicarum, Pachnobia, 180
saliceti, Sphinx, 55
salicis, Apatela, 157
saligneana, Eucosma, 418
Sallow; Angle-striped, 217; Anointed, 218; Even-lined, 220; Lost, Moffat's, 218; Red-winged, 215; Roadside, 218; Round-loaf, 219; Silky, 218; Sloping, Smudged, 219; Unsated, Walker's, 218
Salobrana, genus; tecomæ, 401
saltusaria, Racheospila, 336
sambuci, Zotheca, 219
Sambucus, 212, 219
Samea, genus; castellalis, disertalis, ecclesialis, luccusalis, 393
Samia, genus, 83; californica, ceanothi, 84; cecropia, 83, 84; columbia, euryalus, gloveri, rubra, 84
sanborni, Acoloithus, 371
sanguineola, Ptychoglene, 110
sanguivenosa, Æmilia, 137
saniaria, Hæmatopsis, 332
saniptri, Hyloicus, 52
Sannina, genus; quinquecaudatus, uroceriformis, 382
Sanninoidea, genus; exitiosa, pepsidiformis, persica, xiphiæformis, 384
saporis, Triocnemis, 225
sappho, Catocala, 260
satellitia, Pholus, 65
saturata, Schinia, 227
Saturnia, genus, 89; mendocino, 89
Saturniidæ, Family, 9, 12, 24, 31, 80
Saturniinæ, 80, 81, 86
satyricus, Ufeus, 191
satyriniformis, Melittia, 380
saucia, Peridroma, 182
Sauer-kraut, 239
saundersi, Apantesis, 129; Homoptera, 278
sauzælitæ, Ochria, 214
saxea, Syneda, 259
scabra, Plathypena, 287

scabriuscula, Dipterygia, 172
Scale insects, fed upon by larvæ, 6
Scape-moth, The Yellow-collared, The White-collared, 101
scapha, Prolimacodes, 367
Scarce Bordered Straw, 222
scardina, Anaphora, 443
scarletina, Palada, 229
Scepsis, genus, 100; fulvicollis, matthewi, packardi, semidiaphana, wrighti, 101
Schaus, W , 33
Schidax, genus, 356
Schinia, genus, 226; acutilinea, 227; albafascia, 228; aleucis, 227; arcifera, atrites, brevis, 228; brucei, chrysellus, 227; contracta, 228; cumatilis, 227; designata, divergens, 228; exaltata, 227; jaguarina, 228; lineata, lynx, 227; marginata, mortua, 228; nigrirena, 227; nobilis, 228; nundina, 227; packardi, rivulosa, 228; roseitincta, saturata, separata, simplex, 227; spraguei, tertia, thoreaui, 228; trifascia, 227
Schizura, genus; badia, 229; cinereofrons, concinna, conspecta, edmandsi, humilis, ipomœæ, 298; leptinoides, mustelina, 299; nitida, 298; significata, 299; unicornis, 298
schlægeri, Stenoma, 428
schœnherri, Anarta, 199
Schœnobiinæ, Subfamily, 402
schwarziorum, Illice, 109
Sciagraphia, genus; duplicata, granitata, heliothidata, mellistrigata, ocellinata, restorata, subcolumbata, 339
sciata, Therina, 348
scintillans, Catocala, 266
Scirpophaga, genus; macrinellus, perstrialis, serriradiellus, 402
scissa, Canidia, 226
scitipennis, Hyperæschra, 294
scitiscripta, Cerura, 299
scitula, Synanthedon, 387
scobialis, Epizeuxis, 281
Scolecocampa, genus; liburni, ligni, 244
Scoliopteryx, genus; libatrix, 215
scolopendrina, Harpyia, 299
Scoparia, genus, 399
Scopariinæ, Subfamily, 399
Scopelosoma, genus, 217; ceromatica, devia, moffatiana, walkeri, 218
Scotchmen, 80
Scotogramma, genus; inconcinna, infuscata, submarina, 198
Scribbler, The, 324
scribonia, Ecpantheria, 120
scripta, Habrosyne, 303
scriptipennis, Epizeuxis, 280
scudderiana, Eucosma, 418
sculptus, Anytus, 191
scutellaris, Bomolocha, 286
scutosus, Heliothis, 224
Sebastiania, 417
Seckel pear, 410
sectilis, Morrisonia, 196
sectomaculata, Philobia, 339
sedata, Tarache, 251
Seirarctia, genus; echo, niobe, 122
selecta, Autographa, 239
Selenis, genus; monotropa, 277
Selicanis, genus; cinereola, 216
semiaperta, Tricholita, 205
semiauratus, Sthenopis, 443
semiclarata, Feltia, 186; Orthofidonia, 337
semiclusaria, Nepytia, 343
semicrocea, Exyra, 248
semidiaphana, Scepsis, 101
semifascia, Monoleuca, 365

semiflava, Xanthoptera, 249
semifusellus, Crambus, 402
semilineata, Hyamia, 254
semilunata, Hadena, 169
seminudaria, Therina, 348
seminudata, Therina, 348
Semiophora, genus; badicollis, catharina, dilucidula, elimata, janualis, manifesto-labes, opacifrons, tenebrifera, 180
Semioscopis, genus; merricella, 429
semiplaga, Heterocampa, 297
semipurpurea, Prothymia, 248
senatoria, Anisota, 94
senta, Hæmorrhagia, 64
sentinaria, Leptomeris, 333
separata, Schinia, 227
separatus, Hyloicus, 50
septentrionalis, Gluphisia, 300; Porosagrotis, 187
sepulchralis, Citheronia, 97; Thyris, 374
Sequoia, 52
sequoiæ, Hyloicus 52; Vespamima, 384
serena, Catocala, 267
sericea, Glæa, 218
sericeiferata, Paleacrita, 324
serinaria, Plagodis, 349
serrata, Euchlæna, 350; Trichopolia, 199
serrataria, Euchlæna, 350
serriradiellus, Scirpophaga, 402
Sesia, genus, 61, 379; fadus, tantalus, titan 62
Sesiidæ, Family, 379
Sesiinæ, Subfamily, 57
sesquilinea, Syssaura, 352
sesquistriaris, Agnomonia, 274
Setagrotis, genus; terrifica, 181
Setting-board, 20
Setting-needle, 19
severa, Gluphisia, 300
sevorsa, Fenaria, 233
sexatilis, Euxoa, 190
sexfasciata, Synanthedon, 385
sexmaculata, Celama, 357
sexpunctata, Hyamia, 254
sexsignata, Litocala, 272
sexta, Protoparce, 45
Shakespeare, quoted, 94, 103, 356, 379, 423
Sharp, David, quoted, 3, 17, 30
shastaensis, Apantesis, 131; Pseudohazis, 93
Sheep-moth, Nuttall's, 93
Siavana, genus; auripennis, repanda, 273
Sibine, genus; ephippiatus, stimulea, 364
siccaria, Therina, 348
Sicya, genus; macularia, 347
Sideraria, Eois, 336
sigmaria, Cymatophora, 340
sigmoides, Eueretagrotis, 179
signata, Dasylophia, 296; Tricholita, 203
signataria, Melanolophia, 344
signifera, Laphygma, 174
significans, Æmilia, 137
significata, Schizura, 299
silago, Xanthia, 214
Silk-culture, The History of, 316
Silk-moth, The Ailanthus, 82; Ceanothus, Columbian, Glover's, 84; Mendocino, 89; Orizaba, 82; Spice-Bush, 84; Tulip-tree, 86; Zephyr, 89
simalis, Cornifrons, 399
similana, Eucosma, 418
similis, Alypia, 143; Catocala, 268
simplaria, Notodonta, 295; Peridroma, 183
simplex, Autographa, 240; Comacla, 107; Xylomiges, 197
simulans, Memythrus, 383
singula, Pseudanarta, 175
sinualis, Melipotis, 258

Sister, The Little, 269
Sisyrosea, genus; inornata, textula, 366
sitellata, Gypsochroa, 332
Six-plume Moth, The, 417
Skeletonizer, The Apple-leaf, 411
Skinner, Henry, ix
slossoni, Gluphisia, 300
slossoniæ, Alarodia, 366
Slug; Monkey, 366; Nason's, 366; Pygmy, 365; Slosson's, 366, Spiny Oak-, 365
Small Angle Shades, 172
Smerinthus, 54
Smith, Herbert H., 20
Smith, John B., viii, 29, 30, 32, 33, 34, 118, 151
smithi, Grammodes, 274
Smythe, Ellison, 63
Snout-moth, The Meal, 400
snoviaria, Mellilla, 338
snowi, Melittia, 381
sobria, Calpe, 236; Drasteria, 257; Eois, 335; Nephelodes, 199
socia, Syneda, 259
socors, Cænurgia, 257
Solanaceæ, 45
solanella, Phthorimæa, 425
Solenobia, genus, 360
solidaginis, Rancora, 209
Solidago, 101, 117, 126, 252, 418
Solidago Gall-moth, The, 425
solituda, Gæa, 381
Somites, in body of larvæ, 6
somnus, Catocala, 263
sordida, Hyloicus, 49; Phlyctænodes, 395
sordidata, Hydriomena, 331
sororius, Hemileuca, 91
Southey, quoted, 77
stellata, Derrima, 224
stellidaria, Almodes, 354
Stenaspilates, genus; zalissaria, 351
Stenoma, genus; schlægeri, 428
Sthenopis, genus; alni, argentata, argenteo-maculata, quadriguttatus, semiauratus, 443
Stibadium, genus; spumosum, 234
sticticalis, Phlyctænodes, 395
stigma, Anisota, 94
stigmata, Dryobota, 171
stigmosa, Feltia, 186
stimulea, Sibine, 364
Stinging Caterpillars, 90; spines, 9
Stiria, genus; rugifrons, 234
stragula, Hyperæschra, 294
Strawberry-borer, The, 385
Strawberry Leaf-roller, 419
Strecker, Herman, 30, 52
Strenoloma, genus; lunilinea, 147, 276
Stretch, R. H., 32, 35
stretchi, Catocala, 263; Syneda, 260; Utetheisa, 117
Stretchia, genus; muricina, 205
striata, Illice, 109
striatella, Euchalcia, 237
strigata, Calophasia, 170; Euclea, 365; Eucalyptera, 244; Rancora, 209
strigataria, Phigalia, 347
strigicollis, Mamestra, 195
strigilis, Pholus, 67
strigosa, Apantesis, 131; Calidota, 139; Melalopha, 293
strigularia, Cœnocalpe, 332
stygiaria, Azelina, 352
stylata, Cerapoda, 177
stylobata, Campometra, 276
Stylopoda, genus; cephalica, 229
spadix, Cissusa, 256
Span-worm; Goose-berry, 340; Walnut, 345

Sparrows, English, 325
Spear-mark, The, 329
Specimens, capture of, killing, mounting, 19
speciosa, Apantesis, 131
speciosata, Hydriomena, 331
spectanda, Chloridea, 222
spectans, Apatela, 156
Spectre, The, 77
Spencer, Herbert, quoted, 364
sperataria, Lycia, 345
Spermacoce, 75
speyeri, Cucullia, 208
Sphacelodes, genus; floridensis, vulneraria, 354
Sphacelodinæ, Subfamily, 354
Sphecodina, genus, 70; abbotti, 70
Sphida, genus; obliqua, obliquata, 211
Sphingidæ, 12, 25, 30, 41
Sphinx, genus, 54; astarte, 55; cerisyi, 54; geminatus, jamaicensis, 55; ocellata, 54; ophthalmica, pallidulus, saliceti, tripartitus, 55
Sphinx, Abbot's, 70; Abbot's Pine, 53; Achemon, 66; Alope, 58; Ash, 46; Azalea, 68; Bear, 71; Big Poplar, 57; Blinded, 56; Bombyx, 53; Catalpa, 48; Cerisy's, 54; Chersis, 50; Clark's Day-, 73; Colorado, 52; Cramer's, 59; Cypress, 48; Domingo, 59; Ello, 58; Euterpe, 74; Fig, 60; Four-horned, 47; Galium, 76; Gaudy, 67; Gaura, 72; Giant Gray, 57; Gordian, 51; Grote's, 61; Hermit, Hermit-like, 49; Hog, 68; Huckleberry, 56; Hydrangea, 69; Laurel, 51; Lesser Vine, 67; Lettered, 71; Lintner's, 51; Lintner's Pine, 53; Madame Merian's, 58; Mourning, 61; Nessus, 72; Neumœgen's, 50; Obscure, 50; Occult, 45; Œnotrus, 59; Papaw, 46; Phaeton, 74; Pine, 52; Pluto, 75; Rustic, 45; Satellite, 65; Sequoia, 59; Silver-spotted, 60; Small-eyed, 56; Strecker's, 73; Striped Morning, 76; Tersa, 75; Tomato, 45; Twin-spot, 55; Vancouver, 50; Vine, 67; Walnut, 75; Waved, 48; Western Poplar, 57; White-banded Day-, 62; Wild Cherry, 52; Yellow-banded Day-, 73
spilomela, Caradrina, 165
Spinneret, 7
spinosæ, Eupanychis, 226
spinuloides, Adoneta, 365
Spiræa, 237, 366
spissa, Euxoa, 189
"Splitters" and "Lumpers," 112
Sport, The, 152
Spots on wings of noctuid moth, 18
spraguei, Pygarctia, 136; Schinia, 228
Spragueia, genus; dama, guttata, onagrus, plumbifimbriata, trifariana, 252
spumosum, Stibadium, 234
spuraria, Leptomeris, 333
Spurs, tibial, 14, 15
sputatrix, Hadena, 168
squamigera, Almodes, 354
s-signata, Macaria, 339
subæquaria, Apæcasia, 342
subalbicans, Heterocampa, 297
subapicalis, Xylomiges, 197
subatomaria, Paraphia, 343
subcedens, Hadena, 167
subcinctaria, Macaria, 339
subcitrina, Megalopyge, 369
subcolumbata, Sciagraphia, 339
subdolens, Nephelodes, 199
subflava, Nonagria, 211
subgothica, Feltia, 186
subjecta, Illice, 109
subjectalis, Pyrausta, 397

subjuncta, Hadenella, 162; Mamestra, 193
sublunaria, Cleora, 344
submarina, Scotogramma, 198
subnata, Catocala, 266
subolivalis, Pyrausta, 398
subornata, Hypoprepia, 106
subpartita, Galgula, 247
subprivata, Plagodis, 349
subpunctata, Heliophila, 201
Subregions, Faunal, 387
subsequalis, Pyrausta, 398
subsignarius, Ennomos, 348
subsinuaria, Hyperitis, 349
substrigata, Noctua, 184
Subterminal line, 18
subusta, Atethmia, 220
subviridis, Catocala, 261
successaria, Cymatophora, 341; Hæmatopsis, 332
Sudraka, quoted, 269
sueta, Melicleptria, 230
suffusa, Agrotis, 182; Mamestra, 192
suffusalis, Pantographa, 393
Sugar-beet Moth, The, 395
Sugar-cane, 403
Sugaring for moths, 146
sulphuraria, Alcis, 343
sulphurata, Sabulodes, 353
superans, Apatela, 156
superaria, Caberodes, 352
suppressaria, Eois, 335
surrectalis, Epizeuxis, 280
sutrix, Tornacontia, 250
Sweetheart, The, 263
Swift, quoted, 370
Swordgrass; American, Dot and Dash, 208
Sylectra, genus; erycata, 254
sylvaticoides, Malacosoma, 313
Symmerista, genus; albifrons, 296
Sympherta, genus; tripunctaria, 342
Symphoricarpus, 62, 63
Sympistis, genus; proprius, 229
Synanthedon, genus; acericolum, acerni, 386; æmula, albicornis, 387; aureola, 385; aureopurpurea, 387; bassiformis, bolli, brunneipennis, consimilis, eupatorii, 385; gallivorum, 387; hemizonæ, 385; hospes, 387; hyperici, imitata, impropria, infirma, 385; inusitata, 386; kœbelei, 387; lupini, lustrans, madariæ, 385; modesta, 387; neglecta, perplexa, 385; pictipes, 386; proxima, pyri, 387; rileyana, rutilans, 385; scitula, 387; sexfasciata, tipuliformis, washingtonia, 385
Synchlora, genus; liquoraria, tricoloraria, 336
Syneda, genus; adumbrata, alleni, 259; athabasca, 260; capticola, divergens, 259; edwardsi, 260; graphica, 259; howlandi, hudsonica, 260; saxea, socia, 259; stretchi, 260
Synelys, genus; alabastaria, ennucleata, reconditaria, 333
Syngrapha, genus; alticola, devergens, divergens, hochenwarthi, 240
synochitis, Eustrotia, 247
Syntomeida, genus; epilais, euterpe, ferox, ipomeæ, 99
Syntomidæ, 24, 31, 98
syracosia, Æmilia, 137
Syringa, 382
syringæ, Podosesia, 382
syringicola, Phlyctænia, 397
Syssaura, genus; æquosus, biclaria, ephyrata, infensata, juniperaria, œmearia, olyzonaria, puber, sesquilinea, varus, 352
Syssphinx, genus, 96; albolineata, heiligbrodti, raspa, White-lined, 96

Index

Sysyrhypena, genus; harti, orciferalis, pupillaris, 282

T

tabacella, Phthorimæa, 425
tactus, Homopyralis, 256
tædata, Pseudoglæa, 216
talidiformis, Crambodes, 163
tantalus, Sesia, 42, 61, 62
tapayusa, Cocytius, 44
tapetzella, Trichophaga, 434
Tapinostola, genus; variana, 216
Tarache, genus; aprica, binocula, delecta, erastrioides, flavipennis, lactipennis, lanceolata, libedis, metallica, sedata, terminimacula, virginalis, 251
tardigrada, Euclea, 365
Tarsius spectrum, 77
Tarsus, 14, 15
Taylor, J., quoted, 322
tearli, Bombycia, 304
Tecoma, 49, 401
tecomæ, Salobrana, 401
tecta, Amyna, 242; Orthodes, 203
Telea, genus, 87; fenestra, oculea, paphia, polyphemus, 87
telifera, Agrotis, 182
teligera, Mamestra, 195
telum, Apatela, 155
tenebrifera, Semiophora, 180
tenebrosata, Cymatophora, 341
tenera, Pareuchætes, 134
Tennyson, Alfred, quoted, 22, 445
tenuifascia, Illice, 109; Oncocnemis, 176
tenuimargo, Ptychoglene, 110
tenuis, Hæmorrhagia, 63; Isogona, 256
tepida, Xylina, 207
tephra, Olene, 308
Tephroclystis, genus, 327; absinthiata, absynthiata, coagulata, elongata, geminata, minutata, notata, 328
teratophora, Jaspidia, 160
terlooi, Arctonotus, 71
Terminal lunules, 18
terminalis, Pygoctenucha, 111; Utetheisa, 117
terminimacula, Tarache, 251
terraria, Almodes, 354
terrella, Phthorimæa, 425
terrifica, Setagrotis, 181
tersa, Xylophanes, 75
tertia, Schinia, 228
tertialis, Phlyctænia, 397
tessellaris, Halisidota, 137
tessellata, Euxoa, 189
testacea, Tortricidia, 368
Tetanolita, genus, 283; mynesalis, 284
Tetracis, genus; allediusaria, aspilata, crocallata, 353
tetradactylus, Phobetron, 366
tetragonalis, Phlyctænodes, 395
tetraspilaris, Cochlidion, 367
tetrio, Pseudosphinx, 57
texana, Comacla, 107; Harrisina, 372; Horama, 100; Parora, 255; Remigia, 274
textor, Hyphantria, 124
textula, Sisyrosea, 366
thalialis, Noctuelia, 399
Thalpochares, genus; ætheria, 249
thaxteri, Xylina, 207
thecata, Himella, 204
theodori, Polia, 171
Therasea, genus; flavicosta, 251
Therina, genus, 347; æqualiaria, athasiaria, bibularia, 348; endropiaria, 347; fervidaria, fiscellaria, flagitaria, invexata, panisaria, pultaria, sciata, seminudaria, seminudata, siccaria, 348

thesealis, Pyrausta, 397
thetis, Hæmorrhagia, 64; Daritis, 289
Thomas, Edith M., quoted, 358
Thomson, James, quoted, 331, 390
thoracica, Malacosoma, 313
thoracicoides, Malacosoma, 313
thorates, Xylophanes, 75
Thorax, 14, 18
thoreaui, Schinia, 228
thraxalis, Renia, 283
Thyatiridæ, Family, 25, 34, 303
thyatiroides, Eosphoropteryx, 237; Dosylophia, 296
Thyreion, genus; rosea, 222
Thyrididæ, Family, 24, 35, 374
Thyridopteryx, genus; coniferarum, ephemeræformis, 361
Thyris, genus; lugubris, maculata, Mournful, nevadæ, perspicua, sepulchralis, Spotted, 374
Thysania, genus; zenobia, 279
thysbe, Hæmorrhagia, 62
Tibia, 14, 15
Tiger, 78
Tiger-moths, 115; Aulæan, 124; Banded, 132; Bean's, 126; Blake's, 131; Bruce's, 126; Eyed, 120; Figured, 132; Great, 134; Intermediate, 129; Isabella, 125; Labrador, Little Virgin, 131; Many-spotted, 121; Mexican, 131; Nevada, 131; Ornate, 130, Phyllira, 132; Ranchman's, 128; Ruby, 126; Small, 134; St. Lawrence, 128; Straight-lined, 129; Virgin, 129; Virginian, Vestal, 127; Williams', 132; Yarrow's, 127; Zuni, 124
triangulatum, Eustroma, 329
triangulifer, Cirrhophanus, 234
tigris, Diastema, 241
Tilia, 300
tiliaria, Erannis, 347
timais, Xanthopastis, 231
tinctaria, Cleora, 344
Tinea, genus; dubiella, flavescentella, grisella, merdella, pellionella, 433
Tineidæ, Family, 6, 25, 26, 37, 430
Tineola, genus; biselliella, bisselliella, crinella, destructor, lanariella, 432
tipuliformis, Synanthedon, 385
titan, Sesia, 62
Titanio, genus; proximalis, 396
titea, Phigalia, 347
titearia, Phigalia, 347
titubatis, Euxoa, 189
togata, Orthodes, 203; Xanthia, 214
Tolype, genus; velleda, 312
Topsell, "Historie of Serpents," quoted, 114; "Historie of Four-footed Beasts," quoted, 357
toreuta, Bomolocha, 286
Tornacontia, genus; sutrix, 250
torrefacta, Apatelodes, 292
Tortricidæ, Family, 24, 25, 37, 417
Tortricidia, genus; cæsonia, flexuosa, testacea, 368
Tortrix, genus; albicomana, 423
tortuosa, Hyperæschra, 294
Tosale, genus; anthœcioides, nobilis, oviplagalis, 402
Toxocampa, genus; victoria, 273
trabalis, Yuma, 407
trabea, Polychrysia, 236
Trachea, genus; delicata, 172
Tragedy of the Night-moth, 209
tragopoginis, Pyrophila, 173
Trama, genus; arrosa, detrahens, 276
tranquila, Zotheca, 219
transducens, Abbotana, 353

transferens, Abbotana, 353
transfindens, Sabulodes, 353
transfrons, Hadena, 166
translucida, Hemihyalea, 138
transmontana, Arctia, 134
transmutans, Sabulodes, 353
transposita, Sabulodes, 353
transversata, Ellida, 300; Sabulodes, 353
Transverse, anterior line, 18; posterior line, 18
trentonalis, Herculia, 401
Trichoclea, genus; antica, 199
Trichocosmia, genus; inornata, 220
Tricholita, genus; semiaperta, signata, 205
Trichophaga, genus; tapetzella, 434
Trichopolia, genus; serrata, 199
Trichosellus, genus; crotchi, cupes, 226
Trichotarache, genus; assimilis, 246
tricinctus, Memythrus, 382
tricolor, Cerathosia, 253; Hemileuca, 93; Hypoprepia, 106; Kodiosoma, 133
tricoloraria, Synchlora, 336
trifariana, Spragueia, 252
trifascia, Schinia, 227
trifolii, Mamestra, 193
trigona, Bertholdia, 140
Trigonophora, genus; periculosa, v-brunneum, 215
triguttaria, Heterophleps, 327
trilinearia, Metanema, 351; Platea, 343
trilineata, Gluphisia, 300
trimaculata, Alypiodes, 145; Euerythra, 120
trinotata, Celama, 357
Triocnemis, genus; saporis, 225
tripars, Porosagrotis, 187
tripartita, Dasylophia, 296
tripartitus, Sphinx, 55
Triphosa, genus; dubitata, indubitata, progressata, 331
triplipunctaria, Paraphia, 343
Triprocris, genus, 371; constans, latercula, 372; rata, 371; smithsonianus, 372
Tripsacum dactyloides, 405
Tripudia, genus; opipara, 250
tripunctaria, Sympherta, 342
triquetrana, Celama, 357
trisectus, Crambus, 403
tristis, Catocala, 262
Tristyla, genus; alboplagiata, 220
triumphalis, Phlyctænodes, 395
Trochanter, 14, 15
truncataria, Epelis, 337
truncatula, Fruva, 252
truxaliata, Sabulodes, 353
Tubercles, larval, 8
Tuerta, genus; noctuiformis, sabulosa, 143
tumida, Pseudanthœcia, 228
tunicana, Epagoge, 421
turbans, Apantesis, 131
turbatellus, Crambus, 402
turbida, Heterocampa, 297
turbitella, Zophodia, 411
turbulenta, Hadena, 167
Turkeys, Shooting wild, 148
turris, Euxoa, 190
Turuptiana, genus; cæca, permaculata, reducta, 121
Typha latifolia, 211
typhon, Pholus, 65
typica, Pronoctua, 185
tyralis, Pyrausta, 398

U

u-brevis, Autographa, 238
Ufeus, genus; barometricus, plicatus, satyricus, 191

ulmi, Apatela, 155; Ceratomia, 47; Heterocampa, 297
Ulolonche, genus; modesta, 198
Ulosyneda, genus; valens, 257
ultronia, Catocala, 265
umbellana, Depressaria, 428
umbellella, Depressaria, 428
umbra, Pyrrhia, 214
umbrata, Clemensia, 108; Heterocampa, 297
umbrifascia, Hyamia, 254
uncanaria, Platea, 342
Underwings, The, 260; Agrippina, 260; Aholibah, 265; Amasia, 268; American Copper, 173; Andromache, 267; Angus', 262; Augusta, 264; Babayaga, 263; Badia, 267; Bianca, 262; Briseis, 264; California, 263; Carrie's, 261; Celia, 265; Cleopatra, 263; Clouded, 266; Darling, 263; Dejected, 261; Delilah, Desdemona, 267; Epione, 260; Evelina, Faintly Green, 261; Faustina, 264; Glittering, 266; Gloomy, 262; Graceful, 269; Grote's, 264; Hawthorn, 268; Hermia, 264; Hinda, 266; Ilia, 265; Inconsolable, Judith, 262; Little, 269; Luciana, 263; Magdalen, 267; Marbled, 263; Meske's, 264; Mopsa, 265; Mother, 264; Mourning, Obscure, 262; Old-Maid, 268; Oldwife, 266; Olivia, 269; Once-married, 264; Paulina, 261; Phalanga, 266; Pure, 264; Robinson's, 262; Rosalind, 264; Sappho, 260; Scarlet, 265; Serene, 267; Sleepy, Stretch's, 263; Tearful, 261; Ultronia, Verrill's, 265; Wayward, 267; Widow, Widowed, 261; Whitney's, 268; Yellow-banded, 266; Yellow-gray, 262; Youthful, 266
undatifascia, Pachylia, 60
undifera, Prolimacodes, 367
undosus, Cossus, 377
undularis, Ypsia, 278
undulata, Hydria, 329
undulosa, Ceratomia, 48
Ungues, 14, 15
unica, Gonodonta, 236
unicolor, Eudule, 327; Misogada, 297; Noctua, 184
unicornis, Schizura, 298
unifascia, Illice, 109
unifascialis, Pyrausta, 397
uniformis, Crambidia, 104; Hæmatomis, 107; Hæmorrhagia, 63
unijuga, Catocala, 264
unilineata, Homoptera, 278
unimacula, Pyrausta, 398
unimoda, Xylina, 207
unio, Euthisanotia, 232
unipuncta, Heliophila, 200; Leucania, 175; Paraphia, 343
unipunctata, Paraphia, 343
urentis, Abrostola, 240
uroceriformis, Sannina, 382
ursina, Lathosea, 209
Utahensis, Arctia, 134
Utetheisa, genus, 114; The Beautiful, The Ornamented, bella, hybrida, intermedia ornatrix, pura, stretchi, terminalis, 117
uxor, Catocala, 265

V

vaccinii, Autographa, 239
vacciniivorana, Alceris, 421
Vaccinium, 56
vagans, Diacrisia, 128
valens, Ulosyneda, 257
Valeria, genus; opina, 172
vancouverensis, Feltia, 186; Hyloicus, 50
vanella, Pseudotamila, 229

477

Index

varadaria, Caberodes, 352
varia, Automeris, 89; Heterocampa, 297;
  Oligia, 165
variabilis, Pseudorthosia, 216
variana, Tapinostola, 216
variolana, Alceris, 421
variolaria, Deilinea, 338
varus, Syssaura, 352
vashti, Hyloicus, 50
vau, Melalopha, 293
v-brunneum, Trigonophora, 215
vecors, Orthodes, 203; Perigea, 165
vega, Pogocolon, 73
vegeta, Cissusa, 256
velata, Orthodes, 203; Rhynchagrotis, 178
velleda, Tolype, 312
velleripennis, Euxoa, 188
vellifera, Bomolocha, 286
Venation of wings, 16
venerabilis, Feltia, 186
venezuelensis, Pachylia, 60
venosa, Ctenucha, 101
ventilator, Marasmalus, 242
venus, Hyparpax, 299
Venusia, genus; cambrica, comptaria, condensata, duodecimlineata, inclinata, inclinataria, perlineata, 328
venusta, Euchalcia, 237; Hyparpax, 299
verbascoides, Hadena, 169
Verbena, 163
vermiculata, Gnophæla, 290
vernata, Euclea, 365; Nyctobia, 324; Paleacrita, 324
verrilliana, Catocala, 265
verruca, Autographa, 238
versicolor, Darapsa, 69
versuta, Hadena, 167; Pseudorgyia, 245
verticalis, Euxoa, 189
vesca, Galgula, 247
Vespamima, genus; pinorum, sequoiæ, 384
vespiformis, Ægeria, 383
vesta, Philosamia, 82
vestaliata, Orthofidonia, 337
vestalis, Haploa, 118; Mænas, 127
vestitaria, Ania, 349
vesulia, Oxydia, 352
vetusta, Hemerocampa, 306; Porosagrotis,
  187
viatica, Glæa, 218; Orthofidonia, 337
Viburnum, 62, 63
vicaria, Noctua, 184
vicariana, Archips, 422
vicina, Mamestra, 195
victoria, Toxocampa, 273
videns, Platysenta, 163
vidua, Catocala, 261
viduata, Catocala, 261
vinculum, Phurys, 275
vinela, Hadena, 170
vinnula, Apatela, 156
vinesaria, Euchlæna, 350
violacea, Hadena, 167
violans, Nephelodes, 199
viralis, Hadena, 168
virescens, Chloridea, 222
virgata, Ianassa, 298
virginalis, Platyprepia, 128; Tarache, 251
virginaria, Epimecis, 344
virginica, Ctenucha, 102; Diacrisia, 127
virginiensis, Anisota, 94, 95
virgo, Apantesis, 129
virguncula, Apantesis, 131
viridans, Homoptera, 278
viridescens, Psaphidia, 177
viridiclava, Euclea, 365
viridis, Euclea, 365
viridisignata, Autographa, 239

viridoperlata, Metrocampa, 348
viridula, Zotheca, 219
Vitaceæ, 61, 65, 70
vitis, Pholus, 67
vittata, Apantesis, 132; Hypoprepia, 106
vivida, Pygarctia, 136
volubilis, Feltia, 186
volupia, Rhododipsa, 225
voluta, Adoneta, 365
vomerina, Morrisonia, 196
votiva, Pygoctenucha, 111
v-signatana, Archips, 422
vulneraria, Sphacelodes, 354
vulnifica, Bellura, 211
vultuosa, Hadena, 168

W

Wainscot; Comma, 203; Dark-winged,
  False, 201; Heterodox, 202; Lesser, 201;
  Many-lined, 202; White-lined, 201
wakarusa, Yponomeuta, 423
Walker, Francis, 27, 30
walkeri, Philosamia, 82; Scopelosoma, 218
Walking as a Fine Art, 270
Walnut Case-bearer, The, 408
Walnut Span-worm, The, 345
Walshia, genus; amorphella, 430
Walsingham, Lord, 37, 38
walsinghami, Ctenucha, 102
Walton, Izaak, quoted, 374
washingtonia, Synanthedon, 385
washingtoniana, Xylina, 207
Wasp-moth; Double-tufted, 99; Edwards',
  100; Lesser, 99; Polka-dot, 99; Scarlet-
  bodied, 98; Texan, 100; Yellow-banded, 99
Web-worm, The Parsnip, 428
Westwood, J. O., 35, 370, 428
whitneyi, Catocala, 268
Whittier, J. G., quoted, 292 320
Wife, The, 265
williamsi, Apantesis, 132
wilsoni, Ciris, 233
Wings, structure of, p. 15
wiskotti, Arctia, 134
Wittfeldi, Alypia, 143, 144
Wood, Rev. J. G., quoted, 360
woodi, Homoptera, 278
Woodling, Beautiful, Brown, Fletcher's
  Grieving. Hardened, Oregon, Simple, 197
Wood-nymph, Beautiful, Pearly, 232
Woolly bears, 115, 125
Wordsworth, quoted, 415
worthingtoni, Porosagrotis, 187
wrighti, Gluphisia, 300; Scepsis, 101

X

Xanthia, genus; flavago, silago, togata, 214
xanthioides, Perigea, 165
xanthometata, Mellilla, 338
Xanthopastis, genus; regnatrix, timais, 231
Xanthoptera, genus; nigrofimbria, 248;
  semiflava, 249
Xanthothrix, genus; neumœgeni, 231
Xanthotype, genus; cælaria, citrina, crocataria, 349
xiphiæformis, Sanninoidea, 384
Xylina, genus; antennata, 206; baileyi, 207;
  cinerea, disposita, 206; innominata, laticinerea, 207; petulca, 206; pexata, tepida,
  thaxteri, unimoda, washingtoniana, 207
xylina, Alabama, 243
xylinoides, Hyppa, 171
Xylomiges, genus; cognata, crucialis, dolosa
  fletcheri, indurata, patalis, perlubens
  pulchella, simplex, subapicalis, 197

Xylophanes, genus, 75; bœrhaviæ, crœsus
eson, pluto, tersa, thorates, 75
Xylorictidæ, Family, 26, 428

Y

Yarrowi, Phragmatobia, 127
yavapai, Hemileuca, 92
y-inversa, Cochlidion, 367; Prodoxus, 439
yosemitæ, Fishea, 170
Yponomeuta, genus; euonymella, multipunctella, orbimaculella, ordinatellus, wakarusa, 423
Yponomeutidæ, Family, 26, 38, 423
Ypsia, genus; undularis, 278
ypsilon, Agrotis, 140, 182
Yrias, genus; clientis, repentis, 277
Yucca, 437; angustifolia, filamentosa, 442;
whipplei, 440, 442
Yucca-moth, 441
yuccasella, Pronuba
Yuma, genus; adulatalis, trabalis, 407

Z

Zale, genus; horrida, 277
zalissaria, Stenaspilates, 351
Zanclognatha, genus; lævigata, lituralis,
minimalis, ochreipennis, protumnusalis, 281
zeæ, Achatodes, 212; Plodia, 415
zelatella, Mineola, 409
Zeller, P. C., 37
zelleri, Automeris, 89
zenobia, Thysania, 279
zephyria, Automeris, 89
Zeuzera, genus; æsculi, decipiens, hilaris
hypocastrina, pyrina, 376
Zinckenia, genus; albifascialis, angustalis,
diffascialis, fascialis, recurvalis, 392
zonata, Homopyralis, 256
Zophodia, genus; grossulariæ, turbitella, 411
Zosteropoda, genus; hirtipes, 203
Zotheca, genus; sambuci, tranquila, viridula
219
zuni, Arachnis, 124
Zygænidæ, Family, 25, 35, 233, 371